AMERICA

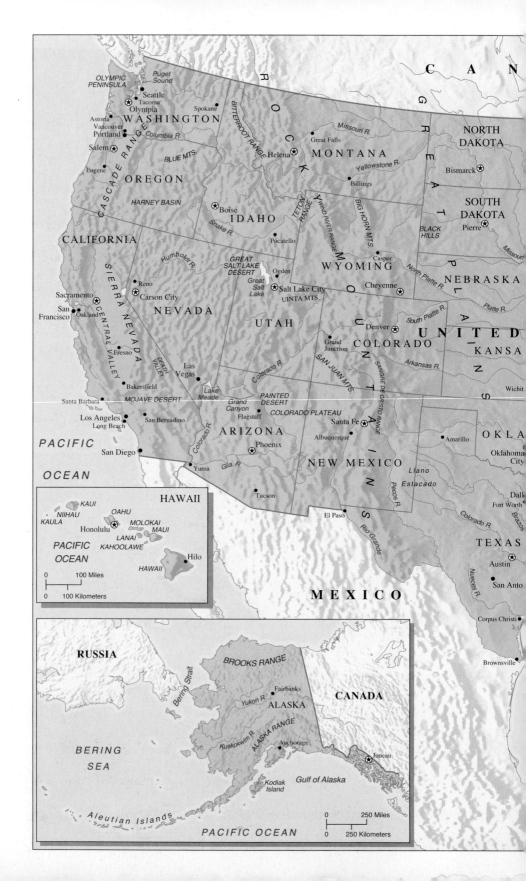

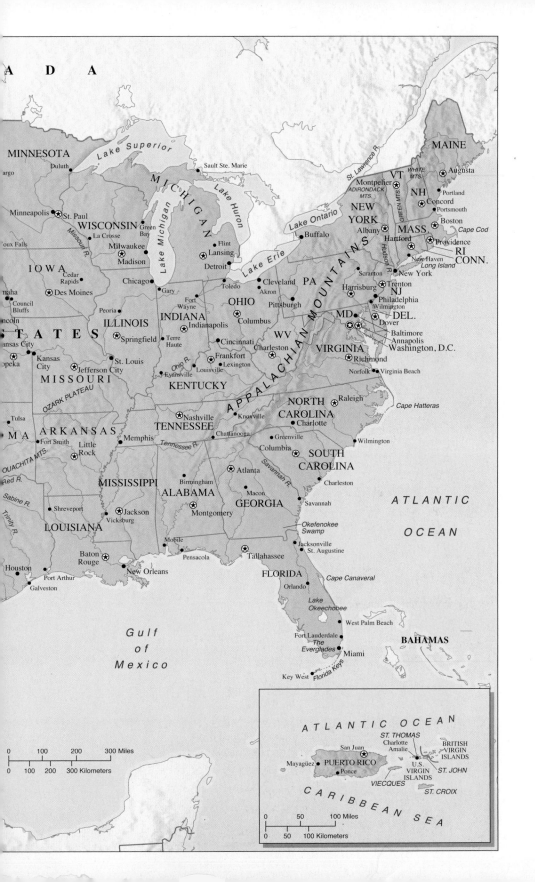

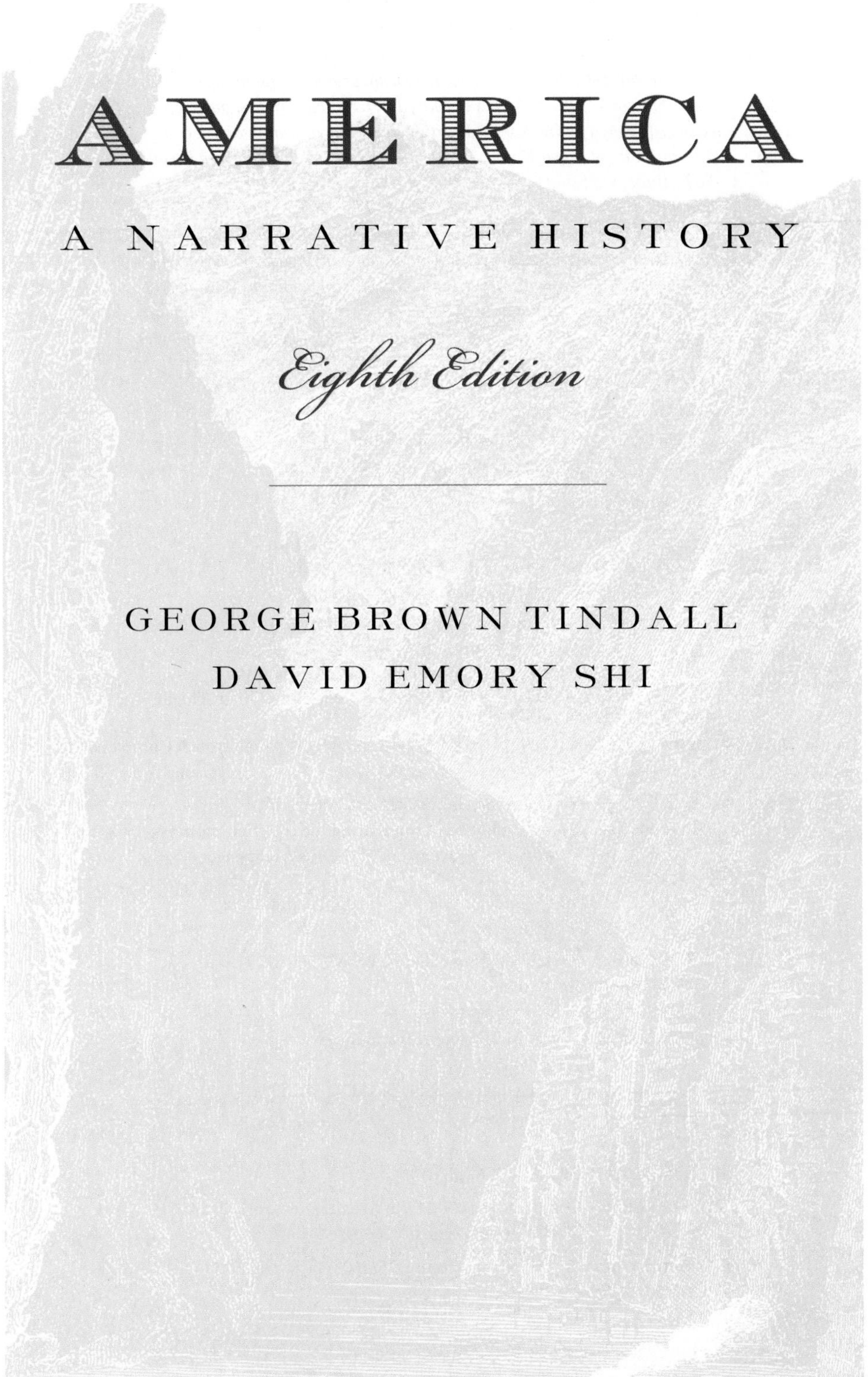

AMERICA

A NARRATIVE HISTORY

Eighth Edition

GEORGE BROWN TINDALL

DAVID EMORY SHI

W · W · NORTON & COMPANY · NEW YORK · LONDON

W. W. Norton & Company has been independent since its founding in 1923, when William Warder Norton and Mary D. Herter Norton first published lectures delivered at the People's Institute, the adult education division of New York City's Cooper Union. The firm soon expanded its program beyond the Institute, publishing books by celebrated academics from America and abroad. By mid-century, the two major pillars of Norton's publishing program—trade books and college texts—were firmly established. In the 1950s, the Norton family transferred control of the company to its employees, and today—with a staff of four hundred and a comparable number of trade, college, and professional titles published each year—W. W. Norton & Company stands as the largest and oldest publishing house owned wholly by its employees.

Editor: Jon Durbin
Manuscript editor: Abby Winograd
Project editor: Melissa Atkin
Emedia editor: Steve Hoge
Print ancillary editor: Rachel Comerford
Production manager: Christine D'Antonio
Editorial assistant: Jason Spears
Book design by Antonina Krass
Composition by TexTech, Inc.
Manufacturing by World Color Press, Inc., Taunton
Cartographer: CARTO-GRAPHICS/Alice Thiede and William Thiede

Library of Congress Cataloging-in-Publication Data

Tindall, George Brown.
   America : a narrative history / George Brown Tindall,
David Emory Shi.—8th ed.
      p.   cm.
   Includes bibliographical references and index.
   ISBN 978-0-393-93405-2
   1. United States—History.   I. Shi, David E.   II. Title.
   E178.1 .T55 2009   2009024625
   973—dc22
   ISBN 978-0-393-93407-6 (pbk.)

W. W. Norton & Company, Inc., 500 Fifth Avenue, New York, NY 10110
www.wwnorton.com

W. W. Norton & Company Ltd., Castle House, 75/76 Wells Street, London W1T 3QT

6 7 8 9 0

FOR BRUCE AND SUSAN
AND FOR BLAIR

FOR
JASON AND JESSICA

GEORGE B. TINDALL recently of the University of North
Carolina, Chapel Hill, was an award-winning historian
of the South with a number of major books to his credit,
including *The Emergence of the New South, 1913–1945* and
The Disruption of the Solid South.

DAVID E. SHI is a professor of history and the president of
Furman University. He is the author of several books on
American cultural history, including the award-winning
*The Simple Life: Plain Living and High Thinking in American
Culture* and *Facing Facts: Realism in American Thought and
Culture, 1850–1920.*

CONTENTS

Part Six / MODERN AMERICA

MAPS

PREFACE

This edition of *America: A Narrative History* marks the twenty-fifth anniversary of the book. I very much regret that George Tindall is not alive to celebrate with me. He died on December 2, 2006, in Chapel Hill, North Carolina. He was eighty-five. George was a meticulous, pathbreaking, award-winning scholar. He was also an eloquent writer, an engaging teacher, and a caring mentor. And, of course, he wrote a wonderful history of America!

George Tindall developed the idea for a distinctive American history textbook nearly four decades ago. He set out to write a compelling narrative history of the American experience, a succinct narrative that would be animated by colorful characters, informed by balanced analysis and social texture, and guided by the unfolding of events. Those classic principles, combined with the book's handy format and low price, have helped make *America: A Narrative History* one of the most popular and well-respected American history textbooks. It was my good fortune to join George in this worthy endeavor beginning with the Second Edition.

Beginning in 1984, George and I sought to improve *America* with each edition. Each subsequent edition has introduced a new theme designed to show how politics, economics, culture, and society interact to shape the American experience. New themes in previous editions have included the role of immigration, the western experience, work, and the environment. This Eighth Edition of *America* features the theme of religion and its myriad effects on history and society. Religion, of course, is one of the most powerful forces in human life, and it has played a crucial role in the development of the United States. Americans have always been a peculiarly religious people. Native American cultures centered their societies on spiritual life. And most of the first European colonists saw themselves as "a chosen people," agents of divine providence with a mission to spread the gospel to the so-called New World. In 1831 and 1832, the astute Frenchman Alexis de Tocqueville toured the United States and reported that there "is no country in the world where the Christian religion retains a greater influence over the souls of men than in America."

Yet Christianity in America has always assumed many forms. Religious freedom has been as valued a principle as religious belief. And in recent years the United States has witnessed a surge in non-Christian religions. "We are a religious people," said Supreme Court Justice William O. Douglas in 1952. Yet thirteen years later he added that America had become "a nation of Buddhists, Confucianists, and Taoists." Islam, in fact, is the nation's fastest-growing faith; there are more Muslims in America than Episcopalians. The United States is fast becoming a pluralistic, multireligious nation in which toleration is an ever-important outlook. More than the members of any other industrialized society, the vast majority of Americans (90 percent) believe in God, pray, and attend religious services at churches, synagogues, temples, and mosques. To a remarkable degree, many Americans fashion their personal conduct upon their religious principles and their social relationships upon their religious beliefs. Thus diversity characterizes American religious life. There are many different faiths and also quite different expressions of the same faith. Although the U.S. Constitution creates a "wall of separation" between religion and government, Americans are also more apt to mix faith and politics than citizens of other countries. In other words, religion continues to be one of the most dynamic—and most contested—elements of American life.

Some of the additions to the Eighth Edition relating to religious history are outlined here:

- Chapter 1 includes discussions of Aztec religious beliefs and rituals, sixteenth-century European religious life, and Spanish efforts to convert Native Americans to Catholicism.
- Chapter 2 examines the English Reformation and the distinctive characteristics of Anglicanism (the faith of the Church of England), the Native Americans' reverence for nature, and Judaism in British North America.
- Chapter 3 describes the important role of women in colonial religious life, the popularity of Deism among many key Revolutionary leaders, and the social aspects of the Great Awakening.
- Chapter 4 details the impact of the Jesuit missionaries in New France.
- Chapter 8 analyzes the logic of the First Amendment's emphasis on the separation of church and state.

- Chapter 13 explores the changes in religious life during the early nineteenth century.
- Chapter 15 includes new material on religious life in the Old South.
- Chapter 16 features the religious revival of 1857–1859.
- Chapter 17 shows that the armies fighting the Civil War engaged in frequent religious services and revivals.
- Chapter 18 details the role played by religious life in the Reconstruction of the South after the Civil War.
- Chapter 22 summarizes the role that religious fervor played in the populist movement of the 1890s.
- Chapter 23 discusses the role of religion in justifying American imperialism at the end of the nineteenth century.
- Chapter 24 highlights the role of religion in the motives of "progressive" social reformers.
- Chapter 32 describes the efforts of Congress and President Dwight Eisenhower to reaffirm America's belief in God.
- Chapter 33 stresses the crucial role played by religion in the development of the civil rights movement of the 1950s and 1960s.
- Chapter 36 explains the rise of the Republican conservatives and the role that the major revival of evangelical religion played in the conservative ascendancy in American politics.

Beyond those explorations of religious history, I have introduced other new material throughout the Eighth Edition, including new segments on Native Americans, African Americans, and women. In addition, I have incorporated fresh insights from important new scholarly works.

America is a book that students like to read and teachers like to teach. *America*'s consistent narrative voice provides a clear path through the complexities of American history. New, carefully crafted pedagogical features have been added to the Eighth Edition to further help guide students through the narrative. New focus questions and chapter summaries work together seamlessly to highlight core content. Other text features include easy-to-read full-color maps, new chapter chronologies, and new lists of key terms.

Also revised is the outstanding support package that supplements the text. *For the Record: A Documentary History of America,* Fourth Edition, by David E. Shi and Holly A. Mayer (Duquesne University), is the perfect companion reader for *America: A Narrative History*. The new edition has been brought into closer alignment with the main text, and the price has been reduced by nearly 50 percent. *For the Record* now has 225 primary-source readings from diaries, journals, newspaper articles, speeches, government documents, and novels, including a number of readings that highlight the new theme of religion in *America*. If you haven't looked at *For the Record* in a while, now would be a good time to take a look.

America: A Narrative History StudySpace (http://wwnorton.com/study space) provides a proven assignment-driven plan for each chapter. Highlights include chapter outlines, quizzes in the the new Quiz Plus format, iMaps and new iMap quizzes, map worksheets, flashcards, interactive timelines, new U.S. History Tours powered by Google Earth map technology, research topics, and several hundred multimedia primary-source documents. The *Norton Instructor's Resource Disk* provides enhanced PowerPoint lecture outlines with images from the text, four-color maps, the U.S. History Tours in a slide-show format, additional images from the Library of Congress archives, and audio files of historic speeches.

W. W. Norton is pleased to offer adopters the *Norton American History Digital Archive,* a set of seven DVDs, including a new DVD on religion that will help instructors visually tell the story of religion in the American experience.

The *Instructor's Manual and Test Bank,* by Stephen Davis (Kingwood College), Edward Richey (University of North Texas), Michael Krysko (Kansas State University), Brian McKnight (Angelo State University), and David Dewar (Angelo State University), includes a test bank of short-answer and essay questions, as well as detailed chapter outlines, lecture suggestions, and bibliographies. Finally, Norton coursepacks deliver all the instructional materials in a ready-to-use format for your course management system (Blackboard, WebCT, Angel, Moodle, and so on).

It's clear why *America* continues to set the standard when it comes to providing a low-cost book with high-value content. Your students will read it, and they will save money.

In preparing the Eighth Edition, I have benefited from the insights and suggestions of many people. Some of those insights have come from student readers of the text, and I encourage such feedback. I'd particularly like to thank Eirlys Barker (Thomas Nelson Community College), who was a reviewer for us and worked on the wonderful new student pedagogy in the text. Likewise, I'd like to thank Stephen Davis for his work on the *Instructor's*

Manual and Test Bank. I'd like to give special thanks to Brandon Franke (Blinn College, Bryan) for his work on the new PowerPoint lectures. Numerous scholars and survey instructors advised me on the new edition:

Heather Abdelnur (Augusta State University), Alan Autrey (Lamar University), Frank Baglione (Tallahassee Community College), Mario Bennekin (Georgia Perimeter College), William Bush (University of Nevada, Las Vegas), David Castle (Ohio University, Eastern), Craig Coenen (Mercer County Community College), Alice Connally (Purdue University, North Central), Scott Cook (Motlow State Community College), Amy Darty (University of Central Florida), Wade Derden (Pulaski Technical College), Brandon Franke (Blinn College, Bryan), Mark Goldman (Tallahassee Community College), James Good (North Harris College), Shane Hamilton (University of Georgia), Gene Hatfield (Clayton State University), Marc Horger (Ohio State University), Charles Killinger (Valencia Community College), Margaret (Peggy) Lambert (Lone Star College, Kingwood), Pat Ledbetter (North Central Texas College), Robby Luckett (University of Georgia), Lisa Morales (North Central Texas College, Corinth), Bret Nelson (San Jacinto College, North), Michael Nichols (Tarrant County College, Northwest), Yolanda Orizondo-Harding (University of Central Florida), George Pabis (Georgia Perimeter College), Thomas Price (State University of New York, Ulster County Community College), Brooks Simpson (Arizona State University), Alice Taylor-Colbert (University of Arkansas, Fort Smith), John Wegner (Eastern Michigan University), Joseph Whitehorne (Lord Fairfax Community College)

Once again, I thank my friends at W. W. Norton, especially Steve Forman, Jon Durbin, Steve Hoge, Karl Bakeman, Nicole Netherton, Melissa Atkin, Christine D'Antonio, Abigail Winograd, Rachel Comerford, Stephanie Romeo, and Jason Spears for their care and attention along the way.

AMERICA

18

RECONSTRUCTION: NORTH AND SOUTH

FOCUS QUESTIONS

 wwnorton.com/studyspace

- What were the different approaches to Reconstruction?
- How did white southerners respond to the end of the old order in the South?
- To what extent did blacks function as citizens in the reconstructed South?
- What were the main issues in national politics in the 1870s?
- Why did Reconstruction end in 1877?

In the spring of 1865, the Civil War was finally over. At a frightful cost of 630,000 lives and the destruction of the southern economy and much of its landscape, the Union had emerged triumphant, and some 4 million enslaved Americans had seized their freedom. Ratification of the Thirteenth Amendment in December 1865 abolished slavery throughout the Union. Now the nation faced the task of reuniting, coming to terms with the abolition of slavery, and "reconstructing" a ravaged and resentful South.

THE WAR'S AFTERMATH

In the war's aftermath difficult questions faced the victors: Should the Confederate leaders be tried for treason? How should new governments be formed? How and at whose expense was the South's economy to be rebuilt?

Should debts incurred by the Confederate state governments be honored? Who should pay to rebuild the South's railroads and public buildings, dredge the clogged southern harbors, and restore damaged levees? What was to be done for the freed slaves? Were they to be given land? social equality? education? voting rights? Such complex questions required sober reflection and careful planning, but policy makers did not have the luxury of time or the benefit of consensus. Some northerners wanted the former Confederate states returned to the Union with little or no changes in the region's social, political, and economic life. Others wanted southern society punished and transformed. The editors of the nation's foremost magazine, *Harper's Weekly*, expressed this vengeful attitude when they declared at the end of 1865 that "the forgive-and-forget policy . . . is mere political insanity and suicide."

DEVELOPMENT IN THE NORTH   To some Americans the Civil War had been more truly a social revolution than the War of Independence, for it reduced the once-dominant influence of the South's planter elite in national politics and elevated the power of the northern "captains of industry." Government, both federal and state, became more friendly to business leaders and more unfriendly to those who would probe into their activities. The wartime Republican Congress had delivered on the party's major platform promises of 1860.

In the absence of southern members, the wartime Congress had centralized national power and enacted the Republican economic agenda. It passed the Morrill Tariff, which doubled the average level of import duties. The National Banking Act created a uniform system of banking and bank-note currency and helped finance the war. Congress also decided that the first transcontinental railroad would run along a north-central route, from Omaha, Nebraska, to Sacramento, California, and it donated public land and sold bonds to ensure its financing. In the Homestead Act of 1862, moreover, Congress provided free federal homesteads of 160 acres to settlers, who had only to occupy the land for five years to gain title. No cash was needed. The Morrill Land Grant Act of the same year conveyed to each state 30,000 acres of federal land per member of Congress from the state. The sale of some of the land provided funds to create colleges of "agriculture and mechanic arts." Such measures helped stimulate the North's economy in the years after the Civil War.

DEVASTATION IN THE SOUTH   The postwar South offered a sharp contrast to the victorious North. Along the path of General William T. Sherman's Union army, one observer reported in 1866, the countryside

A street in the "burned district"

Ruins of Richmond, Virginia, in the spring of 1865.

"looked for many miles like a broad black streak of ruin and desolation."
Columbia, South Carolina, said another witness, was "a wilderness of ruins";
Charleston, a place of "vacant houses, of widowed women, of rotting
wharves, of deserted warehouses, of weed-wild gardens, of miles of grass-
grown streets, of acres of pitiful and voiceless barrenness."

Throughout the South, property values had collapsed. Confederate bonds
and paper money were worthless; most railroads were damaged or destroyed.
Cotton that had escaped destruction was seized by federal troops. Emancipation wiped out $4 billion invested in human flesh and left the labor system
in disarray. The great age of expansion in the cotton market was over. Not
until 1879 would the cotton crop again equal the record harvest of 1860;
tobacco production did not regain its prewar level until 1880; the sugar crop
of Louisiana did not recover until 1893; and the old rice industry of the
Tidewater and the hemp industry of the Kentucky Bluegrass never regained
their prewar status.

A TRANSFORMED SOUTH   The defeat of the Confederacy transformed much of southern society. The freeing of slaves, the destruction of
property, and the collapse of land values left many planters destitute and
homeless. Amanda Worthington, a planter's wife from Mississippi, saw her

whole world destroyed. In the fall of 1865, she assessed the damage: "None of us can realize that we are no longer wealthy—yet thanks to the yankees, the cause of all unhappiness, such is the case."

Union soldiers who fanned out across the defeated South to impose order were cursed and spat upon. A Virginia woman expressed a spirited defiance common among her circle of friends: "Every day, every hour, that I live increases my hatred and detestation, and loathing of that race. They [Yankees] disgrace our common humanity. As a people I consider them vastly inferior to the better classes of our slaves." Fervent southern nationalists, both men and women, implanted in their children a similar hatred of Yankees and a defiance of northern rule. One mother said that she trained her children to "fear God, love the South, and live to avenge her."

LEGALLY FREE, SOCIALLY BOUND   In the former Confederate states the newly freed slaves often suffered most of all. A few northerners argued that what the ex-slaves needed most was their own land. But even abolitionists shrank from proposals to confiscate white-owned land and distribute it to the freed slaves. Citizenship and legal rights were one thing, wholesale confiscation of property and land redistribution quite another. Nonetheless, discussions of land distribution fueled false rumors that freed slaves would get "forty acres and a mule," a slogan that swept the

Freed slaves in Richmond, Virginia

According to a former Confederate general, freed slaves had "nothing but freedom."

South at the end of the war. Instead of land or material help, the freed slaves more often got advice about proper behavior.

THE FREEDMEN'S BUREAU   On March 3, 1865, while the war was still raging, Congress set up within the War Department the Bureau of Refugees, Freedmen, and Abandoned Lands to provide "such issues of provisions, clothing, and fuel" as might be needed to relieve "destitute and suffering refugees and freedmen and their wives and children." It was the first federal experiment in social welfare, albeit temporary. Agents of what came to be called the Freedmen's Bureau negotiated labor contracts (something new for both blacks and white planters), provided medical care, and set up schools. The bureau had its own courts to deal with labor disputes and land titles, and its agents were authorized to supervise trials involving blacks in other courts. The intensity of racial prejudice in the South thwarted the efforts of Freedmen's Bureau agents to protect and assist the former slaves.

Freedmen's school in Virginia

Throughout the former Confederate states the Freedmen's Bureau set up schools such as this one.

THE BATTLE OVER RECONSTRUCTION

The question of how to reconstruct the South's political structure centered on deciding which governments would constitute authority in the defeated states. As Union forces advanced into the South, President Lincoln in 1862 named military governors for conquered Tennessee, Arkansas, and Louisiana. By the end of the following year, he had formulated a plan for regular governments in those states and any others that might be liberated from Confederate rule.

LINCOLN'S PLAN AND CONGRESS'S RESPONSE   In late 1863, President Lincoln had issued a Proclamation of Amnesty and Reconstruction, under which any former Rebel state could form a Union government whenever a number equal to 10 percent of those who had voted in 1860 took an oath of allegiance to the Constitution and the Union and had received a presidential pardon. Participants also had to swear support for laws and proclamations dealing with emancipation. Certain groups, however, were excluded from the pardon: Confederate officials; senior officers of the Confederate army and navy; judges, congressmen, and military officers of the United States who had left their federal posts to aid the rebellion; and those accused of failure to treat captured African American soldiers and their officers as prisoners of war.

Under this plan, governments loyal to the Union appeared in Tennessee, Arkansas, and Louisiana, but Congress recognized neither their representatives nor their 1864 electoral votes. In the absence of specific provisions for Reconstruction in the Constitution, politicians disagreed as to where authority to restore Rebel states properly rested. Lincoln claimed the right to direct Reconstruction under the clause that set forth the presidential power to grant pardons and under the constitutional obligation of the United States to guarantee each state a republican form of government. Republican congressmen, however, argued that this obligation implied that Congress, not the president, should supervise Reconstruction.

A few conservative and most moderate Republicans supported Lincoln's program of immediate restoration. The small but influential group of Radical Republicans, however, favored a sweeping transformation of southern society based upon granting freed slaves full-fledged citizenship. The Radicals hoped to reconstruct southern society so as to dismantle the old planter class and the Democratic party.

The Radical Republicans were talented, earnest legislators who insisted that Congress control the Reconstruction program. To this end in 1864 they helped pass the Wade-Davis Bill, sponsored by Senator Benjamin Wade of Ohio and Representative Henry Winter Davis of Maryland. In contrast to Lincoln's 10 percent plan, the Wade-Davis Bill required that a majority of white male citizens declare their allegiance and that only those who could take an "ironclad" oath (required of federal officials since 1862) attesting to their *past* loyalty could vote or serve in the state constitutional conventions. The conventions, moreover, would have to abolish slavery, exclude from political rights high-ranking civil and military officers of the Confederacy, and repudiate debts incurred during the conflict.

Passed during the closing day of the session, the Wade-Davis Bill never became law: Lincoln vetoed it. In retaliation furious Republicans penned the Wade-Davis Manifesto, which accused the president of usurping power and attempting to use readmitted states to ensure his reelection, among other sins. Lincoln offered his last view of Reconstruction in his final public address, on April 11, 1865. Speaking from the White House balcony, he pronounced that the Confederate states had never left the Union. Those states were simply "out of their proper practical relation with the Union," and the object was to get them back "into their proper practical relation." At a cabinet meeting, Lincoln proposed the creation of new southern state governments before Congress met in December. He shunned the vindictiveness of the Radicals. He wanted "no persecution, no bloody work," no radical restructuring of southern social and economic life.

THE ASSASSINATION OF LINCOLN   On the evening of April 14, 1865, Lincoln went to Ford's Theatre and his rendezvous with death. With his trusted bodyguard called away to Richmond and the policeman assigned to his box away from his post, Lincoln was helpless as John Wilkes Booth slipped into the unguarded presidential box. Booth, a crazed actor and Confederate zealot, fired his derringer point-blank at the president's head. He then stabbed Lincoln's aide and jumped from the box to the stage, crying "*Sic semper tyrannis*" (Thus always to tyrants), the motto of Virginia. The president died nine hours later. Accomplices of Booth had also targeted Vice President Andrew Johnson and Secretary of State William Seward. Seward and four others, including his son, were victims of severe but not fatal stab wounds. Johnson escaped injury, however, because his would-be assassin got cold feet and wound up tipsy in the barroom of the vice president's hotel.

The nation extracted a full measure of vengeance from the conspirators. Booth was pursued into Virginia and killed in a burning barn. Three of his

Mourning a fallen president

President Lincoln's funeral procession on Pennsylvania Avenue.

collaborators were convicted by a military court and hanged, along with the woman at whose boardinghouse they had plotted. Three others got life sentences, including a Maryland doctor who set the leg Booth had broken when he jumped to the stage. President Johnson eventually pardoned them all, except one who died in prison.

JOHNSON'S PLAN   Lincoln's death elevated to the White House Andrew Johnson of Tennessee, a combative man who lacked most presidential virtues. Essentially illiterate, Johnson was provincial and bigoted—he harbored fierce prejudices. He was also short-tempered and impetuous. At the inaugural ceremonies in early 1865, he had delivered his vice-presidential address in a state of slurring drunkenness that embarrassed Lincoln and the nation. Johnson was a war (pro-Union) Democrat who had been put on the National Union ticket in 1864 as a gesture of unity. Of origins as humble as Lincoln's, Johnson was an orphan who had moved as a youth from his birthplace in Raleigh, North Carolina, to Greeneville, Tennessee, where he became the proprietor of a tailor shop. Self-educated with the help of his wife, he

Andrew Johnson

A pro-Union Democrat from Tennessee.

had served as mayor, congressman, governor, and senator, then as the Unionist military governor of Tennessee before he became vice president. In the process he had become an advocate of the small farmers in opposition to the privileges of the large planters—"a bloated, corrupted aristocracy." He also shared the racist attitudes of most white yeomen. "Damn the negroes," he exclaimed to a friend during the war, "I am fighting those traitorous aristocrats, their masters."

Some Radicals at first thought Johnson, unlike Lincoln, to be one of them. Johnson had, for example, once asserted that treason "must be made infamous and traitors must be impoverished." Senator Benjamin Wade loved such vengeful language. "Johnson, we have faith in you," he promised. "By the gods, there will be no trouble now in running this government." But Wade would soon find Johnson as unsympathetic as Lincoln, if for different reasons.

Johnson's loyalty to the Union sprang from a strict adherence to the Constitution and a fervent belief in limited government. When discussing what to do with the former Confederate states, Johnson preferred the term *restoration* to *reconstruction*. In 1865, Johnson declared that "there is no such thing as reconstruction. Those States have not gone out of the Union. Therefore reconstruction is unnecessary." Like many other whites he also opposed the growing Radical sentiment to grant the vote to African Americans.

Johnson's plan to restore the Union thus closely resembled Lincoln's. A new Proclamation of Amnesty, issued in May 1865, excluded not only those Lincoln had excluded from pardon but also everybody with taxable property worth more than $20,000. Those wealthy planters, bankers, and merchants were the people Johnson believed had led the South to secede. Those in the excluded groups might make special applications for pardon directly to the president, and before the year was out Johnson had issued some 13,000 pardons.

Johnson followed up his amnesty proclamation with his own plan for readmitting the former Confederate states. In each state a native Unionist became provisional governor, with authority to call a convention of men elected by loyal voters. Lincoln's 10 percent requirement was omitted. Johnson called upon the state conventions to invalidate the secession ordinances, abolish slavery, and repudiate all debts incurred to aid the Confederacy. Each state, moreover, must ratify the Thirteenth Amendment. In his final public address, Lincoln had endorsed a limited black suffrage. Johnson repeated Lincoln's advice. He reminded the provisional governor of Mississippi, for example, that the state conventions might "with perfect safety" extend suffrage to African Americans with education or with military service so as to "disarm the adversary," the adversary being "radicals who are wild upon" giving all African Americans the right to vote.

The state conventions for the most part met Johnson's requirements. But Carl Schurz, a German immigrant and war hero who became a prominent Missouri politician, found during a visit to the South "an *utter absence of national feeling* . . . and a desire to preserve slavery . . . as much and as long as possible." Southern whites had accepted the situation because they thought so little had changed after all. Emboldened by Johnson's indulgence, they ignored his pleas for moderation and conciliation. Suggestions of black suffrage were scarcely raised in the state conventions and promptly squelched when they were.

SOUTHERN INTRANSIGENCE   When Congress met in December 1865, for the first time since the end of the war it faced the fact that the new state governments in the postwar South were remarkably like the old ones. Southern voters had acted with extreme disregard for northern feelings. Among the new members presenting themselves to Congress were Georgia's Alexander Stephens, former vice president of the Confederacy, now claiming a seat in the Senate, four Confederate generals, eight colonels, and six cabinet members. The Congress forthwith denied seats to all such officials. It was too much to expect, after four bloody years, that the Unionists in Congress would welcome back ex-Confederate leaders.

Furthermore, the new southern state legislatures, in passing repressive "black codes" restricting the freedom of African Americans, demonstrated that they intended to preserve slavery as nearly as possible. As one white southerner stressed, "The ex-slave was not a free man; he was a free Negro," and the black codes were intended to highlight the distinction.

The black codes varied from state to state, but some provisions were common. Existing marriages, including common-law marriages, were recognized (although interracial marriages were prohibited), and testimony of blacks was accepted in legal cases involving blacks—and in six states in all cases.

"(?) Slavery Is Dead (?)"

Thomas Nast's cartoon suggests that in 1866 slavery was not dead.

Blacks could own property. They could sue and be sued in the courts. On the other hand, they could not own farmland in Mississippi or city lots in South Carolina; they were required to buy special licenses to practice certain trades in Mississippi. Blacks who worked for whites were required to enter into labor contracts with their employers, to be renewed annually. Unemployed ("vagrant") blacks were often arrested and punished with severe fines, and if unable to pay they were forced to labor in the fields of those who paid the courts for this source of cheap labor. In other words, aspects of slavery were simply being restored in another guise.

Faced with such blatant evidence of southern intransigence, moderate Republicans in Congress drifted toward the Radicals' views. The new Congress set up a Joint Committee on Reconstruction, with nine members from the House and six from the Senate, to gather evidence of southern efforts to thwart Reconstruction. Initiative fell to determined Radical Republicans who knew what they wanted: Benjamin Wade of Ohio, George Julian of Indiana, and—most conspicuously of all—Thaddeus Stevens of Pennsylvania and Charles Sumner of Massachusetts.

THE RADICAL REPUBLICANS   Most Radical Republicans had been connected with the anti-slavery cause for decades. In addition, few could escape the bitterness bred by the long war or remain unaware of the partisan advantage that would come to the Republican party from black suffrage. The Republicans needed African American votes to maintain their control of Congress and the White House. They also needed to disenfranchise former Confederates to keep them from helping to elect Democrats who would restore the old southern ruling class to power. In public, however, the Radical Republicans rarely disclosed such partisan self-interest. Instead, they asserted that the Republicans, the party of Union and freedom, could best guarantee the fruits of victory and that extending voting rights to African Americans would be the best way to promote their welfare.

Senator Charles Sumner

A leading Radical Republican.

The growing conflict of opinion over Reconstruction policy brought about an inversion in constitutional reasoning. Secessionists—and Andrew Johnson—were now arguing that the Rebel states had in fact remained in the Union, and some Radical Republicans were contriving arguments that they had left the Union after all. Thaddeus Stevens argued that the Confederate states should be viewed as conquered provinces, subject to the absolute will of the victors, and that the "whole fabric of southern society must be changed." Most Republicans, however, held that the Confederate states continued to exist as entities, but by the acts of secession and war they had forfeited "all civil and political rights under the Constitution." And Congress, not the president, was the proper authority to determine how and when such rights might be restored.

JOHNSON'S BATTLE WITH CONGRESS   A long year of political battling remained, however, before this idea triumphed. By the end of 1865, the Radical Republicans' views had gained a majority in Congress, if one not yet large enough to override presidential vetoes. But the critical year of 1866 saw the gradual waning of Andrew Johnson's power and influence, much of which was self-induced. Johnson first challenged Congress in 1866, when he vetoed a bill to extend the life of the Freedmen's Bureau. The measure, he said, violated the Constitution in several ways: it made the federal government responsible for the care of indigents, it was passed by a Congress in which

"The Cruel Uncle and the Vetoed Babes in the Wood"

A cartoon depicting Andrew Johnson leading two children, "Civil Rights" and "Bureau," into the "Veto Wood."

eleven ex-Confederate states had been denied seats, and it used vague language in defining the "civil rights and immunities" of African Americans. For the time being, Johnson's prestige remained sufficiently intact that the Senate upheld his veto.

Three days after the veto, however, during an impromptu speech, Johnson undermined his already weakening authority with a fiery assault upon the Radical Republican leaders. From that point forward, moderate Republicans deserted a president who had opened himself to counterattack. The Radical Republicans took the offensive. Johnson was "an alien enemy of a foreign state," Stevens declared. Sumner called him "an insolent drunken brute," a charge Johnson was open to because of his behavior at the 1865 inauguration.

In mid-March 1866 the Radical-led Congress passed the Civil Rights Act. A response to the black codes and the neo-slavery system created by unrepentant southern state legislatures, it declared that "all persons born in the United States and not subject to any foreign power, excluding Indians not taxed," were citizens entitled to "full and equal benefit of all laws." The granting of citizenship to native-born blacks, Johnson fumed, exceeded the scope of federal power. It would, moreover, "foment discord among the races." Johnson vetoed the bill, but this time, on April 9, Congress overrode the presidential veto. On July 16 it enacted a revised Freedmen's Bureau Bill, again overriding a veto. From that point on, Johnson steadily lost both public and political support.

THE FOURTEENTH AMENDMENT   To remove all doubt about the constitutionality of the new Civil Rights Act, the joint committee recommended a new constitutional amendment, which passed Congress on June 16, 1866, and was ratified by the states on July 28, 1868. The Fourteenth Amendment went far beyond the Civil Rights Act, however. It reaffirms the state and federal citizenship of persons born or naturalized in the United States,

and it forbids any state (the word *state* would be important in later litiga-
tion) to "abridge the privileges or immunities of citizens," to deprive any
person (again an important term) "of life, liberty, or property, without due
process of law," or to "deny any person . . . the equal protection of the
laws." These three clauses have been the subject of many lawsuits, resulting
in applications not widely, if at all, foreseen at the time. The "due-process
clause" has come to mean that state as well as federal power is subject to the
Bill of Rights, and it has been used to protect corporations, as legal "persons," from "unreasonable" regulation by the states. Other provisions of the
amendment have had less far-reaching effects. One section specified that
the debt of the United States "shall not be questioned" by the former Confederate states and declared "illegal and void" all debts contracted in aid of
the rebellion.

Johnson's home state was among the first to ratify the Fourteenth Amendment. In Tennessee, which had more Unionists than any other Confederate
state, the government had fallen under Radical Republican control. The
state's governor, in reporting the results to the secretary of the Senate, added,
"Give my respects to the dead dog of the White House." His words illustrate
the growing acrimony on both sides of the Reconstruction debates. In May
and July, race riots in Memphis and New Orleans added fuel to the flames.
Both incidents involved indiscriminate massacres of blacks by local police
and white mobs. The carnage, Radical Republicans argued, was the natural
fruit of Andrew Johnson's lenient policy. "Witness Memphis, witness New
Orleans," Senator Sumner cried. "Who can doubt that the President is the
author of these tragedies?"

RECONSTRUCTING THE SOUTH

THE TRIUMPH OF CONGRESSIONAL RECONSTRUCTION   As
1866 drew to an end, the congressional elections promised to be a referendum on the growing split between Andrew Johnson and the Radical Republicans. To win votes, Johnson went on a speaking tour of the Midwest, which
turned into an undignified shouting contest between the president and his
critics. In Cleveland he described the Radical Republicans as "factious, domineering, tyrannical" men, and he foolishly exchanged hot-tempered insults
with a heckler. At another stop, while Johnson was speaking from the back
of a railway car, the engineer mistakenly pulled the train out of the station,
making the president appear quite the fool. Such incidents tended to confirm
his image as a "ludicrous boor" and a "drunken imbecile," which Radical

Republicans promoted. The 1866 congressional elections were a devastating defeat for Johnson; Republicans won more than a two-thirds majority in each house, a comfortable margin with which to override presidential vetoes.

Congress in fact enacted a new program even before the new members took office. Two acts passed in 1867 extended voting rights to African Americans in the District of Columbia and the territories. Another law provided that the new Congress would convene on March 4 instead of the following December, depriving Johnson of a breathing spell. On March 2, 1867, two days before the old Congress expired, it passed, over Johnson's vetoes, three laws promoting congressional Reconstruction: the Military Reconstruction Act, the Command of the Army Act (an amendment to an army appropriation), and the Tenure of Office Act.

The first of the three acts prescribed conditions under which the formation of southern state governments should begin all over again. The other two sought to block any effort by the president to obstruct the process. The Command of the Army Act required that all orders from the commander in chief go through the headquarters of the general of the army, then Ulysses Grant. The Radical Republicans trusted Grant, who was already leaning their way. The Tenure of Office Act required Senate permission for the president to remove any federal officeholder whose appointment the Senate had confirmed. The purpose of at least some congressmen was to retain Secretary of War Edwin Stanton, the one Radical Republican sympathizer in Johnson's cabinet. But an ambiguity had crept into the wording of the act. Cabinet officers, it said, should serve during the term of the president who appointed them—and Lincoln had appointed Stanton, although, to be sure, Johnson was serving out Lincoln's term.

The Military Reconstruction Act was hailed—or denounced—as the triumphant victory of Radical Reconstruction. The act declared that "no legal state governments or adequate protection for life and property now exists in the rebel States." One state, Tennessee, which had ratified the Fourteenth Amendment, was exempted from the application of the new act. The other ten southern states were divided into five military districts, and the commanding officer of each was authorized to keep order and protect the "rights of persons and property." The Johnson governments remained intact for the time being, but new constitutions were to be framed "in conformity with the Constitution of the United States," in state conventions elected by male citizens aged twenty-one and older "of whatever race, color, or previous condition." Each state constitution had to provide the same universal male suffrage. Then, once the constitution was ratified by a majority of voters and accepted by Congress, other criteria had to be met. The new state legislature had to ratify the Fourteenth Amendment, and once the amendment became part of the Constitution, any given state would be entitled to representation in Congress. Persons excluded from officeholding by the proposed amendment were also excluded from participation in the process.

Johnson reluctantly appointed military commanders under the new act, but the situation remained uncertain for a time. Some people expected the Supreme Court to strike down the act, and no process existed for the new elections. Congress quickly remedied that on March 23, 1867, with the Second Reconstruction Act, which directed the army commanders to register all adult men who swore they were qualified. A Third Reconstruction Act, passed on July 19, directed registrars to go beyond the loyalty oath and determine each person's eligibility to take it and authorized district army commanders to remove and replace officeholders of any existing "so-called state" or division thereof. Before the end of 1867, new elections had been held in all the states but Texas.

Having clipped the president's wings, the Republican Congress moved a year later to safeguard its Reconstruction program from possible interference by the Supreme Court. On March 27, 1868, Congress simply removed the power of the Supreme Court to review cases arising under the Military Reconstruction Act, which Congress clearly had the right to do under its power to define the Court's appellate jurisdiction. The Court accepted this curtailment of its authority on the same day it affirmed the principle of an "indestructible Union" in *Texas v. White* (1869). In that case the Court also asserted the right of Congress to reframe state governments, thus endorsing the Radical Republican point of view.

THE IMPEACHMENT AND TRIAL OF JOHNSON   By 1868, Radical Republicans were convinced not only that the power of the Supreme Court and the president needed to be curtailed but also that Andrew Johnson himself had to be removed from office. Johnson, though hostile to the congressional Reconstruction program, had gone through the motions required of him. He continued to pardon former Confederates, however, and transferred several of the district military commanders who had displayed Radical sympathies. Johnson lacked Lincoln's resilience and pragmatism and allowed his temper to get the better of his judgment. He castigated the Radical Republicans as "a gang of cormorants and bloodsuckers who have been fattening upon the country."

The Republicans unsuccessfully tried to impeach Johnson early in 1867, alleging a variety of flimsy charges, none of which represented an indictable crime. Then Johnson himself provided the occasion for impeachment when

he deliberately violated the Tenure of Office Act in order to test its constitutionality. Secretary of War Edwin Stanton had become a thorn in Johnson's
side, refusing to resign despite his disagreements with the president's Reconstruction policy. On August 12, 1867, during a congressional recess, Johnson
suspended Stanton and named General Ulysses S. Grant in his place. When
the Senate refused to confirm Johnson's action, however, Grant returned the
office to Stanton.

The Radical Republicans now saw their chance to remove the president.
On February 24, 1868, the Republican-dominated House passed eleven articles of impeachment by a party-line vote of 126 to 47. Of the eleven articles,
eight focused on the charge that Johnson had unlawfully removed Secretary
of War Stanton. Article 9 accused the president of issuing orders in violation
of the Command of the Army Act. The last two articles of impeachment in
effect claimed that the president had undermined Congress by "inflammatory and scandalous harangues." Article 11 also accused him of "unlawfully
devising and contriving" to violate the Reconstruction Acts, contrary to his
obligation to execute the laws. At the very least, it stated, Johnson had tried to
obstruct Congress's will while observing the letter of the law.

The trial of Andrew Johnson

House of Representatives managers of the impeachment proceedings. Among
them were Benjamin Franklin Butler (Republican of Massachusetts, seated left)
and Thaddeus Stevens (Republican of Pennsylvania, seated with cane).

The Senate trial began on March 5, 1868, and continued until May 26, with Chief Justice Salmon P. Chase presiding. It was a great spectacle before a packed gallery. As the five-week trial ended and the voting began in May 1868, seven moderate Republicans and all twelve Democrats voted to acquit. The final tally was 35 to 19 for conviction, only one vote short of the two thirds needed for removal from office. Although the Senate failed to remove Johnson, the trial crippled his already weakened presidency. During the remaining ten months of his term, he initiated no other clashes with Congress. In 1868, Johnson sought the Democratic presidential nomination but lost to New York governor Horatio Seymour, who then lost to the Republican, Ulysses Grant, in the general election. The impeachment of Johnson was in the end a great political mistake, for the failure to remove the president damaged Radical Republican morale and support. Nevertheless, the Radical cause did gain something: to stave off impeachment, Johnson agreed not to obstruct the process of Reconstruction. Thereafter Radical Reconstruction began in earnest.

REPUBLICAN RULE IN THE SOUTH In June 1868, Congress agreed that seven southern states, all but Virginia, Mississippi, and Texas, had met the more stringent conditions for readmission to the Union. Congress rescinded Georgia's admission, however, when the state legislature expelled twenty-eight African American members and seated former Confederate leaders. The federal military commander in Georgia then forced the legislature to reseat the black members and remove the Confederates, and the state was compelled to ratify the Fifteenth Amendment before being admitted in July 1870. Mississippi, Texas, and Virginia had returned earlier in 1870, under the added requirement that they, too, ratify the Fifteenth Amendment. That amendment, submitted to the states in 1869 and ratified in 1870, forbids the states to deny any person the vote on grounds of "race, color, or previous condition of servitude."

Long before the new governments were established, Republican groups had begun to spring up in the South, chiefly sponsored by the Union League, founded in Philadelphia in 1862 to promote support for the Union. League recruiters in the South enrolled African Americans and loyal whites, initiated them into the secrets and rituals of the order, and instructed them "in their rights and duties." Their recruiting efforts were so successful that in 1867, on the eve of South Carolina's choice of convention delegates, the league reported eighty-eight chapters, which claimed to have enrolled almost every adult black male in the state.

The Reconstructed South

THE FREED SLAVES   African Americans in the postwar South were active agents in affecting the course of Reconstruction. It was not an easy road, though. Many former Confederates displayed deeply ingrained racial prejudices. During the era of Reconstruction, whites used terror, intimidation, and violence to suppress black efforts to gain social and economic equality. In July 1866, for instance, a black woman in Clinch County, Georgia, was arrested and given sixty-five lashes for "using abusive language" during an encounter with a white woman. The Civil War had brought freedom to enslaved African Americans, but it did not bring them protection against exploitation or abuse.

Participation in the Union army or navy had provided many freedmen with training in leadership. Black military veterans would form the core of the first generation of African American political leaders in the postwar South. Military service provided many former slaves with the first opportunities to learn to read and write. Army life also alerted them to new opportunities for economic advancement, social respectability, and civic leadership. Fighting for the Union cause also instilled a fervent sense of nationalism. A Virginia freedman explained that the United States was "now *our* country— made emphatically so by the blood of our brethren."

Former slaves established churches after the war, which quickly formed the foundation of African American community life. Blacks preferred the Baptist denomination, in part because its decentralized structure allowed each congregation to worship in its own way. By 1890 over 1.3 million African Americans in the South had become Baptists, nearly three times as many as had joined any other black denomination. In addition to forming viable new congregations, freed African Americans organized thousands of fraternal, benevolent, and mutual-aid societies, as well as clubs, lodges, and associations. Memphis, for example, had over 200 such organizations; Richmond boasted twice that number.

Freed slaves also hastened to reestablish their families. Marriages that had been prohibited during slavery were now legitimized through the assistance of the Freedmen's Bureau. By 1870 a preponderant majority of former slaves were living in two-parent households. With little money or technical training, freed slaves faced the prospect of becoming wage laborers. Yet many husbands and wives instead chose sharecropping, in which the crop produced was divided between the tenant and the landowner. This choice enabled mothers and wives to devote more of their time to domestic duties while contributing to the family's income.

The First African Church

On the eve of its move to a new building, the First African Church of Richmond, Virginia, was featured in a short article, including illustrations such as the one above, in *Harper's Weekly*, in June 1874.

African American communities in the postwar South also sought to establish schools. The antebellum planter elite had denied education to blacks because they feared that literate slaves would read abolitionist literature and organize uprisings. After the war the white elite worried that formal education would encourage poor whites and poor blacks to leave the South in search of better social and economic opportunities. Economic leaders wanted to protect the competitive advantage afforded by the region's low-wage labor market. "They didn't want us to learn nothin'," one former slave recalled. "The only thing we had to learn was how to work." White opposition to education for blacks made education all the more important to African Americans. South Carolina's Mary McLeod Bethune, the fifteenth child of former slaves, reveled in the opportunity to gain an education: "The whole world opened to me when I learned to read." She walked five miles to school as a child, earned a scholarship to college, and went on to become the first black woman to found a school that became a four-year college, Bethune-Cookman, in Daytona Beach, Florida. African American churches and individuals helped raise the money and often built the schools and paid the teachers. Soldiers who had acquired some literacy skills often served as the teachers, and the students included adults as well as children.

AFRICAN AMERICANS IN SOUTHERN POLITICS   In the post-war South the new role of African Americans in politics caused the most controversy. If largely illiterate and inexperienced in the rudiments of politics, southern blacks were little different from the millions of newly enfranchized propertyless whites in the age of Andrew Jackson's political reforms or immigrants in postwar cities. Some freedmen frankly confessed their disadvantages. Beverly Nash, an African American delegate to the South Carolina convention of 1868, told his colleagues: "I believe, my friends and fellow-citizens, we are not prepared for this suffrage. But we can learn. Give a man tools and let him commence to use them, and in time he will learn a trade. So it is with voting."

Several hundred African American delegates participated in the statewide political conventions. Most had been selected by local political meetings or churches, fraternal societies, Union Leagues, or black army units from the North, although a few simply appointed themselves. The African American delegates "ranged all colors and apparently all conditions," but free mulattoes from the cities played the most prominent roles. At Louisiana's Republican

Freedmen voting in New Orleans

The Fifteenth Amendment, ratified in 1870, guaranteed at the federal level the right of citizens to vote regardless of "race, color, or previous condition of servitude." But former slaves had been registering to vote—and voting in large numbers—in state elections since 1867, as in this scene.

state convention, for instance, nineteen of the twenty black delegates had been born free.

By 1867, however, former slaves had begun to gain political influence and vote in large numbers, and this development revealed emerging tensions within the African American community. Some southern blacks resented the presence of northern brethren who moved south after the war, while others complained that few ex-slaves were represented in leadership positions. Northern blacks and the southern free black elite, most of whom were urban dwellers, often opposed efforts to redistribute land to the rural freedmen, and many insisted that political equality did not mean social equality. As a black Alabama leader stressed, "We do not ask that the ignorant and degraded shall be put on a social equality with the refined and intelligent." In general, however, unity rather than dissension prevailed, and African Americans focused on common concerns such as full equality under the law.

Brought suddenly into politics in times that tried the most skilled of statesmen, many African Americans served with distinction. Nonetheless, the derisive label "black Reconstruction," used by later critics, exaggerates

African American political figures of Reconstruction

Blanche K. Bruce (left) and Hiram Revels (right) served in the U.S. Senate. Frederick Douglass (center) was a major figure in the abolitionist movement.

African American political influence, which was limited mainly to voting. Such criticism also overlooks the political clout of the large number of white Republicans, especially in the mountain areas of the Upper South, who also favored the Radical plan for Reconstruction. Only one of the new state conventions, South Carolina's, had a black majority, seventy-six to forty-one. Louisiana's was evenly divided racially, and in only two other conventions were more than 20 percent of the members black: Florida's, with 40 percent, and Virginia's, with 24 percent. The Texas convention was only 10 percent black, and North Carolina's was 11 percent—but that did not stop a white newspaper from calling it a body consisting of "baboons, monkeys, mules . . . and other jackasses."

In the new state governments any African American participation was a novelty. Although some 600 blacks—most of them former slaves—served as state legislators, no black man was ever elected governor, and only a few served as judges. In Louisiana, however, Pinckney Pinchback, a northern black and former Union soldier, won the office of lieutenant governor and served as acting governor when the white governor was indicted for corruption. Several African Americans were elected lieutenant governor, state treasurer, or secretary of state. There were two black senators in Congress, Hiram Revels and Blanche K. Bruce, both Mississippi natives who had been educated in the North, and fourteen black members of the House of Representatives during Reconstruction.

CARPETBAGGERS AND SCALAWAGS   The top positions in postwar southern state governments went for the most part to white Republicans, whom the opposition whites labeled carpetbaggers and scalawags, depending upon their place of birth. Northerners who allegedly rushed South with all their belongings in carpetbags to grab the political spoils were more often than not Union veterans who had arrived as early as 1865 or 1866, drawn South by the hope of economic opportunity and other attractions that many of them had seen in their Union service. Many other so-called carpetbaggers were teachers, social workers, or preachers animated by a sincere missionary impulse.

The scalawags, or native white Republicans, were even more reviled and misrepresented. A Nashville newspaper editor called them the "merest trash." Most scalawags had opposed secession, forming a Unionist majority in many mountain counties as far south as Georgia and Alabama and especially in the hills of eastern Tennessee. Among the scalawags were several distinguished figures, including the former Confederate general James Longstreet, who decided after Appomattox that the Old South must change its ways. He became a successful cotton broker in New Orleans, joined the Republican party, and supported the Radical Reconstruction program. Other scalawags were former Whigs attracted by the Republican party's economic program of industrial and commercial expansion.

THE RADICAL REPUBLICAN RECORD Former Confederates resented the new state constitutions because of their provisions allowing for black voting and civil rights. Yet most of those constitutions remained in effect for some years after the end of Radical Republican control, and later constitutions incorporated many of their features. Conspicuous among the Radical innovations were such steps toward greater democracy as requiring

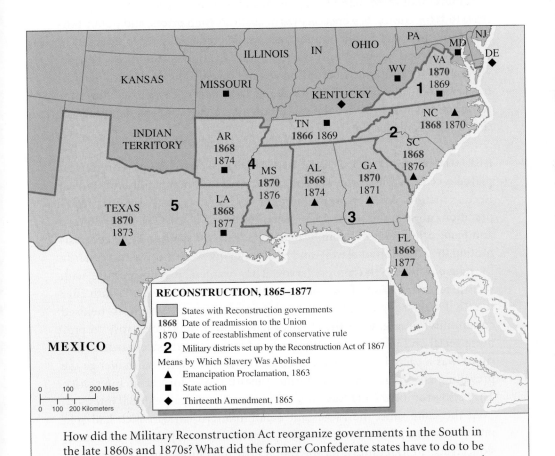

RECONSTRUCTION, 1865–1877

	States with Reconstruction governments
1868	Date of readmission to the Union
1870	Date of reestablishment of conservative rule
2	Military districts set up by the Reconstruction Act of 1867

Means by Which Slavery Was Abolished
- ▲ Emancipation Proclamation, 1863
- ■ State action
- ◆ Thirteenth Amendment, 1865

How did the Military Reconstruction Act reorganize governments in the South in the late 1860s and 1870s? What did the former Confederate states have to do to be readmitted to the Union? Why did "Conservative" parties gradually regain control of the South from the Republicans in the 1870s?

universal manhood suffrage, reapportioning legislatures more nearly according to population, and making more state offices elective.

Given the hostile circumstances under which the Radical governments operated, their achievements were remarkable. They constructed an extensive railroad network and established state-supported public school systems. Some 600,000 black pupils were enrolled in southern schools by 1877. State governments under the Radicals also gave more attention to the poor and to orphanages, asylums, and institutions for the deaf and the blind of both races. Public roads, bridges, and buildings were repaired or rebuilt. African Americans achieved rights and opportunities that would never again be taken away, at least in principle: equality before the law and the rights to own property, carry on business, enter professions, attend schools, and learn to read and write.

Yet several of these Republican state regimes also engaged in corrupt practices. Bids for contracts were accepted at absurdly high prices, and public officials took their cut. Public money and public credit were often awarded to privately owned corporations, notably railroads, under conditions that invited influence peddling. Corruption was not invented by the Radical Republican regimes, nor did it die with them. Louisiana's "carpetbag" governor recognized as much. "Why," he said, "down here everybody is demoralized. Corruption is the fashion."

RELIGION AND RECONSTRUCTION The religious community played a critical role in the implementation and ultimate failure of Radical Reconstruction. And religious commentators offered quite different interpretations of what should be done with the defeated South. Thaddeus Stevens and many other Radical Republican leaders who had spent their careers promoting the abolition of slavery and racial equality were motivated primarily by religious ideals and moral fervor. They wanted no compromise with racism. Likewise, most of the Christian missionaries who headed south after the Civil War brought with them a progressive vision of a biracial "beloved community" emerging in the reconstructed South, and they strove to promote social and political equality for freed slaves. For these crusaders, civil rights was a sacred cause. They used Christian principles to challenge the prevailing theological and "scientific" justifications for racial inferiority. They also promoted Christian solidarity across racial and regional lines.

At the same time, the Protestant denominations, all of which had split into northern and southern branches over the issues of slavery and secession, struggled to reunite after the war. A growing number of northern ministers promoted reconciliation between the warring regions after the Civil War. These "apostles of forgiveness" prized white unity over racial equality.

For example, the Reverend Henry Ward Beecher, the powerful New York minister whose sister Harriet Beecher Stowe wrote *Uncle Tom's Cabin*, wanted white southern planters—rather than federal officials or African Americans themselves—to oversee Reconstruction. Not surprisingly, Beecher's views gained widespread support among evangelical ministers in the South.

The collapse of the Confederacy did not prompt southern whites to abandon their belief that God was on their side. In the wake of defeat and emancipation, white southern ministers reassured their congregations that they had no reason to question the moral foundations of their region or their defense of white racial superiority. For African Americans, the Civil War and emancipation demonstrated

The "white republic"

This cartoon illustrates white unity over racial equality.

that God was on their side. Emancipation was in their view a redemptive act through which God wrought national regeneration. African American ministers were convinced that the United States was indeed a divinely inspired nation and that blacks had a providential role to play in its future. Yet neither black nor idealistic white northern ministers could stem the growing chorus of whites who were willing to abandon goals of racial equality in exchange for national religious reconciliation. By the end of the nineteenth century, mainstream American Protestantism promoted the image of a "white republic" that conflated whiteness, godliness, and nationalism.

THE GRANT YEARS

THE ELECTION OF 1868 Ulysses S. Grant, who presided during the collapse of Republican rule in the South, brought to the White House little political experience. But in 1868 northern voters supported the Lion of Vicksburg because of his record as the Union army commander. He was the most popular man in the nation. Both parties wooed him, but his falling-out with President Johnson had pushed him toward the Republicans. They were,

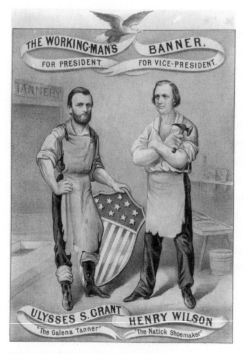

"The Working-Man's Banner"

This campaign banner makes reference to the working-class origins of Ulysses S. Grant and his vice-presidential candidate, Henry Wilson, by depicting Grant as a tanner and Wilson as a shoemaker.

as Thaddeus Stevens said, ready to "let him into the church."

The Republican party platform of 1868 endorsed congressional Reconstruction. One plank cautiously defended black suffrage as a necessity in the South but a matter each northern state should settle for itself. Another urged payment of the national debt "in the utmost good faith to all creditors," which meant in gold. More important than the platform were the great expectations of a soldier-president and his slogan, "Let us have peace."

The Democrats took opposite positions on both Reconstruction and the debt. The Republican Congress, the Democratic party platform charged, instead of restoring the Union had "so far as in its power, dissolved it, and subjected ten states, in the time of profound peace, to military despotism and Negro supremacy." As for the federal debt, the party endorsed Representative George H. Pendleton's "Ohio idea" that, since most war bonds had been bought with depreciated greenbacks, they should be paid off in greenbacks rather than in gold. With no conspicuously available candidate in sight, the Democratic Convention turned to Horatio Seymour, wartime governor of New York. Seymour neither sought nor embraced the nomination, leading opponents to call him the Great Decliner. Yet the Democrats made a closer race of it than the electoral vote revealed. While Grant swept the Electoral College by 214 to 80, his popular majority was only 307,000 out of a total of over 5.7 million votes. More than 500,000 African American voters accounted for Grant's margin of victory.

Grant had proved himself a great military leader, but as the youngest president ever (forty-six years old at the time of his inauguration), he was often blind to the political forces and influence peddlers around him. He was awestruck by men of wealth and unaccountably loyal to some who betrayed his trust, and he passively followed the lead of Congress. This approach at first endeared him to Republican party leaders, but at last it left him ineffective and others disillusioned with his leadership.

At the outset, Grant consulted nobody on his seven cabinet appointments. Some of his choices indulged personal whims; others simply displayed bad judgment. In some cases, appointees learned of their nomination from the newspapers. As time went by, Grant betrayed a fatal gift for losing men of talent and integrity from his cabinet. Secretary of State Hamilton Fish of New York turned out to be a happy exception; he guided foreign policy throughout the Grant presidency. Other than Fish, however, the Grant cabinet overflowed with incompetents.

THE GOVERNMENT DEBT   Financial issues dominated Grant's presidency. After the war the Treasury had assumed that the $432 million worth of greenbacks issued during the conflict would be retired from circulation and that the nation would revert to a "hard-money" currency—gold coins. Many agrarian and debtor groups resisted any contraction of the money supply resulting from the elimination of greenbacks, believing that it would mean lower prices for their crops and more difficulty repaying long-term debts. They were joined by a large number of Radical Republicans who thought that a combination of high tariffs and inflation would generate more rapid economic growth. As Senator John Sherman explained, "I prefer gold to paper money. But there is no other resort. We must have money or a fractured government." In 1868 congressional supporters of such a "soft-money" policy halted the retirement of greenbacks. There matters stood when Grant took office.

The "sound-money" (or hard-money) advocates, mostly bankers and merchants, claimed that Grant's election was a mandate to save the country from the Democrats' "Ohio idea" of using greenbacks to repay government bonds. Quite influential in Republican circles, the hard-money advocates also reflected the deeply ingrained popular assumption that gold coins were morally preferable to paper currency. Grant agreed as well, and in his inaugural address he endorsed payment of the national debt in gold as a point of national honor. On March 18, 1869, the Public Credit Act, which endorsed that principle, became the first act of Congress that Grant signed. The following year, under the Refunding Act of 1870, the Treasury was able to replace 6 percent Civil War bonds with a new bond issue promising purchasers a return of 4 to 5 percent in gold.

SCANDALS   The complexities of the "money question" exasperated Grant, but that was the least of his worries, for his administration soon fell into a cesspool of scandal. In the summer of 1869, two unscrupulous financial buccaneers, Jay Gould and James Fisk, connived with the president's brother-in-law to corner the nation's gold market. That is, they would create a public craze for gold by purchasing massive quantities of the precious yellow metal and convincing traders and the general public that the price would keep climbing. As more buyers joined the frenzy, the value of gold would soar. The only danger to the scheme lay in the federal Treasury's selling large amounts of gold, which would deflate its value.

Grant apparently smelled a rat from the start, but he was seen in public with the speculators. As the rumor spread on Wall Street that the president had bought the argument, gold rose from $132 to $163 an ounce. Finally, on Black Friday, September 24, 1869, Grant ordered the Treasury to sell a large quantity of gold, and the bubble burst. Fisk got out by repudiating his agreements and hiring thugs to intimidate his creditors. "Nothing is lost save honor," he said.

The plot to corner the gold market was only the first of several scandals that rocked the Grant administration. During the campaign of 1872, the public learned about the financial crookery of the Crédit Mobilier, a sham construction company composed of directors of the Union Pacific Railroad who had milked the Union Pacific for exorbitant fees in order to line the pockets of the insiders who controlled both firms. Union Pacific shareholders were left holding the bag. The schemers bought political support by giving congressmen stock in the enterprise. This chicanery had transpired before Grant's election in 1868, but it now touched a number of prominent Republicans. The beneficiaries included Speaker of the House Schuyler Colfax, later vice president, and Representative James A. Garfield, later president. Of the thirteen members of Congress involved, only two were censured.

Even more odious disclosures soon followed, some involving the president's cabinet. The secretary of war, it turned out, had accepted bribes from merchants who traded with Indians at army posts in the West. He was impeached, but he resigned in time to elude a Senate trial. Post-office contracts, it was revealed, went to carriers who offered the highest kickbacks. The secretary of the Treasury had awarded a political friend a commission of 50 percent for the collection of overdue taxes. In St. Louis a "whiskey ring" bribed tax collectors to bilk the government out of millions of dollars in revenue. Grant's private secretary was enmeshed in that scheme, taking large sums of money and other valuables in return for inside information. There is no evidence that Grant himself was ever involved in, or personally profited from, any of the fraud, but his poor choice of associates and his gullibility earned him widespread criticism.

"Worse Than Slavery"

This Thomas Nast cartoon chides the Ku Klux Klan and the White League for promoting conditions "worse than slavery" for southern blacks after the Civil War.

WHITE TERROR President Grant initially fought hard to enforce the federal efforts to reconstruct the postwar South. By the time he became president, southern resistance to "Radical rule" had turned violent. In Grayson County, Texas, three whites murdered three former slaves because they felt the need to "thin the niggers out and drive them to their holes."

The prototype of all the terrorist groups was the Ku Klux Klan (KKK), organized in 1866 by some young men of Pulaski, Tennessee, as a social club, with the costumes and secret rituals common to fraternal groups. At first a group of pranksters, its members soon turned to intimidation of blacks and white Republicans. The KKK and its imitators, like Louisiana's Knights of the White Camelia, spread rapidly across the South in answer to the Republican party's Union League. Klansmen rode about the countryside, hiding behind masks and under robes, spreading horrendous rumors, issuing threats, harassing African Americans, and occasionally wreaking violence and destruction. "We are going to kill all the Negros," a white supremacist declared during one massacre.

Klansmen focused their terror on prominent Republicans, black and white. Racial violence was widespread and horrific. In Mississippi they killed a black Republican leader in front of his family. Three white "scalawag" Republicans were murdered in Georgia in 1870. That same year an armed mob of whites assaulted a Republican political rally in Alabama, killing four blacks and wounding fifty-four. In South Carolina white supremacists were especially active—and violent. Virtually the entire white male population of York County joined the Klan, and they were responsible for eleven murders and hundreds of whippings. In 1871 some 500 masked men laid siege to the Union County jail and eventually lynched eight black prisoners.

At the urging of President Grant, who showed true moral courage in trying to protect the former slaves, Congress struck back with three Enforcement Acts (1870–1871) to protect black voters. The first of these measures levied penalties on anyone who interfered with any citizen's right to vote. A second placed the election of congressmen under surveillance by federal election supervisors and marshals. The third (the Ku Klux Klan Act) outlawed the characteristic activities of the Klan—forming conspiracies, wearing disguises, resisting officers, and intimidating officials—and authorized the president to suspend habeas corpus where necessary to suppress "armed combinations." In 1871 the federal government singled out nine counties in up-country South Carolina as an example, suspended habeas corpus, and pursued mass prosecutions. In general, however, the Enforcement Acts suffered from weak and inconsistent execution. As time passed, President Grant vacillated between clamping down on the Klan and capitulating to racial intimidation. The strong tradition of states' rights and local autonomy in the South, as well as racial prejudice, resisted federal force. The unrelenting efforts of white racists to use violence to thwart Reconstruction continued into the 1870s. On Easter Sunday in 1873 in Colfax, Louisiana, a mob of white vigilantes attacked a group of black Republicans, slaughtering eighty-one. White southerners had lost the war, but during the 1870s they were winning the peace with their reactionary behavior. In the process, the goals of racial justice and civil rights were blunted.

REFORM AND THE ELECTION OF 1872 Long before President Grant's first term ended, a reaction to Radical Reconstruction and incompetence and corruption in the administration had incited mutiny within the Republican ranks. A new faction, called Liberal Republicans, favored free trade, the redemption of greenbacks with gold, a stable currency, an end to federal Reconstruction efforts in the South, the restoration of the rights of former Confederates, and civil service reform. In 1872 the Liberal Republicans held their own national convention, in which they produced a compromise platform condemning the Republicans' Reconstruction policy and favoring civil service reform, but they remained silent on the protective tariff. The delegates embraced a quixotic presidential candidate: Horace Greeley, the prominent editor of the *New York Tribune*, a longtime champion of just about every reform available. Greeley had promoted vegetarianism, socialism, and spiritualism. His image as an eccentric was complemented by his record of hostility to the Democrats, whose support the Liberals needed. The Democrats nevertheless swallowed the pill and gave their nomination to Greeley as the only hope of beating Grant.

"What I Know about Raising the Devil"

With the tail and cloven hoof of the devil, Horace Greeley (center) leads a small band of Liberal Republicans in pursuit of incumbent president Ulysses S. Grant and his supporters in this 1872 cartoon.

The result was a foregone conclusion. Republican regulars duly endorsed Grant, Radical Reconstruction, and the protective tariff. Greeley, despite an exhausting tour of the country—still unusual for a presidential candidate—carried only six southern and border states and none in the North. Grant won by 3,598,235 votes to Greeley's 2,834,761.

CONSERVATIVE RESURGENCE   The Klan's impact on southern politics varied from state to state. In the Upper South it played only a modest role in facilitating a Democratic resurgence. But in the Deep South, Klan violence and intimidation had more substantial effects. In overwhelmingly black Yazoo County, Mississippi, vengeful whites used violence to reverse the political balance of power. In the 1873 elections the Republicans cast 2,449 votes and the Democrats 638; two years later the Democrats polled 4,049 votes, the Republicans 7. Throughout the South the activities of the Klan and other white supremacists weakened black and Republican morale, and in the North they encouraged a growing weariness with the whole "southern question." "The plain truth is," noted *The New York Herald*, "the North has got tired of the Negro."

The erosion of northern interest in civil rights resulted from more than weariness, however. Western expansion, Indian wars, new economic opportunities, and political controversy over the tariff and the currency distracted attention from southern outrages against Republican rule and black rights. In addition, after a business panic that occurred in 1873 and an ensuing depression, desperate economic circumstances in the North and the South created new racial tensions that helped undermine federal efforts to promote racial justice in the former Confederacy. Republican control in the South gradually loosened as "Conservative" parties—a name used by Democrats to mollify former Whigs—mobilized the white vote. Prewar political leaders reemerged to promote the antebellum Democratic goals of limited government, states' rights, and free trade. They politicized the race issue to excite the white electorate and intimidate black voters. The Republicans in the South became increasingly an organization limited to African Americans and federal officials. Many scalawags and carpetbaggers drifted away from the Radical Republican ranks under pressure from their white neighbors. Few of them had joined the Republicans out of concern for black rights in the first place. And where persuasion failed to work, Democrats were willing to use chicanery. As one enthusiastic Democrat boasted, "The white and black Republicans may outvote us, but we can outcount them."

Republican political control collapsed in Virginia and Tennessee as early as 1869; in Georgia and North Carolina it collapsed in 1870, although North Carolina had a Republican governor until 1876. Reconstruction lasted longest in the Deep South states with the largest black population, where whites abandoned Klan masks for barefaced intimidation in paramilitary groups such as the Mississippi Rifle Club and the South Carolina Red Shirts. By 1876, Radical Republican regimes survived only in Louisiana, South Carolina, and Florida, and those collapsed after the elections of that year.

PANIC AND REDEMPTION   Economic distress followed close upon the public scandals besetting the Grant administration. Such developments help explain why northerners lost interest in Reconstruction. A contraction of the nation's money supply resulting from the withdrawal of greenbacks and investments in new railroads helped precipitate a financial crisis. During 1873 the market for railroad bonds turned sour as some twenty-five railroads defaulted on their interest payments. The prestigious investment bank of Jay Cooke and Company went bankrupt on September 18, 1873. The ensuing stampede of investors eager to exchange securities for cash forced the stock market to close for ten days. The panic of 1873 set off a depression that lasted six years, the longest and most severe that Americans had yet suffered.

Thousands of businesses went bankrupt, millions of people lost their jobs, and as usually occurs, voters blamed the party in power for their economic woes.

Hard times and political scandals hurt Republicans in the midterm elections of 1874. The Democrats won control of the House of Representatives and gained seats in the Senate. The new Democratic House launched inquiries into the scandals and unearthed further evidence of corruption in high places. The financial panic, meanwhile, focused attention once more on greenback currency.

Since the value of greenbacks was lower than that of gold, greenbacks had become the chief circulating medium. Most people spent greenbacks first and held their gold or used it to settle foreign accounts, thereby draining much gold out of the country. The postwar reduction of greenbacks in circulation, from $432 million to $356 million, had made for tight money. To relieve the currency shortage and stimulate business expansion, the Treasury issued more greenbacks. As usually happened during economic hard times in the nineteenth century, debtors, the people hurt most by depression, called upon the federal government to inflate the money supply so as to make it easier for them to pay their obligations.

For a time the advocates of paper money were riding high. But in 1874, Grant vetoed a bill to issue more greenbacks. Then, in his annual message, he called for the redemption of greenbacks in gold, making greenbacks "good as gold" and raising their value to a par with that of the gold dollar. Congress obliged by passing the Specie Resumption Act of 1875. The payment in gold to people who turned in their paper money began on January 1, 1879, after the Treasury had built a gold reserve for that purpose and reduced the value of the greenbacks in circulation. This act infuriated those promoting an inflationary monetary policy and prompted the formation of the Greenback party, which elected fourteen congressmen in 1878. The much-debated and very complex "money question" was destined to remain one of the most divisive issues in American politics.

THE COMPROMISE OF 1877   President Grant, despite the controversies swirling around him, wanted to run again in 1876, but many Republicans balked at the prospect of the nation's first three-term president. After all, the Democrats had devastated the Republicans in the 1874 congressional elections: the decisive Republican majority in the House had evaporated, and the Democrats had taken control. In the summer of 1875, Grant acknowledged the growing opposition to his renomination and announced his retirement. James Gillespie Blaine of Maine, former Speaker of the House and one of the

The Compromise of 1877

This illustration represents the compromise between Republicans and southern Democrats that ended Radical Reconstruction.

nation's favorite orators, emerged as the Republican front-runner, but he, too, bore the taint of scandal. Letters in the possession of James Mulligan of Boston linked Blaine to dubious railroad dealings, and the "Mulligan letters" found their way into print.

The Republican Convention therefore eliminated Blaine and several other hopefuls in favor of Ohio's favorite son, Rutherford B. Hayes. Elected governor of Ohio three times, most recently as an advocate of gold rather than greenbacks, Hayes had also made a name for himself as a civil service reformer. But his chief virtue was that he offended neither Radicals nor reformers. As a journalist put it, he was "a third rate nonentity, whose only recommendation is that he is obnoxious to no one."

The Democratic Convention was abnormally harmonious from the start. The nomination went on the second ballot to Samuel J. Tilden, a millionaire corporation lawyer and reform governor of New York who had directed a campaign to overthrow the notorious Tweed ring controlling New York City politics.

The 1876 campaign generated no burning issues. Both candidates favored the trend toward relaxing federal authority and restoring white conservative rule in the South. In the absence of strong differences, Democrats aired the Republicans' dirty linen. In response, Republicans waved "the bloody shirt," which is to say that they linked the Democratic party to secession and the outrages committed against Republicans in the South. As one Republican speaker insisted, "The man that assassinated Abraham Lincoln was a Democrat. . . . Soldiers, every scar you have on your heroic bodies was given you by a Democrat!"

Early election returns pointed to a Tilden victory. Tilden enjoyed a 254,000-vote edge in the balloting and had won 184 electoral votes, just one short of a majority. Hayes had only 165 electoral votes, but the Republicans also claimed 19 doubtful votes from Florida, Louisiana, and South Carolina. The Democrats laid a counterclaim to 1 of Oregon's 3 electoral votes, but the Republicans had clearly carried that state. In the South the outcome was less certain, and given the fraud and intimidation perpetrated on both sides, nobody will ever know what might have happened if, to use a slogan of the day, "a free ballot and a fair count" had prevailed.

In all three of the disputed southern states, rival canvasing boards sent in different returns. The Constitution offered no guidance in this unprecedented situation. Finally, on January 29, 1877, the Congress decided to set up a special Electoral Commission with fifteen members, five each from the House, the Senate, and the Supreme Court. The commission's decision went by a vote of 8 to 7 along party lines, in favor of Hayes. After much bluster and the threat of a filibuster by the Democrats, the House voted on March 2 to accept the report and declared Hayes elected by an electoral vote of 185 to 184.

Critical to this outcome was the defection of southern Democrats, who had made several informal agreements with the Republicans. On February 26, 1877, prominent Ohio Republicans (including future president James A. Garfield) and powerful southern Democrats struck a secret bargain at Wormley's Hotel in Washington. The Republicans promised that if Hayes were elected, he would withdraw the last federal troops from Louisiana and South Carolina, letting the Republican governments there collapse. In return, the Democrats promised to withdraw their opposition to Hayes, accept in good faith the Reconstruction amendments (including civil rights for blacks), and refrain from partisan reprisals against Republicans in the South.

Southern Democrats could now justify deserting Tilden because this so-called Compromise of 1877 ended Radical Reconstruction and brought a return to "home rule," which actually meant rule by white Democrats. As a former slave observed in 1877, "The whole South—every state in the South—has got [back] into the hands of the very men that held us as slaves." Other, more informal promises, less noticed by the public, were made at the "Wormley Conference." Hayes's friends pledged more support for rebuilding Mississippi River

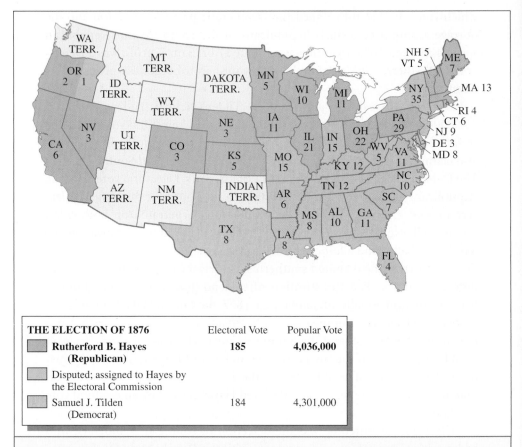

THE ELECTION OF 1876	Electoral Vote	Popular Vote
Rutherford B. Hayes (Republican)	**185**	**4,036,000**
Disputed; assigned to Hayes by the Electoral Commission		
Samuel J. Tilden (Democrat)	184	4,301,000

Why did the Republicans pick Rutherford Hayes as their presidential candidate? Why were the electoral votes of several states disputed? What was the Compromise of 1877?

levees and other internal improvements, including a federal subsidy for a transcontinental railroad along a southern route. Southerners extracted a further promise that Hayes would name a white southerner as postmaster general, the cabinet position with the most patronage jobs at hand. In return, southerners would let the Republicans make James Garfield the Speaker of the new House. Such a deal illustrates the relative weakness of the presidency compared with Congress during the postwar era.

THE END OF RECONSTRUCTION In 1877 the new president withdrew federal troops from Louisiana and South Carolina, and those states'

Republican governments collapsed soon thereafter—along with much of Hayes's claim to legitimacy. The president chose a Tennessean and former Confederate as postmaster general. But most of the other Wormley Conference promises were either renounced or forgotten. As for southern promises to protect the civil rights of African Americans, only a few Democratic leaders, such as the new governors of South Carolina and Louisiana, remembered them for long. Over the next three decades the protection of black civil rights crumbled under the pressure of restored white rule in the South and the force of Supreme Court decisions narrowing the application of the Reconstruction amendments.

Radical Reconstruction never offered more than an uncertain commitment to black civil rights and social equality. Yet it left an enduring legacy—the Thirteenth, Fourteenth, and Fifteenth Amendments—not dead but dormant, waiting to be awakened. If Reconstruction did not provide social equality or substantial economic opportunities for African Americans, it did create the foundation for future advances. It was a revolution, sighed former governor of North Carolina Jonathan Worth, and "nobody can anticipate the action of revolutions."

End of Chapter Review

- **Reconstruction** Abraham Lincoln and his successor, the southerner Andrew Johnson, wanted a lenient and quick plan for Reconstruction. Lincoln's assassination made many northerners favor the Radical Republicans, who wanted to end the grasp of the old planter class on the South's society and economy. Congressional Reconstruction included the stipulation that to reenter the Union, former Confederate states had to ratify the Fourteenth and Fifteenth Amendments. Congress also passed the Military Reconstruction Act, which attempted to protect the voting rights and civil rights of African Americans.

- **Southern Violence** Many white southerners blamed their poverty on freed slaves and Yankees. White mobs attacked blacks in 1866 in Memphis and New Orleans. That year the Ku Klux Klan was formed as a social club; its members soon began to intimidate freedmen and white Republicans. Despite government action, violence continued and even escalated in the South.

- **Freed Slaves** Newly freed slaves suffered economically. Most did not have the resources to succeed in the aftermath of the war's devastation. There was no redistribution of land; former slaves were given their freedom but nothing else. The Freedmen's Bureau attempted to educate and aid freed slaves and reunite families. Many former slaves found comfort in their families and the independent churches they established. Some took part in state and local government under the last, radical phase of Reconstruction.

- **Grant Administration** During Ulysses Grant's administration fiscal issues dominated politics. Paper money (greenbacks) was regarded as inflationary; and agrarian and debtor groups opposed its withdrawal from circulation. Many members of Grant's administration were corrupt; scandals involved an attempt to corner the gold market, construction of the intercontinental railroad, and the whiskey ring's plan to steal millions of dollars in tax revenue.

- **End of Reconstruction** Most southern states had completed the requirements of Reconstruction by 1876. The presidential election returns of that year were so close that a special commission was established to count contested electoral votes. A decision hammered out at a secret meeting gave the presidency to the Republican, Rutherford B. Hayes; in return, the Democrats were promised that the last federal troops would be withdrawn from Louisiana and South Carolina, putting an end to the Radical Republican administrations in the southern states.

CHRONOLOGY

1862	Congress passes the Morrill Land Grant Act
	Congress guarantees the construction of a transcontinental railroad
	Congress passes the Homestead Act
1864	Lincoln refuses to sign the Wade-Davis Bill
1865	Congress sets up the Freedmen's Bureau
April 14, 1865	Lincoln is assassinated
1866	Ku Klux Klan is organized
	Congress passes the Civil Rights Act
1867	Congress passes the Military Reconstruction Act
	Congress passes the Tenure of Office Act
1868	Fourteenth Amendment is ratified
	Congress impeaches President Andrew Johnson; the Senate fails to convict him
1877	Compromise of 1877 ends Reconstruction

KEY TERMS & NAMES

Part Five

GROWING

PAINS

The Federal victory in 1865 restored the Union and in the process helped accelerate America's transformation into a modern nation-state. A distinctly national consciousness began to displace the sectional emphases of the antebellum era. During and after the Civil War the Republican-led Congress pushed through legislation to foster industrial and commercial development and western expansion. In the process the United States abandoned the Jeffersonian dream of a decentralized agrarian republic and began to forge a dynamic new industrial economy nurtured by an increasingly national and even international market.

After 1865 many Americans turned their attention to the unfinished business of settling a continent and completing an urban-industrial revolution begun before the war. Huge corporations based upon mass production and mass marketing began to dominate the economy. As the prominent social theorist William Graham Sumner remarked, the process of industrial development "controls us all because we are all in it. It creates the conditions of our own existence, sets the limits of our social activity, and regulates the bonds of our social relations."

The Industrial Revolution was not only an urban phenomenon; it transformed rural life as well. Those who got in the way of the new emphasis on large-scale, highly mechanized commercial agriculture and ranching were brusquely pushed aside. Farm folk, as one New Englander stressed, "must understand farming as a business; if they do not it will go hard with them." The friction between new market forces and traditional folkways generated political revolts and social unrest during the last quarter of the nineteenth century. Fault lines appeared throughout the social order, and they unleashed tremors that exerted what one writer called "a seismic shock, a cyclonic violence" upon the body politic.

The clash between tradition and modernity peaked during the 1890s, one of the most strife-ridden decades in American history. A deep depression, agrarian unrest, and labor violence unleashed fears of class warfare. This turbulent situation transformed the presidential-election campaign of 1896 into a clash between rival visions of America's future. The Republican candidate, William McKinley, campaigned on behalf of modern urban-industrial values. By contrast, William Jennings Bryan, the nominee of the Democratic and Populist parties, was an eloquent defender of America's rural past. McKinley's victory proved to be a watershed in American political and social history. By 1900 the United States would emerge as one of the world's greatest industrial powers, and it would thereafter assume a new leadership role in world affairs.

19

THE SOUTH AND THE WEST TRANSFORMED

FOCUS QUESTIONS

 wwnorton.com/studyspace

- How did life in the South change for blacks and whites politically, economically, and socially after the Civil War?
- What happened to Native Americans as whites settled the West?
- What were the experiences of farmers, cowboys, and miners in the West?
- How did mining affect the development of the West?
- How important was the concept of the frontier to America's political and diplomatic development?

After the Civil War the South and the West provided enticing opportunities for American inventiveness and entrepreneurship. The two regions were ripe for development. The devastated South had to be rebuilt; the trans-Mississippi West beckoned entrepreneurs and farmers. In both cases, undeveloped regions would prove to be fertile catalysts for urbanization and industrialization. This was particularly true of the West, where before 1860 most Americans had viewed the region between the Mississippi River and California as a barren landscape unfit for human habitation or cultivation, an uninviting land suitable only for Indians and animals. Half the state of Texas, for instance, was still not settled at the end of the Civil War. After 1865, however, the federal government encouraged western settlement and economic exploitation. The construction of transcontinental railroads, the military conquest of the Indians, and a liberal land-distribution policy combined to help lure thousands of pioneers and expectant capitalists westward. Charles Goodnight, a Texas cattleman, recalled that "we were adventurers in a great land as fresh and full of the zest of darers."

Although the first great wave of railroad building occurred in the 1850s, the most spectacular growth took place during the quarter century after the Civil War. From about 35,000 miles of track in 1865, the national rail network grew to nearly 200,000 miles by 1897. The transcontinental rail lines led the way, and they helped populate the plains and the Far West. Of course, such a sprawling railroad system was expensive, and the long-term debt required to finance it would become a major cause of the financial panic of 1893 and the ensuing depression.

In the postwar South, rail lines were rebuilt and supplemented with new branch lines. The former Confederacy was ripe for investment and industrial development. After 1865, proponents of a "New South" argued that the region must abandon its single-minded preoccupation with agriculture and pursue industrial and commercial development. As a result, the South also experienced dramatic social and economic changes during the last third of the nineteenth century. By 1900 the South and the West had been transformed in ways that few could have predicted, and twelve new states were created out of the western territories.

The New South

A FRESH VISION   Amid the pains of defeat and the ruins of war, many southerners looked wistfully to the plantation life that had dominated their region before the firing on Fort Sumter in 1861. A few prominent leaders, however, insisted that the postwar South must liberate itself from nostalgia and create a modern society of small farms, thriving industries, and bustling cities. The major prophet of this New South during the 1880s was Henry W. Grady, editor of the *Atlanta Constitution*. "The Old South," he said, "rested everything on slavery and agriculture, unconscious that these could neither give nor maintain healthy growth." The New South, on the other hand, "presents a perfect democracy" of small farms and diversifying industries. The postwar South, Grady believed, held the promise of a real democracy, one no longer run by the planter aristocracy and no longer dependent upon slave labor.

Henry Grady's compelling vision of a New South attracted many supporters, who preached with evangelical fervor the gospel of industrial development.

The Confederacy, they reasoned, had lost the war because it had relied too much upon King Cotton. In the future the South must follow the North's example and industrialize. From that central belief flowed certain corollaries: that a more diversified, efficient agriculture would be a foundation for economic growth, that more widespread education, especially vocational training, would promote material success, and that sectional peace and racial harmony would provide a stable environment for economic growth.

ECONOMIC GROWTH   The chief accomplishment of the New South movement was a dramatic expansion of the region's textile production. From 1880 to 1900, the number of cotton mills in the South grew from 161 to 400, the number of mill workers (among whom women and children outnumbered men) increased fivefold, and the demand for cotton went up eightfold. By 1900 the South had surpassed New England as the largest producer of cotton fabric in the nation.

Tobacco growing also increased significantly. Essential to the rise of the tobacco industry was the Duke family of Durham, North Carolina. At the end

"The Heroes of the Civil War"

Ulysses S. Grant and Robert E. Lee share this 1889 album cover, issued by W. Duke, Sons, and Company to promote their cigarettes.

of the Civil War, the story goes, Washington Duke took a barnful of tobacco and, with the help of his two sons, beat it out with hickory sticks, stuffed it into bags, hitched two mules to his wagon, and set out across the state, selling tobacco in small pouches as he went. By 1872 the Dukes had a factory producing 125,000 pounds of tobacco annually, and Washington Duke prepared to settle down and enjoy success.

His son Buck (James Buchanan Duke) wanted even greater success, however. He recognized that the tobacco industry was "half smoke and half ballyhoo," so he poured large sums into advertising schemes and perfected the mechanized mass production of cigarettes. Duke also undersold competitors in their own markets and cornered the supply of ingredients needed to make cigarettes. Eventually his competitors agreed to join forces, and in 1890 Duke brought most of them into the American Tobacco Company, which controlled nine tenths of the nation's cigarette production and, by 1904, about three fourths of all tobacco production. In 1911 the Supreme Court ruled that the massive company was in violation of the Sherman Anti-Trust Act and ordered it broken up, but by then Duke had found new worlds to conquer, in hydroelectric power and aluminum.

Systematic use of other natural resources helped revitalize the region along the Appalachian Mountain chain from West Virginia to Alabama. Coal production in the South (including West Virginia) grew from 5 million tons in 1875 to 49 million tons by 1900. At the southern end of the mountains, Birmingham, Alabama, sprang up during the 1870s in the shadow of Red Mountain, so named for its iron ore, and boosters soon tagged the steel-making city the Pittsburgh of the South.

Industrial growth spawned a need for housing, and after 1870 lumbering became a thriving industry in the South. Lumber camps sprouted up across the mountains and flatlands. By the turn of the century, their product, mainly southern pine, had outdistanced textiles in value. Tree cutting seemed to know no bounds, despite the resulting ecological devastation. In time the lumber industry would be saved only by the warm climate, which fostered quick growth of replanted forests, and the rise of scientific forestry.

The South still had far to go to achieve the diversified industry that Henry Grady envisioned in the mid-1880s, but a profusion of other products poured from southern plants: phosphate fertilizers from coastal South Carolina and Florida; oysters, vegetables, and fruits from widespread canneries; ships, including battleships, from the Newport News Shipbuilding and Drydock Company; leather products; liquors and other beverages; and goods made from clay, glass, and stone.

AGRICULTURE OLD AND NEW   At the start of the twentieth century, however, most of the South remained undeveloped, at least by northeastern standards. Despite the optimistic rhetoric of Henry Grady and other New South spokesmen, the typical southerner was less apt to be tending a textile loom or iron forge than, as the saying went, facing the eastern end of a west-bound mule. King Cotton survived the Civil War and expanded over new acreage even as its export markets leveled off. Louisiana cane sugar, probably the most war-devastated of all crops, was flourishing again by the 1890s.

In the old rice belt of coastal South Carolina and elsewhere, vegetable farming blossomed with the advent of the railroads and refrigerated railcars. But the majority of southern farmers were not flourishing. A prolonged

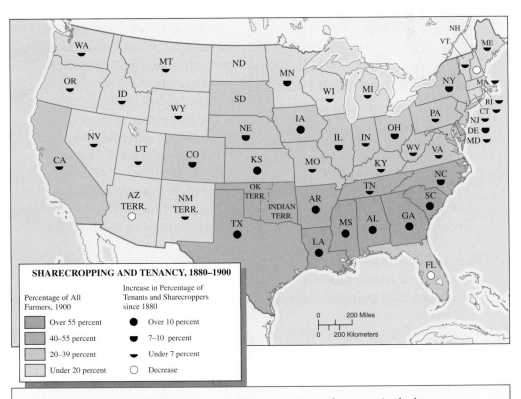

SHARECROPPING AND TENANCY, 1880–1900

Percentage of All Farmers, 1900	Increase in Percentage of Tenants and Sharecroppers since 1880
Over 55 percent	● Over 10 percent
40–55 percent	◗ 7–10 percent
20–39 percent	◡ Under 7 percent
Under 20 percent	○ Decrease

0   200 Miles

0   200 Kilometers

Why was there a dramatic increase in sharecropping and tenancy in the late nineteenth century? Why did the South have more sharecroppers than other parts of the country? Why, in your opinion, was the rate of sharecropping low in the western territories of New Mexico and Arizona?

Picking cotton in Mississippi, 1870

Tenant farming was extremely inefficient, as the tenant lacked incentive to care for the land and the owner was largely unable to supervise the work.

deflation in crop prices affected the entire Western world during the last third of the nineteenth century. Sagging prices for farm crops made it more difficult than ever to own land. Sharecropping and tenancy among blacks and whites grew increasingly prevalent. By 1890 most southern farms were worked by people who did not own the land. Rates of farm ownership in the Deep South belied Henry Grady's dream of a southern democracy of small landowners: South Carolina, 39 percent; Georgia, 40 percent; Alabama, 42 percent; Mississippi, 38 percent; and Louisiana, 42 percent.

How did sharecropping and tenancy work? Sharecroppers, who had nothing to offer the landowner but their labor, worked the owner's land in return for supplies and a share of the crop, generally about half. Tenant farmers, hardly better off, might have their own mule, plow, and line of credit with the country store. They were entitled to claim a larger share of the crops. The sharecropper-tenant system was horribly inefficient and corrupting. It was in essence a post–Civil War version of land slavery. Tenants and landowners developed an intense suspicion of each other. Landlords often swindled the farmworkers by not giving them their fair share of the crops.

The postwar South suffered from an acute shortage of capital; people had to devise ways to operate without cash. One innovation was the crop-lien system: country merchants furnished supplies to small farmers in return for liens (or mortgages) on their crops. The credit offered a way out of dependency for some farmers, but to most it offered only a hopeless cycle of perennial debt. The merchant, who assumed great risks, generally charged interest that ranged, according to one publication, "from 24 percent to grand larceny." The merchant, like the planter (and often the same man), required his farmer clients to grow a cash crop, which could be readily sold at harvesttime. So for all the wind and ink expended by promoters of a New South based upon diversified agriculture, the routines of tenancy and sharecropping geared the marketing, supply, and credit systems to a staple crop, usually cotton. The stagnation of rural life thus held millions, white and black, in bondage to privation and ignorance.

TENANCY AND THE ENVIRONMENT The pervasive use of tenancy and sharecropping unwittingly caused profound environmental damage. Growing commercial row crops like cotton on the same land year after year leached the nutrients from the soil. Tenants had no incentive to take care of farmland by manuring or rotating crops because it was not their own. They used fertilizer to accelerate the growing cycle, but the extensive use of phosphate fertilizers only accelerated soil depletion, by enabling multiple plantings each year. Fertilizer, said an observer, seduced southern farmers into believing that there was a "short cut to prosperity, a royal road to good crops of cotton year after year. The result has been that their lands have been cultivated clean year after year, and their fertility has been exhausted." Once the soil had lost its fertility, the tenants moved on to another farm, leaving behind rutted fields whose topsoil washed away with each rain. The silt and mud flowed into creeks and rivers, swamping many lowland fields and filling millponds and lakes. By the early twentieth century much of the rural South resembled a ravaged land: deep gullies sliced through eroded hillsides, and streams and deep lakes were clogged with silt. As far as the eye could see, red clay devoid of nutrients dominated the landscape.

THE BOURBONS AND THE REDEEMERS In post–Civil War southern politics, habits of social deference and political elitism still prevailed. "Every community," one Union officer noted in postwar South Carolina, "had its great man, or its little great man, around whom his fellow citizens gather when they want information, and to whose monologues they listen with a respect akin to humility." After Reconstruction, southern politics was dominated by small groups of such men. The supporters of these postwar Democratic leaders referred to them as redeemers because they supposedly saved the South from Yankee domination, as well as from the straitjacket of a purely rural economy. The redeemers included a rising class of lawyers, merchants, and entrepreneurs who were eager to promote a more diversified economy based upon industrial development and railroad expansion. The opponents of the redeemers labeled them Bourbons in an effort to depict them as reactionaries. Like the French royal family that Napoléon had said forgot nothing and learned nothing in the ordeal of revolution, the

Bourbons of the postwar South were said to have forgotten nothing and to have learned nothing in the ordeal of the Civil War.

The Bourbons of the New South perfected a political alliance with northern conservatives and an economic alliance with northern capitalists. They generally pursued a government fiscal policy of retrenchment and frugality, except for the tax exemptions and other favors they offered business. The Bourbon governors and legislators slashed state expenditures, including those for the public-school systems started during Reconstruction. Illiteracy rates in the South at the time were about 12 percent among the native-born white population and 50 percent among the black population.

The urge to reduce state expenditures created one of the darkest blots on the Bourbon record: convict leasing. The wartime destruction of prisons and the poverty of state treasuries combined with the demand for cheap labor to make the leasing of convict workers a way for southern states to avoid penitentiary expenses and generate revenue. White political and economic leaders often used a racial argument to rationalize the leasing of convicts, most of whom were African American. An "inferior" and "shiftless" race, they claimed, required the regimen of such coercion to elevate it above its idle, undisciplined ways.

The Bourbons reduced not only state expenditures but also the public debt, and by a simple means: they repudiated a vast amount of it. The corruption and extravagance of Radical rule were commonly advanced as justification for the process, but repudiation did not stop with Reconstruction debts. Altogether, nine states repudiated more than half of what they owed to bondholders and creditors.

The penny-pinching Bourbon regimes did create commissions to regulate the rates charged by railroads for commercial transport. They also established boards of agriculture and public health, stations for agricultural experimentation, agricultural and mechanical colleges, teacher-training schools and women's colleges, and even state colleges for African Americans.

Nor can any simplistic interpretation encompass the variety of Bourbon leaders. The Democratic party of the time was a mongrel coalition that threw Unionists, secessionists, businessmen, small farmers, hillbillies, planters, and even some Republicans together in an alliance against the Reconstruction Radicals. Democrats, therefore, even those who bore the Bourbon label, often marched to different drummers. And once they gained control, Bourbon regimes never achieved complete unity in philosophy or government.

Perhaps the ultimate paradox of the Bourbons' rule was that these paragons of white supremacy tolerated a lingering black voice in politics and showed no haste to raise the barriers of racial separation in public places. In the 1880s

The effects of Radical and Bourbon rule in the South

This 1880 cartoon shows the South staggering under the oppressive weight of military Reconstruction (left) and flourishing under the "Let 'Em Alone Policy" of President Rutherford B. Hayes and the Bourbons (right).

southern politics remained surprisingly open and democratic, with 64 percent of eligible voters, blacks and whites, participating in elections. African Americans sat in the state legislature of South Carolina until 1900 and in the state legislature of Georgia until 1908; some of them were Democrats. The South sent African American congressmen to Washington in every election except one until 1900, though they always represented gerrymandered districts in which most of the state's African American voters had been placed. Under the Bourbons the disenfranchisement of African American voters remained inconsistent, a local matter brought about mainly by fraud and intimidation, but it occurred often enough to ensure white control of the southern states.

A like flexibility applied to other aspects of race relations. The color line was drawn less strictly immediately after the Civil War than it would be in the twentieth century. In some places, to be sure, racial segregation appeared before the end of Reconstruction, especially in schools, churches, hotels, and rooming houses and in private social relations. In places of public accommodation such as trains, depots, theaters, and diners, discrimination was more sporadic.

The ultimate achievement of the New South promoters and their allies, the Bourbons, was that they reconciled tradition with innovation. Their relative moderation in racial policy, at least before the 1890s, allowed them to embrace just enough of the new to disarm adversaries and keep control. By promoting the growth of industry, the Bourbons led the South into a new economic era, but without sacrificing a mythic reverence for the Old South. Bourbon rule left a permanent mark on the South. As the historian C. Vann Woodward noted, "It was not the Radicals nor the Confederates but the Redeemers who laid the lasting foundations in matters of race, politics, economics and institutions for the modern South."

DISENFRANCHISING AFRICAN AMERICANS   During the 1890s the attitudes that had permitted moderation in race relations evaporated. A violent "Negrophobia" swept across the South and much of the nation at the end of the century. One reason for it was that many whites resented signs of black success and social influence. An Alabama newspaper editor declared that "our blood boils when the educated Negro asserts himself politically."

Education did bring enlightenment—as it was supposed to do. A new generation of African Americans born and educated since the end of the Civil War was determined to gain true equality. This generation was more assertive and less patient than their parents. "We are not the Negro from whom the chains of slavery fell a quarter century ago, most assuredly not," a black editor announced. A growing number of young white adults, however, were equally determined to keep "Negroes in their place."

Racial violence and repression surged to the fore during the last decade of the nineteenth century and the first two decades of the twentieth. By the end of the nineteenth century, the so-called New South had come to resemble the racially segregated Old South. Ruling whites ruthlessly imposed their will over all areas of black life, imposing racial subjugation and segregation by preventing blacks from voting and by enacting "Jim Crow" laws mandating separation of the races in various public places. This development was not the logical culmination of the Civil War and emancipation but rather the result of a calculated campaign by white elites and racist thugs to limit African American political, economic, and social life.

The political dynamics of the 1890s exacerbated racial tensions. The rise of Populism, a farm-based protest movement that crystallized into a third political party in the 1890s, divided the white vote to such an extent that in some places the black vote became the balance of power. Some Populists courted black votes and brought African Americans prominently into their leadership councils. In response the Bourbons revived the race issue, which they exploited with seasoned finesse, all the while controlling for their ticket a good part of the black vote in plantation areas. Nevertheless, the Bourbons soon reversed themselves and began arguing in the 1890s that the black vote should be eliminated from southern elections. The affluent, well-educated Democrats in southern counties with large African American populations promoted disenfranchisement. They wanted to eliminate the voting of poor whites as well as blacks. Some farm leaders hoped that disenfranchisement of blacks would make it possible for whites to divide politically without raising the specter of "Negro domination." But since the Fifteenth Amendment made it impossible simply to deny African Americans the right to vote, disenfranchisement was accomplished indirectly, through such devices as poll taxes (or head taxes) and literacy tests.

Mississippi led the way to near-total disenfranchisement of blacks and many poor whites as well. The state called a constitutional convention in 1890 to change the suffrage provisions of the Radical constitution of 1868. The Mississippi plan set the pattern that seven more states would follow over the next twenty years. First, a residence requirement—two years in the state, one year in an election district—struck at those African American tenant farmers who were in the habit of moving yearly in search of better opportunities. Second, voters were disqualified if convicted of certain crimes. Third, all taxes, including a poll tax, had to be paid before a person could vote. This proviso fell most heavily on poor whites and blacks. Fourth and finally, all

"Jim Crow" laws

In this wood engraving, African Americans are depicted leaving Mississippi from the wharves of Vicksburg.

Jim Crow

This stock character in old minstrel shows became a synonym for racial segregation in the twentieth century.

voters had to be literate. The alternative, designed as a loophole for otherwise-disqualified whites, was an "understanding" clause. The voter, if unable to read the Constitution, could qualify by being able to "understand" it—to the satisfaction of the registrar. Not surprisingly, registrars declared far more blacks ineligible than whites.

Other states added variations on the Mississippi plan. In 1898, Louisiana invented the "grandfather clause," which allowed illiterates to vote if their fathers or grandfathers had been eligible to vote on January 1, 1867, when African Americans were still disenfranchised. By 1910, Georgia, North Carolina, Virginia, Alabama, and Oklahoma had adopted the grandfather clause. Every southern state, moreover, adopted a statewide Democratic primary between 1896 and 1915, which became the only meaningful election outside isolated areas of Republican strength. With minor exceptions the Democratic primaries excluded African American voters altogether. The effectiveness of these measures can be seen in a few sample figures. Louisiana in 1896 had 130,000 registered black voters. By 1900 the number was only 5,320. In Alabama in 1900, 121,159 black men over twenty-one were literate, according to the census; only 3,742, however, were registered to vote.

THE SPREAD OF SEGREGATION   What came to be called Jim Crow social segregation followed political disenfranchisement and in some states came first. The symbolic first target was the railway train. In 1885 the novelist George Washington Cable noted that in South Carolina, blacks "ride in first class [rail] cars as a right" and "their presence excites no comment." From 1875 to 1883, in fact, any racial segregation violated a federal Civil Rights Act, which forbade discrimination in places of public accommodation. But in 1883 the Supreme Court ruled on seven civil rights cases involving discrimination against blacks by corporations or individuals. The Court held, with only one dissent, that the force of federal law could not extend to individual action because the Fourteenth Amendment, which provided that "no State" could deny citizens equal protection of the law, stood as a prohibition only against *state* action; individuals were free to discriminate as they saw fit.

This interpretation left as an open question the validity of state laws *requiring* separate public facilities under the rubric of "separate but equal," a slogan popular with the New South prophets. In 1881, Tennessee had required railroads in the state to maintain separate first-class railcars for blacks and whites. In 1888, Mississippi went a step further by requiring passengers to occupy the car set aside for their race. When Louisiana followed suit in 1890, dissidents challenged the law in the case of *Plessy v. Ferguson,* which the Supreme Court decided in 1896.

The test case originated in New Orleans when Homer Plessy, an octoroon (a person having one-eighth African ancestry), refused to leave a whites-only railroad car when told to do so. He was convicted of violating the law, and the case rose on appeal to the Supreme Court. The Court ruled in 1896 that segregation laws "have been generally, if not universally recognized as within the competency of state legislatures in the exercise of their police power."

Very soon the principle of racial segregation extended to every area of southern life, including streetcars, hotels, restaurants, hospitals, parks, sports stadiums, and places of employment. In 1900 the editor of the *Richmond Times* expressed the prevailing view:

> It is necessary that this principle be applied in every relation of Southern life. God Almighty drew the color line and it cannot be obliterated. The negro must stay on his side of the line and the white man must stay on his side, and the sooner both races recognize this fact and accept it, the better it will be for both.

Unashamed and unregulated violence accompanied the Jim Crow laws. From 1890 to 1899, lynchings in the United States averaged 188 per year, 82 percent of which occurred in the South; from 1900 to 1909, they averaged 93 per year, with 92 percent in the South. Whites constituted 32 percent of the victims during the former period but only 11 percent in the latter. By the end of the nineteenth century, legalized racial discrimination—segregation of public facilities, political disenfranchisement, and vigilante justice punctuated by brutal public lynchings and race riots—had elevated government-sanctioned bigotry to an official way of life in the South. South Carolina senator Benjamin Tillman, an outspoken racist, declared in 1892 that blacks "must remain subordinate or be exterminated."

How did African Americans respond to the resurgence of racism and statutory segregation? Some left the South in search of equality and opportunity, but the vast majority stayed in their native region. In the face of overwhelming force and prejudicial justice, most accommodated themselves to the realities of white supremacy and segregation. "Had to walk a quiet life," explained James Plunkett, a Virginia black. "The least little thing you would do, they [whites] would kill ya."

Yet accommodation did not mean total submission. Excluded from the dominant white world and eager to avoid confrontations, black southerners after the 1890s increasingly turned inward and constructed their own culture and nurtured their own pride. A young white visitor to Mississippi in 1910 noticed that nearly every black person he met had "two distinct social selves, the one he reveals to his own people, the other he assumes among the whites."

African American churches continued to serve as the hub for black community life. Often the only public buildings available for African Americans, churches were used not only for worship but also for activities that had nothing to do with religion: social gatherings, club meetings, political rallies. For men especially, churches offered leadership roles and political status. Serving as a deacon was often one of the most prestigious roles an African American man could achieve. Churches fostered racial pride and personal dignity and enabled African Americans of all classes to interact and exercise roles denied them in the larger society. Religious life provided great comfort to people worn down by the daily hardships and abuses associated with segregation.

One irony of state-enforced segregation is that it opened up economic opportunities for blacks. A new class of African American entrepreneurs emerged to provide services—insurance, banking, funeral, barbering—to the black community in the segregated South. At the same time, African Americans formed their own social and fraternal clubs and organizations, all of which helped bolster black pride and provide fellowship and opportunities for service.

Middle-class black women formed a network of thousands of racial-uplift organizations across the South and around the nation. The women's clubs were engines of social service in their communities. Members cared for the aged and the infirm, the orphaned and the abandoned. They created homes for single mothers and provided nurseries for working mothers. They sponsored health clinics and classes in home economics for women. In 1896 the leaders of such women's clubs from around the country converged to form the National Association of Colored Women, an organization meant to combat racism and segregation. Its first president, Mary Church Terrell, told members that they had an obligation to serve the "lowly, the illiterate, and even the vicious to whom we are bound by the ties of race and sex, and put forth every effort to uplift and reclaim them."

IDA B. WELLS One of the most outspoken African American activists of the time was Ida B. Wells. Born into slavery in 1862 in Mississippi, she attended a school staffed by white missionaries. In 1878 an epidemic of yellow fever killed her parents as well as an infant brother. At age sixteen, Wells assumed responsibility for her five younger siblings and secured a job as a country schoolteacher. In about 1880 she moved to nearby Memphis, where she taught in segregated schools and gained entrance to the social life of the city's striving African American middle class.

Ida B. Wells

While raising four children, Wells sustained her commitment to ending racial and gender discrimination.

In 1883, Wells confronted the reality and power of white supremacy. After being denied a seat on a railroad car because she was black, she became the first African American to file suit against such discrimination. The circuit court decided in her favor and fined the railroad, but the Tennessee Supreme Court overturned the ruling. Wells thereafter discovered "[my] first and [it] might be said, my only love"—journalism—and, through it, a weapon with which to wage her crusade for justice. Writing under the pen name Iola, she became a prominent editor of *Memphis Free Speech*, a newspaper focusing on African American issues.

In 1892, when three of her friends were lynched by a white mob, Wells launched a lifelong crusade against lynching. Angry whites responded by destroying her office and threatening to lynch her. She moved to New York and continued to use her fiery journalistic talent to criticize Jim Crow laws and demand that blacks have their voting rights restored. In the spring of 1898, the lynching of an African American postmaster in South Carolina so incensed Wells that she spent five weeks in Washington, D.C., fruitlessly trying to persuade the federal government to intervene. She helped found the National Association for the Advancement of Colored People (NAACP) in 1909 and worked to promote women's suffrage. In promoting full equality, Wells often found herself in direct opposition to the accommodationist views of Booker T. Washington.

WASHINGTON AND DU BOIS Booker T. Washington, born in Virginia of a slave mother and a white father, fought extreme adversity to get an

Booker T. Washington

Founder of the Tuskegee Institute.

education at Hampton Institute, one of the postwar missionary schools, and went on to build at Tuskegee, Alabama, a leading college for African Americans. By the 1890s, Washington had become the foremost black educator in the nation. He argued that blacks should first establish an economic base for their advancement before striving for social equality. In a speech at the Cotton States and International Exposition in Atlanta in 1895 that propelled him to fame, Washington advised fellow African Americans: "Cast down your bucket where you are—cast it down in making friends . . . of the people of all races by whom we are surrounded. Cast it down in agriculture, mechanics, in commerce, in domestic service, and in the professions." He conspicuously omitted politics from that list and offered an oblique endorsement of segregation: "In all things that are purely social we can be as separate as the five fingers, yet one as the hand in all things essential to mutual progress."

Some people bitterly criticized Washington, and have since, for making a bad bargain: the sacrifice of broad educational and civil rights for the dubious acceptance of white conservatives and economic opportunities. W. E. B. Du Bois led this criticism. A native of Massachusetts, Du Bois first experienced southern racial practices as an undergraduate at Fisk University in Nashville. Later he was the first African American to earn a doctorate from Harvard (in history) and briefly attended the University of Berlin. In addition to an active career in racial protest, he left a distinguished record as a scholar, authoring over twenty books. Trim and dapper in appearance, sporting a goatee, carrying a cane, and often wearing gloves, Du Bois possessed a combative spirit. Not long after he began his teaching career, at Atlanta University in 1897, he began to assault Booker T. Washington's accommodationist philosophy and put forward his own program of "ceaseless agitation" for civil rights. He became the architect of the twentieth-century civil rights movement.

Washington, Du Bois argued, preached "a gospel of Work and Money to such an extent as . . . to overshadow the higher aims of life." The education of blacks, Du Bois maintained, should not be merely vocational but should nurture bold leaders willing to challenge segregation and discrimination through political action. He demanded that disenfranchisement and legalized segregation cease immediately and that the laws of the land be enforced. Du Bois called Washington's 1895 speech "the Atlanta Compromise" and said that he would not "surrender the leadership of this race to cowards." The dispute between Washington and Du Bois came to define the tensions that would divide the civil rights movement: militancy versus conciliation, separatism versus assimilation, social justice versus economic advances.

W. E. B. Du Bois

A fierce advocate for black education.

THE NEW WEST

Like the South, the West is a region wrapped in myths and constricted by stereotypes. The vast land west of the Mississippi River contains remarkable geographic extremes: majestic mountains, roaring rivers, searing deserts, sprawling grasslands, and dense forests. For vast reaches of western America, the great epics of the Civil War and Reconstruction were remote events hardly touching the lives of the Indians, Mexicans, Asians, trappers, miners, and Mormons scattered through the plains and mountains. There the march of settlement and exploitation continued, propelled by a lust for land and a passion for profit. Between 1870 and 1900, Americans settled more land in the West than had been occupied by all Americans up to 1870. On one level western settlement beyond the Mississippi River constitutes a colorful drama of determined pioneers and two-fisted gunslingers overcoming all obstacles to secure their vision of freedom and opportunity amid the region's awesome vastness. The post–Civil War West offered the promise of democratic individualism, economic opportunity, and personal freedom that had long before come to define the American dream. On another level, however, the colonization of the Far West was a tragedy of shortsighted greed and irresponsible behavior, a story of reckless exploitation that scarred the land, decimated its wildlife, and nearly exterminated the culture of Native Americans.

In the second tier of trans-Mississippi states—Iowa, Kansas, Nebraska— and in western Minnesota, farmers began spreading across the Great Plains after midcentury. From California, miners moved east through the mountains with one new strike after another. From Texas nomadic cowboys migrated northward onto the plains and across the Rockies into the Great Basin.

The settlers encountered climates and landscapes markedly different from those they had left behind. The Great Plains were arid, and the scarcity of water and timber rendered useless or impossible the familiar trappings of the pioneer: the ax, the log cabin, the rail fence, and the accustomed methods of tilling the soil. For a long time the region had been called the Great American Desert and thought of only as a barren barrier to cross on the way to the Pacific, unfit for human habitation and therefore, to white Americans, the perfect refuge for Indians. But that view changed in the last half of the nineteenth century as a result of newly discovered deposits of gold, silver, and other minerals, the completion of the transcontinental railroads, the destruction of the buffalo, the collapse of Indian resistance, the rise of the range-cattle industry, and the dawning realization that the arid region need not be a sterile desert. With the use of what water was available, new techniques of dry farming and irrigation could make the land fruitful after all.

THE MIGRATORY STREAM   During the second half of the nineteenth century, an unrelenting stream of migrants flowed into the largely Indian and Hispanic West. Millions of Anglo-Americans, African Americans, Mexicans, and European and Chinese immigrants transformed the patterns of western society and culture. Most of the settlers were relatively prosperous white, native-born farm folk. Because of the expense of transportation, land, and supplies, the very poor could not afford to relocate. Three quarters of the western migrants were men.

The largest number of foreign immigrants came from northern Europe and Canada. In the northern plains, Germans, Scandinavians, and Irish were especially numerous. In the new state of Nebraska in 1870, a quarter of the 123,000 residents were foreign-born. In North Dakota in 1890, 45 percent of the residents were immigrants. Compared with European immigrants, those from China and Mexico were much less numerous but nonetheless significant. More than 200,000 Chinese arrived in California between 1876 and 1890.

AFRICAN AMERICAN MIGRATION   In the aftermath of the collapse of Radical Republican rule in the South, thousands of African Americans began migrating west from Kentucky, Tennessee, Louisiana, Arkansas, Mississippi, and Texas. Some 6,000 southern blacks arrived in Kansas in 1879 alone, and as many as 20,000 may have come the following year. These migrants

Nicodemus, Kansas

A colony founded by southern blacks in the 1860s.

came to be known as Exodusters, because they were making their exodus from the South—in search of a haven from racism and poverty.

The foremost promoter of black migration to the West was Benjamin "Pap" Singleton. Born a slave in Tennessee in 1809, he escaped to Detroit. After the Civil War he returned to Tennessee, convinced that God was calling him to rescue his brethren. When Singleton learned that land in Kansas could be had for $1.25 an acre, he led his first party of 200 colonists to Kansas in 1878, bought 7,500 acres that had been an Indian reservation, and established the Dunlop community. Over the next several years, thousands of African Americans followed Singleton into Kansas, leading many southern leaders to worry about the loss of black laborers in the region. In 1879 whites closed access to the Mississippi River and threatened to sink all boats carrying black colonists from the South to the West. An army officer reported to President Rutherford B. Hayes that "every river landing is blockaded by white enemies of the colored exodus; some of whom are mounted and armed, as if we are at war."

The black exodus to the West died out by the early 1880s. Many of the settlers were unprepared for the living conditions on the plains. Their Kansas homesteads were not large enough to allow self-sufficiency, and most of the black farmers were forced to supplement their income by hiring themselves out to white ranchers. Drought, grasshoppers, prairie fires, and dust storms led to crop failures. The sudden influx of so many people taxed resources and patience. Many of the African American pioneers in Kansas soon abandoned their land and moved to the few cities in the state. Life on the frontier was not the "promised land" that settlers had been led to expect. Nonetheless, by 1890 some 520,000 African Americans lived west of the Mississippi River. As many as 25 percent of the cowboys who participated in the Texas cattle drives were African Americans.

In 1866, Congress passed legislation establishing two "colored" cavalry units and dispatched them to the western frontier. Nicknamed buffalo soldiers by the Indians, the men were mostly Civil War veterans from Louisiana and Kentucky. They built and maintained forts, mapped vast areas of the Southwest, strung hundreds of miles of telegraph lines, protected railroad construction crews, subdued hostile Indians, and captured outlaws and rustlers. Eighteen of the buffalo soldiers won Congressional Medals of Honor for their service.

MINING THE WEST   Valuable mineral deposits continued to lure people to the West after the Civil War. The California miners of 1849 (forty-niners) set the typical pattern, in which the sudden, disorderly rush of prospectors to a new find was quickly joined by camp followers—a motley crew of peddlers, saloon keepers, prostitutes, cardsharps, hustlers, and assorted desperadoes eager to mine the miners. If a new field panned out, the forces of respectability and more subtle forms of exploitation slowly worked their way in. Lawlessness gave way to vigilante rule and, finally, to a stable community.

Deadwood, Dakota Territory

A gold-rush town in 1876, before the Dakotas became states.

The drama of the 1849 gold rush was reenacted time and again in the following three decades. Along the South Platte River, not far from Pikes Peak in Colorado, a prospecting party found gold in 1858, and stories of success brought perhaps 100,000 "fifty-niners" into the country by the next year. New discoveries in Colorado kept occurring: near Central City in 1859, at Leadville in the 1870s, and the last important strikes in the West, again gold and silver, at Cripple Creek in 1891 and 1894. During those years, farming and grazing had given the economy a stable base, and Colorado, the Centennial State, entered the union in 1876.

While the early miners were crowding around Pikes Peak, the Comstock Lode was discovered near Gold Hill, Nevada. H. T. P. Comstock, a Canadian-born fur trapper, had drifted to the Carson River diggings, which opened in 1856. He talked his way into a share in a new discovery made by two other prospectors in 1859 and gave it his own name. The lode produced gold and silver. Within twenty years it had yielded more than $300 million from shafts that reached hundreds of feet into the mountainside. In 1861, largely on account of the settlers attracted to the Comstock Lode, Nevada became a territory, and in 1864 the state of Nevada was admitted to the Union in time to give two electoral votes to Abraham Lincoln (the new state's third electoral voter got caught in a snowstorm).

The growing demand for orderly government in the West led to the hasty creation of new territories and eventually the admission of a host of new states. After Colorado's admission in 1876, however, there was a long hiatus because of party divisions in Congress: Democrats were reluctant to create states out of territories that were heavily Republican. After the sweeping Republican victory in the 1888 legislative races, however, Congress admitted the Dakotas, Montana, and Washington in 1889 and Idaho and Wyoming in 1890. Utah entered the Union in 1896 (after the Mormons abandoned the practice of polygamy) and Oklahoma in 1907, and in 1912 Arizona and New Mexico rounded out the forty-eight contiguous states.

MINING AND THE ENVIRONMENT   During the second half of the nineteenth century, the nature of mining changed drastically. It became a mass-production industry as individual prospectors gave way to large companies. The first wave of miners who rushed to California in 1849 sifted gold dust and nuggets out of riverbeds by means of "placer" mining, or "panning." But once the placer deposits were exhausted, efficient mining required large-scale operations and huge investments. Companies shifted from surface digging to hydraulic mining, dredging, or deep-shaft "hard-rock" mining.

Hydraulicking, dredging, and shaft mining transformed vast areas of vegetation and landscape. Huge hydraulic cannons shot an enormous stream of water under high pressure, stripping the topsoil and gravel from the bedrock and creating steep-sloped barren canyons that could not sustain plant life. The tons of dirt and debris unearthed by the water cannons covered rich farmland downstream and created sandbars that clogged rivers and killed fish. All told, some 12 billion tons of earth were blasted out of the

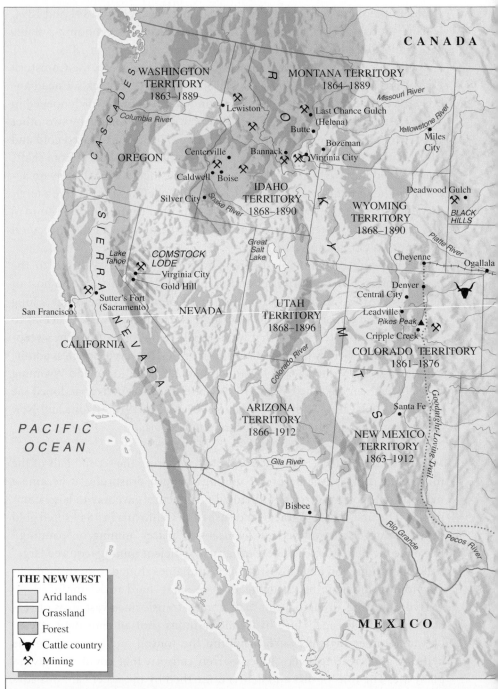

THE NEW WEST

- Arid lands
- Grassland
- Forest
- Cattle country
- Mining

What were the main industries of the New West? How did mining transform its ecology?

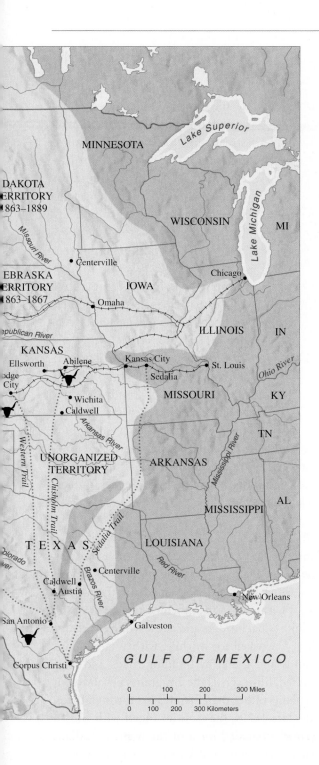

Yuba County, California, 1866

Miners look on as water pours into a sluice.

Sierra Nevadas and washed into local rivers.

Irate California farmers in the fertile Central Valley bitterly protested the damage done downstream by the industrial mining operations. In 1878 they formed the Anti-Debris Association, with its own militia, to challenge the powerful mining companies. Efforts to pass state legislation restricting hydraulic mining repeatedly failed because mining companies controlled the votes. The Anti-Debris Association then turned to the courts. On January 7, 1884, the farmers won their case when federal judge Lorenzo Sawyer, a former miner, outlawed the dumping of mining debris where it could reach farmland or navigable rivers. Thus *Woodruff v. North Bloomfield Gravel Mining Company* became the first major environmental ruling in the nation. As a result of the ruling, hydraulic mining dried up, leaving a legacy of abandoned equipment, ugly ravines, ditches, gullies, and mountains of discarded rock and gravel.

THE INDIAN WARS   As the frontier pressed in from east and west, Native Americans were forced into what was supposed to be their last refuge. Perhaps 250,000 Indians on the Great Plains and in the mountain regions lived mainly off the buffalo herds, which provided food and, from their hides, clothing and shelter. The 1851 Fort Laramie Treaty, in which the chiefs of the Plains tribes agreed to accept definite tribal borders and allow white emigrants to travel on their trails unmolested, worked for a while, with wagon trains passing safely through Indian lands and the army building roads and forts without resistance. Fighting resumed, however, as the emigrants began to encroach upon Indian lands on the plains rather than merely pass through them.

From the early 1860s until the late 1870s, the frontier raged with Indian wars. In 1864, Colorado's governor persuaded most of the warring Indians in his territory to gather at Fort Lyon, on Sand Creek, where they were promised protection. Despite that promise, Colonel John M. Chivington's untrained militia attacked an Indian camp flying a white flag of truce, slaughtering 200 peaceful Indians—men, women, and children—in what one general called the "foulest and most unjustifiable crime in the annals of America."

With other scattered battles erupting, a congressional committee in 1865 gathered evidence on the grisly Indian wars and massacres. Its 1867 "Report on the Condition of the Indian Tribes" led to the creation of an Indian Peace Commission charged with removing the causes of the Indian wars. Congress decided that this would be best accomplished at the expense of the Indians, by persuading them to take up life on out-of-the-way reservations. Yet the persistent encroachment on Indian hunting grounds continued. In 1870, Indians outnumbered whites in the Dakota Territory by two to one; in 1880, whites outnumbered Indians by more than six to one.

In 1867 a conference at Medicine Lodge, Kansas, ended with the Kiowas, Comanches, Arapahos, and Cheyennes reluctantly accepting land in western Oklahoma. The following spring the Sioux agreed to settle within the Black Hills Reservation in Dakota Territory. But Indian resistance in the southern plains continued until the Red River War of 1874–1875, when General Philip Sheridan forced the Indians to disband in the spring of 1875. Seventy-two Indian chiefs were imprisoned for three years.

Meanwhile, trouble was brewing again in the north. In 1874, Lieutenant Colonel George A. Custer, a reckless, glory-seeking officer, led an exploratory expedition into the Black Hills. Miners were soon filtering onto the Sioux hunting grounds despite promises that the army would keep them out. The army had done little to protect Indian land, but when ordered to move against wandering bands of Sioux hunting on the range according to their treaty rights, it moved vigorously.

What became the Great Sioux War was the largest military event since the end of the Civil War and one of the largest campaigns against Indians in American history. The war lasted fifteen months and entailed fifteen battles in present-day Wyoming, Montana, South Dakota, and Nebraska. The Sioux were ably led by the heroic Chief Sitting Bull. In 1876, after several indecisive encounters, Custer found the main encampment of Sioux and their Northern Cheyenne allies on the Little Bighorn River. Separated from the main body of soldiers and surrounded by 2,500 warriors, Custer's detachment of 210 men was annihilated.

Instead of following up their victory, the Indians celebrated and renewed their hunting. The army quickly regained the offensive and compelled the Sioux to give up their hunting grounds and goldfields in return for payments. Forced onto reservations situated on the least valuable land in the

The Battle of Little Bighorn, 1876

A painting by Amos Bad Heart Bull, an Oglala Sioux.

region, the Indians soon found themselves struggling to subsist under harsh conditions. Many of them died of starvation or disease. When a peace commission imposed a settlement, Chief Spotted Tail said: "Tell your people that since the Great Father promised that we should never be removed, we have been moved five times. . . . I think you had better put the Indians on wheels and you can run them about wherever you wish."

In the Rocky Mountains and to the west, the same story of hopeless resistance was repeated. Indians were the last obstacle to white western expansion, and they suffered as a result. The Blackfeet and Crows had to leave their homes in Montana. In a war along the California-Oregon boundary, the Modocs held out for six months in 1871–1872 before they were overwhelmed. In 1879 the Utes were forced to give up their vast territories in western Colorado. In Idaho the peaceful Nez Perce bands refused to surrender land along the Salmon River, and prolonged fighting erupted there and in eastern Oregon. Joseph, one of several Nez Perce chiefs, delivered an eloquent speech of surrender that served as an epitaph to the Indians' efforts to withstand the march of American empire: "I am tired of fighting. Our chiefs are killed. . . . The old men are all dead. . . . I want to have time to look for my children, and see how many of them I can find. . . . Hear me, my chiefs! I am tired. My heart is sick and sad. From where the sun now stands I will fight no more forever."

A generation of Indian wars virtually ended in 1886 with the capture of Geronimo, a chief of the Chiricahua Apaches, who had fought white settlers

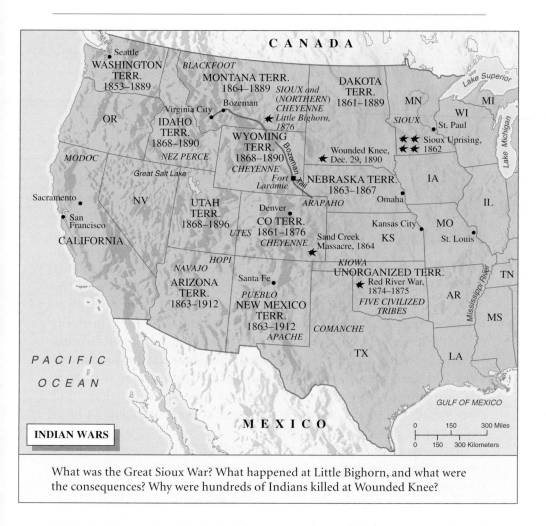

What was the Great Sioux War? What happened at Little Bighorn, and what were the consequences? Why were hundreds of Indians killed at Wounded Knee?

in the Southwest for fifteen years. But there would be a tragic epilogue. Late in 1888, Wovoka (or Jack Wilson), a Paiute in western Nevada, fell ill and in a delirium imagined he had visited the spirit world, where he learned of a deliverer coming to rescue the Indians and restore their lands. To hasten their deliverance, he said, the Indians must take up a ceremonial dance at each new moon. The Ghost Dance craze fed upon old legends of a coming messiah and spread rapidly. In 1890 the Lakota Sioux adopted it with such fervor that it alarmed white authorities. They banned the Ghost Dance on Lakota reservations, but the Indians defied the order and a crisis erupted. On December 29, 1890, a bloodbath occurred at Wounded Knee, South Dakota. An accidental rifle discharge led nervous soldiers to fire into a group of Indians who had come to surrender. Nearly 200 Indians and 25 soldiers died in the Battle of

Indian wars

Chief Joseph of the Nez Perce.

Wounded Knee. The Indian wars had ended with characteristic brutality and misunderstanding.

THE DEMISE OF THE BUFFALO Over the long run the collapse of Indian resistance in the face of white settlement on the Great Plains resulted as much from the decimation of the buffalo herds as from the actions of federal troops. In 1750 there were an estimated 30 million buffalo; by 1850 there were less than 10 million; by 1900 only a few hundred were left. What happened to them? The conventional story focuses on intensive harvesting of buffalo by white hunters after the Civil War. Americans east of the Mississippi River developed a voracious demand for buffalo robes and buffalo leather. The average white commercial hunter killed 100 animals a day, and the hides and bones (to be ground into fertilizer) were shipped east on railroad cars. Some army officers encouraged the slaughter. "Kill every buffalo you can!" Colonel Richard Dodge told a sport hunter in 1867. "Every buffalo dead is an Indian gone."

This conventional explanation tells only part of a more complicated story, however. The buffalo disappeared from the western plains for a variety of environmental reasons, including a significant change in climate; competition for forage with horses, sheep, and cattle; and cattle-borne disease. A prolonged drought on the Great Plains during the late 1880s and 1890s, the same drought that would help spur the agrarian political revolt and the rise of populism, also devastated the buffalo herds by reducing the grasslands upon which the animals depended. At the same time, the buffalo had to compete for forage with other grazing animals. By the 1880s over 2 million horses were roaming buffalo lands. In addition, the Plains Indians themselves, empowered by horses and guns and spurred by the profits reaped from selling hides and meat to white traders, accounted for much of the devastation of the buffalo herds after 1840. White hunters who killed buffalo by the millions in the 1870s and 1880s played a major role in the animals' demise, but only as the final catalyst. If there had been no white hunters, the buffalo would probably have lasted only another thirty years because their numbers had been so greatly reduced by other factors.

INDIAN POLICY   The slaughter of buffalo and Indians ignited wide-spread criticism. Politicians and religious leaders spoke out against the persistent mistreatment of Indians. In his annual message of 1877, President Rutherford B. Hayes joined the protest: "Many, if not most, of our Indian wars have had their origin in broken promises and acts of injustice on our part." Helen Hunt Jackson, a novelist and poet, focused attention on the Indian cause in *A Century of Dishonor* (1881). Indian policy gradually became more benevolent, but this change did little to ease the plight of the Indians and actually helped destroy the remnants of their culture. The reservation policy inaugurated by the Peace Commission in 1867 did little more than extend a practice that dated from colonial Virginia. Partly humanitarian in motive, it also saved money: housing and feeding Indians on reservations cost less than fighting them.

Well-intentioned reformers sought to "Americanize" Indians by dealing with them as individuals rather than tribes. The fruition of such reform efforts came with the Dawes Severalty Act of 1887. Sponsored by Senator Henry L. Dawes of Massachusetts, the act divided the land of any tribe, granting 160 acres to each head of a family and lesser amounts to others. To protect the Indians' property, the government held it in trust for twenty-five years, after which the owner won full title and became a U.S. citizen. Under the Burke Act of 1906, Indians who took up life apart from their tribes became citizens immediately. Members of the tribes who were granted land titles were subject to state and federal laws like all other residents of the United States. In 1901, citizenship was extended to the Five Civilized Tribes of Oklahoma and, in 1924, to all Indians.

But the more it changed, the more Indian policy remained the same. Despite the best of intentions, the Dawes Act created opportunities for more white plundering of Indian land and disrupted what remained of the traditional culture. The Dawes Act broke up reservations and often led to the loss of Indian land to whites. Land not distributed to Indian families was sold, and some of the land the Indians did receive they lost to land sharks because of the Indians' inexperience with private ownership or simply their weakness in the face of fraud. Between 1887 and 1934, Indians lost an estimated 86 million of their 130 million acres. Most of what remained was unsuited for agriculture.

CATTLE AND COWBOYS   While the West was being taken from the Indians, cattle entered the grasslands where the buffalo had roamed. Much of the romance of the open-range cattle industry derived from its Mexican roots. The Texas longhorns and the cowboys' horses had in large part descended from stock brought to the New World by the Spaniards, and many of the industry's trappings had been worked out in Mexico first: the cowboy's saddle, chaps (*chaparreras*) to protect the legs, spurs, and lariat.

For many years wild cattle competed with the buffalo in the Spanish borderlands. Natural selection and contact with Anglo-American cattle produced the Texas longhorns: lean and rangy, they were noted more for speed and endurance than for yielding a choice steak. They had little value, moreover, because the largest markets for beef were too far away. At the end of the Civil War, as many as 5 million cattle roamed the grasslands of Texas, still neglected—but not for long. In the upper Mississippi Valley, where herds had been depleted by the war, cattle were in great demand, and the Texas cattle could be had just for the effort of rounding them up.

New opportunities arose as railroads pushed farther west, where cattle could be driven through relatively vacant lands. Joseph G. McCoy, an Illinois livestock dealer, recognized the possibilities of moving the cattle trade west.

The cowboy era

Cowboys herd cattle near Cimarron, Colorado, 1905.

In 1867 in Abilene, Kansas, he bought 250 acres for a stockyard; he then built a barn, an office building, livestock scales, a hotel, and a bank and sent an agent into Indian territory to cultivate owners of herds bound north. Over the next few years, Abilene flourished as the first successful Kansas cowtown. But as the railroads moved west, so did the cowtowns—Ellsworth, Wichita, Caldwell, and Dodge City in Kansas; farther north to Ogallala, Nebraska; Cheyenne, Wyoming; and Miles City, Montana—and the trails.

During the twenty years after the Civil War, some 40,000 cowboys roamed the Great Plains. They were young—the average age was twenty-four—and from diverse backgrounds. Some 30 percent were Mexican or African American, and hundreds were Indians. Many others were Civil War veterans from the North and the South, and still others were immigrants from Europe. The life of a cowboy, for the most part, was rarely as exciting as has been depicted by movies and television shows. Working as a ranch hand involved grueling, dirty wage labor interspersed with drudgery and boredom, often amid terrible weather conditions.

The thriving cattle industry spurred rapid growth in the region, however. The population of Kansas increased from 107,000 in 1860 to 365,000 ten years later and reached almost 1 million by 1880. Nebraska witnessed similar increases. During the 1860s, cattle would be delivered to rail depots, loaded onto freight cars, and shipped east. By the time the animals arrived in New York or Massachusetts, some would be dead or dying, and all would have lost significant weight. The secret to higher profits in the cattle industry was to devise a way to slaughter the cattle in the Midwest and ship the dressed carcasses east and west. That process required refrigeration to keep the meat from spoiling. In 1869, G. H. Hammond, a Chicago meat packer, shipped the first refrigerated beef in an air-cooled railroad car from Chicago to Boston. Eight years later Gustavus Swift developed a more efficient system of mechanical refrigeration, an innovation that earned him a fortune and provided the cattle industry with a major stimulus.

The flush times of the cowtown soon passed, however, and the long cattle drives played out too, because they were economically unsound. The dangers of the trail, the wear and tear on men and cattle, the charges levied on drives across Indian territory, and the advance of farms across the trails combined to persuade cattlemen that they could function best near railroads. As railroads spread out into Texas and across the plains, the cattle business spread with them over the High Plains as far as Montana and on into Canada.

In the absence of laws governing the open range, cattle ranchers at first worked out a code of behavior largely dictated by circumstances. As cattle often wandered onto other ranchers' claims, cowboys would "ride the line"

Langtry, Texas, 1900
Judge Roy Bean's courthouse and saloon.

to keep as many of the animals as they could off the adjoining ranches. In the spring they would "round up" the herds, which invariably got mixed up, and sort out ownership by identifying the distinctive ranch symbols "branded," or burned, into the cattle. All that changed in 1873, when Joseph Glidden, an Illinois farmer, invented the first effective barbed wire, which ranchers used to fence off their claims at relatively low cost. Ranchers rushed to buy the new wire fencing, and soon the open range was no more. Cattle raising, like mining, evolved from a romantic adventure into a big business dominated by giant enterprises.

THE END OF THE OPEN RANGE   A combination of factors put an end to the open range. Farmers kept crowding in and laying out homesteads and waging "barbed-wire wars" with ranchers by cutting the ranchers' fences or policing their own. The boundless range was being overstocked with cattle by 1883, and expenses mounted as stock breeders formed associations to keep intruders off overstocked ranges, establish and protect land titles, deal with railroads and buyers, fight prairie fires, and cope with rustlers and wolves and cougars. The rise of sheepherding by 1880 caused still another conflict with the cattle ranchers. A final blow to the open-range industry came with two unusually severe winters, in 1886 and 1887, followed by ten long years of drought.

Surviving the hazards of the range required ranchers to establish legal title and fence in the land, limit the herds to a reasonable size, and provide shelter and hay during the rigors of winter. Moreover, as the long cattle drives gave way to more rail lines and refrigerated railcars, the cowboy settled into a more sedentary existence. Within merely two decades, from 1866 to 1886, the era of the cowboy had come and gone.

RANGE WARS Conflicting claims over land and water rights triggered violent disputes between ranchers and farmers. Ranchers often tried to drive off neighboring farmers, and farmers in turn tried to sabotage the cattle barons, cutting their fences and spooking their herds. The cattle ranchers also clashed with sheepherders over access to grassland. A strain of ethnic and religious prejudice heightened the tension between ranchers and herders. In the Southwest, shepherds were typically Mexican Americans; in Idaho and Nevada they were from the Basque region of Spain, or they were Mormons. Many Anglo-American cattle ranchers and cowboys viewed those ethnic and religious groups as un-American and inferior, adopting an attitude that helped them rationalize the use of violence against sheepherders. Warfare gradually faded, however, as the sheep for the most part found refuge in the high pastures of the mountains, leaving the grasslands of the plains to the cattle ranchers.

Yet there also developed a perennial tension between large and small cattle ranchers. The large ranchers fenced in huge tracts of public land, leaving the smaller ranchers with too little pasture. To survive, the smaller ranchers cut the fences. In central Texas this practice sparked the Fence-Cutters' War of 1883–1884. Several ranchers were killed and dozens wounded before the state ended the conflict by passing legislation outlawing fence cutting.

FARMERS AND THE LAND Among the legendary figures of the West, the sodbusters projected an unromantic image in contrast to the images of the cowboys, cavalrymen, and Indians. Farming has always been a hard life, and it was made more so on the Great Plains by the region's unforgiving environment and mercurial weather. After 1865, on paper at least, the federal land laws offered farmers favorable terms. Under the Homestead Act of 1862, a settler could gain title to federal land simply by staking out a claim and living on it for five years, or he could buy land at $1.25 an acre after six months. But such land legislation was predicated upon the tradition of farming the fertile lands east of the Mississippi River, and the laws were never adjusted to the fact that much of the prairie was suited only for cattle raising. Cattle ranchers were forced to obtain land by gradual acquisition from homesteaders or land-grant railroads.

As so often happens, environmental forces shaped development. The unchangeable fact of aridity, rather than new land laws, shaped institutions in the West after the Civil War. Where farming was impossible, ranchers simply

The construction of Hoover Dam

When completed in 1936, Hoover Dam was the world's largest concrete structure.

established dominance by control of the water, regardless of the law. Belated legislative efforts to develop irrigable land finally achieved a major success when the 1901 Newlands Reclamation Act (after the aptly named Senator Francis G. Newlands of Nevada) set up the Bureau of Reclamation. The proceeds of public land sales in sixteen states created a fund for irrigation projects, and the Reclamation Bureau set about building such major projects as the Boulder (later the Hoover) Dam on the Nevada-Arizona line, the Roosevelt Dam in Arizona, the Elephant Butte Dam in New Mexico, and the Arrowrock Dam in Idaho.

The lands of the New West, like those on previous frontiers, passed to their ultimate owners more often from private hands than directly from the government. Many of the 274 million acres claimed under the Homestead Act passed quickly to ranchers or speculators and thence to settlers. The land-grant railroads got some 200 million acres of the public domain between 1851 and 1871 and sold much of it to create towns along the lines. The West of ranchers and farmers was in fact largely the product of the railroads.

The first arrivals on the sod-house frontier faced a grim struggle against danger, adversity, and monotony. Though land was relatively cheap, horses, livestock, wagons, wells, lumber, fencing, seed, and fertilizer were not. Freight rates and interest rates on loans seemed criminally high. As in the South, declining crop prices produced chronic indebtedness, leading strapped western farmers to embrace virtually any plan to inflate the money supply. The virgin land itself, although fertile, resisted planting; the heavy sod broke many a plow. Since wood was almost nonexistent on the prairie, pioneer families used buffalo chips (dried dung) for fuel.

Farmers and their families also fought a constant battle with the elements: tornadoes, hailstorms, droughts, prairie fires, blizzards, and pests. Swarms of locusts would cloud the horizon, occasionally covering the ground six inches deep. A Wichita newspaper reported in 1878 that the grasshoppers devoured "everything green, stripping the foliage off the bark and from the tender twigs of the fruit trees, destroying every plant that is good for food or pleasant to the eyes, that man has planted."

As the railroads arrived bearing lumber from the East, farmers could leave their sod houses (homes built of sod) to build more comfortable frame dwellings. New machinery helped provide fresh opportunities. In 1868, James Oliver, a Scottish immigrant living in Indiana, made a successful chilled-iron plow. This "sodbuster" plow greatly eased the task of breaking the tough grass roots of the plains. Improvements and new inventions in threshing machines, hay mowers, planters, manure spreaders, cream separators, and other devices lightened the burden of farm labor but added to the farmers' capital outlay. In Minnesota, the Dakotas, and central California the gigantic "bonanza farms," with machinery for mass production, became the marvels of the age. On one farm in North Dakota, 13,000 acres of wheat made a single field. Another bonanza farm employed over 1,000 migrant workers to tend 34,000 acres.

While the overall value of farmland and farm products increased in the late nineteenth century, small farmers did not keep up with the march of progress. Their numbers grew but decreased in proportion to the population at large. Wheat, like cotton in the antebellum period, was the great export crop that spurred economic growth. For a variety of reasons, however, few small farmers prospered. By the 1890s they were in open revolt against the "system" of corrupt processors and "greedy" bankers who they believed conspired against them.

PIONEER WOMEN   The West remained a largely male society throughout the nineteenth century. Women were not only a numerical minority; they also continued to face traditional legal barriers and social prejudice. A wife could not sell property without her husband's approval, for example. Texas women could not sue except for divorce, nor could they serve on juries, act as lawyers, or witness a will.

Women of the frontier

A woman and her family in front of their sod house. The difficult life on the prairie led to more egalitarian marriages than were found in other regions of the country.

But the fight for survival in the trans-Mississippi West made men and women more equal partners than were their eastern counterparts. Many women who lost their mates to the deadly toil of sod busting thereafter assumed complete responsibility for their farms. In general, women on the prairie became more independent than women leading domestic lives back East. Explained one Kansas woman: "The outstanding fact is that the environment was such as to bring out and develop the dominant qualities of individual character. Kansas women of that day learned at an early age to depend on themselves—to do whatever work there was to be done, and to face danger when it must be faced, as calmly as they were able."

THE END OF THE FRONTIER American life reached an important juncture at the end of the nineteenth century. After the 1890 population count the superintendent of the national census noted that he could no longer locate a continuous frontier line beyond which population thinned out to fewer than two people per square mile. This fact inspired the historian Frederick Jackson Turner to develop his influential frontier thesis, first outlined in "The Significance of the Frontier in American History," a paper delivered to the American Historical Association in 1893. "The existence of an area of free land," Turner wrote, "its continuous recession, and the advance of American settlement westward, explain American development." The frontier, he added, had shaped the national character in fundamental ways. It was

> to the frontier [that] the American intellect owes its striking characteristics. That coarseness and strength combined with acuteness and acquisitiveness; that practical, inventive turn of mind, quick to find expedients; that masterful grasp of material things, lacking in the artistic but powerful to effect great ends; that restless, nervous energy; that dominant individualism, working for good and for evil, and withal that buoyancy and exuberance which comes with freedom—these are traits of the frontier, or traits called out elsewhere because of the existence of the frontier.

In 1893, Turner concluded, "four centuries from the discovery of America, at the end of a hundred years under the Constitution, the frontier has gone and with its going has closed the first period of American history."

Turner's "frontier thesis" guided several generations of scholars and students in their understanding of the distinctive characteristics of American history. His view of the frontier as the westward-moving source of the nation's democratic politics, open society, unfettered economy, and rugged individualism, far removed from the corruptions of urban life, gripped the popular imagination as well. But it left out much of the story. The frontier experience Turner described exaggerated the homogenizing effect of the frontier environment and virtually ignored the role of women, African Americans, Native Americans, Mormons, Hispanics, and Asians in shaping the diverse human geography of the western United States. Turner also implied that the West would be fundamentally different after 1890 because the frontier experience was essentially over. But in many respects that region has retained the qualities associated with the rush for land, gold, timber, and water rights during the post–Civil War decades. The mining frontier, as one historian has recently written, "set a mood that has never disappeared from the West: the attitude of extractive industry—get in, get rich, get out."

End of Chapter Review

- **Southern Segregation** By 1900 elite southern whites had regained control of state governments; prominent black Republicans had been squeezed out of political positions; and black men were being kept from exercising their right to vote. Segregation became the social norm. Some African American leaders, most prominently Booker T. Washington, believed that by showing deference to whites, blacks could avoid violence while quietly acquiring an education and property. Others, like Ida B. Wells and W. E. B. Du Bois, wanted to fight segregation and lynching through the courts.

- **Indian Wars and Policies** By 1900, Native Americans in the West were no longer free to roam the plains. Disease and the influx of farmers and miners reduced their numbers and curtailed their way of life. Instances of resistance, such as the Great Sioux War, were dealt with harshly. Initially, Indian tribes were forced to sign treaties and were confined to reservations. From 1887 the American government's Indian policy was aimed at forcing Indians to relinquish their traditional culture and adopt individual land ownership, settled agriculture, and Christianity.

- **Life in the West** Life in the West was harsh and violent, but the promise of cheap land or wealth from mining drew settlers from the East. Most cowboys and miners did not acquire wealth, however, because raising cattle and mining became large-scale enterprises that enriched only a few. Although most westerners were white Protestant Americans or northern European immigrants, Mexicans, African Americans, and Chinese contributed to the West's diversity. As a consequence of the region's rugged isolation, women achieved greater equality in everyday life than did most women elsewhere in the country.

- **Growth of Mining** Mining lured settlers to largely uninhabited regions, thereby hastening the creation of new territories and the admission of new states into the Union. By the 1880s, when mining became a big business employing large-scale equipment, its environmental impact could be seen in the blighted landscape.

- **The American Frontier** The historian Frederick Jackson Turner believed that the enduring presence of the frontier was responsible for making Americans individualistic, materialistic, practical, democratic, and energetic. In 1893 he declared that the closing of the frontier had ended the first stage of America's history.

CHRONOLOGY

1859	Comstock Lode is discovered
1862	Congress passes the Homestead Act
1864	Sand Creek Massacre
1873	Joseph Glidden invents barbed wire
1876	Battle of Little Bighorn
1877	With the Compromise of 1877, Rutherford B. Hayes becomes president and Reconstruction comes to an end
1886	Surrender of Geronimo marks the end of the Indian wars
1887	Congress passes the Dawes Severalty Act
1890	Battle of Wounded Knee
1890	Mississippi Plan
1895	Booker T. Washington delivers his Atlanta Compromise speech
1896	Supreme Court issues *Plessy v. Ferguson* decision
1909	National Association for the Advancement of Color People is created

KEY TERMS & NAMES

New South p. 748

sharecropping p. 752

Bourbons p. 753

Redeemers p. 753

"Jim Crow" laws p. 756

Mississippi Plan p. 757

"separate but equal" p. 759

Booker T. Washington p. 761

W. E. B. Du Bois p. 761

Ida B. Wells p. 761

panning p. 767

George A. Custer p. 771

Great Sioux War p. 771

Ghost Dance movement p. 773

range wars p. 779

20

BIG BUSINESS AND ORGANIZED LABOR

FOCUS QUESTIONS wwnorton.com/studyspace

- What fueled the growth of the post–Civil War economy?
- What roles were played by leading entrepreneurs like John D. Rockefeller, Andrew Carnegie, and J. Pierpont Morgan?
- Who composed the labor force of the period, and what were labor's main grievances?
- What led to the rise of labor unions?

America emerged as an industrial and agricultural giant in the late nineteenth century. Between 1869 and 1899 the nation's population nearly tripled, farm production more than doubled, and the value of manufactures grew sixfold. Within three generations after the Civil War, the predominantly rural nation burst forth as the world's preeminent industrial power. Bigness became the prevailing standard of corporate life, and social tensions and political chicanery worsened with the rising scale of business enterprise.

THE RISE OF BIG BUSINESS

The Industrial Revolution created huge corporations that came to dominate the economy—as well as political and social life—during the late nineteenth century. As businesses grew, their owners sought to integrate all the processes of production and distribution into single companies, thus creating even larger firms. Others grew by mergers, joining forces with their competitors in an effort to dominate entire industries. This process of industrial combination and concentration transformed the nation's economy and social order. It also sparked widespread dissent and the emergence of an organized labor movement.

Many factors converged to help launch the dramatic economic growth after the Civil War. The nation's unparalleled natural resources—forests, mineral wealth, rivers—along with a rapidly expanding population, were crucial ingredients. At the same time, inventors and business owners developed more efficient, labor-saving machinery and mass-production techniques that spurred dramatic advances in productivity and efficiency. As the volume and efficiency of production increased, the larger businesses and industries expanded into numerous states and in the process developed standardized machinery and parts, which became available nationwide. Innovative, bold leadership was crucial. A group of shrewd, determined, and energetic entrepreneurs took advantage of fertile business opportunities to create huge enterprises. Federal and state politicians after the Civil War actively encouraged the growth of business by imposing high tariffs on foreign manufacturers as a means of blunting competition and by providing land and cash to finance railroads and other internal improvements. At the same time that the federal government was issuing massive land grants to railroads and speculators, it was also distributing land to farmers through the Homestead Act of 1862.

The American agricultural sector, by 1870 the world's leader, fueled the rest of the economy by providing wheat and corn to be milled into flour and meal. With the advent of the cattle industry, the processes of slaughtering and packing meat themselves became major industries. So the farm sector directly stimulated the industrial sector of the economy. A national government-subsidized network of railroads connecting the East and West Coasts played a crucial role in the development of related industries and in the evolution of a national market for goods and services. Industry in the United States also benefited from an abundance of power sources—water, wood, coal, oil, and electricity—that were inexpensive compared with those of the other nations of the world.

THE SECOND INDUSTRIAL REVOLUTION   The Industrial Revolution "controls us all," said Yale sociologist William Graham Sumner, "because we are all in it." Sumner and other Americans living during the second half of the nineteenth century experienced what economic historians have termed the Second Industrial Revolution. The First Industrial Revolution began in Britain during the late eighteenth century. It was propelled by the convergence of three new technologies: the coal-powered steam engine, textile machines for spinning thread and weaving cloth, and blast furnaces to produce iron.

The Second Industrial Revolution began in the mid–nineteenth century and was centered in the United States and Germany. It was spurred by three related developments. The first was the creation of an interconnected national transportation and communication network, which facilitated the emergence of a national and even an international market for American goods and services. Contributing to this development were the completion of the national telegraph and railroad systems, the emergence of steamships, and the laying of the undersea telegraph cable, which spanned the Atlantic Ocean and connected the United States with Europe.

During the 1880s a second major breakthrough—the use of electric power—accelerated the pace of industrial change. Electricity created dramatic advances in the power and efficiency of industrial machinery. It also spurred urban growth through the addition of electric trolleys and subways, and it greatly enhanced the production of steel and chemicals.

The third major aspect of the Second Industrial Revolution was the systematic application of scientific research to industrial processes. Laboratories staffed by graduates of new research universities sprouted up across the country, and scientists and engineers discovered dramatic new ways to improve industrial processes. Researchers figured out, for example, how to

"The Hand of Man" (1902)

Photogravure by Alfred Stieglitz.

refine kerosene and gasoline from crude oil and how to improve steel production. Inventors developed new products—telephones, typewriters, adding machines, sewing machines, cameras, elevators, and farm machinery—that resulted in lower consumer prices. These advances in turn expanded the scope and scale of industrial organizations. Capital-intensive industries such as steel and oil, as well as processed food and tobacco, took advantage of new technologies to gain economies of scale that emphasized maximum production and national as well as international marketing and distribution.

BUILDING THE TRANSCONTINENTAL RAILROADS   Railroads were the first big business, the first magnet for the great financial markets, and the first industry to develop a large-scale management bureaucracy. The railroads opened the western half of the nation to economic development and transported raw materials to factories and retailers, and in so doing they created an interconnected national market. At the same time, the railroads were themselves gigantic consumers of iron, steel, lumber, and other capital goods.

Transcontinental railroads

Using picks, shovels, wheelbarrows, and horse-drawn carts, Chinese laborers largely helped to construct the Central Pacific track.

The renewal of railroad building after the Civil War filled out the rail network east of the Mississippi River. Gradually, tracks in the South that had been destroyed during the war, were rebuilt, and a spiderweb of new trunk lines was added throughout the country. But the most spectacular exploits were the monumental transcontinental lines built west of the Mississippi through granite mountains, over roaring rivers and deep canyons, and across desolate plains. Running through sparsely settled land, the western railroads promised little quick return on investment but served the national purpose of binding the country together and so received generous government support in the form of huge loans, land grants, and cash subsidies. The transcontinental railroads were feats of daring, engineering, construction and politics.

Before the Civil War, sectional differences over the choice of routes had held up the start of a transcontinental line. Secession and the departure of southern congressmen finally permitted passage of the Pacific Railroads Act, which Abraham Lincoln signed into law in 1862, authorizing a line along a north-central route, to be built by the Union Pacific Railroad westward from Omaha, Nebraska, and by the Central Pacific Railroad eastward from Sacramento, California. Both railroads began construction during the war, but most of the work was done after 1865 as the companies raced to get the most out of the generous federal subsidy, paid per mile of track. The Union Pacific pushed across the plains at a rapid pace, avoiding the Rocky Mountains by going through Evans Pass in Wyoming. Construction of the 2,000-mile rail line and hundreds of trestles was hasty, and much of it had to be redone later. The executives and financiers directing the transcontinental railroads often cut corners and bribed legislators. They also ruthlessly used federal troops to suppress the Plains Indians. But their shenanigans do not diminish the heroic efforts of the workers and engineers who built the rail lines, erected the bridges, and gouged out the tunnels under terrible conditions. Building the transcontinental railroads was an epic feat that tied a nation together, changed the economic and political landscape, and enabled the United States to emerge as a world power.

It took armies of laborers to build the railroads. The Union Pacific work crews, composed of former Union and Confederate soldiers, former slaves, and Irish and German immigrants, coped with bad roads, water shortages, extreme weather conditions, Indian attacks, and frequent accidents and injuries. The Central Pacific crews were composed mainly of courageous, disciplined Chinese workers lured to America first by the California gold rush and then by railroad jobs. Most of these "coolie" laborers were single men intent upon accumulating money and returning to their homeland, where they could then afford to marry and buy a parcel of land. Their temporary status and dream of a good life back in China apparently made them more willing than American laborers to endure the low pay of railroad work and the dangerous working conditions. Many railroad construction workers died on the job.

All sorts of issues delayed the effort to finish the transcontinental line. Iron prices spiked. Broken treaties prompted Indian raids. Blizzards shut down work for weeks. Fifty-seven miles east of Sacramento, construction crews encountered the towering Sierra Nevadas, through which they had to cut before reaching more level terrain in Nevada. The Union Pacific had built 1,086 miles compared with the Central Pacific's 689 when the race ended on the salt plains at Promontory, Utah. There, on May 10, 1869, former California governor Leland Stanford drove a gold spike symbolizing the railroad's completion.

The next transcontinental line, completed in 1881, linked the Atchison, Topeka, and Santa Fe Railroad with the Southern Pacific Railroad at Needles in southern California. The Southern Pacific, which had absorbed the

The Union Pacific meets the Central Pacific

The celebration of the completion of the first transcontinental railroad, Promontory, Utah, May 10, 1869.

Central Pacific, pushed through Arizona to Texas in 1882, where it made connections to St. Louis and New Orleans. To the north the Northern Pacific had connected Lake Superior with Oregon by 1883, and ten years later the Great Northern, which had slowly and carefully been building westward from St. Paul, Minnesota, thrust its way to Tacoma, Washington. Thus, before the turn of the century, five major trunk lines existed, supplemented by connections that afforded other transcontinental routes.

FINANCING THE RAILROADS   The railroads were built by private companies that raised money for construction primarily by selling bonds to American and foreign investors. Until 1850 constitutional scruples had

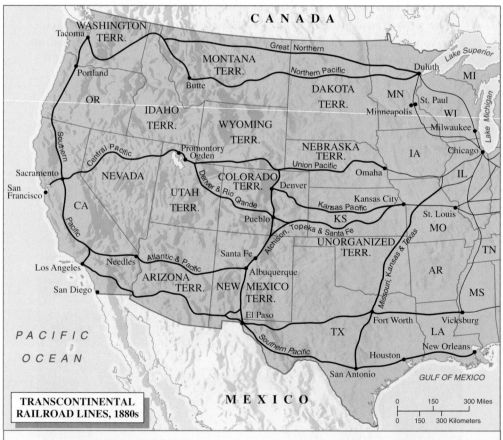

TRANSCONTINENTAL RAILROAD LINES, 1880s

What was the route of the first transcontinental railroad, and why was it not in the South? Who built the railroads? How were they financed?

constrained the granting of federal aid for internal improvements, although many states had subsidized railroads within their borders. But in 1850, Illinois senator Stephen Douglas secured from Congress a grant of public lands to subsidize a north-south railroad connecting Chicago and Mobile, Alabama. Over the next twenty years, federal land grants, mainly to transcontinental railroad companies, totaled 129 million acres. In addition to land, the railroads received massive financial aid from federal, state, and local governments.

In the long run, the federal government recovered much of its investment in transcontinental railroads and accomplished the purpose of linking the country together. As farms, ranches, and towns sprouted up around the rail lines, the value of the government land on either side of the tracks skyrocketed. The railroads also benefited the public by hauling government freight, soldiers, and equipment, as well as the mail, at half fare or free of charge. Moreover, by helping to accelerate the creation of a national market, the railroads spurred economic growth and thereby increased government tax revenues.

But that is only part of the story. The shady financial practices of railroad executives earned them the label of "robber barons," an epithet soon extended to other "captains of industry" as well. These were shrewd, determined, often dishonest men. The building of both the Union Pacific and the Central Pacific—as well as other transcontinental lines—induced shameless profiteering by construction companies controlled by insiders who overcharged the railroad companies. One such company, Crédit Mobilier of America, according to congressional investigators, bribed congressmen and charged the Union Pacific $94 million for a construction project that cost at most $44 million.

The prince of the railroad robber barons was Jay Gould, a secretive trickster who mastered the fine art of buying rundown railroads, making cosmetic improvements, and selling out at a profit, meanwhile using corporate funds for personal investment and judicious bribes for politicians and judges. Ousted by a reform group

Jay Gould

Prince of the railroad buccaneers.

"Commodore" Cornelius Vanderbilt

Vanderbilt consolidated control of the vast New York Central Railroad in the 1860s.

after looting New York's Erie Railroad, Gould moved on to richer spoils in western railroads. Nearly every enterprise he touched was compromised or ruined; Gould, meanwhile, was building a fortune that amounted to $100 million upon his death, at age fifty-six.

Few railroad fortunes were amassed in those freewheeling times by purely honest methods, but compared with opportunistic rogues such as Gould, most railroad owners were saints. They at least took some interest in the welfare of their companies, if not always in that of the public. Cornelius Vanderbilt, called Commodore by virtue of his early exploits in steamboating, stands out among the railroad barons. Already rich before the Civil War, he decided to give up the hazards of wartime shipping in favor of land transport. Under his direction the first of the major eastern railroad consolidations took form.

Vanderbilt merged separate trunk lines connecting Albany and Buffalo, New York, into a single powerful rail network led by the New York Central. This accomplished, he forged connections to New York City and then tried to corner the stock of his chief competitor, the Erie Railroad. But the directors of that line fended him off by printing new Erie stock faster than Vanderbilt could buy it. In 1873, however, he bought a midwest rail company that gave his lines connections to the lucrative Chicago market. After the Commodore's death, in 1877, his son William Henry extended the Vanderbilt railroads to include more than 13,000 miles in the Northeast. The consolidation trend was nationwide: about two thirds of the nation's railroad mileage were under the control of only seven major groups by 1900.

INVENTIONS SPUR MANUFACTURING The story of manufacturing after the Civil War shows much the same pattern of expansion and merger in old and new industries. Technological innovations spurred phenomenal increases in productivity. The U.S. Patent Office, which had recorded only 276 inventions during its first decade of existence, the 1790s, registered almost 235,000 in the 1890s. New processes in steelmaking and oil refining enabled those industries to flourish. The refrigerated railcar allowed the beef, mutton, and pork of the New West to reach a national market, giving rise to great packinghouse enterprises. Corrugated rollers that could crack the hard, spicy wheat of the Great Plains provided impetus to the flour milling industry that centered in Minneapolis under the control of the Pillsbury Company and others.

The list of innovations after the Civil War can be extended nearly indefinitely: barbed wire, farm implements, George Westinghouse's air brake for trains (1868), steam turbines, gas distribution and electrical devices, Christopher Sholes's typewriter (1867), Ives McGaffey's vacuum cleaner (1869), and countless others. Before the end of the century, the internal-combustion engine and the motion picture were stimulating new industries that would emerge in the twentieth century.

These technological advances transformed daily life. In no field was this more true than in the application of electricity to power and communications. Few if any inventions of the time could rival the importance of the telephone, which Alexander Graham Bell patented in 1876. To promote the new device, the inventor and his supporters formed the Bell Telephone Company. Its stiffest competition came from Western Union, which after turning down a chance to buy Bell's "toy," employed Thomas Edison to develop an improved version. Bell sold its rights and properties for a tidy sum, clearing the way for the creation of the American Telephone and Telegraph Company. By 1899 it was a huge holding company controlling forty-nine licensed subsidiaries and an operating company for long-distance lines.

New technologies

Alexander Graham Bell being observed by businessmen at the New York end of the first long-distance telephone call to Chicago, 1892.

In the development of electrical industries, the name Thomas Alva Edison stands above those of other inventors. Edison invented the phonograph in 1877 and the first lightbulb in 1879. Altogether he created or perfected hundreds of new devices and processes, including the storage battery, Dictaphone, mimeograph, electric motor, electric transmission, and the motion picture.

Until 1880 or so the world was lit by flickering oil and gas lamps. In 1882, with the backing of J. P. Morgan, the Edison Electric Illuminating Company supplied electrical current to eighty-five customers in New York City, beginning the great electric utility industry. A number of companies making lightbulbs merged into the Edison General Electric Company in 1888. But the use of direct current limited Edison's lighting system to a radius of about two miles. To cover greater distances required an alternating current, which could be transmitted at high voltage and then stepped down by transformers. George Westinghouse, inventor of the air brake for railroads, developed the first alternating-current electric system in 1886 and set up the Westinghouse Electric Company to manufacture the equipment. Edison resisted the new method as too risky, but the Westinghouse system won the "battle of the currents," and the Edison companies had to switch over. After the invention of the alternating-current motor by a Serbo-Croatian immigrant named Nikola Tesla, Westinghouse improved upon it. This invention enabled factories to locate wherever they wished; they no longer had to cluster around waterfalls and coal deposits for a ready supply of energy.

ENTREPRENEURS

Thomas Edison and George Westinghouse were rare examples of inventors with the luck and foresight to get rich from the industries they created. The great captains of commerce were more often pure entrepreneurs rather than inventors, men skilled mainly in organizing and promoting big business. Several post–Civil War entrepreneurs stand out for both their achievements and their special contributions: John D. Rockefeller and Andrew Carnegie for their innovations in organization, J. Pierpont Morgan for his development of investment banking, and Richard Sears and Alvah Roebuck for their creation of mail-order retailing.

John D. Rockefeller

His Standard Oil Company dominated the oil industry.

ROCKEFELLER AND THE OIL TRUST Born in New York State, the son of a flamboyant con-man father and a devout Baptist mother, John D. Rockefeller moved as a youth to Cleveland, Ohio. Soon thereafter his father abandoned the family and started a new life under an assumed name with a second wife. Raised by his mother, John Rockefeller developed a passion for systematic organization and self-discipline. He was obsessed with precision, order, and tidiness. And early on he decided to bring order and rationality to the chaotic oil industry.

The railroad and shipping connections around Cleveland made it a strategic location for servicing the oil fields of western Pennsylvania. The first oil well had been struck in 1859 in Titusville, Pennsylvania, and led to the Pennsylvania oil rush of the 1860s. As oil could be refined into kerosene, which could be used in lighting, heating, and cooking, the economic importance of the oil rush soon outstripped that of the California gold rush of just ten years before. Well before the end of the Civil War, derricks checkered western Pennsylvania, and refineries sprang up in Pittsburgh and Cleveland. Of the two cities, Cleveland had the edge in transportation, and Rockefeller focused his energies there.

Rockefeller recognized the potential profits in refining oil, and in 1870 he incorporated his various interests, naming the enterprise the Standard Oil Company of Ohio. Although Rockefeller was the largest refiner, he wanted all of the oil business. So he decided to weed out the competition, which he

The rise of oil

Wooden derricks crowd the farm of John Benninghoff in Oil Creek, Pennsylvania, in the 1860s.

perceived as flooding the market with too much refined oil, bringing down prices and reducing profits. Rockefeller approached his Cleveland competitors and offered to buy them out. Those who resisted were forced out. In less than six weeks, Rockefeller had taken over twenty-two of his twenty-six rivals. By 1879, Standard Oil was controlling 90 to 95 percent of the oil refining in the country.

Much of Rockefeller's success was based upon his determination to "pay nobody a profit." Instead of depending upon the products or services of other firms, known as middlemen, Standard Oil produced its own barrels, cans, staves, and whatever else it needed—in economic terms this is called vertical integration. The company also kept large amounts of cash reserves to make it independent of banks in case of a crisis. Furthermore, Rockefeller set out to control his transportation needs. With Standard Oil owning most of the pipelines leading to railroads, plus the railroad tank cars and the oil-storage facilities, it was able to dissuade the railroads from serving its eastern competitors. Those rivals that had insisted upon holding out then faced a giant marketing organization capable of driving them to the wall with price wars.

To consolidate their scattered business interests under more efficient control, Rockefeller and his advisers resorted to a new legal device: in 1882 they organized the Standard Oil Trust. All thirty-seven stockholders in various Standard Oil enterprises conveyed their stock to nine trustees, receiving "trust certificates" in return. The nine trustees thereby controlled all the varied Standard Oil companies.

But the trust device, widely copied by other companies in the 1880s, proved vulnerable to prosecution under state laws against monopoly or restraint of trade. In 1892, Ohio's supreme court ordered the Standard Oil Trust dissolved. For a while the company managed to unify control by the simple device of interlocking directorates, through which the board of directors of one company was made identical or nearly so to the boards of the others. Gradually, however, Rockefeller perfected the idea of the holding company: a company that controlled other companies by holding all or at least a majority of their stock. He was convinced that such big business was a natural result of capitalism at work. "It is too late," he declared in 1899, "to argue about the advantages of [huge] industrial combinations. They are a necessity." That year, Rockefeller brought his empire under the direction of the Standard Oil Company of New Jersey, a gigantic holding company. Though less vulnerable to prosecution under state law, some holding companies were broken up by the Sherman Anti-Trust Act of 1890.

Rockefeller not only made a colossal fortune, but he also gave much of it away, mostly to support advances in education and medicine. A man of simple tastes who opposed the use of tobacco and alcohol and believed his fortune was a public trust awarded by God, he became the world's leading philanthropist. He donated more than $500 million during his ninety-eight-year lifetime. "I have always regarded it as a religious duty," Rockefeller said late in life, "to get all I could honorably and to give all I could."

CARNEGIE AND THE STEEL INDUSTRY   Andrew Carnegie, like Rockefeller, experienced an atypical rise from poverty to riches. Born in Scotland, he migrated in 1848 with his family to Allegheny County, Pennsylvania. Then thirteen, he started work as a bobbin boy in a textile mill. In 1853 he became personal secretary and telegrapher to Thomas Scott, then district superintendent of the Pennsylvania Railroad and later its president. When Scott moved up, Carnegie took his place as superintendent. During the Civil War, when Scott became assistant secretary of war in charge of transportation, Carnegie went with him and developed a military telegraph system.

Carnegie kept on moving—from telegraphy to railroading to bridge building and then to steelmaking and investments. Until the mid–nineteenth century, steel could be made only from wrought iron—itself expensive—and only in small quantities. Then, in 1855, Briton Sir Henry Bessemer invented what became known as the Bessemer converter, a process by which steel could be produced directly and quickly from pig iron (crude iron made in a blast furnace). In 1873, Carnegie resolved to concentrate on steel. Steel was the miracle material of the post–Civil War era, not because it was new but because Bessemer's process had made it suddenly cheap. As more steel was produced, its price dropped and uses soared. In 1860 the United States had produced only 13,000 tons of steel. By 1880, production had reached 1.4 million tons.

Carnegie was never a technical expert on steel. He was a promoter, salesman, and organizer with a gift for hiring men of expert ability. He insisted upon up-to-date machinery and equipment and used times of recession to expand cheaply by purchasing struggling companies. He also preached to his

Andrew Carnegie

Steel magnate and business icon.

Carnegie's empire

The huge Carnegie steel plant at Homestead, Pennsylvania.

employees a philosophy of continual innovation in order to reduce operating costs.

Carnegie stood out from other business titans as a thinker who fashioned a philosophy of big business, a conservative rationale that became deeply ingrained in the conventional wisdom of some Americans. He believed that however harsh their methods at times, he and other captains of industry were on the whole public benefactors. In his best-remembered essay, "The Gospel of Wealth" (1889), he argued that in the evolution of society the contrast between the millionaire and the laborer measures the distance society has come. "Not evil, but good, has come to the race from the accumulation of wealth by those who have the ability and energy that produces it." The process had been costly in many ways, but the law of human competition is "best for the trade, because it insures the survival of the fittest in every department."

When Carnegie retired from business, at age sixty-five, he devoted himself to dispensing his fortune for the public good, out of a sincere desire to promote social welfare and further world peace. He called himself a "distributor" of wealth (he disliked the term *philanthropy*). He gave money to many universities, built 1,700 libraries, and helped fund numerous hospitals, parks, halls for meetings and concerts, swimming pools, and church buildings. He also donated 800 organs to churches around the world.

J. P. MORGAN, FINANCIER   Unlike Rockefeller and Carnegie, J. Pierpont Morgan was born to wealth, increasing it enormously through his bold innovations. His father was a partner in a London banking house, which he later came to direct. Young Pierpont attended boarding school in Switzerland and university in Germany. After a brief apprenticeship he was sent in 1857 to work in a New York firm representing his father's interests and in 1860 set himself up as its New York agent under the name J. Pierpont Morgan and Company. That firm, under various names, channeled European capital into the United States and grew into a financial power in its own right.

Morgan was an investment banker, which meant that he would buy corporate stocks and bonds wholesale and sell them at a profit. The growth of large corporations put investment firms such as Morgan's in an increasingly strategic position in the economy. Since the investment business depended upon the general good health of client companies, investment bankers became involved in the operation of their clients' firms, demanding seats on the boards of directors so as to influence company policies.

Like John Rockefeller, J. P. Morgan sought to consolidate rival firms into giant trusts. Morgan early realized that railroads were the key to the times, and he acquired and reorganized one line after another. By the 1890s he alone controlled a sixth of the nation's railway system. To Morgan, an imperious, domineering man, the stability brought by his operations helped the economy and the public. His crowning triumph was consolidation of the steel industry. After a rapid series of mergers in the iron and steel industry, he bought out Andrew Carnegie's huge steel and iron holdings in 1901. In rapid succession, Morgan added other steel interests as well as the Rockefeller iron ore holdings in Minnesota's Mesabi Range and a Great Lakes shipping fleet. The new United States Steel Corporation, a holding

J. Pierpont Morgan

Morgan is shown here in a famous 1903 portrait by Edward Steichen.

company for these varied interests, was a marvel of the new century, the first billion-dollar corporation, the climactic event in the age of relentless business consolidation.

SEARS AND ROEBUCK American inventors helped manufacturers after the Civil War produce a vast number of new products, but the most important challenge was extending the reach of national commerce to the millions of people who lived on isolated farms and in small towns. In the aftermath of the Civil War, a traveling salesman from Chicago named Aaron Montgomery Ward decided that he could reach more people by mail than on foot and in the process could eliminate the middlemen whose services increased the retail price of goods. Beginning in the early 1870s, Montgomery Ward and Company began selling goods at a 40 percent discount through mail-order catalogs.

By the end of the century, a new retailer had come to dominate the mail-order industry: Sears, Roebuck and Company, founded by two young midwestern entrepreneurs, Richard Sears and Alvah Roebuck, who began offering a cornucopia of goods by mail in the early 1890s. The Sears, Roebuck catalog in 1897 was 786 pages long. It featured groceries, drugs, tools, bells, furniture,

The rise of business

A lavish dinner celebrated the merger of the Carnegie and Morgan interests in 1901. The shape of the table is meant to symbolize a rail.

iceboxes, stoves, household utensils, musical instruments, farm implements, boots and shoes, clothes, books, and sporting goods. The company's ability to buy goods in high volume from wholesalers enabled it to sell items at prices below those offered in rural general stores. By 1907, Sears, Roebuck and Company had become one of the largest business enterprises in the nation.

Cover of the 1897 Sears, Roebuck and Company catalog

Sears, Roebuck's extensive mail-order business and discounted prices allowed its many products to reach customers in cities and in the backcountry.

The Sears catalog helped create a truly national market and in the process transformed the lives of millions of people. With the advent of free rural mail delivery in 1898 and the widespread distribution of Sears catalogs, families on farms and in small towns and villages could purchase by mail the products that heretofore were either prohibitively expensive or available only to city dwellers. By the turn of the century, 6 million Sears catalogs were being distributed each year, and the catalog had become the single most widely read book in the nation after the Bible.

LABOR CONDITIONS AND ORGANIZATION

SOCIAL TRENDS Accompanying the spread of huge corporations during the so-called Gilded Age was a rising standard of living for most people. If the rich were still getting richer, a lot of other people were at least better off. But disparities in the distribution of wealth had hardly disappeared. One set of estimates reveals that in both 1860 and 1900 the richest 2 percent of American families owned more than a third of the nation's wealth, while the top 10 percent owned almost three fourths of it. Studies of social mobility in towns across the country, however, show that while the rise from rags to riches was rare, "upward mobility both from blue-collar to white-collar callings and from low-ranked to high-ranked manual jobs was quite common."

The continuing demand for unskilled or semiskilled workers, meanwhile, attracted new groups entering the workforce at the bottom: immigrants above all, but also growing numbers of women and children. Because of a long-term decline in prices and the cost of living, real wages and earnings in manufacturing went up about 50 percent between 1860 and 1890 and another 37 percent from 1890 to 1914. By modern-day standards, however, working conditions were dreary—and often dangerous. At the turn of the century, the average hourly wage in manufacturing was about $3.50 in 2009 constant dollars. The average workweek was fifty-nine hours, or nearly six ten-hour days, but that was only an average. Most steelworkers put in a twelve-hour day, and as late as the 1920s a great many worked a seven-day, eighty-four-hour week.

Although wage levels were rising overall, working and living conditions remained precarious. In the crowded tenements and immigrant neighborhoods of major cities, the death rate was much higher than that in the countryside. Factories often maintained poor health and safety conditions. American industry had the highest accident rate in the world. In 1913, for instance, there were some 25,000 workplace fatalities and 700,000 job-related injuries that required at least four weeks' disability. The United States was the only industrial nation in the world that had no workmen's compensation program to provide support for workers injured on the job. The new industrial culture after the Civil War was also increasingly impersonal. Ever-larger numbers of people were dependent upon the machinery and factories of owners whom they seldom if ever saw. In the simpler world of small shops, workers and employers could enter into close relationships; the new large factories and corporations, on the other hand, were governed by a bureaucracy in which ownership was separate from management. Much of the social history of the modern world in fact turns upon the transition from a world of personal relationships to one of impersonal, contractual relationships.

CHILD LABOR   A growing number of wage laborers after the Civil War were children—boys and girls who worked full-time for meager wages under unhealthy conditions. Young people had of course always worked in America: farms required everyone to pitch in. After the Civil War, however, millions of children took up work outside the home, operating machines, sorting coal, stitching clothes, shucking oysters, peeling shrimp, canning food, blowing glass, and tending looms. Parents desperate for income believed they had no choice but to put their children to work. By 1880 one out of every six children in the nation was working full-time. And by 1900 there were almost

2 million child laborers in the United States. In southern cotton mills, where few African Americans were hired, a fourth of the employees were below the age of fifteen, with half of the children younger than twelve. Children as young as eight were laboring alongside adults twelve hours a day, six days a week. This meant they received little or no education and had little time for play or parental nurturance.

Factories, mills, mines, and canneries were dangerous places, especially for children. Few machines had safety devices, and few factories or mills had ventilating fans or fire escapes. Throughout Appalachia, soot-smeared boys worked deep in the coal mines. In New England and the South, thousands of young girls worked in dusty textile mills, brushing away lint from the clacking machines and retying broken threads. Children suffered three times as many accidents as adult workers, and respiratory diseases were common in the unventilated buildings. A child working in a textile mill was only half as likely to reach the age of twenty as a child outside a mill. Although some states passed laws limiting the number of hours children could work and establishing minimum-age requirements, they were rarely enforced and often ignored. By 1881 only seven states, mostly in New England, had laws requiring children to be at least twelve before they worked for

Children in industry

Four young boys who did the dangerous work of mine helpers in West Virginia in 1900.

wages. Yet the only proof required by employers in such states was a statement from a child's parents. Working-class and immigrant parents were often so desperate for income that they forged work permits for their children or taught them to lie about their age to keep a job.

DISORGANIZED PROTEST   Under these circumstances it was very difficult for workers to organize unions. Civic leaders respected property rights more than the rights of labor. Many businessmen believed that a "labor supply" was simply another commodity to be procured at the lowest possible price. Among workers recently removed from an agrarian world of independent farmers, the idea of labor unions was slow to take hold. And much of the workforce was made up of immigrant workers from a variety of cultures. They spoke different languages and harbored ethnic animosities. Nonetheless, with or without unions, workers staged impromptu strikes in response to wage cuts and other grievances. Such action often led to violence, however, and three incidents of the 1870s colored much of the public's view of labor unions thereafter.

THE MOLLY MAGUIRES   The decade's early years saw a reign of terror in the Pennsylvania coalfields, attributed to an Irish group called the Molly Maguires. The Mollies took their name from an Irish patriot who had led violent resistance against the British. They were motivated by the dangerous working conditions in the mines and the owners' brutal efforts to suppress union activity. Convinced of the justness of their cause, the Mollies used intimidation, beatings, and killings to right perceived wrongs against Irish workers. Later investigations have shown that agents of the mine operators themselves stirred up some of the trouble. The terrorism reached its peak in 1874–1875, and mine owners hired Pinkerton detectives to stop the movement. One of the agents who infiltrated the Mollies produced enough evidence to have the leaders indicted. At trials in 1876, twenty-four of the Molly Maguires were convicted; ten were hanged. The trials also resulted in a wage reduction in the mines and the final destruction of the Miners' National Association, a weak union the Mollies had dominated.

THE RAILROAD STRIKE OF 1877   A far more widespread labor incident was the Great Railroad Strike of 1877, the first major interstate strike in American history. After the financial panic of 1873 and the ensuing depression, the major rail lines in the East had cut wages. In 1877 they made another 10 percent cut, which led most of the railroad workers at Martinsburg, West Virginia, to walk off the job and block the tracks. Without organized direction, however, the group of picketers degenerated into a mob that burned and plundered railroad property.

Walkouts and sympathy demonstrations spread spontaneously from Maryland to San Francisco. The railroad strike engulfed hundreds of cities and towns, leaving in its wake over 100 people dead and millions of dollars in property destroyed. Militiamen called in from Philadelphia managed to disperse one crowd at the cost of twenty-six lives but then found themselves besieged in the railroad's roundhouse, where they disbanded and shot their way out.

Federal troops finally quelled the violence. Looting, rioting, and burning went on for another day until the frenzy wore itself out. A reporter described the scene as "the most horrible ever witnessed, except in the carnage of war. There were fifty miles of hot rails, ten tracks side by side, with as many miles of ties turned into glowing coals and tons on tons of iron car skeletons and wheels almost at white heat." Eventually the strikers, lacking organized bargaining power, had no choice but to drift back to work. Everywhere, the strikes failed.

For many Americans the railroad strike raised the specter of a worker-based social revolution. As a Pittsburgh newspaper warned, "This may be the beginning of a great civil war in this country between labor and capital." Equally disturbing to those in positions of corporate and political power was the presence of many women among the protesters. A Baltimore journalist noted that the "singular part of the disturbances is the very active part taken by the women, who are the wives and mothers of the [railroad] firemen." From the point of view of organized labor, however, the Great Railroad Strike demonstrated potential union strength and the need for tighter organization.

THE SAND-LOT INCIDENT   In California the railroad strike indirectly gave rise to a working-class political movement. At a San Francisco sand lot a meeting to express sympathy for the railroad strikers ended with attacks on some passing Chinese. Within a few days sporadic anti-Chinese riots had led to a mob attack on Chinatown. The depression of the 1870s had hit the West Coast especially hard, and the Chinese were handy scapegoats for frustrated white laborers who believed the Asians had taken their jobs.

Soon an Irish immigrant, Denis Kearney, had organized the Workingmen's Party of California, whose platform called for ending Chinese immigration. A gifted agitator, himself only recently naturalized, Kearney harangued the "sand lotters" about the "foreign peril" and assaulted the rich railroad barons for exploiting the poor. In 1878 his new party won a hefty number of seats to a state constitutional convention. The Workingmen's

Denis Kearney

This cartoon shows support for Denis Kearney, who organized the Workingmen's Party of California, and his Chinese labor exclusion policy.

movement peaked in 1879, when it elected many members to the state legislature and the mayor of San Francisco. Kearney lacked the gift for building a durable movement, but as his party went to pieces, his anti-Chinese theme became a national issue—in 1882, Congress voted to prohibit Chinese immigration for ten years.

TOWARD PERMANENT UNIONS   Meanwhile, efforts to build a national labor union movement were gaining momentum. Earlier efforts, in the 1830s and 1840s, had largely been dominated by reformers with schemes that ranged from free homesteads to utopian socialism. But the 1850s had seen the beginning of "job-conscious" unions in selected skilled trades. By 1860 there were about twenty such craft unions. During the Civil War, because of the demand for skilled labor, those unions grew in strength and number.

Yet there was no overall federation of such groups until 1866, when the National Labor Union convened in Baltimore. The NLU comprised delegates from labor and reform groups more interested in political and social reform than in bargaining with employers. The groups espoused such ideas as the eight-hour workday, workers' cooperatives, greenbackism (the printing of paper money to inflate the currency and thereby relieve debtors), and equal rights for women and African Americans. After the head of the union died suddenly, its support fell away quickly, and by 1872 the NLU had disbanded. The National Labor Union was not a total failure, however. It was influential in persuading Congress to enact an eight-hour workday for federal employees and to repeal the 1864 Contract Labor Act, passed during the Civil War to encourage the importation of laborers by allowing employers to pay for their passage to America. Employers had taken advantage of the Contract Labor Act to recruit foreign laborers willing to work for lower wages than their American counterparts.

THE KNIGHTS OF LABOR Before the National Labor Union collapsed, another labor group of national standing had emerged: the Noble Order of the Knights of Labor, a name that evoked the aura of medieval guilds. The founder of the Knights of Labor, Uriah S. Stephens, a Philadelphia tailor, was a habitual joiner involved with several secret orders, including the Masons. His early training for the Baptist ministry also affected his outlook. Secrecy, he felt, along with a semireligious ritual, would protect members from retaliation by employers and create a sense of solidarity.

Members of the Knights of Labor

This national union was more egalitarian than most of its contemporaries.

The Knights of Labor, started in 1869, grew slowly, but during the depression of the 1870s, as other unions collapsed, it spread more rapidly. In 1878 its first general assembly established it as a national organization. Its preamble and platform endorsed the reforms advanced by previous workingmen's groups, including the creation of bureaus of labor statistics and mechanics' lien laws (to ensure payment of salaries), elimination of convict-labor competition, establishment of the eight-hour day, and use of paper currency. One plank in the platform, far ahead of the times, called for equal pay for equal work by men and women. Throughout its existence the Knights of Labor emphasized reform measures and preferred boycotts to strikes as a way to put pressure on employers. The Knights of Labor also proposed to organize worker cooperatives that would enable members, collectively, to own their own large-scale manufacturing and mining operations. The Knights allowed as members all who had ever worked for wages, except lawyers, doctors, bankers, and those who sold liquor. Theoretically it was one big union of all workers, skilled and unskilled, regardless of race, color, creed, or sex.

In 1879, Stephens was succeeded as head of the Knights of Labor by Terence V. Powderly, the thirty-year-old mayor of Scranton, Pennsylvania. Born of Irish immigrant parents, Powderly had started working for a railroad at age sixteen. In many ways he was unsuited to his new job as head of the Knights of Labor. He was frail, sensitive to criticism, and indecisive at critical moments. He was temperamentally opposed to strikes, and when they did occur, he did not always support the local groups involved. Yet the Knights owed their greatest growth to strikes that occurred under his leadership. In the 1880s the Knights increased their membership from about 100,000 to more than 700,000. In 1886, however, the organization peaked and went into rapid decline after the failure of a railroad strike.

ANARCHISM The tensions between labor and management during the late nineteenth century in the United States and Europe helped generate the doctrine of anarchism. Anarchists believed that government—any government—was in itself an abusive device used by the rich and powerful to oppress and exploit the working poor. Anarchists dreamed of the eventual disappearance of government altogether, and many of them believed that the transition to such a stateless society could be hurried along by promoting revolutionary action among the masses. One favored tactic was the use of dramatic acts of violence against representatives of the government. Many European anarchists emigrated to the United States during the last quarter of the nineteenth century, bringing with them their belief in the impact of "propaganda of the deed."

THE HAYMARKET AFFAIR   Labor-related violence increased during the 1880s. The Haymarket affair, for instance, grew indirectly out of agitation for an eight-hour workday. In 1884, Knights of Labor organizers set May 1, 1886, as the deadline for adopting the eight-hour workday in all trades. Chicago became the center of the movement, and on May 3, 1886, the International Harvester plant became the site of a clash between strikers and policemen in which one striker was killed.

Leaders of a minuscule anarchist movement in Chicago scheduled an open meeting the following night at Haymarket Square to protest the killing. After listening to long speeches promoting socialism and anarchism, the crowd was beginning to break up when a group of policemen arrived and called upon the meeting to disperse. At that point somebody threw a bomb at the police, killing one officer and wounding others. The police then fired into the crowd. Subsequently, in a trial marked by prejudice and hysteria, seven anarchist leaders were sentenced to death despite the lack of any evidence linking them to the bomb thrower, whose identity was never established. Of these, two were reprieved, one committed suicide in prison, and four were hanged. All but one of the group were German speaking, and that one held a membership card in the Knights of Labor.

The violent incident at Haymarket Square triggered widespread revulsion at the Knights of Labor and labor groups in general. Despite his best efforts, Terence Powderly could never dissociate in the public mind the Knights from the anarchists. He clung to leadership until 1893, but after that the union evaporated. By the turn of the century, it was but a memory. Several factors accounted for the Knights' decline, besides fear of their supposed radicalism: a leadership devoted more to reform than to the nuts and bolts of organization, the failure of the Knights' cooperative enterprises, and a preoccupation with politics that led the Knights to sponsor labor candidates in hundreds of local elections.

The Knights nevertheless attained some lasting achievements, among them the creation of the federal Bureau of Labor Statistics in 1884 as well as several state labor bureaus; the Foran Act of 1885, which, though weakly enforced, penalized employers who imported contract labor (an arrangement similar to the indentured servitude of colonial times, in which workers were committed to a term of labor in exchange for transportation to America); and an 1880 federal law providing for the arbitration of labor disputes. The Knights by example also spread the idea of unionism and initiated a new type of union organization: the industrial union, an industrywide union of skilled and unskilled workers.

GOMPERS AND THE AFL   The craft unions (skilled workers) opposed industrial unionism. Leaders of the craft unions feared that joining with unskilled laborers would mean a loss of their craft's identity and a loss of the skilled workers' greater bargaining power. Thus in 1886, delegates from twenty-five craft unions organized the American Federation of Labor (AFL). Its structure differed from that of the Knights of Labor in that it was a federation of national organizations, each of which retained a large degree of autonomy and exercised greater leverage against management.

Samuel Gompers served as president of the AFL from its start until his death, in 1924, with only one year's interruption. Born in England of Dutch Jewish ancestry, Gompers came to the United States as a teenager, joined the Cigarmakers' Union in 1864, and became president of his New York local in 1877. Unlike Terence Powderly and the Knights of Labor, Gompers focused on concrete economic gains—higher wages, shorter hours, better working conditions—and avoided involvement with utopian ideas or politics.

Gompers was temperamentally more suited than Powderly to the rough-and-tumble world of unionism. He had a thick hide, liked to talk and drink with workers in the back room, and willingly used strikes to achieve favorable trade agreements, including provisos for union recognition in the form of closed shops (which could hire only union members) or union-preference shops (which could hire others only if no union members were available).

Samuel Gompers

Head of the American Federation of Labor striking an assertive pose.

The AFL at first grew slowly, but by 1890 it had surpassed the Knights of Labor in membership. By the turn of the century, it claimed 500,000 members in affiliated unions; in 1914, on the eve of World War I, it had 2 million; and in 1920 it reached a peak of 4 million. But even then it embraced less than 15 percent of the nation's nonagricultural workers. All unions, including the unaffiliated railroad brotherhoods, accounted for little more than 18 percent of those workers. Organized labor's strongholds

Union workers

A cigar-box label celebrating union workers, ca. 1898.

were in transportation and the building trades. Most of the larger manufacturing industries—including steel, textiles, tobacco, and packinghouses—remained almost untouched. Gompers never frowned upon industrial unions, and several became important affiliates of the AFL: the United Mine Workers, the International Ladies Garment Workers, and the Amalgamated Clothing Workers. But the AFL had its greatest success in organizing skilled workers.

THE HOMESTEAD STRIKE   Two violent incidents in the 1890s stalled the emerging industrial-union movement and set it back for the next forty years: the Homestead steel strike of 1892 and the Pullman strike of 1894. Those dramatic labor conflicts in several respects represented the culminating events of the Gilded Age, a bewildering era during which huge corporations came to exercise overweening influence over American life. Both events pitted organized labor in a bitter contest against two of the nation's largest and most influential corporations. In both cases the stakes were enormous. The two strikes not only represented a test of strength for the organized labor movement but also served to reshape the political landscape at the end of the nineteenth century.

The Amalgamated Association of Iron and Steel Workers, founded in 1876, had by 1891 a membership of more than 24,000 and was probably the largest craft union at the time. But it excluded unskilled steelworkers and had failed to organize the larger steel plants. The massive Homestead Works near Pittsburgh was an important exception. There the union, which included about a fourth of Homestead's 3,800 workers, had enjoyed friendly relations with Andrew Carnegie's company until Henry Clay Frick became its president in 1889. A showdown was delayed until 1892, however, when the union contract came up for renewal. Carnegie, who had expressed sympathy for unions in the past, had gone hunting in his native Scotland and left matters in Frick's hands. Yet Carnegie knew what was afoot: a cost-cutting reduction in the number of highly paid skilled workers through the use of labor-saving machinery and a deliberate attempt to smash the union. "Am with you to the end," he wrote to Frick.

As negotiations dragged on, the company announced on June 25 that it would treat workers as individuals unless an agreement with the union was reached by June 29. A strike—or, more properly, a lockout of unionists—began on that date. In no mood to negotiate, Frick built a twelve-foot fence around the entire plant and hired 300 union-busting Pinkerton detectives to protect what was soon dubbed Fort Frick. On the morning of July 6, 1892, when the Pinkertons floated up the Monongahela River on barges, unionists were waiting behind breastworks on shore. Who fired the first shot remains unknown, but a fourteen-hour battle broke out in which seven workers and three Pinkertons died. In the end the Pinkertons surrendered and were marched away, subjected to taunts and beatings from crowds in the street. Six days later Pennsylvania's governor dispatched 8,500 state militia to protect the strikebreakers hired by Frick to restore production.

The strike dragged on until November, but by then the union was dead at Homestead, its leaders charged with murder and treason. Its cause was not helped when an anarchist, a Lithuanian immigrant named Alexander Berkman, tried to assassinate Frick on July 23, shooting him twice and stabbing him four times. Much of the local sympathy for the strikers evaporated. Penniless and demoralized, the defeated workers ended their walkout on November 20 and accepted the company's terms. Only a fifth of the strikers were hired back. Carnegie and Frick, with the support of local, state, and national government officials, had eliminated the union. Across the nation in 1892, state militias intervened to quash twenty-three labor disputes. In the ongoing struggles between workers and owners, big business held sway—in the workplace and in state governments. The Homestead strike was symptomatic of the overweening power of industrial capitalism. By 1899, Andrew Carnegie could report to a friend: "Ashamed to tell you [of my] profits these days. Prodigious!"

THE PULLMAN STRIKE   Even more than Homestead, the Pullman strike of 1894 was a notable walkout in American history. It paralyzed the economies of the twenty-seven states and territories making up the western half of the nation. It involved a dispute at Pullman, Illinois, a model industrial town built on 4,000 acres outside Chicago, where workers of the Pullman Palace Car Company were housed. The town's idyllic appearance was deceptive, however. Employees were required to live there, pay rents and utility costs that were higher than those in nearby towns, and buy goods from company stores. During the depression of 1893, George Pullman laid off 3,000 of his 5,800 employees and cut wages 25 to 40 percent, but not his rents and other charges. After Pullman fired three members of a workers' grievance committee, a strike began on May 11, 1894.

During this tense period, Pullman workers had been joining the new American Railway Union, founded the previous year by Eugene V. Debs. The tall, gangly Debs was a man of towering influence and charismatic appeal.

The Pullman strike

Troops guarding the railroads, 1894.

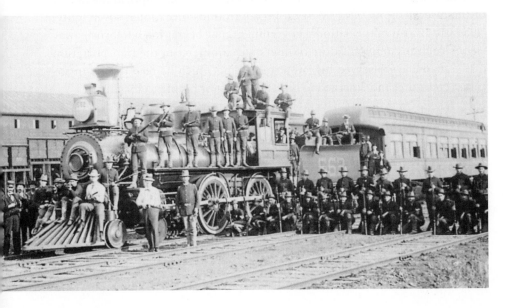

A child of working-class immigrants, he quit school at age fourteen and began working for an Indiana railroad. By the early 1890s Debs had become a tireless spokesman for labor radicalism, and he strove to organize *all* railway workers—skilled or unskilled—into the American Railway Union. Soon he was in charge of a powerful new labor organization, and he quickly turned his attention to the controversy in Pullman, Illinois.

In June 1894, after George Pullman refused Debs's plea for arbitration, the union workers stopped handling Pullman railcars. By the end of July they had tied up most of the railroads in the Midwest. Railroad executives then hired strikebreakers to connect mail cars to Pullman cars so that interference with Pullman cars would entail interference with the federal mail. The U.S. attorney general, a former railroad attorney himself, swore in 3,400 special deputies to keep the trains running. When clashes occurred between those deputies and some of the strikers, angry workers ignored Debs's plea for an orderly boycott. They assaulted strikebreakers ("scabs") and destroyed property.

Finally, on July 3, 1894, President Grover Cleveland sent federal troops into the Chicago area, where the strike was centered. The Illinois governor insisted that the state could keep order, but Cleveland claimed authority and a duty to ensure delivery of the mail. Meanwhile, the attorney general won an injunction forbidding any interference with the mail or any effort to restrain interstate commerce; the principle was that a strike or boycott violated the 1890 Sherman Anti-Trust Act. On July 13 the union called off the strike. A few days later the district court cited Debs for violating the injunction, and he served six months in jail. The Supreme Court upheld the decree in the case of *In re Debs* (1895) on broad grounds of national sovereignty: "The strong arm of the national government may be put forth to brush away all obstructions to the freedom of interstate commerce or the transportation of the mails." Debs served his jail term, during which he read deeply in socialist literature, and emerged to devote the rest of his life to socialism.

MOTHER JONES   One of the most colorful and beloved labor agitators at the end of the nineteenth century was a remarkable woman known simply as Mother Jones. White haired, pink cheeked, and dressed in matronly black dresses and hats, she was a tireless champion of the working poor who used fiery rhetoric to excite crowds and attract media attention. She led marches, dodged bullets, served jail terms, and confronted business titans and police with disarming courage. In 1913 a district attorney called her the "most dangerous woman in America."

Born in Cork, Ireland, in 1837, Mary Harris was the second of five children in a poor Catholic family that fled the Irish potato famine at midcentury and settled in Toronto. In 1861 she moved to Memphis and began teaching. There, as the Civil War was erupting, she met and married George Jones, an iron molder and staunch union member. They had four children, and then disaster struck. In 1867 a yellow fever epidemic devastated Memphis, killing Mary Jones's husband and four children. The grief-stricken thirty-seven-year-old widow moved to Chicago and took up dressmaking, only to see her shop, home, and belongings destroyed in the great fire of 1871. Having lost her family and her finances and angry at the social inequality and injustices she saw around her, Mary Jones drifted into the labor movement and soon emerged as its most passionate advocate. Chicago was then the seedbed of labor radicalism, and the union culture nurtured in Mary Jones a lifelong dedication to the cause of wage workers and their families.

The gritty woman who had lost her family now declared herself the "mother" of the fledgling labor movement. She joined the Knights of Labor as an organizer and public speaker. In the late 1880s she became an ardent speaker for the United Mine Workers (UMW), various other unions, and the Socialist party. For the next thirty years she crisscrossed the nation, recruiting union members, supporting strikers (her "boys"), raising funds, walking picket lines, defying court injunctions, berating politicians, and spending time in prison.

Wherever Mother Jones went, she promoted higher wages, shorter hours, safe workplaces, and restrictions on child labor. Coal miners, said the UMW president, "have had no more staunch supporter, no more able defender than the one we all love to call Mother." During a miners' strike in West Virginia, Jones was arrested, convicted of "conspiracy that resulted in murder," and sentenced to twenty years in prison. The outcry over her plight helped spur a Senate committee to investigate conditions in the coal mines; the governor set her free.

Mother Jones was especially determined to end the exploitation of children in the workplace. In 1903 she organized a highly publicized week-long march of child workers from Pennsylvania to the New York home of President Theodore Roosevelt. The children were physically stunted and

Mother Jones

A pioneer of the labor movement.

mutilated, most of them missing fingers or hands from machinery accidents. President Roosevelt refused to see the ragtag children, but as Mother Jones explained, "Our march had done its work. We had drawn the attention of the nation to the crime of child labor." Soon the Pennsylvania state legislature raised the legal working age to fourteen.

Mother Jones lost most of the strikes she participated in, but over the course of her long life she saw average wages increase, working conditions improve, and child labor diminish. Her commitment to the cause of social justice never wavered. At age eighty-three she was arrested after joining a miners' strike in Colorado and jailed in solitary confinement. At her funeral, in 1930, one speaker urged people to remember her famous rallying cry: "Pray for the dead and fight like hell for the living."

SOCIALISM AND THE UNIONS   The major unions for the most part never allied themselves with socialists, as many European labor movements did. But socialist ideas had been circulating in the United States at least since the 1820s. Marxism, one strain of socialism, was imported mainly by German immigrants. Karl Marx's International Workingmen's Association, founded in 1864 and later called the First International, inspired only a few affiliates in the United States. In 1872, at Marx's urging, the headquarters was moved from London to New York. In 1877, followers of Marx in America organized the Socialist Labor party, a group so dominated by immigrants that German was initially its official language.

The movement gained little notice before the rise of Daniel De Leon in the 1890s. As editor of a Marxist newspaper, the *People,* he became the dominant figure in the Socialist Labor party. He proposed to organize socialist industrial unions and to build a political party that would abolish the government once it gained power, after which the unions of the Socialist Trade and Labor Alliance, formed under his supervision, would become the units of control. De Leon preached revolution at the ballot box, not by violence.

Eugene Debs was more successful than De Leon at building a socialist movement in America, however. In 1897, Debs announced that he was a socialist and organized the Social Democratic party from the remnants of the American Railway Union; he won over 96,000 votes as its candidate for president in 1900. The next year his followers joined a number of secessionists from De Leon's party to set up the Socialist Party of America. Debs polled over 400,000 votes as the party's candidate for president in 1904 and more than doubled that, to more than 900,000 votes, or 6 percent of the popular vote, in 1912. In 1910, Milwaukee elected a socialist mayor and congressman.

Eugene V. Debs

Founder of the American Railway Union and later candidate for president as head of the Socialist Party of America.

By 1912 the Socialist party seemed well on the way to becoming a permanent fixture in American politics. Thirty-three cities had socialist mayors. The party sponsored five English-language daily newspapers, eight foreign-language dailies, and a number of weeklies and monthlies. In the Southwest the party built a sizable grassroots following among farmers and tenants. Oklahoma, for instance, had more paid-up party members in 1910 than any other state except New York and in 1912 gave 16.5 percent of its popular vote to Debs, a greater proportion than any other state ever gave him. But the Socialist party reached its peak in 1912. It would be racked by disagreements over America's participation in World War I and was split thereafter by desertions to the new Communist party.

THE WOBBLIES   During the years of Socialist party growth, a parallel effort to revive industrial unionism emerged, led by the Industrial Workers of the World (IWW). The chief base for this group was the Western Federation of Miners, organized at Butte, Montana, in 1893. Over the next decade the Western Federation was the storm center of violent confrontations with unyielding mine operators who mobilized private armies against it in Colorado, Idaho, and elsewhere. In 1905 the founding convention of the IWW drew a variety of delegates who opposed the AFL's philosophy of organizing unions made up only of skilled workers. Eugene Debs participated, although many of his comrades preferred to work within the AFL. Daniel De Leon seized this chance to strike back at craft unionism. He argued that the IWW "must be founded on the class struggle" and "the irrepressible conflict between the capitalist class and the working class."

But the IWW waged class war better than it articulated class ideology. Like the Knights of Labor, it was designed to be "one big union," including all workers, skilled or unskilled. Its roots were in the mining and lumber camps of the West, where unstable conditions of employment created a large number of nomadic workers, to whom neither the AFL's pragmatic approach nor the socialists' political appeal held much attraction. The revolutionary goal of the Wobblies, as they came to be called, was an idea labeled syndicalism by its French supporters: the ultimate destruction of the government and its replacement by one big union. But just how that union would govern remained vague.

Like other radical groups, the IWW was split by sectarian disputes. Because of policy disagreements all the major founders withdrew, first the Western Federation of Miners, then Debs, then De Leon. William D. "Big Bill" Haywood of the Western Federation remained, however, and as its leader he held the group together. Haywood was an imposing figure. Well over six feet tall, handsome and muscular, he commanded the attention and respect of his listeners. This hard-rock miner, union organizer, and socialist from Salt Lake City despised the AFL and its conservative labor philosophy. He called Samuel Gompers "a squat specimen of humanity" who was "conceited, petulant, and vindictive." Instead of following Gompers's advice to organize only skilled workers, Haywood promoted the concept of one all-inclusive union dedicated to a socialism "with its working clothes on."

Haywood and the Wobblies, however, were reaching out to the fringe elements of the labor force with the least power and influence, chiefly the migratory workers of the West and the ethnic groups of the East. Always ambivalent about diluting their revolutionary principles, Wobblies scorned the usual labor agreements even when they participated in them. As a consequence, they engaged in spectacular battles with employers but scored few victories. The largest was a textile strike at Lawrence, Massachusetts, in 1912 that garnered wage raises, overtime pay, and other benefits. But the next year a strike of silk workers at Paterson, New Jersey, ended in disaster, and the IWW entered a rapid decline.

The fading of the Wobblies was accelerated by the hysterical opposition they aroused. Its members were branded anarchists, bums, and criminals. The IWW was effectively destroyed during World War I, when most of its leaders were jailed for conspiracy because of their militant opposition to the war. Big Bill Haywood fled to the Soviet Union, where he married a Russian woman, died in 1928, and was honored by burial in the Kremlin wall. The short-lived Wobblies left behind a rich folklore of nomadic workingmen and a gallery of heroic agitators, such as Elizabeth Gurley Flynn, a dark-haired Irishwoman who at age eighteen chained herself to a lamppost to impede her arrest during a strike. The movement also bequeathed martyrs such as the Swedish American singer and labor organizer Joe Hill, framed (so the faithful assumed) for murder and executed by a Utah firing squad. His last words were written to Haywood: "Goodbye, Bill. I die like a true blue rebel. Don't waste any time mourning. Organize." The intensity of conviction and devotion to a cause shown by Hill, Flynn, and others ensured that the IWW's ideal of a classless society did not die.

CHAPTER SUMMARY

- **Second Industrial Revolution** The postwar economy was characterized by large-scale industrial development and a burgeoning agriculture sector. The Second Industrial Revolution was fueled by the creation of national transportation and communications systems, the use of electric power, and the application of scientific research to industrial processes. The federal government encouraged growth by imposing high tariffs and granting the railroad companies public land.

- **Rising Big Business** The leading entrepreneurs were extraordinarily skilled at organizing and controlling industry. John D. Rockefeller eventually controlled nearly every facet of the oil industry, consolidating that control through trusts and holding companies. Andrew Carnegie, who believed that competition benefited both society and business, came to dominate the steel industry by buying struggling companies. J. Pierpont Morgan, an investment banker, not only controlled most of the nation's railroads but also bought Carnegie's steel interests in 1901, thereby creating the nation's first billion-dollar company.

- **Labor Conditions and Organizations** The labor force was largely composed of unskilled workers, including recent immigrants and growing numbers of women and children. Some children as young as eight years of age worked twelve hours a day in coal mines and southern mills. In hard times, business owners cut wages without discounting the rents they charged for company housing or the prices they charged in company stores.

- **Rising Labor Unions** It was difficult for unskilled workers to organize effectively. Strikebreakers were plentiful because new immigrants were desperate for work. Business owners often had recourse to state and local militias, which would be mobilized against strikers in the face of perceived anarchy. Craft unions became more successful at organizing as the American Federation of Labor focused on concrete economic gains and better working conditions and avoided involvement in politics.

CHRONOLOGY

1855	Bessemer converter process allows steel to be made quickly and inexpensively
1859	First oil well is struck in Titusville, Pennsylvania
1869	First transcontinental railroad is completed at Promontory, Utah
1876	Alexander Graham Bell patents his telephone
1876	Thomas A. Edison makes the first successful incandescent lightbulb
1877	Great Railroad Strike
1882	John D. Rockefeller organizes the Standard Oil Trust
1886	In the Haymarket incident, a bomb set off at a Chicago labor rally kills and wounds police officers
1886	American Federation of Labor is organized
1892	Homestead Strike
1894	Pullman Strike
1901	J. Pierpont Morgan creates the U.S. Steel Corporation

KEY TERMS & NAMES

21

THE EMERGENCE
OF URBAN AMERICA

FOCUS QUESTIONS wwnorton.com/studyspace

- What accounted for the rise of cities in America?
- How did the "new immigration" change America at the end of the nineteenth century?
- What new forms of mass entertainment had emerged by 1900?
- What was the impact of Darwinian thought on social sciences?
- What were some of the literary and philosophical trends of the late nineteenth century?

Cities are humanity's greatest creation. And in America during the second half of the nineteenth century, cities grew at a rate unparalleled in world history. The late nineteenth century, declared an economist in 1899, was "not only the age of cities, but the age of great cities." Between 1860 and 1910 the urban population mushroomed from 6 million to 44 million. By 1920 more than half the nation's population lived in urban areas. This rise of big cities created a distinctive urban culture. People from different ethnic and religious backgrounds and every walk of life poured into the high-rise apartment buildings and ramshackle tenements springing up in every major city. They came in search of jobs, wealth, and excitement.

Not surprisingly, the rise of metropolitan America created an array of new social problems. Rapid urban development produced widespread poverty and political corruption. How to feed, clothe, shelter, and educate the new arrivals taxed the imagination—and the patience—of urban leaders. Further complicating efforts to improve the quality of life in the nation's cities was increasing residential segregation according to racial and ethnic background and social class.

AMERICA'S MOVE TO TOWN

The prospect of good jobs and social excitement in the cities lured workers by the millions from the countryside and overseas. City people became distinctively urban in demeanor and outlook, and the contrasts between farm and city life grew more vivid with each passing year.

EXPLOSIVE URBAN GROWTH   The frontier was a societal safety valve, the historian Frederick Jackson Turner said in his influential thesis on American development. Its cheap lands afforded a release for the population pressures mounting in the cities. If there was such a thing as a safety valve in the nineteenth century, however, Turner had it exactly backward. The flow of population toward the cities was greater than the flow toward the West. Much of the westward movement, in fact, was itself an urban movement, spawning new towns near the mining digs or at the railheads. On the Pacific coast a greater portion of the population was urbanized than anywhere else; its major concentrations were around San Francisco Bay at first and then in Los Angeles, which became a boomtown after the arrival of the Southern Pacific and Santa Fe Railroads in the 1880s. In the Northwest, Seattle grew quickly, first as the terminus of three transcontinental railroad lines and, by the end of the century, as the staging area for the Yukon gold rush. Minneapolis, St. Paul, Omaha, Kansas City, and Denver experienced rapid growth as well. The South, too, produced new cities: Durham, North Carolina, and Birmingham, Alabama, which were centers of tobacco and iron production, and Houston, Texas, which handled cotton and cattle and, later, oil.

While the Far West had the greatest proportion of urban dwellers, the Northeast had far more people in its teeming cities. These city dwellers were increasingly landless and homeless: they had nothing but their labor to sell. By 1900 more than 90 percent of the residents in New York City's Manhattan lived in rented houses or congested multi-story apartment buildings, called tenements.

Several technological innovations allowed cities to expand vertically to accommodate their surging populations. In the 1870s, developments in heating, such as steam circulating through radiators, enabled the construction of large apartment buildings, since fireplaces were no longer needed. In

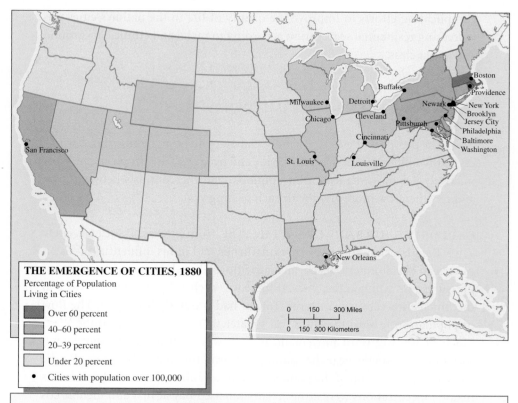

THE EMERGENCE OF CITIES, 1880
Percentage of Population
Living in Cities

- Over 60 percent
- 40–60 percent
- 20–39 percent
- Under 20 percent
- Cities with population over 100,000

Which states had the largest urban population in 1880? What drove the growth of western cities? How were western cities different from eastern cities?

1889 the Otis Elevator Company installed the first electric elevator, which made possible the erection of taller buildings—before the 1860s few structures had risen beyond three or four stories. And during the 1880s, engineers developed cast-iron and steel-frame construction techniques. Because such materials were stronger than brick, they allowed developers to erect highrise buildings, called skyscrapers.

Cities also expanded horizontally after the introduction of important transportation innovations. Before the 1890s the chief power sources of urban transport were either animals or steam. Horse- and mule-drawn streetcars had appeared in antebellum cities, but they were slow and cumbersome, and cleaning up after the animals added to the cost. In 1873, San Francisco became the first city to use cable cars that clamped onto a moving underground cable driven by a central power source. Some cities used steam-powered trains on

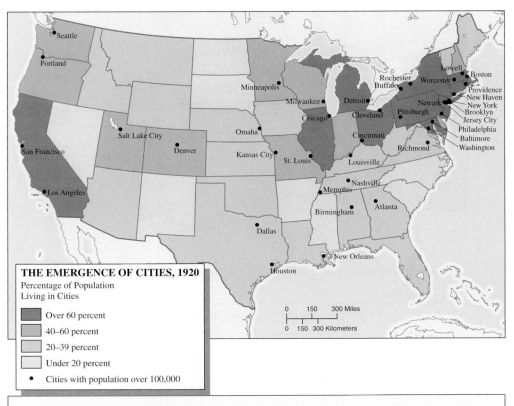

THE EMERGENCE OF CITIES, 1920
Percentage of Population
Living in Cities

- Over 60 percent
- 40–60 percent
- 20–39 percent
- Under 20 percent
- • Cities with population over 100,000

How did technology change urban life in the early twentieth century? What was the role of mass transit in expanding the urban population? How did the demographics of the new cities change between 1880 and 1920?

elevated tracks, but by the 1890s electric trolleys were preferred. Mass transit received an added boost when subways were built in Boston, New York City, and Philadelphia.

The spread of mass transit allowed large numbers of people to become commuters, and a growing middle class retreated from downtown to live in quieter tree-lined "streetcar suburbs," whence they could travel into the central city for business or entertainment (though working folk generally stayed put, unable to afford even the nickel fare). Urban growth often became a sprawl, since it usually took place without plan, in the interest of a fast buck, and without thought to the need for parks and public services.

The use of horse-drawn railways, cable cars, and electric trolleys helped transform the social character of cities. After the Civil War, the emergence of

Urban mass transit

A horse-drawn streetcar moving along rails in New York City.

suburbs began to segregate people according to their wealth. The more affluent moved outside the city, leaving behind the working folk, many of whom
were immigrants or African Americans. The poorer districts of a city became more congested and crime ridden as the population grew, fueled by
waves of newcomers from abroad.

THE ALLURE AND PROBLEMS OF THE CITIES   The wonders of
the cities—their glittering new electric lights, their streetcars, telephones,
department stores, vaudeville shows and other amusements, newspapers
and magazines, and a thousand other attractions—cast a magnetic lure on
rural youth. In times of rural depression, thousands left farms for the cities
in search of opportunity and personal freedom. The exodus from the countryside was especially evident in the East, where the census documented the
shift in population from country to city. Yet those who moved to the city
often traded one set of problems for another. Workers in the big cities often
had no choice but to live in crowded apartments, most of which were poorly
designed. In 1900, Manhattan's 42,700 tenements housed almost 1.6 million
people. Such unregulated urban growth created immense problems of sanitation, health, and morale.

During the last quarter of the nineteenth century, cities became so
cramped and land so scarce that designers were forced to build upward. In

New York City this resulted in tenement houses, shared buildings with multiple housing units. These structures were usually six to eight stories tall and jammed tightly against one another. Twenty-four to thirty-two families would cram into each building. Some city blocks housed almost 4,000 people. Shoehorned into their quarters, families living in tenements had no privacy, free space, or sunshine; children had few places to play except in the streets; infectious diseases and noxious odors were rampant. Not surprisingly, the mortality rate among the urban poor was much higher than that of the general population. In one poor Chicago district at the end of the century, three out of five babies died before their first birthday.

CITY POLITICS   After the Civil War the sheer size of the cities helped create a new form of politics. Because local government was often fragmented and beset by parochial rivalries, a need grew for a central organization to coordinate citywide services such as public transportation, sanitation, and utilities. Urban political machines thus developed, consisting of local committeemen and district captains led by a political boss. While the city bosses granted patronage favors (awarding city jobs to supporters) and engaged in graft, buying and selling votes, taking kickbacks and payoffs, they also provided needed services. They distributed food, coal, and money to the poor; found jobs for those who were out of work; sponsored English-language classes for immigrants; organized sports teams, social clubs, and neighborhood gatherings; and generally helped newcomers adjust to their new life. In return the political professionals felt entitled to some reward for having done the grubby work of the local organization.

CITIES AND THE ENVIRONMENT   Nineteenth-century cities were filthy and disease ridden, noisy and smelly. They overflowed with garbage, contaminated water, horse urine and manure, roaming pigs, and untreated sewage. Providing clean water was a chronic problem, and raw sewage was dumped into streets and waterways. Epidemics of water-related diseases such as cholera, typhoid fever, and yellow fever ravaged urban populations. Animal waste was pervasive. In 1900, for example, there were over 3.5 million horses in American cities, each of which generated 20 pounds of manure and several gallons of urine daily. In Chicago alone, 82,000 horses produced 300,000 tons of manure each year. The life expectancy of urban draft horses was only two years, which meant that thousands of horse carcasses had to be disposed of each year. In New York City, 15,000 dead horses were removed annually.

During the late nineteenth century, municipal reformers organized to clean up the cities. The "sanitary reformers"—public health officials and

Urbanization and the environment

A garbage cart retrieves trash in New York City, ca. 1890.

municipal engineers—persuaded city governments to banish hogs and cattle, mount cleanup campaigns, build water and sewage systems, institute trash collection, and replace horses with electric streetcars. By 1900, 94 percent of American cities had developed regular trash-collection services.

Yet such improvements in public health involved important social and ecological trade-offs and caused unanticipated problems. Waste that once had been put into the land was now dumped into waterways. Similarly, solving the horse-manure problem involved trade-offs. The manure dropped on city streets caused stench and bred countless flies, many of which carried diseases such as typhoid fever. But urban horse manure also had benefits. Farmers living on the outskirts of cities used it to fertilize hay and vegetable crops. City-generated manure was the agricultural lifeblood of the vegetable farms outside New York, Baltimore, Philadelphia, and Boston.

Ultimately, however, the development of public water and sewer systems and flush toilets separated urban dwellers and their waste from the agricultural cycle at the same time that the emergence of refrigerated railcars and massive meatpacking plants separated most people from their sources of food. While the advances provided great benefits, a flush-and-forget-it mentality emerged. Well into the twentieth century, people presumed that running water purified itself, so they dumped massive amounts of untreated waste into rivers and bays. What they failed to calculate was the carrying capacity of the waterways. The high phosphorous content of bodily waste dumped into streams led to algae blooms that sucked the oxygen out of the water and unleashed a string of environmental reactions that suffocated fish and affected marine ecology. In sum, city growth had unintended consequences.

THE NEW IMMIGRATION

The Industrial Revolution brought to American shores waves of new immigrants from every part of the globe. Between 1860 and 1920 about one in seven Americans was foreign-born. Immigrants were even more numerous in cities. By 1900 nearly 30 percent of the residents of major cities were foreign-born. These newcomers provided much-needed labor, but their arrival sparked ugly racial and ethnic tensions.

AMERICA'S PULL   The migration of foreigners to the United States has been one of the most powerful forces shaping American history, and this was especially true between 1860 and 1920. In steadily rising numbers, immigrants moved from the agricultural areas of eastern and southern Europe directly to the largest cities of America. Once in the United States, they wanted to live with others who shared their language, customs, and religion. Ethnic neighborhoods in American cities preserved familiar folkways and shielded newcomers from the shocks of a strange culture. In 1890 four out of five New Yorkers were foreign-born, a higher proportion than in any other city in the world. New York had twice as many Irish as Dublin, as many Germans as Hamburg, and half as many Italians as Naples. In 1893, Chicago claimed the largest Bohemian (Czech) community in the world, and by 1910 the size of its Polish population ranked behind only the populations of Warsaw and Lodz.

This nation of immigrants continued to draw new inhabitants for much the same reasons as before and from much the same segments of society. Immigrants took flight from famine or the dispiriting lack of opportunity in their native lands. They fled racial, religious, and political persecution and compulsory military service. Yet more immigrants were probably pulled by America's promise than were pushed out by conditions at home. American industries, seeking cheap labor, sent recruiting agents abroad. Railroads, eager to sell land and build up the traffic on their lines, distributed tempting propaganda in Europe in a medley of languages. Under the Contract Labor Act of 1864, the federal government helped pay an immigrant's passage. The

Steerage deck of the S.S. *Pennland*, 1893

These immigrants are about to arrive at Ellis Island in New York Harbor. Many newcomers to America settled in cities because they lacked the means to take up farming.

law was repealed in 1868, but not until 1885 did the government forbid companies to import contract labor, a practice that put immigrant workers under the control of their employers.

After the Civil War the tide of immigration rose from just under 3 million in the 1870s to more than 5 million in the 1880s, then fell to a little over 3.5 million in the depression decade of the 1890s and rose to its high-water mark of nearly 9 million in the first decade of the twentieth century. The numbers declined to 6 million from 1910 to 1920 and to 4 million in the 1920s, after which official restrictions nearly cut the flow of immigrants.

Before 1880, immigrants were mainly from northern and western Europe. By the 1870s, however, that pattern had begun to change. The proportion of Slavs and Jews from southern and eastern Europe rose sharply. After 1890 these groups made up a majority of the newcomers, and by the first decade of the new century they formed 70 percent of the immigrants to this country. Among the new immigrants were Italians, Hungarians, Czechs, Slovaks, Poles, Serbs, Croats, Slovenes, Russians, Romanians, and Greeks—all people whose culture and language were markedly different from those of western Europe and whose religion for the most part was Judaism or Catholicism.

ELLIS ISLAND   As the number of immigrants passing through the port of New York soared during the late nineteenth century, the state-run Castle Garden receiving center overflowed with corruption. Money changers cheated new arrivals, railroad agents overcharged them for tickets, and baggage handlers engaged in blackmail. With reports of such abuses filling the newspapers, Congress ordered an investigation, which resulted in the closure of Castle Garden in 1890. Thereafter the federal government's new Bureau of Immigration took over the business of admitting newcomers to New York City.

To launch this effort, Congress funded the construction of a new reception center on a tiny island off the New Jersey coast, a mile south of Manhattan, near the Statue of Liberty. In 1892, Ellis Island opened its doors to the "huddled masses" of the world. In 1907, the reception center's busiest year, more than 1 million new arrivals passed through the receiving center, an average of about 5,000 per day; in one day alone, immigration officials processed some 11,750. These were the immigrants who crammed into the steerage compartments deep in the ships' hulls. Those refugees who could afford first- and second-class cabins did not have to visit Ellis Island; they were examined

The Registry Room at Ellis Island

Inspectors asked arriving passengers twenty-nine probing questions, including "Are you a polygamist?"

on board, and most of them simply walked down the gangway onto the docks in lower Manhattan.

MAKING THEIR WAY   Once on American soil, immigrants felt exhilaration, exhaustion, and usually a desperate need for work. Many were greeted by family and friends who had come over before them, others by representatives of immigrant-aid societies or by hiring agents offering jobs in mines, mills, or sweatshops. Since most immigrants knew little if any English and nothing about American employment practices, they were easy subjects for exploitation. In exchange for a bit of whiskey and a job, obliging hiring agents claimed a healthy percentage of their wages. Among Italians and Greeks these agents were known as padrones, and they dominated the labor market in New York. Other contractors provided train tickets to inland cities such as Buffalo, Pittsburgh, Cleveland, Chicago, Milwaukee, Cincinnati, and St. Louis.

As strangers in a new land, most of the immigrants naturally gravitated to neighborhoods populated by their own kind. The immigrant enclaves—nicknamed Little Italy, Little Hungary, Chinatown, and so on—served as crucial transitional communities between the newcomers' Old World past and their New World future. By 1920, Chicago had some seventeen separate Little Italy colonies scattered across the city, representing various home provinces. In such kinship communities, immigrants practiced their native religion, clung to their native customs, and conversed in their native tongue. But they paid a price for such community solidarity. When the "new immigrants" moved into an area, older residents typically moved out, taking with them whatever social prestige and political influence they had achieved. The quality of living conditions quickly deteriorated as housing and sanitation codes went unenforced.

THE NATIVIST RESPONSE   Then, as now, many native-born Americans saw the wave of new immigrants as a threat to their way of life and their jobs. "Immigrants work for almost nothing," groused one laborer. Other "nativists" felt that the newcomers threatened traditional American culture. A Stanford University professor called them "illiterate, docile, lacking in self-reliance and initiative, and not possessing the Anglo-Teutonic conceptions of law, order, and government." Cultural differences confirmed in the minds of nativists the assumption that the Nordic peoples of the old immigration were superior to the Slavic, Italian, Greek, and Jewish peoples of the new immigration. Many of the new immigrants were illiterate, and more appeared so because they could not speak English. Some resorted to crime, encouraging suspicions that criminals were being quietly helped out of Europe just as they had once been transported from England to the colonies.

Mulberry Street, Little Italy, New York City, ca. 1900

Immigrants established ethnic enclaves in which they could carry on Old World traditions.

Religious prejudice, mainly anti-Catholic, anti-Buddhist, and anti-Semitic sentiments, also underlay hostility toward the latest newcomers. During the 1880s nativist groups emerged to stop the flow of immigrants. The most successful of the nativist groups, the American Protective Association (APA), operated mainly in Protestant strongholds of the upper Mississippi Valley. Its organizer harbored paranoid fantasies of Catholic conspiracies and was especially eager to keep public schools free from Jesuit control. The association grew slowly from its start in 1887 until 1893, when leaders took advantage of a severe depression to draw large numbers of the frustrated to its ranks. The APA promoted government restrictions on immigration, more stringent naturalization requirements, workplaces that refused to employ aliens or Catholics, and the teaching of the "American" language in the schools.

IMMIGRATION RESTRICTION   In 1891 the prominent politician Henry Cabot Lodge of Massachusetts took up the cause of excluding illiterate foreigners, a measure that would have affected much of the new wave of immigrants even though literacy in English was not required. Bills embodying the restriction were vetoed by three presidents on the grounds that they penalized people for lack of opportunity: Grover Cleveland in 1897, William H. Taft in 1913, and Woodrow Wilson in 1915 and 1917. The last time, however, Congress overrode the veto.

Proponents of immigration restriction during the late nineteenth century did succeed in excluding the Chinese, who were victims of every act of discrimination the European immigrants suffered and more. They were not white; they were not Christian; many were not literate. By 1880 there were some 75,000 Chinese in California, about a ninth of the state's population. Many white workers resented the Chinese for accepting lower wages, but the Asians' greatest sin, the editor of the *New York Nation* opined with tongue-in-cheek irony, was perpetuating "those disgusting habits of thrift, industry, and self-denial."

In 1882, Congress overturned President Chester A. Arthur's veto of the Chinese Exclusion Act. It thus became the first federal law to restrict immigration on the basis of race and class, shutting the door to Chinese immigrants for ten years. The discriminatory legislation received overwhelming support. One congressman explained that because the "industrial army of Asiatic laborers" was increasing the tension between workers and management, "the gate must be closed." The Chinese Exclusion Act was periodically renewed

Anti-Chinese protest, California, 1880

Widespread racism and prejudice against the Chinese resulted in the Chinese Exclusion Act (1882), which banned Chinese immigration.

before being extended indefinitely in 1902. Not until 1943 were barriers to Chinese immigration finally removed.

Although the Chinese Exclusion Act sharply reduced the flow of Chinese immigrants, it did not stop the influx completely. In 1910 the West Coast counterpart of Ellis Island opened on rugged Angel Island, six miles offshore from San Francisco, to process tens of thousands of Asian immigrants, most of them Chinese. Those arrivals from China who could claim a Chinese American parent were allowed to enter, as were certain officials, teachers, merchants, and students. The powerful prejudice that the Chinese immigrants encountered helps explain why over 30 percent of the arrivals at Angel Island were denied entry.

POPULAR CULTURE

The influx of people into large towns and cities created new patterns of recreation and leisure. Whereas people in rural areas were tied to the rituals of the harvest season and intimately connected to their neighbors and extended families, most middle-class urban whites had enough money to be more mobile; they were primarily connected to the other members of their nuclear family (made up only of parents and children), and their affluence enabled them to enjoy greater leisure time and an increasing discretionary income. Middle- and upper-class urban families spent much of their leisure time together at home, usually in the parlor, singing around a piano, reading novels, or playing cards, dominoes, backgammon, chess, and checkers.

In the congested metropolitan areas, politics became as much a form of public entertainment as it was a means of providing civic representation and public services. People flocked to hear visiting candidates speak. In cities such as New York, Philadelphia, Boston, and Chicago, membership in a political party was akin to belonging to a social club. In addition, labor unions provided activities that were more social than economic in nature, and members often visited the union hall as much to socialize as to discuss working conditions. The sheer number of city dwellers also helped generate new forms of mass entertainment, such as traveling Wild West shows, vaudeville shows, and spectator sports.

VAUDEVILLE Growing family incomes and innovations in urban transportation—cable cars, subways, electric streetcars and streetlights—enabled more people to take advantage of urban cultural life. Attendance at theaters, operas, and dance halls soared after the Civil War. But by far the most popular—and most diverse—form of theatrical entertainment in the late

Vaudeville

For as little as one cent, Vaudeville offered customers entertainment.

nineteenth century was vaudeville. The term derives from a French word for a play accompanied by music.

Vaudeville "variety" shows featured comedians, singers, musicians, black-face minstrels, farcical plays, animal acts, jugglers, gymnasts, dancers, mimes, and magicians. Vaudeville houses attracted all social classes and types—men, women, and children. The shows included something to please every taste and, as such, reflected the heterogeneity of city life. To commemorate the opening of a palatial new Boston theater in 1894, an actress read a dedicatory poem in which she announced that "all are equals here"; the vaudeville house was the people's theater: it knew "no favorites, no class." She promised the spectators that the producers would "ever seek the new" in providing entertainers who epitomized "the spice of life, Variety," with its motto "ever to please—and never to offend."

SALOON CULTURE   The most popular destinations for the urban working class were saloons and dance halls. The saloon was the poor-man's social club during the late nineteenth century. By 1900 there were more saloons in the United States than there were grocery stores and meat markets. New York

City alone had 10,000, or one for every 500 residents. Often sponsored by beer brewers and frequented by local politicians, saloons offered a free lunch to encourage patrons to visit and buy 5¢ beer or 15¢ whiskey.

Saloons provided much more than food and drink, however; they were in effect public homes, offering haven and fellowship to people who often worked ten hours a day, six days a week. Saloons were especially popular among male immigrants seeking companionship in a new land. Saloons served as busy social hubs and were often aligned with local political machines. In New York City in the 1880s, most of the primary elections and local political caucuses were conducted in saloons.

Men went to saloons to learn about jobs, engage in labor union activities, cash paychecks, mail letters, read newspapers, and gossip about neighborhood affairs. Because saloons were heated and offered public restrooms, they also served as places of refuge for poor people whose own slum tenements or cramped lodging houses were not as accommodating. Many saloons included gymnasiums. Patrons could play handball, chess, billiards, darts, cards, or dice.

Saloons were defiantly male enclaves. Although women and children occasionally entered a saloon—through a side door—in order to carry home a pail of beer (called "rushing the growler") or to drink at a backroom party, the main bar at the front was for men only. Some saloons provided "snugs," small separate rooms for female patrons.

A workingman's social center

Men gather at a neighborhood saloon in New York City, ca. 1895.

Saloons aroused intense criticism. Anti-liquor societies such as the Women's Christian Temperance Union and the Anti-Saloon League charged that saloons contributed to alcoholism, divorce, crime, and absenteeism from work. The reformers demanded that saloons be closed down. Yet drunkenness in saloons was the exception rather than the rule. To be sure, most patrons of working-class saloons had little money to waste, and recent studies have revealed that the average amount of money spent on liquor was no more than 5 percent of a man's annual income. Saloons were the primary locus of the workingman's leisure time and political activity. As a journalist observed, "The saloon is, in short, the social and intellectual center of the neighborhood."

OUTDOOR RECREATION   The congestion and disease associated with city life led many people to participate in forms of outdoor recreation intended to restore their vitality and improve their health. A movement to create urban parks flourished after the construction of New York's Central Park in 1858. Its designer, Frederick Law Olmsted, went on to design parks for Boston, Brooklyn, Chicago, Philadelphia, San Francisco, and many other cities. Although originally intended as places where people could walk and commune with nature, parks soon offered more vigorous forms of exercise and recreation—for men and women.

Croquet and tennis courts were among the first additions to city parks because they took up little space and required little maintenance. Lawn tennis was invented by an Englishman in 1873 and arrived in the United States a year later. By 1885, Central Park had thirty courts. Even more popular than croquet or tennis was cycling, or "wheeling." In the 1870s, bicycles began to be manufactured in the United States, and by the end of the century a bicycle craze had swept the country. Bicycles were especially popular with women who chafed at the restricting conventions of the Victorian era. The new vehicles offered exercise, freedom, and access to the countryside.

The urban working poor could not afford to acquire a bicycle or join a croquet club, however. Nor did they have as much free time as the affluent. At the end of their long days and on Sundays, they sought recreation and fellowship on street corners or on the front stoops of their apartment buildings. Organ-grinders and other musicians would perform on the sidewalks among the food vendors. Many ethnic groups, especially the Germans and the Irish, formed male singing, drinking, or gymnastic clubs. Working folk also attended bare-knuckle boxing matches or baseball games and on Sundays would gather for picnics. By the end of the century, large-scale amusement parks such as the one at Brooklyn's Coney Island provided entertainment for

Tandem tricycle

In spite of the danger and discomfort of early bicycles, "wheeling" became a popular form of recreation and mode of transportation.

the entire family. Yet many inner-city youth could not afford the trolley fare, so the crowded streets and dangerous alleys remained their playgrounds.

WORKINGWOMEN AND LEISURE   In contrast to the male public culture centered in saloons, the leisure activities of working-class women, many of them immigrants, were more limited at the end of the nineteenth century. Married women were so encumbered by housework and maternal responsibilities that they had little free time. As a social worker noted, "The men have the saloons, political clubs, trade-unions or [fraternal] lodges for their recreation . . . while the mothers have almost no recreation, only a dreary round of work, day after day, with occasionally doorstep gossip to vary the monotony of their lives." Married working-class women often used the streets as their public space. Washing clothes, supervising children, or shopping at the local market provided opportunities for fellowship with other women.

Steeplechase Park, Coney Island, Brooklyn, New York

Members of the working class could afford the inexpensive rides at this popular amusement park.

Single women had more opportunities for leisure and recreation than did working mothers. They flocked to dance halls, theaters, amusement parks, and picnic grounds. On hot summer days many working-class folk went to public beaches. With the advent of movie theaters during the second decade of the twentieth century, the cinema became the most popular form of entertainment for women.

Young single women participated in urban amusements for a variety of reasons: escape, pleasure, adventure, companionship, and autonomy. As a promotional flyer for a movie theater promised, "If you are tired of life, go to the movies. If you are sick of troubles rife, go to the picture show. You will forget your unpaid bills, rheumatism and other ills, if you stow your pills and go to the picture show." Urban recreational and entertainment activities also allowed opportunities for romance and sexual relationships. Not surprisingly, young women eager for such recreation encountered far more obstacles than did young men. Just as reformers sought to shut down saloons, parents and authorities tried to restrict the freedom of young women to engage in "cheap amusements." Yet many young women followed their own wishes and in so doing helped carve out their own social sphere.

SPECTATOR SPORTS   In the last quarter of the nineteenth century, new spectator sports such as college football and basketball and professional baseball gained mass appeal, reflecting the growing urbanization of life. People could gather easily for sporting events in the large cities. Spectator sports became urban extravaganzas, unifying the diverse ethnic groups in the large cities and attracting people with the leisure time and cash to spend on watching others perform—or bet on the outcome.

Football emerged as a modified form of soccer and rugby. The College of New Jersey (Princeton) and Rutgers played the first college football game in 1869. Basketball was invented in 1891, when Dr. James Naismith, a physical education instructor, nailed two peach baskets to the walls of the Young Men's Christian Association training school in Springfield, Massachusetts. Naismith wanted to create an indoor winter game that could be played between the fall football and spring baseball seasons. Basketball quickly grew in popularity among boys and girls. Vassar and Smith Colleges added the sport in 1892. In 1893, Vanderbilt University, in Nashville, became the first college to field a men's team.

Baseball laid claim to being America's national pastime at midcentury. Contrary to popular opinion, Abner Doubleday did not invent the game. Instead, Alexander Cartwright, a New York bank clerk and sportsman, is recognized as the father of organized baseball. In 1845 he gathered a group of merchants, stockbrokers, and physicians to form the Knickerbocker Base Ball Club of New York.

The first professional baseball team was the Cincinnati Red Stockings, which made its appearance in 1869. In 1900 the American League was organized, and two years later the first World Series was held. Baseball became the national pastime and the most democratic sport in America. People from all social classes (mostly men) attended the games, and ethnic immigrants were among the most faithful fans. The *St. Louis*

Baseball card, 1887

The excitement of rooting for the home team united all classes.

Post-Dispatch reported in 1883 that "a glance at the audience on any fine day at the ball park will reveal . . . telegraph operators, printers who work at night, travelling [sales]men . . . men of leisure . . . men of capital, bank clerks who get away at 3 P.M., real estate men . . . barkeepers . . . hotel clerks, actors and employees of the theater, policemen and firemen on their day off . . . butchers and bakers." Cheering for a city baseball team gave rootless people a common loyalty and a sense of belonging.

Only white players were allowed in the major leagues. African Americans played on "minor league" teams or in all-black Negro leagues. In 1887, the Cuban Giants, an exhibition team made up of black players, traveled the country. A few major league white teams agreed to play them. An African American–owned newspaper announced in early 1888 that the Cuban Giants "have defeated the New Yorks, 4 games out of 5, and are now virtually champions of the world." But, it added, "the St. Louis Browns, Detroits and Chicagos, afflicted by Negrophobia and unable to bear the odium of being beaten by colored men, refused to accept their challenge."

By the end of the nineteenth century, sports of all kinds had become a major cultural phenomenon in the United States. A writer for *Harper's Weekly* announced in 1895 that "ball matches, football games, tennis tournaments, bicycle races, [and] regattas, have become part of our national life." They "are watched with eagerness and discussed with enthusiasm and understanding by all manner of people, from the day-laborer to the millionaire." One reporter in the 1890s referred to the "athletic craze" that was sweeping the American imagination. Moreover, it was in 1892 that a Frenchman, Pierre de Coubertin, called for the revival of the ancient Olympic Games, and the first modern olympiad was held four years later.

EDUCATION AND THE PROFESSIONS

THE SPREAD OF PUBLIC EDUCATION The spread of public education, spurred partly by the determination to "Americanize" immigrant children, helped quicken the emergence of a new urban culture. In 1870 there were 7 million pupils in public schools; by 1920 the number had risen to 22 million. The percentage of school-age children in attendance went from 57 to 78 during those years.

The spread of secondary schools accounted for much of the increased enrollment in public schools. In antebellum America private academies prepared those who intended to enter college. At the beginning of the Civil

War, there were only about 100 public high schools in the whole country, but their number grew to about 800 in 1880 and to 6,000 at the turn of the century. Their curricula at first copied the academies' emphasis on higher mathematics and classical languages, but the public schools gradually accommodated their programs to those not going on to college, devising vocational training in such arts as bookkeeping, typing, drafting, and the use of tools.

VOCATIONAL TRAINING   Vocational training was most intensely promoted after the Civil War by missionary schools for African Americans in the South, such as the Hampton Institute in Virginia, which trained Booker T. Washington. Congress had supported vocational training at the college level for many years. The Morrill Act of 1862 granted each state 30,000 acres per representative and senator, the income from which was to be applied to teaching agriculture and the mechanic arts in what came to be known as the land-grant colleges. Among the new land-grant institutions were Clemson

Vocational education

Students in a current-events class at Virginia's Hampton Institute, 1899.

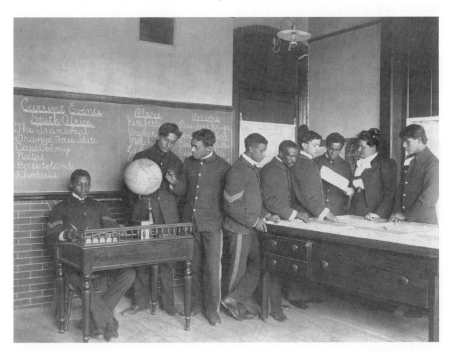

University, Pennsylvania State University, and Iowa State University. In 1890 a second Morrill Act provided federal grants to these colleges.

HIGHER EDUCATION   The demand for higher learning after the Civil War led to an increase in the college-student population, from 52,000 in 1870 to 157,000 in 1890 and 600,000 in 1920. To accommodate the diverse needs of these growing numbers, colleges moved from rigidly prescribed courses toward an elective system. The new approach allowed students to favor their strong points and colleges to expand their scope. But as Henry Cabot Lodge complained, it also allowed students to "escape without learning anything at all by a judicious selection of unrelated subjects taken up only because they were easy or because the burden imposed by those who taught them was light."

Colleges remained largely male bastions, but women's access to higher education improved markedly in the late nineteenth century. Before the Civil War a few men's colleges had admitted women, and most state universities in the West were open to women from the start. But colleges in the South and the East fell in line very slowly. Vassar, opened in 1865, was the first women's

Women as students

An astronomy class at Vassar College, 1880.

college to teach by the same standards as the best of the men's colleges. In the 1870s two more excellent women's schools appeared in Massachusetts: Wellesley and Smith, the latter being the first to set the same admission requirements as men's colleges. By the end of the century, women made up more than a third of all college students.

The dominant new trend in American higher education after the Civil War was the rise of the graduate school. The versatile professors of the antebellum era had a knowledge more broad than deep. They engaged in little research, nor were they expected to advance the frontiers of knowledge. But gradually more and more Americans experienced a different system at the German universities, where training was more systematic and focused. After the Civil War the German system became the basis for the modern American university. Yale awarded its first doctorate of philosophy in 1861, and Harvard awarded its in 1872. The Johns Hopkins University, opened in Baltimore in 1876, set a precedent by making graduate work its chief concern.

THE RISE OF REALISM

Much as popular culture was transformed as a result of the urban-industrial revolution, intellectual life also adapted to new social realities. Before the Civil War various forms of idealism dominated American thought. Although quite diverse in motive and means of expression, idealists shared a basic conviction that fundamental truths rest in the unseen world of ideas and spirit or in the distant past rather than in the tangible world of fact and contemporary experience. The most prominent writers, artists, and philosophers were more concerned with Romantic or biblical themes than with exploring aspects of "real" life.

At midcentury and after, however, a more realistic sensibility began to challenge the idealistic tradition. The new urban culture relished new knowledge and immediate experience. This realistic movement matured into a full-fledged cultural force in Europe and America during the second half of the nineteenth century. The horrors of the Civil War eroded Romanticism. And the growth of urban-industrial civilization reinforced an emphasis on everyday concerns and empirical evidence. A growing number of writers, artists, and intellectuals focused on the emerging realities of scientific research and technology, factories and railroads, cities and immigrants, wage labor and social tensions.

The prestige and premises of modern science increased enormously during the second half of the nineteenth century as researchers explored electromagnetic induction, the conservation of matter, the laws of thermo-dynamics, and the relationship between heat and energy. Breakthroughs in chemistry led to new understandings about the formation of compounds and the nature of chemical reactions. Discoveries of fossils opened up new horizons in geology and paleontology, and greatly improved microscopes enabled zoologists to decipher cell structures.

THEORIES OF SOCIAL CHANGE   Every field of thought in the post–Civil War years felt the impact of Charles Darwin's *On the Origin of Species* (1859). Darwin used extensive observations and cast-iron logic to argue that existing species, including humanity itself, have slowly evolved, through a long, random process of "natural selection," from less complex forms of life: those species that adapted to survival by reason of quickness, shrewdness, or other advantages reproduced their kind, while others fell by the wayside.

The idea of species evolution shocked people who embraced a literal in-terpretation of the biblical creation stories. Heated arguments arose between scientists and clergymen. Some of the faithful rejected Darwin's doctrine while others found their faith severely shaken not only by evolutionary the-ory but also by the urging of professional scholars to apply the critical stan-dards of scholarship to the Bible itself. Most of the faithful, however, came to reconcile science and religion. They viewed evolution as the divine will, one of the secondary causes through which God worked.

Charles Darwin

Darwin's theories influenced more than a century of political debate.

SOCIAL DARWINISM   Although Charles Darwin's theory of evolution applied only to biological phenom-ena, other thinkers drew broader in-ferences from it. The temptation to apply evolutionary theory to the so-cial (human) world proved irre-sistible. Darwin's fellow Englishman Herbert Spencer became the first ma-jor prophet of social Darwinism and an important influence on American thought. Spencer argued that human society and institutions, like organisms, passed through the process of natural selection, which resulted, in Spencer's chilling phrase, in the "survival of the fittest." For Spencer, social evolution was the engine of progress, ending "only in the establishment of the greatest perfection and the most complete happiness."

If, as Spencer believed, society naturally evolved for the better, then government interference with the process of social evolution was a serious mistake. Social Darwinism implied a government policy of hands off; it decried the regulation of business, the graduated income tax, and sanitation and housing regulations. Such intervention, Spencer charged, would help the "unfit" survive and thereby impede progress. The only acceptable charity was voluntary, and even that was of dubious value. Spencer warned that "fostering the good-for-nothing [people] at the expense of the good, is an extreme cruelty."

For Spencer and his many American supporters, successful businessmen and corporations promoted social progress. If small businesses were crowded out by trusts and monopolies, that too was part of the evolutionary process. The oil tycoon John D. Rockefeller told his Baptist Sunday-school class that the "growth of a large business is merely a survival of the fittest. . . . This is not an evil tendency in business. It is merely the working-out of a law of nature and a law of God."

The ideas of Charles Darwin and Herbert Spencer spread quickly. *Popular Science Monthly*, founded in 1872, became the chief medium for popularizing Darwinism. That year, Spencer's chief academic disciple, William Graham Sumner, began teaching at Yale and preached the gospel of natural selection. Sumner's most lasting contribution, made in his book *Folkways* (1907), was to argue that it would be a mistake for government to interfere with established customs in the name of ideals of equality or natural rights.

Lester Frank Ward

Proponent of reform Darwinism.

REFORM DARWINISM Sumner's efforts to use Darwinism to promote "rugged individualism" provoked strong criticism. Reform Darwinism found its major philosopher in an obscure Washington civil servant, Lester Frank Ward, who fought his way up from poverty and never lost his empathy for the underdog. Ward's book

Dynamic Sociology (1883) singled out one product of evolution that Darwin and Spencer had neglected: the human brain. People, like animals, compete, but they also collaborate; they have minds that shape social evolution. And humans also show compassion for others. Far from being the helpless pawn of evolution, Ward argued, humanity could control the process. Ward's progressive reform Darwinism challenged Sumner's conservative social Darwinism, holding that cooperation, not competition, would better promote progress. According to Ward, Sumner's "irrational distrust of government" might have been justified in an earlier day of autocracy but was not applicable under a representative system. Government could become the agency of progress by promoting two main goals: ameliorating poverty, which impeded the development of the mind, and promoting the education of the masses. "Intelligence, far more than necessity," Ward wrote, "is the mother of invention," and "the influence of knowledge as a social factor, like that of wealth, is proportional to the extent of its distribution." Intellect, rightly informed by science, could promote social improvement.

PRAGMATISM   Around the turn of the century, the concept of evolutionary development found expression in a philosophical principle set forth in mature form by William James in his book *Pragmatism: A New Name for Some Old Ways of Thinking* (1907). James, a professor of philosophy and psychology at Harvard, shared Lester Frank Ward's focus on the role of ideas in the process of evolution. Pragmatists, said James, believed that ideas gain their validity not from their inherent truth but from their social consequences and practical applications. Thus scientists could test the validity of their ideas in the laboratory and judge their import by their applications. Pragmatism reflected a quality often looked upon as genuinely American: the inventive, experimental spirit that judged ideas on their results and their ability to adapt to changing social needs and environments.

John Dewey, who would become the chief philosopher of pragmatism after James, preferred the term *instrumentalism*, by which he meant that ideas were instruments for action, especially social

William James

The conceptual founder of pragmatism.

reform. Dewey, unlike James, threw himself into movements for the rights of labor and women, the promotion of peace, and the reform of education. He believed that education was the process through which society would gradually progress toward the goal of economic democracy.

CLEMENS   What came to be called the local-color movement expressed the nostalgia of people moving from a rural culture to an urban one and longing for those places where the old folkways survived. The best of the local colorists could find universal truths in common life, and Samuel Langhorne Clemens (Mark Twain) transcended them all. A native of Missouri, he was impelled to work at age twelve, becoming first a printer and then a Mississippi riverboat pilot. When the Civil War shut down the river traffic, he briefly joined a Confederate militia company, then left with his brother, Orion, for Nevada. He moved on to California in 1864 and first gained widespread notice with his tall tale of the gold country, "The Celebrated Jumping Frog of Calaveras County" (1865). In 1867 the San Francisco *Alta Californian* staked him to a tour of the Mediterranean, and his humorous reports on the trip, revised and collected as *The Innocents Abroad* (1869), established him as a comic writer much in demand on the lecture circuit. With the success of *Roughing It* (1872), an account of his western years, he moved to Hartford, Connecticut, and was able to support himself as an irreverent author and hilarious lecturer.

Clemens was the first great American writer born and raised west of the Appalachians. His early writings accentuate his western background, but for his greatest books he drew heavily upon his boyhood in a border slave state and the tall-tale tradition of southwestern humor. In *The Adventures of Tom Sawyer* (1876), he evoked in fiction the prewar Hannibal, Missouri, where his own boyhood was cut so short. Clemens's masterpiece, *The Adventures of Huckleberry Finn* (1884), created unforgettable characters in Huck Finn, his shiftless father, the slave Jim, the Widow Douglas,

A Tramp Abroad (1880)

Mark Twain in the frontispiece to his travel narrative.

"the King," and "the Duke." The product of an erratic upbringing, Huck Finn embodied the instinct of every red-blooded American boy to "light out for the territory" whenever polite society set out to civilize him. Huck's effort to help his friend Jim escape bondage expressed well the moral dilemmas imposed by slavery on everyone. Many years later another great American writer, Ernest Hemingway, would claim that "all modern American literature comes from one book by Mark Twain, called *Huckleberry Finn.*"

LITERARY NATURALISM   During the 1890s a new literary school, known as naturalism, shocked genteel sensibilities. The naturalists were young literary rebels who imported scientific determinism to literature, viewing humanity as part of the animal world, prey to natural forces and internal drives without control over them or even a full understanding of them.

Stephen Crane in *Maggie: A Girl of the Streets* (1893) and *The Red Badge of Courage* (1895) portrayed people caught up in environments that were beyond their control. *Maggie* depicts a tenement girl driven to prostitution and death amid scenes so sordid and controversial that Crane had to finance the book's publication himself. *The Red Badge of Courage*, his masterpiece, tells of a young man going through his baptism of fire in the Civil War.

Two naturalists who achieved a degree of popular success were Jack London and Theodore Dreiser. London was both a professed socialist and a believer in the German philosopher Friedrich Nietzsche's doctrine of the superman. In adventure stories such as *The Call of the Wild* (1903) and *The Sea Wolf* (1904), London celebrated the triumph of brute force and the will to survive. He reinforced his point about animal force in *The Call of the Wild*, whose protagonist is not a superman but a superdog that reverts to the wild in Alaska and runs with a wolf pack.

Theodore Dreiser shocked the genteel public probably more than the others, presenting protagonists who sinned without remorse and without punishment. *Sister Carrie* (1900), a counterpoint to Crane's *Maggie*, departed from it by having Carrie Meeber survive illicit loves and go on to success on the stage. In *The Financier* (1912) and *The Titan* (1914), Dreiser's main character is a sexual athlete, a man of elemental force who rises to a dominant position in business and society.

SOCIAL CRITICISM   Behind their dogma of determinism, the naturalists harbored intense outrage at human misery and social injustice. Other writers shared their indignation but addressed themselves more directly to protest and reform. One of the most influential of these activists was Henry

George, a California printer and journalist. During a visit to New York City, he was shocked by the contrast between wealth and poverty. The basic social problem, he reasoned, was the "unearned increment" in wealth that came to those who owned land. The fruit of his thought, *Progress and Poverty* (1879), a thick and difficult book, sold slowly at first but by 1905 had sold about 2 million copies in several languages.

George held that everyone had as much right to the use of the land as to the air. Nobody had a right to the value that accrued from the land, since that was created by the community, not by its owner. George proposed simply to tax the "unearned" increment in the value of the land, or the rent. His idea was widely propagated and actually affected tax policy here and there, but his influence on the thinking of the day came less from his "single-tax" panacea than from the paradox he posed in his title, *Progress and Poverty*.

Another prominent social critic, Thorstein Veblen, brought to his work a background of formal training in economics and the purpose of making that subject more an evolutionary or historical science. By all accounts he taught miserably, even inaudibly, and seldom held a job for long, but he wrote brilliantly. In his best-known work, *The Theory of the Leisure Class* (1899), he examined the pecuniary values of the middle classes and introduced phrases that have since become almost clichés: *conspicuous consumption* and *conspicuous leisure*. With the advent of industrial society, Veblen argued, property became the conventional basis of reputation. For the upper classes, moreover, it became necessary to consume time nonproductively as evidence of the ability to afford a life of leisure. In this and later works, Veblen held that the division between industrial experts and business managers was widening to a dangerous point. The businessman's interest in profits, combined with his ignorance of efficiency, produced wasteful organization and a failure to realize the full potential of modern technology.

THE SOCIAL GOSPEL

During the late nineteenth century more and more people took action to address the complex social problems generated by rapid urban and industrial growth. Some reformers focused on legislative solutions to social problems; others stressed philanthropy or organized charity. A few militants promoted socialism or anarchism. Whatever the method or approach, however, social reformers were on the march at the turn of the century, and their activities gave to American life a new urgency and energy.

Social service

A Salvation Army group in Flint, Michigan, 1894.

THE RISE OF THE INSTITUTIONAL CHURCH   Churches responded slowly to the mounting social concerns of urban America, for American Protestantism had become one of the main props of the established order. The Reverend Henry Ward Beecher, pastor of the fashionable Plymouth Congregational Church in Brooklyn, preached success, social Darwinism, and the unworthiness of the poor. As the middle classes moved out to the streetcar suburbs, their churches followed. From 1868 to 1888, for instance, seventeen Protestant churches abandoned the area below Fourteenth Street in Manhattan. In the center of Chicago, 60,000 residents had no church, Protestant or Catholic. Where churches became prosperous, they fell easily under the spell of respectability and do-nothing social Darwinism.

Many churches responded to the human needs of the time, however, by devoting their resources to community service and care of the unfortunate. The Young Men's Christian Association (YMCA) entered the United States from England in the 1850s and grew rapidly after 1870; the Salvation Army, founded in London in 1878, came to the United States a year later. Churches in urban districts began to develop institutional features that were more social than strictly religious in function. After the Civil War, churches acquired gymnasiums, libraries, lecture rooms, and other facilities for social programs. Russell Conwell's Baptist church in Philadelphia included, among other features, a night school for working people that grew into Temple University.

RELIGIOUS REFORMERS   Church reformers who feared that Christianity was losing influence in the cities preached what came to be called the social gospel. Washington Gladden of Columbus, Ohio, argued that true Christianity lies not in rituals, dogmas, or even the mystical experience of God but in the principle that "thou shalt love thy neighbor as thyself." Christian law should govern the workplace, with worker and employer united in serving each other's interests. Gladden endorsed labor's right to organize and complained that class distinctions split congregations as well.

The acknowledged intellectual leader of the social gospel movement, however, was the Baptist Walter Rauschenbusch, professor at the Colgate-Rochester Theological Seminary. In *Christianity and the Social Crisis* (1907) and other works, he developed a theological basis for the movement in the kingdom of God. The church was indispensable to religion, he insisted, but "the greatest future awaits religion in the public life of humanity."

EARLY EFFORTS AT URBAN REFORM

THE SETTLEMENT HOUSE MOVEMENT   While preachers of the social gospel dispensed inspiration, other dedicated reformers attacked the problems of the slums from residential community centers called settlement houses. By 1900 perhaps 100 settlement houses existed in the United States, some of the best known being Jane Addams and Ellen Starr's Hull-House in Chicago (1889), Robert A. Woods's South End House in Boston (1891), and Lillian Wald's Henry Street Settlement (1893) in New York.

The settlement houses were staffed mainly by young middle-class idealists, a majority of them college-trained women who had few other outlets for meaningful work outside the home. Settlement workers sought to broaden the horizons and improve the lives of slum dwellers in diverse ways. At Hull-House, for instance, Jane Addams rejected the "do-goodism" spirit of religious reformers and tried to avoid the assumption that she and the other social workers knew what was best for the poor immigrants. Her approach used pragmatism rather than preaching, focusing on the practical needs of the working poor. She and her staff helped enroll neighborhood

Jane Addams

By the end of the century, religious groups were taking up the settlement house movement.

children in clubs and kindergartens and set up a nursery to care for the infant children of working mothers. The program gradually expanded as Hull-House sponsored health clinics, lectures, music and art studios, an employment bureau, men's clubs, training in skills such as bookbinding, a gymnasium, and a savings bank.

Settlement house leaders realized, however, that the spreading slums made their work as effective as bailing out the ocean with a teaspoon. They therefore organized political support for housing laws, public playgrounds, juvenile courts, mothers' pensions, workers' compensation laws, and legislation prohibiting child labor. Lillian Wald promoted the establishment of the federal Children's Bureau in 1912, and Jane Addams, for her work in the peace movement, received the Nobel Peace Prize for 1931. When Addams died, in 1935, she was the most venerated woman in America.

WOMEN'S EMPLOYMENT AND ACTIVISM Settlement house workers, insofar as they were paid, made up but a fraction of all gainfully employed women. With the rapid growth of the general population, the number of employed women steadily increased, as did the percentage of women in the labor force. The greatest leaps forward came in the 1880s and the first decade of the new century, which were also peak decades of immigration, a correlation that can be explained by the immigrants' need for income. The number of employed women went from over 2.6 million in 1880 to 4 million in 1890, then from 5.1 million in 1900 to 7.8 million in 1910. The employment of women in large numbers was the most significant event in women's history. Through all those years domestic work remained the largest category of employment for women; teaching and nursing also remained among the leading fields. The main change was that clerical work (bookkeeping, stenography, and the like) and sales jobs became increasingly available to women.

Elizabeth Cady Stanton

In this 1870s engraving, Stanton speaks at a meeting of the National Woman Suffrage Association.

These changes in occupational status had little connection to the women's rights movement, which increasingly focused on the issue of suffrage. Immediately after the Civil War, Susan B. Anthony, a seasoned veteran of the movement, demanded that the Fifteenth Amendment guarantee the vote for women as well as black men. She made little impression on the defenders of a man's prerogative, however, who insisted that women belonged in the domestic sphere.

In 1869 the unity of the women's movement was broken in a manner reminiscent of the anti-slavery rift three decades before. The question once again was whether the movement should concentrate on one overriding issue. Susan B. Anthony and Elizabeth Cady Stanton founded the National Woman Suffrage Association to promote a women's suffrage amendment to the Constitution, but they looked upon the vote as but one among many feminist causes to be promoted. Later that year, activists formed the American Woman Suffrage Association, which focused single-mindedly on the suffrage as the first and basic reform.

It would be another half century before the battle would be won, and the long struggle focused the women's cause ever more on the primary objective

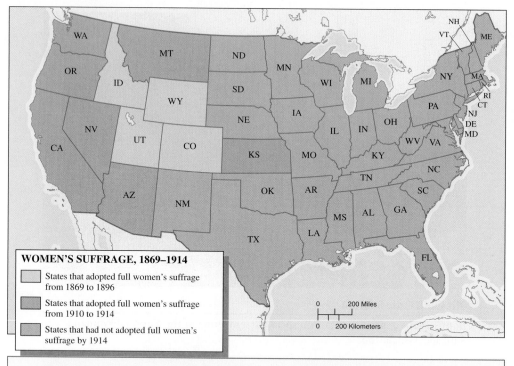

WOMEN'S SUFFRAGE, 1869–1914

☐ States that adopted full women's suffrage from 1869 to 1896

■ States that adopted full women's suffrage from 1910 to 1914

■ States that had not adopted full women's suffrage by 1914

Which states first gave women the right to vote? Why did it take fifty-one years, from Wyoming's grant of full suffrage to women until ratification of the Nineteenth Amendment, for women to receive the right to vote? How was suffrage part of a larger women's reform movement?

of the vote. In 1890, after three years of negotiation, the rival groups united as the National American Woman Suffrage Association, with Elizabeth Cady Stanton as president for two years, to be followed by Susan B. Anthony until 1900. The work thereafter was carried on by a new generation of activists, led by Anna Howard Shaw and Carrie Chapman Catt. Over the years the movement achieved some local and partial victories as a few states granted women suffrage in school board or municipal elections or bond referenda. In 1869 the territory of Wyoming granted full suffrage to women, and after 1890 it retained women's suffrage when it became a state. Three other western states soon followed suit: Colorado in 1893, Utah and Idaho in 1896. But women's suffrage lost in a California referendum in 1896.

The suffrage movement remained in the doldrums until the cause easily won a Washington State referendum in 1910 and then carried California by a close majority in 1911. The following year three more western states—Arizona, Kansas, and Oregon—joined in to make a total of nine western states with full suffrage. In 1913, Illinois granted women suffrage in presidential and municipal elections. Yet not until New York acted in 1917 did a state east of the Mississippi adopt universal suffrage. In 1878, California's Senator A. A. Sargent introduced the "Anthony amendment," a women's suffrage provision that remained before Congress until 1896 and then vanished until 1919, when it was finally passed by Congress and ratified a year later.

Despite the focus on the vote, women did not confine their public work to that issue. In 1866 the Young Women's Christian Association (YWCA), a parallel to the YMCA, appeared in Boston and spread elsewhere. The New England Women's Club, started in 1868 by Julia Ward Howe and others, was an early example of the women's clubs that proliferated to such an extent that a General Federation of Women's Clubs was established in 1890 to tie them all together. Many women's clubs focused solely on "literary" and social activities, but others became deeply involved in charities and reform. The New York Consumers' League, formed in 1890, and the National Consumers' League, formed nine years later, sought to make the buying public, chiefly women, aware of unfair labor conditions. One of its devices was the "White List" of firms that met its minimum standards. The National Women's Trade Union League, founded in 1903, performed a similar function of bringing educated and middle-class women together with workingwomen for the benefit of women unionists.

These and the many other women's groups of the time may have aroused the fear in opponents to women's suffrage that voting women would tilt the nation toward reform. That was the fear of the brewing and liquor interests, large business interests generally, and political-machine bosses. Others, mainly in the South, opposed national women's suffrage on the ground that black women would be enfranchised or that it would violate states' rights.

TOWARD A WELFARE STATE Even without the support of voting women in most places, many states during the late nineteenth century adopted rudimentary measures to regulate big business and labor conditions in the public interest. By the end of the century, nearly every state had begun to regulate railroads, if not always effectively, and had moved to supervise banks and insurance companies. By one count the states and territories passed over 1,600 laws between 1887 and 1897 relating to conditions of work: limiting the number of hours required of workers, providing special protection for women, limiting or forbidding child labor, requiring that wages be paid regularly and in cash, and calling for factory inspections. Nearly all states had boards or commissioners of labor, and some had boards of conciliation and arbitration. Still, conservative judges limited the practical impact of the laws.

In thwarting new regulatory efforts, the Supreme Court used a revised interpretation of the Fourteenth Amendment clauses forbidding the states to "deprive any person of life, liberty, or property, without due process of law" or to deny any person "the equal protection of the laws." Two significant steps of legal reasoning turned the due-process clause into a bulwark of private property. First, the judges reasoned that the word *person* in the clause included corporations. Second, the courts moved away from the old view that "due process" referred only to correct procedures, adopting instead the doctrine of "substantive due process," which allowed courts to review the substance of an action. The principle of substantive due process enabled judges to overturn laws that deprived persons (and corporations) of property to an unreasonable degree and thereby violated due process.

From the due-process clause the Court also derived a new doctrine of "liberty of contract," defined as being within the liberties protected by the due-process clause. Liberty, the Court ruled in 1897, involved the right of the citizen "to enter into all contracts." When it came to labor laws, this translated into an employee's "liberty" to contract for work under the most oppressive conditions without interference from the state. The courts continued to apply such a business-friendly interpretation well into the twentieth century.

At the end of the nineteenth century, opinion in the country stood poised between such conservative rigidities and a growing sense that new corporate structures and social problems required more progressive action. "By the last two decades of the century," wrote one observer, "many thoughtful men had begun to march under various banners declaring that somewhere and somehow the promise of the American dream had been lost—they often said 'betrayed'—and that drastic changes needed to be made to recapture it."

The last two decades of the nineteenth century had already seen a slow erosion of laissez-faire values, which had found their most secure home in the courts. By 1900 a concept of the general-welfare state had emerged, which, in the words of one historian, sought "to promote the general welfare . . . by taking such positive action as is deemed necessary to improve the condition under which its citizens live and work." The reformers supplied no agreed-upon blueprint for a general-welfare utopia, but "simply assumed that government could promote the public interest by appropriate positive action . . . whenever the circumstances indicated that such action would further the common weal." The conflict between this notion and conservative laissez-faire values went on into the new century, but by the mid–twentieth century, after the Progressive movement, the New Deal, and the Fair Deal, the conflict would be "resolved in theory, in practice, and in public esteem in favor of the general-welfare state."

CHAPTER SUMMARY

- **Rise of Cities** America's cities grew in all directions. Electric elevators and new steel-frame construction allowed architects to extend buildings upward. Mass transit allowed the middle class to retreat to suburbs. Crowded tenements bred disease and crime and created an opportunity for urban political bosses to accrue power, in part by distributing to the poor the only relief that existed.

- **New Immigration** By 1900, 30 percent of Americans were foreign-born, with many immigrants coming from eastern and southern Europe rather than western and northern Europe, like most immigrants of generations past. Thus their languages and culture were vastly different from those of native-born Americans. They tended to be Catholic or Jewish rather than Protestant. Beginning in the 1880s, nativists advocated immigration laws to exclude the Chinese and the poor and demanded that immigrants pass a literacy test. A federal immigration station on Ellis Island, in New York Harbor, opened in 1892 to process immigrants arriving by ship from across the Atlantic.

- **Mass Entertainment** Cities began to create urban parks, like New York's Central Park, as places for all citizens to stroll, ride bicycles, or play games such as tennis. Vaudeville shows emerged as a popular form of entertainment. Saloons served as local social and political clubs for men. It was in this era that football, baseball, and basketball emerged as spectator sports.

- **Social Darwinism** Charles Darwin's *On the Origin of Species* shocked people who believed in a literal interpretation of the Bible's account of creation. Darwin's scientific theory was applied to human society and social institutions by Herbert Spencer and William Graham Sumner, who equated economic and social success with "survival of the fittest" and advanced the idea that government should not interfere to promote equality.

- **Rise of Realism** American literature responded to the changes in society at this time. Samuel L. Clemens (Mark Twain) wrote humorously about his experiences and observations and later created masterpieces that playfully comment on social issues. The movement known as naturalism shocked many readers in the 1890s by depicting individuals as victims of a brutal world. Social critics such as Henry George were shocked by the vast disparities between rich and poor. The social gospel movement, in which the religious community reached out to the poor, was another response to America's poverty.

CHRONOLOGY

1858	Construction of New York's Central Park begins
1859	Darwin's *On the Origin of Species* is published
1882	Congress passes the Chinese Exclusion Act
1889	Hull-House, a settlement house, opens in Chicago
1889	Otis Elevator Company installs the first electric elevator
1890	National American Woman Suffrage Association is formed
1891	Basketball is invented
1892	Ellis Island, a federal center for processing immigrants, opens
1900	Baseball's National League is formed

KEY TERMS & NAMES

22

GILDED AGE POLITICS AND AGRARIAN REVOLT

FOCUS QUESTIONS wwnorton.com/studyspace

- What were the major features of American politics during the Gilded Age?
- What were the major issues in politics during this period?
- What were the main problems facing farmers in the South and the Midwest after the Civil War?
- How and why did farmers become politicized?
- What was significant about the election of 1896?

In 1873 the writers Mark Twain and Charles Dudley Warner created an enduring label for the post–Civil War era when they collaborated on a novel titled *The Gilded Age*, a depiction of widespread political corruption and corporate greed. Generations of political scientists and historians have since reinforced the two novelists' judgment. As a young college graduate in 1879, future president Woodrow Wilson described the state of the political system after the Civil War: "No leaders, no principles; no principles, no parties." Indeed, the real movers and shakers of the Gilded Age were not the men who sat in the White House or Congress but the captains of industry who crisscrossed the continent with railroads and adorned its cities with plumed smokestacks and gaudy mansions.

PARADOXICAL POLITICS

Political life in the Gilded Age, the thirty-five years between the end of the Civil War and the end of the nineteenth century, had several distinctive elements. Local politics, especially in cities crowded with waves of new immigrants, was usually controlled by "rings"—small groups of political insiders who managed the nomination and election of candidates, conducted primaries, and influenced policy. Each ring typically had a powerful "boss" who ran things, using his "machine"—a network of neighborhood activists and officials—to govern the town or city. Bosses organized neighborhoods (precincts), mediated disputes, picked candidates, helped the needy, and distributed patronage (municipal jobs and contracts) to loyal followers and corporate contributors. The various city rings and bosses were usually corrupt and rarely efficient, but they did bring structure, stability, and services to rapidly growing and often chaotic inner-city communities. Colorful figures such as New York City's William "Boss" Tweed shamelessly ruled, plundered, and occasionally improved municipal government, often through dishonest means and frequent bribes. Until his arrest in 1871 and his conviction in 1873, Tweed used the Tammany Hall ring to dominate the nation's largest city.

National political parties during the Gilded Age were much more dominant forces than they are today. Party loyalty was powerful, often extending over many generations. Parties also were the nexus of political activity. They controlled access to political offices, dominated elections, and shaped policy making. Another distinctive element was the close division between Republicans and Democrats in Congress, which created the sense of a stalemate. Neither party was willing to embrace controversial issues or take bold initiatives because each one's relative strength was so precarious. Many observers then and since considered this a time of political mediocrity, in which the parties refused to confront "real issues" such as the runaway growth of an unregulated economy and its attendant social injustices. Voters of

William "Boss" Tweed

Tweed is represented here as having a money-bag face and a $15,500 diamond stickpin.

the time nonetheless thought politics was very important, making widespread political participation the third distinctive element of post-Civil War politics. Voter turnout during the Gilded Age was commonly about 70 to 80 percent, even in the South, where the disenfranchisement of African Americans was not yet complete. (By contrast, the turnout for the 2008 presidential election was almost 57 percent.) The paradox of such a high rate of voter participation in the face of the inertia at the national political level raises an obvious question: how was it that leaders who failed to address the "real issues" of the day presided over the most highly organized and politically active electorate in U.S. history?

The answer is partly that the politicians and the voters believed that they *were* dealing with crucial issues: tariff rates, the regulation of corporations, monetary policy, Indian disputes, civil service reform, and immigration. But the answer also reflects the extreme partisanship of the times and the essentially local nature of political culture during the Gilded Age.

PARTISAN POLITICS Most Americans after the Civil War were intensely loyal to one of the two major parties, Democratic or Republican. Political parties gave people an anchor for their activity and their loyalty in an unstable world. Local party officials took care of those who voted their way and distributed appointive public offices and other favors to party loyalists. These "city machines" used patronage and favoritism to keep the loyalty of business supporters while providing jobs or food or fuel to working-class voters who had fallen on hard times. The party faithful eagerly took part in rallies and picnics, deriving from them a sense of camaraderie as well as an opportunity for recreation that offered a welcome relief from their usual workday routine.

Party loyalties and voter turnout in the late nineteenth century reflected religious and ethnic divisions as well as geographic differences. The Republican party attracted mainly Protestants of British descent. The party was dominant in New England, and its other strongholds were New York and the Upper Midwest. The Republicans, the party of Abraham Lincoln, could also rely upon the votes of African Americans and Union veterans of the Civil War.

The Democrats, by contrast, tended to be a heterogeneous, often unruly coalition embracing southern whites, immigrants and Catholics of any origin in the northern states, Jews, freethinkers, skeptics, and all those repelled by the "party of morality." As one Chicago Democrat explained, "A Republican is a man who wants you t' go t' church every Sunday. A Democrat says if a man wants to have a glass of beer on Sunday he can have it."

Republicans pressed nativist policies, calling for restrictions on both immigration and the employment of foreigners and promoting the teaching of the "American" language in the schools. Prohibitionism revived along with nativism in the 1880s. Among the immigrants who crowded into the growing cities were many Irish, Germans, and Italians, who tended to enjoy alcoholic beverages. Republicans increasingly saw saloons as the central social evil around which all others revolved, including vice, crime, political corruption, and neglect of families, and they associated these problems with the ethnic groups that frequented saloons.

POLITICAL STALEMATE AT THE NATIONAL LEVEL Between 1869 and 1913, from the presidency of Ulysses S. Grant through that of William Howard Taft, Republicans monopolized the White House except for the two nonconsecutive terms of the New York Democrat Grover Cleveland, but Republican domination was more apparent than real. Between 1872 and 1896 no president won a majority of the popular vote. In each of those presidential elections, sixteen states invariably voted Republican and fourteen voted Democratic, leaving a pivotal six states whose results might change. The important swing-vote role played by two of those states, New York and Ohio, helps explain the election of eight presidents from those states from 1872 to 1908.

No chief executive between Abraham Lincoln and Theodore Roosevelt could be described as a "strong" president. None challenged the prevailing view that Congress, not the White House, should formulate policy. Senator John Sherman of Ohio expressed the widely held notion that the legislative branch should predominate in a republic: "The President should merely obey and enforce the law."

Republicans controlled the Senate and Democrats controlled the House during the Gilded Age. Only during 1881 to 1883 and 1889 to 1891 did a Republican president coincide with a Republican Congress, and only between 1893 and 1895 did a Democratic president enjoy a Democratic Congress.

Political stasis thus led Congress to postpone making major decisions or launching new programs and to concentrate instead on partisan maneuvering over procedural issues. Because most bills required bipartisan support to pass both houses and legislators tended to vote along party lines, the Democrats and the Republicans pursued a policy of evasion on the national issues of the day. Only the tariff created clear-cut divisions, between protectionist Republicans and low-tariff Democrats, but there were individual exceptions even on that. On the important questions of the currency, regulation of big business, farm problems, civil service reform, and immigration, the parties differed very little. As a result, they primarily became vehicles for seeking office and dispensing patronage in the form of government jobs and contracts.

STATE AND LOCAL INITIATIVES   Unlike those of today, Americans during the Gilded Age expected little direct support from the federal government; most significant political activity occurred at the state and local levels. Residents of the western territories were largely forced to fend for themselves rather than rely upon federal authorities. They formed towns, practiced vigilante justice, and made laws on their own. Once incorporated into the Union, the former territories retained much of their autonomy.

Thus state governments after the Civil War were dynamic centers of political activity and innovation. Over 60 percent of the nation's spending and taxing was exercised by state and local authorities. Then, unlike today, the large cities spent far more on local services than did the federal government. And three fourths of all public employees worked for state and local governments. Local issues such as prohibition, Sunday closing laws, and parochial-school funding generated far more excitement than complex debates over tariffs and monetary policies. It was the state and local governments that first sought to curb the power and restrain the abuses of corporate interests.

CORRUPTION AND REFORM: HAYES TO HARRISON

After the Civil War, states sought to regulate big business; most of that regulation was overturned by the courts, however. A close alliance thus developed between business and political leaders at every level. As a congressman, for example, James G. Blaine of Maine, and many of his supporters saw nothing wrong in his accepting stock certificates from an Arkansas railroad after helping it win a land grant from Congress. Railroad passes, free entertainment, and a host of other favors were freely provided to politicians, newspaper editors, and other leaders in positions to influence public opinion or affect legislation.

Both Republican and Democratic leaders also squabbled over the "spoils" of office, the appointive offices at the local and the national levels. After each election it was expected that the victorious party would throw out the defeated party's appointees and appoint its own men to office. The patronage system of awarding government jobs to supporters invited corruption. It also was so time-consuming that it distracted elected officials from more important issues. Yet George Washington Plunkitt, a Democratic boss in

"The Bosses of the Senate"

This 1889 cartoon bitingly portrays the period's corrupt alliance between big business and politics.

New York City, spoke for many Gilded Age politicians when he explained that "you can't keep an organization together without patronage. Men ain't in politics for nothin'. They want to get somethin' out of it." Each party had its share of corrupt officials willing to buy and sell government appointments or congressional votes, yet each also witnessed the emergence of factions promoting honesty in government. The struggle for "cleaner" government soon became one of the foremost issues of the day.

HAYES AND CIVIL SERVICE REFORM   In the aftermath of Reconstruction, President Rutherford B. Hayes embodied the "party of morality." Hayes brought to the White House in 1877 a new style of uprightness, in sharp contrast to the graft and corruption practiced by members of the Grant administration. The son of an Ohio farmer, Hayes in the 1850s became one of the early Republicans; he was wounded four times in the Civil War and was promoted to the rank of major general. Elected governor of Ohio in 1867, he served three terms.

Hayes's presidency suffered from the supposed secret deal that awarded him victory over the New York Democrat Samuel Tilden in the contested 1876 election. Snide references to him as "His Fraudulence" denied him any chance at a second term, which he renounced from the beginning. Hayes's own party was split between so-called Stalwarts and Half-Breeds, led respectively by Senators Roscoe Conkling of New York and James G. Blaine of Maine. The difference between these Republican factions was murkier than that between the two major parties. The Stalwarts had been stalwart in their support of President Grant during the furor over the misbehavior of his cabinet members. They also promoted Radical Reconstruction of the South and the "spoils system" of distributing federal political jobs to party loyalists. The Half-Breeds acquired their name because they were only half-loyal to Grant and half-committed to reform of the spoils system.

For the most part the two Republican factions were loose alliances designed to advance the careers of Conkling and Blaine. The two men could not abide each other. Tall and lordly, Conkling boasted good looks, fine clothes, and an arrogant manner. Yet underneath his glamorous facade he was a ruthless power broker willing to reward friends and punish enemies. Conkling viewed politics as a brute struggle for control. Politics "is a rotten business," he declared. "Nothing counts except to win."

By contrast, Hayes aligned himself with the growing public discontent over political corruption. American leaders were just learning about the merit system for public employees, which was long established in the bureaucracies of France and Germany, and the new British practice in which civil service jobs were filled by competitive examination rather than awarded as political favors. Hayes had raised the issue of civil service reform during the campaign of 1876.

Although Hayes failed to get civil service legislation through the Congress, he did make political appointments based on merit: those already in office would be dismissed only for the good of the government and not for political reasons; party members would have no more influence in appointments than other respectable citizens; no assessments of government employees for political contributions would be permitted; and no officeholder could manage election campaigns for political organizations, although all could vote and express their opinions.

For all of Hayes's efforts to clean house, his vision of government's role remained limited. On the economic issues of the day, he held to a conservative line that would guide his successors for the rest of the century. His solution to labor troubles, demonstrated in the Great Railroad Strike of 1877, was to send in federal troops and break the strike. His answer to demands for an expansion of the currency was to veto the 1878 Bland-Allison Act, which provided for a limited expansion of silver money through the government's purchase of $2 million to $4 million worth of silver coins per month. (The act passed anyway when Congress overrode Hayes's veto.) A bruised president confided in his diary that he had lost the support of his own party. In 1879, with a year still left in his term, Hayes was ready to leave the White House. "I am now in my last year of the Presidency," he wrote a friend, "and look forward to its close as a schoolboy longs for the coming vacation."

GARFIELD AND ARTHUR   With Hayes out of the running for a second term, the Stalwarts, led by Conkling, brought Ulysses S. Grant forward for a third time, still a strong contender despite the tarnish of his administration's scandals. For two days the Republican Convention in Chicago was deadlocked, with Grant holding a slight lead over Blaine. When Wisconsin's delegates suddenly switched their votes to Senator-elect James A. Garfield, the convention stampeded to the dark-horse Ohio candidate, carrying him to the nomination. As a sop to the Stalwarts, the convention named Chester A. Arthur, the deposed collector of the New York Customhouse, as the candidate for vice president.

The Democrats selected Winfield Scott Hancock, a Union commander at Gettysburg, to counterbalance the Republicans' "bloody-shirt" attacks on their party as the vehicle of rebellion. Former Confederates nevertheless advised their constituents to "vote as you shot"—that is, against the Republicans. In an election characterized by widespread bribery, Garfield eked out a plurality

Invitation to the inaugural reception for President James A. Garfield

Garfield, on the left, and Chester Arthur, on the right, flank a portrait of George Washington.

of only 39,000 votes, or 48.5 percent of the vote, but with a comfortable margin of 214 to 155 in the Electoral College.

A native of Ohio and an early foe of slavery, Garfield had distinguished himself during the Civil War and was mustered out as a major general when he went to Congress in 1863. Noted for his oratorical and parliamentary skills, he became one of the outstanding leaders in the House.

On July 2, 1881, after only four months in office, President Garfield was walking through the Washington, D.C., railroad station when a deranged man, Charles Guiteau, shot him in the back. "I am a Stalwart," Guiteau explained to the arresting officers. "Arthur is now President of the United States," an announcement that would prove crippling to the Stalwarts. Garfield lingered near death for two months. On September 19 he died of complications resulting from the shooting and inept medical care. Chester Arthur was now president.

Little in Arthur's past raised hopes that he would rise above customhouse politics. But Arthur proved to be a surprisingly competent president. He distanced himself from Conkling and the Stalwarts and established a genuine independence. He vigorously prosecuted the Star Route postal frauds, a kickback scheme on contracts for postal routes that involved his old political cronies. The president further surprised old-guard Republicans in 1882 with the veto of an $18 million river and harbors bill, a pork-barrel measure that included something for most congressional districts. He also vetoed the Chinese Exclusion Act (1882), which in his view violated the Burlingame Treaty of 1868 by excluding Chinese immigrants for twenty years. Congress overturned both vetoes.

Most startling of all was Arthur's emergence as something of a civil service and tariff reformer. The assassin Guiteau had unwittingly stimulated widespread public support of reform. In 1883 a reform bill sponsored by "Gentleman George" Pendleton, a Democratic senator from Ohio, set up a three-member Civil Service Commission independent of the cabinet departments, the first such federal agency established on a permanent basis. About 14 percent of all government jobs would now be filled on the basis of competitive examinations rather than political favoritism. What was more, the president could enlarge the class of affected jobs at his discretion. This development would have important consequences over the years because after each of the next four presidential elections the party out of power emerged as the victor. Each new president thus had a motive to enlarge this category of government jobs, because it would shield his own appointees from political removal. The Pendleton Act was thus a vital step in a new approach to government administration that valued merit over partisanship.

The high protective tariff, a heritage of the Civil War designed to deter foreign imports by taxing them, had by the early 1880s raised federal revenues to a point where the government was enjoying an embarrassment of riches, a surplus that drew money into the Treasury and out of circulation, thus constricting economic growth. Some argued that lower tariff rates would reduce consumer prices by enabling foreign competition and at the same time leave more money in circulation to fuel economic growth. In 1882 a special presidential commission recommended a 20 to 25 percent rate reduction, which gained Arthur's support, but any attempt at tariff reform ran up against swarms of lobbyists representing different industries determined to keep the rate on their particular commodity high. The resulting "mongrel tariff" of 1883, so called because of its different rates for different commodities, provided for a slight rate reduction overall.

THE SCURRILOUS CAMPAIGN   When the 1884 presidential campaign began, Chester Arthur's record might have attracted voters, but it did not please leaders of his party. So the Republicans dumped Arthur and turned to the glamorous senator James Gillespie Blaine of Maine, longtime leader of the Republican Half-Breeds. Blaine was the consummate politician. He inspired the party faithful with his oratory, and at the same time he knew how to wheel and deal in the backrooms. Blaine did have his enemies, however. Democratic newspapers, for example, turned up evidence of his corruption. Based on references in the "Mulligan letters," they once again claimed that Blaine was in the pocket of the railroad barons and that while Speaker of the House he had sold his votes on measures favorable to their interests.

During the campaign, more letters surfaced with disclosures embarrassing to Blaine. For the reform element of the Republican party, this was too much, and prominent leaders and supporters of the party bolted the ticket. Party regulars scorned them as "goo-goos"—the good-government crowd, who ignored partisan realities—and the editor of the *New York Sun* jokingly called them Mugwumps, after an Algonquian word for a self-important chieftain. The Mugwumps were centered in the large cities and

Senator James G. Blaine of Maine

The Republican candidate in 1884.

major universities. Mostly educators or editors, they opposed tariffs and championed free trade. They disdained efforts to inflate the money supply by coining more silver, were hostile to efforts at regulating railroads, and were suspicious of excessive democracy. Their foremost goal was to enact civil service reform by removing the ability to distribute federal jobs to party supporters.

The rise of the Mugwumps influenced the Democrats to nominate the New Yorker Stephen Grover Cleveland as a reform candidate. Cleveland rose rapidly from obscurity to the White House. One of many children in the family of a small-town Presbyterian minister, he had first attracted national attention when, in 1881, he was elected as the anti-corruption mayor of Buffalo. In 1882 he was elected governor, and he continued to build a reform record by fighting New York City's corrupt Tammany Hall ring. As mayor and as governor, he repeatedly vetoed what he considered special-privilege bills serving selfish interests.

A stocky 270-pound man, Cleveland seemed the stolid opposite of Blaine. He possessed little charisma but impressed the public with his stubborn

"Another Voice for Cleveland"

This 1884 cartoon attacks "Grover the Good" for fathering an illegitimate child.

integrity. Then a scandal erupted when the *Buffalo Evening Telegraph* revealed that as a bachelor, Cleveland had had an affair with an attractive Buffalo widow, who had named him as the father of a child born to her in 1874. Cleveland had responded by providing financial support for the child. The respective escapades of Blaine and Cleveland provided some of the most colorful battle cries in political history: "Blaine, Blaine, James G. Blaine, the continental liar from the state of Maine," Democrats chanted; Republicans countered with "Ma, ma, where's my pa? Gone to the White House, ha, ha, ha!"

Near the end of the brutal campaign, Blaine and his supporters committed two fateful blunders. The first occurred at New York's fashionable Delmonico's restaurant, where Blaine went to a private dinner with several millionaire bigwigs to discuss campaign finances. Cartoons and accounts of "Belshazzar's feast" festooned the opposition press for days. The second fiasco occurred when one member of a delegation of Protestant ministers visiting Republican headquarters in New York referred to the Democrats as the party of "rum, Romanism, and rebellion." Blaine, who was present, let pass the implied insult to Catholics—a fatal oversight, since he had always cultivated Irish American support with his anti-English talk and public reminders that his mother was Catholic. Democrats spread the word that Blaine was at heart anti-Irish and anti-Catholic. The two incidents may have tipped the election. The electoral vote, in Cleveland's favor, stood at 219 to 182, but the popular vote ran far closer: Cleveland's plurality was fewer than 30,000 votes.

CLEVELAND AND THE SPECIAL INTERESTS   For all of Cleveland's hostility to the spoils system and politics as usual, he represented no sharp break with the conservative policies of his predecessors, except in opposing government favors to business. "A public office is a public trust" was one of his favorite mottoes. He held to a strictly limited view of government's role in both economic and social matters, a rigid philosophy illustrated by his 1887 veto of the Texas seed bill, an effort to appropriate funds to meet drought victims' urgent need for seed grain. Back to Congress it went, with a lecture on the need to limit the powers and functions of government. "Though the people support the government, the government should not support the people," Cleveland asserted.

Cleveland's stubborn courage and concern for protecting the public Treasury led him into conflicts with special-interest groups that eventually cost him the White House. Cleveland incurred the wrath of Union war veterans with his firm stand against their pension raids on the Treasury. Congress had passed the first Civil War pension law in 1862 to provide for Union veterans disabled in service and for the widows, orphans, and dependents of veterans. By 1882 the Grand Army of the Republic, an organization of Union veterans and a powerful pressure group, was trying to get pensions paid for any disability, even if unrelated to military service. Meanwhile, many veterans succeeded in pushing private pension bills through an obliging Congress. Insofar as time permitted, Cleveland examined such bills critically and vetoed the dubious ones. A climax came in 1887 when Congress passed the dependents pension bill, which provided funds for veterans dependent upon manual labor and unable to work, whether or not the reason was connected to military service. Cleveland sent it back with a ringing veto, declaring that the pension list would become a refuge for frauds rather than a "roll of honor."

In about the middle of his term, Cleveland urged Congress to adopt an important new policy: railroad regulation. Since the late 1860s, states had adopted laws regulating railroads, and from the early 1870s Congress had debated federal legislation. In 1886 a Supreme Court decision finally spurred action. In the case of *Wabash, St. Louis, and Pacific Railroad Company v. Illinois*, the Court denied the state's power to regulate rates on interstate traffic. Cleveland thereupon urged that since this "important field of control and regulation [has] thus been left entirely unoccupied," Congress should act.

It did, and in 1887 Cleveland signed into law an act creating the Interstate Commerce Commission (ICC), the first such independent federal regulatory commission. The law empowered the ICC's five members to investigate railroads and prosecute violators of federal regulations. All freight rates had to be "reasonable and just." Railroads were forbidden to grant secret rebates to preferred shippers or enter into pools (secret agreements among competing companies to fix rates). The commission's actual powers proved to be weak, however, when first tested in the courts.

THE TARIFF President Cleveland's most dramatic challenge to the power of special interests focused on tariff reform. Why was the tariff such an important and controversial issue? During the late nineteenth century, Republicans and business leaders assumed that prosperity and high tariffs were tightly linked. Others disagreed. Many observers had concluded that the formation of huge corporate "trusts" was not a natural development of a maturing capitalist system. Instead, critics charged that government tariff policies had fostered big business at the expense of small producers and retailers by effectively shutting out foreign imports, thereby enabling corporations to dominate their American markets and charge higher prices for their products.

Cleveland agreed that tariff rates were too high and too often inequitable. Near the end of 1887, the president devoted his entire annual message to Congress to the subject. Congress, Cleveland argued, should reduce the tariff rates. Blaine and other Republicans denounced Cleveland's message as pure "free trade," a doctrine all the more suspect because it was also British policy. The stage was set for the election of 1888 to highlight a difference between the major parties on an issue of substance.

Grover Cleveland

As president, Cleveland made the issue of tariff reform central to the politics of the late 1880s.

THE ELECTION OF 1888 Cleveland was the obvious nominee of his party for reelection. The Republicans, now calling themselves the GOP (Grand Old Party), turned to the obscure Benjamin Harrison, who had all the attributes of availability. The grandson of President William Henry Harrison, he resided in a pivotal state and had a good war record. There was little in his political record to offend any voter. He had lost a race for governor and served one term in the Senate (1881–1887). The Republican platform accepted Cleveland's challenge to make the tariff the chief issue.

The Republicans enjoyed a huge advantage over the Democrats in funding and organization. To fend off Cleveland's efforts to reduce the tariff, business owners contributed over $3 million to the Republican campaign. On the eve of the election, Cleveland suffered a more devastating blow. A California Republican had written the British minister to the United States, Sir Lionel Sackville-West, using the false name Charles F. Murchison. Posing as an English immigrant, he asked advice on how to vote in the presidential election. Sackville-West, engaged at the time in sensitive negotiations over British and U.S. access to Canadian fisheries, hinted that the man should vote for Cleveland. The letter aroused a storm of protest against foreign intervention and suggested a further link between Cleveland and British free traders. The Democrats' explanations never caught up with the public's sense of outrage.

Still, the outcome was incredibly close. Cleveland won the popular vote by 5,538,000 to 5,447,000, but Harrison carried the Electoral College by 233 to 168.

REPUBLICAN REFORM UNDER HARRISON As president, Benjamin Harrison was a competent figurehead overshadowed by his flamboyant secretary of state, James G. Blaine. Harrison owed a heavy debt to Union Civil War veterans, which he discharged by signing the Dependent Pension Act, substantially the same measure that Cleveland had vetoed. The pension rolls almost doubled between 1889 and 1893.

During the first two years of Harrison's term, the Republicans controlled the presidency and both houses of Congress for only the second time since 1875. They were positioned to have pretty much their own way, and in 1890 they passed some of the most significant legislation enacted in the entire period. In addition to the Dependent Pension Act, Congress and the president approved the Sherman Anti-Trust Act, the Sherman Silver Purchase Act, the McKinley Tariff Act, and the admission of Idaho and Wyoming as new states, which followed the admission of the Dakotas, Montana, and Washington in 1889.

Both parties had pledged to do something about the growing power of trusts and monopolies. The Sherman Anti-Trust Act, named for Ohio senator John Sherman, chairman of the committee that drafted it, forbade contracts, combinations, or conspiracies in restraint of trade or in the effort to establish monopolies in interstate or foreign commerce. A broad consensus put the vague law through, but its passage turned out to be largely symbolic. During the next decade successive administrations rarely enforced the new law, in part because of the ambiguity about what constituted "restraint of trade." From 1890 to 1901, only eighteen lawsuits were instituted, and four of those were against labor unions.

A billion-dollar hole

In an attack on Benjamin Harrison's spending policies, Harrison is shown pouring Cleveland's huge surplus down a hole.

Congress, meanwhile, debated currency legislation against the backdrop of growing economic distress in the farm regions of the

West and the South. Hard-pressed farmers demanded increased coinage of silver to inflate the currency and raise commodity prices, making it easier for them to earn the money they needed to pay their debts.

The farmers found allies, especially in the Senate, among members from the new western states. All six of the states admitted to the Union in 1889 and 1890 had substantial silver mines, and their new congressional delegations— largely Republican—wanted the federal government to mint more silver. Thus Congress passed the Sherman Silver Purchase Act in 1890, replacing the Bland-Allison Act of 1878. The new act required the Treasury to purchase 4.5 million ounces of silver each month and to issue in payment paper money redeemable in gold or silver.

"King of the World"

Republican reform targeted the growing power of monopolies, such as that of Rockefeller's Standard Oil.

Although the amount of silver purchased doubled, that was still too little to inflate the economy substantially. Yet eastern business and financial groups saw a threat to the gold reserve in the growth of paper currency that holders could redeem for gold at the Treasury. The stage was set for the currency issue to eclipse all others during the financial panic that would sweep the country three years later.

Republicans viewed their victory over Cleveland and the Democrats in 1888 as a mandate not just to maintain the protective tariff but to raise it. Piloted through Congress by Ohio representative William McKinley, chairman of the Committee on Ways and Means, and by Senator Nelson W. Aldrich, the McKinley Tariff of 1890 raised duties on manufactured goods to their highest level ever. Critics charged that the new tariff would raise prices for all consumers. In the 1890 midterm elections, voters repudiated the McKinley Tariff with a landslide of Democratic votes. In the new House, Democrats outnumbered Republicans by almost three to one; in the Senate the Republican majority was reduced to eight. One of the election casualties was Congressman McKinley himself. But there was more to the election than the tariff. Voters also reacted to the Republican Congress's extravagant expenditures on military pensions and other programs. With expenditures rising and revenues dropping, largely because the McKinley Tariff was so high as to discourage imports, the nation's Treasury surplus was rapidly shrinking.

The large Democratic vote in 1890 may also have been a reaction to Republican efforts to legislate against alcohol. Between 1880 and 1890 sixteen out of twenty-one states outside the South held referenda on a constitutional ban of alcoholic beverages, although only six states voted for prohibition. Teetotaling Republicans were playing a losing game, arousing wets (anti-prohibitionists) on the Democratic side. Another issue that served to mobilize Democratic resistance was the Republican attempt to eliminate funding for state-supported Catholic (parochial) schools. In 1889, Wisconsin Republicans pushed through a law that held that a school could be accredited only if it taught the basic subjects in English. That was the last straw: it turned large numbers of outraged immigrants into Democratic activists. In 1889 and 1890 the Democrats swept state after state.

THE FARM PROBLEM AND AGRARIAN PROTEST MOVEMENTS

The 1890 election reflected more than a reaction against the Republican tariff, patronage politics, extravagant spending, and moralizing. The Democratic victory revealed a deep-seated unrest in the farming communities of the South and the western Midwest, as well as in the mining towns of the Rocky Mountain region. People used the term revolution to describe the rapid growth of grassroots support for populism. In drought-devastated Kansas, Populists took over five Republican congressional seats. As the congressional Democrats took power, the beginnings of an acute economic crisis appeared on the horizon: farmers' debts mounted as crop prices plummeted.

Frustrated by the unwillingness of Congress to meet their demands and ease their plight, disgruntled farmers concentrated on political action. Like so many of their counterparts laboring in urban factories, they realized that social change required demonstrations of power, and power lay in numbers. Unlike labor unions, however, the farm organizations faced a more complex array of economic variables affecting their livelihood. They had to deal with more than just management. Bankers, food processors, railroad and grain-elevator operators, as well as the world commodities market, all affected the agricultural sector. So, too, did unpredictable forces of nature: droughts, blizzards, insects, and erosion.

There were also important obstacles to collective action by farmers. Farmers' rugged individualism and physical isolation made communication

"I Feed You All!"

This 1875 poster shows the farmer at the center of society.

and organization especially difficult. American farmers had long prided themselves on their self-reliant hardihood, and many balked at sacrificing their independence. Another hurdle was that agricultural interests had diverged after the Civil War and in some cases conflicted with one another. On the Great Plains, for example, the railroads were the largest landowners. In addition, there were large absentee landowners, some foreign, who leased out vast tracts of land. There were also huge "bonanza" farms that employed hundreds of seasonal workers. Yet the majority of farmers were simple rural folk in the South and West who were moderate-size landowners, small land speculators, tenant farmers, sharecroppers, and hourly wage workers. It was the middle-size landowners who were most affected by rapidly rising land values and rising indebtedness. Those farmers were concerned with land values and crop prices, while tenants, sharecroppers, and farmhands supported land-distribution schemes that would give them access to their own land.

Given such a diversity of interests, farm activists discovered that it was often difficult to develop and maintain a cohesive grassroots organization.

Yet for all the difficulties, they persevered, and the results were dramatic, if not completely successful. Thus, for example, the deep-seated unrest in the farming communities of the South and the West began to find voice in the Granger movement, the Farmers' Alliances, and the new People's party, agrarian movements of considerable political and social significance.

ECONOMIC CONDITIONS   Since the end of the Civil War, farmers in the South and Midwest suffered from worsening economic and social conditions. The source of their problems was a long decline in commodity prices, from 1870 to 1898, the result of domestic overproduction and growing international competition for world markets. The vast new land brought under cultivation in the West poured an ever-increasing supply of farm products into the market, driving prices down. This effect was reinforced as innovations in transportation and communications brought American farmers ever more into international competition, further increasing the supply of farm commodities. Considerations of abstract economic forces puzzled many farmers, however. How could one speak of overproduction when so many remained in need? Instead, they reasoned, there must be a screw loose somewhere in the system.

The railroads and the food processors who handled the farmers' products were seen as the prime villains. Farmers resented the high railroad freight rates that prevailed in farm regions with no alternative forms of transportation. Individual farmers could not get the rebates on freight charges that the big corporations could extract from the railroads, and they could not exert the political influence wielded by the railroad lobbies. In other ways, farmers found themselves with little bargaining power as either buyers or sellers. When they tried to sell wheat or cotton, the buyer set the price; when they went to buy a plow point, the seller set the price.

High tariffs also operated to farmers' disadvantage, because they protected manufacturers from foreign competition, allowing them to raise the prices of factory goods upon which farmers depended. Farmers, however, had to sell their wheat, cotton, and other staples in foreign markets, where competition lowered prices. Tariffs inflicted a double blow on farmers because, insofar as they hampered imports, they indirectly hampered exports, by making it harder for foreign buyers to get the U.S. currency necessary to purchase American crops.

Debt, too, had been a perennial problem of agriculture. After the Civil War, farmers had become ever more enmeshed in debt, usually to local banks or merchants: western farmers incurred mortgages to cover the costs of land and machinery, while southern farmers used crop liens. As commodity prices dropped, the burden of debt grew because farmers had to cultivate more wheat or cotton to raise the same amount of money; and by growing more, they furthered the vicious cycle of surpluses and price declines.

THE GRANGER MOVEMENT   When the Department of Agriculture sent Oliver H. Kelley on a tour of the South in 1866, it was the isolation of farm folk that most impressed him. To address the problem, Kelley and some government clerks in 1867 founded the National Grange of the Patrons of Husbandry, better known as the Grange (an old word for granary), as each chapter was called. In the next few years the Grange mushroomed, reaching a membership as high as 1.5 million by 1874. The Grange started as a social and educational response to the farmers' isolation, but as it grew, it began to promote farmer-owned cooperatives for the buying and selling of crops. The Grangers' long-range ideal was to free themselves from the high fees charged by grain-elevator operators and food processors.

The Grange soon became indirectly involved in politics, through independent third parties, especially in the Midwest during the early 1870s. The Grange's chief political goal was to regulate the rates charged by railroads and warehouses. In five states, Grangers brought about the passage of "Granger laws," which at first proved relatively ineffective but laid a foundation for stronger legislation. Owners subject to their regulation challenged the laws in cases that soon advanced to the Supreme Court, where the plaintiffs in the "Granger cases" claimed to have been deprived of property without due process of law. In a key case involving warehouse regulation, *Munn v. Illinois* (1877), the Supreme Court ruled that the state, according to its "police powers," had the right to regulate property that was clothed in a public interest. If regulatory power were abused, the ruling said, "the people must resort to the polls, not the courts." Later, however, the courts would severely restrict state regulatory powers.

"Gift for the Grangers"

A promotional print for Grange members showing scenes of farming and farm life.

The Granger movement gradually declined (but never vanished) as members' energies were drawn off into both cooperatives, many of which failed, and political action. In 1875, out of the independent political movements, grew a party calling itself the Independent National party, more commonly known as the Greenback party because of its emphasis on the virtues of paper money. In the 1878 midterm elections the Greenbacks polled over 1 million votes and elected fifteen congressmen. But in 1880 the party's fortunes declined, and it disintegrated after 1884.

FARMERS' ALLIANCES   As the Grange lost energy, other farm organizations, known as Farmers' Alliances, grew in size and significance. Like the Grange, the Farmers' Alliances organized social and recreational activities, but they also emphasized political action. Struggling farmers throughout the South and Midwest, where tenancy rates were highest, rushed to join the Alliance movement. They saw in collective action a way to seek relief from the hardships created by chronic indebtedness, declining prices, and devastating droughts. Yet unlike the Grange, which was a national organization that tended to attract larger and more prosperous farmers, the Alliance was a grassroots organization that would become the largest and most dynamic farmers' movement in American history.

The Alliance movement swept across the cotton belt in the South and established strong positions in Kansas and the Dakotas. In 1886 a white minister in Texas, which had one of the largest and most influential Alliance movements, responded to the appeals of African American farmers by organizing the Colored Farmers' National Alliance. The white leadership of the Alliance movement in Texas endorsed this development because the Colored Alliance stressed that its objective was economic justice, not social equality. By 1890 the Alliance movement had members from New York to California, numbering about 1.5 million, and the Colored Farmers' National Alliance claimed over 1 million members.

A powerful attraction for many isolated, struggling farmers and their families was the sense of community provided by the Alliance. The Alliance movement welcomed rural women and men over sixteen years of age who displayed a "good moral character," believed in God, and demonstrated "industrious habits." Lawyers and blacks were excluded. The slogan of the Southern Alliance was "equal rights to all, special privileges to none." Women embraced the chance to engage in economic and political issues. One North Carolina woman relished the "grand opportunities" the Alliance provided women, allowing them to emerge from traditional domesticity. "Drudgery, fashion, and gossip," she declared, "are no longer the bounds of woman's sphere." One Alliance publication made the point explicitly: "The Alliance has come to redeem woman from her enslaved condition, and place her in her proper sphere." The number of women in the movement grew rapidly, and many assumed key leadership roles in the "grand army of reform."

The Alliance movement sponsored some 1,000 rural newspapers to spread the word about the farm problem. It also recruited 40,000 lecturers, who fanned out across the countryside to help people understand the tyrannical forces arrayed against the farm sector: bankers and creditors, Wall Street, railroads, and corporate giants who controlled both the markets and the political process. Unlike the Grange, however, the Alliance proposed an elaborate economic program. In 1890, Alliance agencies and exchanges in some eighteen states claimed a business of $10 million, but they soon went the way of the Granger cooperatives, victims of discrimination by wholesalers, manufacturers, railroads, and bankers—as well as their own inexperienced management and overextended credit.

In 1887, Charles W. Macune, the new Alliance president, proposed that Texas farmers create their own Alliance Exchange in an effort to free themselves

Members of the Texas Farmers' Alliance, 1880s

Alliances united local farmers, fostered a sense of community, and influenced political policies.

from their dependence upon food processors and banks. Members of the exchange would sign joint notes, borrow money from banks, and purchase their goods and supplies from a new corporation created by the Alliance in Dallas. The exchange would also build its own warehouses to store and market members' crops. While their crops were being stored, member farmers would be able to obtain credit from the warehouse cooperative so that they could buy household goods and supplies.

This grand cooperative scheme collapsed when Texas banks refused to accept the paper money from Alliance members. Macune and others then focused their energies on what Macune called a "subtreasury plan." Under this plan, farmers would be able to store their crops in new government warehouses and obtain government loans for up to 80 percent of the value of their crops at 1 percent interest. Besides providing immediate credit, the plan would allow the farmer the leeway to hold a crop for a better price later, since he would not have to sell it at harvesttime to pay off debts. The plan would also promote inflation because the loans to farmers would be made in new legal-tender notes.

The subtreasury plan went before Congress in 1890 but was never adopted. Its defeat, as well as setbacks to other Alliance proposals, convinced many farm leaders that they needed more political power in order to secure railroad regulation, currency inflation, state departments of agriculture, anti-trust laws, and farm credit.

FARM POLITICS   In the farm states west of the Mississippi River, where hard times had descended after the blizzards of 1887, farmers agitated for third-party political action to address their economic concerns. In the South, however, white Alliance members hesitated to bolt the Democratic party, seeking instead to influence or control it. Both approaches gained startling success. Independent parties under various names upset the political balance in western states, almost electing a governor under the banner of the People's party (also known as the Populist party) in Kansas (where a Populist was elected governor in 1892) and taking control of one house of the state legislature there and both houses in Nebraska. In South Dakota and Minnesota, Populists gained a balance of power in the state legislatures, and Kansas sent a Populist to the Senate.

The farm protest movement produced colorful leaders, especially in Kansas, where Mary Elizabeth Lease emerged as a fiery speaker. Born in Pennsylvania, Lease migrated to Kansas, taught school, raised a family, and failed at farming in the mid-1880s. She then studied law, "pinning sheets of notes above her wash tub," and became one of the state's first female lawyers. At the same time, she took up public speaking on behalf of various causes, including freedom for her ancestral Ireland, temperance, and women's suffrage. By the end of the 1880s, Lease had joined the Alliance as well as the Knights of Labor, and she soon applied her gifts as a speaker to the cause of free silver. A tall, proud, and imposing woman, Lease drew attentive audiences. "The people are at bay," she warned in 1894; "let the bloodhounds of money beware." She urged angry farmers to obtain their goals "with the ballot if possible, but if not that way

Mary Elizabeth Lease, 1890

A charismatic leader in the farm protest movement.

then with the bayonet." Like so many of the Populists, Lease viewed the urban-industrial East as the enemy of the working classes. "The great common people of this country," she shouted, "are slaves, and monopoly is the master. The West and South are bound and prostrate before the manufacturing East."

Jeremiah Simpson was an equally charismatic agrarian radical. Born in Canada, he served as a seaman on Great Lakes steamships before buying a farm in northern Kansas. He, his wife, and their young daughter made a go of the farm, but when he saw his child crushed to death in a sawmill accident, he and his wife relocated to the southern part of the state. There Simpson raised cattle for several years before losing his herd in a blizzard. Simpson embraced the Alliance movement, and in 1890 he campaigned for Congress. A shrewd man with huge, callused hands, he simplified the complex economic and political issues of the day. "Man must have access to the land," he maintained, "or he is a slave." He warned Republicans: "You can't put this movement down by sneers or by ridicule, for its foundation was laid as far back as the foundation of the world. It is a struggle between the robbers and the robbed." Simpson dismissed his Republican opponent, a wealthy railroad lawyer, as an indulgent pawn of the corporations whose "soft white hands" and "silk hosiery" betrayed his true priorities. His outraged opponent thereupon shouted that it was better to have silk socks than none at all, providing Simpson with his folksy nickname. Sockless Jerry won a seat in Congress, and so, too, did many other friends of "the people" in the Midwest.

In the South the Alliance won equal if not greater success by forcing the Democrats to nominate candidates pledged to their program. The southern states elected four pro-Alliance governors, seven pro-Alliance legislatures, forty-four pro-Alliance congressmen, and several senators. Among the most respected of the southern Alliance leaders was Thomas E. Watson of Georgia. The son of prosperous slaveholders who had lost everything after the Civil War, Watson became a successful lawyer and orator on behalf of the Alliance cause. He took the lead in urging African American tenant farmers and sharecroppers to join with their white counterparts in ousting the white political elite. "You are kept apart," he told black and white farmers, "that you may be separately fleeced of your earnings."

THE POPULIST PARTY AND THE ELECTION OF 1892 The success of the Alliances led to the formation of a third political party on the national level. In 1891 a conference in Cincinnati brought together delegates from farm, labor, and reform organizations to discuss strategy. The meeting endorsed a national third party and formed a national executive committee of the People's party. Few southerners attended the Cincinnati conference, but many approved of the third-party idea after their failure to move the Democratic party toward the subtreasury plan. In 1892 a larger meeting in St. Louis called for a national convention of the People's party at Omaha to adopt a platform and choose candidates.

The Populist party

A Populist gathering in Callaway, Nebraska, 1892.

The Populist Convention opened on July 4, 1892. Delegates drafted a platform that focused on issues of finance, transportation, and land. Its financial program demanded implementation of the subtreasury plan, unlimited coinage of silver, an increase in the money supply, a graduated income tax, whose rates would rise with personal income levels, and postal savings banks to protect depositors who otherwise risked disastrous losses in small-town banks vulnerable to farm depressions. As for transportation, the time had come "when the railroad corporations will either own the people or the people must own the railroads." Let government therefore nationalize the railroads, and the telephone and telegraph systems as well. The Populists called for the government to reclaim from railroads and other corporations lands "in excess of their actual needs" and to forbid land ownership by immigrants who had not gained citizenship. Finally, the platform endorsed the eight-hour workday and restriction of immigration. The party took these last positions to win support from urban workers, whom Populists looked upon as fellow "producers." The party's platform turned out to be more exciting than its candidate. Iowa's James B. Weaver, an able, prudent man, carried the stigma of his defeat on the Greenback ticket twelve years before. To attract southern voters who might be distanced by Weaver's service as a Union general, the party named a former Confederate general for vice president.

The Populist party was the startling new feature of the 1892 campaign. The major parties renominated the candidates of 1888: Democrat Grover Cleveland and Republican Benjamin Harrison. The tariff issue monopolized their attention. Both major candidates polled over 5 million votes, but Cleveland carried a plurality of the popular votes and a majority of the Electoral College. Weaver polled over 1 million votes and carried Colorado, Kansas, Nevada, and Idaho, for a total of twenty-two electoral votes. Alabama was the banner Populist state of the South, with 37 percent of its vote going to Weaver.

POPULISM AND RELIGION   Religion played a crucial role in the rise of Populism. At the new party's 1892 convention, one of the delegates said the gathering was like "a religious revival, a crusade, a Pentecost of politics in which a tongue of flame sat upon every man, and each spoke as the spirit gave him utterance." Populists believed that God was on their side in the fight to "save our republican institutions and common Christianity from decay and death." A Populist flyer promoting the new political party declared that "we are men that fear God and love his commands." Alliance meetings and Populist rallies often occurred in evangelical Protestant churches. They began with prayers and included the singing of hymns, the passing of an offering plate, and a period of instruction, or "exhortation." Speakers promoted the "conversion" of voters to the sacred cause. Evangelical ministers and lay leaders were in the vanguard of the agrarian social and political organizations. A leading evangelical Populist, the Reverend Thomas Dixon, argued that the farm revolt was "the result of divine inspiration." It constituted "a great social and moral revolution" that "would elevate mankind" and "purify politics."

THE ECONOMY AND THE SILVER SOLUTION

While the farmers were funneling their discontent into politics and businessmen were consolidating their holdings, a fundamental weakness in the economy was about to cause a major collapse.

INADEQUATE CURRENCY   The nation's money supply in the late nineteenth century lacked the flexibility to grow along with the expanding economy. From 1865 to 1890, the amount of currency in circulation per capita decreased about 10 percent. Currency deflation raised the cost of borrowing money, as a tight money supply caused bankers to hike interest rates on loans.

Metallic money dated from the Mint Act of 1792, which authorized free and unlimited coinage of silver and gold at a ratio of 15 to 1, meaning that the amount of precious metal in a silver dollar weighed fifteen times as much as that in a gold dollar, a reflection of the relative value of gold and silver at the time. "Free and unlimited coinage" simply meant that owners of precious metals could have any quantity of their gold or silver coined free, except for a nominal fee to cover costs.

A fixed ratio of values of gold and silver did not reflect fluctuations in the shifting market value of the metals, however. When gold rose to a market value higher than that reflected in the official ratio, owners ceased to present it for coinage. The country was actually on a silver standard until 1837, when Congress changed the ratio to 16 to 1, which soon reversed the situation. Silver became more valuable in the open market than in coinage, and the country drifted to a gold standard. This state of affairs prevailed until 1873, when Congress passed a general revision of the coinage laws and dropped the then-unused provision for the coinage of silver.

This occurred just when silver production in the western states began to increase, however, reducing its market value through the growth in supply. Soon advocates of currency inflation began to denounce the "crime of '73," which they had scarcely noticed at the time. Gradually suspicion grew that bankers and merchants had conspired in 1873 to stop coining silver so as to ensure a nationwide scarcity of money. But the pro-silver forces had little more legislative success than the advocates of greenback inflation. The Bland-Allison Act of 1878 and the Sherman Silver Purchase Act of 1890 provided for some silver coinage, but too little in each case to offset the overall contraction of the currency as the population and the economy grew.

THE DEPRESSION OF 1893 Just ten days before Grover Cleveland started his second term, in 1893, the Philadelphia and Reading Railroad declared bankruptcy, setting off a national panic. Other overextended railroads collapsed, taking many banks with them. Not only was business affected, but entire farm regions were also devastated by the spreading depression. A quarter of the cities' unskilled workers lost their jobs, and by the fall of 1893 over 600 banks had closed and 15,000 businesses had failed. Farm foreclosures soared. By 1894 the nation's economy had reached bottom. The catastrophic depression lasted another four years, with unemployment hovering at 20 percent. In New York some 35 percent were unemployed, and 20,000 homeless people camped out at police stations and other makeshift shelters. Violent labor strikes at Pullman, Illinois, and at the Homestead Works outside Pittsburgh symbolized the fracturing of the social order. In 1894 some 750,000 workers went on strike, millions found themselves unemployed, and railroad construction workers, laid off in the West, began tramping east and talked of marching on Washington, D.C.

National panic

The New York Stock Exchange on the morning of Friday, May 5, 1893.

One protest group that reached Washington was Coxey's Army, led by Jacob S. Coxey, a wealthy Ohio quarry owner turned Populist who demanded that the federal government provide the unemployed with meaningful work. Coxey, his wife, and their son, Legal Tender Coxey, rode in a carriage ahead of some 400 hardy protesters who finally straggled into Washington. There Coxey was arrested for walking on the grass. Although his ragtag army dispersed peacefully, the march on Washington, as well as the growing political strength of Populism, struck fear into the hearts of many Americans. Critics portrayed Populists as "hayseed socialists" whose election would endanger property rights.

The 1894 congressional elections, taking place amid this climate of mushrooming anxiety, produced a severe setback for the Democrats, who paid politically for the economic downturn, and the Republicans were the chief beneficiaries. The third-party Populists emerged with six senators and seven representatives. They had polled 1.5 million votes for their congressional candidates and expected the festering discontent to carry them to national power in 1896.

SILVERITES VERSUS GOLDBUGS   The course of events would dash that hope, however. In the mid-1890s, events conspired to focus all concerns on the currency issue. One of the causes of the 1893 depression was the failure of a major British bank, which had led many British investors to sell their American holdings in return for gold. Soon after Grover Cleveland's inauguration, the U.S. gold reserve had fallen below $100 million. To plug the drain on the Treasury by stopping the issuance of silver notes redeemable in gold, the president sought repeal of the Sherman Silver Purchase Act. Cleveland won the repeal in 1893, but at the cost of an irreparable division in his own party. One embittered pro-silver Democrat labeled the president a Benedict Arnold.

Western silver interests now escalated their demands for silver coinage, presenting a strategic dilemma for Populists: should the party promote the long list of varied reforms it had originally advocated, or should it try to ride the silver issue into power? The latter seemed the practical choice. As a consequence, the Populist leaders decided, over the protests of more radical members, to hold their 1896 nominating convention last, confident that the two major parties would at best straddle the silver issue and they would then reap a harvest of bolting silverite Republicans and Democrats.

THE ELECTION OF 1896   Contrary to those expectations, the major parties took opposite positions on the currency issue. The Republicans, as expected, chose William McKinley on a gold-standard platform. McKinley, a former congressman and governor of Ohio, symbolized the mainstream Republican values that had served the party well. After the convention, a friend told McKinley that the "money question" would determine the election. The Republican candidate dismissed that notion, insisting that the tariff would continue to govern national elections. But one of McKinley's advisers disagreed. "In my opinion," said Judge William Day of Ohio, "in thirty days you won't hear of anything else" but the money question. He was right.

On the Democratic side the pro-silver forces captured the convention for their platform. Thirty-six-year-old William Jennings Bryan arranged to give the closing speech for the silver plank. A fervent evangelical moralist, Bryan was a two-term congressman from Nebraska who had been defeated in the Senate race in 1894, when Democrats were swept out of office by the dozens. In the months before the convention, he had traveled throughout the South and the West, speaking eloquently for free silver and against Cleveland's "do-nothing" response to the depression. Bryan was an extraordinary public speaker, a minister masquerading as a politician, self-infatuated and self-dramatizing, who used his theatrical speaking skills to infuse religion into politics. At the 1896 Democratic Convention, his carefully rehearsed phrases and gestures swept the delegates into a frenzy. Bryan reiterated that he spoke for the "producing masses of this nation" against the Eastern "financial magnates" who enslaved them with high interest rates. He was the first major candidate to champion the poor and the oppressed. As his speech reached a crescendo, Bryan fused Christian imagery with Populist anger:

> I come to speak to you in defense of a cause as holy as the cause of liberty—the cause of humanity. . . . We have petitioned, and our petitions have been scorned. We have entreated, and our entreaties have been disregarded. We have begged, and they have mocked when our calamity came. We beg no longer; we entreat no more; we petition no more. We defy them!

The messianic Bryan then stretched his fingers across his forehead and reached his free-silver conclusion: "You shall not press down upon the brow of labor this crown of thorns. You shall not crucify mankind upon a cross of gold!" Bryan extended his arms straight out from his sides, posing as if being crucified. As he strode triumphantly off the stage, the delegates erupted in a frenzy of adulation. It was pure theater, but it worked better than even Bryan had imagined. "Everybody seemed to go mad at once," reported the *New York World*. The whole face of the convention was broken by the tumult—hills and valleys of shrieking men and women."

William Jennings Bryan

His "cross of gold" speech at the 1896 Democratic Convention roused the delegates and secured him the party's presidential nomination.

The day after his riveting speech, Bryan won the nomination on the fifth ballot, and in the process the Democratic party was fractured—for the time being. Disappointed pro-gold, pro-Cleveland Democrats were so alienated by Bryan's inflationary program and Jacksonian rhetoric that they walked out of the convention and nominated their own candidate, Senator John M. Palmer of Illinois. "Fellow Democrats," Palmer announced, "I will not consider it any great fault if you decide to cast your vote for [the Republican] William McKinley."

When the Populists met in St. Louis two weeks later, they faced an impossible choice. They could name their own candidate and divide the silver vote, or they could endorse Bryan and probably lose their identity as an independent party. In the end they backed Bryan but chose their own vice-presidential candidate, former representative Thomas E. Watson of Georgia, and invited the Democrats to drop their vice-presidential nominee, an action that Bryan refused to countenance.

Bryan crisscrossed the country, exploiting his spellbinding eloquence and relentless good cheer on behalf of "the struggling masses" of workers, farmers, and small-business owners and promising the panacea of the unlimited coinage of silver. In his self-appointed role as a pious paladin crusading on behalf of "the people," Bryan demonstrated that politics should be a moral enterprise. He was the first major-party leader, a "godly hero," to advocate the social gospel and the expansion of federal powers to promote the welfare of ordinary Americans. He said that strikes should be legalized, farmers should be given federal subsidies, the rich should be taxed, corporate campaign contributions should be banned, and liquor should be outlawed. Bryan's populist crusade was for whites only, however. Like so many otherwise progressive Democratic leaders, he never challenged the pattern of racial segregation and violence against blacks in the solid Democratic South.

McKinley, meanwhile, conducted a "front-porch campaign," receiving select delegations of supporters at his home in Canton, Ohio, and giving only prepared responses. McKinley's campaign manager, Mark Hanna, shrewdly portrayed Bryan as a radical whose "communistic spirit" would ruin the capitalist system. Many observers agreed with the portrait. The *New York Tribune* denounced Bryan as a "wretched rattle-pated boy, posing in vapid vanity and mouthing resounding rottenness." Theodore Roosevelt had equally strong opinions. "The silver craze surpasses belief," he wrote a friend. "Bryan's election would be a great calamity."

By preying upon such fears, the McKinley campaign raised vast sums of money to finance an army of 1,400 Republican speakers who traveled the country in his support. In the end the Democratic-Populist-silverite candidates were overwhelmed by the well-organized and well-financed Republican campaign. McKinley won the popular vote by 7.1 million to 6.5 million and the Electoral College vote by 271 to 176.

Bryan carried most of the West and the South but found little support in the metropolitan centers east of the Mississippi and north of the Ohio and Potomac Rivers. In the critical midwestern battleground, from Minnesota and Iowa eastward to Ohio, Bryan carried not a single state. Many Catholic voters, normally drawn to the Democrats, were repelled by Bryan's evangelical style. Farmers in the Northeast, moreover, were less attracted to agrarian radicalism than were farmers in the wheat and cotton belts, where there were higher rates of tenancy and a narrower range of crops. Among factory workers in the cities, Bryan found even less support. Wage laborers found it easier to identify with McKinley's "full dinner pail" pledge than with Bryan's free-silver panacea. Some workers, moreover, may have been intimidated by business owners' threats to close shop if the "Demopop" heresies triumphed.

A NEW ERA   The election of 1896 was a climactic political struggle that generated intense interest. Over 79 percent of eligible voters participated. Urban-industrial values had indeed taken firm hold of the political system. The first important act of the McKinley administration was to call a special session of Congress to raise the tariff again. The Dingley Tariff of 1897 became the highest ever. By 1897 economic prosperity was returning, helped along by inflation of the currency, which bore out the arguments of the Greenbackers and silverites. But the inflation came, in one of history's many ironies, not from greenbacks or silver but from a new flood of gold onto the market and into the mints. During the 1880s and 1890s, discoveries of gold in South Africa, the Canadian Yukon, and Alaska led to spectacular new gold rushes. In 1900, Congress passed a Gold Standard Act, which marked an end to the silver movement.

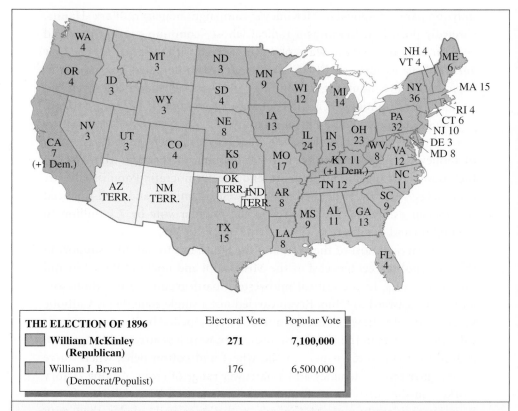

THE ELECTION OF 1896	Electoral Vote	Popular Vote
William McKinley **(Republican)**	**271**	**7,100,000**
William J. Bryan (Democrat/Populist)	176	6,500,000

How did Bryan's "cross of gold" speech divide the Democratic party? How did McKinley's strategy differ from Bryan's? Why was Bryan able to carry the West and the South but unable to win in cities and the Northeast?

At the close of the nineteenth century, the old issues of tariff and currency policy, which had dominated national politics since the Civil War, gave way to global concerns: the outbreak of the War of 1898 and the acquisition of territories outside the Western Hemisphere. At the same time the advent of a new century brought new social and political developments. Even though the Populist movement faded with William Jennings Bryan's defeat, most of the progressive agenda promoted by Bryan Democrats and Populists, dismissed as too radical and controversial in 1896, would be implemented over the next two decades. Bryan's impassioned candidacy helped transform the Democratic party into a vigorous instrument of "progressive" reform during the early twentieth century. Democrats began to promote anti-trust prosecutions, state laws to limit the working hours of women and children, the establishment of a minimum wage, and measures to support farmers and protect labor union organizers. As the United States looked ahead to a new century, it began to place more emphasis on the role of the national government in society and the economy.

End of Chapter Review

CHAPTER SUMMARY

- **Guilded Age Politics** Americans were intensely loyal to the two major parties, which operated on a local level by distributing favors. "City machines" also provided working-class men with jobs and gave relief (money or necessities) to the poor, thereby winning votes. New York's Tammany Hall ring under the boss William Tweed best exemplifies the corruption resulting from this system. The major political parties shared power nearly equally during the Gilded Age, and neither party was willing to embrace bold initiatives.

- **National Politics** Politicians focused on tariff reform, the regulation of corporations, Indian wars and Indian policy, civil service reform, and immigration. In the 1884 presidential election, Republicans favoring reform, dubbed Mugwumps, bolted their party to support the Democrat, Grover Cleveland, a reformer.

- **Farm Problems** Farmers had serious grievances at the end of the nineteenth century. Commodity prices were falling because of domestic overproduction and international competition, and many farmers had gone into debt: they had bought new machinery on credit at high interest rates and were paying the railroads exorbitant rates to ship their goods to market without receiving the rebates that large corporations had the leverage to demand. In addition, high tariffs allowed manufacturers to raise the price of goods that farmers needed.

- **Farm Movements** Despite farmers' traditional reluctance to organize, many reacted to their difficulties by joining the Granger movement, which promoted farmer-owned cooperatives and, subsequently, Farmers' Alliances, grassroots social organizations that also promoted political action. The Alliances became a major force in the Midwest and the South. Influenced by their success, delegates from farm, labor, and reform organizations in 1892 established the People's party, also known as the Populist party. Populists sought greater regulation of business by the federal government and the free coinage of silver (because they hoped that the ensuing inflation would make it easier for them to repay their debts). To appeal to urban voters, they endorsed the eight-hour workday and restrictions on immigration.

- **Rise of Populism** The Populists did well in 1892 and, with the depression of 1893, had high hopes for the next presidential election. But the Democrat, William Jennings Bryan stole the silver issue from the Populists. The Populists thus fused with the Democrats, but Bryan lost the election to the Republicans, who in a well-organized, well-financed campaign won the urban northeastern vote by portraying the Democratic candidate as a dangerous radical. The People's party did not recover from the blow.

CHRONOLOGY

1877	Rutherford B. Hayes is inaugurated president
1877	Supreme Court issues *Munn v. Illinois* decision
1881	President James A. Garfield is assassinated
1881	Chester Arthur becomes president
1883	Congress passes the Pendleton Civil Service Reform Act
1885	Grover Cleveland, a Democrat, begins his first term as president
1886	Supreme Court issues *Wabash, St. Louis, and Pacific Railroad Company v. Illinois* decision
1887	Interstate Commerce Commission is created
1888	Grover Cleveland loses the presidency to Benjamin Harrison
1890	Congress passes the Sherman Anti-Trust Act, the Sherman Silver Purchase Act, and the McKinley Tariff
1892	People's party drafts its Omaha platform
1892	Grover Cleveland wins a second term as president
1893	Economic depression affects a substantial proportion of the population
1896	In the presidential election, Republicans defeat the Democrats, who have the support of the Populists

KEY TERMS & NAMES

Part Six

MODERN AMERICA

he United States entered the twentieth century on a wave of unrelenting change. In 1800 the nation was a rural, agrarian society largely detached from the concerns of international affairs. By 1900 the United States had become a highly industrialized urban culture with a growing involvement in world politics and international commerce. In other words, the nation was on the threshold of modernity.

The prospect of modernity both excited and scared Americans. Old truths and beliefs clashed with unsettling scientific discoveries and social practices. People debated the legitimacy of Darwinism, the existence of God, the dangers of jazz, and the federal effort to prohibit the sale of alcoholic beverages. The automobile and airplane helped shrink distance, and such communications innovations as radio and film contributed to a national consciousness. In the process the United States began to emerge from its isolationist shell. Throughout most of the nineteenth century, policy makers had sought to isolate America from the intrigues and conflicts of the great European powers. As early as 1780, John Adams had warned Congress against involving the United States in the affairs of Europe. "Our business with them, and theirs with us," he wrote, "is commerce, not politics, much less war."

With only a few exceptions, statesmen during the nineteenth century followed such advice. Noninvolvement in foreign wars and nonintervention in the internal affairs of foreign governments formed the pillars of American foreign policy until the end of the century. During the 1890s, however, expanding commercial interests around the world led Americans to expand the horizons of their concerns. Imperialism was the order of the day among the great European powers, and a growing number of American expansionists demanded that the United States also adopt a global ambition and join in the hunt for new territories and markets. Such mixed motives helped spark the War of 1898 and helped to justify the resulting acquisition of colonies outside the continental United States. Entangling alliances with European powers soon followed.

The outbreak of the Great War in Europe in 1914 posed an even greater challenge to the tradition of isolation and nonintervention. The prospect of a German victory over the French and the British threatened the European balance of power, which had long ensured the security of the United States. By 1917 it appeared that Germany might emerge triumphant and begin to menace the Western Hemisphere. Woodrow Wilson's crusade to use American intervention in World War I to transform the world order in accordance with his idealistic principles dislodged foreign policy from its isolationist moorings. It also spawned a prolonged debate about the role of the United States in world affairs, a debate that World War II would resolve for a time on the side of internationalism.

While the United States was entering the world stage as a formidable military power, it was also settling into its role as a great industrial power. Cities and factories sprouted across the landscape. An abundance of new jobs served as a magnet attracting millions of immigrants from nearly every landmass on the globe. They were not always welcomed, nor were they readily assimilated. Ethnic and racial strife, as well as labor agitation, increased at the turn of the century. In the midst of such social turmoil and unparalleled economic development, reformers made their first sustained attempt to adapt their political and social institutions to the realities of the industrial age. The worst excesses and injustices of urban-industrial development—corporate monopolies, child labor, political corruption, hazardous working conditions, urban ghettos—were finally addressed in a comprehensive way. During the Progressive Era (1890–1917), local, state, and federal governments sought to rein in the excesses of industrial capitalism and develop a more rational and efficient public policy.

A conservative Republican resurgence challenged the notion of the new regulatory state during the 1920s. Free enterprise and corporate capitalism witnessed a dramatic revival. But the stock market crash of 1929 helped propel the United States and the world into the worst economic downturn in history. The unprecedented severity of the Great Depression renewed public demands for federal programs to protect the general welfare. "This nation asks for action," declared President Franklin D. Roosevelt in his 1933 inaugural address. The  many New Deal initiatives and agencies instituted by Roosevelt and his Democratic administration created the framework for a welfare state that has since served as the basis for public policy.

The New Deal helped revive public confidence and put people back to work, but it did not end the Great Depression. It took a world war to restore full employment. The necessity of mobilizing the nation in support of the Second World War also accelerated the growth of the federal government. And the unparalleled scope of the war helped catapult the United States into a leadership role in world politics. The use of atomic bombs ushered in a new era of nuclear diplomacy that held the fate of the world in the balance. For all of the new creature comforts associated with modern life, Americans in 1945 found themselves living amid an array of new anxieties.

23

AN AMERICAN EMPIRE

FOCUS QUESTIONS

wwnorton.com/studyspace

- What motivated America's "new imperialism"?
- What was the role of religion as a motive for American territorial expansion?
- What were the causes of the War of 1898?
- What did America gain from the War of 1898?
- What were the main achievements of President Roosevelt's foreign policy?

Throughout the nineteenth century most Americans displayed what one senator called "only a languid interest" in foreign affairs. The overriding priorities were industrial development, western settlement, and domestic politics. Foreign relations simply were not important to the vast majority of Americans. After the Civil War an isolationist mood swept across the United States as the country basked in its geographic advantages: wide oceans as buffers, the British navy situated between America and the powers of Europe, and militarily weak neighbors in the Western Hemisphere.

Yet the notion of America's having a Manifest Destiny ordained by God to expand its territory and its democratic values remained alive in the decades after the Civil War. Several prominent political and business leaders argued that the rapid industrial development of the United States required the acquisition—or conquest—of foreign territories in order to gain easier access to vital raw materials. In addition, as their exports grew, American companies and farmers became increasingly intertwined in the world economy. This involvement, in turn, required an expanded naval force to protect the shipping lanes. And a modern steam-powered navy needed bases where its ships could replenish their supplies of coal and water. For these and other reasons the United States during the last quarter of the nineteenth century began to expand its military presence and territorial possessions beyond the Western Hemisphere, often at the expense of other nations' sovereignty.

Toward the New Imperialism

By the late nineteenth century, European powers had already unleashed a new surge of imperialism in Africa and Asia, where they had seized territory, established colonies, and promoted economic exploitation, racial superiority, and Christian evangelism. Writing in 1902, the British economist J. A. Hobson declared that imperialism was "the most powerful factor in the current politics of the Western world."

IMPERIALISM IN A GLOBAL CONTEXT Western imperialism had economic roots and racist overtones. The new phase of global expansion was primarily a quest for new markets and sources of raw materials. The Second Industrial Revolution generated such dramatic increases in production that business leaders felt compelled to find new markets for their burgeoning supply of goods and new sources of investment for their growing supply of capital. Manufacturers, on the other hand, were eager to find new sources of raw materials to supply their expanding needs. At the same time, the aggressive nationalism and bitter rivalries of the European powers made all of them compete with one another as they expanded their far-flung empires.

The result was a widespread process of imperial expansion into Africa and Asia. Beginning in the 1880s, the British, French, Belgians, Italians, Dutch, Spanish, and Germans used military force and political guile to conquer those continents. Each of the imperial nations, including the United States, dispatched Christian missionaries to convert native peoples. By 1900 some 18,000 Christian missionaries were scattered around the world. Often the conversion to Christianity was the first step in the loss of a culture's indigenous traditions. Western religious efforts also influenced the colonial power structure. A British nationalist explained the global ambitions of the imperialist nations: "Today, power and domination rather than freedom and independence are the ideas that appeal to the imagination of the masses— and the national ideal has given way to the imperial." This imperial outlook triggered clashes among the Western powers that would lead to unprecedented conflict in the twentieth century.

AMERICAN IMPERIALISM   As the European nations expanded their control over much of the rest of the world, the United States also began to acquire new territories. Most Americans became increasingly aware of world markets as developments in transportation and communication quickened the pace of commerce and diplomacy. From the first, agricultural exports had been the basis of economic growth. Now the conviction grew that industrial manufacturers had matured to the point where they could outsell foreign competitors in the world market. But should the expansion of markets lead to territorial expansion as well—or to intervention in the internal affairs of other countries? On such points, Americans disagreed, but a small yet vocal and influential group of public officials embraced the idea of acquiring overseas possessions, regardless of the implications. These expansionists included Senators Albert J. Beveridge of Indiana and Henry Cabot Lodge of Massachusetts, Theodore Roosevelt, and not least of all, naval captain Alfred Thayer Mahan.

During the 1880s, Captain Mahan had become a leading advocate of sea power and Western imperialism. In 1890 he published *The Influence of Sea Power upon History, 1660–1783*, in which he argued that national greatness and prosperity flowed from maritime power. Mahan insisted that modern economic development required a powerful navy, a strong merchant marine, foreign commerce, colonies, and naval bases. A self-described imperialist, Mahan championed America's "destiny" to control the Caribbean, build an isthmian canal to connect the Pacific and the Caribbean, and spread Western civilization in the Pacific. His ideas were widely circulated in popular journals and within the U.S. government. Theodore Roosevelt, the assistant secretary of the navy, ordered a copy of Mahan's book for every American ship. Yet even before Mahan's writings became influential, a gradual expansion of the navy had begun. In 1880 the nation had fewer than 100 seagoing vessels, many of them rusting or rotting at the docks. By 1896 eleven powerful new steel battleships had been built or authorized.

IMPERIALIST THEORY   Claims of racial superiority bolstered the new imperialist spirit. Spokesmen in each Western country, including the United States, used the arguments of social Darwinism to justify economic exploitation and territorial conquest. Among nations as among individuals, expansionists claimed, the fittest survive and prevail. John Fiske, a historian and popular lecturer on Darwinism, developed racial corollaries from Darwin's ideas. In *American Political Ideas Viewed from the Standpoint of Universal History* (1885), he stressed the superior character of "Anglo-Saxon" institutions and peoples. The English-speaking "race," he argued, was destined to dominate the globe and transform the institutions, traditions, language—even the blood—of the world's peoples. Josiah Strong, a Congregationalist minister, added the sanction of religion to theories of racial and national superiority. In his book *Our Country: Its Possible Future and Its Present Crisis* (1885), Strong asserted that the "Anglo-Saxon" embodied two great ideas: civil liberty and "a pure spiritual Christianity." The Anglo-Saxon was "divinely commissioned to be, in a peculiar sense, his brother's keeper."

EXPANSION IN THE PACIFIC

For Josiah Strong and other expansionists, Asia offered an especially alluring target for American imperialism. President Andrew Johnson's secretary of state, William H. Seward, had predicted in 1866 that the United States must inevitably exercise commercial domination "on the Pacific Ocean, and its islands and continents." Eager for American manufacturers to exploit Asian markets, Seward believed the United States first had to remove all foreign interests from the northern Pacific coast and gain access to that region's valuable ports. To that end, he cast covetous eyes on the British colony of British Columbia, sandwiched between Russian America (Alaska) and the Washington Territory.

Late in 1866, while encouraging British Columbians to consider making their colony a U.S. territory, Seward learned of Russia's desire to sell Alaska. He leaped at the opportunity, in part because its acquisition might influence British Columbia to join the union. In 1867 the United States bought Alaska for $7.2 million, thus removing Russia, the most recent colonial power, from the New World. Critics scoffed at "Seward's folly" of buying the Alaskan "icebox," but it proved to be the biggest bargain since the Louisiana Purchase. Seward's successors at the State Department sustained his expansionist vision. Acquiring key ports in the Pacific Ocean was the major focus of overseas activity through the rest of the nineteenth century. Two island groups occupied especially strategic positions: Samoa and Hawaii (the Sandwich Islands). Both had major harbors, Pago Pago and Pearl Harbor, respectively. In the years after the Civil War, American interest in those islands deepened.

SAMOA   In 1878 the Samoans signed a treaty with the United States that granted a naval base at Pago Pago and extraterritoriality for Americans

American expansion

In a critical comment on William Seward's 1867 purchase of Alaska, this cartoon
represents the territory as a block of ice labeled "Russian America."

(meaning that in Samoa, Americans remained subject only to U.S. law), exchanged trade concessions, and called for the United States to extend its
good offices in case of a dispute with another nation. The Senate ratified this
accord, and in the following year the German and British governments
worked out similar arrangements with other islands in the Samoan group.
There matters rested until civil war broke out in Samoa in 1887. A peace
conference in Berlin in 1889 established a protectorate over Samoa, with
Germany, Great Britain, and the United States in an uneasy partnership.

HAWAII   In Hawaii the Americans had a clearer field to exploit. The islands, a united kingdom since 1795, had a sizable settlement of American
missionaries and planters and were strategically more important to the
United States than Samoa. In 1875 the kingdom had signed a reciprocal
trade agreement, according to which Hawaiian sugar would enter the United
States duty-free and Hawaii promised that none of its territory would be
leased or granted to a third power. This agreement resulted in a boom in
sugar production, and American settlers in Hawaii soon formed an economic
elite. American planters in Hawaii built their fortunes on cheap immigrant
labor, mainly Chinese and Japanese. By the 1890s the native population had
been reduced to a minority by smallpox and other foreign diseases, and
Asians quickly became the most numerous group.

Queen Liliuokalani

The Hawaiian queen sought to preserve her nation's independence.

In 1885, President Grover Cleveland called the Hawaiian Islands "the stepping-stone to the growing trade of the Pacific." Two years later Americans in Hawaii forced the king to accept a constitutional government, which they dominated. In 1890, however, the McKinley Tariff destroyed Hawaii's favored position in the sugar trade by putting the sugar of all countries on the duty-free list and granting growers in the continental United States a 2¢ subsidy per pound of sugar. This change led to an economic crisis in Hawaii and brought political turmoil as well.

In 1891, when Liliuokalani, the king's sister, ascended the throne, she tried to eliminate white control of the government. Two years later Hawaii's white population revolted and seized power. The American ambassador brought in marines to support the coup. As he cheerfully reported to Washington, "The Hawaiian pear is now fully ripe, and this is the golden hour for the United States to pluck it." Within a month a committee of the new government in Hawaii turned up in Washington with a treaty calling for the island nation to be annexed to the United States.

The treaty appeared just weeks before President Benjamin Harrison left office, however, and Democratic senators blocked its ratification. President Cleveland then withdrew it and sent a special commissioner to investigate. The commissioner removed the marines and reported that the Americans in Hawaii had acted improperly. Most Hawaiians opposed annexation to the United States, the commissioner found. He concluded that the revolution had been engineered mainly by the American planters hoping to take advantage of the subsidy for sugar grown in the United States. Cleveland proposed to restore the queen to power in return for amnesty to the revolutionists. The provisional government controlled by the sugar planters refused to give up power, however, and on July 4, 1894, it proclaimed the islands the Republic of Hawaii, which included in its constitution a standing provision for American annexation. In 1897, when William McKinley became president, he was looking for an excuse to annex the islands. "We need Hawaii," he claimed, "just as much and a good deal more than we did California. It is manifest destiny." When the Japanese, also hoping to take over the islands, sent a naval flotilla to Hawaii, McKinley responded by sending U.S. warships and asked the Senate to approve a treaty to annex the islands. When the Senate could not muster the two-thirds majority needed to approve the treaty, McKinley used a joint resolution of the House and the Senate to achieve his aims. The resolution passed by simple majorities in both houses, and Hawaii was annexed in the summer of 1898.

THE WAR OF 1898

Until the 1890s, a certain ambivalence about overseas possessions had checked America's drive to expand. Suddenly, in 1898 and 1899, such inhibitions collapsed, and the United States aggressively thrust its way to the far reaches of the Pacific. The spark for this explosion of imperialism lay neither in the Pacific nor in the quest for bases and trade but to the south, in Cuba. Ironically, the chief motive was a sense of outrage at another country's imperialism.

"CUBA LIBRE" Throughout the second half of the nineteenth century, Cubans had repeatedly revolted against Spanish rule, only to be ruthlessly suppressed. One of Spain's oldest colonies, Cuba was a major export market for the mother country. Yet American investments in Cuba, mainly in sugar and mining, were steadily increasing. The United States in fact traded more with Cuba than Spain did.

On February 24, 1895, insurrection broke out again. Cubans waged guerrilla warfare against Spanish troops and business interests. Americans sympathized with the rebellion, often comparing the insurrection to their own War of Independence. In 1896 the Spanish commanding general adopted a policy of gathering Cubans behind Spanish lines, often in detention (*reconcentrado*) centers so that no one could join the insurrections by night and appear peaceful by day. In some of the centers, a combination of tropical climate, poor food, and unsanitary conditions quickly produced a heavy toll of disease and death. The American press christened the Spanish commander a butcher.

Events in Cuba supplied exciting copy for newspapers and magazines. William Randolph Hearst's *New York Journal* and Joseph Pulitzer's *New York World* were at the time locked in a monumental competition for readers. "It was a battle of gigantic proportions," one journalist later wrote, "in which the sufferings of Cuba merely chanced to furnish some of the most convenient

José Martí y Perez

Leader of the Cuban revolt against Spanish rule.

ammunition." The newspapers' sensationalism came to be called yellow journalism.

At the outset of the rebellion, the Cleveland administration tried to protect American rights in Cuba while avoiding involvement beyond an offer of mediation. Mounting public sympathy for the rebel cause prompted concern in Congress, however. By concurrent resolutions on April 6, 1896, the two houses endorsed official recognition of the Cuban rebels and urged the president to help them gain independence. Cleveland, however, offered only to cooperate with Spain in bringing peace on the basis of allowing Cubans a measure of self-governance. The Spanish politely refused.

PRESSURE FOR WAR America's posture of neutrality changed sharply when William McKinley became president. He had been elected in 1896 on a platform that endorsed Cuban independence as well as American control of Hawaii and the construction of an isthmian canal connecting the Caribbean Sea to the Pacific Ocean. In 1897, Spain offered Cuba autonomy (self-government without formal independence) in return for peace. The Cubans rejected the offer. Spain was impaled on the horns of a dilemma, unable to end the rebellion and unready to give up Cuba.

Early in 1898, events moved rapidly to arouse American opinion against Spain. On January 25 the U.S. battleship *Maine* docked in Havana Harbor, ostensibly on a courtesy call. On February 9 the *New York Journal* released the text of a letter from the Spanish ambassador Depuy de Lôme to a friend in Havana, stolen from the post office by a Cuban spy. In the letter, de Lôme called President McKinley "weak and a bidder for the admiration of the crowd, besides being a would-be politician who tries to leave a door open behind himself while keeping on good terms with the jingoes of his party." De Lôme resigned to prevent further embarrassment to his government.

Six days later, during the night of February 15, 1898, the *Maine* exploded and sank in Havana Harbor, with a horrible loss of 260 men. The ship's captain, one of only 84 survivors, scribbled a telegram to Washington: "*Maine*

The sinking of the *Maine* in Havana Harbor

The uproar created by the incident and its coverage in the "yellow press" helped to push President William McKinley to declare war.

blown up in Havana Harbor at nine forty tonight and destroyed. Many wounded and doubtless more killed or drowned. . . . Public opinion should be suspended until further report."

But those eager for a war with Spain saw no need to withhold judgment. Assistant secretary of the navy Theodore Roosevelt called the sinking "an act of dirty treachery on the part of the Spaniards." The United States, he claimed, "needs a war." A naval court of inquiry reported that an external mine had set off an explosion in the ship's munitions magazine. Lacking hard evidence, the court made no effort to fix the blame, but the yellow press had no need of evidence. The outcry against Spain rose in a crescendo with the words "Remember the *Maine*!" Never mind that Spain could have derived little benefit from such an act. (A comprehensive study in 1976 concluded that the sinking of the *Maine* was an accident, the result of an internal explosion triggered by a fire in its coal bunker.)

The weight of outraged public opinion and the influence of Republican militants such as Theodore Roosevelt and the president's closest friend, Senator Henry Cabot Lodge, eroded McKinley's neutrality. On March 9 the president asked Congress for a $50 million appropriation for defense. Still McKinley sought to avoid war, as did most business leaders. Their caution infuriated Roosevelt. "We will have this war for the freedom of Cuba," he fumed on March 26, "in spite of the timidity of the commercial interests."

The Spanish government, sensing the growing militancy in the United States, announced a unilateral cease-fire in early April. On April 10 the Spanish ambassador to the United States gave the State Department a message that amounted to a surrender: Cubans could form an autonomous government, and the question of the sinking of the *Maine* would go to arbitration. The U.S. minister to Spain then cabled from Madrid: "I hope nothing will now be done to humiliate Spain, as I am satisfied that the present government is going, and is loyally ready to go, as fast and as far as it

News announcements, 1898

A crowd watches men post news announcements outside the New York Tribune building, during the War of 1898.

can." McKinley, he predicted, could win a settlement by August 1 on any terms: autonomy, independence, or cession of Cuba to the United States.

But the message came too late to change American minds. The following day, McKinley asked Congress for power to use armed forces in Cuba to protect U.S. property and trade. On April 20 a joint resolution of Congress declared Cuba independent and demanded withdrawal of Spanish forces. The Teller Amendment, added on the Senate floor, disclaimed any U.S. designs on Cuban territory. McKinley signed the war resolution, and a copy went off to the Spanish government, with notice that McKinley would execute it unless Spain gave a satisfactory response by noon on April 23. Meanwhile, on April 22 the president announced a blockade of Cuba's northern coast and the port of Santiago de Cuba. Under international law this was an act of war. Rather than give in to an ultimatum, the Spanish government declared war on April 24. Determined to be first, Congress declared war on April 25, retroactive to April 21, 1898.

Why such a rush to war after the American ambassador had predicted that Spain would cave in before the summer was out? Chiefly because too much momentum and popular pressure had built up for a confidential message to change the course of events. Also, leaders of the business community were now demanding a quick resolution of the problem. Many of them lacked faith in the willingness or ability of the Spanish government to carry out a moderate policy in the face of hostile public opinion. Still, it is fair to ask why McKinley did not take a stronger stand for peace. He might have defied Congress and public opinion, but in the end he decided that the political risk was too high. The ultimate blame for war, if blame must be levied, belongs to the American people for letting themselves be whipped into such a hostile frenzy.

MANILA   The war itself lasted only 114 days. John Hay, soon to be secretary of state, called it "a splendid little war." The conflict's end was also the end of Spain's once-great New World empire. It marked as well the emergence of the United States as a world power. The United States liberated Spain's colonies, yet in some cases it would substitute its own oppression for Spain's. If war with Spain saved many lives by ending the insurrection in Cuba, it also led to brutal efforts by the United States to suppress another insurrection, in the Philippines, and created a host of festering problems that persisted into the twentieth century.

The war was barely under way before the U.S. Navy produced a spectacular victory in an unexpected quarter in the Pacific Ocean: Manila Bay in the Philippines. While public attention focused on Cuba, young Theodore Roosevelt was thinking of the Spanish-controlled Philippines in the western

Pacific Ocean: the assistant secretary of the navy had ordered Commodore George Dewey, commander of the small squadron in Asia, to engage Spain in the Philippines in case of war in Cuba. President McKinley had approved the orders.

Arriving late on April 30 with four cruisers and two gunboats, Dewey destroyed or captured all the Spanish warships in Manila Bay. Without an occupation force, Dewey was now in awkward possession of the bay. Promised reinforcements, he stayed while German and British warships hung about the scene like watchful vultures, ready to take over the Philippines if the United States did not do so. In the meantime, Emilio Aguinaldo, whom Dewey had brought back from exile to make trouble for the Spanish in Luzon, declared the Philippines independent on June 12. At last, American troops arrived, and with the help of Filipino insurrectionists under Aguinaldo, Dewey's forces entered Manila on August 13. The Spanish forces preferred to surrender to the Americans than to the vengeful Filipino forces.

THE CUBAN CAMPAIGN   While these events transpired halfway around the world, the fighting in Cuba reached a surprisingly quick climax. The U.S. Navy blockaded the Spanish navy at Santiago while some 17,000 American troops hastily assembled at Tampa, Florida. One significant unit was the First Volunteer Cavalry, better known as the Rough Riders and best remembered because Lieutenant Colonel Theodore Roosevelt was second in command. Eager to get "in on the fun" and "to act up to my preachings," Roosevelt had quit the Navy Department soon after war was declared. He ordered a custom-fitted powder-blue army uniform from Brooks Brothers and rushed to help organize a volunteer regiment of Ivy League athletes, leathery ex-convicts, Indians, and southwestern sharpshooters. Their landing at the southeastern tip of Cuba was a mad scramble, as the horses were mistakenly sent elsewhere, leaving the Rough Riders to become the "Weary Walkers." Only Roosevelt had a horse.

Land and sea battles around Santiago quickly broke Spanish resistance. On July 1, about 7,000 U.S. soldiers took the fortified village of El Caney. While a much larger force attacked San Juan Hill, a smaller unit, including the dismounted Rough Riders together with African American soldiers from two cavalry units, seized the enemy position atop nearby Kettle Hill. Roosevelt later claimed that he "would rather have led that charge than [have] served three terms in the U.S. Senate." A friend wrote to Roosevelt's wife that her husband was "revelling in victory and gore." Roosevelt's oversized ego and penchant for self-promotion led him to lobby Congress—unsuccessfully—to award him a Congressional Medal of Honor for his headlong gallop at the

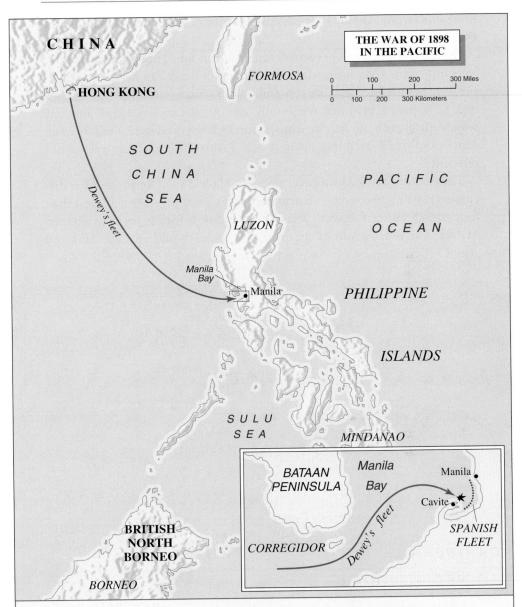

THE WAR OF 1898 IN THE PACIFIC

CHINA

FORMOSA

HONG KONG

SOUTH CHINA SEA

Dewey's fleet

LUZON

PACIFIC OCEAN

Manila Bay

Manila

PHILIPPINE ISLANDS

SULU SEA

MINDANAO

BRITISH NORTH BORNEO

BORNEO

BATAAN PENINSULA

Manila Bay

Manila

Cavite

Dewey's fleet

CORREGIDOR

SPANISH FLEET

Why did Theodore Roosevelt order Commodore Dewey to take Manila? What role did Emilio Aguinaldo play? Why were many Americans opposed to the acquisition of the Philippines?

head of his troops in Cuba. (President Bill Clinton finally awarded Roosevelt the medal in 2001.)

On July 3 the Spanish navy made a gallant run for it, but its decrepit ships were little more than sitting ducks for the newer American fleet. The casualties were as one-sided as those at Manila: 474 Spanish were killed or wounded and 1,750 taken prisoner, while only one American was killed and one wounded. Spanish officials in Santiago surrendered on July 17. On July 25 an American force moved into Spanish-held Puerto Rico, meeting only minor resistance.

The next day the Spanish government in Madrid sued for peace. After discussions lasting two weeks, an armistice was signed on August 12, less than four months after the war's start and the day before Americans entered Manila. The peace protocol specified that Spain should give up Cuba and

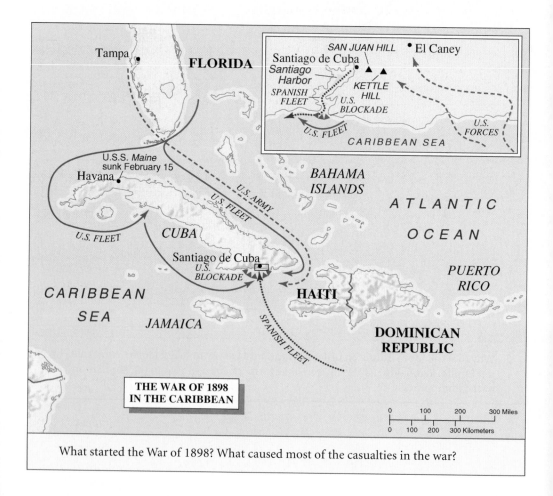

THE WAR OF 1898
IN THE CARIBBEAN

What started the War of 1898? What caused most of the casualties in the war?

that the United States should annex Puerto Rico and occupy Manila pending the transfer of power in the Philippines.

In all, over 60,000 Spanish soldiers died of disease or wounds in the four-month war. Among the Americans who served during the war and the ensuing demobilization, more than 274,000, 5,462 died, but only 379 in battle. Most succumbed to malaria, typhoid, dysentery, or yellow fever. At such a cost the United States was launched onto the world scene as a great power, with all the benefits—and burdens—of a new colonial power.

THE DEBATE OVER ANNEXATION   The United States and Spain signed the Treaty of Paris on December 10, 1898, but the status of the Philippines remained unresolved. There had been no demand for annexation of the Philippines before the war, but Commodore Dewey's victory quickly aroused expansionist fever. Business leaders began thinking of the commercial possibilities in the nearby continent of Asia, such as selling oil for the lamps of China and clothing for its millions of inhabitants. Missionary societies saw the chance to bring Christianity to "the little brown brother." The Philippines promised to provide a useful base for all such activities. It would be neither the first nor the last time that Americans would get caught up in self-serving fantasies of "saving" the teeming populations of Asia or getting rich there. McKinley pondered the alternatives and later explained his reasoning to a group of fellow Methodists:

> And one night late it came to me this way—I don't know how it was, but it came: (1) that we could not give them back to Spain—that would be cowardly and dishonorable; (2) that we could not turn them over to France or Germany—our commercial rivals in the Orient—that would be bad business and discreditable; (3) that we could not leave them to themselves—they were unfit for self-government—and they would soon have anarchy and misrule over there worse than Spain's was; and (4) that there was nothing left for us to do but to take them all, and to educate the Filipinos, and uplift and civilize and Christianize them, and by God's grace do the very best we could by them, as our fellowmen for whom Christ also died. And then I went to bed, and went to sleep and slept soundly.

In one brief statement, McKinley had summarized the motivating ideas of imperialism: (1) national glory, (2) commerce, (3) racial superiority, and (4) Christian altruism. Spanish negotiators raised the delicate point that American forces had no claim by right of conquest and had even occupied Manila after the armistice. American negotiators finally offered the Spanish compensation of $20 million. The treaty thus added to U.S. territory Puerto Rico, Guam (a Spanish-controlled island in the Pacific), and the Philippines.

Meanwhile, Americans had taken other giant steps in the Pacific. Congress had annexed Hawaii in the midst of the war. In 1899, after another outbreak of fighting over the royal succession in Samoa, Germany and the United States agreed to partition the Samoa Islands. The United States annexed the easternmost islands; Germany took the rest, including the largest. Meanwhile, in 1898 the United States had laid claim to Wake Island, located between Guam and the Hawaiian Islands, which would become a vital link in a future transpacific cable line.

The Treaty of Paris had yet to be ratified in the Senate, where most Democrats and Populists and some Republicans opposed it. Anti-imperialists argued that acquisition of the Philippines would corrupt American values and undermine democracy. They stressed traditional isolationism, American principles of self-government, the inconsistency of liberating Cuba and annexing the Philippines, and the danger that the Philippines would become impossible to defend. The prospect of incorporating into the United States so many alien peoples was not the least of some Americans' worries. Some critics insisted that the former Spanish colonies were not capable of establishing self-sustaining democracies. "Bananas and self-government cannot grow on the same piece of land," one senator claimed.

The opposition might have been strong enough to kill the treaty had not the Democrat William Jennings Bryan influenced the vote for approval. Ending the war, he argued, would open the way for the future independence of Cuba and the Philippines. Finally, ratification came on February 6, 1899, by the narrowest of margins: only one vote more than the necessary two thirds. Senator Henry Cabot Lodge of Massachusetts described his efforts to gain approval of the treaty as "the closest, hardest fight" he had witnessed in the Senate. He also admitted that if U.S. troops had not provoked a clash with Filipino insurgents the weekend before, the treaty would have been rejected and the Philippines would have been set free.

But McKinley had no intention of granting the Philippines independence. He insisted that the United States take control of the islands as an act of "benevolent assimilation." In February 1899, in the incident Senator Lodge referred to, an American soldier outside Manila fired on Filipino nationalists, and the United States found itself in a new war. Since Aguinaldo's forces were more or less in control of the islands outside Manila, what followed was largely a brutal American war of conquest that lasted more than two years.

THE PHILIPPINE-AMERICAN WAR   The American effort to suppress Filipino nationalism lasted three years, eventually involved some

Turmoil in the Philippines

Emilio Aguinaldo (seated third from right) and other leaders of the Filipino insurgence.

126,000 U.S. troops, and took the lives of hundreds of thousands of Filipinos (most of them civilians) and 4,234 American soldiers. The nature of the war also cost the United States much of its professed benevolence. It was a sordid conflict, with massacres committed by both sides.

Within the first year of the war in the Philippines, American newspapers had begun to report an array of atrocities committed by U.S. forces—villages burned, prisoners tortured and executed. A favorite means of torture was the "water cure," whereby a Filipino would be placed on his back on the ground. While American soldiers stood on his outstretched arms and feet, salted water would be poured into the captive's mouth and nose until his stomach was bloated, whereupon the soldiers would stomp on the prisoner's abdomen, forcing all of the water out. This process would be repeated until the captive told the soldiers what they wanted to know—or he died. A Senate investigation revealed the scope of such atrocities, but in the end the senators did nothing. Their attitude resembled that of President Theodore Roosevelt, who was convinced that "nobody was seriously damaged" by the "water cure," whereas "Filipinos had inflicted terrible tortures upon our own people." Still, he wrote, "torture is not a thing that we can tolerate." Yet he did tolerate such torture, in large part because he believed that the American army was bringing peace and order and freedom to the Philippines. The "dark abuses"

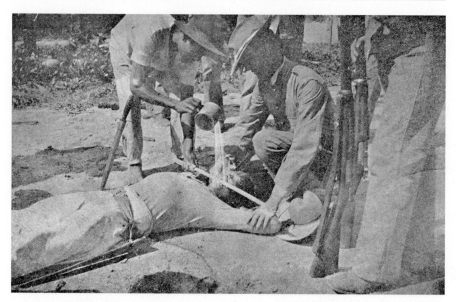

"The water cure"

A prisoner of war being tortured during the Philippine-American War.

were the price Americans paid for the "progress of humanity." Thus did the United States alienate and destroy a Filipino independence movement modeled after America's own struggle for independence from Great Britain. Organized Filipino resistance had collapsed by the end of 1899, but even after the American capture of Aguinaldo in 1901, sporadic guerrilla action lasted until mid-1902.

Against the backdrop of this nasty guerrilla war, the great debate over imperialism continued in the United States. In 1899 several anti-imperialist groups combined to form the American Anti-Imperialist League. The league attracted members representing many shades of opinion. Andrew Carnegie footed the bills; and on imperialism, at least, the union leader Samuel Gompers agreed with the steel king. Presidents Charles Eliot of Harvard and David Starr Jordan of Stanford University supported the group, along with the social reformer Jane Addams. The drive for imperialism, said the philosopher William James, had caused the nation to "puke up its ancient soul."

RELIGION AND EMPIRE   Among those supporting the war against Spain and the imperial conquest of Spain's Caribbean and Pacific colonies were many religious leaders. In Boston, for example, the *Herald* reported that

Protestant ministers were the most rabid supporters of America's new imperialism. The time was ripe for "evangelization of the world." Foreign missionary activity had soared after the Civil War as Protestants asserted that Christianity was the "highest and purest form of religion in the world" and evangelicals eagerly spread the blessings of Christianity around the globe.

Protestant missionaries and their supporting organizations unabashedly promoted the global superiority of the Anglo-Saxon "race" and the Christian religion, and they were often virulently anti-Catholic. The *California Christian Advocate*, for example, cheered the declaration of war with Catholic Spain: "The war is the Kingdom of God coming!" Another Protestant magazine, the *Pacific Advocate*, announced that "the cross will follow the flag" as "righteous" American soldiers prepared to liberate Cuba from Spanish control. Another evangelical declared that missionary activity was itself "a war of conquest." For Catholic Americans, however, the war against Spain, one of the oldest and most intensely Catholic nations in the world, was more problematic. They objected to Protestant plans to evangelize the Catholic Cubans. A Catholic official warned that efforts to convert the Catholics of Cuba, Puerto Rico, and the Philippines "would be the speediest and most effective way to make the inhabitants of those islands discontented and opposed to America."

In the debate over America's annexing the Spanish colonies, religious arguments held sway. Senator Albert Beveridge, an ardent imperialist, declared that "we are God's chosen people." The United States, he added, had a "sacred duty" to bring the blessings of American Christianity to the lands acquired from Spain. Others shared this notion of providential responsibility for the "backward" peoples of the world. Lyman Abbott, a prominent Protestant clergyman and editor, said that America was a divine instrument of Christian imperialism. It was, he said, "the function of the Anglo-Saxon race to confer these gifts of civilization, through law, commerce, and education, on the uncivilized people of the world." Abbott lambasted the anti-imperialists:

> It is said that we have no right to go to a land occupied by barbaric people and interfere with their life. It is said that if they prefer barbarism they have a right to be barbarians. I deny the right of a barbaric people to retain possession of any quarter of the globe. What I have already said I reaffirm: barbarism has no rights which civilization is bound to respect. Barbarians have rights which civilized people are bound to respect, but they have no right to their barbarism.

Abbott and others insisted that the United States could not shirk its providential duty to "save" the former Spanish colonies from barbarism.

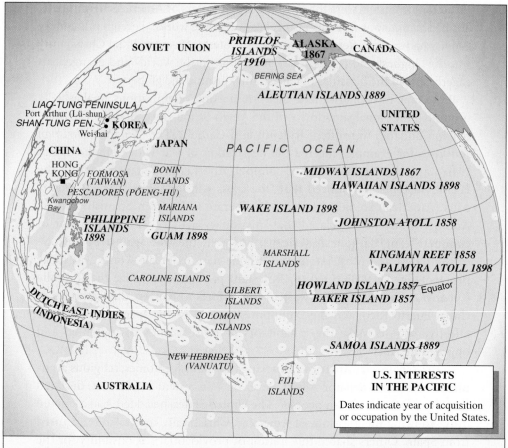

SOVIET UNION
PRIBILOF ISLANDS 1910
ALASKA 1867
CANADA
BERING SEA
ALEUTIAN ISLANDS 1889
LIAO-TUNG PENINSULA
Port Arthur (Lü-shun)
SHAN-TUNG PEN.
Wei-hai
KOREA
UNITED STATES
JAPAN
PACIFIC OCEAN
CHINA
HONG KONG
FORMOSA (TAIWAN)
BONIN ISLANDS
MIDWAY ISLANDS 1867
HAWAIIAN ISLANDS 1898
PESCADORES (PŌENG-HÚ)
Kwangchow Bay
WAKE ISLAND 1898
JOHNSTON ATOLL 1858
PHILIPPINE ISLANDS 1898
MARIANA ISLANDS
GUAM 1898
MARSHALL ISLANDS
KINGMAN REEF 1858
PALMYRA ATOLL 1898
CAROLINE ISLANDS
GILBERT ISLANDS
HOWLAND ISLAND 1857
BAKER ISLAND 1857
Equator
DUTCH EAST INDIES (INDONESIA)
SOLOMON ISLANDS
SAMOA ISLANDS 1889
NEW HEBRIDES (VANUATU)
AUSTRALIA
FIJI ISLANDS

U.S. INTERESTS IN THE PACIFIC

Dates indicate year of acquisition or occupation by the United States.

Why was President McKinley eager to acquire territory in the Pacific and the Caribbean? What kind of political system did the U.S. government create in Hawaii and in the Philippines? How did Filipinos and Hawaiians resist the Americans?

ORGANIZING THE ACQUISITIONS In the end the imperialists won the debate. Senator Beveridge boasted in 1900: "The Philippines are ours forever. And just beyond the Philippines are China's illimitable markets. We will not retreat from either. . . . The power that rules the Pacific is the power that rules the world."

On July 4, 1901, the U.S. military government in the Philippines came to an end, and Judge William Howard Taft became the civil governor. The Philippine Government Act, passed by Congress in 1902, declared the Philippine Islands an "unorganized territory" and made the inhabitants citizens of the Philippines. In 1917 the Jones Act affirmed America's intention

"Well, I Hardly Know Which to Take First!"

At the end of the nineteenth century, it seemed that Uncle Sam had developed a considerable appetite for foreign territory.

to grant the Philippines independence on an unspecified date. Finally, the Tydings-McDuffie Act of 1934 offered independence after ten more years. The Philippines would finally become independent on July 4, 1946.

Closer to home, Puerto Rico had been acquired in part to serve as a U.S. outpost guarding the approach to the Caribbean and any future isthmian canal. On April 12, 1900, the Foraker Act established a government on the island. The president appointed a governor and eleven members of an executive council, and an elected House of Delegates made up the lower house of the legislature. Residents of the island were declared citizens of Puerto Rico; they were not made citizens of the United States until 1917, when the Jones Act granted them U.S. citizenship and made both houses of the legislature elective. In 1947 the governor also became elective, and in 1952 Puerto Rico became a commonwealth with its own constitution and elected officials, a unique status. Like a state, Puerto Rico is free to change its constitution insofar as it does not conflict with the U.S. Constitution.

Finally, there was Cuba. Having liberated the Cubans from Spanish rule, the Americans found themselves propping up a shaky new government whose economy was in shambles. Clashes between U.S. soldiers and Cubans erupted almost immediately. When President McKinley set up a military government for the island late in 1898, it was at odds with rebel leaders from the start. The United States finally fulfilled the promise of independence after the military regime had restored order, organized schools, and improved sanitary conditions. The problem of disease in Cuba prompted the work of Dr. Walter Reed, who made an outstanding contribution to health in tropical climates around the world. Named head of the Army Yellow Fever Commission in 1900, he proved that yellow fever was carried by mosquitoes. The commission's experiments led the way to effective control of the worldwide disease.

In 1900, on President McKinley's order, Cubans drafted a constitution modeled on that of the United States. The Platt Amendment, added to an army appropriations bill passed by Congress in 1901, sharply restricted the new government's independence, however. The amendment required that Cuba never impair its independence by signing a treaty with a third power, that it keep its debt within the government's power to repay it out of ordinary revenues, and that it acknowledge the right of the United States to intervene in Cuba for the preservation of Cuban independence and the maintenance of "a government adequate for the protection of life, property, and individual liberty." Finally, Cuba had to sell or lease to the United States lands to be used for coaling or naval stations, a proviso that led to a U.S. naval base at Guantánamo Bay.

Under pressure, the Cuban delegates added the Platt Amendment to their constitution. But resentments against America festered. As early as 1906, an insurrection arose against the new government, and President Theodore Roosevelt responded by sending Secretary of War William Howard Taft to suppress the rebels. Backed by U.S. armed forces, Taft assumed full government authority, as he had in the Philippines, and the American army stayed until 1909, when a new Cuban president was peacefully elected. Sporadic interventions by U.S. troops would follow for more than two decades.

IMPERIAL RIVALRIES IN EAST ASIA

During the 1890s the United States was not the only nation to emerge as a world power. Another was Japan. Commodore Matthew Perry's voyage of 1853–1854 had opened Japan to Western ways, and the country had expanded in earnest after the 1860s. Flexing its new muscles, Japan defeated China's stagnant empire in the First Sino-Japanese War (1894–1895) and as a result picked up the Pescadores Islands and the island of Formosa (modern-day Taiwan).

China's weakness, demonstrated in the war, brought the European powers into a scramble for control of that remaining frontier of imperialist expansion. Russia secured the privilege of building a railroad across Manchuria and established itself in Port Arthur (Lü-shun) and on the Liao-tung Peninsula. The Germans moved into Shan-tung, the French into Kwangchow Bay, the British into Wei-hai.

The bright prospect of massive American trade with China dimmed with the possibility that the great powers would throw up tariff barriers in their own spheres of influence. The British, embroiled in Hong Kong since 1840, had more to lose than the Americans, though, for they already had the largest foreign trade with China. Just before the War of 1898 started, the British suggested joint action with the United States to preserve the integrity of China against Western imperialism, and they renewed the proposal early in 1899. Both times the Senate rejected the request because it risked an entangling alliance.

THE "OPEN DOOR" What soon came to be known as the Open Door policy was outlined in Secretary of State John Hay's Open Door Note, dispatched in 1899 to London, Berlin, and St. Petersburg (Russia) and a little later to Tokyo, Rome, and Paris. It proposed to keep China open to trade with all countries on an equal basis. More specifically, it called upon foreign powers, within their spheres of influence, (1) to refrain from interfering with any treaty port (a port open to all by treaty) or any vested interest, (2) to permit Chinese authorities to collect tariffs on an equal basis, and (3) to show no favors to their own nationals in the matter of harbor dues or railroad charges. As it turned out, none of the European powers except Britain accepted Hay's principles, but none rejected them either. So Hay simply announced that all powers had accepted the policy.

The Open Door policy, if rooted in the self-interest of American businesses eager to exploit Chinese markets, also tapped the deep-seated sympathies of those who opposed

"The Open Door"

Cartoon depicting Uncle Sam propping open a door for China with a brick labeled "U.S. Army and Navy Prestige," as colonial powers look on.

imperialism, especially as the policy pledged to protect China's territorial integrity. But it had little legal standing. When the Japanese, concerned about Russian pressure in Manchuria, asked how the United States intended to enforce the policy, Hay replied that America was "not prepared . . . to enforce these views." So it would remain for forty years, until continued Japanese expansion in China would bring America to war in 1941.

THE BOXER REBELLION A new Asian crisis arose in 1900 when a group of Chinese nationalists known to the Western world as Boxers (Fists of Righteous Harmony) rebelled against foreign encroachments on China, especially Christian missionary efforts, and laid siege to foreign embassies in Peking. An international expedition of British, German, Russian, Japanese, and American forces mobilized to relieve the embassy compound. Hay, fearful that the intervention might become an excuse to dismember China, took the opportunity to further refine the Open Door policy. The United States, he said in a letter of July 3, 1900, sought a solution that would "preserve Chinese territorial and administrative integrity" as well as "equal and impartial

Trade with China

U.S. troops marching in Peking after quelling the Boxer Rebellion.

trade with all parts of the Chinese Empire." Six weeks later the expedition reached Peking and quelled the Boxer Rebellion.

BIG-STICK DIPLOMACY

More than any other American of his time, Theodore Roosevelt transformed the role of the United States in world affairs. The nation had emerged from the War of 1898 a world power, and he insisted that this status entailed major new responsibilities. To ensure that the United States accepted its international obligations, Roosevelt stretched both the Constitution and executive power to the limit. In the process he pushed a reluctant nation onto the center stage of world affairs.

ROOSEVELT'S RISE   Born in 1858, the son of a wealthy New York merchant and a Georgia belle, Roosevelt had grown up in Manhattan in cultured comfort, had visited Europe as a child, spoke German fluently, and had graduated from Harvard with honors in 1880. A sickly, scrawny boy with poor eyesight and chronic asthma, he built himself up into a physical and intellectual athlete, a lifelong practitioner of the "strenuous life." Roosevelt loved rigorous exercise and outdoor activities. A boxer, wrestler, mountain climber, hunter, and outdoorsman, he also displayed extraordinary intellectual curiosity. He became a dedicated bird-watcher, a renowned historian and essayist, and a zealous moralist. He wrote thirty-eight books on a wide variety of subjects. His boundless energy and fierce competitive spirit were inexhaustible and infectious, and he was ever willing to express an opinion on any subject. Within two years of graduating from Harvard, Roosevelt won election to the New York legislature. "I rose like a rocket," he later observed.

But with the world seemingly at his feet, disaster struck. In 1884, Roosevelt's beloved mother, only forty-eight years old, died. Eleven hours later, in the same house, his twenty-two-year-old wife struggled with kidney failure and died in his arms, having recently given birth to their only child. The double funeral was so wrenching that the officiating minister wept throughout his prayer. In an attempt to recover from this "strange and terrible fate," a distraught Roosevelt turned his baby daughter over to his sister, quit his political career, sold the family house, and moved west to take up cattle ranching in the Dakota Territory. The blue-blooded New Yorker relished hunting, leading roundups, capturing outlaws, fighting Indians—and reading novels by the campfire. When a drunken cowboy, a gun in each hand, tried to bully the tinhorn Roosevelt, teasing him about his glasses, the feisty Harvard dude laid him out with one punch. Although his western career lasted only two years, he never got over being a cowboy.

Back in New York City, Roosevelt remarried and ran unsuccessfully for mayor in 1886; he later served six years as civil service commissioner and two years as New York City's police commissioner. In 1896, Roosevelt campaigned hard for McKinley, and the new president was asked to reward him with the position of assistant secretary of the navy. McKinley initially balked, saying that young Roosevelt was too "hotheaded" and "too pugnacious. I want peace." But he eventually relented and appointed the war-loving aristocrat. After fighting in Cuba and hastening into print his self-promoting account of the Rough Riders, Roosevelt easily won the governorship of New York, arousing audiences with his impassioned speeches and powerful personality.

In the 1900 presidential contest, the Democrats turned once again to the Nebraskan William Jennings Bryan, who sought to make imperialism the "paramount issue" of the campaign. The Democratic platform condemned the Philippine conflict as "an unnecessary war" that had "placed the United States, previously known and applauded throughout the world as the champion of freedom, in the false and un-American position of crushing with military force the efforts of our former allies to achieve liberty and self-government."

The Republicans welcomed the chance to disagree. They renominated McKinley and named Roosevelt, now virtually Mr. Imperialism, his running mate. McKinley outpolled Bryan by 7.2 million to 6.4 million popular votes and 292 to 155 electoral votes. Less than a year later, on September 6, 1901, at a reception at the Pan-American Exposition in Buffalo, an anarchist named Leon Czolgosz (pronounced chole-gosh) approached the fifty-eight-year-old president with a gun concealed in a bandaged hand and

Mr. Imperialism

This 1900 cartoon shows the Republican vice-presidential candidate, Theodore Roosevelt, overshadowing his running mate, President William McKinley.

fired at point-blank range. McKinley died eight days later, and Theodore Roosevelt was elevated to the White House. "Now look," erupted Mark Hanna, the Ohio businessman and politico, "that damned cowboy is President of the United States!"

Six weeks short of his forty-third birthday, Roosevelt was the youngest man ever to reach the White House, but he had more experience in public affairs than most and perhaps more vitality than any. One observer compared him to Niagara Falls, "both great wonders of nature." Roosevelt's glittering spectacles, glistening teeth, and overflowing gusto were a godsend to the cartoonists, who added another trademark when he pronounced the adage "Speak softly, and carry a big stick."

Along with Roosevelt's boundless energy went an unshakable righteousness, which led him to cast every issue in moral and patriotic terms. He considered the presidency his "bully pulpit," and he delivered fist-pumping speeches on the virtues of righteousness, honesty, civic duty, and strenuosity. Nowhere was President Roosevelt's forceful will more evident than in his conduct of foreign affairs.

THE PANAMA CANAL   After the 1898 War, the United States became more deeply involved in the Caribbean. One issue overshadowed every other in the region: the Panama Canal. The narrow isthmus of Panama had first become a major concern of the United States in the late 1840s, when it became an important route to the California goldfields. Two treaties dating from that period loomed years later as obstacles to the construction of a canal. The Bidlack Treaty (1846) with Colombia (then New Granada) guaranteed both Colombia's sovereignty over Panama and the neutrality of the isthmus. In the Clayton-Bulwer Treaty (1850) the British agreed to acquire no more Central American territory, and the United States joined them in agreeing to build or fortify a canal only by mutual consent.

After the War of 1898, Secretary of State John Hay commenced talks with the British ambassador to establish such consent. The outcome was the Hay-Pauncefote Treaty of 1900, but the Senate rejected it on the grounds that it forbade fortification of the canal and required that the canal be neutral even in time of war. By then a bill for a Nicaraguan canal was pending in Congress, and the British apparently decided to accept the inevitable. In 1901 the Senate ratified a second Hay-Pauncefote Treaty, which simply omitted reference to the former limitations.

Other obstacles remained, however. From 1881 to 1887, a French company under Ferdinand de Lesseps, who had engineered the Suez Canal in Egypt between 1859 and 1869, had spent nearly $300 million and some 20,000 lives to dig less than a third of a canal through Panama, still under the control of Colombia. The company now wanted $109 million for its holdings. An Isthmian Canal Commission, appointed by President McKinley, reported in 1901 that a Nicaraguan route would be cheaper. When the House of Representatives quickly passed an act for construction there, the French company lowered its price to $40 million, and the Canal Commission switched its focus to Panama.

Meanwhile, Secretary Hay had opened negotiations with Ambassador Tomás Herrán of Colombia. In return for a canal zone six miles wide, the United States agreed to pay $10 million in cash and a rental fee of $250,000 a year. The U.S. Senate ratified the Hay-Herrán Treaty in 1903, but the Colombian senate held out for $25 million in cash. In response to this act by those "foolish and homicidal corruptionists in Bogotá," Theodore Roosevelt, by then president, flew into a rage punctuated by references to "dagos" and "contemptible little creatures." Meanwhile in Panama, an isolated province long at odds with the remote Colombian authorities in Bogotá, by Colombia's rejection of the treaty inspired new ideas. Manuel Amador Guerrero, an employee of the French canal company, hatched a plot in close collusion with the company's wily representative, Philippe Bunau-Varilla. After Bunau-Varilla visited Roosevelt and Hay and apparently obtained inside information, Amador informed his conspirators that American warships would arrive at Colón, Panama, on November 2.

With an army of some 500 Panamanians, Amador staged a revolt the next day. Colombian troops, who could not penetrate the overland jungle, found U.S. ships blocking the sea-lanes. On November 13 the Roosevelt administration received its first

Digging the canal

President Theodore Roosevelt operating a steam shovel during his 1906 visit to the Panama Canal.

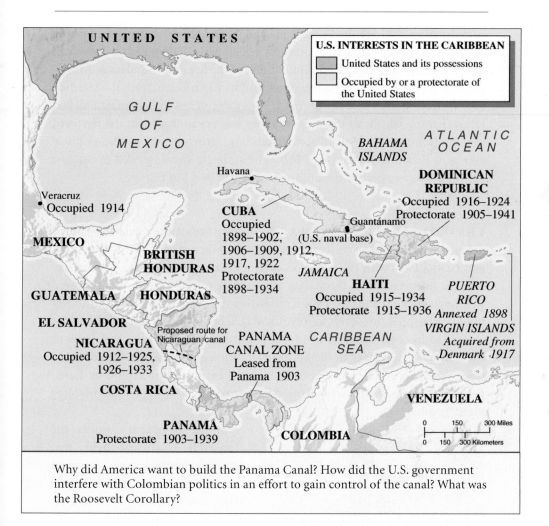

UNITED STATES

U.S. INTERESTS IN THE CARIBBEAN

United States and its possessions

Occupied by or a protectorate of the United States

GULF
OF
MEXICO

BAHAMA
ISLANDS

ATLANTIC
OCEAN

Havana

**DOMINICAN
REPUBLIC**
Occupied 1916–1924
Protectorate 1905–1941

Veracruz
Occupied 1914

CUBA
Occupied
1898–1902,
1906–1909, 1912,
1917, 1922
Protectorate
1898–1934

Guantánamo
(U.S. naval base)

MEXICO

**BRITISH
HONDURAS**

JAMAICA

HAITI
Occupied 1915–1934
Protectorate 1915–1936

*PUERTO
RICO*
Annexed 1898

GUATEMALA

HONDURAS

EL SALVADOR

NICARAGUA
Occupied 1912–1925,
1926–1933

Proposed route for
Nicaraguan canal

**PANAMA
CANAL ZONE**
Leased from
Panama 1903

*CARIBBEAN
SEA*

VIRGIN ISLANDS
*Acquired from
Denmark 1917*

COSTA RICA

VENEZUELA

PANAMA
Protectorate 1903–1939

COLOMBIA

0   150   300 Miles

0   150   300 Kilometers

Why did America want to build the Panama Canal? How did the U.S. government interfere with Colombian politics in an effort to gain control of the canal? What was the Roosevelt Corollary?

ambassador from Panama, who happened to be Philippe Bunau-Varilla, and Bunau-Varilla signed a treaty that extended the Canal Zone from six to ten miles in width. For $10 million down and $250,000 a year, the United States received "in perpetuity the use, occupation and control" of the Canal Zone. The U.S. attorney general, asked to supply a legal opinion upholding Roosevelt's actions, responded wryly, "No, Mr. President, if I were you I would not have any taint of legality about it."

In 1904, Congress created a new Isthmian Canal Commission to direct construction, and Roosevelt instructed its members to make the "dirt fly." He later explained, "I took the Canal Zone and let Congress debate; and while the debate goes on the Canal does also." By needlessly offending Latin American sensibilities, Roosevelt had committed one of the greatest blunders in American foreign policy. Colombia eventually got its $25 million, from the Harding administration in 1921, but only once America's interest in Colombian oil had lubricated the wheels of diplomacy. There was no apology, but the payment was made to remove "all misunderstandings growing out of the political events in Panama, November, 1903." The strategic canal opened on August 15, 1914, two weeks after the outbreak of World War I in Europe.

THE ROOSEVELT COROLLARY   Even without the canal the United States would have been concerned with the stability of the Caribbean region, and particularly with the activities of any hostile power there. A prime excuse for intervention in those days was to force the collection of debts owed to foreign corporations. In 1904 a crisis over the debts of the Dominican Republic prompted Roosevelt to formulate U.S. policy in the Caribbean. In his annual address to Congress in 1904, he outlined what came to be known as the Roosevelt Corollary to the Monroe Doctrine: the principle, in short, that since the Monroe Doctrine prohibited intervention in the region by Europeans, the United States was justified in intervening first to forestall involvement by outsiders.

The world's constable

President Theodore Roosevelt wields "the big stick," symbolizing his aggressive diplomacy.

In the president's words the Roosevelt Corollary held that "chronic wrongdoing . . . may in America, as elsewhere, ultimately require intervention by some civilized nation, and in the Western Hemisphere the adherence of the United States to the Monroe Doctrine may force the United States, however reluctantly, in flagrant cases of such wrongdoing or impotence, to the exercise of an international police power." As put into practice by mutual agreement with the Dominican Republic in 1905, the Roosevelt Corollary called for the United States to appoint a collector of customs, who would apply 55 percent of the nation's revenues to debt payments owed to American companies.

THE RUSSO-JAPANESE WAR   In east Asia, meanwhile, the principle of equal trading rights embodied in the Open Door policy was tested when rivalry between Russia and Japan flared into a fight. By 1904 the Japanese had decided that the Russians threatened their ambitions in China and Korea. On February 8, Japanese warships devastated the Russian fleet. The Japanese then occupied Korea and drove the Russians back into Manchuria. But neither side could score a knockout blow, and neither relished a prolonged war. Roosevelt offered to mediate their conflict. When the Japanese signaled that they would welcome a negotiated settlement, Roosevelt sponsored a peace conference in Portsmouth, New Hampshire. With the Treaty of Portsmouth, signed on September 5, 1905, the concessions all went to the Japanese. Russia acknowledged Japan's "predominant political, military, and economic interests in Korea" (Japan would annex the kingdom in 1910), and both powers agreed to evacuate Manchuria.

RELATIONS WITH JAPAN   Japan's show of strength against Russia raised doubts among American leaders about the security of the Philippines. During the Portsmouth talks, Roosevelt sent William Howard Taft to meet with the Japanese foreign minister in Tokyo. The two men negotiated the Taft-Katsura Agreement of July 29, 1905, in which the United States accepted Japanese control of Korea, and Japan disavowed any designs on the Philippines. Three years later the Root-Takahira Agreement, negotiated by Secretary of State Elihu Root and the Japanese ambassador, endorsed the status quo and reinforced the Open Door policy by supporting "the independence and integrity of China" and "the principle of equal opportunity for commerce and industry in China."

Behind the diplomatic facade of goodwill, however, lay mutual distrust. For many Americans the Russian threat in east Asia now gave way to concerns about the "yellow peril" (a term apparently coined by Kaiser Wilhelm II of Germany). Racial animosities on the West Coast helped sour relations with Japan. In 1906, San Francisco's school board ordered students of Asian descent to attend a separate public school. The Japanese government sharply protested such prejudice, and President Roosevelt persuaded the school board to change its policy, but only after making sure that Japanese authorities would not issue "visas" to "laborers," except former residents of the United States; the parents, wives, or children of residents; or those who already possessed an interest in an American farming enterprise. This "Gentlemen's Agreement" of 1907, the precise terms of which have never been revealed, halted the influx of Japanese immigrants and brought some respite to racial agitation in California.

THE UNITED STATES AND EUROPE   At the same time that the United States was expanding into Asia and the Caribbean, tensions in Europe were boiling over. While Roosevelt was moving toward mediation of the Russo-Japanese War in 1905, a dangerous crisis was brewing in Morocco. There, on March 31, 1905, the German kaiser, Wilhelm II, stepped ashore at Tangier and gave a saber-rattling speech criticizing French and British interests in North Africa. The kaiser's speech aroused a diplomatic firestorm. Roosevelt felt that the United States had a huge stake in preventing the outbreak of a major war. At the kaiser's behest he talked the French and the British into attending an international conference at Algeciras, Spain, with U.S. delegates present. Roosevelt then maneuvered the Germans into accepting his compromise proposal.

The Act of Algeciras, signed in 1906, affirmed the independence of Morocco and guaranteed an open door for trade there but provided for the training and control of Moroccan police by France and Spain. The U.S. Senate ratified the agreement, but stipulated that America remain committed to neutrality in European affairs. Roosevelt received the Nobel Peace Prize in 1906 for his diplomacy at Portsmouth and Algeciras. Despite his bellicosity on other occasions, he had earned it.

Before Roosevelt left the White House, he celebrated America's rise to the status of a world power with one great flourish. In 1907 he sent the entire U.S. Navy, by then second in strength only to the British fleet, on a grand tour around the world, announcing that he was ready for "a feast, a frolic, or a fight." He got mostly the first two and none of the last. At every port of call down the Atlantic coast of South America, up the west coast, out to Hawaii, and down to New Zealand and Australia, the "Great White Fleet" received rousing welcomes. The triumphal procession continued home by way of the Mediterranean and steamed back into American waters in early 1909, just in time to close out Roosevelt's presidency on a note of success.

Yet it was a success that would have mixed consequences. Roosevelt's ability to deploy American power abroad was accompanied by a racist ideology shared by many prominent political figures of the time. He once told the graduates of the Naval War College that all "the great masterful races have been fighting races, and the minute that a race loses the hard fighting virtues . . . it has lost the right to stand as equal to the best." On another occasion he called warfare the best way to promote "the clear instinct for race selfishness" and insisted that "the most ultimately righteous of all wars is a war with savages." Such a belligerent and bigoted attitude would come back to haunt the United States in world affairs—and at home.

End of Chapter Review

CHAPTER SUMMARY

- **New Imperialism** By the beginning of the twentieth century, the idea of a manifest destiny and American industrialists' need for new markets for their goods fueled America's "new imperialism." The ideology of social Darwinism was used to justify the colonization of less industrially developed nations as white Americans held that their own industrial superiority proved their racial superiority and, therefore, the theory of the survival of the fittest. White Americans rationalized further that they had a duty to Christianize and uplift "backward" peoples.

- **Religion and Imperialism** Protestant missionaries felt impelled to take Christianity to native peoples throughout the world. An indigenous people's acceptance of Christianity was the first step toward the loss of their indigenous culture.

- **War of 1898** Spain still had an extensive empire, and Cuba was one of its oldest colonies. When Cubans revolted against Spain in 1895, many Americans were sympathetic to their demand for independence. The insurrection was harshly suppressed, and sensational coverage in certain New York newspapers further aroused Americans' sympathy. Early in 1898, the publication of a letter by Spain's minister to the United States, Depuy de Lôme, which criticized President McKinley, and then the explosion of the U.S. battleship *Maine* in Havana Harbor propelled America into a war with Spain despite the reluctance of President McKinley and many business interests.

- **Results of the War of 1898** Although the Teller Amendment declared that the United States had no intention of annexing Cuba, America curtailed Cuba's freedom and annexed other territories taken from Spain in the War of 1898. Insurrection followed in the Philippines when insurgents saw that the islands would be administered by the United States. In the treaty that ended the war, the United States gained Puerto Rico as well as Guam and other islands in the Pacific. Meanwhile, Hawaii had been annexed during the war.

- **Big-Stick Diplomacy** As president, Theodore Roosevelt actively pursued an imperialist foreign policy, confirming the United States' new role as a world power. With his Big-Stick Diplomacy, he arbitrated the treaty that ended the Russo-Japanese War, proclaimed the Open Door policy with China, allowed his administration to engage in dealings that made possible American control over the Panama Canal, and sent the navy's entire fleet around the world as a symbol of American might. He articulated an extension of the Monroe Doctrine whereby the United States might intervene in disputes between North and South America and other world powers.

CHRONOLOGY

1894	Republic of Hawaii is proclaimed
1895	Cuban insurrection breaks out against Spanish rule
1898	U.S. battleship *Maine* explodes in Havana Harbor
1898	War of 1898
1898	United States annexes Hawaii
1899	U.S. Senate ratifies the Treaty of Paris, ending the War of 1898
1899–1902	Filipino insurgents resist U.S. domination
1900	Army Yellow Fever Commission confirms the cause of yellow fever
1900	International alliance quells the Boxer Rebellion
1903	Panamanians revolt against Colombia
1905	Russo-Japanese War
1907	Great White Fleet circumnavigates the globe in a demonstration of America's rise to world-power status
1914	Panama Canal opens

KEY TERMS & NAMES

24

THE PROGRESSIVE ERA

FOCUS QUESTIONS

wwnorton.com/studyspace

- Who were the progressives, and what were their major causes?
- Who were the muckrakers, and what impact did they have?
- What were Theodore Roosevelt's and William Taft's progressive programs, and what were those programs' goals?
- Why was the election of 1912 significant?
- How was Woodrow Wilson's progressivism different from Roosevelt's?

Theodore Roosevelt's emergence as a national leader coincided with the onset of what historians have labeled the Progressive Era (1890–1917). Progressivism was very diverse in its motives and methods. It was less an organized movement than a multifaceted response to the problems created by unregulated industrialization, unplanned urbanization, and unrelenting immigration. Progressives believed that American life was threatened by social instability, economic injustice, and political corruption. But progressives were not despondent. They were convinced that society could be improved through creative initiatives and concerted action. By working together in a spirit of community, individuals, organizations, and governments could ensure the "progress" of American society. And in fact they did so through an array of reforms and initiatives, some of which conflicted with one another. By the 1920s, progressives had implemented significant changes at all levels of government and across all levels of society.

The progressive impulse arose in response to many societal changes, the most powerful of which were the devastating depression of the 1890s and its attendant social unrest. The depression brought hard times to the cities, worsened already-dreadful factory conditions, deepened distress in rural areas, and aroused both the fears and the conscience of the rapidly growing middle and upper-middle classes. Although the United States boasted the highest per capita income in the world, it also harbored some of the poorest people. In 1900 an estimated 10 million of the 82 million Americans lived in desperate poverty. Most of the destitute were immigrants living in the major cities.

By the turn of the century, so many activists were at work seeking to improve social conditions that people began to speak of a Progressive Era, a time of fermenting idealism and sweeping social, economic, and political change. The scope of the social crisis was so vast and complex that new remedies were needed. Old prejudices toward the poor and needy had to be changed. Reform needed to become more pragmatic and scientific. "The conditions of life forced by our civilization upon the poor in our great cities are undemocratic, unchristian, and unrighteous," said Vida Scudder, a settlement house leader. But the efforts to address widespread poverty had to be "wholly free from the spirit of social dogmatism and doctrinaire assertion. . . . As we become more practical, we also become better idealists."

Elements of Reform

Political progressives crusaded against the abuses of urban political bosses and corporate robber barons. Their goals were greater democracy, honest and efficient government, more effective regulation of business, and greater social justice for working people. Only by expanding the scope of local, state, and federal government authority, they believed, could these goals be accomplished. The "real heart of the movement," declared one reformer, was "to use the government as an agency of human welfare."

Progressivism contained an element of conservatism. In some cases the regulation of business turned out to be regulation proposed *by* business leaders who preferred regulated stability to the chaos and uncertainty of unrestrained competition. In addition, many reformers were motivated by religious beliefs that led them to emphasize moral reforms such as the prohibition of alcoholic beverages and Sunday closing laws.

In sum, progressivism was diverse in both its origins and its agenda. Few people embraced all of the progressive causes. What reformers shared was a common assumption that the complex social ills and tensions generated by the urban-industrial revolution required new responses. Governments were now called upon to provide a broad range of direct public services: schools, good roads (a movement propelled first by cyclists and then by automobilists), environmental conservation, public health and welfare, care of the disabled, and farm loans and demonstration agents (county workers who visited farms to demonstrate new technology), among others. Such initiatives represented the first tentative steps toward what would become known during the 1930s and thereafter as the welfare state.

THE ANTECEDENTS OF PROGRESSIVISM   Populism was one of the catalysts of progressivism. The Populist platform of 1892 outlined many reforms that would be accomplished in the Progressive Era. After the collapse of the farmers' movement and the revival of the agricultural economy at the turn of the century, the reform spirit shifted to the cities, where middle-class activists had for years attacked the problems of political corruption and urban development. The Mugwumps, those gentlemen reformers who had fought the spoils system and insisted that government jobs be awarded on the basis of merit, supplied progressivism with an important element of its thinking: the honest-government ideal. Over the years the honest-government outlook had been broadened to include urban problems such as crime, vice, and the efficient provision of gas, electricity, water, sewers, mass transit, and garbage collection.

Finally, another significant force in fostering the most radical wing of progressivism was the influence of socialist doctrines. The Socialist party served as the left wing of progressivism. Most progressives found socialist remedies unacceptable, and the progressive impulse arose in part from a desire to counter the growing influence of socialist doctrines by promoting more mainstream reforms. More important in spurring progressive reform were social critics who dramatized the need for reform through investigative journalism.

THE MUCKRAKERS   Chronic urban poverty, unsafe working conditions, and child labor in mills, mines, and factories were complex social issues; remedying them required raising public awareness, which would in turn spur political action. The "muckrakers," investigative journalists, who thrived on exposing social ills, got their name when Theodore Roosevelt compared them to a character in John Bunyan's *Pilgrim's Progress:* "A man that could look no way but downwards with a muckrake in his hands."

"Muckrakers are often indispensable to . . . society," Roosevelt said, "but only if they know when to stop raking the muck."

Henry Demarest Lloyd was one of the first muckrakers. His book *Wealth against Commonwealth* (1894) provided a critical examination of the Standard Oil Company and other monopolies. Another early muckraker was Jacob Riis, a Danish immigrant who exposed New York City slum conditions in *How the Other Half Lives* (1890). The chief outlets for these social critics were the inexpensive popular magazines that began to flourish in the 1890s, such as the *Arena* and *McClure's*.

The golden age of muckraking is sometimes dated from 1902, when *McClure's* began to run articles by Lincoln Steffens on municipal corruption, later collected into a book,

Cover of McClure's Magazine, 1902

This cover features Ida Tarbell's muckracking series on the Standard Oil Company.

The Shame of the Cities (1904). *McClure's* also published Ida M. Tarbell's devastating *History of the Standard Oil Company* (1904). Tarbell's revelations of predatory practices and rigged railroad rates helped convince the Supreme Court in 1911 to rule that the Standard Oil Company must be dismantled. Other reform-minded books that began as magazine articles exposed corruption in the stock market, the meat-processing industry, the life-insurance business, and the political world.

Without the muckrakers, progressivism would never have achieved widespread popular support. In feeding the public's appetite for sordid social facts, the muckrakers demonstrated one of the salient features of the Progressive movement, and one of its central failures: the progressives were stronger on diagnosis than on remedy. They professed a naive faith in the power of democracy. Give the people the facts, expose corruption, and bring government close to the people, reformers believed, and the correction of evils would follow automatically. The cure for the ills of democracy, it seemed, was a more informed and a more active democracy.

FEATURES OF PROGRESSIVISM

DEMOCRACY   The most important reform that political progressives promoted to democratize government and encourage greater political participation was the direct primary, or the nomination of candidates by the vote of all party members rather than an inner circle of activists. Under the traditional convention system, only a small proportion of voters attended the local caucuses or precinct meetings that sent delegates to county, and in turn to state and national, conventions. While this traditional method allowed seasoned leaders to sift the candidates, it also lent itself to domination by political professionals. Direct primaries at the local level had been held sporadically since the 1870s, but after South Carolina adopted the first statewide primary in 1896, the movement spread within two decades to nearly every state.

The party primary was but one expression of a broad progressive movement for greater public participation in the political process. In 1898, South Dakota became the first state to adopt the initiative and referendum, procedures that allow voters to enact laws directly. If a designated number of voters petitioned to have a measure put on the ballot (the initiative), the electorate could then vote it up or down (the referendum). Oregon adopted a spectrum of reform measures, including a voter-registration law (1899), the initiative and referendum (1902), the direct primary (1904), a sweeping corrupt-practices act (1908), and the recall (1910), whereby corrupt or incompetent public officials could be removed by a public petition and vote. Within a decade nearly twenty states had adopted the initiative and referendum, and nearly a dozen had accepted the recall.

Most states adopted the party primary even in the choice of U.S. senators, heretofore selected by state legislatures. Nevada was first, in 1899, to let voters express a choice that state legislators of their party were expected to follow in choosing senators. The popular election of senators required a constitutional amendment, and the House of Representatives, beginning in 1894, four times adopted such an amendment, only to see it defeated in the Senate, which came under increasing attack as a "millionaires' club." In 1912 the Senate finally accepted the inevitable and agreed to the Seventeenth Amendment, authorizing popular election of senators. The amendment was ratified in 1913.

EFFICIENCY   A second major theme of progressivism was the "gospel of efficiency." In the business world during the early twentieth century, Frederick

W. Taylor, the original "efficiency expert," was developing the techniques he summed up in his book *The Principles of Scientific Management* (1911). Taylorism, as scientific industrial management came to be known, promised to reduce waste through the scientific analysis of labor processes. By breaking down the production of goods into sequential steps and meticulously studying the time it took each worker to perform a task, Taylor prescribed the optimum technique for the average worker and establish detailed performance standards for each job classification. The promise of higher wages, he believed, would motivate workers to exceed "average" expectations.

Instead, many workers resented Taylor's innovations. They saw in scientific management a tool for employers to make people work faster than was healthy or fair. Yet Taylor's controversial system brought concrete improvements in productivity, especially among those industries whose production processes were highly standardized and whose jobs were rigidly defined. "In the future," Taylor predicted in 1911, "the system [rather than the individual workers] will be first."

In government the efficiency movement demanded the reorganization of agencies to eliminate redundancy, to establish clear lines of authority, and to assign responsibility and accountability to specific officials. Two progressive ideas for making municipal government more efficient gained headway in the first decade of the new century. One, the commission system, was first adopted by Galveston, Texas, in 1901, when local government there collapsed in the aftermath of a devastating hurricane and tidal wave. The system placed ultimate authority in a board composed of elected administrative heads of city departments—commissioners of sanitation, police, utilities, and so on. The more durable idea, however, was the city-manager plan, under which a professional administrator ran the municipal government in accordance with policies set by the elected council and mayor. Staunton, Virginia, first adopted the plan in 1908. By 1914 the National Association of City Managers had heralded the arrival of a new profession.

When America was a pre-industrial society, Andrew Jackson's notion that any reasonably intelligent citizen could perform the duties of any public office may have been true. By the early twentieth century, however, many complex functions of government and business had come to require specialists. This principle of government by experts was promoted by progressive Governor Robert M. La Follette of Wisconsin, who established a Legislative Reference Bureau to provide research, advice, and help in the drafting of legislation. The "Wisconsin idea" of efficient and more scientific government was widely publicized and copied. La Follette also pushed for such reforms

Robert M. La Follette

A progressive proponent of expertise in government.

as the direct primary, stronger railroad regulation, the conservation of natural resources, and workmen's compensation programs to support laborers injured on the job.

REGULATION Of all the problems facing American society at the turn of the century, one engaged a greater diversity of progressive reformers and elicited more solutions than any other: the regulation of giant corporations, which became a third major theme of progressivism. Bipartisan concern over the concentration of economic power had brought passage of the Sherman Anti-Trust Act in 1890, but the act had turned out to be more symbolic than effective.

The problem of concentrated economic power and its abuse offered a dilemma for progressives. Four broad solutions were available, but of these, two were extremes that had limited support: letting business work out its own destiny under a policy of laissez-faire or adopting a socialist program of public ownership of big businesses. At the municipal level, however, the socialist alternative was rather widely adopted for public utilities and transportation— so-called gas and water socialism; otherwise, it was not seriously considered as a general policy. The other choices were either to adopt a policy of trust-busting in the belief that restoring old-fashioned competition would best prevent economic abuses or to accept big business in the belief that it brought economies of scale but to regulate it to prevent abuses.

Efforts to restore the competition of small firms proved unworkable, however, partly because breaking up large corporations was a complicated process. To some extent, regulation and "stabilization" won acceptance among business leaders; whatever respect they paid to competition in the abstract, they preferred not to face it in practice. As time passed, however, regulatory agencies often came under the influence or control of those they were supposed to regulate. Railroad executives, for instance, generally had more intimate knowledge of the intricate details involved in their business, giving them the advantage over the outsiders who might be appointed to the Interstate Commerce Commission.

SOCIAL JUSTICE   A fourth important feature of the Progressive spirit was the impulse toward social justice, which manifested itself in an array of activities: the promotion of private charities; efforts by sanitation reformers to clean up cities through personal hygiene, municipal sewers, and public-awareness campaigns; and campaigns aimed at regulating child labor and the consumption of alcohol.

Led by women, the settlement house movement of the late nineteenth century had spawned a corps of social workers and reformers devoted to the uplift of slum dwellers. By 1910 there were over 400 settlement houses in cities across the country. The settlement house movement, led by Jane Addams, Ellen Gates Starr, and Lillian Wald, manifested an important aspect of progressivism: women, mostly middle-class married, Christian women, were the driving force behind the grassroots progressive movement. In massive numbers they fanned out to address social ills.

The Women's Christian Temperance Union (WCTU), founded in 1874, was the largest women's group in the nation at the end of the nineteenth century, boasting 300,000 members. Frances Willard, the dynamic president of the WCTU between 1879 and 1898, adopted the motto "do everything" to emphasize that all social problems were interconnected. Members of the WCTU strove to close saloons, improve prison conditions, shelter prostitutes and abused women and children, support female labor unions, and champion women's suffrage. The WCTU also lobbied for the eight-hour workday, the regulation of child labor, better nutrition, the federal inspection of food processors and drug manufacturers, free kindergartens and public playgrounds, and uniform marriage and divorce laws across the states.

With time it became apparent that social evils extended beyond the reach of private charities and grassroots organizations and demanded government intervention. Labor legislation was perhaps the

Child labor

A young girl working as a spinner in a cotton mill in Vermont, 1910.

Frances Elizabeth Willard

Willard founded the WCTU and lobbied for women's suffrage.

most significant reform to emerge from the drive for social justice. It emerged first at the state level. The National Child Labor Committee, organized in 1904, led a movement for laws banning the still-widespread employment of young children. Within ten years, through the organization of state and local committees and a graphic documentation of the evils of child labor by the photographer Lewis W. Hine, the committee pushed through legislation in most states banning the labor of underage children (the minimum age varying from twelve to sixteen) and limiting the hours older children might work.

Closely linked to the child-labor reform movement was a concerted effort to regulate the hours of work for women. Spearheaded by Florence Kelley, the head of the National Consumers' League, this progressive crusade promoted state laws to regulate the long working hours imposed on women who were wives and mothers. Many states also outlawed night work and labor in dangerous occupations for both women and children. But numerous exemptions and inadequate enforcement often nullified the intent of those laws.

The Supreme Court pursued a curiously erratic course in ruling on state labor laws. In *Lochner v. New York* (1905), the Court voided a ten-hour-workday law because it violated workers' "liberty of contract" to accept any terms they chose. But in *Muller v. Oregon* (1908), the high court upheld a ten-hour-workday law for women largely on the basis of sociological data regarding the effects of long hours on the health and morals of women. In *Bunting v. Oregon* (1917), the Court accepted a ten-hour day for both men and women but for twenty more years held out against state minimum-wage laws.

Legislation to protect workers against avoidable accidents gained impetus from disasters such as the 1911 fire at the Triangle Shirtwaist Company in New York City, in which 146 workers died, mostly Jewish and Italian immigrants, most of them women and many of them in their teens, because the owner kept the stairway doors locked to prevent theft. Workers trapped on the three upper floors of the ten-story building died in the fire or leaped to their death. Stricter local building codes and factory-inspection acts followed. One of the most important advances along these lines was the series of workers' compensation laws enacted after Maryland led the way in 1902. Accident-insurance systems replaced the old common-law principle that an injured worker was entitled to compensation only if employer negligence could be proved, a costly and capricious procedure from which the worker was likely to win nothing or be granted excessive awards from an overly sympathetic jury.

PROGRESSIVISM AND RELIGION   Religion was a crucial source of energy for progressive reformers. Christians and Jews embraced the social gospel, seeking to express their faith through aid to the less fortunate. Jane Addams called the impulse to found settlement houses for the waves of immigrants arriving in American cities "Christian humanitarianism." She and others often used the phrase "social righteousness" to explain the connection between social activism and religious belief. Protestants, Catholics, and Jews worked closely together to promote state laws providing for minimum-wage levels and shorter workdays. Some of the reformers applied their crusade for social justice to organized religion itself. Frances Willard, who spent time as a traveling evangelist, lobbied church organizations to allow women to become ministers. As she said, "If women can organize missionary societies, temperance societies, and every kind of charitable organization . . . why not permit them to be ordained to preach the Gospel and administer the sacraments of the Church?"

PROHIBITION   For many activists with strong religious convictions, the cause of liquor prohibition was a fifth area of action. Opposition to strong drink was an ideal cause in which to merge the older religious-based ethics with the new social ethics promoting reforms. Given the importance of saloons as arenas for local politics, prohibitionists could equate the "liquor traffic" with Progressive suspicion of bossism and "special interests." When reform pressures mounted, prohibition offered an easy outlet, bypassing the complexities of corporate regulation.

The battle against booze dated to the nineteenth century. The WCTU had promoted the cause since 1874, and a Prohibition party had entered the elections in 1876. But the most successful political action followed the formation in 1893 of the Anti-Saloon League, an organization that pioneered the strategy of the single-issue pressure group. Through its singleness of purpose, it forced the prohibition issue into the forefront of state and local elections. At its "Jubilee Convention" in 1913, the bipartisan Anti-Saloon League endorsed a prohibition amendment to the Constitution, adopted by Congress in 1917.

By the time it was ratified, two years later, state and local action had already dried up areas occupied by nearly three fourths of the nation's population.

ROOSEVELT'S PROGRESSIVISM

While most progressive initiatives originated at the state and local levels, national reform efforts emerged around 1900. Theodore Roosevelt brought to the White House in 1901 an expansive vision of the presidency that well suited the cause of progressive reform. In one of his first addresses to Congress, he stressed the need for a new political approach. When the Constitution was drafted in 1787, he explained, the nation's social and economic conditions were quite unlike those at the dawn of the twentieth century. "The conditions are now wholly different and wholly different action is called for."

More than any other president since Abraham Lincoln, Roosevelt possessed an activist bent. Still, his initial approach to reform was cautious. He sought to avoid the extremes of socialism on the one hand and laissez-faire individualism on the other. A skilled political maneuverer, Roosevelt greatly expanded the role and visibility of the presidency, as well as the authority and scope of the federal government. He cultivated party leaders in Congress and steered away from such divisive issues as the tariff and regulation of the banks. And when he did approach the explosive issue of regulating the trusts, he took care to reassure the business community. For him politics was the art of the possible. Unlike the more radical progressives and the doctrinaire "lunatic fringe," as he called it, he would take half a loaf rather than none at all.

EXECUTIVE ACTION   In 1901, at the outset of his presidency, Roosevelt promised to sustain William McKinley's policies. He worked with Republican leaders in Congress, against whom the minority of new progressives was as yet powerless. Yet Roosevelt would accomplish more by vigorous executive action than by passing legislation, and in the exercise of presidential power he would not be inhibited by points of legal detail. He argued that as president he might do anything not expressly forbidden by the Constitution.

In 1902, Roosevelt endorsed a "Square Deal" for all, calling for more rigorous enforcement of existing anti-trust laws and stricter controls on big business. "Of all forms of tyranny," Roosevelt asserted, "the least attractive and the most vulgar is the tyranny of mere wealth." From the outset, however, Roosevelt balked at wholesale trust-busting. Effective regulation of corporate giants was better than a futile effort to restore small business, which might be achieved only at a cost to the efficiencies of scale gained in larger operations. Because

Congress balked at regulatory legislation, Roosevelt sought to force the issue by a more vigorous prosecution of the 1890 Sherman Anti-Trust Act. He chose his target carefully. In the case against the sugar trust (*United States v. E. C. Knight and Company,* 1895), the Supreme Court had declared manufacturing strictly an intrastate activity. Railroads, however, were beyond question engaged in interstate commerce and thus subject to federal authority.

So in 1902, Roosevelt ordered the U.S. attorney general to break up the Northern Securities Company, a giant conglomerate of railroads. The company, formed the previous year, had taken shape during a gigantic battle over the Northern Pacific, which was crucial to shipping in the Northwest. The titanic battle to control the railroad, waged between E. H. Harriman of the Union Pacific and James J. Hill and J. P. Morgan of the Great Northern, had raised the threat of a panic on the New York Stock Exchange and so led to a settlement in which the chief contenders made peace by forming Northern Securities, a holding company that controlled the Great Northern and the Northern Pacific. The merger of such rival rail lines essentially ended competition by forging a monopoly. In 1904 the Supreme Court ordered the railroad combination dissolved.

THE 1902 COAL STRIKE   Roosevelt also used the "big stick" against corporations in the coal strike of 1902. On May 12 some 150,000 members of the United Mine Workers walked off the job in Pennsylvania and West Virginia, demanding a 20 percent wage increase, a reduction in daily working hours from ten to nine, and official recognition of the union by the mine owners. The mine operators, having granted a 10 percent raise two years before, shut down the mines in preparation for a long struggle to starve out the miners, many of whom were immigrants from eastern Europe. One mine owner expressed the prejudices of many others when he proclaimed, "The miners don't suffer—why, they can't even speak English."

Previous presidents such as Rutherford Hayes and Grover Cleveland had responded to labor unrest by dispatching federal troops. But the coal strike had not become violent when Roosevelt aggressively intervened. He was concerned about the approach of winter amid a nationwide coal shortage and the effects of the strike on the fall congressional elections—he told a friend that the public would blame the Republicans if coal were in short supply. By October 1902 the strike had caused the price of coal to soar, and hospitals and schools reported empty coal bins. Roosevelt thus decided upon a bold move: he invited leaders of both sides to a conference in Washington, where he appealed to their "patriotism, to the spirit that sinks personal considerations and makes individual sacrifices for the public good." The mine

Roosevelt's duality

Theodore Roosevelt as an "apostle of prosperity" (top) and as a Roman tyrant (bottom). Roosevelt's energy, self-righteousness, and impulsiveness elicited sharp reactions.

owners attended the conference but arrogantly refused even to speak to the UMW leaders. The "extraordinary stupidity and temper" of the "wooden-headed" owners infuriated Roosevelt. The president wanted to grab the spokesman for the mine owners "by the seat of his breeches" and "chuck him out" a window. With the conference ending in an impasse, Roosevelt reluctantly threatened to take over the mines and send in the army to run them. When a congressman questioned the constitutionality of such a move, an exasperated Roosevelt roared, "To hell with the Constitution when the people want coal!" Militarizing the mines would have been an act of dubious legality, but the owners feared that Roosevelt might do it and that public opinion would support him.

The coal strike ended on October 23 with an agreement to submit the issues to an arbitration commission named by the president. The agreement enhanced Roosevelt's prestige, although it produced only a partial victory for the miners. By the arbitrators' decision in 1903, the miners won a nine-hour day but only a 10 percent wage increase and no union recognition by the owners.

EXPANDING FEDERAL POWER   Roosevelt continued to use his executive powers to enforce the Sherman Anti-Trust Act (1890), but he shrank from further anti-trust legislation. Altogether, his administration initiated about twenty-five anti-trust suits; the most notable victory came in *Swift and Company v. United States* (1905), a decision against the "beef trust" through which most of the meat packers had avoided competitive bidding in the purchase of livestock. In this decision the Supreme Court put forth the "stream-of-commerce" doctrine, which overturned its previous holding that manufacturing was strictly intrastate. Since both livestock and the meat products of the packers moved in the stream of interstate commerce, the Court reasoned, both were subject to

"The Lion-Tamer"

Theodore Roosevelt confronts the beasts of the steel trust, the oil trust, the beef trust, and others in the arena of Wall Street.

federal regulation. This interpretation of the interstate commerce power would be broadened in later years until few enterprises would remain beyond the reach of federal regulation.

In 1903, Congress passed the Elkins Act, which made it illegal for railroads to take, as well as to give, secret rebates on freight charges to their favorite customers. All shippers would pay the same price. That same year, Congress created a new Bureau of Corporations to monitor the activities of interstate corporations. Its findings could lead to anti-trust suits, but its purpose was rather to help corporations correct malpractices and avoid the need for lawsuits. Many companies, including United States Steel and International Harvester, worked closely with the bureau, but others held back. When Standard Oil refused to turn over its records, the government brought an anti-trust suit that resulted in the breakup of the huge company in 1911. The Supreme Court broke up the American Tobacco Company at the same time. This approach fell short of the direct regulation that Roosevelt preferred, but lacking congressional support for such laws, little more was possible. Trusts that cooperated were left alone; others had to run the gauntlet of anti-trust suits.

ROOSEVELT'S SECOND TERM

Roosevelt's policies built a coalition of progressive- and conservative-minded voters who assured his election in his own right in 1904. The Republican Convention chose him by acclamation. The Democrats, having lost with William Jennings Bryan twice, turned to Alton B. Parker, who as chief justice of New York had upheld labor's right to the closed shop (requiring that all employees be union members) and the state's right to limit hours of work. Despite Parker's liberal record, party leaders presented him as a safe conservative, and his acceptance of the gold standard as "firmly and irrevocably established" bolstered such a view. The effort to present a candidate more conservative than Roosevelt proved a futile gesture for the party that had twice nominated Bryan. Despite Roosevelt's trust-busting proclivities, most business executives, according to the *New York Sun,* preferred the "impulsive candidate of the party of conservatism to the conservative candidate of the party which the business interests regard as permanently and dangerously impulsive." Even business tycoons J. P. Morgan and E. H. Harriman contributed handsomely to Roosevelt's campaign chest.

Roosevelt's invincible popularity plus the sheer force of his personality swept the president to an impressive victory by a popular vote of 7.6 million to 5.1 million. Parker carried only the solidly Democratic South of the former Confederacy and two border states, Kentucky and Maryland. With an electoral vote of 336 for the president and 140 for Parker, Roosevelt savored his lopsided victory. The president told his wife that he was "no longer a political accident." He now had a popular mandate. On the eve of his inauguration in March 1905, Roosevelt announced: "Tomorrow I shall come into office in my own right. Then watch out for me!"

LEGISLATIVE LEADERSHIP   Elected in his own right, Roosevelt approached his second term with heightened confidence and a stronger commitment to progressive reform. In 1905 he devoted most of his annual message to the regulation and control of big business. His comments irked many of his corporate contributors and congressional Republican leaders. Said steel baron Henry Frick, "We bought the son of a bitch and then he did not stay bought." The independent-minded Roosevelt took aim at the railroads first. The Elkins Act of 1903, finally outlawing rebates, had been a minor step. Railroad executives themselves welcomed it as an escape from shippers clamoring for special favors.

But a new proposal for railroad regulation endorsed by Roosevelt was something else again. It sought to extend the authority of the Interstate Commerce Commission, giving it effective control over railroad freight rates. Enacted in 1906, the Hepburn Act for the first time gave the ICC the power to set maximum freight rates. The commission no longer had to go to court to enforce its decisions. In other ways, too, the Hepburn Act enlarged the mandate of the ICC. Its reach now extended beyond railroads, to oil pipelines, sleeping-car companies, bridges, and ferries, and it could prescribe a uniform system of bookkeeping to provide uniform statistics.

Regulating railroads was Roosevelt's first priority, but he also embraced the regulation of meat packers, food processors, and makers of drugs and patent medicines. Discontent with abuses in those industries had grown rapidly as a result of muckrakers' revelations. Journalists supplied evidence of harmful preservatives and adulterants in the preparation of "embalmed meat" and other food products. The *Ladies' Home Journal* and *Collier's* published evidence of false claims and dangerous ingredients in patent medicines. One of the more notorious "medicines," Lydia Pinkham's vegetable compound, was advertised to work wonders in the relief of "female complaints"; that was no wonder, for the compound was 18 percent alcohol.

Perhaps the most telling blow against such abuses was struck by Upton Sinclair's novel *The Jungle* (1906). Sinclair meant the book to promote socialism, but its main impact came from its portrayal of filthy conditions in Chicago's meatpacking industry:

> It was too dark in these storage places to see well, but a man could run his hand over these piles of meat and sweep off handfuls of the dried dung of rats. These rats were nuisances, and the packers would put poisoned bread out for them, they would die, and then rats, bread, and meat would go into the hoppers together.

Roosevelt read *The Jungle*—and reacted quickly. He sent two agents to Chicago, and their report confirmed all that Sinclair had said: "We saw meat shovelled from filthy wooden floors, piled on tables rarely washed, pushed from room to room in rotten box carts, in all of which processes it was in the way of gathering dirt, splinters, floor filth, and the expectoration of tuberculous and other diseased workers."

Congress and Roosevelt responded by creating the Meat Inspection Act of 1906. It required federal inspection of meats destined for interstate commerce and empowered officials in the Agriculture Department to impose sanitation standards in processing plants. The Pure Food and Drug Act, enacted the same day, placed restrictions on the makers of prepared foods and patent medicines and forbade the manufacture, sale, or transportation of adulterated, misbranded, or harmful foods, drugs, and liquors.

The meat industry

Pigs strung up along the hog-scraping rail at Armour's packing plant in Chicago, ca. 1909.

CONSERVATION One of the most enduring legacies of Roosevelt's leadership was his energetic support for the emerging environmental conservation movement. Roosevelt was the first president to challenge the long-standing myth of America's having inexhaustible natural resources. In fact, Roosevelt pronounced that conservation was the "great material question of the day." He and other early conservationists were convinced that the tradition of free-wheeling individual and corporate exploitation of the environment must be supplanted by the scientific management of the nation's natural resources for the *long-term* public benefit. "The things that will destroy America," he said, "are prosperity at any price, peace at any price, safety first instead of duty first, the love of soft living and the get-rich-quick theory of life."

After the Civil War a growing number of individual activists and conservation organizations had begun to oppose the unregulated exploitation of natural resources and sought to preserve wilderness areas. Just as reformers promoted the regulation of business and industry for the public welfare, conservationists championed efforts to manage and preserve the natural environment for future generations. The first promoters of resource conservation were ardent sportsmen among the social elite (including Theodore Roosevelt), who worried that unregulated commercial hunters and trappers were killing game animals to the point of extermination. In 1886, for example, the sportsman-naturalist George Bird Grinnell, editor of *Forest and Stream*, founded the Audubon Society to protect wild birds from being killed for their plumage. Two years later Grinnell, Roosevelt, and a dozen other recreational hunters formed the Boone and Crockett Club, named in honor of Daniel Boone and Davy Crockett, the legendary frontiersmen. The club's goal was to ensure that big-game animals were protected for posterity. Those goals were shared and promoted by national monthly newspapers such as *American Sportsman*, *Forest and Stream*, and *Field and Stream*. By 1900 most states had enacted laws regulating game hunting and had created game refuges and wardens to enforce the new rules, much to the chagrin of local hunters, including Native Americans, who now were forced to abide by state laws designed to protect the interests of wealthy recreational hunters.

Roosevelt and the sportsmen conservationists formed a powerful coalition promoting rational government management of natural resources: rivers and streams, forests, minerals, and natural wonders. Those concerns, as well as the desire of railroad companies to transport tourists to destinations featuring majestic scenery, led the federal government to displace Indians in order to establish the 2-million-acre Yellowstone National Park in 1872 at the junction of the Montana, Wyoming, and Idaho Territories (the National Park Service would be created in 1916 after other parks had been established). In 1881, Congress created a Division of Forestry (now the U.S. Forest Service) within the Department of the Interior. At the same time, New York State officials established a Forest Commission in 1885 to manage

Nathaniel Pitt Langford

The first superintendent of Yellowstone National Park, on Jupiter Terrace at Mammoth Hot Springs, ca. 1875.

timber in the vast state-owned acreage of the Adirondack Mountains. Seven years later the legislature created the 5-million-acre Adirondack Park. The legislature also imposed restrictions on hunting in state forests and created a "forest police" to enforce the new regulations. As president, Theodore Roosevelt created fifty federal wildlife refuges, approved five new national parks, and designated as national monuments unfit for economic use such natural treasures as the Grand Canyon.

In 1898, while serving as vice president, Roosevelt had endorsed the appointment of Gifford Pinchot, a close friend and the nation's first professional forester, as the head of the Division of Forestry. Pinchot and Roosevelt believed that conservation entailed the scientific management of natural resources to serve the public interest. Pinchot explained that the conservation movement sought to promote the "greatest good for the greatest number for the longest time."

Roosevelt and Pinchot championed the progressive notion of efficiency and government regulation. They were not romantics about nature, nor were they ecologists; they did not understand the complex interdependence of trees, plants, insects, and animals, nor did they appreciate the environmental benefits of natural fires. Instead, they were utilitarian progressives determined to ensure that entrepreneurs and industrialists exploited nature in appropriate ways. As Pinchot insisted, "The first principle of conservation is development." He sought to ensure the wisest "use of the natural resources now existing on this continent for the benefit of the people who live here now."

The president and Pinchot were especially concerned about the millions of acres still owned by the federal government. Over the years vast tracts of public land had been given away or sold at discount prices to large business enterprises. Roosevelt and Pinchot were determined to end such carelessness and exploitation. They championed the systematic management of natural resources by government experts trained to promote the most efficient public use of the environment. "Forestry," Pinchot explained, "is handling trees so that one crop follows another." He and Roosevelt opposed the mindless clear-cutting of entire forests for short-term profit and sought to restrict particular forests from any economic development. In fact, Roosevelt as president used the Forest Reserve Act (1891) to protect some 172 million acres of timberland. Lumber companies were furious, but Roosevelt held firm. As he bristled, "I hate a man who skins the land."

Gifford Pinchot

Pinchot is seen here with two children at the edge of a larch grove.

Congressional resistance to Roosevelt and Pinchot's environmental proposals led them to publicize the cause through a White House Conference on Conservation in 1908 and later that year by setting up a National Conservation Commission, which proposed a thorough survey of the nation's mineral, water, forest, and soil resources. Within eighteen months some forty-one state conservation commissions had been organized. The infant environmental movement remained divided, however, between those who wanted to conserve resources for continuous human use and those who wanted to set aside areas as wilderness preserves.

Theodore Roosevelt's far-flung conservation efforts also encompassed reclamation and irrigation projects. In 1902 the president signed the Reclamation

Roosevelt's western tour

Roosevelt visited Yellowstone National Park in 1903.

Act (also known as the Newlands Act, after its sponsor, Nevada senator Francis Newlands). The Reclamation Act established a new federal agency within the Interior Department, called the Reclamation Service (renamed the Bureau of Reclamation in 1923), to administer a massive new program designed to bring water to arid western states. Using funds from the sale of federal lands in sixteen states in the West, the Reclamation Service constructed dams and irrigation systems to transform barren desert acreage into farmland.

Federal and state initiatives to conserve the nation's natural resources and manage them for the public welfare brought many improvements during the Progressive Era but also generated unexpected consequences. The efforts to set aside national parks and forests, for example, often came at the expense of Indians and whites who were pushed off the property and denied traditional hunting rights. Conservation efforts to satisfy the desires of affluent Americans, as one historian has written, meant for poorer Americans "fines and jail time, and empty bellies." Government efforts to suppress fires in national forests and destroy predators such as mountain lions, wolves, coyotes, and bobcats that preyed upon popular game animals unwittingly disrupted natural ecological cycles and often caused more harm than good. Yet the progressive conservation movement, for all its unexpected complexities and ironies, did succeed in reining in the unregulated exploitation of natural resources for private gain. As Pinchot recalled late in life, "Launching the Conservation movement was the most significant achievement of the T. R. Administration, as he himself believed."

FROM ROOSEVELT TO TAFT

Toward the end of his second term, Roosevelt declared, "I have had a great time as president." Although eligible to run again, he opted for retirement. He decided that the heir to the White House should be Secretary of

War William Howard Taft, and the Republican Convention ratified the choice on its first ballot in 1908. The Democrats, whose conservative strategy had backfired in 1904, decided to give William Jennings Bryan one more chance at the highest office. Still vigorous at forty-eight, Bryan retained a faithful following but struggled to attract national support. Roosevelt advised Taft: "Do not answer Bryan; *attack* him. Don't let him make the issues." Taft followed Roosevelt's advice, declaring that Bryan's election would result in a "paralysis of business."

The Republican platform declared its support for Roosevelt's policies, including conservation and further strengthening of the Interstate Commerce Commission. The Democratic platform hardly differed on regulation, but it endorsed a lower tariff and opposed court injunctions against labor actions. In the end, voters opted for Roosevelt's chosen successor: Taft swept the Electoral College, 321 to 162. The real surprise of the election, however, was the strong showing of the Socialist party candidate, labor hero Eugene V. Debs. His 421,000 votes revealed the depth of working-class resentment in the United States.

Out of office, the fifty-year-old Roosevelt set off in 1909 on a prolonged safari in Africa, prompting his old foe J. P. Morgan to mutter, "Let every lion do his duty." The new president he left behind was an entirely different political

William Howard Taft

Speaking at Manassas, Virginia, in 1911.

animal—in fact, he was hardly a political animal at all. The offspring of a prominent Cincinnati family—his father had been Ulysses Grant's attorney general—Taft had progressed through appointive offices, from judge in Ohio to solicitor in the Justice Department, federal judge, commissioner and governor general in the Philippines, and secretary of war. As secretary of war, Taft had overseen construction of the Panama Canal. The presidency was the only elective office he ever held. Later he would be chief justice of the Supreme Court (1921–1930), a job more suited to his temperament.

Taft detested the give-and-take of backroom politics and never felt comfortable in the White House. He once observed that whenever someone said "Mr. President," he looked around for Roosevelt. The political dynamo in the family was his wife, Helen, who had wanted the White House more than he. One of the major tragedies of Taft's presidency was that Nellie Taft suffered a debilitating stroke soon after they entered the White House, and for most of his term she remained unable to serve as his political adviser.

TARIFF REFORM   Taft's domestic policies generated a storm of controversy within his own party. Contrary to Republican tradition, Taft preferred a lower tariff, and he made this the first important issue of his presidency. But if Taft, in pressing an issue that Roosevelt had skirted, seemed the bolder of the two, he proved less skillful in dealing with Congress. A tariff bill passed the House with surprising ease. It lowered rates less than Taft would have preferred but made some important reductions and enlarged the number of duty-free items. But the chairman of the Senate Finance Committee, Nelson W. Aldrich, guided through the upper chamber a drastically revised bill, one that included more than 800 changes. What came out of the conference committee was a measure close to the final Senate version, although Taft did get some reductions on particular items.

In response to the higher rates in Aldrich's bill, a group of midwestern Republicans took the Senate floor to fight what they considered a corrupt throwback to the days when the Republican party had done the bidding of big business. In all, ten progressive Republicans joined the Democrats in an unsuccessful effort to defeat the bill. Taft at first agreed with them; then, fearful of a party split, he backed the majority and agreed to an imperfect bill. He lacked Roosevelt's love of a grand battle as well as his gift for working both sides of the street. Temperamentally conservative, inhibited by scruples about interfering too much with the legislative process, he drifted into the orbit of the Republican Old Guard and quickly alienated the progressive wing of his party, whom he tagged "assistant Democrats."

BALLINGER AND PINCHOT   In 1910, president Taft's policies drove the wedge deeper between the conservative and progressive Republican factions. What came to be called the Ballinger-Pinchot controversy made Taft appear to be a less reliable custodian of Roosevelt's conservation policies than he actually was. The strongest conservation leaders, such as Roosevelt and Gifford Pinchot, a Pennsylvanian, were often easterners, and Taft's secretary of the interior, Richard A. Ballinger of Seattle, was well aware that many westerners opposed conservation programs on the grounds that they held back full development of the region. Ballinger therefore threw open to commercial use more than 1 million acres of waterpower sites that Roosevelt had withdrawn in the guise of ranger stations. Ballinger's reasoning was that the withdrawal had "gone far beyond legal limitations," and Taft agreed. At about the same time, Ballinger turned over certain federal coal lands in Alaska to a group of Seattle tycoons, some of whom he had represented as a lawyer. Apparently without Ballinger's knowledge, this group had already agreed to sell part of the land for commercial development.

As chief of forestry, Pinchot reported the collusion to Taft, who refused to intervene. When Pinchot went public with the controversy early in 1910, Taft fired him for insubordination. A joint congressional investigation exonerated Ballinger of all charges of fraud or corruption, but lingering suspicions created such pressure that he resigned in 1911. In firing Pinchot, Taft had acted according to the strictly legal view that his training had taught him to value, but circumstances tarnished his image in the public mind. "In the end," one historian has written, "the Ballinger-Pinchot affair had more impact on politics than it did on conservation." Taft had been elected to carry out Roosevelt's policies, his opponents said, and he was carrying them out— "on a stretcher."

Meanwhile, in the House of Representatives, the more progressive Republicans rebelled against Taft and the party leaders. When the regular session opened in 1910, the insurgents joined Democrats in voting to investigate Ballinger. Flushed with that victory, they resolved to clip the wings of House Speaker Joseph G. Cannon, Republican of Illinois, a conservative who held almost a stranglehold on procedures with his power to appoint all committee members and their chairmen and especially with his control of the Rules Committee, of which he was a member. A coalition of Democrats and progressive Republicans overrode a ruling by the Speaker and proceeded to adopt new rules offered by George W. Norris, Republican of Nebraska, that enlarged the Rules Committee from five to fifteen members, made them elective by the House, and excluded the Speaker as a member. About forty

Joseph Cannon

Caricature of Cannon enjoying too much decision-making power as House Speaker.

Republicans joined the Democratic minority in the move. In the next Congress the rules would be further changed to make all committees elective.

Events had conspired to cast Taft in a conservative role at a time when progressive sentiment was riding high in the country. The result was a severe rebuke of the president in the congressional elections of 1910, first by the widespread defeat of pro-Taft candidates in the Republican primaries and then by the election of a Democratic majority in the House and enough Democrats in the Senate to allow progressive Republicans to wield the balance of power.

TAFT AND ROOSEVELT In 1910, Theodore Roosevelt returned from his extended travels abroad. He had been reading news accounts and letters about Taft's "betrayal," but unlike some of his supporters, he refused to break with his successor. With rather severe politeness, however, Roosevelt refused an invitation to visit the White House. He wrote Taft, "I shall keep my mind open as I keep my mouth shut." Neither was easy for Roosevelt, whose followers urged him to act. Roosevelt was finding it much less fulfilling to be a former president than to be a president. He also was growing increasingly concerned about Taft's administration. His handpicked successor had replaced many of Roosevelt's cabinet members with corporate attorneys, and Taft's dismissal of Pinchot infuriated Roosevelt, who eventually decided that Taft had fallen under the spell of the Republican Old Guard leadership. During the fall of 1910, Roosevelt made several speeches promoting "sane and progressive" Republican candidates in the congressional elections. In Kansas he gave a catchy name to his latest principles, the "New Nationalism." Roosevelt issued a stirring call for an array of new federal regulatory laws, a social-welfare program, and new measures of direct democracy, including the old Populist demands for the initiative, recall, and referendum at the federal level. His purpose was not to revolutionize the political system but to save it from the threat of revolution. "What I have advocated," he explained a few days later, "is not wild radicalism. It is the highest and wisest kind of conservatism."

Relations between Roosevelt and Taft remained tense, but it was another year before they came to an open break. The split happened in the fall of 1911, when the Taft administration announced an anti-trust suit against United States Steel, citing specifically as its cause the company's acquisition of the Tennessee Coal and Iron Company in 1907, a move to which Roosevelt had given tacit approval in the belief that it would avert a business panic. In mid-November, Roosevelt published a sharp attack on Taft's "archaic" attempt to restore competition. The only sensible response to the problem, he argued, was to accept business combinations under modern circumstances but to enlarge the government's power to regulate them. Roosevelt's entry into the next presidential campaign was now only a matter of time.

Many progressive Republicans who assumed that Roosevelt would not run again proposed to back Wisconsin senator Robert La Follette in 1912, but they were ready to switch if Roosevelt entered the race. An opening came on February 2, 1912, when La Follette showed signs of nervous exhaustion in

Political giants

A cartoon showing Roosevelt charging through the air at Taft, who is seated on a mountain top.

a rambling speech in Philadelphia. As his following began to drop away, a group of seven Republican governors met in Chicago and called upon Roosevelt to become a candidate. On February 24, Roosevelt decided to enter the race. "I hope that so far as possible the people may be given the chance, through direct primaries," Roosevelt wrote the governors, "to express their preference." He had decided that Taft had "sold the Square Deal down the river," and he now dismissed Taft as a "hopeless fathead."

The rebuke implicit in Roosevelt's decision to run against Taft, his chosen successor, was in many ways undeserved. During Taft's first year in office, one political tempest after another had left his image irreparably damaged. The three years of solid achievement that followed came too late to restore its luster or reunite his divided party. Taft had at least attempted tariff reform, which Roosevelt had never dared. He replaced Ballinger and Pinchot with men of impeccable credentials as conservationists. He won from Congress the power to protect public lands for any reason and was the first president to withdraw federal oil reserves from use. Under the Appalachian Forest Reserve Act (1911), he enlarged the national forest by purchasing land in the East. In the end his administration withdrew more public land in four years than Roosevelt's had in nearly eight and brought more anti-trust suits, by a score of eighty to twenty-five.

In 1910, with Taft's support, Congress passed the Mann-Elkins Act, which for the first time empowered the Interstate Commerce Commission to initiate changes in railroad freight rates, extended regulation to telephone and telegraph companies, and set up the Commerce Court to expedite appeals of ICC rulings. Taft also established the Bureau of Mines and the federal Children's Bureau (1912), and he called for statehood for Arizona and New Mexico and territorial government for Alaska (1912). The Sixteenth Amendment (1913), authorizing a federal income tax, was ratified with Taft's support before he left office, and the Seventeenth Amendment (1913), providing for the popular election of senators, was ratified soon after he left office.

Despite Taft's progressive record, Roosevelt turned on him. Senator Elihu Root, formerly Roosevelt's secretary of state and one of Taft's closest advisers and the chairman of the Republican Convention, told a friend that Roosevelt would not gain the party's nomination but would "succeed in so damaging Taft that he can't be elected." In all but two of the thirteen states that held presidential primaries, Roosevelt won, even in Taft's Ohio. But the groundswell of popular support was no match for Taft's decisive position as sitting president and party leader. In state nominating conventions the party regulars held the line, and so Roosevelt entered the Republican National Convention about 100 votes short of victory. The Taft forces proceeded to nominate their man by the same steamroller tactics that had nominated Roosevelt in 1904.

Outraged at such "naked theft," the Roosevelt delegates—mostly social workers, reformers, intellectuals, and executives who favored Roosevelt's leadership—assembled in a rump convention. "If you wish me to make the fight I will make it," Roosevelt told the delegates, who then issued a call for a Progressive party convention, which assembled in Chicago on August 5. Roosevelt appeared before the delegates, feeling "fit as a bull moose." He was "stripped to the buff and ready for the fight," he said. "We stand at Armaged-

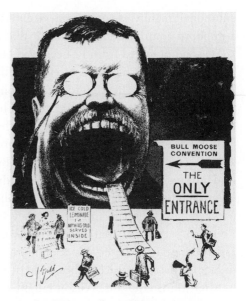

The "Bull Moose" candidate in 1912

A skeptical view of Theodore Roosevelt.

don, and we battle for the Lord." But few professional politicians turned up. Progressive Republicans decided to preserve their party credentials and fight another day. For the time being, with the disruption of the Republican party caused by the rift between Taft and Roosevelt, the progressive torch was about to be passed to the Democrats.

WOODROW WILSON'S PROGRESSIVISM

WILSON'S RISE   The emergence of Thomas Woodrow Wilson as the Democratic nominee in 1912 climaxed a political rise even more rapid than that of Grover Cleveland. In 1910, before his nomination and election as governor of New Jersey, Wilson had been president of Princeton University, but he had never run for public office. Born in Staunton, Virginia, in 1856, the son of a "noble-saintly mother" and a stern Presbyterian minister, he had grown up in Georgia and the Carolinas during the Civil War and Reconstruction.

Young Wilson, tall and slender with a lean, long, sharply chiseled face, inherited his father's unquestioning piety, once declaring that "so far as religion is concerned, argument is adjourned." Wilson also developed a consuming ambition to "serve" humankind. Driven by a sense of providential destiny and self-righteous moralism, he coupled a rigid sense of rectitude with chronic emotional fragility. He once confessed that "I am too intense." Wilson nurtured a stubborn commitment to principle that would prove to be his undoing.

Wilson graduated from Princeton in 1879, and after law school at the University of Virginia he had a brief, unfulfilling, and profitless legal practice in Atlanta. From there he went to the new Johns Hopkins University in Baltimore, where he found his calling in the study of history and political science. As a college student he had said that he loved nothing more than "writing and talking."

Wilson's doctoral dissertation, *Congressional Government,* published in 1885, argued that the president, like the British prime minister, should be the leader of party government, as active in directing legislation as in the administration and enforcement of laws. In calling for a stronger presidency, he expressed views closer to those of Roosevelt than those of Taft. He also shared Roosevelt's concern that government should promote the general welfare rather than narrowly serve special interests. And like Roosevelt he was critical of big business, organized labor, socialists, and agrarian radicalism.

After Johns Hopkins, Wilson taught at Bryn Mawr College, in Pennsylvania, and then at Wesleyan University, in Connecticut, before moving to Princeton in 1890. There he quickly earned renown for his polished lectures, vigorous mind, and sharp debating skills. In 1902 he was unanimously elected president of the university. In that position he showed the first evidence of reform views. "We are not put into this world to sit still and know," he stressed in his inaugural address. "We are put into it to act." And act he did. At Princeton, Wilson modernized the curriculum, expanded and improved the faculty, introduced the tutorial system, and raised admissions standards. But he failed in his attempt to restructure the elitist student social clubs.

Wilson's reforms

Woodrow Wilson campaigning from a railroad car.

Wilson's urge for reform increasingly antagonized university administrators and alumni, however, and when the Democratic party boss of New Jersey offered Wilson his support for the 1910 gubernatorial nomination, Wilson accepted. The party leaders sought a respectable candidate to help them ward off progressive challengers, but they discovered too late that the professor actually had an iron will of his own. Like Roosevelt, Wilson had come to shed some of his original conservatism and view progressive reform as a necessary expedient in order to stave off more radical social change. Elected as a reform candidate, Governor Wilson promoted progressive measures and pushed them through the New Jersey legislature. He pressured lawmakers to enact a workers' compensation law, a corrupt-practices law, measures to regulate public utilities, and ballot reforms. Such strong leadership in a state known as the home of the trusts because of its lenient incorporation laws brought Wilson to national attention.

In the spring of 1911, a group of southern Democrats in New York opened a Wilson presidential campaign headquarters, and Wilson set forth on strenuous tours across the country, denouncing special privilege and political bossism. Despite a fast start, however, the Wilson campaign seemed headed for defeat by Speaker of the House Champ Clark of Missouri. Clark had enough support for a majority in the early ballots, but the Wilson forces combined with supporters of Oscar Underwood of Alabama to prevent the required two-thirds majority. On the fourteenth ballot, William Jennings Bryan went over to Wilson. When the Democratic boss of Illinois deserted Clark on the forty-second ballot and the Underwood delegates went over to Wilson on the forty-sixth, he clinched the nomination.

THE ELECTION OF 1912   The 1912 presidential campaign involved four candidates: Wilson and Taft represented the two major parties, while Eugene Debs ran as a Socialist, and Roosevelt headed the Progressive party ticket. They all shared a basic progressive assumption that the old notion of do-nothing government was bankrupt; modern conditions required active measures to promote the general welfare. The rise of big business, in other words, required a bigger role for government. But they differed in the nature and extent of their activism.

No sooner did the formal campaign open than Roosevelt's candidacy almost ended. While entering a car on his way to deliver a speech in Milwaukee, he was shot by John Schrank, a mentally disturbed New Yorker who believed any president seeking a third term should be shot. The bullet went through Roosevelt's overcoat, spectacles case, and fifty-page speech, then fractured a rib before lodging just below his right lung, an inch from his heart. "Stand back, don't hurt the man," he yelled at the crowd as they mobbed the attacker. Roosevelt demanded that he be driven to the auditorium to deliver his speech. In a dramatic gesture he showed the audience his bloodstained shirt and punctured text and vowed, "It takes more than this to kill a bull moose."

As the campaign developed, Taft quickly lost ground. "There are so many people in the country who don't like me," he lamented. The contest settled down to a running debate over the competing ideologies of the two front-runners: Roosevelt's New Nationalism and Wilson's New Freedom. The inchoate ideas that Roosevelt fashioned into his New Nationalism had first been presented systematically in *The Promise of American Life* (1909) by Herbert Croly, a then-obscure New York journalist. Its central point was often summarized in a useful catchphrase: "Hamiltonian means to achieve Jeffersonian ends," meaning that Alexander Hamilton's program of government activism on behalf of business interests should be used to achieve democratic and egalitarian Jeffersonian goals. The times required Americans to give up Jeffersonian prejudices against big government and use a strong central government to achieve democratic ends in the interest of the people. Big business necessitated big government.

The old nationalism had been used "by the sinister . . . special interests," Roosevelt said. His New Nationalism would enable government to promote social justice and effect such reforms as graduated income and inheritance taxes, workers' compensation, regulations to protect women and children at work, and a stronger Bureau of Corporations. These ideas and more went into the platform of the Progressive party, which called for a federal trade commission with sweeping authority over business and a tariff commission to set rates on a "scientific basis."

Before the end of his administration, Wilson would be swept into the current of New Nationalism, too. But initially he adhered to the decentralizing anti-trust traditions of his party. Before the start of the campaign, Wilson conferred with Louis D. Brandeis, a progressive lawyer from Boston who focused Wilson's thought much as Croly had focused Roosevelt's. Brandeis's design for Wilson's New Freedom program differed from Roosevelt's New Nationalism in its belief that the federal government should restore the competition among small economic units rather than regulate huge monopolies. Where Roosevelt admired the power and efficiency of large corporations that behaved themselves, Wilson was convinced that all huge industries needed to be broken up. Such a policy required a vigorous anti-trust policy, lower tariffs to allow more foreign goods to compete in American markets, and dissolution of the concentration of financial power in Wall Street. But Brandeis and Wilson saw the vigorous expansion of federal power as only a temporary necessity, not a permanent condition. Roosevelt, who was convinced that both giant corporations and an expanding federal government were permanent developments, dismissed the New Freedom as mere fantasy. For his part, Taft attacked his two progressive opponents by reminding them that the federal government "cannot create good times. It cannot make the rain to fall, the sun to shine or the crops to grow," but too many "meddlesome" regulations could deny the nation the prosperity it deserved.

The Republican schism between Taft and Roosevelt opened the way for Woodrow Wilson to win, by 435 electoral votes to 88 for Roosevelt and 8 for

Taft. But in popular votes, Wilson had only 42 percent of the total. Roosevelt received 27 percent, Taft 23 percent, and Debs 6 percent. After learning of his election, Wilson told the chairman of the Democratic party that "God ordained that I should be the next president of the United States." Perhaps. But had the Republican party not been split in two, Wilson would have been trounced. His was the victory of a minority over a divided opposition.

The 1912 election was significant in several ways. First, it was a high-water mark for progressivism. The election was the first to feature presidential primaries. The two leading candidates debated the basic issues of progressivism in a campaign unique in its focus on vital alternatives and in its highly philosophical tone. Taft, too, despite his temperament and associations, showed his own progressive instincts. And the Socialist party, the left wing of

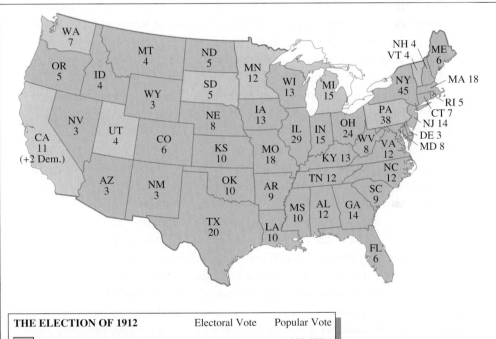

THE ELECTION OF 1912	Electoral Vote	Popular Vote
Woodrow Wilson (Democrat)	**435**	**6,300,000**
Theodore Roosevelt (Progressive)	88	4,100,000
William H. Taft (Republican)	8	3,500,000

Why was Taft so unpopular? How did the division between Roosevelt and Taft give Wilson the victory? Why was Wilson's victory in 1912 significant?

progressivism, polled over 900,000 votes for Eugene V. Debs, its highest proportion ever. Debs called his version of socialism "Christianity in action."

Second, the election gave Democrats effective national power for the first time since the Civil War. For two years during the second administration of Grover Cleveland, from 1893 to 1895, they had held the White House and majorities in both houses of Congress, but they had fallen quickly out of power during the severe economic depression of the 1890s. Now, under Wilson, they again held the presidency and were the majority in both the House of Representatives and the Senate.

Third, the election of Wilson brought southerners back into the orbit of national and international affairs in a significant way for the first time since the Civil War. Five of Wilson's ten cabinet members were born in the South, three still resided there, and William Jennings Bryan, the secretary of state, was an idol of the southern masses. At the president's right hand, and one of the most influential members of the Wilson circle, at least until 1919, was "Colonel" Edward M. House of Texas. Wilson described House as "my second personality. He is my independent self." On Capitol Hill, southerners, by virtue of their seniority, held the lion's share of committee chairmanships. As a result, much of the Progressive legislation of the Wilson era would bear the names of the southern Democrats who guided it through Congress.

Fourth and finally, the election of 1912 had begun to alter the character of the Republican party. The defection of the Bull Moose Progressives had weakened the party's progressive wing. The leaders of the Republican party that would return to power in the 1920s would be more conservative in tone and temperament.

WILSONIAN REFORM Wilson's inaugural address in 1913 voiced in eloquent tones the ideals of social justice that animated many progressives. "We have been proud of our industrial achievements," he said, "but we have not hitherto stopped thoughtfully enough to count the human cost . . . the fearful physical and spiritual cost to the men and women and children upon whom the dead weight and burden of it all has fallen pitilessly the years through." He promised specifically a lower tariff and a new nationally regulated banking system. "This is not a day of triumph; it is a day of dedication. Here muster, not the forces of party, but the forces of humanity."

If Roosevelt had been a strong president by force of personality, Wilson became a strong president by force of conviction. The president, he had written in *Congressional Government*, "is . . . the political leader of the nation, or has it in his choice to be. The nation as a whole has chosen him, and is conscious that it has no other political spokesman. His is the only national voice in affairs." Wilson courted popular support, but he also courted members of Congress through personal contacts, invitations to the White House, and speeches in the Capitol. He used patronage power to reward friends and punish enemies. He might have acted through a progressive coalition but chose instead to rely upon party loyalty. "I'd rather trust a machine Senator when he is committed to your program," he told his navy secretary, "than a talking Liberal who can never quite go along with others because of his admiration of his own patented plan of reform." Wilson therefore made use of the party caucus, in which disagreements among Democrats were settled.

THE TARIFF   Wilson's leadership faced its first big test on the issue of tariff reform. Tariffs were originally needed to protect infant industries from foreign competition. Now, however, Wilson believed, tariffs were being abused by corporations to suppress foreign competition and keep prices high. He often claimed that the "tariff made the trusts," believing that tariffs had encouraged the growth of American industrial monopolies and degraded the political process by producing armies of paid lobbyists who invaded Congress each year. In attacking high tariffs, Wilson sought to strike a blow for consumers and honest government. He acted quickly and boldly, summoning Congress to a special session and addressing it in person—the first president to do so since John Adams. (Roosevelt was said to have asked, "Why didn't I think of that?") And Congress acted vigorously on tariff reductions. Only four Democrats crossed the party line, and the new bill passed the House easily.

The crunch came in the Senate, the traditional graveyard of tariff reform. Swarms of lobbyists got so thick in Washington, Wilson said, that "a brick couldn't be thrown without hitting one of them." The president turned the tables with a public statement that focused the spotlight on the "industrious and insidious" tariff lobby.

The Underwood-Simmons Tariff became law in 1913. It reduced import duties on most goods and lowered the overall average duty from about 37 percent to about 29 percent. The act lowered tariff rates but raised federal revenues with the first income tax levied under the newly ratified Sixteenth Amendment: 1 percent on income over $3,000 ($4,000 for married couples) and a surtax graduated from 1 percent on income of about $20,000 to 6 percent on income above $500,000. The highest total tax rate would thus be 7 percent.

THE FEDERAL RESERVE ACT   Before the new tariff had cleared the Senate, the administration proposed the first major banking and currency

"Reading the Death Warrant"

Woodrow Wilson's plan for banking and currency reform spells the death of the "money trust," according to this cartoon.

reform since the Civil War. Ever since Andrew Jackson had killed the second Bank of the United States in the 1830s, the nation had been without a central bank. Instead, the country's money supply was administered by hundreds of private banks. Such a decentralized system fostered instability and inefficiency. By 1913 virtually everyone had agreed that the banking system needed restructuring. Wilson told Congress that a federal banking system was needed to ensure that "the banks may be the instruments, not the masters, of business and of individual enterprise and initiative."

The Federal Reserve Act of 1913 created a new national banking system, with regional reserve banks supervised by a central board of directors. There would be twelve Federal Reserve banks, each owned by member banks in its district, which could issue Federal Reserve notes (currency) to member banks. All national banks became members; state banks and trust companies could join if they wished. Each member bank had to transfer 6 percent of its capital to the Federal Reserve bank and deposit a portion of its reserves there. This arrangement made it possible to expand both the money supply and bank credit in times of high business activity or as the level of borrowing increased.

The new system corrected three great defects in the previous arrangement: now bank reserves could be pooled, affording greater security; both the nation's currency supply and bank credit became more elastic; and the concentration of reserves in New York City was decreased. The new national banking system represented a new step in active government intervention and control in one of the most sensitive segments of the economy.

ANTI-TRUST LAWS While promoting banking and tariff reforms, Wilson made trust-busting the central focus of the New Freedom. The concentration of economic power had continued to grow despite the Sherman Anti-Trust Act and the federal watchdog agency, the Bureau of Corporations.

Wilson's solution to the problem was a revision of the Sherman Act to define more explicitly what counted as restraint of trade. He decided to make a strong Federal Trade Commission (FTC) the cornerstone of his anti-trust program. Created in 1914, the five-member commission replaced Roosevelt's Bureau of Corporations and assumed new powers to define "unfair trade practices" and issue "cease-and-desist" orders when it found evidence of unfair competition.

Henry D. Clayton, a Democrat from Alabama on the House Judiciary Committee, drafted an anti-trust bill in 1914 that outlawed practices such as price discrimination (charging different customers different prices for the same goods); "tying" agreements, which limited the right of dealers to handle the products of competing manufacturers; and corporations' acquisition of stock in competing corporations. In every case, however, conservative forces in the Senate qualified these provisions by tacking on the weakening phrase "where the effect may be to substantially lessen competition" or words of similar effect. And conservative southern Democrats and northern Republicans amended the Clayton Anti-Trust Act to allow for broad judicial review of the FTC's decisions, thus further weakening its freedom of action. In accordance with the president's recommendation, however, corporate officials were made individually responsible for any violations.

Agrarian activists in alliance with organized labor won a stipulation that declared farm-labor organizations were not unlawful combinations in restraint of trade. Injunctions in labor disputes, moreover, were not to be handed down by federal courts unless "necessary to prevent irreparable injury to property." Though hailed by union leaders as labor's Magna Carta, these provisions were actually little more than pious affirmations, as later court decisions would demonstrate. Wilson himself remarked that the act did little more than affirm the right of unions to exist by forbidding their dissolution for acting in restraint of trade.

Administration of the anti-trust laws generally proved disappointing to the more vehement progressives under Wilson. The president reassured business that his purposes were friendly. As his secretary of commerce put it later, Wilson hoped to "create in the Federal Trade Commission a counsellor and friend to the business world." But its first chairman lacked forcefulness, and under its next head, a Chicago industrialist, the FTC practically abandoned its function as watchdog. The Justice Department, meanwhile, offered help and advice to businessmen interested in arranging matters so as to avoid anti-trust prosecutions. The appointment of conservative men to the Interstate Commerce Commission and the Federal Reserve won plaudits from the business world and profoundly disappointed progressives.

SOCIAL JUSTICE   Wilson had never been a strong progressive of the social-justice persuasion. He carried out promises to lower the tariff, reorganize the banking system, and strengthen the anti-trust laws. Swept along by the course of events and the pressures of more far-reaching progressives, he was pushed further than he intended to go on some points. The New Freedom was now complete, he wrote late in 1914; the future would be "a time of healing because [it would be] a time of just dealing." Although Wilson endorsed state action for women's suffrage, he declined to support a federal suffrage amendment because his party platform had not done so. He withheld support from federal child-labor legislation because he regarded it as a state matter. He opposed a bill for federal support of rural credits (low-interest loans to farmers) on the grounds that it was "unwise and unjustifiable to extend the credit of the government to a single class of the community."

Not until the second anniversary of his inauguration (March 4, 1915) did Wilson sign an important piece of social-justice legislation, the La Follette Seamen's Act. The product of stubborn agitation by the eloquent president of the Seamen's Union, the act strengthened shipboard safety requirements,

The privileged elite

President Wilson and the First Lady ride in a carriage.

reduced the power of ship captains, set minimum food standards, and required regular wage payments. Seamen who jumped ship before their contracts expired, moreover, were relieved of the charge of desertion.

PROGRESSIVISM FOR WHITES ONLY   Like many other progressives, Woodrow Wilson showed little interest in the plight of African Americans. In fact, he shared many of the racist attitudes prevalent at the time. Although Wilson denounced the Ku Klux Klan's "reign of terror," he sympathized with its motives of restoring white rule in the postwar South and relieving whites of the "ignorant and hostile" power of the black vote. As a student at Princeton, Wilson had detested the enfranchisement of blacks, arguing that Americans of Anglo-Saxon origin would always resist domination by "an ignorant and inferior race."

Later, as a politician, Wilson courted African American voters, but he rarely consulted black leaders and repeatedly avoided opportunities to associate with them in public. Many of the southerners he appointed to his cabinet were uncompromising racists who systematically began segregating the employees in their agencies even though the agencies had been integrated for over fifty years. Federal offices were segregated by race, as were toilets, drinking fountains, and areas for work breaks. When black leaders protested these actions, Wilson replied that such racial segregation was intended to eliminate "the possibility of friction."

PROGRESSIVE RESURGENCE   The need to weld a winning political coalition in 1916 pushed Wilson back onto the road of reform. Progressive Democrats were restless, and after war broke out in Europe in August 1914, further divisions arose over defense preparedness and foreign policy. At the same time the Republicans were repairing their own rift, as the "Bull Moose" Progressive party showed little staying power in the midterm elections and Roosevelt showed little will to preserve it. Wilson could gain reelection only by courting progressives of all parties. In 1916 the president scored points with them when he nominated Louis D. Brandeis to the Supreme Court. Conservatives waged a vigorous battle against Brandeis, but Senate progressives rallied to win confirmation of the social-justice champion, the first Jewish member of the Court.

Meanwhile, Wilson began to promote a broad program of farm and labor reforms. The agricultural sector continued to suffer from a shortage of capital. To address the problem, Wilson supported a proposal to set up special rural banks to sponsor long-term farm loans. The Federal Farm Loan Act became law in 1916. Under the control of the Federal Farm Loan

Board, twelve Federal Land banks paralleled the regional Federal Reserve banks and offered farmers loans of five to forty years' duration at low interest rates.

Thus the dream of federal loans to farmers, sponsored by a generation of Alliance members and Populists, finally came to fruition. Democrats had never embraced the Populist subtreasury plan, but they made a small step in that direction with the Warehouse Act of 1916. This measure authorized federal licensing of private warehouses, and federal backing made their receipts for stored produce more acceptable as collateral for short-term bank loans to farmers. Other concessions to farm demands came in the Smith-Lever Act of 1914 and the Smith-Hughes Act of 1917, both of which passed with little controversy. The first provided federal grants-in-aid for farm-demonstration agents under the supervision of land-grant colleges: agents fanned out to educate farmers about new equipment and new ideas related to agricultural efficiency. The second measure extended agricultural and mechanical education to high schools, also through grants-in-aid.

Farmers with the newfangled automobiles had more than a passing interest as well in the Federal Highways Act of 1916, which provided dollar-matching contributions to states with highway departments that met certain federal standards. The measure authorized the distribution of $75 million over five years and marked a sharp departure from Jacksonian opposition to internal improvements at federal expense, just as the Federal Reserve System departed from Jacksonian banking principles. Although the argument that highways were one of the nation's defense needs had weakened constitutional scruples against the act, it still restricted support to "post roads" used for the delivery of mail. A renewal act in 1921 would mark the beginning of a systematic network of numbered U.S. highways.

The progressive resurgence of 1916 broke the logjam on workplace reforms as well. Advocates of child-labor legislation persuaded Wilson that social-justice progressives would regard his stand on the issue an important test of his humanitarian concerns. Wilson thus overcame doubts about its constitutionality to support and sign the Keating-Owen Act, which excluded from interstate commerce goods manufactured by children under the age of fourteen. Both the Keating-Owen Act and a later act of 1919 that achieved the same purpose with a prohibitory tax were ruled unconstitutional by the Supreme Court on the grounds that regulation of interstate commerce could not extend to the conditions of labor. Effective action against child labor abuses had to await the New Deal of the 1930s.

Another important accomplishment was the eight-hour workday for railroad workers, a measure that the Supreme Court upheld. The Adamson Act of 1916 was brought about by a threatened strike of railroad unions demanding an eight-hour workday and other concessions. Wilson, who objected to some of the demands, nevertheless went before Congress to request action on the hours limitation. The resulting Adamson Act required an eight-hour work-day, with time and a half for overtime, and appointed a commission to study the problem of working conditions in the railroad industry.

In Wilson's first term, progressivism reached its zenith. The president and his supporters had conquered the old dictum that the government is best that governs least. From two decades of ferment (three if the Populist years are counted), the great contribution of progressive politics was the firm establishment and general acceptance of the public-service concept of government.

LIMITS OF PROGRESSIVISM

The Progressive Era was an optimistic age in which all sorts of reformers assumed that no problem lay beyond solution. But like all great historic movements, progressivism displayed elements of paradox and irony. Despite its talk of greater democracy, it was the age of disenfranchisement for southern blacks—an action seen ironically by many whites as progressive. The first two decades of the twentieth century also witnessed a new round of anti-immigrant prejudice. The initiative and referendum, supposedly democratic reforms, proved subject to manipulation by well-financed publicity campaigns. And much of the public policy of the time came to be formulated by experts and members of appointed boards, not by broad segments of the population. There is a fine irony in the fact that the drive to increase the political role of ordinary people paralleled efforts to strengthen executive leadership and exalt government expertise. This "progressive" age of efficiency and bureaucracy, in business as well as government, brought into being a society in which more and more of the decisions affecting people's lives were made by unelected policy makers.

Progressivism was largely a middle-class movement in which the poor and unorganized had little influence. The supreme irony was that a movement so dedicated to the rhetoric of democracy should experience so steady a decline in voter participation. In 1912, the year of Roosevelt's Bull Moose campaign, voting dropped off by between 6 and 7 percent. The new politics of issues and charismatic leaders proved to be less effective in turning out voters than traditional party organizations and bosses had been. And by 1916 the optimism of an age that looked to infinite progress was already confronted by a vast slaughter. Europe had stumbled into a horrific war, and America would soon be drawn in. The twentieth century, which dawned with such bright hopes, held in store episodes of unparalleled brutality and holocaust.

End of Chapter Review

CHAPTER SUMMARY

- **Progressivism** Progressives believed that industrialization and urbanization were negatively affecting American life. They were middle-class idealists in both political parties who sought reform and regulation in order to ensure social justice. Many progressives wished to curb the powers of local political machines and establish honest and efficient government. They also called for an end to child labor, laws promoting safety in the workplace, a ban on the sale of alcoholic beverages, legislation curbing trusts, and women's suffrage.

- **Muckrakers** Theodore Roosevelt named the journalists whose works exposed social ills "muckrakers." New inexpensive popular magazines, such as *McClure's*, published articles about municipal corruption, horrendous conditions in meatpacking plants and urban slums, and predatory business practices. By raising public awareness of these issues, muckrakers contributed to major changes in the workplace and in governance.

- **Square Deal Program** President Roosevelt used his executive position to promote his progressive Square Deal program, which included regulating trusts, arbitrating the 1902 coal strike, regulating the railroads, and cleaning up the meat and drug industries. President Taft continued to bust trusts and reform the tariff, but Republican party bosses, reflecting their big business interests, ensured that the tariff reductions were too few to satisfy the progressives in the party. Roosevelt decided to seek the Republican presidential nomination in 1912 because of progressives' disillusionment with Taft.

- **Presidential Election of 1912** In 1912, after the Republicans renominated Taft, Roosevelt's supporters bolted the convention, formed the Progressive party, and nominated Roosevelt. Although some Democratic progressives supported Roosevelt, the split in the Republican party led to Woodrow Wilson's success. Having won a majority in both houses of Congress as well as the presidential election, the Democrats effectively held national power for the first time since the Civil War.

- **Wilsonian Progressivism** Although Wilson was a progressive, his approach was different from Roosevelt's. His New Freedom program promised less federal intervention in business and a return to such traditional Democratic policies as a low tariff. Wilson began a rigorous anti-trust program and oversaw the establishment of the Federal Reserve System. He opposed federal programs promoting social justice and initially withheld support for federal regulation of child labor and a constitutional amendment guaranteeing women's suffrage. A southerner, he believed blacks were inferior and supported segregation.

CHRONOLOGY

1902	Theodore Roosevelt attempts to arbitrate the coal strike
1902	Justice Department breaks up Northern Securities Company
1903	Congress passes the Elkins Act
1906	Upton Sinclair's *The Jungle* is published
1906	Congress passes the Meat Inspection Act and the Pure Food and Drug Act
1908	Supreme Court issues *Muller v. Oregon* decision
1909	William Taft is inaugurated president
1910	Congress passes the Mann-Elkins Act
1911	Triangle Shirtwaist Company fire
1913	Congress passes the Federal Reserve Act
1914	Congress passes the Clayton Anti-Trust Act
1916	Louis Brandeis is nominated to fill a seat on the Supreme Court

KEY TERMS & NAMES

25

AMERICA AND
THE GREAT WAR

FOCUS QUESTIONS

 wwnorton.com/studyspace

- Why did Woodrow Wilson involve the United States in Mexico's affairs?
- What were the causes of World War I in Europe?
- Why did the United States enter the Great War in Europe?
- How did Wilson promote his peace plan?
- Why did the United States fail to ratify the Treaty of Versailles?
- What were the consequences of the war at home and abroad?

Throughout the nineteenth century the United States reaped the benefits of its distance from the wars that plagued Europe. The Atlantic Ocean provided a welcome buffer. During the early twentieth century, however, the nation's comfortable isolation ended. Ever-expanding world trade entwined American interests with the fate of Europe. In addition, the development of steam-powered ships and submarines meant that foreign navies could threaten American security. At the same time, the election of Woodrow Wilson in 1912 brought to the White House a stern and often self-righteous moralist determined to impose his standards for right conduct on renegade nations. This combination of circumstances made the outbreak of war in Europe in 1914 a profound crisis for the United States, a crisis that would transform the nation's role in international affairs.

WILSON AND FOREIGN AFFAIRS

Woodrow Wilson had no experience or expertise in international relations. The former college professor admitted before taking office, "It would be an irony of fate if my administration had to deal chiefly with foreign affairs." But events in Latin America and Europe were to make the irony all too real. From the summer of 1914, when a catastrophic world war erupted in Europe, foreign relations increasingly overshadowed all else, including Wilson's ambitious domestic program.

AN IDEALIST'S DIPLOMACY   Although devoid of international experience, Wilson did not lack ideas or convictions about global issues. He saw himself as a man of providential destiny who would help create a new world order governed by morality and idealism rather than selfish national interests. Both Wilson and Secretary of State William Jennings Bryan believed that America had a religious duty to advance democracy around the world. As Wilson had declared a few years before becoming president, "Every nation of the world needs to be drawn into the tutelage of America." Wilson and Bryan thus developed a diplomatic policy based on pious idealism. During 1913 and 1914, Bryan negotiated some thirty "cooling-off" treaties, under which participating nations pledged not to go to war over any disagreement for a period of twelve months pending discussion by an international arbitration panel. The treaties were of little consequence, however. They were soon forgotten in the revolutionary sweep of world events that would make the twentieth century the bloodiest in recorded history.

INTERVENTION IN MEXICO   Mexico, which had been in the throes of revolutions for nearly three years, presented a thorny problem for Wilson soon after he took office in 1913. Between 1876 and 1910, Porfirio Díaz had dominated Mexico as military dictator. But in 1910 popular resentment boiled over into revolt. Revolutionary armies occupied Mexico City, and in 1911, Díaz fled.

The leader of the rebellion, a progressive reformer named Francisco Madero, proved to be tragically naive; he was unable to manage the tough adversaries attracted by the scramble for power. In 1913, Madero's chief of staff, General Victoriano Huerta, assumed power, and his henchmen murdered Madero soon afterward. President Wilson refused to recognize any government that used force to gain power: "We hold . . . that just government rests upon the consent of the governed." Official recognition by the U.S. government, formerly extended routinely to governments that exercised de facto power, now would depend upon judgments of their legality; an immoral government would not pass muster.

Wilson expressed sympathy with the revolutionary movement in Mexico and put diplomatic pressure on the "desperate brute" Huerta. Early in 1914 he removed an arms embargo against Mexico in order to help an insurgent faction under Venustiano Carranza of the Constitutionalist party. He also stationed U.S. warships off Veracruz to halt arms shipments to Huerta. "I am going to teach the South American republics to elect good men," Wilson vowed to a British diplomat. On April 9, 1914, several American sailors gathering supplies in Tampico, Mexico, strayed into a restricted area and were arrested. Mexican officials quickly released them and apologized to the U.S. naval commander. There the incident might have ended, but the pompous naval officer demanded that the Mexicans salute the American flag. Wilson backed him up and won from Congress authority to use force to bring Huerta to terms. William Borah, a Republican senator from Idaho, was one of many outraged legislators who demanded retribution from the Mexicans and implied that the United States was prepared to take control of Mexico and Central America. "If the flag of the United States is ever run up in Mexico," he declared, "it will never come down. This is the beginning of the march of the United States to the Panama Canal!" Before the Tampico incident could be resolved, Wilson sent some 6,000 U.S. marines and sailors ashore at Veracruz on April 21, 1914. They occupied the city at a cost of 19 American lives; at least 200 Mexicans were killed.

The military intervention in Mexico by the United States played out like many such interventions in the Caribbean and Central America. The public and the Congress readily endorsed the decision to send troops because the cause was just and American firepower and virtue were assumed to be superior, but the complex realities of U.S. troops fighting in a foreign country eventually led to a prolonged stay and public disillusionment. Wilson assumed the Mexican people would welcome the Americans as liberators. Instead, the American occupation of Veracruz aroused the opposition of all factions against the Yankee imperialists, and Huerta rallied support against a foreign invasion. At this juncture, Wilson accepted an offer of mediation by the ABC (Argentina, Brazil, and Chile) powers, which proposed the withdrawal of U.S. forces, the removal of Huerta, and the installation of a provisional government sympathetic to democratic reforms. Huerta refused to step down, but the moral effect of the proposal and the growing strength of his foes soon forced him to leave office. The Carranzistas entered Mexico

"Pancho" Villa

Villa (center) and his followers rebelled against the president of Mexico and antagonized the United States with attacks against "gringos."

City, and the American troops left Veracruz in late 1914. A year later the
United States and several Latin American governments recognized Carranza
as president of Mexico.

Still the troubles south of the border continued. Bickering among various
Mexican factions erupted in chaotic civil war. The prolonged upheaval
spawned independent gangs of bandits, Francisco "Pancho" Villa's among
the wildest. All through 1915 the forces of Villa and the forces of Carranza
attacked each other, killing thousands and committing numerous atrocities.
In 1916 the charismatic Villa and his men seized a train and murdered sixteen American mining engineers in a deliberate attempt to trigger U.S. intervention, discredit Carranza, and build himself up as an opponent of
the "gringos." That failing, he crossed the border on raids into Texas and
New Mexico. On March 9 he audaciously entered Columbus, New Mexico,
burned the town, and killed seventeen Americans.

A furious Woodrow Wilson abandoned his policy of "watchful waiting."
With the reluctant consent of Carranza, he sent General John J. Pershing across
the border with a force of 11,000 soldiers and mobilized 150,000 national
guardsmen. For nearly a year, Pershing's troops chased Villa through northern

Mexico. They had no luck and were ordered home in 1917. Carranza then pressed his own war against Villa and his bandits and in 1917 put through a new liberal constitution. Mexico was on its way to a more orderly government, in spite of Wilson's actions rather than because of them.

OTHER PROBLEMS IN LATIN AMERICA   In the Caribbean, Wilson found it as hard to act on his democratic ideals as it was in Mexico. The "dollar diplomacy" practiced by the Taft administration had encouraged American bankers to aid debt-plagued governments in Haiti, Guatemala, Honduras, and Nicaragua. Despite Wilson's public stand against using military force to back up American investments, he kept U.S. marines in Nicaragua, where they had been sent by President Taft in 1912 to prevent renewed civil war. Then, in 1915, he dispatched more marines to Haiti after that country experienced two successive revolutions and subsequent government disarray. The American troops stayed in Nicaragua until 1933 and in Haiti until 1934. Disorders in the Dominican Republic brought U.S. marines to that country in 1916; they remained until 1924. The repeated use of military force only exacerbated the hatred many Latin Americans felt toward the United States, then and since. As the *New York Times* charged, Wilson's frequent interventions made Taft's dollar diplomacy look like "ten cent diplomacy."

AN UNEASY NEUTRALITY

During the summer of 1914, problems in Latin America and the Caribbean, as well as family tragedy, loomed larger in Wilson's thinking than the gathering storm in Europe. During his first year as president, his wife, Ellen, had contracted kidney disease, and she died on August 6, 1914. President Wilson was devastated. "Oh, my God! What am I to do?" he exclaimed. His family doctor said the president is a "man with his heart torn out." Yet six months later the president fell in love with Edith Bolling Galt, a Washington widow, and in December 1915 they were married.

Ellen Wilson had died just as another tragedy was erupting overseas. When the thunderbolt of war struck Europe in the summer of 1914, most Americans, one North Carolinian wrote, saw it "as lightning out of a clear sky." Whatever the troubles in Mexico, whatever disorders and interventions agitated other countries, it seemed unreal that civilized Europe could descend into an orgy of destruction. At the beginning of the twentieth century, Europe had been peaceful and prosperous. No one imagined a new—and unnecessary—industrialized form of war erupting that would assume such horrible proportions and involve such unprecedented ruthlessness. Between 1914 and 1921 the war was directly responsible for the deaths of over 9 million combatants and the horrible wounding of 15 million more; it would produce at least 3 million widows and 6 million orphans. The war's sheer horror and destructiveness, its obscene butchery and ravaged landscapes, defied belief.

World War I erupted when an Austrian citizen of Serbian descent who wanted an independent Serbia assassinated the Austrian archduke Franz Ferdinand. Austria-Hungary's determination to punish Serbia for the murder led Russia to mobilize its army in sympathy with its Slavic friends in Serbia. That in turn triggered reactions by a European system of alliances: the Triple Alliance, or Central Powers (Germany, Austria-Hungary, and Italy), and the Triple Entente, or Allied Powers (France, Great Britain, and Russia). When Russia refused to stop its army's mobilization, Germany, which backed Austria-Hungary, declared war on Russia on August 1, 1914, and on Russia's ally France two days later. Germany then invaded Belgium to get at France, an action that brought Great Britain into the war on August 4. Japan, eager to seize German holdings in the Pacific, declared war on August 23, and Turkey entered on the side of the Central Powers in October. Although allied with the Central Powers, Italy initially stayed out of the war and then struck a bargain under which it joined the Allied Powers in 1915.

The First World War was unlike any previous conflict in its scope and carnage. Machine guns, high-velocity rifles, aerial bombing, poison gas, flame throwers, land mines, long-range artillery, and armored tanks changed the nature of warfare and produced horrific casualties and widespread destruction. The battlefields were surreal in their horrors. What began as a war of quick movement bogged down into a stalemated war of senseless attrition. During the Battle of Verdun, in northeast France, which lasted from February to December 1916, some 32 million artillery shells were fired—1,500 shells for every square meter of the battlefield. Such devastating firepower ravaged the landscape, turning farmland and forests into wasteland. The casualties were staggering. Some 162,000 French soldiers died at Verdun; German losses were 143,000.

Trench warfare gave the First World War its lasting character. Most of the great battles involved hundreds of thousands of men crawling out of their muddy, rat-infested trenches and crossing a no-man's-land to attack enemy positions, only to be pushed back a day or a week later. In addition to the dangers of enemy fire, soldiers on both sides were forced to deal with flooded trenches and terrible diseases such as trench fever and trench foot, which could lead to amputation. Lice and rats were constant companions.

Verdun

A landscape image from Verdun, taken immediately after the battle, shows how the firepower ravaged the land.

The stench was unbearable. Soldiers on both sides ate, slept, and fought among the dead and amid the reek of death.

INITIAL REACTIONS   As the trench war along the western front in Belgium and France stalemated, casualties soared and pressure for American intervention increased. On July 1, 1916, the first day of the Battle of the Somme, 20,000 British soldiers were killed and 40,000 others were wounded—in less than twenty-four hours. Shock in the United States over the devastating war in Europe gave way to gratitude that an ocean stood between America and the killing fields. "Our isolated position and freedom from entangling alliances," said the *Literary Digest,* ensure that "we are in no peril of being drawn into the European quarrel." President Wilson repeatedly urged the public to remain "neutral in thought as well as in action."

That was more easily said than done. More than a third of the nation's citizens were "hyphenated Americans," first- or second-generation immigrants who retained strong ties to their old country. Among the 13 million immigrants from the countries at war, German Americans were by far the largest group, numbering 8 million. And the 4 million Irish Americans harbored a deep-rooted enmity toward England. These groups instinctively leaned toward the Central Powers. But old-line Americans, largely of British origin, supported the Allied Powers. American leaders were pro-British from the outset of the war. Robert Lansing, first counselor of the State Department; Walter Hines Page, ambassador to London; and "Colonel" Edward House, Wilson's closest adviser— all saw in German militarism a potential danger to America.

A STRAINED NEUTRALITY

At first the war in Europe brought a slump in American exports and the threat of a depression, but by the spring of 1915 the Allies' demand for food and war supplies generated an economic boom. To finance their purchases of Ameri-

The Samson-like "War" pulls down the temple of "Civilization"

Most Americans tended to support the Allied Powers, but everyone was shocked by the carnage of the Great War.

can supplies, the Allies, especially Britain and France, needed loans. Early in the war, Secretary of State William Jennings Bryan, a strict pacifist, declared that loans to any warring nation were "inconsistent with the true spirit of neutrality." Yet Wilson quietly began approving short-term credit to sustain trade with the desperate Allies. When in the fall of 1915 it became apparent that the Allies could no longer carry on without long-term credit, Wilson removed all restrictions, and American investors would eventually advance over $2 billion to the Allies before the United States entered the war, and only $27 million to Germany.

The administration nevertheless clung to neutrality through two and a half years of warfare in Europe and tried to uphold the traditions of "freedom of the seas," which had guided American policy since the Napoleonic Wars of the early nineteenth century. As the German army's advance through Belgium toward Paris bogged down into the stalemate of trench warfare, transatlantic trade with the United States assumed a new importance. In a war of attrition, survival depended upon access to supplies, and in such a war British naval power counted for a great deal.

WORLD WAR I IN EUROPE, 1914

- Central Powers (Triple Alliance)
- Allied Powers (Triple Entente)
- Neutral countries

How did the European system of alliances spread conflict across all of Europe? How was World War I different from previous wars? How did the war in Europe lead to ethnic tensions in the United States?

On August 6, 1914, Secretary of State Bryan called upon the belligerents to accept the Declaration of London, drafted and signed in 1909 by leading powers but never ratified by the British. That document reduced the list of contraband (war-related) trade items and specified that a blockade was legal only when effective just outside an enemy port. The Central Powers promptly accepted the declaration. The British almost as promptly refused to, lest they lose some of their advantage in sea power. Britain gradually extended the list of contraband goods to include all sorts of items formerly excluded, such as food, cotton, wood, and certain ores. In November 1914 the British declared the whole North Sea a war zone, sowed it with mines, and ordered neutral ships to submit to searches. In March 1915 they announced that they would seize ships carrying goods to Germany. American protests were ignored.

NEUTRAL RIGHTS AND SUBMARINES   British actions, including blacklisting American companies that traded with the enemy and censoring the mail, raised old issues of neutral rights, but the German reaction introduced an entirely new question. With the German fleet bottled up by the British blockade, the German government proclaimed a war zone around the British Isles. Enemy merchant ships in those waters would be attacked by submarines, the Germans declared, and "it may not always be possible to save crews and passengers." As the chief advantage of U-boat (*Unterseeboot*) warfare was in surprise, the German decision violated the established procedure of stopping an enemy vessel and providing for the safety of passengers and crew before sinking it. Since the British sometimes flew neutral flags as a ruse, neutral ships in this war zone would also be in danger.

The United States pronounced the new German submarine policy "an indefensible violation of neutral rights" and warned that Germany would be

The *Lusitania*

Americans were outraged when a German torpedo sank the *Lusitania* on May 7, 1915.

held to "strict accountability" for any destruction of American lives and property. Then, on May 7, 1915, a German submarine sank a huge ocean-liner moving slowly through the Irish Sea. Only as it tipped into the waves was the German commander able to make out the name *Lusitania* on the stern. Before that ship had left New York, bound for Liverpool, the German embassy had published warnings in the American press against travel to the war zone, but 128 Americans were nonetheless among the 1,198 persons lost.

Americans were outraged. The sinking of the *Lusitania* was an act of piracy, Theodore Roosevelt declared. To quiet the uproar, Wilson urged patience: "There is such a thing as a man being too proud to fight. There is such a thing as a nation being so right that it does not need to convince others by force that it is right." Wilson immediately knew he had misspoken. Critics lambasted his lame response to the deaths of 128 Americans. "I have a bad habit of thinking out loud," he confessed to a friend the day after his "too proud to fight" speech. The language, he admitted, had "occurred to me while I was speaking, and I let it out. I should have kept it in." But his previous demand for "strict accountability" forced him to make a stronger response. On May 13, Secretary of State Bryan reluctantly signed a note demanding that the Germans abandon unrestricted submarine warfare and pay reparations for the sinking of the *Lusitania*. The Germans responded that the ship was armed (which it was not) and secretly carried a cargo of rifles and ammunition (which it did). A second note, on June 9, repeated American demands in stronger terms. The United States, Wilson asserted, was "contending for nothing less high and sacred than the rights of humanity." Bryan, unwilling to risk war over the issue, resigned in protest. He groused to Wilson that Colonel House "has been [acting as] secretary of state, not I, and I have never had your full confidence." Edith Galt, not yet Wilson's wife, took great delight in Bryan's resignation. "Hurrah! Old Bryan

Stand by the president

In this 1915 cartoon, Woodrow Wilson holds to the middle course between the pacifism of Bryan (whose sign reads, "Let Us Avoid Unnecessary Risks") and the belligerence of Roosevelt (whose sign reads, "Let Us Act without Unnecessary Delay").

is out!" she told the president. "I could shout and sing that at last the world will *know* just what he is." Bryan's successor, Robert Lansing, signed the note to the Germans.

In response to the uproar over the *Lusitania,* the German government had secretly ordered U-boat captains to avoid sinking large passenger vessels. When, despite the order, two American lives were lost in the sinking of the New York–bound British liner *Arabic,* the Germans paid an indemnity and offered a public assurance on September 1, 1915: "Liners will not be sunk by our submarines without warning and without safety of the lives of non-combatants, provided that the liners do not try to escape or offer resistance." With this so-called Arabic Pledge, Wilson's resolute stand seemed to have resulted in a victory for his policy.

During early 1916, Wilson's trusted adviser Colonel House visited London, Paris, and Berlin in an effort to negotiate an end to the war but found neither side ready to begin serious negotiations. On March 24, 1916, a U-boat torpedoed the French steamer *Sussex,* injuring two Americans. When Wilson threatened to break off relations, Germany renewed its pledge that U-boats would not torpedo merchant and passenger ships. This Sussex Pledge implied the virtual abandonment of submarine warfare.

THE DEBATE OVER PREPAREDNESS   The *Lusitania* incident and, more generally, the quarrels over neutral commerce contributed to a growing demand in the United States for a stronger army and navy. On December 1, 1914, champions of preparedness organized the National Security League to promote their cause. After the *Lusitania* sinking, Wilson asked the War and Navy Departments to draft proposals for military expansion.

Progressives and pacifists, however, as well as many residents of the rural South and West, were opposed to a defense buildup. Their anti-war sentiments tapped into the traditional American suspicion of military establishments, especially of standing armies, which dated back to the colonial period. The new Democratic leader in the House spoke for many Americans when he declared his opposition to "the big Navy and big Army program of the jingoes and war traffickers." The administration's plan to enlarge the regular army and create a national reserve force of 400,000 ran into such stubborn opposition in Congress that Wilson was forced to accept a compromise between advocates of an expanded force under federal control and advocates of a traditional citizen army. The National Defense Act of 1916 expanded the regular federal army from 90,000 to 175,000 and permitted gradual enlargement to 223,000. It also increased the National Guard to 440,000, made provision for training, and gave federal funds for summer training camps for civilians.

The bill for an increased navy aroused less opposition because of the general feeling expressed by the navy secretary that there was "no danger of militarism from a relatively strong navy such as would come from a big standing army." The Naval Construction Act of 1916 authorized between $500 million and $600 million for a three-year expansion program.

Forced to relent on military preparedness, opponents of a buildup insisted that the financial burden should rest upon the wealthy people they held responsible for promoting the military expansion and profiting from trade with the Allies. The income tax became their weapon. Supported by a groundswell of popular support, legislators wrote into the Revenue Act of 1916 changes that doubled the basic income tax rate from 1 to 2 percent, lifted the surtax to a maximum of 13 percent (for a total of 15 percent) on income over $2 million, added an estate tax, levied a 12.5 percent tax on gross receipts of munitions makers, and added a new tax on excess corporate profits. The new taxes amounted to the most clear-cut victory for radical progressives in the entire Wilson period, a victory further consolidated and advanced after America entered the war. It was the capstone to the progressive legislation that Wilson supported in preparation for the upcoming presidential election.

THE ELECTION OF 1916   As the 1916 election approached, Republicans hoped to regain their normal electoral majority, and Theodore Roosevelt hoped to be their leader again. But he had committed the deadly sin of bolting his party in 1912. His eagerness for the United States to enter the war also scared many voters. Needing somebody who would draw Bull Moose Progressives back into the fold, the Republican regulars turned to Supreme Court Justice Charles Evans Hughes, who had a progressive record as governor of New York from 1907 to 1910. The remnants of the Progressive party gathered in Chicago at the same time as the Republicans. Roosevelt had held out the vain hope of getting both nominations, but he now declined to lead a third party. Two weeks later the Progressive National Committee disbanded the party and endorsed Hughes.

The Democrats, as expected, chose Woodrow Wilson again. Their platform endorsed a program of social-welfare legislation and prudent military preparedness. The party referred the idea of women's suffrage to the states and pledged support for a postwar league of nations to enforce peace with collective-security measures against aggressors. The Democrats' most popular issue, however, was an insistent pledge to keep the nation out of the war in Europe. The peace theme, refined in the slogan "He kept us out of war," became the rallying cry of the Wilson campaign.

Peace with honor

Woodrow Wilson's policies of neutrality proved popular in the 1916 campaign.

The candidates in the 1916 presidential election were remarkably similar. Both Wilson and Hughes were the sons of preachers; both were attorneys and former professors; both had been progressive governors; both were known for their pristine integrity. Theodore Roosevelt highlighted the similarities between them when he called the bearded Hughes a "whiskered Wilson." Wilson, however, proved to be the better campaigner. In the end, his twin pledges to keep America out of war and promote progressivism brought a narrow victory. The final vote showed a Democratic sweep of the Far West and the South, enough for narrow victories in the Electoral College, by 277 to 254, and in the popular vote, by 9 million to 8.5 million.

LAST EFFORTS FOR PEACE   Immediately after the election, Wilson again offered to mediate an end to the war in Europe, but neither side was willing to abandon its major war aims. Wilson then made one more appeal, in the hope that public opinion would force the hands of the warring governments. Speaking before the Senate on January 22, 1917, he asserted the right of the United States to propose a lasting peace, which would have to be a "peace without victory," for only a "peace among equals" could endure. Wilson's peace plan would be based upon the principles of democratic government, freedom of the seas, and disarmament, and those ideals must be enforced by an international league for peace established to make another such catastrophe impossible.

Although Wilson did not know it, he was already too late. Exactly two weeks before he spoke, impatient German military leaders had decided to wage unrestricted submarine warfare on Allied shipping. They took the calculated risk of arousing American anger in the hope of scoring a quick knockout. On January 31 the new policy was announced, effective the next day. All vessels would be sunk without warning. "Freedom of the seas," said the *Brooklyn Eagle*, "will now be enjoyed [only] by icebergs and fish."

On February 3, 1917, Wilson told a joint session of Congress that the United States had broken diplomatic relations with the German government. Three weeks later he asked for authority to arm merchant ships and "to employ any other instrumentalities or methods" necessary and "to protect our ships and our people." There was little quarrel with arming merchant ships, but there was bitter opposition to Wilson's vague reference to "any other instrumentalities or methods." A group of eleven or twelve die-hard noninterventionists in Congress filibustered the measure until the legislative session expired on March 4. A furious Wilson decided to outflank Congress. On March 12 the State Department announced that a forgotten law of 1792 allowed the arming of merchant ships regardless of congressional inaction.

On February 25, Wilson learned that the British had intercepted an important message from the German foreign minister Arthur Zimmermann to his ambassador in Mexico. The note offered an alliance and financial aid to Mexico in case of war between the United States and Germany. In return for attacking the United States, Mexico would recover "the lost territory in Texas, New Mexico, and Arizona." On March 1, news of the Zimmermann telegram broke in the American press and infuriated the public. Then, later in March 1917, on the other side of the world, a revolution overthrew Russia's czarist government and established the provisional government of a Russian republic. The fall of the czarist autocracy gave Americans the illusion that all the major Allied powers were now fighting for constitutional democracy—an illusion that was shattered in November 1917, when the Bolsheviks, led by Vladimir Lenin, seized power in Russia and established a Communist dictatorship.

AMERICA'S ENTRY INTO THE WAR

In March 1917, German submarines sank five U.S. merchant vessels in the North Atlantic. On April 2, Wilson asked Congress to recognize that imperial Germany and the United States were at war. He insisted that "the world must be made safe for democracy." The war resolution passed the Senate by a vote of 82 to 6 on April 4. The House concurred, 373 to 50, and Wilson signed the measure on April 6, 1917.

How had matters come to this less than three years after Wilson's proclamation of neutrality? Prominent among the various explanations of America's entrance into the war were the effects of British propaganda in the United States and America's deep involvement in trade with the Allies, which some observers credited to the intrigues of war profiteers and munitions makers. Some proponents of war thought German domination of Europe would be a threat to American security, especially if it meant the destruction of the British navy. Such factors, however, would not have been decisive without the issue of submarine warfare. Once Wilson had taken a stand for the traditional rights of neutral nations and noncombatants on the high seas, he was to some extent at the mercy of decisions by the German high command.

AMERICA'S EARLY ROLE War had been declared, but the scope of America's role in the European conflict remained unclear. Few on either side of the Atlantic expected more than a token U.S. military effort. Despite Congress's preparedness measures, the army remained small and untested. The navy also was largely undeveloped. The Americans made two important contributions to Allied naval strategy, however. Merchant ships had previously survived submarine attacks by means of speed and evasive action. Now, Rear Admiral William S. Sims, commander of American ships in European waters, persuaded the Allies to adopt a system of escorting merchant ships in convoy groups. The result was a sharp decrease in Allied shipping losses. As its second contribution, the U.S. Navy laid a gigantic minefield across the North Sea, limiting U-boat access to the North Atlantic.

Within a month of the declaration of war in April 1917, British and French officials arrived in the United States. They first requested money for buying more American supplies, a request Congress had anticipated in the Liberty Loan Act, which added $5 billion to the national debt in "liberty bonds." Of this amount, $3 billion could be lent to the Allied Powers. The United States was also willing to furnish naval support, financial credits, supplies, and munitions. But to recruit and train a large army, equip it, and send it across a submarine-infested ocean seemed out of the question. The French nevertheless insisted that the United States send a token military force to bolster morale, and on June 26, 1917, the first contingent of U.S. soldiers, about 14,500 men commanded by the mediocre general John J. Pershing, disembarked on the

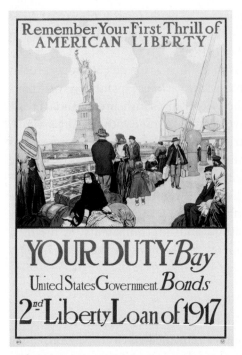

The thrill of American liberty

This Liberty Loan poster urges immigrants to do their duty for their new country by buying government bonds.

French coast. Pershing and his troops reached Paris by July 4. Pershing soon advised the War Department to send 1 million American troops by the following spring. It was done—but only through strenuous efforts.

When the United States entered the war, the combined strength of the regular army and National Guard was only 379,000; at the end it would be 3.7 million. The need for such large numbers of troops forced Wilson to implement a military draft. Under the Selective Service Act of 1917, all men aged twenty-one to thirty (later, eighteen to forty-five) could be drafted for military service. All told, about 2 million American troops crossed the Atlantic, and about 1.4 million saw at least some combat.

MOBILIZING A NATION   One of the most obvious effects of American entry into the war was a dramatic increase in the size and power of the federal government. Complete economic mobilization on the home front was necessary to conduct the war efficiently. The Army Appropriation Act of 1916 had created a Council of National Defense, which in turn led to the creation of other wartime agencies. The Lever Food and Fuel Control Act of 1917 created a Food Administration, headed by Herbert Hoover, a future president, who sought to raise agricultural production while reducing civilian consumption of foodstuffs. "Food will win the war" was the slogan. Hoover directed a conservation campaign promoting "meatless Tuesdays," "wheatless Wednesdays," "porkless Saturdays," the planting of victory gardens, and the creative use of leftovers.

The War Industries Board (WIB), established in 1917, soon became the most important of all the mobilization agencies. It was headed by Bernard Baruch, a brilliant financier who exercised a virtual dictatorship over the economy. Under Baruch the purchasing bureaus of the United States and Allied governments submitted their needs to the board, which set priorities and issued production quotas to industries. The board could allocate raw materials, tell manufacturers what to produce, order construction of new plants, and with the approval of the president, fix prices. Despite such efforts, however, the unprecedented mobilization effort was often chaotic. Men were drafted only to discover there were no uniforms, weapons, or housing for them. Most of the artillery used by the American army in France had to be acquired from the Allies.

A NEW LABOR FORCE   The closing off of foreign immigration and the movement of 4 million men from the workforce into the armed services created a labor shortage. To meet it, women, African Americans, and other ethnic minorities were encouraged to enter industries and engage in agricultural activities heretofore dominated by white men. Northern businesses sent recruiting agents into the Deep South to find workers for their factories and mills, and over 400,000 southern blacks began the Great Migration northward during the war years, a mass movement that continued unabated through the 1920s and changed the political and social dynamics of northern cities. Mexican Americans followed the same migratory pattern. Recruiting agents and newspaper editors portrayed the North as the "land of promise" for southern blacks suffering from their region's depressed agricultural economy and rising racial intimidation and violence. The African American *Chicago Defender* exclaimed: "To die from the bite of frost is far more glorious than at the hands of a mob." By 1930 the number of African Americans living in the North was triple that of 1910.

But the newcomers were not always welcomed above the Mason-Dixon line. Many white workers resented the new arrivals, and racial tensions sparked clashes across the country. In 1917 over forty African Americans and nine whites were killed during a riot over employment in a defense plant in East St. Louis, Illinois. Two years later the toll of a Chicago race riot was nearly as high, with twenty-three African Americans and fifteen whites left dead. In these and other incidents of racial violence, the pattern was the same: whites angered by the influx of southern blacks into their communities would seize upon an incident as an excuse to rampage through black neighborhoods, killing, burning, and looting while white policemen looked the other way or encouraged the hooliganism.

For women, intervention in World War I had more positive effects. Initially women supported the war effort in traditional ways. They helped organize war-bond and war-relief drives, conserved foodstuffs and war-related materials, supported the Red Cross, and joined the army nurse corps. But as

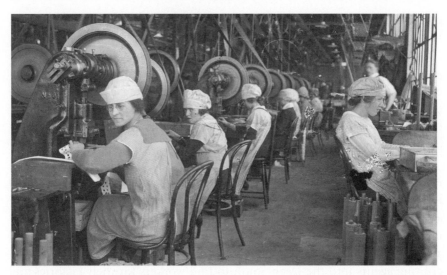

Women aid the war effort

Women working at the Bloomfield International Fuse Company, New Jersey, 1918.

the scope of the war widened, both government and industry sought to mobilize women workers for service on farms, loading docks, and railway crews, as well as in the armaments industry, machine shops, steel and lumber mills, and chemical plants. Many women leaders saw such opportunities as a breakthrough. "At last, after centuries of disabilities and discrimination," said a speaker at a Women's Trade Union League meeting in 1917, "women are coming into the labor [force] and festival of life on equal terms with men."

In fact, however, war-generated changes in female employment were limited and brief. About 1 million women participated in "war work," but most of them were young and single and already working outside the home. Most returned to their previous jobs once the war ended. In fact, male-dominated unions encouraged women to revert to their stereotypical domestic roles after the war ended. The Central Federated Union of New York insisted that "the same patriotism which induced women to enter industry during the war should induce them to vacate their positions after the war." The anticipated gains of women in the workforce failed to materialize. In 1920 the 8.5 million working women made up a smaller percentage of the labor force than had working women in 1910. Still, one lasting result of women's contributions to the war effort was Woodrow Wilson's decision to endorse women's suffrage. In the fall of 1918, he told the Senate that giving women the vote was "vital to the winning of the war."

WAR PROPAGANDA   The war effort led the government to mobilize more than economic life: the progressive gospel of efficiency suggested mobilizing public opinion as well. On April 14, 1917, eight days after the declaration of war, President Wilson established the Committee on Public Information, composed of the secretaries of state, war, and the navy. Its executive head, George Creel, a Denver newsman, sold Wilson on the idea that the best approach to influencing public opinion was propaganda instead of censorship. Creel organized a propaganda machine to convey the Allies' war aims to the people and, above all, to the enemy, where it might help sap their morale. To sell the war, Creel gathered a remarkable group of journalists, photographers, artists, entertainers, and others useful to his purpose. A film division produced such pictures as *The Beast of Berlin*. Hardly any public group escaped a harangue by one of the 75,000 "four-minute men" organized to give short speeches on liberty bonds, the need to conserve food and fuel, and other timely topics.

The Beast of Berlin

A scene from the movie *The Beast of Berlin*, which gave audiences a propagandistic view of World War I.

CIVIL LIBERTIES   By arousing public opinion to such a frenzy, the war effort spawned grotesque campaigns of "Americanism" and witch-hunting. Wilson had foreseen these consequences. "Once lead this people into war," he said, "and they'll forget there ever was such a thing as tolerance." Popular prejudice equated anything German with disloyalty. Symphonies refused to perform Bach and Beethoven, schools dropped courses in the German language, and patriots translated *sauerkraut* into "liberty cabbage," *German measles* into "liberty measles," and *dachshunds* into "liberty pups."

Under the Espionage and Sedition Acts, Congress suppressed criticism of government leaders and war policies. The Espionage Act of 1917 imposed penalties of up to $10,000 and twenty years in prison for anyone who gave aid to the enemy; who tried to incite insubordination, disloyalty, or refusal of duty in the armed services; or who sought to interfere with the war effort. The Sedition Act of 1918 extended the penalties to those who did or said anything to obstruct the government sale of war bonds or to advocate cutbacks in production, and—just in case something had been overlooked—for saying, writing, or printing anything "disloyal, profane, scurrilous, or abusive" about the American form of government, the Constitution, or the army and navy.

The Espionage and Sedition Acts generated more than 1,000 convictions. Socialists and other radicals were the primary targets. Victor Berger, a Socialist congressman from Milwaukee, received a twenty-year sentence for editorials in the Milwaukee *Leader* that called the war a capitalist conspiracy. Eugene V. Debs, who had polled over 900,000 votes for president in 1912, repeatedly urged men to refuse to serve in the military, even though he knew he could be prosecuted for such remarks under the Espionage Act. "I would a thousand times rather be a free soul in jail than a sycophant and a coward in the streets," he told a Socialist gathering in 1918. He received his wish. Debs was arrested and given a ten-year prison sentence for encouraging draft resistance. In 1920, still in jail, he polled nearly 1 million votes for president.

In two important decisions just after the war, the Supreme Court upheld the Espionage and Sedition Acts. *Schenck v. United States* (1919) reaffirmed the conviction of a man for circulating anti-draft leaflets among members of the armed forces. In this case, Justice Oliver Wendell Holmes said, "Free speech would not protect a man in falsely shouting fire in a theater, and causing a panic." The act applied where there was "a clear and present danger" that speech in wartime might create evils Congress had a right to prevent. In *Abrams v. United States* (1919), the Court upheld the conviction of a man who circulated pamphlets opposing American intervention in Russia to oust the Bolsheviks. Here, Holmes and Louis Brandeis dissented from the majority view. The "surreptitious publishing of a silly leaflet by an unknown man," they argued, posed no danger to government policy.

AMERICA AT WAR

American troops played little more than a token role in the European fighting until early 1918. Before that they were parceled out in quiet sectors mainly for training purposes. All through 1917 the Allied armies remained on the defensive, and late in the year their situation turned desperate. In October the Italian lines collapsed and were overrun by Austrian forces. With the help of troops from France, the Italians finally held their ground. In November the Bolshevik Revolution overthrew the infant Russian republic, and the new government dropped out of the war. With the Central Powers victorious over Russia, they were free to concentrate their forces on the western front. The American war effort thus became a "race for France," to restore the balance of strength. The French premier Georges Clemenceau appealed to the Americans to accelerate their mobilization. "A terrible blow is imminent," he predicted to a journalist. "Tell your Americans to come quickly."

Fighting on the western front

A gun crew firing on entrenched German positions, 1918.

THE WESTERN FRONT   On March 21, 1918, Clemenceau's prediction came true when the Germans began the first of several offensives in France and Belgium to try to end the war before the Americans arrived in force. By May 1918 there were 1 million fresh but untested and undertrained U.S. troops in Europe, and for the first time they made a difference. During the first week in June, a marine brigade blocked the Germans at Belleau Wood, and army troops took Vaux and opposed the Germans at Château-Thierry. Though these relatively modest actions had limited military significance, their effect on Allied morale was significant.

The turning point in France came on July 15, 1918, in the Second Battle of the Marne. On both sides of Reims, the Germans assaulted the French lines. Within three days, however, they had stalled, and soon the British, French, and Americans began to roll the German front back into Belgium. Then, on August 10, the U.S. First Army attacked the Germans at St.-Mihiel, southeast of Verdun. There, on September 12, an army of more than 500,000 staged the first strictly American offensive of the war. Within three days the out-numbered Germans had pulled back. The great Meuse-Argonne offensive, begun on September 26, then employed American divisions in a drive toward

The Meuse-Argonne offensive

U.S. soldiers fire an artillery gun in Argonne, France.

**WORLD WAR I,
THE WESTERN FRONT, 1918**

--- Western front, March 1918

— German offensive, spring 1918

→ Allied counteroffensive

— Western front, November 1918

Why was the war on the western front a stalemate for most of World War I? What was the effect of the arrival of the American troops? Why was the Second Battle of the Marne the turning point of the war?

Sedan and its railroad, which supplied the entire German front. The largest American action of the war, it involved 1.2 million U.S. troops and resulted in 117,000 American casualties, including 26,000 dead. But along the entire front from Sedan to Flanders, the Germans were in retreat. "America," wrote German general Erich Ludendorff, "thus became the decisive power in the war."

American casualties

A Salvation Army worker writing a letter home for a wounded soldier.

THE BOLSHEVIKS When the war broke out in 1914, Russia was one of the Allied Powers. Over the next three years the Russians suffered some 6.6 million casualties. By 1917 there were shortages of ammunition for the Russian troops and food for the Russian people. The czarist government was in disarray. After the czar's abdication the new provisional republican government succumbed, in November 1917, to a revolution led by Vladimir Lenin and his Bolshevik party, who promised war-weary Russians "peace, land, and bread."

The Bolsheviks were a small but determined sect of ruthless ideologues, convinced that they were in the irresistible vanguard of historical change as described by Karl Marx. They found themselves in the right place at the right time—a backward country devastated by prolonged war, besieged by invading armies, and burdened by a mediocre government. As Lenin observed, power was lying in the streets, waiting to be picked up. Once in control of the government, the Bolsheviks unilaterally stopped fighting in World War I. With German troops deep in Russian territory and armies of "White" Russians (anti-Bolsheviks) organizing resistance to their power, the Bolsheviks concluded a separate peace with Germany, the Treaty of Brest-Litovsk, on March 3, 1918. To prevent military supplies from falling into German hands and encourage anti-Bolshevik forces in the developing Russian Civil War, President Wilson sent American forces into Russia's Arctic ports. Troops were also sent to eastern Siberia, where they remained until April 1920 in an effort to curb growing Japanese ambitions there. The Allied intervention in Russia failed because the Bolsheviks were able to consolidate their power. Russia took no further part in World War I and did not participate in the peace settlement. The failed Allied intervention largely served to generate among Soviets a long-lasting suspicion of the West.

THE FOURTEEN POINTS As the conflict in Europe was ending, neither the Allies nor the Central Powers, despite Wilson's prodding, had stated openly what they hoped to gain from the fighting. Wilson repeated that the Americans had no selfish war aims. "We desire no conquest, no dominion," he stressed in his war message of 1917. "We seek no indemnities for ourselves, no material compensation for the sacrifices we shall freely make. We are but one of the champions of the rights of mankind." Unfortunately for his idealistic purpose, after the Bolsheviks seized power in Russia in 1917, they published copies of secret treaties in which the British and French had promised territorial gains in order to win Italy, Romania, and Greece to their side. When an Interallied Conference in Paris late in 1917 failed to agree on a statement of war aims, Colonel House advised Wilson to formulate his own.

During 1917 a group of American experts, called the Inquiry, began formulating plans for peace. With advice from these experts, Wilson himself developed what would come to be called the Fourteen Points. These he presented to a joint session of Congress on January 8, 1918, "as the only possible program" for peace. The first five points called for open diplomacy rather than secret treaties, freedom of the seas, removal of trade barriers, reduction of armaments, and an impartial adjustment of the victors' colonial claims based upon the desires of the populations involved. Most of the remaining points dealt with territorial claims: they called on the Central Powers to evacuate occupied lands and to allow political self-determination for various nationalities, a crucial principle for Wilson. Point 13 proposed an independent Poland with access to the sea. Point 14, the capstone in Wilson's thinking, called for the creation of a "league" of nations to protect global peace. When the Fourteen Points were made public, African American leaders asked the president to add a fifteenth point: an end to racial discrimination. Wilson did not respond.

The Fourteen Points embodied Wilson's sincere commitments, but they also served the purpose of psychological warfare. One of their aims was to keep Russia in the war by stating a more liberal purpose—a vain hope, as it turned out. Another was to reassure the citizens of the Allied Powers that they were involved in a noble cause. A third was to drive a wedge between the governments of the Central Powers and their people by offering a reasonable peace.

On October 3 a new German chancellor made the overtures for peace on the basis of the Fourteen Points. The Allies accepted the Fourteen Points as a basis of negotiations, but with two significant reservations: the British insisted on the right to discuss limiting freedom of the seas, and the French demanded reparations for war damages.

Meanwhile the German home front was being torn apart by a loss of morale, culminating in a naval mutiny at Kiel. Germany's allies dropped out of the

Allied victory

Celebration of the armistice ending World War I, New York City, November 1918.

war: Bulgaria on September 29, 1918, Turkey on October 30, and Austria-Hungary on November 3. On November 9 the kaiser abdicated, and a German republic was proclaimed. On November 11 at 5 A.M., an armistice was signed. Six hours later, at the eleventh hour of the eleventh day of the eleventh month, the guns fell silent. Under the armistice the Germans had to evacuate occupied territories, pull their troops back behind the Rhine River, and surrender their naval fleet and railroad equipment. The Germans were assured that Wilson's Fourteen Points would be the basis for the peace conference.

During its nineteenth months of participation in the Great War, the United States saw 126,000 of its servicemen killed. Germany's war dead totaled over 2 million, including civilians; France lost nearly 1.4 million combatants, Great Britain lost 703,000 soldiers, and Russia lost 1.7 million. The new Europe emerging from the carnage would be much different: more violent, more polarized, more cynical, less sure of itself, and less capable of decisive action. The United States, for good or ill, would be sucked into the vacuum of power created by the destructiveness of the Great War.

THE FIGHT FOR THE PEACE

DOMESTIC UNREST Woodrow Wilson made a fateful decision to attend the peace conference that convened in Paris on January 18, 1919. It shattered all precedent for a president to leave the country for so long. Because no U.S. president had ever before traveled abroad while in office, Wilson's decision dramatized all the more his messianic vision and his desire for a lasting peace. From one viewpoint it was a shrewd move, for his prestige and determination made a difference at the Paris peace talks. But during his prolonged trip abroad he lost touch with political developments at home. His progressive political coalition was already unraveling under the pressures of wartime discontent. Western farmers complained about the government's control of wheat prices while southern cotton producers rode the wartime inflation. Eastern businessmen chafed at federal revenue policies designed, according to the *New York Sun*, "to pay for the war out of taxes raised north of the Mason and Dixon Line." Organized labor, despite manifest gains during the war, was unhappy with inflation and the problems of reconversion to a peacetime economy.

In the midterm elections of 1918, Wilson defied his advisers and urged voters to elect a Democratic Congress to support his foreign policies. Republicans, who for the most part had supported Wilson's war measures, now took affront. In elections held on November 5, a week before the armistice, the Democrats lost control of both houses of Congress. With an opposition majority in the new Congress, Wilson further weakened his standing by failing to appoint a prominent Republican to the staff of peace commissioners. Former president Taft groused that Wilson's real intention in going to Paris was "to hog the whole show."

When Wilson reached Paris in December 1918, enthusiastic demonstrations greeted him. The cheering millions saw in the American idealist a prophet of peace and a spokesman for humanity. Their heartfelt support no doubt strengthened his hand at the conference, but Wilson had to deal with some tough-minded statesmen who did not share his utopian zeal.

The Paris Peace Conference lasted from January to June 1919. It included delegates from all countries that had declared war or broken diplomatic relations with Germany. It was controlled by the Big Four: the prime ministers of Britain, France, and Italy and the president of the United States. Japan restricted its interests to Asia and the Pacific. French premier Georges Clemenceau was a stern realist who had little patience with Wilson's utopianism. "God gave us the Ten Commandments and we broke them," Clemenceau sneered. "Wilson gave us the Fourteen Points—we shall see." The French insisted on harsh provisions in the peace treaty to weaken Germany. So did the British prime minister David Lloyd George. He had campaigned on the slogan, "Hang the kaiser." Vittorio Orlando, prime minister of Italy, focused his efforts on picking up the spoils promised in the secret 1915 Treaty of London, in which the Allies had promised Italy the Austrian province of Dalmatia in exchange for its entry into the war.

The Paris Peace Conference

Woodrow Wilson (second from left) with Georges Clemenceau of France (center) and Arthur Balfour of Great Britain (second from right) during the Paris Peace Conference in 1919.

THE LEAGUE OF NATIONS As the negotiations began, Woodrow Wilson insisted that his cherished League of Nations come first in the treaty making. Whatever compromises he might have to make regarding territorial boundaries and financial claims, whatever mistakes might result, Wilson believed that a league of nations committed to collective security would ensure international stability. Wilson presided over the commission set up to draft its charter. Article X of the charter, which Wilson called "the heart of the League," pledged member nations to impose military and economic sanctions against aggressors. The use of armed force would be a last (and an improbable) resort. The League, it was assumed, would exercise enormous moral influence, making military action unnecessary. Its structure would allow each member an equal voice in the Assembly; the Big Five (Britain, France, Italy, Japan, and the United States) and four other nations would make up the executive Council; the administrative staff, with headquarters in Geneva, Switzerland, would make up the Secretariat; and a Permanent Court of International Justice (set up in 1921 and usually called the World Court) could "hear and determine any dispute of an international character."

On February 14, 1919, Wilson presented the finished draft of the League covenant to the Allies and departed Paris for a visit home. Already he faced opposition. Wilson's proposed League of Nations, Theodore Roosevelt grumbled, would revive German militarism and undermine American morale. "To substitute internationalism for nationalism," the former president argued, "means to do away with patriotism." Roosevelt's close friend and fellow Republican Henry Cabot Lodge, powerful chairman of the Senate Foreign Relations Committee, also scorned Wilson's naive idealism. He announced that the League's covenant was unacceptable. Lodge's statement bore the signatures of thirty-nine Republican senators or senators-elect, more than enough to block ratification.

"The League of Nations Argument in a Nutshell"

Jay N. "Ding" Darling's summation of the League controversy.

TERRITORY AND REPARATIONS   Back in Paris in the spring of 1919, Wilson grudgingly acceded to French demands for territorial concessions and reparations payments by Germany that would keep it weak. Yet the petulant and vain Wilson clashed sharply with the French premier Clemenceau, and after the American president threatened to leave the conference, they decided that the Rhineland (up to thirty-one miles beyond the Rhine River) would be a "demilitarized" zone for fifteen years. France could also exploit Germany's Saar coal mines for fifteen years, after which the region's residents would vote to determine their national allegiance.

In other territorial matters, Wilson had to compromise his principle of national self-determination. As a result of the Great War, four long-standing multinational empires had disintegrated: the Russian, Austro-Hungarian, German, and Ottoman (Turkish). Hundreds of millions of people had to be reorganized into new nations. There was in fact no way to make Europe's boundaries correspond to its tangled ethnic groupings. The folk wanderings of centuries had left mixed populations scattered throughout Central Europe. In some areas, moreover, national self-determination yielded to other interests: the Polish Corridor, for instance, gave Poland its much-needed outlet to the sea through German territory, and the South Tyrol, home to some 200,000 German-speaking Austrians, gave Italy a more defensible northern frontier at the Brenner Pass. One part of the Austro-Hungarian Empire became Czechoslovakia, which included the German-speaking Sudetenland, an area favored with good natural defenses. Another part united with Serbia to create the kingdom of Yugoslavia. Still other substantial parts of the former empire passed to Poland (Galicia), Romania (Transylvania), and Italy (Trentino–Alto Adige and Trieste). All in all, the new boundaries more nearly followed the ethnic divisions of Europe than had the prewar lines.

The discussion of reparations (payments by the vanquished to the victors) triggered the most bitter exchanges at the conference. Despite a pre-armistice agreement that Germany would be liable only for civilian damages, Clemenceau and Lloyd George proposed reparations for the entire financial cost of the war, including the payment of veterans' pensions. On this point, Wilson made perhaps his most fateful concessions. He accepted a clause in the treaty in which Germany confessed responsibility for the war and thus took responsibility for its entire expense. The "war guilt" clause offended Germans and made for persistent bitterness.

On May 7, 1919, the victorious powers presented the treaty to the German delegates, who returned three weeks later with 443 pages of criticism. A few changes were made, but when the Germans still refused to sign, the French prepared to move their army across the Rhine River. Finally, on June 28, 1919, the Germans gave up and signed the treaty in the Hall of Mirrors at Versailles.

WILSON'S LOSS AT HOME   On July 8, 1919, Woodrow Wilson returned home with the Versailles Treaty amid a great clamor of popular support. A third of the state legislatures had endorsed the League of Nations, as had thirty-three of the nation's forty-eight governors. Two days later Wilson called upon the Senate to accept "this great duty." With typical disdain, he dismissed critics of the League as "blind and little provincial people."

Yet Senator Henry Cabot Lodge denounced the Versailles Treaty's foolish "scheme of making mankind suddenly virtuous by a statute or a written constitution." Wilson, thought Lodge, was too filled with prophetic certitude, too prone to promise more than he could deliver when great principles entailed great sacrifices. A staunch Republican with an intense dislike for

EUROPE AFTER THE TREATY OF VERSAILLES, 1918

- ········ 1914 boundaries
- New nations
- Plebiscite areas
- Occupied area

Why was self-determination difficult for states in Central Europe? How did territorial concessions weaken Germany? Why might territorial changes like the creation of the Polish Corridor or the concession of the Sudetenland to Czechoslovakia have created problems that would surface in the future?

Wilson, Lodge sharpened his partisan knives. He knew the undercurrents already stirring up opposition to the treaty: the resentment of German, Italian, and Irish groups in the United States, the disappointment of liberals with Wilson's compromises on reparations and territories, the distractions of demobilization and the resulting domestic problems of converting quickly to a peacetime economy, and the revival of isolationism. Some Republicans claimed that Wilson's preoccupation with his cherished League of Nations revealed that he really wanted to be president of the world.

Others agreed. In the Senate a group of "irreconcilables," fourteen Republicans and two Democrats, refused to join the League of Nations on any terms. They were mainly western and midwestern progressives who feared that such sweeping foreign commitments threatened domestic reforms. The irreconcilables would be useful to Lodge's purpose, but he belonged to a larger group, "reservationists," who insisted upon limiting American participation in the League. Wilson pointed out to them that the League Council included veto power; the United States could not be obligated to do anything against its will. Lodge proposed a set of amendments—his reservations. Wilson responded by agreeing to interpretive reservations but to nothing that would reopen the negotiations in Europe. He especially opposed weakening Article X of the League covenant, which provided for collective action against aggression.

By September 1919, with momentum for the treaty slackening, Wilson decided to go to the people and, as he put it, "purify the wells of public opinion." Against the advice of doctors and friends, he set forth on a grueling railroad tour through the Midwest to the West Coast. In all he traveled 8,000 miles in twenty-two days, giving thirty-two major speeches. For a while, Wilson seemed to be regaining the initiative, but on October 2, 1919, he suffered a severe stroke that left him paralyzed on his left side and an invalid for the rest of his life. For seventeen months his protective wife, Edith, kept him isolated from all but the most essential business. Wilson's disability intensified his stubbornness. He might have done better to secure the best compromise possible, but now he refused to yield and continued to be needlessly confrontational. As he scoffed to an aide, "Let Lodge compromise." The president's hardened arteries seemed to have hardened his outlook.

Lodge strove to amend the Versailles Treaty before it was ratified. The Senate adopted fourteen of his reservations, most having to do with the League of Nations. Wilson especially opposed the revision of Article X, which, he said, "does not provide for ratification but, rather, for the nullification of the treaty." As a result, his supporters found themselves thrown into an unlikely combination with the irreconcilables, who opposed the treaty under any circumstances. The Senate vote on the revised treaty was 39 for and 55 against. On the question of approving the original treaty without reservations, irreconcilables and reservationists combined to defeat ratification again, with 38 for and 53 against.

In the face of public reaction, however, the Senate voted to reconsider. But the stricken Wilson remained adamant: "Either we should enter the League fearlessly, accepting with responsibility and not fearing the role of leadership which we now enjoy, contributing our efforts toward establishing a just and permanent peace, or we should retire as gracefully as possible from the great concert of powers by which the world was saved." On March 19, 1920, twenty-one Democrats deserted the intransigent Wilson and joined the reservationists, but the treaty once again fell short of a required two-thirds majority. In the end, the real winner was the smallest of the three groups in the Senate, neither the Wilsonians nor the reservationists but the irreconcilables.

When Congress declared the war at an end by a joint resolution on May 20, 1920, Wilson vetoed the action; it was not until July 2, 1921, after he had left office, that a joint congressional resolution ended the state of war with Germany and Austria-Hungary. Peace treaties with Germany, Austria, and Hungary were ratified on October 18, 1921, but by then Warren G. Harding was president of the United States.

LURCHING FROM WAR TO PEACE

The Versailles Treaty, for all the time it spent in the Senate, was but one issue clamoring for public attention in the turbulent period after the war. The year 1919 began with ecstatic victory parades that soon gave way to widespread labor unrest, race riots, domestic terror, and government tyranny. Demobilization of the armed forces and war industries proceeded in haphazard fashion. The sudden cancellation of war-related contracts left workers and business leaders to cope with reconversion to a peacetime economy on their own. Wilson's leadership was missing. He had been preoccupied by the war and the League, and once bedridden by the stroke, he became grim and peevish. His administration floundered through its last two years.

THE SPANISH FLU   Amid the confusion of postwar life, many Americans confronted a virulent menace that produced far more casualties than the war itself. It became known as the Spanish flu, and its contagion spread around the globe. Erupting in the spring of 1918 and lasting a year, the pandemic killed more than 22 million people worldwide, twice as many as died in World War I. In the United States alone it accounted for 675,000 deaths, nearly seven times the number of American combat deaths in France.

Americans returning from France brought the flu with them, and it raced through the congested army camps and naval bases. Some 43,000 servicemen died of influenza in 1918. By September the epidemic had spread to the civilian population. In that month alone 10,000 Americans died from the

Influenza epidemic

Office workers wearing gauze masks during the Spanish flu epidemic of 1918.

disease. "Nobody seemed to know what the disease was, where it came from or how to stop it," observed the editors of *Science* magazine in 1919. In Philadelphia, 528 people were buried in a single day. Life-insurance companies nearly went bankrupt, hospitals were besieged, and cemeteries ran out of burial space.

By the spring of 1919, the pandemic had finally run its course. It ended as suddenly—and as inexplicably—as it had begun. Although another outbreak occurred in the winter of 1920, the population had grown more resistant to its assaults. No plague, war, famine, or natural catastrophe in world history killed so many people in such a short time.

THE ECONOMIC TRANSITION   Disease was only one of many challenges confronting postwar America. Consumer prices continued to rise after the war, and discontented workers, released from wartime constraints, were more willing to strike for their demands. In 1919 more than 4 million workers went on strike in thousands of disputes with management. Some workers in the East won their demands early in the year, but after a general strike in Seattle, public opinion began to turn against labor's demands. Seattle's mayor denounced the walkout of 60,000 workers as evidence of Bolshevik influence. The strike lasted only five days, but public alarm over the affair damaged the cause of unions across the country.

An American Federation of Labor campaign to organize steelworkers suffered from charges of radicalism against its leader, William Z. Foster, who had joined the Socialists in 1900 and later emerged as a Communist. The focus on

Foster's radicalism obscured the squalid conditions and long hours that had marked the steel industry since the Homestead strike of 1892: the twelve-hour day, often combined with a seven-day week, was common. On September 22, 1919, after U.S. Steel refused to talk, some 340,000 workers walked out. When information about working conditions became widely known, public opinion turned in favor of the steelworkers, but too late: the strike had ended after four months. Steelworkers remained unorganized until the 1930s.

The most celebrated postwar labor dispute was the Boston police strike. Though less significant than the steel strike in the numbers involved, it inadvertently launched a presidential career. On September 9, 1919, most of Boston's police force went out on strike. Massachusetts governor Calvin Coolidge was furious; he mobilized the National Guard to keep order, and after four days the police strikers offered to return, but the commissioner refused to take them back. When labor leader Samuel Gompers appealed for their reinstatement, Coolidge responded in words that suddenly turned him into a national figure: "There is no right to strike against the public safety by anybody, anywhere, any time."

RACIAL FRICTION   The summer of 1919 also sparked a season of deadly race riots across the nation. What the African American leader James Weldon Johnson called the Red Summer (*red* here signifying blood) began in July, when whites invaded the black section of Longview, Texas, in search of a teacher who had allegedly accused a white woman of dating a black man. They burned shops and houses and ran several African Americans out of town. A week later in Washington, D.C., reports of black assaults on white women aroused white mobs, and for four days gangs of white and black rioters waged a race war in the streets until soldiers and driving rains ended the fighting. These were but preliminaries to the Chicago riot of late July, in which 38 people were killed and 537 injured. The

Domestic unrest

A victim of racial rioting in Chicago, July 1919.

climactic disorders of the summer occurred in the rural area around Elaine, Arkansas, where African American tenant farmers tried to organize a union. According to official reports, 5 whites and 25 blacks died in the rioting, but the death toll may have actually included more than 100 blacks. Altogether, twenty-five race riots erupted in 1919, and there were eighty racial lynchings.

THE RED SCARE   Public reaction to the wave of labor strikes and race riots reflected the impact of the Bolshevik Revolution. Some radicals thought America's domestic turbulence, like that in Russia, was the first scene in a drama of world revolution. Many Americans decided that they might be right. After all, a tiny faction in Russia, the Bolsheviks, had exploited confusion to impose its will over a huge nation. In 1919 left-wing members of the Socialist party formed the Communist party (U.S.A.) and the short-lived Communist Labor party. Wartime hysteria against all things German was readily transformed into a postwar Red Scare against Communists.

Fears of revolution in America were fueled by the actions of militants. In April 1919 the post office intercepted nearly forty homemade letter bombs addressed to prominent citizens. One slipped through and blew off the hands of a Georgia senator's maid. In June another bomb destroyed the front of Attorney General A. Mitchell Palmer's house in Washington. The explosion killed the terrorist and almost killed Palmer. Although the bombings were probably the work of a small group of Italian anarchists, the attorney general and many other Americans concluded that a well-organized Communist terror campaign was "sweeping over every American institution of law and order."

Soon the government organized witch hunts. In 1919 the Justice Department decided to deport radical aliens, and Attorney General Palmer appointed the young J. Edgar Hoover to collect files on radicals. Raids began on November 7, 1919, when federal agents swooped down on offices of the Union of Russian Workers in twelve cities. On December 22 the transport ship *Buford*, dubbed the Soviet ark, left New York for Finland with 249 passengers, including assorted anarchists and criminals. All were deported to Russia without a court hearing. On January 2, 1920, police raids in dozens of cities swept up some 5,000 suspects, many taken from their homes without arrest warrants. That same month the New York State legislature expelled five duly elected Socialist members.

Basking in popular approval, Palmer continued to exaggerate the Red menace, but like other fads and alarms, the panic subsided. By the summer of 1920, the Red Scare had begun to evaporate. Communist revolutions in Europe died out, leaving Bolshevism isolated in Russia. Bombings in the United

States tapered off; the wave of strikes and race riots receded. The paranoid attorney general began to seem more threatening to civil liberties than the handful of radicals he uncovered. By September 1920, when a bomb explosion at the corner of Broad and Wall Streets in New York City killed thirty-eight people, Americans were ready to take it for what it was: the work of a crazed mind and not the start of a revolution. The Red Scare nonetheless left a lasting mark on American life. Part of its legacy was the continuing crusade for "100 percent Americanism" and restrictions on immigration. It left a stigma on labor unions and contributed to the anti-union open-shop campaign—the American plan, its sponsors called it. But for many Americans the chief residue of the Great War, President Wilson's physical collapse, and its disordered aftermath was a profound disillusionment that pervaded cultural life in the 1920s.

End of Chapter Review

CHAPTER SUMMARY

- **Wilson and Mexico** Woodrow Wilson wanted to foster democratic governments in Latin America; he got the United States involved in Mexican politics after Mexico experienced several military coups. The popular Pancho Villa tried to gain power in Mexico by promoting an anti-American program, even making raids across the border into New Mexico.

- **Causes of WWI** Europe had developed a system of alliances that divided the continent in two. Democratic Britain and France, along with the Russian Empire, had formed the Triple Entente. Central Powers were comprised of the new German Empire, Austria-Hungary, and Italy. The assassination of the heir to the Austro-Hungarian throne by a Serbian nationalist triggered the world war.

- **U.S. Enters WWI** Most Americans supported the Triple Entente, or Allied Powers, at the outbreak of World War I. The Wilson administration declared the nation neutral but allowed businesses to extend credit to the Allies to purchase food and military supplies. Americans were outraged by the Germans' use of unlimited submarine warfare, especially after the 1915 sinking of the British liner *Lusitania*. In 1917 unrestricted submarine activity and the revelation of the Zimmermann telegram, in which the Germans sought to incite the Mexicans to wage war against the United States, led the United States to enter the Great War.

- **Wilson's Peace Plan** Wilson insisted that the United States wanted no selfish gains from the war, only a new, democratic Europe to emerge from the old empires. His famous Fourteen Points speech outlined his ideas for the establishment of continent-wide democratic nation-states and a league of nations.

- **Treaty of Versailles** The United States did not ratify the Treaty of Versailles because Wilson had alienated the Republican senators whose support he needed for ratification. A coalition of "irreconcilables" formed in the Senate: midwestern and western progressives who feared that involvement in a league of nations would stifle domestic reforms and that ratification would necessitate involvement in future wars. The irreconcilables were joined by "reservationists," who would accept the treaty with certain limitations on America's involvement in the League of Nations. Wilson's illness and his refusal to compromise ensured failure of ratification.

- **Consequences of WWI** As a result of the war, four European empires were dismantled, replaced by smaller nation-states. The reparations imposed on Germany and the "war guilt" clause laid the foundations for German bitterness. The presence of a Communist regime in the old Russian Empire had major consequences in America.

CHRONOLOGY

1914	United States intervenes in Mexico
1914	World War I begins in Europe
1915	British liner *Lusitania*, with Americans aboard, is torpedoed without warning by a German submarine
1916	Congress passes the National Defense Act
March 1917	Zimmermann telegram reveals that Germany is attempting to incite Mexico to enter the war against the United States
April 1917	United States enters the Great War
January 1918	Woodrow Wilson delivers his Fourteen Points speech
November 11, 1918	Representatives of warring nations sign armistice
1919	Supreme Court issues *Schenck v. United States* decision
May 1919	Treaty of Versailles is presented to the Germans
1919	Race riots break out in Chicago
1919	U.S. attorney general launches Red Scare
July 1921	Joint resolution of Congress officially ends the war among the United States, Germany, and Austro-Hungary

KEY TERMS & NAMES

26

THE MODERN TEMPER

FOCUS QUESTIONS wwnorton.com/studyspace

- What accounted for the nativism of the 1920s?
- What was meant by the Jazz Age?
- How did the new social trends of the 1920s challenge traditional attitudes?
- What was modernism, and how did it influence American culture?

The horrors of World War I dealt a shattering blow to the widespread belief that Western civilization was progressing. The editors of *Presbyterian* magazine announced in 1919 that the "world has been convulsed" by the terrible war, and "every field of thought and action has been disturbed." The war's colossal carnage disillusioned young intellectuals and spurred a new "modernist" sensibility among artists and writers.

At once a mood and a movement, modernism appeared first in Europe at the end of the nineteenth century and had become a pervasive international force by 1920. It arose out of a widespread recognition that Western civilization had entered an era of bewildering change and disorienting upheavals. New technologies, new modes of transportation and communication, and new scientific discoveries such as quantum mechanics, relativity theory, and Freudian psychology combined to rupture traditional perceptions of reality, herald new ways of understanding human behavior and consciousness, and generate new forms of artistic expression. "One must never forget," declared

Gertrude Stein, the experimentalist poet, "that the reality of the twentieth century is not the reality of the nineteenth century, not at all." Modernism spawned an array of intellectual and artistic movements: impressionism, futurism, dadaism, surrealism, Freudianism. As the French painter Paul Gauguin acknowledged, the upheavals of modernism produced "an epoch of confusion."

Just as the war, with its turbulent aftermath, provided an accelerant for modernism, so it stimulated political and social radicalism. The postwar wave of strikes, bombings, anti-Communist hysteria, and race riots symbolized a frightening new era of turmoil and change that led many people to cling to old ideas and ways of life. Defenders of tradition located the germs of radicalism in the polyglot cities teeming with immigrants and foreign ideas. The reactionary mood of the 1920s fed on a growing tendency to connect American nationalism with nativism, Anglo-Saxon racism, and militant Protestantism. In sum, postwar American culture was fraught with contradictory impulses and seething tensions.

REACTION IN THE TWENTIES

NATIVISM   The foreign connections of so many political radicals strengthened the sense that the seeds of sedition were foreign-born. In the early 1920s over half of the white men and a third of the white women working in industry were immigrants, most of them from central or eastern Europe. That socialism and anarchism were popular in those regions made immigrant workers especially suspect in the eyes of "old stock" Americans.

The most celebrated criminal case of the times seemed to prove the connection between immigrants and radicalism. It involved two Italian immigrant anarchists: shoemaker Nicola Sacco and fish peddler Bartolomeo Vanzetti. They were arrested on May 5, 1920, for stealing $16,000 and killing a paymaster and his guard. Both were armed when arrested, both lied to police about their activities, and both were identified by eyewitnesses. The Sacco and Vanzetti case occurred at the height of Italian immigration to the United States and against the backdrop of numerous terror attacks by anarchists, including the 1920 bombing that killed thirty-eight people on Wall Street in New York City. At the trial of Sacco and Vanzetti the judge was openly prejudicial. He privately referred to the defendants as "anarchist bastards." Sacco and Vanzetti were convicted and ordered executed, but appeals of the verdict lasted seven years. People then and since claimed that Sacco

Sacco and Vanzetti

Painting from a series (1931–1932) by Ben Shahn.

and Vanzetti were sentenced for their political ideas and ethnic origin rather than for any crime they had committed. The case became a great radical and liberal cause célèbre of the 1920s, but despite public demonstrations around the world on behalf of the two men, the evidence convicting them was compelling; they were executed on August 23, 1927.

The surging postwar nativism generated new efforts to restrict immigration. The flow of immigrants, slowed by the war, rose again at its end. From June 1920 to June 1921, more than 800,000 immigrants entered the country, 65 percent of them from southern and eastern Europe, and more were on the way. An alarmed Congress passed the Emergency Immigration Act of 1921, which restricted European arrivals each year to 3 percent of the foreign-born of any nationality as shown in the 1910 census. The Immigration Act of 1924 reduced the number to 2 percent based on the 1890 census, which included fewer of the "new" immigrants from southern and eastern Europe. This law set a permanent limitation, which became effective in 1929, of slightly over 150,000 new arrivals per year based on the "national origins" of the U.S. population as of 1920. However inexact the quotas, their purpose was clear: to tilt the balance in favor of immigrants from northern and western Europe, who were assigned about 85 percent of the total. The law completely excluded people from east Asia—a gratuitous insult to the Japanese, who were already kept out of the United States by their Gentlemen's Agreement with Theodore Roosevelt.

On the other hand, the Immigration Act of 1924 left the gate open to new arrivals from Western Hemisphere countries, so that an ironic consequence was a substantial increase in the Hispanic Catholic population of the United States. Legal arrivals from Mexico peaked at 89,000 in 1924. Lower figures after that date reflect the Mexican government's policies of clamping down on the outflow. Waves of illegal immigrants continued to flow across the border, however, in response to southwestern agriculture's demand for "stoop" labor. People of Latin American descent (chiefly Mexicans, Puerto Ricans, and Cubans) became the fastest-growing ethnic minority in the country.

THE KLAN   During the postwar years the tradition of nativist prejudice against "foreigners" took on a new form: a revived Ku Klux Klan modeled on the vigilante group founded during Reconstruction. The new Klan was devoted to "100 percent Americanism" and restricted its membership to native-born white Protestants. It was determined to protect its warped notion of the American way of life not only from African Americans but also from Roman Catholics, Jews, and immigrants. The United States was no melting pot, the twentieth-century Klan's founder, William J. Simmons, warned: "It is a garbage can! . . . When the hordes of aliens walk to the ballot box and their votes outnumber yours, then that alien horde has got you by the throat." A habitual joiner and promoter of fraternal orders, Simmons had gathered a hooded group of bigots near Atlanta on Thanksgiving night 1915. There, "bathed in the sacred glow of

Klan rally

In 1925 the Ku Klux Klan staged a huge parade down Pennsylvania Avenue in Washington, D.C.

the fiery cross, the invisible empire was called from its slumber of half a century to take up a new task."

The revived Klan was no longer restricted to the South. Its appeal to bigotry thrived in small towns and cities in the North and especially in the Midwest. The robes, the flaming crosses, the eerie processionals, the kneeling recruits, the occult liturgies—all tapped a deep urge toward mystery and brought drama into the dreary routine of a thousand small communities. The Klan was a vicious reaction to shifting moral standards, the declining influence of churches, and the broad-mindedness of city dwellers and college students. Although the Klan was very successful at raising money and electing Klan-backed local politicians, it rarely succeeded in its goal of coercing African Americans and immigrants to leave its members' communities. In the mid-1920s the Klan's peak membership may have been as high as 4 million, but its influence evaporated after passage of the 1924 immigration law. The Klan also suffered from recurrent factional quarrels and schisms, and its willing use of violence tarnished its moral pretensions.

FUNDAMENTALISM   While the Klan saw a threat mainly in the "alien menace," many adherents of the old-time religion saw threats from modernism in the churhes: new ideas held that the Bible should be studied in the light of modern scholarship (the "higher criticism") or that it could be reconciled with biological theories of evolution. Such "modern" notions surfaced in schools and even pulpits. In resisting the inroads of modernism, orthodox Christians took on a militant new fundamentalism, which was distinguished less by a faith that many others shared than by a posture of hostility toward any other belief.

Among rural fundamentalist leaders only former secretary of state William Jennings Bryan had the following, prestige, and eloquence to make the movement a popular crusade. The aging Bryan continued to espouse a unique blend of progressive populism and religious fundamentalism. In 1921 Bryan promoted state laws to prohibit the teaching of evolution in the public schools. He denounced Charles Darwin with the same zeal he had once used in opposing William McKinley. "Evolution," he said, "by denying the need or possibility of spiritual regeneration, discourages all reforms, for reform is always based upon the regeneration of the individual." Anti-evolution bills emerged in legislatures, but the only victories came in the South—and there were few of those. Some officials took direct action without legislation. Governor Miriam "Ma" Ferguson of Texas outlawed textbooks upholding

Courtroom scene during the Scopes trial

The media, food vendors, and others flocked to Dayton, Tennessee, for the case against John Scopes, the teacher who taught evolution.

Darwinism. "I am a Christian mother," she declared, "and I am not going to let that kind of rot go into Texas schoolbooks."

The climax came in Tennessee, where in 1925 the state legislature passed a bill outlawing the teaching of evolution in public schools and colleges. The governor, unwilling to endanger a pending school program, signed the bill with the hope that it would probably never be applied. He was wrong. In Dayton, Tennessee, citizens persuaded a young high-school science teacher, John T. Scopes, to accept an offer from the American Civil Liberties Union to defend a test case—chiefly to put their town on the map. They succeeded beyond their wildest hopes: the publicity was worldwide and enduring. Before the opening of the twelve-day "monkey trial" on July 10, 1925, the streets of Dayton swarmed with publicity hounds, curiosity seekers, evangelists, atheists, hot-dog and soda-pop hucksters, and a miscellany of reporters.

The two stars of the show—William Jennings Bryan, who had offered his services to the prosecution, and Clarence Darrow, renowned trial lawyer of

Chicago and articulate agnostic—united at least in their determination to make the trial an exercise in public education. When the judge ruled out scientific testimony, however, the defense called Bryan as an expert witness on biblical interpretation. In his dialogue with Darrow, he repeatedly trapped himself in literal-minded interpretations and revealed his ignorance of biblical history and scholarship. He insisted that a "great fish" had swallowed Jonah and that Joshua had made the sun stand still—both, according to Darrow, "fool ideas that no intelligent Christian on earth believes." It was a bitter scene. At one point the two men, their patience exhausted in the broiling summer heat, lunged at each other, shaking their fists, prompting the judge to adjourn court.

At the end of the trial, the only issue before the court, the judge ruled, was whether Scopes had taught evolution, and no one denied that he had. He was found guilty, but the Tennessee Supreme Court, while upholding the state's anti-evolution statute, overruled the $100 fine on a technicality. The chief prosecutor accepted the higher court's advice against "prolonging the life of this bizarre case" and dropped the issue. With more prescience than he knew, Bryan had described the trial as a "duel to the death." Five days after it closed, he died of a heart condition aggravated by heat and fatigue.

PROHIBITION The reaction against new social attitudes took many forms. Prohibition of alcoholic beverages offered another example of reforming zeal channeled into a drive for moral righteousness and social conformity. Around 1900 the leading temperance organizations, the Women's Christian Temperance Union and the Anti-Saloon League, had launched a campaign for a national prohibition law. By the 1910s the Anti-Saloon League had become one of the most effective pressure groups in history, mobilizing Protestant churches behind its single-minded battle to elect "dry" candidates. Proponents of prohibition often displayed blatant ethnic and social prejudices. The head of the Anti-Saloon League castigated German Americans because they "eat like gluttons and drink like swine." For many anti-alcohol crusaders, the primary goal of eliminating alcoholic beverages seemed to be policing the behavior of the poor, the foreign-born, and the working class. One prohibitionist referred to Italian immigrants as "Dagos, who drink excessively [and] live in a state of filth."

At its Jubilee Convention in 1913, the league endorsed a prohibition amendment to the Constitution. The 1916 elections finally produced two-thirds majorities for prohibition in both houses of Congress. Soon the wartime spirit of sacrifice, the need to use grain for food rather than booze, and wartime hostility to German-American brewers transformed the cause of prohibition into a virtual test of patriotism. On December 18, 1917, Congress sent to the states the Eighteenth Amendment, which one year after ratification, on January 16, 1919, banned the manufacture, sale, and transportation of intoxicating liquors.

But the new amendment did not persuade people to stop drinking. Instead, it motivated them to use ingenious—and illegal—ways to satisfy their thirst for alcohol. Congress never supplied adequate enforcement, if such was indeed possible given the public thirst, the spotty support of local officials, and the profits to be made in bootlegging. In Detroit the liquor industry during the Prohibition era was second in size only to the auto industry. Speakeasies, hip flasks, and cocktail parties were among the social innovations of Prohibition, along with increased drinking by women. As the popular humorist Will Rogers quipped, "Prohibition is better than no liquor at all."

It would be too much to say that Prohibition gave rise to organized crime, but it supplied criminals with an enormous source of new income while the automobile and the submachine gun provided criminals greater mobility and firepower. Organized crime leaders showed remarkable gifts for exploiting loopholes in the law when they did not simply bribe policemen and politicians.

The most celebrated gangster was "Scarface" Al Capone. In 1927 his Chicago-based bootlegging, prostitution, and gambling empire brought him an income of $60 million, which he flaunted with expensive suits and silk pajamas, a custom-upholstered bulletproof Cadillac, an entourage of bodyguards,

Prohibition

A 1926 police raid on a speakeasy, where illegal "bootleg" liquor was sold.

and lavish support for city charities. Capone insisted that he was merely providing the public with the goods and services it demanded: "They say I violate the prohibition law. Who doesn't?" He neglected to say that he had also bludgeoned to death several police lieutenants and ordered the execution of dozens of his rival criminals. Law-enforcement officials led by Federal Bureau of Investigation agent Eliot Ness began to smash his bootlegging operations in 1929, but they were unable to pin anything on him until a Treasury agent infiltrated his gang and uncovered evidence that nailed him for tax evasion. Tried in 1931, Capone was sentenced to eleven years in prison.

THE ROARING TWENTIES

In many ways the reactionary temper of the 1920s and the repressive movements it spawned arose as reactions to a social and intellectual revolution that threatened to rip America from its old moorings. As described by various labels given to the times, it was an era of excess, the Jazz Age, and the Roaring Twenties. During those years a cosmopolitan urban America confronted an insular, rural America, and cultural conflict reached new levels of tension.

Leading young urban intellectuals disdained the old-fashioned rural and small-town values of the hinterlands. Sinclair Lewis's novel *Main Street* (1920), for example, portrayed the stifling, mean, cramped life of a prairie town, depicting a "savorless people, gulping tasteless food, and sitting afterward, coatless and thoughtless, in rocking chairs prickly with inane decorations, listening to mechanical music, saying mechanical things about the excellence of Ford automobiles, and viewing themselves as the greatest race in the world." The Baltimore journalist H. L. Mencken was the most merciless in his attacks on the "booboisie." The daily panorama of America, he wrote, had become "so inordinately gross and preposterous . . . that only a man who was born with a petrified diaphragm can fail to laugh himself to sleep every night, and to awake every morning with all the eager, unflagging expectation of a Sunday-school superintendent touring the Paris peep-shows." The hinterlands responded to such criticism of rural folkways with images of cities infested with vice, crime, corruption, and foreigners.

THE JAZZ AGE   The writer F. Scott Fitzgerald dubbed the postwar era the Jazz Age because daring young people were willing to experiment with new forms of recreation and sexuality. The new music bubbling to the surface in New Orleans, Kansas City, Memphis, New York City, and Chicago

Frankie "Half Pint" Jackson and his band at the Sunset Cafe, Chicago, in the 1920s
Jazz emerged in the 1920s as an especially American expression of the modernist spirit. African American artists bent musical conventions to give fuller rein to improvisation and sensuality.

blended African and European traditions to form a distinctive sound. The syncopated rhythms of jazz were immensely popular among rebellious young adults and helped create carefree new dance steps such as the Charleston and the black bottom, whose gyrations shocked guardians of morality.

THE NEW MORALITY   Much of the shock to old-timers during the Jazz Age came from the revolution in manners and morals, evidenced first among young people, and especially on college campuses. In *This Side of Paradise* (1920), a novel of student life at Princeton, F. Scott Fitzgerald wrote of "the great current American phenomenon, the 'petting party.'" None of the Victorian mothers, he said, "had any idea how casually their daughters were accustomed to be kissed." From such novels and from magazine pieces, the heartland learned about the wild parties, bathtub gin, promiscuity, speakeasies, "shimmy dancers," and new uses to which automobiles were put on secluded lovers' lanes.

Writers also informed the nation about the "new woman" eager to exercise new freedoms. These independent women discarded corsets and sported bobbed hair, heavy makeup, and skirts above the ankle; they smoked cigarettes

The "new woman" of the 1920s

Two flappers dance atop the Hotel Sherman in Chicago, 1926.

and drank beer, drove automobiles, and in general defied Victorian expectations of feminine behavior.

Sex came to be discussed with a new frankness during the 1920s. Much of the talk derived from a spreading awareness of Dr. Sigmund Freud, the Viennese father of psychoanalysis. When in 1909 Freud visited Clark University in Massachusetts, he was surprised to find himself so well known "even in prudish America." By the 1920s, his ideas had begun to percolate among the public, and books and magazines discussed libido, inhibitions, Oedipus complexes, and repression.

Fashion also reflected the rebellion against prudishness and a loosening of inhibitions. In 1919 women's skirts were typically six inches above the ground; by 1927 they were at the knee, and the "flapper" was providing a shocking model of the new feminism. The name derived from the way fashionable young women allowed their galoshes to flap around their ankles. Conservative moralists saw the flappers as just another sign of a degenerating society. Others saw in the "new women" an expression of American individualism. "By sheer force of violence," explained the *New York Times* in 1929, the flapper has "established the feminine right to equal representation in such hitherto masculine fields of endeavor as smoking and drinking, swearing, petting, and upsetting the community peace."

MARGARET SANGER AND BIRTH CONTROL   Perhaps the most controversial women's issue of the Jazz Age was birth control. Margaret Sanger, a New York nurse and midwife in the working-class tenements of Manhattan, saw many young mothers struggling to provide for their growing families. She also witnessed firsthand the consequences of unwanted pregnancies, tragic miscarriages, and amateur abortions. Sanger began to distribute birth-control information to working-class women in 1912 and resolved to spend the rest of her life helping women gain control of their bodies.

In 1921 Sanger organized the American Birth Control League, which in 1942 changed its name to Planned Parenthood. The Birth Control League distributed birth-control information to doctors, social workers, women's clubs, and the scientific community, as well as to thousands of women. In the 1920s, however, Sanger alienated supporters of birth control by endorsing sterilization for the mentally incompetent and for people with certain hereditary conditions. Birth control, she stressed, was "the most constructive and necessary of the means to racial health." In 1928 Sanger angrily resigned as president of the American

Margaret Sanger

The birth-control activist opened the nation's first family-planning clinic in Brooklyn in 1916.

Birth Control League over issues related to the eugenics movement and her own autocratic style of leadership. Although Sanger did not succeed in legalizing the distribution of contraceptives and contraceptive information through the mail, she had laid the foundation for such efforts. In 1936 a federal court ruled that physicians could prescribe contraceptives—a vital step in Sanger's efforts to realize her slogan, "Every child a wanted child."

THE WOMEN'S MOVEMENT   Federal voting rights for women arrived in 1920. The suffrage movement, which had been in the doldrums since 1896, sprang back to life in the second decade of the new century. In 1912, Alice Paul, a Quaker social worker, returned from an apprenticeship with the militant suffragists of England and became head of the Congressional Committee of the National American Woman Suffrage Association (NAWSA). Paul instructed female activists to picket state legislatures, target and "punish" politicians who failed to endorse suffrage, chain themselves to public buildings, incite police to arrest them, and undertake hunger strikes. In 1913 Paul and Lucy Burns organized the Congressional Union for Woman Suffrage in an effort to gain a constitutional amendment to secure the right to vote for women. Four years later Paul helped form the National Woman's Party. She encouraged members to adopt many of the tactics used by British suffragists. By 1917 she and her followers were picketing the White House and deliberately provoking arrests, after which they went on hunger strikes in prison. The authorities cooperated in making martyrs; they arrested them by the hundreds.

For several years, President Woodrow Wilson had evaded the issue of an amendment, but he supported a plank in the 1916 Democratic platform encouraging states to allow women's suffrage. He also addressed NAWSA that year, which was once again headed by Carrie Chapman Catt, and thereafter worked closely with its leaders to promote voting rights for women.

The courageous proponents of women's suffrage put forth several arguments in favor of voting rights. Many assumed that the right to vote and hold office was a matter of simple justice: women were just as capable as men in exercising the rights and responsibilities of citizenship. Others insisted that women were morally superior to men and therefore would raise the quality of the political process by their participation in it. They also would be less prone to use warfare as a solution to international disputes and national differences. Women voters, advocates argued, would also promote the welfare of society rather than partisan or selfish gains. Allowing women to vote would create a great engine for progressive social change. One activist explicitly linked women's suffrage with the social gospel, declaring that women embraced Christ more readily than men and if they were elected to public office, they would "far more effectively guard the morals of society and the sanitary conditions of cities."

Yet the women's suffrage movement was not immune from the prevailing social, ethnic, and racial prejudices of the day. Carrie Chapman Catt echoed the fears of many middle- and upper-class urban dwellers when she warned of the danger that "lies in the votes possessed by the males in the slums of the cities, and the ignorant foreign [immigrant] vote." She added that the nation, with "ill-advised haste" had enfranchised "the foreigner, the Negro and the Indian" but still balked at women voting. In the South, suffragists catered to generations of deeply embedded racism. One of them declared in 1903 that giving white women the vote "would insure immediate and durable white supremacy."

Whatever the motives, President Wilson finally endorsed the "Susan B. Anthony amendment" in speeches to the House and Senate in 1918. In a speech on September 18, he said, "We have made partners of the women in this war. Shall we admit them only to a partnership of suffering and sacrifice and toil and not to a partnership of right?" After six months of delay, debate, and failed votes, the Congress passed the Nineteenth Amendment in the

Votes for women

Suffragettes march in New York City in 1912, their children by their side.

spring of 1919 and sent it to the states for ratification. Tennessee's legislature was the last of thirty-six state assemblies to approve the amendment, and it did so in dramatic fashion. The initial vote was deadlocked 48–48. Then a twenty-four-year-old legislator named Harry Burn changed his vote to yes at the insistence of his mother. The Nineteenth Amendment was ratified on August 18, 1920. It was the climactic achievement of the Progressive Era.

Women thereafter engaged in politics and voted in elections in growing numbers, but they did not have the transformative effect that boosters had predicted. As it turned out, women tended to vote like men on most issues. One group, however, wanted something more. Alice Paul set a new goal for women: an equal rights amendment to the Constitution that would eliminate all remaining legal distinctions between the sexes. In 1923, Alice Paul saw the equal rights amendment introduced in Congress, and forty-nine years later she would see her amendment adopted. After her death, however, it would fall short of ratification.

Although the sharp increase in the number of women in the workforce during World War I proved short-lived, in the longer view a steady increase in the number of employed women occurred in the 1920s and 1930s. By 1910, women made up almost a quarter of all nonagricultural workers, and in 1920 women were found in all but 35 of the 572 job categories listed by the census. The continued entry of women into the workforce brought their numbers up from 8 million in the 1920 census to 10 million in 1930 and to 13 million in 1940. Still, women remained concentrated in traditional occupations, finding employment primarily as domestics, office workers, teachers, clerks, salespeople, dressmakers, milliners, and seamstresses. On the eve of World War II, women's work was little more diversified than it had been at the beginning of the century, but by 1940 it was on the verge of a major transformation.

THE "NEW NEGRO"   The most significant development in African American life during the early twentieth century was the Great Migration northward from the South. The movement of blacks to the North began in

"A Negro Family Just Arrived in Chicago from the Rural South," 1922

Between 1910 and 1930 almost 1 million African Americans left the South.

1915–1916, when rapidly expanding war industries and restrictions on immigration together created a labor shortage; legal restrictions on immigration continued the movement in the 1920s. Altogether between 1910 and 1920 the Southeast lost some 323,000 African Americans, or 5 percent of the native black population, and by 1930 it had lost another 615,000, or 8 percent of the native black population in 1920. With the migration, a slow but steady growth in black political influence in northern cities set in. African Americans were freer to speak and act in a northern setting; they also gained political leverage by settling in large cities in states with many electoral votes.

Along with political activity came a bristling spirit of protest, a spirit that received cultural expression in a literary and artistic movement known as the Harlem Renaissance. Claude McKay, a Jamaican immigrant, was the first significant writer of the movement, which featured a rediscovery of black folk culture and bolder treatment of controversial topics. Poems collected in McKay's *Harlem Shadows* (1922) expressed defiance in such titles as "If We Must Die" and "To the White Fiends." Other emergent writers included Langston Hughes, Zora Neale Hurston, Countee Cullen, and James Weldon Johnson. Perhaps the greatest single creation of the time was Jean Toomer's novel *Cane* (1923), which pictured the lives of simple folk in Georgia's black belt and the sophisticated African American middle class in Washington, D.C.

The spirit of the "new Negro" also found expression in what came to be called Negro nationalism, which exalted blackness, black cultural expression, and black exclusiveness. The leading spokesman for such views was the flamboyant Marcus Garvey. In 1916, Garvey brought to New York City the Universal Negro Improvement Association (UNIA), which he had started in his native Jamaica two years before. His organization grew rapidly amid the racial tensions of the postwar years. Garvey exhorted African Americans to liberate themselves from the surrounding white culture. He saw every white person as

Marcus Garvey

Garvey was the founder of the Universal Negro Improvement Association and a leading spokesman for "Negro nationalism" in the 1920s.

a "potential Klansman" and therefore endorsed the "social and political separation of all peoples to the extent that they promote their own ideals and civilization."

Such a separatist message appalled other African American leaders. W. E. B. Du Bois, for example, labeled Garvey "the most dangerous enemy of the Negro race. . . . He is either a lunatic or a traitor." Garvey and his aides created their own black version of Christianity, organized their own fraternal lodges and community cultural centers, started their own businesses, and published their own newspaper. Garvey's message of racial pride and self-reliance appealed to many blacks who had arrived in the northern cities during the Great Migration and had grown frustrated and embittered with the hypocrisy of American democracy during the postwar economic slump.

In 1920, Garvey declared that the only lasting hope for blacks was to flee America and build their own republic in Africa. Garvey quickly enlisted half a million members in the UNIA and claimed as many as 6 million by 1923. At that point he was charged with mail fraud for his fund-raising activities. Found guilty, he was sent to prison in 1925, where he remained until President Calvin Coolidge pardoned him, deporting him to Jamaica in 1927. Garvey died in obscurity in London in 1940, but the memory of his movement kept alive an undercurrent of racial nationalism that would reemerge later under the slogan of black power.

A more lasting force for racial equality was the National Association for the Advancement of Colored People (NAACP), founded in 1910 by white progressives and black activists. Black participants came mainly from the Niagara movement, a group associated with W. E. B. Du Bois that had met each year since 1905 at places associated with the anti-slavery movement (Niagara Falls; Oberlin, Ohio; Boston; Harpers Ferry) and issued defiant statements against discrimination.

Although most white progressives did not embrace the NAACP, the new group took seriously the progressive idea that the solution to social problems begins with informing the people, and it planned an active press bureau to accomplish this. Du Bois became its director of publicity and research and editor of its journal, the *Crisis*. The NAACP's main strategy was to focus on legal action designed to bring the Fourteenth and Fifteenth Amendments back to life. One early victory came with *Guinn v. United States* (1915), in which the Supreme Court struck down Oklahoma's grandfather clause, used to deprive African Americans of the vote. In *Buchanan v. Worley* (1917) the Court invalidated a residential segregation ordinance in Louisville, Kentucky.

In 1919 the NAACP launched a campaign against lynching, then a still-common form of vigilante racism. An anti-lynching bill to make mob murder a federal offense passed the House in 1922 but lost to a filibuster by southern senators. The bill stayed before the House until 1925, and NAACP field secretary James Weldon Johnson believed the continued agitation on the issue did more than the bill's passage would have to reduce lynchings, which decreased to a third of what they had been in the previous decade. But even one lynching was too many for a so-called progressive society.

THE CULTURE OF MODERNISM

After 1920, changes in the realms of science and social thought were perhaps even more dramatic than those affecting women and African Americans. As the twentieth century advanced, the faith in progress and reform expressed by progressives fell victim to a series of frustrations and disasters, including the Great War, the failure of the League of Nations to win approval in the United States, Woodrow Wilson's physical and political collapse, and the failure of Prohibition. On a grander scale, startling new findings in physics further shook prevailing assumptions of order and certainty.

SCIENCE AND SOCIAL THOUGHT   Physicists of the early twentieth century altered the image of the cosmos in bewildering ways. Since the eighteenth century, conventional wisdom had held that the universe was governed by laws that the scientific method could ultimately uncover. This rational world of order and certainty disintegrated at the beginning of the new century when Albert Einstein, a young German physicist, announced his theory of relativity, which maintained that space, time, and mass were not absolutes but instead were relative to the location and motion of the observer. Sir Isaac Newton's laws of mechanics, according to Einstein's relativity theories, worked well enough at relatively slow speeds, but the more nearly one approached the velocity of light (about 186,000 miles per second), the more all measuring devices would change accordingly, so that yardsticks would become shorter, clocks and heartbeats would slow down, even the aging process would ebb.

The farther one reached out into the universe and the farther one reached inside the minute world of the atom, the more certainty dissolved. The discovery of radioactivity in the 1890s showed that atoms were not irreducible

Albert Einstein

Widely regarded as one of the most influential scientists of the twentieth century, Einstein was awarded a Nobel Prize in 1921.

units of matter and that some of them emitted particles of energy. This meant, Einstein noted, that mass and energy were not separate phenomena but interchangeable. By 1921, when Einstein was awarded the Nobel Prize, his abstract concept of relativity had become internationally recognized—and popularized. Hundreds of books about relativity had been published. His theories also had consequences that Einstein had not foreseen. Younger physicists built upon them to further transform notions of reality and the universe.

The pace of theoretical physics quickened as the twentieth century unfolded. The German physicist Max Planck discovered that electromagnetic emissions of energy, whether as electricity or light, come in little bundles that he called quanta. The development of quantum theory suggested that atoms were far more complex than once believed and, as stated in 1927 in the uncertainty principle of the German physicist Werner Heisenberg, ultimately indescribable. One could never know both the position and the velocity of an electron, Heisenberg concluded, because the very process of observation would inevitably affect the behavior of the particle, altering its position or its velocity. The observer, in other words, changes what is being observed.

Heisenberg's simple, yet startling thesis meant that human knowledge had limits. "The physicist thus finds himself in a world from which the bottom has dropped clean out," a Harvard mathematician wrote in 1929. The scientist had to "give up his most cherished convictions and faith. The world is not a world of reason, understandable by the intellect of man, but as we penetrate ever deeper, the very law of cause and effect, which we had thought to be a formula to which we could force God Himself to subscribe, ceases to have any meaning." Hard for the public to grasp, such findings proved too troubling even for Einstein, who spent much of the rest of his life in the search for an explanation that would unify the relativity and quantum theories. "I shall never believe that God plays dice with the world," Einstein asserted.

Just as Enlightenment thinkers had drawn on Isaac Newton's laws of gravitation two centuries before to formulate their views on the laws governing society, the ideas of relativity and uncertainty in the twentieth century led people to deny the relevance of absolute values in any sphere of society, thus undermining the concepts of personal responsibility and absolute standards. Anthropologists aided the process by transforming the word *culture*, which had before meant "refinement," into a term for the whole system of ideas, folkways, and institutions within which any group lives. Even the most primitive groups had a culture, and all things being relative, one culture should not impose its value judgments upon another. Two anthropologists, Ruth Benedict and Margaret Mead, were especially effective in spreading this viewpoint.

MODERNIST ART AND LITERATURE   The cluster of scientific ideas associated with Charles Darwin, Sigmund Freud, and Albert Einstein inspired a revolution in the minds of intellectuals and creative artists, which they expressed in the new modernism. The modernist world was one in which, as Karl Marx said, "all that is solid melts into air." Whereas nineteenth-century writers and artists took for granted an accessible world that could be readily observed and accurately represented, self-willed modernists viewed reality as something to be created rather than copied, expressed rather than reproduced. They thus concluded that the subconscious regions of the psyche were more interesting and more potent than reason, common sense, and logic.

Gertrude Stein

Pablo Picasso's 1906 portrait of the writer.

In the various arts, related technical features appeared: abstract painting that represented an inner mood rather than a recognizable image of an object, atonal music, free verse, stream-of-consciousness narrative, and interior monologues in stories and novels. Writers showed an intense concern with new forms in language in an effort to avoid outmoded forms and structures and to violate expectations and shock their audiences.

The search for the new centered in America's first major artistic bohemias, in Chicago and New York, especially in the area of lower Manhattan known as Greenwich Village. In 1913 the Armory Show, an international art exhibition that opened in a National Guard building in New York and went on to Chicago, Philadelphia, and Boston, shocked traditionalists with its display of the latest works by experimental and nonrepresentational artists: postimpressionists, expressionists, primitives, and cubists. Pablo Picasso's work made its American debut there. The show aroused shock, indignation, and not a little good-natured ridicule, but it was a huge success.

The chief prophets of modernism were neither in Chicago nor in New York but were American expatriates in Britain and Europe: Ezra Pound and T. S. Eliot in London and Gertrude Stein in Paris were all deeply concerned with creating new and often difficult styles of modernist expression. Pound, as foreign editor of *Poetry,* became the conduit through which many American poets achieved publication. Eliot's *The Waste Land* (1922) made few concessions to readers in its arcane allusions, its juxtaposition of unexpected metaphors, its deep sense of postwar disillusionment and melancholy, and its suggestion of a burned-out civilization, but it became for a generation almost the touchstone of the modern temper, along with the Irishman James Joyce's stream-of-consciousness novel *Ulysses,* published the same year. As poet and critic writing for the *Criterion,* which he founded in 1922, Eliot became the arbiter of modernist taste in Anglo-American literature.

Gertrude Stein, in voluntary exile since 1903, was, with her brother, Leo, an early champion of modern art and a collector of works by Paul Cézanne, Henri Matisse, and Picasso. Long regarded as no more than the literary eccentric who wrote, "Rose is a rose is a rose is a rose," Stein came to be recognized as one of the chief promoters of the modernist prose style, beginning with *Three Lives* (1909). She sought to capture interior moods in her writing, developing in words the equivalent of nonrepresentational painting.

But Stein was long known chiefly through her influence on other expatriates, such as Ernest Hemingway, whom she told, "All of you young people who served in the war, you are the lost generation." The earliest chronicler of that generation, F. Scott Fitzgerald, blazed up brilliantly and then quickly flickered out like all the tinseled, sad young characters who people his novels. Successful and famous at age twenty-four, having published *This Side of Paradise* in 1920, Fitzgerald, along with his wife, Zelda, lived in and wrote about the "greatest, gaudiest spree in history," and then both had their crack-ups during the Great Depression. What gave depth to the best of Fitzgerald's work was what a character in *The Great Gatsby* (1925), Fitzgerald's finest novel, called "a sense of the fundamental decencies" amid all the surface gaiety—and almost always a sense of impending doom.

Ernest Hemingway's novels *The Sun Also Rises* (1926) and *A Farewell to Arms* (1929) depict a desperate search for "real" life and the doomed, war-tainted love affairs of young Americans of the "lost" generation. These novels feature the frenetic, hard-drinking lifestyle and the cult of athletic masculinity (epitomized by the bullfighter) that became the stuff of the public image Hemingway cultivated for himself. Hundreds of writers tried to imitate Hemingway's terse style,

The Fitzgeralds celebrate Christmas

F. Scott Fitzgerald and his wife, Zelda, lived in and wrote about the "greatest, gaudiest spree in history."

but few had his gift, which lay less in what he had to say than in the way he said it.

THE SOUTHERN RENAISSANCE As modernist literature arose in response to the changes taking place in the United States and Europe, so southern literature of the twenties reflected a mythic world in the midst of rebirth. A southern renaissance in writing emerged from the conflict between the dying world of tradition and the modern commercial world struggling to come to life in the aftermath of the Great War. While in the South the onset of modernism aroused the Ku Klux Klan and fundamentalist furies, both of which tried desperately to bring back the world of tradition, it also inspired the vitality and creativity of the South's young writers.

"One may reasonably argue," wrote a critic in 1930, "that the South is the literary land of promise today." Just the previous year two vital figures had emerged: Thomas Wolfe, with *Look Homeward, Angel,* and William Faulkner, with *Sartoris* and *The Sound and the Fury.* Fame rushed in first on Wolfe and his native Asheville, North Carolina, which became in the 1920s a classic example of the scandalized community. "Against the Victorian morality and the Bourbon aristocracy of the South," Wolfe had "turned in all his fury," wrote newspaper editor Jonathan Daniels, a former classmate. Daniels's reaction was not an uncommon response to the works of the southern renaissance, created by authors who had outgrown their "provincial" hometowns and looked back from new perspectives acquired through travel and education.

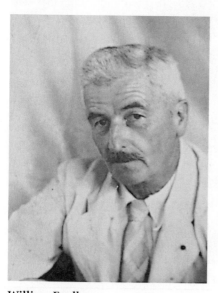

William Faulkner

Faulkner discovered that his "own little postage stamp of native soil was worth writing about."

William Faulkner's achievement, more than Wolfe's, was rooted in the coarsely textured social world that produced him. Born near Oxford, Mississippi, Faulkner transmuted his hometown into the fictional town of Jefferson, in Yoknapatawpha County. With *The Sound and the Fury,* Faulkner created one of the triumphs of the modernist style.

Modernism and the southern literary renaissance, both of which emerged from the crucible of the Great War and its aftermath, were products of the 1920s. But the widespread cultural alienation of the 1920s did not survive the decade. The onset of the Great Depression in 1929 sparked a renewed sense of commitment and affirmation in the arts, as if people could no longer afford the art-for-art's-sake affectations of the 1920s. Alienation would give way to social activism in the decade to come.

End of Chapter Review

CHAPTER SUMMARY

- **Nativism** With the end of the Great War, race riots and the fear of communism ushered in a wave of virulent nativism. With many "old stock" Americans fearing that many immigrants were socialists, Communists, or anarchists, Congress passed laws to restrict immigration. The revived Ku Klux Klan was devoted to "100 percent Americanism" and regarded Catholics, Jews, immigrants, and African Americans as threats to America.

- **Jazz Age** The fads and attitudes of the 1920s, perhaps best represented by the frantic rhythms of jazz music and the fast-paced, sexy movies from Hollywood, led F. Scott Fitzgerald to dub the decade the Jazz Age. The hemlines of women's dresses rose, and sex was openly discussed. The Harlem Renaissance gave voice to black literature and music, and African Americans in northern cities felt freer to speak out against racial injustice and express pride in their race.

- **Reactionary Mood** Many white Americans felt that their religion and way of life were under attack by modern trends. They feared that women's newly earned right to vote might destabilize the family and that scientific scholarship would undermine biblical truth. These modern and traditional forces openly clashed at the Scopes trial in Dayton, Tennessee, in 1925, where the right to teach evolution in public schools was tested in court.

- **Modernism** The carnage of the Great War shattered Americans' belief in the progress of Western civilization. In the movement known as modernism, young artists and intellectuals reflected this disillusionment. For modernists, no longer could the world be easily observed through reason, common sense, and logic; instead, reality was something to be created and expressed through new artistic and literary forms, like abstract painting, atonal music, free verse in poetry, and stream-of-conscious narrative and interior monologues in stories and novels.

CHRONOLOGY

1910	National Association for the Advancement of Colored People is founded
1916	Marcus Garvey brings to New York the Universal Negro Improvement Association
1920	Prohibition begins
1920	Nineteenth Amendment, guaranteeing women's suffrage, is ratified
1920	F. Scott Fitzgerald's *This Side of Paradise* is published
1921	Albert Einstein receives the Nobel Prize in physics
1921	Congress passes the Emergency Immigration Act
1922	T. S. Eliot's *The Waste Land* is published
1923	Alice Paul's equal rights amendment is introduced in Congress
1924	Congress passes the Immigration Act
1925	Scopes "monkey trial" tests the teaching of evolution in Tennessee public schools

KEY TERMS & NAMES

27

REPUBLICAN RESURGENCE AND DECLINE

FOCUS QUESTIONS

 wwnorton.com/studyspace

- To what extent were the policies of the 1920s a rejection of progressivism?
- Why were the 1920s an era of conservatism?
- What drove the growth of the American economy in the 1920s?
- What were the causes of the stock market crash and the Great Depression?

By 1920 the progressive political coalition that elected Theodore Roosevelt in 1904 and reelected Woodrow Wilson in 1916 had fragmented. It unraveled for several reasons. For one thing, its leaders were no more. Roosevelt died in 1919 at the age of sixty, just as he was beginning a campaign for the 1920 Republican presidential nomination and Wilson was finishing out his second term in office broken physically and mentally. Even more significant was public disaffection with progressive leadership. Radicals and other opponents of the war were disaffected by America's participation in the conflict and the war's aftermath. Organized labor resented the Wilson administration's unsympathetic attitude toward the strikes of 1919–1920. Farmers of the Great Plains and the West thought that wartime price controls on commodities had discriminated against them. Liberal intellectuals also drifted away from their former support of progressivism. They became disillusioned with grassroots democracy because of popular support for Prohibition, the Ku Klux Klan, and religious fundamentalism. The larger middle class became preoccupied with building a new business civilization "based not upon monopoly and restriction," in the words of one historian, "but upon a whole new set of business values— mass production and consumption, short hours and high wages, full employment, welfare capitalism." Progressivism's final triumphs at the national level were already pretty much foregone conclusions before the war's end: the Eighteenth Amendment, ratified in 1919, which outlawed alcoholic beverages, and the Nineteenth Amendment, ratified in 1920, which allowed women nationwide to vote.

Progressivism did not disappear in the 1920s, however. Progressives dominated key leadership positions in Congress during much of the decade even while conservative Republicans occupied the White House. The progressive impulse for "good government" and broader public services remained strong, especially at the state and local levels, where movements for better roads, education, public health, and social-welfare programs gained momentum during the decade.

"Normalcy"

THE ELECTION OF 1920 After World War I most Americans had grown weary of Woodrow Wilson's crusading idealism and were suspicious of leaders promoting widespread reforms. Wilson himself recognized the shifting public mood. "It is only once in a generation," he remarked, "that a people can be lifted above material things. That is why conservative government is in the saddle two-thirds of the time."

At the Republican Convention in 1920, the three strongest contenders for president canceled each other out in the balloting. The party leaders then turned to a stunning mediocrity, the affable Ohio senator Warren G. Harding, who set the tone of his campaign when he told a Boston audience: "America's present need is not heroics, but healing; not nostrums, but normalcy; not revolution, but restoration; not agitation, but adjustment; not surgery, but serenity; not the dramatic, but the dispassionate." In contrast to Wilson's grandiose internationalism, Harding promised to "safeguard America first . . . to exalt America first, to live for and revere America first."

Harding's vanilla promise of a "return to normalcy" reflected his own conservative values and folksy personality. The son of an Ohio farmer, he described himself as "just a plain fellow" who was "old-fashioned and even reactionary in matters of faith and morals." But far from being an old-fashioned moralist in his personal life, Harding drank bootleg liquor in the midst of Prohibition, smoked and chewed tobacco, relished weekly poker games, and had numerous affairs and several children with women other than his austere wife, whom he called "the Duchess." The general public, however, remained unaware of Harding's escapades. Instead, voters saw him as a handsome, charming, lovable politician. A man of self-confessed limitations in vision, leadership, and intellectual power, he once admitted that "I cannot hope to be one of the great presidents, but perhaps I may be remembered as one of the best loved."

The Democrats in 1920 hoped that Harding would not be president at all. James Cox, a former newspaper publisher and former governor of Ohio, won the presidential nomination of an increasingly fragmented Democratic party on the forty-fourth ballot. For vice president the convention named New Yorker Franklin D. Roosevelt, who as assistant secretary of the navy occupied the same position his Republican cousin Theodore Roosevelt had once held.

The Democrats suffered from the breakup of the Wilsonian coalition and the conservative postwar mood. In the words of the progressive journalist William Allen White, Americans in 1920 were "tired of issues, sick at heart of ideals, and weary of being noble." The country voted overwhelmingly for Harding's promised "return to normalcy." Harding polled 16 million votes to 9 million for Cox, who carried no state outside the Democratic South.

EARLY APPOINTMENTS AND POLICY Harding in office had much in common with Ulysses Grant. His cabinet, like Grant's, mixed some of the "best minds" in the party, whom he had promised to seek out, with a few of the worst, cronies who sought him out. Charles Evans Hughes, like Grant's Hamilton Fish, became a distinguished secretary of state. Herbert Hoover in the Commerce Department, Andrew Mellon in the Treasury Department, and Henry C. Wallace in the Agriculture Department functioned efficiently and made policy on their own. Other cabinet members and administrative appointees, however, were not so conscientious. The secretary of the interior landed in prison, and the attorney general narrowly escaped serving time. Many lesser offices went to members of the "Ohio gang," a group with which Harding met in a house on K Street to get away from the pressures of the White House.

Until he became president, Harding had loved politics. He was the party hack par excellence, "bloviating" (a favorite verb of his, which means "speaking with gaseous eloquence") at public events, jollying it up in the clubhouse and cloakroom, hobnobbing with the great and near great in Washington. As president, however, Harding was simply in over his head, and self-doubt overwhelmed him. "I don't think I'm big enough for the Presidency," he confided to a friend. Harding much preferred to relax with the Ohio gang, who shared his taste for whiskey, poker, and women.

Still, Harding and his friends had an agenda. They set about dismantling or neutralizing many of the social and economic components of progressivism. The president's four Supreme Court appointments were all conservatives, including Chief Justice William Howard Taft, who announced that he had been "appointed to reverse a few decisions." During the

MR. MELLON GETS THE PAN
—Fitzpatrick in the St. Louis Post-Dispatch

Andrew Mellon

Mellon was accused of allowing his Aluminium Company of America to become a monopoly.

1920s the Taft court struck down a federal child-labor law and a minimum-wage law for women, issued numerous injunctions against striking unions, and passed rulings limiting the powers of federal regulatory agencies.

The Harding administration established a pro-business tone reminiscent of the McKinley White House in the 1890s. To deal with the postwar recession and generate economic growth, Secretary of the Treasury Mellon reduced government spending and lowered taxes. To get a better handle on expenditures, he persuaded Congress to pass the Budget and Accounting Act of 1921, which created a new Bureau of the Budget to prepare a unified federal budget and a General Accounting Office to audit spending by federal agencies. This act realized a long-held progressive desire to bring greater efficiency and nonpartisanship to the budget preparation process. General tax reductions from the wartime level were warranted, but Mellon insisted that they should go mainly to the rich, on the principle that wealth in the hands of the few would spur economic growth through increased capital investment. Mellon's admirers tagged him the greatest secretary of the Treasury since Alexander Hamilton in the late eighteenth century.

In Congress a group of western Republicans and southern Democrats fought a dogged battle to preserve the graduated scale (higher rates on higher income) built into wartime taxes, but Mellon, in office through the 1920s, eventually won out. At his behest, Congress in 1921 repealed the wartime excess-profits tax and lowered the maximum rate on personal income from 65 to 50 percent. Subsequent revenue acts lowered the maximum rate to 40 percent in 1924 and to 20 percent in 1926. The Revenue Act of 1926 extended further benefits to high-income groups by lowering estate taxes and repealing the gift tax. Unfortunately, much of the tax money released to the wealthy seems to have fueled the speculative excess of the late 1920s as much as it fostered gainful enterprise. Mellon, however, did balance the federal budget for a time. Government expenditures fell, as did the national debt.

In addition to tax cuts, Mellon—the third richest man in the United States, after John D. Rockefeller and Henry Ford—favored the time-honored Republican policy of high tariffs on imported goods. The Fordney-McCumber Tariff of 1922 increased rates on chemical and metal products as a safeguard against the revival of German industries that had previously commanded the field. To please the farmers, who historically benefited little from tariffs, the new act further extended the duties on agricultural imports.

Higher tariffs had unexpected consequences, however. During the war the United States had been transformed from a debtor nation to a creditor nation. Foreign capital had long flowed into the United States, playing an important role in the economic expansion of the nineteenth century. But the private and public credits given the Allies to purchase American supplies during the war had reversed the pattern. Mellon insisted that the European powers repay all that they had borrowed. But the high American tariffs made it all the harder for other nations to sell their products in the United States and thus acquire the dollars or credits with which to repay their war debts. For nearly a decade further extensions of American loans and investments sent more dollars abroad, postponing the reckoning.

Rounding out the Republican economic program of the 1920s was a more lenient attitude toward government regulation of corporations. Neither Harding nor his successor, Calvin Coolidge, could dissolve the regulatory agencies, but they named commissioners who promoted "friendly" regulation. Harding appointed conservatives to the Interstate Commerce Commission, the Federal Reserve Board, and the Federal Trade Commission. Senator George Norris characterized the new appointments as "the nullification of federal law by a process of boring from within." Senator Henry Cabot Lodge agreed, boasting that "we have torn up Wilsonism by the roots."

In one area, however, Warren Harding proved to be much more progressive than Woodrow Wilson. He reversed the Wilson administration's policy of excluding African Americans from federal positions. He also spoke out against vigilante racism. In his first speech to a joint session of Congress in 1921, Harding insisted that the nation must deal with the festering "race question." The horrific racial incidents during and after World War I were a stain on American ideals. The new president, unlike his Democratic predecessor, attacked the Ku Klux Klan for fomenting "hatred and prejudice and violence," and he urged Congress "to wipe the stain of barbaric lynching from the banners of a free and orderly, representative democracy." The Senate, however, failed to pass the bill Harding promoted.

ADMINISTRATIVE CORRUPTION   Republican conservatives such as Lodge, Mellon, Coolidge, and Hoover operated out of a philosophical conviction that was intended to benefit the nation. Members of the Ohio gang, however, used White House connections to line their own pockets. Early in 1923, Harding learned that the head of the Veterans Bureau was systematically looting medical and hospital supplies. In February, realizing he had been found out, the official resigned. A few weeks later the legal adviser to the bureau committed suicide. Not long afterward a close friend of Attorney General Harry Daugherty also shot himself. The corrupt crony held no government appointment but had set up an office in the Justice Department from which he peddled influence for a fee. The attorney general himself was implicated in the fraudulent handling of German assets seized after the war. When discovered, he refused to testify on the grounds that he might

"Juggernaut" of corruption

This 1924 cartoon alludes to the dimensions of the Teapot Dome scandal.

incriminate himself. Twice brought to court, he was never indicted, for want of evidence, possibly because he had destroyed pertinent records. These were but the most visible among the many scandals that touched the Justice Department, the Prohibition Bureau, and other federal agencies under Harding.

One major scandal rose above all the others, however. Teapot Dome, like the Watergate break-in fifty years later, became the catchphrase for the climate of corruption surrounding the Harding administration. A government-owned oil deposit under the sandstone in Wyoming, Teapot Dome had been set aside as a naval oil reserve administered by the Interior Department under Albert B. Fall. At the time the move seemed a sensible attempt to unify control of public reserves. But once Fall had control, he signed sweetheart contracts letting petroleum companies exploit the deposits. Fall argued that these contracts were in the government's interest, but suspicions lingered when Fall's standard of living suddenly rose. It turned out that he had taken bribes of about $400,000 (which came in "a little black bag") from oil tycoons.

Harding himself avoided public disgrace. How much he knew of the scandals swirling about him is unclear, but he knew enough to give the appearance of being troubled. "My God, this is a hell of a job!" he confided to a journalist. "I have no trouble with my enemies, I can take care of my enemies all right. But my damn friends, my God-damn friends. . . . They're the ones that keep me walking the floor nights!" In 1923, Harding left on what would be his last journey, a speaking tour to the West Coast and a trip to the Alaska Territory. In Seattle he suffered an attack of food poisoning, recovered briefly, then died in a San Francisco hotel.

The nation was heartbroken. Not since the death of Abraham Lincoln had there been such an outpouring of grief for a "beloved president," for the kindly, ordinary man who found it in his heart (as Woodrow Wilson had not) to pardon Eugene Debs, the Socialist who had been jailed for opposing U.S. entry into World War I. As the black-streamered funeral train moved toward Washington, D.C., then back to Ohio, millions stood by the tracks to honor their lost leader. Eventually, however, grief yielded to scorn and contempt. For nearly a decade, the revelations of scandal within the Harding administration were paraded before investigating committees and then the courts. In 1927 an Ohio woman named Nan Britton published a sensational book in which she claimed that she had had numerous trysts with Harding in the White House and that he was the father of her daughter. Harding's love letters to another man's wife also surfaced.

As a result of Harding's amorous detours and corrupt associates, his foreshortened administration came to be viewed as one of the worst in American history. More recent assessments of Harding's presidency, however, suggest that the scandals obscured accomplishments. Some historians credit Harding with leading the nation out of the turmoil of the postwar years and creating the foundation for the decade's remarkable economic boom. These revisionists also stress that Harding was a hardworking president who played a far more forceful role than previously assumed in shaping his administration's economic and foreign policies and in shepherding legislation through Congress. Harding also promoted diversity and civil rights. He appointed Jews to key federal positions. No previous president had promoted women's rights as forcefully as he did. But even Harding's foremost scholarly defender admits that he lacked good judgment and "probably should never have been president."

"SILENT CAL" The news of Harding's death found Vice President Calvin Coolidge visiting his father in the isolated mountain village of Plymouth, Vermont, his birthplace. There, at 2:47 A.M. on August 3, 1923, by the light of a kerosene lamp, Colonel John Coolidge administered the oath of office to his son. The rustic simplicity of Plymouth, the very name itself, evoked just the image of traditional roots and solid integrity that the country

Conservatives in the White House

Warren Harding (left) and Calvin Coolidge (right).

would long for amid the coming disclosures of corruption and carousing in the Harding administration.

Coolidge brought to the White House his provincial background and a clear conviction that the presidency should revert to its Gilded Age stance of passive deference to Congress. "Four-fifths of our troubles," Coolidge predicted, "would disappear if we would sit down and keep still." He abided by this rule, insisting on twelve hours of sleep and an afternoon nap. The satirist H. L. Mencken asserted that Coolidge "slept more than any other president, whether by day or by night. Nero fiddled, but Coolidge only snored."

Americans embraced the unflappability and unstained integrity of Silent Cal. He was simple and direct, a smugly self-righteous man of strong principles, intense patriotism, pinched frugality, and few words. After being re-elected president of the Massachusetts State Senate, he delivered that office's shortest inaugural address ever. His four-sentence speech urged his colleagues: "Conserve the foundations of our institutions. Do your work with the spirit of a soldier in the public service. Be loyal to the Commonwealth, and to yourselves. And be brief—above all things, be brief." Although a man of few words, he was not as bland or as dry as critics claimed. Yet he was conservative. Even more than Harding, Coolidge identified the nation's welfare with the success of big business. "The chief business of the American people is business," he preached. "The man who builds a factory builds a temple. The man who works there worships there." Where Harding had sought to balance the interests of labor, agriculture, and industry, Coolidge focused on industrial development. He strove to end government regulation of business and industry and reduce taxes as well as the national debt. His fiscal frugality and pro-business stance led the *Wall Street Journal* to exult: "Never before, here or anywhere else, has a government been so completely fused with business."

THE ELECTION OF 1924 In filling out Harding's unexpired term, Calvin Coolidge distanced himself from the scandals of the administration and put in charge of the prosecutions two lawyers of undoubted integrity. A man of honesty and ability, a good administrator who delegated well and managed Republican factions adroitly, Coolidge quietly took control of the party machinery and seized the initiative in the campaign for the nomination, which he won with only token opposition.

Meanwhile, the Democrats again fell victim to dissension, prompting the humorist Will Rogers's classic statement that "I am a member of no organized political party. I am a Democrat." The Democratic party's fractiousness illustrated the deep divisions between the new urban culture of the 1920s and the more traditional hinterland. It took the Democrats 103 ballots to bestow the tarnished nomination on John W. Davis, a Wall Street lawyer from West Virginia who could nearly outdo Coolidge in conservatism.

While the Democrats bickered, a new farm-labor coalition was forming. Meeting in Cleveland, Ohio, on July 4, 1924, activists reorganized the Progressive party and nominated Robert M. La Follette for president. The Wisconsin reformer also won the support of the Socialist party and the American Federation of Labor.

In the 1924 campaign, Coolidge focused on La Follette, whom he called a dangerous radical who would turn America into a "communistic and socialistic state." The voters preferred to "keep cool with Coolidge," who swept both the popular and the electoral votes by decisive majorities. Davis took only the solidly Democratic South, and La Follette carried only his native Wisconsin. The popular vote went 15.7 million for Coolidge, 8.4 million for Davis, and 4.8 million for La Follette—the largest popular vote ever polled by a third-party candidate. The Electoral College result was 382 to 136 to 13, respectively.

The New Era

Business executives interpreted the Republican victory in 1924 as a vindication of their leadership, and Coolidge saw the economy's surging prosperity as a confirmation of his efforts to promote the interests of big business. In fact, the prosperity and technological achievements of the time known as the New Era had much to do with Coolidge's victory over the Democrats and Progressives. Those in the large middle class who had formed an important segment of the Progressive party coalition were now absorbed instead into the prosperous New Era created by advances in communications, transportation, and business organization. The 1920s were years of extraordinary innovation and inventiveness.

THE GROWING CONSUMER CULTURE   Economic and social life was transformed during the 1920s. More people than ever before had the money and leisure to indulge their consumer fancies, and a growing advertising industry fueled the appetites of this expanding moneyed class. By the mid-1920s advertising had become a huge enterprise with powerful social significance. Old-time values of thrift and saving gave way to a new ethic of consumption that made spending a virtue. The innovation of installment buying made an increase in consumption feasible for many. A newspaper editorial

Motion pictures

A dispirited Charlie Chaplin in a still image from his classic 1921 film *The Kid*.

insisted that the American's "first importance to his country is no longer that of citizen but that of consumer. Consumption is a new necessity in response to dramatic increases in productivity."

Consumer-goods industries fueled much of the economic boom from 1922 to 1929. Moderately priced creature comforts, including items such as handheld cameras, wristwatches, cigarette lighters, vacuum cleaners, washing machines, and linoleum, became more widely available. Inventions in communications and transportation, such as motion pictures, radio, telephones, and automobiles, fueled the boom and triggered social transformations.

In 1896 a New York audience viewed the first moving-picture show. By 1908 there were nearly 10,000 movie theaters scattered across the nation. Hollywood, California, became the center of movie production, grinding out cowboy Westerns and the timeless comedies of Mack Sennett's Keystone Company, where a raft of slapstick comedians, most notably Charlie Chaplin, perfected their art, transforming it into a form of social criticism. By the mid-1930s every city and most small towns had movie theaters, and movies became the nation's chief form of mass entertainment. A further advancement in technology came with the "talkies"—movies with soundtracks.

Radio broadcasting had an even more spectacular growth. Except for experimental broadcasts, radio served only for basic communication until 1920. In that year, station WWJ in Detroit began transmitting news bulletins from the *Detroit Daily News,* and KDKA in Pittsburgh, owned by the Westinghouse Electric and Manufacturing Company, began broadcasting regularly scheduled programs. The first radio commercial aired in New York in 1922. By the end of that year, there were 508 stations and some 3 million receivers in use. In 1926 the National Broadcasting Company (NBC), a subsidiary of the Radio Corporation of America (RCA), began linking stations into a network; the Columbia Broadcasting System (CBS) entered the field the next year. In 1927 a Federal Radio Commission was established to regulate the industry; in 1934 it became the Federal Communications Commission, with

The rise of radio

The radio brought this farm family together and connected them to the outside world. By the end of the 1930s, millions would tune in to newscasts, soap operas, sports events, and church services.

authority over other forms of communication as well. Calvin Coolidge was the first president to address the nation by radio, and he did so monthly, paving the way for Franklin Roosevelt's influential "fireside chats."

AIRPLANES, AUTOMOBILES, AND THE ECONOMY Advances in transportation were equally significant. Wilbur and Orville Wright of Dayton, Ohio, owners of a bicycle shop, built and flew the first airplane at Kitty Hawk, North Carolina, in 1903. But the use of planes advanced slowly until the outbreak of war in 1914, after which the Europeans rapidly developed the airplane as a military weapon. When the United States entered the war, it had no combat planes—American pilots flew British or French planes. An American aircraft industry developed during the war but foundered in the postwar demobilization. Under the Kelly Act of 1925, however, the federal government began to subsidize the industry through airmail contracts. The Air Commerce Act of 1926 provided federal funds to aid in

First flight

Orville Wright pilots the first flight of a power-driven airplane while his brother, Wilbur, runs alongside.

the advancement of air transportation and navigation; among the projects it supported was the construction of airports.

The infant aviation industry received a psychological boost in 1927 when Charles A. Lindbergh Jr. made the first solo transatlantic flight, traveling from New York to Paris in thirty-three and a half hours. The heroic deed, which won him $25,000, was dramatic. He flew through a dense fog for part of the way and dropped to within ten feet of the ocean's surface before sighting the Irish coast and regaining his bearings. The New York City parade in Lindbergh's honor surpassed even the celebration of the armistice.

Five years later New York honored another pioneering aviator—Amelia Earhart, who in 1932 became the first woman to fly solo across the Atlantic Ocean. Born in Kansas in 1897, she made her first solo flight in 1921 and began working as a stunt pilot at air shows across the country. Earhart's popularity soared after her transatlantic solo flight. The fifteen-hour feat led Congress to award her the Distinguished Flying Cross, and she was named Outstanding American Woman of the Year in 1932.

In 1937 Earhart and a navigator left Miami, Florida, heading east on a round-the-world flight. The voyage went smoothly until they attempted the most difficult leg: from New Guinea to a tiny Pacific island 2,556 miles away.

The plane disappeared, and despite extensive searches, no trace of it or the aviators was ever found. It remains the most intriguing mystery in aviation history. The accomplishments of Lindbergh and Earhart helped catapult aviation industry to prominence. By 1930 there were forty-three airline companies in operation in the United States.

Nonetheless, by far the most significant economic and social development of the early twentieth century was the automobile. The first motor car had been manufactured for sale in 1895, but the founding of the Ford Motor Company in 1903 revolutionized the infant industry. Ford's reliable Model T (the celebrated Tin Lizzie) came out in 1908 at a price of $850 (in 1924 it would sell for $290). Henry Ford vowed "to democratize the automobile. When I'm through everybody will be able to afford one, and about everyone will have one."

He was right. In 1916 the total number of cars manufactured passed 1 million; by 1920 more than 8 million were registered, and in 1929 there were more than 23 million. The production of automobiles stimulated other industries by consuming large amounts of steel, rubber, glass, and textiles, among other materials. It gave rise to a gigantic market for oil products just as the Spindletop gusher (drilled in 1901 in Texas) heralded the opening of vast southwestern oil fields. It quickened the movement for good roads, financed in large part from a gasoline tax; speeded transportation; encouraged suburban sprawl; and sparked real estate booms in California and Florida.

The automobile industry became the leading example of modern mass-production techniques and efficiency. When the Model T first came out, demand ran far ahead of production. Henry Ford then hired a factory expert who, by rearranging the plant and installing new equipment, met Ford's production goal of 10,000 cars in twelve months. The next year, 1909, Ford's new Highland Park plant outside Detroit was planned with job analysis in mind. In 1910, gravity slides were installed to move parts from one workbench to the next, and by the end of 1913 the system was complete, with seemingly endless chain conveyors pulling the parts along feeder lines and the chassis down the final assembly line.

STABILIZING THE ECONOMY During the 1920s, the drive for efficiency, which had been a prominent feature of the progressive impulse, powered the wheels of mass production and consumption and became a cardinal belief of Republican leaders. Herbert Hoover, who served as secretary of commerce in the Harding and Coolidge cabinets, was an engineer who had made a fortune in mining operations in Australia, China, Russia, and elsewhere.

Ford Motor Company's Highland Park plant, 1913

Gravity slides and chain conveyors contributed to the mass production of automobiles.

Out of his experiences in business and his management of the Food Administration and other wartime activities, he had developed a philosophy that he set forth in the book, *American Individualism* (1922). Hoover prescribed a kind of middle way between the regulatory and trust-busting traditions, a way of government's encouraging voluntary cooperation among competing businesses.

As secretary of commerce, Hoover transformed the trifling Commerce Department into the government's most dynamic agency. He sought out new markets for business, promoted more efficient design, production, and distribution, and created a Bureau of Aviation and the next year established the Federal Radio Commission.

Hoover's priority was the burgeoning trade-association movement. Through trade associations, business leaders competing in a given industry shared information on every aspect of the industry: sales, purchases, shipments, production, and prices. That information allowed them to make plans with more confidence and thereby more accurately predict costs, set prices, and assess markets while maintaining a more stable workforce and paying steadier wages. Sometimes abuses crept in as associations engaged in price-fixing and other monopolistic practices, but the Supreme Court in 1925 held the practice of sharing information as such to be within the law.

THE BUSINESS OF FARMING   During the 1920s, agriculture remained the weakest sector in the economy. Briefly after the war, farmers' hopes soared on wings of prosperity. The wartime boom fed by sales abroad lasted into 1920, and then commodity prices collapsed as world agricultural production returned to prewar levels. Overproduction brought lower prices for crops. Wheat went in eighteen months from $2.50 a bushel to less than $1; cotton from 35¢ per pound to 13¢. Low crop prices persisted into 1923, especially in the wheat and corn belts, and after that improvement was spotty. A bumper cotton crop in 1926 resulted only in a price collapse and an early taste of depression in much of the South, where foreclosures and bankruptcies spread.

Yet the most successful farms, like the most successful corporations, were getting larger, more efficient, and more mechanized. By 1930 about 13 percent of all farmers had tractors, and the proportion was even higher on the western plains. Better plows, harvesters, combines, and other machines were part of the mechanization process that accompanied improved crop yields, fertilizers, and methods of animal breeding.

Yet most farmers in the 1920s were simply struggling to survive. And like their predecessors they sought political remedies. In 1924, Senator Charles L. McNary of Oregon and Representative Gilbert N. Haugen of Iowa introduced the first McNary-Haugen bill, which sought to secure "equality for agriculture in the benefits of the protective tariff." Complex as it would have

Farming technology

Mechanization became increasingly important in early-twentieth-century agriculture. Here, a silo leader, or grain pump, stands at the center of this Wisconsin farm.

been in operation, it was simple in conception: in short, it was a plan to dump farm surpluses on the world market in order to raise prices in the home market. The goal was to achieve "parity"—that is, to raise domestic farm prices to a point where they would have the same purchasing power relative to other prices that they had enjoyed between 1909 and 1914, a time viewed in retrospect as a golden age of American agriculture.

A McNary-Haugen bill passed both houses of Congress in 1927, only to be vetoed by President Coolidge, who dismissed the bill as unsound and unconstitutional. The process was repeated in 1928, when Coolidge pronounced the measure an unsound effort at price-fixing and un-American and unconstitutional to boot. In a broader sense, however, McNary-Haugenism did not fail. The debates over the bill made the farm problem a national policy issue and defined it as a problem of surpluses. Moreover, the evolution of the McNary-Haugen plan revived the idea of a political alliance between the rural South and the West, a coalition that in the next decade became a dominant influence on national farm policy.

SETBACKS FOR UNIONS   Urban workers more than farmers shared in the affluence of the 1920s. "A workman is far better paid in America than anywhere else in the world," a French visitor wrote in 1927, "and his standard of living is enormously higher." Nonfarm workers gained about 20 percent in real wages between 1921 and 1928 while farm income rose only 10 percent.

Organized labor, however, did no better than organized agriculture in the 1920s. Even though President Harding had endorsed collective bargaining and tried to reduce the twelve-hour workday and the six-day workweek so that the working class "may have time for leisure and family life," he ran into stiff opposition in Congress. Overall, unions suffered a setback after the growth years of the war. The Red Scare and strikes of 1919 created concerns that unions practiced subversion, an idea that the enemies of unions promoted. The brief postwar depression of 1921 further weakened the unions, and they felt the severe impact of open-shop associations that proliferated across the country after the war, led by chambers of commerce and other business groups. In 1921 business groups in Chicago designated the open shop the "American plan" of employment. Although the open shop in theory implied only an employer's right to hire anyone, in practice it meant discrimination against unionists and a refusal to recognize unions even in shops where most of the workers belonged to one.

To suppress unions, employers often required "yellow-dog" contracts, which forced workers to agree to stay out of a union. Owners also used labor spies, blacklists, intimidation, and coercion. Some employers tried to kill the unions with kindness. They introduced programs of "industrial democracy" guided by company unions or various schemes of "welfare capitalism," such as profit sharing, bonuses, pensions, health programs, recreational activities, and the like. The benefits of such programs were often considerable.

Prosperity, propaganda, welfare capitalism, and active hostility combined to cause union membership to drop from about 5 million in 1920 to 3.5 million in 1929. Samuel Gompers, founder and longtime president of the AFL, died in 1924; William Green of the United Mine Workers, who took his place, embodied the conservative, even timid, attitude of unions during the period. The outstanding exception to the anti-union policies of the decade was the passage of the Railway Labor Act in 1926, which abolished the Railway Labor Board and substituted a new Board of Mediation. The act also provided for the formation of railroad unions "without interference, influence, or coercion," a statement of policy not extended to other workers until the 1930s.

THE GASTONIA STRIKE OF 1929 Anti-union sentiment was fiercest in the South during the 1920s. In 1929 a wave of violent strikes swept across the region. Most of the unrest centered in the large textile mills that had come to dominate the southern economy. During World War I the desperate need for military clothing brought rapid expansion and high profits to the textile industry. After the war, however, demand for cotton cloth sagged and prices plummeted. Military demobilization, changing women's fashions—rising hemlines—and foreign competition eroded the profit margins of the textile companies. In response, owners closed mills, slashed wages, and raised production quotas. They operated the mills around the clock and established rigid production quotas (piecework) for each worker.

This onerous "stretch-out" system finally provoked workers to rebel. Many of them joined the AFL's United Textile Workers (UTW). Strikes and work stoppages followed, and the powerful mill owners, supported by security guards, local police, and state militias, forcefully suppressed the union efforts. Few of the strikes lasted more than a week, but the 1929 walkout at the huge Loray Mill in Gastonia, North Carolina, escalated into a prolonged conflict that involved two deaths.

The mill's managers refused to negotiate or even meet with the strikers. As tensions rose, the North Carolina governor, himself a textile-mill owner, dispatched National Guard units to break the strike. Vigilante groups took matters into their own hands. A gang of masked men destroyed the union's strike headquarters and assaulted workers. When police entered the strikers'

The Gastonia strike

These female textile workers pit their strength against that of a national guardsman during the strike at the Loray Mill in Gastonia, North Carolina, in 1929.

tent city to search for weapons, a skirmish erupted and someone shot and killed Gastonia's police chief. Police then arrested seventy-five of the strike leaders, thirteen of whom were eventually charged with murder. Reporters from across the nation and around the world descended on Gastonia. Vigilantes again attacked the union headquarters and later assaulted a convoy of strikers headed to a rally. Shots were fired, and twenty-nine-year-old Ella May Wiggins, a folk-singing labor organizer and mother of nine, was killed.

Despite a lack of concrete evidence, seven strikers were eventually convicted of conspiracy to commit murder in the death of the police chief and sentenced to long prison terms. By contrast, those accused of shooting Ella May Wiggins were found not guilty. The Loray strike begun on April 1, 1929, had collapsed by the end of May. Within a few months the mill's owners were sponsoring an essay contest, inviting workers to compete for prizes by describing "Why I Enjoy Working at the Loray."

PRESIDENT HOOVER, THE ENGINEER

HOOVER VERSUS SMITH   On August 2, 1927, while on vacation in the Black Hills of South Dakota, President Coolidge, without consulting anyone, passed out to reporters slips of paper with the curious statement "I do not choose to run for President in 1928." His retirement surprised the nation and cleared the way for Herbert Hoover to mount an active campaign for the nomination. He was the party's only strong candidate. The platform took credit for prosperity, cost cutting, debt and tax reduction, and the protective tariff ("as vital to American agriculture as it is to manufacturing"). It rejected the McNary-Haugen program but promised to create a federal farm board to manage surpluses more efficiently.

The Democratic nomination went to Governor Alfred E. Smith of New York. The party's farm plank, while not endorsing the McNary-Haugen plan, did pledge "economic equality of agriculture with other industries." Like the Republicans the Democrats promised to enforce the Volstead Act, which provided for the enforcement of Prohibition, and, aside from calling for

Campaign sheet music

The sheet music for the Democratic nominee, Alfred Smith (left) and the Republican nominee, Herbert Hoover (right) drew on popular tunes and motifs of the time.

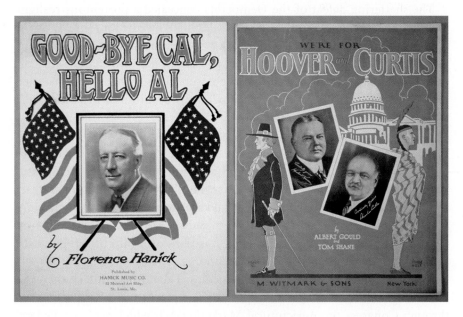

stricter regulation of water power, promised nothing that departed from the conservative position of the Republicans.

The two candidates' sharply different images obscured the essential similarities of their programs. Hoover was the Quaker son of middle America, the successful engineer and businessman, the architect of Republican prosperity, while Smith was the prototype of those things rural and small-town America distrusted: the son of Irish immigrants, Catholic, and anti-Prohibition. Outside the large cities all those attributes were handicaps that Smith could scarcely surmount, for all his affability and wit. Militant members of the religious right launched a furious assault on him. The Ku Klux Klan, for example, mailed thousands of postcards proclaiming that the Catholic New Yorker was the Antichrist.

In the election of 1928, more people voted than ever before. Hoover won in the third consecutive Republican landslide, with 21 million popular votes to Smith's 15 million and an even more top-heavy electoral-vote majority of 444 to 87. Hoover even cracked the Democrats' Solid South, leaving Smith only six Deep South states plus Massachusetts and Rhode Island. The election was above all a vindication of Republican prosperity, although Calvin Coolidge was skeptical that his successor could sustain the good times. He derisively called Hoover the Wonder Boy, and had quipped in 1928 that the new president had "offered me unsolicited advice for six years, all of it bad."

The shattering defeat of the Democrats concealed a portentous realignment in the making. Al Smith had nearly doubled the vote for John W. Davis, the Democratic candidate of four years before. Smith's image, though a handicap in the hinterlands, swung big cities back into the Democratic column. In the farm states of the West, there were signs that some disgruntled farmers had switched over to the Democrats. A coalition of urban workers and unhappy farmers was in the making.

HOOVER IN CONTROL   The milestone year 1929 dawned with high hopes. Business seemed good, income was rising, and the chief architect of Republican prosperity was about to enter the White House. "I have no fears for the future of our country," Hoover told the audience at his inauguration. "It is bright with hope."

Hoover's program to stabilize business carried over into his program for agriculture, the weakest sector of the economy. To treat the malady of glutted markets, he offered two main remedies: federal help for cooperative marketing and higher tariffs on imported farm products. In 1929 he pushed through Congress the Agricultural Marketing Act, which set up a Federal

Farm Board to help farm cooperatives market the major commodities. The act also provided for the Farm Board to set up "stabilization corporations" empowered to buy surpluses so as to raise crop prices. Unluckily for any chance of success the plan might have had, it got under way almost simultaneously with the onset of the Great Depression that fall.

Farmers gained even less from tariff revision. What Hoover won after fourteen months of struggle with competing local interests in Congress was in fact a generally upward revision of duties on manufactures as well as farm goods. The Hawley-Smoot Tariff of 1930 carried duties to an all-time high. Rates went up on some 70 farm products and more than 900 manu-

Herbert Hoover

"I have no fears for the future of our country," Hoover told the nation at his inauguration in 1929.

factured items. More than 1,000 economists petitioned Hoover to veto the bill because, they said, it would raise prices paid by consumers, damage the export trade and thus hurt farmers, promote inefficiency, and incite foreign reprisals. Events proved them right, but Hoover felt that he had to go along with his party in an election year.

THE ECONOMY OUT OF CONTROL   The tariff did nothing to check a deepening crisis of confidence in the economy. After the postwar slump of 1921, the idea grew that the economy had entered a new era of *permanent* growth. Greed then propelled a growing contagion of get-rich-quick schemes. Speculative mania fueled the Florida real estate boom that had begun when the Coolidge prosperity combined with Henry Ford's Tin Lizzies to give people extra money and make Florida an accessible playground. Thousands of people invested in Florida real estate, eager for quick profits in the nation's fastest-growing state. In the fanfare of fast turnover, the reckless speculator was, if anything, more likely to gain than the prudent investor. In mid-1926, however, the Florida real estate bubble burst.

For the losers it was a sobering lesson, but it proved to be but an audition for the great bull market in stocks. Until 1927 stock values had gone up with profits, but then they began to soar on wings of pure speculation. Treasury

Secretary Andrew Mellon's tax reductions had given people more discretionary income, which with the help of aggressive brokerage houses, found its way to Wall Street. Instead of speculating in real estate, one could buy stock on margin—that is, make a small down payment (the "margin") and borrow the rest from a broker, who held the stock as security against a down market. If the stock declined and the buyer failed to meet a margin call for more funds, the broker could sell the stock to cover his loan. Brokers' loans more than doubled from 1927 to 1929.

Gamblers in the market ignored warning signs. By 1927 residential construction and automobile sales were catching up to demand, business inventories had risen, and the rate of consumer spending had slowed. By mid-1929, production, employment, and other measures of economic activity were declining. Still the stock market rose.

By 1929 the stock market had entered a fantasy world. Conservative financiers and brokers who counseled caution were ignored. President Hoover voiced concern about the "orgy of mad speculation," and he urged stock exchange and Federal Reserve officers to discourage speculation in stocks. But to no avail. On September 4 stock prices wavered, and the day after that they dropped, opening a season of fluctuations. The great bull market staggered on into October, trending downward but with enough good days to keep hope alive. On October 22 a leading bank president assured reporters, "I know of nothing fundamentally wrong with the stock market or with the underlying business and credit structure."

THE CRASH AND ITS CAUSES   The next day, stock values tumbled, and the day after that a wild scramble to unload stocks lasted until word arrived that leading bankers had formed a pool to buy stocks to halt the slide. Prices steadied for the rest of the week, but after a weekend to think the situation over, people began to sell their stocks. On Tuesday, October 29, the most devastating single day in the market's history to that point, brokers reported sales of 16.4 million shares (at the time the trading of 3 million shares was a busy day). The plunge in prices fed on itself as brokers sold the shares they held for buyers who failed to meet their margin calls. During October, stocks on the New York Stock Exchange fell in value by an average of 37 percent.

Business and government leaders initially expressed confidence that the markets would rebound. According to President Hoover, "the fundamental business of the country" was sound. Some speculators who had gotten out of the market went back in for bargains but found themselves caught in a slow, tedious erosion of values. By March 1933, the value of stocks on the

Stock market crash

Apprehensive crowds gather on the steps of the Subtreasury Building, opposite the New York Stock Exchange, as news of a stock collapse spreads on October 29, 1929.

New York Stock Exchange was less than a fifth of the value at the market's peak. The *New York Times* stock average, which stood at 452 in September 1929, bottomed at 52 in July 1932.

The collapse of the stock market revealed that the much-trumpeted economic prosperity of the 1920s had been built on weak foundations. From 1929 to 1932, personal income declined by more than half. Unemployment soared. Farmers, already in trouble, faced catastrophe. More than 9,000 banks closed during this period, hundreds of factories and mines shut down, and thousands of farms were foreclosed for debt and sold at auction. A cloak of gloom fell over the nation.

The stock market crash did not cause the Great Depression, but it did reveal major structural flaws in the economy and in government policies. Too many businesses had maintained retail prices and taken large profits while holding down wages. As a result, about a third of personal income went to only 5 percent of the population. By plowing most profits back into expansion rather than wage increases, the business sector brought on a growing imbalance between rising productivity and declining purchasing power. As public consumption of goods declined, the rate of investment in new plants also plummeted. For a time the erosion of consumer purchasing power was concealed by an increase in installment buying, and the deflationary effects of the high tariffs were concealed by the volume of foreign loans and investments, which supported foreign demand for American goods. But the flow of American capital abroad began to dry up when the stock market began to look more attractive. Swollen profits and corporate dividends, together with the Treasury Secretary Mellon's business-friendly tax policies, enticed the rich into stock market speculation. When trouble came, the bloated corporate structure collapsed.

Government policies also contributed to the economic debacle. The domineering secretary of the Treasury in the 1920s, Andrew Mellon, displayed a supreme confidence in market capitalism. He himself was one of the wealthiest men in the world. To him the appropriate role of government was to promote free enterprise by cutting taxes, reducing regulation, and balancing the budget. Mellon's tax reductions led to oversaving by the general public, which helped diminish the demand for consumer goods. Hostility toward labor unions discouraged collective bargaining and may have worsened the prevalent imbalances in income. High tariffs discouraged foreign trade. Lax enforcement of anti-trust laws also encouraged high prices.

Another culprit was the gold standard. The world monetary system remained fragile throughout the 1920s. When economic output, prices, and savings began dropping in 1929, policy makers—certain that they had to keep their currencies tied to gold at all costs—often tightened money supplies at the very moment that economies needed an expanding money supply to keep growing. The only way to restore economic stability within the constraints of the gold standard was to let prices and wages continue to fall, allowing the downturn, in Andrew Mellon's words, to "purge the rottenness out of the system." What happened instead was that passivity among government and financial leaders turned a recession into the world's worst depression.

THE HUMAN TOLL OF THE DEPRESSION   The devastating collapse of the economy caused immense social hardships. By 1933, 13 million people were out of work. Millions more who kept their jobs saw their hours and wages reduced. Factories shut down, banks closed, farms went bankrupt, and millions of people found themselves not only jobless but also homeless and penniless. Hungry people lined up at soup kitchens; others rummaged through trash cans behind restaurants. Many slept on park benches or in alleys. Others congregated in makeshift shelters in vacant lots. Thousands of desperate men in search of jobs rode the rails. These hobos, or tramps, as they were derisively called, sneaked onto empty railway cars and rode from town to town, looking for work. During the winter homeless people wrapped themselves in newspapers to keep warm, sarcastically refer-ring to their coverings as Hoover blankets. Some grew so weary of their grim fate that they ended their lives. The suicide rate soared during the 1930s. America had never before experienced social distress on such a scale.

HOOVER'S EFFORTS AT RECOVERY Although the policies of pub-lic officials helped to bring on economic collapse, few leaders even acknowl-edged that there was an unprecedented crisis: all that was needed, they claimed, was a slight correction of the market. Those who held to the dogma of lim-ited government thought the economy would cure itself. Nothing should be done; the depression should be allowed to run its course until the economy had purged itself of its excesses. The best policy, Treasury Secretary Mellon advised, would be to "liquidate labor, liquidate stocks, liquidate the farmers, liquidate real estate." Yet Hoover was unwilling to sit by and let events take their course. He in fact did more than any president had ever done before in such dire economic circumstances. Still, his own philosophy, now hardened into dogma, set firm limits on government action, and he was unready to set that philosophy aside even to meet an unprecedented national emergency.

Hoover believed that the nation's fundamental business structure was sound and that the country's main need was confidence. In speech after speech, he exhorted people to keep up hope, and he asked business owners to keep their mills and shops open, maintain wage rates, and spread out the work to avoid layoffs—in short, to let the first shock of depression fall on corporate profits rather than on wage earners. In return, union leaders, who had little choice, agreed to refrain from making wage demands and staging strikes. As it hap-pened, however, uplifting words were not enough, and the prediction that good times were just around the corner (actually made by the vice president, though attributed to Hoover) eventually became a sardonic joke.

Hoover did more than try to reassure the public, however. He hurried the start of government construction projects in order to provide jobs, but state and local cutbacks more than offset the new federal spending. At Hoover's demand, the Federal Reserve returned to an easier credit policy, and Congress passed a modest tax reduction to put more cash into people's pockets. The Federal Farm Board stepped up its loans and its purchases of farm surpluses, only to face bumper crops in 1930 despite droughts in the Midwest and Southwest. The high Hawley-Smoot Tariff, proposed at first to help farmers, brought reprisals against American exports abroad, thus devastating foreign trade.

As always, a depressed economy hurt the party in power. Democrats ex-ploited Hoover's predicament for all it was worth. The squalid settlements

Impact of the Depression

Two children set up shop in a Hooverville in Washington, D.C.

that sprouted across the country to house the destitute and homeless became known as Hoovervilles; a Hoover flag was an empty pocket turned inside out. In November 1930 the Democrats gained their first national victory since 1916, winning a majority in the House and enough gains in the Senate to control it in coalition with western agrarians.

In the first half of 1931, economic indicators rose, renewing hope for an upswing. Then, as recovery beckoned, another shock occurred. In May 1931 the failure of Austria's largest bank triggered a financial panic in central Europe. To ease concerns, President Hoover proposed a one-year moratorium on both reparations and war-debt payments by the European nations. European leaders accepted the moratorium as well as a later temporary "standstill" on the settlement of private obligations between banks. The general shortage of monetary exchange drove Europeans to withdraw their gold from American banks and dump their American securities. One European country after another abandoned the gold standard and devalued its currency. Even the Bank of England went off the gold standard. The United States, meanwhile, slid into the third bitter winter of deepening depression.

CONGRESSIONAL INITIATIVES   With a new Congress in session, demands for federal action impelled Hoover to stretch his individualistic philosophy to its limits. He was ready now to use government resources to at least shore up the financial institutions of the country. In 1932 the new Congress set up the Reconstruction Finance Corporation (RFC) with $500 million (and authority to borrow $2 billion more) for emergency loans to banks, life-insurance companies, building-and-loan societies, farm-mortgage associations, and railroads. Under Charles G. Dawes, Calvin Coolidge's vice president, the RFC authorized $1.2 billion in loans within six months. It staved off bankruptcies, but Hoover's critics found in it favoritism to business, the most damaging instance of which was a $90 million loan to Dawes's own Chicago bank, made soon after he left the RFC in 1932. The RFC nonetheless remained a key agency through the mid-1940s.

Further help to the financial structure came with the Glass-Steagall Act of 1932, which broadened the definition of commercial loans that the Federal Reserve would support. The new arrangement also released about $750 million in gold formerly used to back Federal Reserve notes, countering the effect of foreign withdrawals and domestic hoarding of gold at the same time that it enlarged the supply of credit. For homeowners the Federal Home Loan Bank Act of 1932 created with Hoover's blessing a series of discount banks for home mortgages. They provided to savings-and-loan and other mortgage agencies a service much like the one that the Federal Reserve System provided to commercial banks.

Hoover's critics said all these measures reflected a dubious "trickle-down" theory. If government could help banks and railroads, asked New York senator Robert F. Wagner, "is there any reason why we should not likewise extend a helping hand to that forlorn American, in every village and every city of the United States, who has been without wages since 1929?" The contraction of credit devastated such debtors as farmers and those who made purchases on the installment plan or held balloon-style mortgages, whose monthly payments increased over time.

By 1932, members of Congress were filling the hoppers with bills for federal measures to provide relief to individuals. At that point, Hoover might have pleaded "dire necessity" and taken the leadership of the relief movement and salvaged his political fortunes. Instead, he held back and only grudgingly edged toward federally directed relief of human distress. On July 21, 1932, he signed the Emergency Relief Act, which avoided a direct federal dole (cash payment) to individuals but gave the RFC $300 million for relief loans to the states, authorized loans of up to $1.5 billion for state and local public works, and appropriated $322 million for federal public works.

FARMERS AND VETERANS IN PROTEST   Government relief for farmers had long since been abandoned. In mid-1931 the government quit buying crop surpluses and helplessly watched prices slide. Faced with the loss of everything, desperate farmers defied the law. Angry mobs stopped fore-closures and threatened to lynch the judges sanctioning them. In Nebraska, farmers burned corn to keep warm. Iowans formed the militant Farmers' Holiday Association, which called a farmers' strike.

In the midst of the crisis, there was even desperate talk of revolution. "Folks are restless," Mississippi governor Theodore Bilbo told reporters in 1931. "Communism is gaining a foothold. . . . In fact, I'm getting a little pink my-self." Across the country the once-obscure Communist party began to draw crowds to its rallies and willing collaborators to its "hunger marches." Yet for all the sound and fury, few Americans embraced communism during the 1930s. Party membership in the United States never rose much above 100,000.

Fears of organized revolt arose when unemployed veterans converged on the nation's capital in the spring of 1932. The "Bonus Expeditionary Force" grew quickly to more than 20,000. Their purpose was to get immediate pay-ment of the cash bonus to 4 million veterans of World War I that Congress

Anger and frustration

Unemployed military veterans, members of the Bonus Expeditionary Force, clash with Washington, D.C. police at Anacostia Flats in July 1932.

had voted in 1924. The House approved a bonus bill, but when the Senate voted it down, most of the veterans went home. The rest, along with their wives and children, having no place to go, camped in vacant government buildings and in a shantytown at Anacostia Flats, within sight of the Capitol.

Eager to disperse the squatters, Hoover persuaded Congress to pay for their tickets home. More left, but others stayed even after Congress adjourned, hoping at least to meet with the president. Late in July the administration ordered the government buildings cleared. In the ensuing melee, a police-man panicked, fired into the crowd, and killed two veterans. The secretary of war then dispatched about 700 soldiers under General Douglas MacArthur, who was aided by junior officers Dwight D. Eisenhower and George S. Patton. The soldiers drove out the unarmed veterans and their families, injuring dozens and killing one, an eleven-week-old boy born at Anacostia, who died from exposure to tear gas.

General MacArthur hysterically claimed that the "mob" was about to seize control of the government. The administration insisted that the Bonus Army consisted mainly of Communists and criminals, but neither a grand jury nor the Veterans Administration could find evidence to support the charge. One observer wrote before the incident: "There is about the lot of them an atmosphere of hopelessness, of utter despair, though not of desperation. . . . They have no enthusiasm whatever and no stomach for fighting."

Their disheartened mood, and the mood of the country, echoed that of the beleaguered Hoover himself. He worked very hard, but the stress took its toll on his health and morale. "I am so tired," he said, "that every bone in my body aches." Presidential news conferences became more strained and less frequent. When friends urged him to seize the reins of leadership, he said, "I can't be a Theodore Roosevelt" or "I have no Wilsonian qualities." Hoover's deepening sense of futility became increasingly evident to the country. In a mood more despairing than rebellious, Americans in 1932 eagerly antici-pated what the next presidential campaign would produce.

End of Chapter Review

CHAPTER SUMMARY

- **"Return to Normalcy"** Although progressivism lost its appeal after the Great War, the Eighteenth Amendment (paving the way for Prohibition) and the Nineteenth Amendment (guaranteeing women's suffrage) marked the culmination of that movement at the national level. Reformers still actively worked for good and efficient government at the local level, but overall the drive was for a "return to normalcy"—conformity and moral righteousness.

- **Era of Conservatism** Many Americans, particularly people in rural areas and members of the middle class, wanted a return to a quieter, more conservative way of life after World War I, and Warren Harding's landslide Republican victory allowed just that. The policies of Harding's pro-business cabinet were reminiscent of those of the McKinley White House more than two decades earlier. Union membership declined in the 1920s as workers' rights were rolled back by a conservative Supreme Court and in response to fears of Communist subversion. Workers, however, shared in the affluence of the 1920s, thereby contributing to the rise of a mass culture.

- **Growth of Economy** The budget was balanced through reductions in spending and taxes, while tariffs were raised to protect domestic industries, setting the tone for a prosperous decade. Harding's successor, Calvin Coolidge, actively promoted the interests of big business. The public responded enthusiastically to the mass marketing of new consumer goods such as radios and affordable automobiles. Agricultural production, however, lagged after the wartime boom evaporated.

- **The Great Depression** The stock market crash revealed the structural flaws in the economy, but it did not cause the Great Depression. Government policies throughout the twenties—high tariffs, lax enforcement of anti-trust laws, an absence of checks on speculation, and adherence to the gold standard—contributed to the onset of the Depression. Hoover's attempts to remedy the problems were too few and too late. Banks failed, businesses closed, homes and jobs were lost.

CHRONOLOGY

1903	Wright Brothers fly the first airplane
1903	Ford Motor Company is founded
1905	First movie house opens
1922	First radio commercial is aired
1923	President Warren Harding dies in office
1927	Charles Lindbergh Jr. makes first solo transatlantic flight
1928	Herbert Hoover is elected president
October 29, 1929	Stock market crashes
1930	Congress passes the Hawley-Smoot Tariff
1932	Congress sets up the Reconstruction Finance Corporation
1932	Congress passes the Glass-Steagall Act
1933	Bonus Expeditionary Force converges on Washington to demand payment of bonuses promised to war veterans

KEY TERMS & NAMES

28

NEW DEAL AMERICA

FOCUS QUESTIONS   wwnorton.com/studyspace

- What were the immediate challenges facing Franklin Roosevelt in March 1933?
- What were the lasting social effects of the New Deal legislation?
- Why did the New Deal draw criticism from conservatives and liberals?
- How did the New Deal expand the federal government's authority?
- What were the major cultural changes of the 1930s?

Upon arriving in the White House in 1933, Franklin Roosevelt inherited an anxious nation mired in the third year of an unprecedented depression. No other business slump had been so deep, so long, or so painful. One out of every four Americans in 1932 was unemployed, and in many large cities nearly half the adults were out of work. Some 500,000 people had lost homes or farms because they could not pay their mortgages. Thousands of banks had failed; millions of depositors had lost their life savings. The worldwide depression had also helped accelerate the rise of fascism and communism. Totalitarianism was on the march. "The situation is critical," the prominent political analyst Walter Lippmann warned President-elect Roosevelt. "You may have to assume dictatorial powers."

Roosevelt did not become a dictator, but he did take decisive action. He and a supportive Congress immediately adopted bold measures to relieve the human suffering and promote economic recovery. Such initiatives provided the foundation for what came to be called welfare capitalism.

FROM HOOVERISM TO THE NEW DEAL

THE ELECTION OF 1932 On June 14, 1932, while the ragtag Bonus Army was still encamped in Washington, D.C., Republicans gathered in Chicago to renominate Herbert Hoover. The delegates went through the motions in a mood of defeat. By contrast, the Democrats converged on Chicago later in June confident that they would nominate the next president. New York governor Franklin D. Roosevelt was already the front-runner, with most of the delegates lined up, and he went over the top on the fourth ballot.

In a bold gesture, Roosevelt appeared in person to accept the nomination instead of awaiting formal notification. "Let it . . . be symbolic that . . . I broke traditions," he told the delegates. "Republican leaders not only have failed in material things, they have failed in national vision, because in disaster they have held out no hope. . . . I pledge you, I pledge myself to a new deal for the American people." What the New Deal would be in practice Roosevelt had little idea as yet, but he was much more willing to experiment than Hoover. What was more, his upbeat personality communicated joy, energy, and hope. Roosevelt's campaign song was "Happy Days Are Here Again."

Born in 1882, the adored only child of wealthy parents, educated by tutors at his father's Hudson River estate in New York, young Roosevelt led a cosmopolitan life. After attending an elite Massachusetts boarding school, he earned degrees from Harvard College and Columbia University Law School. While a law student, he married his distant cousin, Anna Eleanor Roosevelt, a niece of his fifth cousin, Theodore Roosevelt, then president of the United States.

In 1910, Franklin Roosevelt won a Democratic seat in the New York State Senate. As a freshman legislator he displayed the contradictory qualities that would characterize his political career: he was an aristocrat with empathy for common folk, a traditionalist with a penchant for experimentation, an affable charmer with a buoyant smile and upturned chin who harbored profound convictions, and a skilled political tactician with a shrewd sense of timing and a distinctive willingness to listen to and learn from others.

Tall, handsome, and athletic, Roosevelt seemed destined for greatness. In 1912 he backed Woodrow Wilson for president, and for both of Wilson's terms he served as assistant secretary of the navy. Then, in 1920, largely on the strength of his name, he became James Cox's running mate on the Democratic ticket. The following year, at age thirty-nine, his career was cut short by the onset of polio that left him permanently disabled, unable to stand or walk without braces. But the battle for recovery transformed the young aristocrat. He became less arrogant, less superficial, more focused, and more interesting. A friend recalled that Roosevelt emerged from his struggle with polio "completely warm-hearted, with a new humility of spirit" that led him to identify with the poor and the suffering. Justice Oliver Wendell Holmes later summed up his qualities this way: "a second-class intellect—but a first-class temperament."

For seven years, aided by his talented wife, Roosevelt strengthened his body to compensate for his disability, and in 1928 he won the governorship of New York. Reelected by a whopping majority of 700,000 in 1930, Roosevelt became the Democrats' favorite for president in 1932.

Partly to dispel doubts about his health, the Democratic nominee set forth on a grueling campaign tour in 1932. He blamed the Depression on Hoover and the Republicans, and he began to promise Americans a New Deal. Like Hoover, Roosevelt pledged to balance the budget, but he was willing to incur short-term deficits to prevent starvation and revive the economy. On the tariff he was evasive. On farm policy he offered several options pleasing to farmers and ambiguous enough not to alarm city dwellers. He called for strict regulation of utilities and for at least some government development of electricity, and he consistently stood by his party's pledge to repeal the Prohibition amendment. Perhaps most important, he recognized that a revitalized economy would require national planning and new ideas. "The country needs, and, unless I mistake its temper, the country demands bold, persistent experimentation," he said. "Above all, try something."

What came across to voters, however, was less the content of Roosevelt's speeches than his uplifting confidence. By contrast, Hoover lacked vitality and assurance. Democrats, Hoover argued, ignored the international causes of the Depression. They were also taking a reckless course. Roosevelt's proposals, he warned, "would destroy the very foundations of our American system." Pursue them, and "grass will grow in the streets of a hundred cities, a thousand towns." But few were listening. Amid the persistent depression the country wanted a new course, a new leadership, a new deal.

Some disillusioned voters took a dim view of both major candidates. Those who believed that only a radical departure would suffice supported the Socialist party candidate, Norman Thomas, who polled 882,000 votes, and a few preferred the Communist party candidate, who won 103,000.

The "New Deal" candidate

Governor Franklin D. Roosevelt, the Democratic nominee for president in 1932, campaigning in Topeka, Kansas. Roosevelt's confidence inspired voters.

The wonder is that a desperate people did not turn in greater numbers to radical candidates. Instead, they swept Roosevelt into office with 23 million votes to Hoover's 16 million. Hoover carried only four states in New England plus Pennsylvania and Delaware and lost decisively in the Electoral College by 472 to 59.

THE INAUGURATION   For the last time the country waited four months, until March 4, for a new president and Congress to take office. The Twentieth Amendment, ratified on January 23, 1933, provided that presidents would thereafter take office on January 20 and the newly elected Congress on January 3.

The bleak winter of 1932–1933 witnessed spreading destitution and misery. Unemployment increased, and panic struck the banking system. As bank after bank collapsed, people rushed to their own banks to remove their deposits. Many discovered that they, too, were caught short of cash. When the Hoover administration ended, four fifths of the nation's banks were closed, and the country teetered on the brink of economic paralysis.

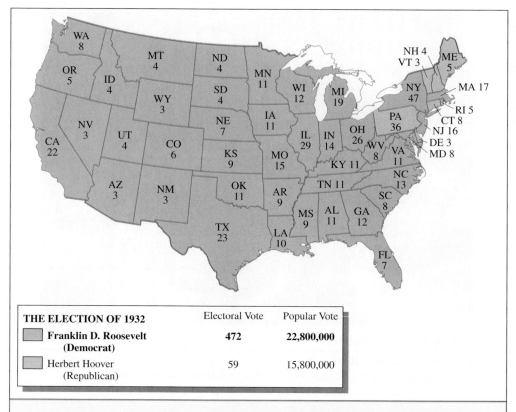

THE ELECTION OF 1932	Electoral Vote	Popular Vote
Franklin D. Roosevelt (Democrat)	472	22,800,000
Herbert Hoover (Republican)	59	15,800,000

Why did Roosevelt appeal to voters struggling during the Depression? What were Hoover's criticisms of Roosevelt's "New Deal"? What policies defined Roosevelt's New Deal during the presidential campaign?

The profound crisis of confidence that greeted Roosevelt when he took the oath of office on March 4, 1933, gave way to a mood of expectancy. The charismatic new president displayed monumental self-assurance when he declared "that the only thing we have to fear is fear itself—nameless, unreasoning, unjustified terror which paralyzes needed efforts to convert retreat into advance." If need be, he said, "I shall ask the Congress for . . . broad executive power to wage a war against the emergency as great as the power that would be given me if we were in fact invaded by a foreign foe." It was a measure of the country's mood that this call for unprecedented presidential power received the loudest applause.

COMPETING SOLUTIONS When Roosevelt and his corps of New Dealers arrived in Washington, they confronted three major challenges:

reviving the economy, relieving the widespread human misery, and rescuing the farm sector and its desperate families. His "brain trust" of advisers offered conflicting opinions about how best to rescue the economy from depression. Some promoted vigorous enforcement of the anti-trust laws as a means of restoring business competition; others argued for the opposite, saying that anti-trust laws should be suspended so as to enable large corporations to collaborate with the federal government and thereby better manage the overall economy. Still others called for a massive expansion of welfare programs and a prolonged infusion of increased government spending to address the profound human crisis and revive the economy.

Roosevelt was willing to try some elements of each approach without ever embracing one completely. In part his flexible outlook reflected the political reality that conservative southern Democrats controlled the Congress and the new president could not risk alienating these powerful proponents of balanced budgets and limited government. Roosevelt's inconsistencies also reflected his own outlook. He was a pragmatist rather than an ideologue. As he once explained, "Take a method and try it. If it fails admit it frankly and try another." Roosevelt's New Deal would therefore take the form of a series of trial-and-error actions, some of which were misguided failures.

Roosevelt and his advisers initially settled on a three-pronged strategy. First, they sought to remedy the banking crisis and to provide short-term emergency relief for the jobless. Second, they tried to promote industrial recovery by increasing federal spending and by facilitating cooperative agreements between management and organized labor. Third, they attempted to raise depressed commodity prices (and thereby farm income) by paying farmers to reduce the size of their crops and herds. By reducing the overall supply of farm products, prices for grain and meat would rise. None of these initiatives worked perfectly, but their combined effect was to restore hope and energy to a nation paralyzed by fear and uncertainty.

STRENGTHENING THE MONETARY SYSTEM On his second day in office, Roosevelt called upon Congress to meet in a special session on March 9 and then declared a four-day bank holiday to allow the financial panic to subside. It took Congress only seven hours to pass the Emergency Banking Relief Act, which permitted sound banks to reopen and provided managers for those that remained in trouble. On March 12, in the first of his radio-broadcast "fireside chats," the president insisted that it was safer to "keep your money in a reopened bank than under the mattress." His reassurances soothed a nervous nation. The following day, deposits in reopened banks exceeded withdrawals. The banking crisis had ended, and the new administration was ready to get on with its broader program.

Roosevelt next followed through on two pledges in the Democratic platform. At his behest, Congress passed an Economy Act, granting the executive branch the power to cut government workers' salaries, reduce payments to military veterans for non-service-connected disabilities, and reorganize federal agencies in the interest of reducing expenses. The Beer-Wine Revenue Act amended the Volstead Act to permit the sale of beverages with an alcohol content of 3.2 percent or less. The Twenty-first Amendment, already submitted by Congress to the states, would be declared ratified on December 5, thus ending the "noble experiment" of Prohibition.

The measures of March were but the beginning of an avalanche of new legislation. During a session that lasted from March 9 to June 16, the so-called Hundred Days, Congress received from the president, and enacted, fifteen major proposals with unprecedented speed:

March 9	Passage of the Emergency Banking Relief Act
March 20	Passage of the Economy Act
March 31	Establishment of the Civilian Conservation Corps
April 19	Abandonment of the gold standard
May 12	Passage of the Federal Emergency Relief Act
May 12	Passage of the Agricultural Adjustment Act, including the Thomas Amendment, which gave the president the power to expand the money supply
May 12	Passage of the Emergency Farm Mortgage Act, providing for the refinancing of farm mortgages
May 18	Passage of the Tennessee Valley Authority Act, providing federal funds for the unified hydroelectric development of the Tennessee Valley
May 27	Passage of the Federal Securities Act, requiring full disclosure in issuing new securities
June 13	Passage of the Home Owners' Loan Act, setting up the Home Owners' Loan Corporation to refinance home mortgages
June 16	Passage of the National Industrial Recovery Act, providing for a system of industrial self-regulation under federal supervision and for a $3.3-billion public-works program
June 16	Passage of the Banking Act, separating commercial and investment banking and establishing the Federal Deposit Insurance Corporation
June 16	Passage of the Farm Credit Act, which reorganized federal agricultural subsidies

With the banking crisis over, an acute debt problem remained for farmers and homeowners, along with a lingering distrust of the banks. By executive decree, Roosevelt reorganized all federal farm credit agencies into the Farm Credit Administration. By the Emergency Farm Mortgage Act and the Farm Credit Act, Congress authorized the extensive refinancing of farm mortgages at lower interest rates to stem the tide of foreclosures.

The Home Owners' Loan Act provided a similar service to city dwellers through the Home Owners' Loan Corporation, which re-

The galloping snail

A vigorous Roosevelt drives Congress to action in this *Detroit News* cartoon from March 1933.

financed mortgage loans at lower monthly payments for strapped homeowners, again helping to slow the rate of foreclosures. The Banking Act further shored up confidence in the banking system. Its Federal Deposit Insurance Corporation guaranteed personal bank deposits up to $5,000. To prevent speculative abuses, the Banking Act separated investment and commercial banking corporations and extended the Federal Reserve Board's regulatory power. The Federal Securities Act required the full disclosure of information about new stock and bond issues, at first by registration with the Federal Trade Commission and later with the Securities and Exchange Commission, which was created to regulate the chaotic stock and bond markets.

RELIEF MEASURES   Another urgent priority in 1933 was relieving the widespread personal distress caused by the Great Depression. Hoover had stubbornly resisted using the federal government to provide direct assistance to the unemployed and homeless. Roosevelt was more flexible. He asked Congress to create the Civilian Conservation Corps (CCC) to provide jobs to unemployed and unmarried young men aged eighteen to twenty-five.

Nearly 3 million men were hired to work at a variety of CCC jobs in forests, parks, and recreational areas and on soil-conservation projects. CCC workers built roads, bridges, campgrounds, and fish hatcheries; planted trees; taught farmers how to control soil erosion; and fought fires. They were paid a nominal

Federal relief programs

Civilian Conservation Corps enrollees in 1933, on a break from work. Directed by army officers and foresters, the CCC adhered to a semi-military discipline.

sum of $30 a month, of which $25 went home to their families. The enrollees could also earn high-school diplomas.

The Federal Emergency Relief Administration (FERA) addressed the broader problems of human distress. Harry L. Hopkins, a tough-talking, big-hearted social worker who had directed Roosevelt's relief efforts in New York State, was appointed director of the FERA. The agency expanded the assistance to the unemployed that had begun under Hoover's RFC, but with a difference. Federal money flowed to the states in outright grants rather than "loans." Hopkins pushed an "immediate work instead of dole" approach on state and local officials, but they preferred the dole (direct cash payments to individuals) as a quicker way to reach the needy.

The first large-scale experiment with *federal* work relief, which put people directly on the government payroll at competitive wages, came with the formation of the Civil Works Administration (CWA). Created in November

1933, when it had become apparent that the state-sponsored programs funded by the FERA were inadequate, the CWA provided federal jobs and wages to those unable to find work that winter. It was hastily conceived and implemented but during its four-month existence put to work over 4 million people. The agency organized a variety of useful projects: making highway repairs and laying sewer lines, constructing or improving more than 1,000 airports and 40,000 schools, and providing 50,000 teaching jobs that helped keep rural schools open. As the number of people employed by the CWA soared, the program's costs skyrocketed to over $1 billion. Roosevelt balked at such expenditures and worried that people would become dependent upon federal jobs. So in the spring of 1934, he ordered the CWA dissolved. By April some 4 million workers were again unemployed.

Roosevelt nevertheless continued to favor providing jobs over doling out cash to the unemployed. He thought the dole was a "narcotic, a subtle destroyer of the human spirit." Real jobs, on the other hand, nurtured "self-respect and self-reliance." In 1935, therefore, he asked for an array of new federal job programs, and Congress responded by passing a $4.8-billion Emergency Relief Appropriation Act, providing work for the jobless. To manage these programs, Roosevelt created the Works Progress Administration (WPA), headed by Harry Hopkins, which replaced the FERA. Hopkins was told to create millions of jobs quickly, and as a result some of the new jobs appeared to be make-work or mere "leaning on shovels." Money was wasted, but by the time the WPA died, during World War II, it had left permanent monuments on the landscape in the form of buildings, bridges, hard-surfaced roads, airports, and schools.

The WPA also employed a wide range of talented Americans in the Federal Theatre Project, the Federal Art Project, the Federal Music Project, and the Federal Writers' Project. Writers such as Ralph Ellison, John Cheever, and Saul Bellow found work writing travel guides to the United States, and Orson Welles directed Federal Theatre Project's productions. Critics charged that these programs were frivolous, but Hopkins replied that writers and artists needed "to eat just like other people." The National Youth Administration (NYA), also under the WPA, provided part-time employment to students, set up technical training programs, and aided jobless youths. Twenty-seven-year-old Lyndon Johnson was director of an NYA program in Texas, and Richard Nixon, a penniless Duke University law student, found work through the NYA at 35¢ an hour. Although the WPA took care of only about 3 million out of some 10 million jobless at any one time, in all it helped some 9 million clients weather desperate times before it expired in 1943.

City Life

This mural, painted by WPA artist Victor Arnautoff, depicts a bustling New Deal–era street scene.

RECOVERY THROUGH REGULATION

In addition to rescuing the banks and providing immediate relief to the unemployed, Roosevelt and his advisers promoted the long-term recovery of agriculture and industry. The languishing economy needed a boost—a big one. There were 13 million people without jobs. Like the earlier progressives, Roosevelt's advisers insisted that the trend toward economic concentration was inevitable. Big businesses were not going to go away. They also believed that the mistakes of the 1920s showed that the only way to operate an integrated economy at capacity and in the public interest was through efficient federal regulation and central planning, not by breaking up huge corporations. The success of government-led economic planning during World War I reinforced such ideas, and new recovery programs sprang from those beliefs.

AGRICULTURAL RECOVERY   The sharp decline in commodity prices after 1929 meant that many farmers could not afford to plant or harvest their crops. Farm income had plummeted from $6 billion in 1929 to $2 billion in 1932. The Agricultural Adjustment Act of 1933 created a new federal agency, the Agricultural Adjustment Administration (AAA), which sought to raise prices for crops and herds by paying farmers to reduce production. The money for such payments came from a tax levied on the processors of certain basic commodities—cotton gins, for example, and flour mills.

By the time Congress acted, however, the growing season was under way. The prospect of another bumper cotton crop forced the AAA to sponsor a plow-under program. To destroy a growing crop was a "shocking commentary on our civilization," Agriculture Secretary Henry A. Wallace lamented. "I could tolerate it only as a cleaning up of the wreckage from the old days of unbalanced production." Moreover, given the oversupply of hogs, some 6 million pigs were slaughtered and buried. It could be justified, Wallace said, only as a means of helping farmers do with pigs what steelmakers did with pig iron—cut production to raise prices.

For a while these farm measures worked. By the end of 1934, Secretary of Agriculture Wallace could report significant declines in wheat, cotton, and corn production and a simultaneous increase in commodity prices. Farm income increased by 58 percent between 1932 and 1935. The AAA was only partially responsible for the gains, however. A devastating drought that settled over the plains states between 1932 and 1935 played a major role in reducing production and creating the epic "dust bowl" migrations so poignantly evoked in John Steinbeck's *The Grapes of Wrath*. Many migrant families had actually been driven off the land by AAA benefit programs that encouraged large farmers to take land worked by tenants and sharecroppers out of cultivation.

Although it created unexpected problems, the AAA achieved successes in boosting the overall farm economy. But conservatives opposed its sweeping powers. On January 6, 1936, in *United States v. Butler,* the Supreme Court, by a vote of six to three, declared the AAA's tax on food processors unconstitutional. The administration hastily devised a new plan in the Soil Conservation and Domestic Allotment Act, which it pushed through Congress in six weeks. The new act omitted processing taxes and acreage quotas but provided benefit payments for soil-conservation practices that reduced the planting of soil-depleting crops, thus indirectly achieving crop reduction.

The act was an almost unqualified success as an engineering and educational project because it helped heal the scars of erosion and the plague of dust storms. But soil conservation nevertheless failed as a device for limiting production. With their worst lands taken out of production, farmers cultivated their fertile acres more intensively. In response, Congress passed the Agricultural Adjustment Act of 1938, which reestablished the earlier programs but left out the processing taxes. Benefit payments would come from general federal funds. By the time the second AAA reached a test in the Supreme Court, changes in the Court's personnel had altered its outlook. This time the law was upheld as a legitimate exercise of federal power to regulate interstate commerce.

INDUSTRIAL RECOVERY   The industrial counterpart to the AAA was the National Industrial Recovery Act (NIRA), the two major parts of which dealt with economic recovery and public-works projects. The latter part created the Public Works Administration (PWA), granting $3.3 billion for government buildings, highway programs, flood control, and other improvements. Under the direction of Interior Secretary Harold L. Ickes, the PWA indirectly served the purpose of relief for the unemployed. Ickes focused it on well-planned permanent improvements, and he used private contractors rather than workers on the government payroll. PWA workers built Virginia's Skyline Drive, New York's Triborough Bridge, the Overseas Highway from Miami to Key West, and Chicago's subway system.

The more controversial and ambitious part of the NIRA created the National Recovery Administration (NRA), headed by Hugh S. Johnson, a colorful retired army general. Its purpose was twofold: (1) to stabilize business by reducing chaotic competition through the implementation of industry-wide codes that set wages and prices and (2) to generate more purchasing power for consumers by providing jobs, defining workplace standards, and raising wages. In each major industry, committees representing management, labor, and government drew up the fair practices codes. The labor standards featured in every code set a forty-hour workweek and minimum weekly wages of $13 ($12 in the South, where living costs were lower), which more than doubled earnings in some cases. Announcement of a proviso prohibiting the employment of children under the age of sixteen did "in a few minutes what neither law nor constitutional amendment had been able to do in forty years," Johnson said.

Labor unions, already hard-pressed by the economic downturn and a loss of members, were understandably concerned about the NRA's efforts to reduce competition by allowing competing businesses to cooperate in fixing wages and prices. To gain their support, the NRA included a provision that guaranteed the right of workers to organize unions. But while prohibiting employers from interfering with union-organizing efforts, the NRA did not create adequate enforcement measures, nor did it require employers to bargain in good faith with labor representatives.

"The Spirit of the New Deal"

In this cartoon, employer and employee agree to cooperate in the spirit of unity that inspired the National Recovery Administration.

For a time the NRA worked, perhaps because an air of confidence had overcome the depression blues, and the downward spiral of wages and prices had subsided. But as soon as economic recovery began, business owners expressed growing hostility toward the constraints of the NRA codes. Charges mounted that the larger companies dominated the code-making activities and that price-fixing robbed small producers of the chance to compete. In 1934 an investigating committee substantiated some of the charges. Moreover, allowing manufacturers to limit production had discouraged capital investment. And because the NRA wage codes excluded agricultural and domestic workers, three out of every four employed African Americans derived no direct benefit from the program. By 1935 the NRA had developed more critics than friends. When it effectively died, in May 1935, struck down by the Supreme Court as unconstitutional, few paused to mourn.

Yet the NRA experiment left an enduring mark. With dramatic suddenness the industrywide codes had set new workplace standards, such as the forty-hour workweek and the abolition of child labor. The NRA's endorsement of collective bargaining spurred the growth of unions. Moreover, the codes advanced trends toward stabilization and rationalization that were becoming the standard practice of business at large and that, despite misgivings about the concentration of power, would be further promoted by trade associations. Yet as 1934 ended, economic recovery was nowhere in sight.

REGIONAL PLANNING   The wide-ranging scope of the New Deal embraced several pathbreaking ideas. The creation of the Tennessee Valley Authority (TVA) was a truly bold venture designed to bring electrical power and jobs to one of the poorest regions in the nation. In May 1933, Congress created the TVA as a multipurpose public corporation. By 1936 it had six dams completed or under way and a master plan to build nine high dams on the Tennessee River, which would create the "Great Lakes of the South," and other dams on the tributaries. The agency, moreover, opened the rivers to boats and barges, fostered soil conservation and forestry, experimented with fertilizers, drew new industries to the region, encouraged the formation of labor unions, improved schools and libraries, and sent cheap electric power pulsating through the valley for the first time. But the construction of dams

Norris Dam

The massive dam in Tennessee, completed in 1936, was essential to the TVA's effort to expand power production.

and the creation of huge power-generating lakes also meant the destruction of homes, farms, and communities. "I don't want to move," said an elderly East Tennessee woman. "I want to sit here and look out over these hills where I was born."

Inexpensive electricity became more and more the TVA's reason for being—a purpose that would become all the more important during World War II. The TVA's success at generating greater power consumption and lowering utility rates in distressed rural areas awakened private utilities to the mass consumer markets. Cheap power transported farmers of the valley from the age of kerosene to the age of electricity. The TVA's first rural cooperative, set up at Corinth, Mississippi, in 1934, pointed the way to the electrification of the nation's farms in the following decade.

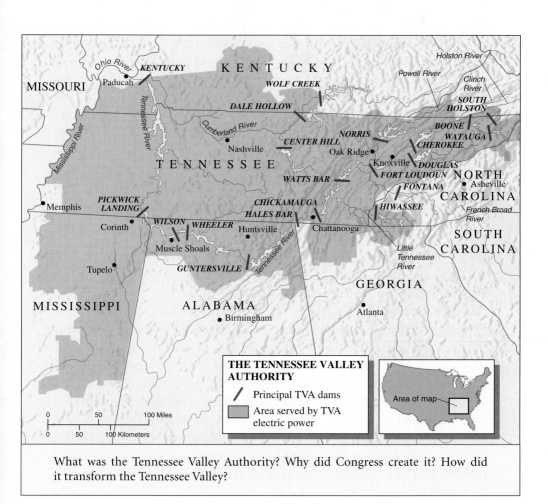

THE TENNESSEE VALLEY AUTHORITY

/ Principal TVA dams

▨ Area served by TVA electric power

What was the Tennessee Valley Authority? Why did Congress create it? How did it transform the Tennessee Valley?

The Social Cost of the Depression

Although New Deal programs helped ease the devastation wrought by the Depression, they did not restore prosperity or end the widespread human suffering. The Depression continued to take a toll on ordinary Americans: factory workers, farmers, bankers, and professionals remained in the throes of a shattered economy that was only slowly working its way back to health during the 1930s.

CONTINUING HARDSHIPS Roosevelt's New Deal programs did not end the Great Depression. As late as 1939, some 9.5 million workers (17 percent of the labor force) remained unemployed. Prolonged economic hardship continued to create personal tragedies and tremendous social strains. Poverty led desperate people to do desperate things. Petty theft soared during the 1930s, as did street-corner begging, homelessness, and prostitution. Although the divorce rate dropped during the decade, in part because couples could not afford to live separately or pay the legal fees to obtain a divorce, all too often husbands down on their luck simply deserted their wives and children. A 1940 survey revealed that 1.5 million husbands had left home. With their future uncertain, married couples often decided not to have children; the birthrate plummeted. Parents sometimes could not support their children. In 1933 the Children's Bureau reported that one out of every five children was not getting enough to eat. Struggling parents sent their children to live with relatives or friends. Some 900,000 children simply left home and joined the army of homeless "tramps."

DUST BOWL MIGRANTS In the southern plains of the Midwest and the Mississippi Valley, a decade-long drought during the 1930s spawned an environmental and human catastrophe known as the dust bowl. Colorado, New Mexico, Kansas, Nebraska, Texas, and Oklahoma were the hardest hit. Crops withered and income plummeted. Unrelenting winds swept across the treeless plains, scooping up millions of tons of parched topsoil into billowing dark clouds that floated east across entire states, engulfing farms and towns in what were called black blizzards. A massive dust storm in May 1934 darkened skies from Colorado to the Atlantic seaboard, depositing silt on porches and rooftops as well as on ships in the Atlantic Ocean. In 1937 there were seventy-two such major dust storms. The worst of them killed livestock and people and caused railroads to derail and automobiles to careen off roads. By 1938 over 25 million acres of prairie land had lost most of its topsoil.

What made these dust storms worse than normal was the transition during the early twentieth century from scattered subsistence farming to widespread commercial agriculture. Huge "factory farms" used dry-farming techniques to plant vast acres of wheat, corn, and cotton. The advent of powerful tractors, deep-furrow plows, and mechanical harvesters greatly increased the scale and intensity of farming—and the indebtedness of farmers. The mercurial cycle of falling crop prices and rising indebtedness led farmers to plant as much and as often as they could. Overfarming and overgrazing disrupted the fragile ecology of the plains by decimating the native prairie grasses that stabilized the nutrient-rich topsoil. Constant plowing loosened vast amounts of dirt, which were easily swept up by powerful winds during the devastating drought of the 1930s. Hordes of grasshoppers followed the gigantic dust storms and devoured what meager crops were left standing.

A sharecropper's family affected by the Oklahoma dust bowl

When the drought and dust storms showed no signs of relenting, many people headed west toward California.

Human misery paralleled the environmental devastation. Parched farmers could not pay mortgages, and banks foreclosed on their property. Suicides soared. With each year, millions of people abandoned their farms. Uprooted farmers and their families formed a migratory stream flowing from the South and the Midwest toward California, buoyed by currents of hope and desperation. The West Coast was rumored to have plenty of jobs. So off they went on a cross-country trek in pursuit of new opportunities. Although frequently lumped together as "Okies," most of the dust bowl refugees were actually from cotton belt communities in Arkansas, Texas, and Missouri, as well as Oklahoma. During the 1930s and 1940s, some 800,000 people left those four states and headed to the Far West. Not all were farmers; many were white-collar workers and retailers whose jobs had been tied to the health of the agriculture sector. Most of the dust bowl migrants were white, and most were adults in their twenties and thirties who relocated with spouses and children. Some traveled on trains or buses; others hopped a freight train or hitched a ride; most rode in their own cars, the trip taking four to five days on average.

Most of the dust bowl migrants who had come from cities gravitated to California's urban areas—Los Angeles, San Diego, or San Francisco. Many

Dust storm approaching, 1930s

When a dust storm blew in, it brought utter darkness, as well as the sand and grit that soon covered every surface, both indoors and out.

of the newcomers, however, moved into the San Joaquin Valley, the agricultural heartland of the state. There they discovered that rural California was no paradise. Only a few of the migrants could afford to buy land. Most found themselves competing with local Hispanics and Asians for seasonal work as pickers in the cotton fields or orchards of large corporate farms. Living in tents or crude cabins and frequently on the move, they suffered from exposure and poor sanitation.

They also felt the sting of social prejudice. The novelist John Steinbeck explained that "Okie us'ta mean you was from Oklahoma. Now it means you're a dirty son-of-a-bitch. Okie means you're scum. Don't mean nothing in itself, it's the way they say it." Such hostility toward the migrants drove a third of them to return to their home states. Most of the farmworkers who stayed tended to fall back upon their old folkways rather than assimilate into their new surroundings. These gritty "plain folk" had brought with them their own prejudices against blacks and ethnic minorities, as well as a potent tradition of evangelical Protestantism and a distinctive style of music variously labeled country, hillbilly, or cowboy. This "Okie" subculture remains a vivid part of California society.

MINORITIES AND THE NEW DEAL   The Great Depression was especially traumatic for the most disadvantaged groups. However progressive Franklin Roosevelt was on social issues, he failed to assault long-standing patterns of racism and segregation for fear of alienating conservative southern Democrats in Congress. As a result, many of the New Deal programs were for whites only. The Federal Housing Administration, for example, refused to guarantee mortgages on houses purchased by blacks in white neighborhoods. In addition, both the CCC and the TVA practiced racial segregation.

The efforts of the Roosevelt administration to raise crop prices by reducing production proved especially devastating for African Americans and Mexican Americans. To earn the federal payments for reducing crops as provided by the AAA and other New Deal agriculture programs, many farm owners would first take out of cultivation the marginal lands worked by tenants and sharecroppers. The effect was to drive the landless off farms and eliminate the jobs of many migrant workers. Over 200,000 black tenant farmers nationwide were displaced by the AAA.

Mexican Americans suffered as well. Thousands of Mexicans had migrated to the United States during the 1920s, most of them settling in California, New Mexico, Arizona, Colorado, Texas, and the midwestern states. But because many of them were unable to prove their citizenship,

Migratory Mexican field worker at home

On the edge of a frozen pea field in Imperial Valley, California, this home to a migratory Mexican family reflects both poverty and impermanence.

either because they were ignorant of the regulations or because their migratory work hampered their ability to meet residency requirements, they were denied access to the new federal relief programs under the New Deal. As economic conditions worsened, government officials called for the deportation of Mexican-born Americans to avoid the cost of providing them with public services. By 1935 over 500,000 Mexican Americans and their American-born children had returned to Mexico. The state of Texas alone returned over 250,000 people.

Deportation became a popular solution in part because of the rising level of involvement of Mexican American workers in union activities. In 1933, Mexican American women in El Paso, Texas, formed the Society of Female Manufacturing Workers to protest wages as low as 75¢ a day. In the same year some 18,000 Mexican cotton pickers went on strike in California's San Joaquin Valley. Police crushed the strike by burning the workers' camps.

Native Americans were also devastated by the Great Depression. They initially were encouraged by Roosevelt's appointment of John Collier as the commissioner of the Bureau of Indian Affairs (BIA). Collier steadily increased the number of Native Americans employed by the BIA and strove to ensure that Indians gained access to the various relief programs. Collier's primary objective, however, was passage of the Indian Reorganization Act. He wanted the new legislation to replace the provisions of the General Allotment Act (1887), known as the Dawes Act, which had sought to "Americanize" Indians by breaking up their tribal land and allocating it to individuals. Collier insisted that the Dawes Act had produced only widespread poverty and demoralization. He hoped to reinvigorate Indian cultural traditions by restoring land to tribes, granting Indians the right to charter business enterprises and establish self-governing constitutions, and providing federal funds for vocational training and economic development. The act that Congress finally passed was a much-diluted version of Collier's original proposal, however, and the "Indian New Deal" brought only a partial improvement to the lives of Native Americans.

COURT DECISIONS AND CIVIL RIGHTS   Although the NAACP's legal campaign against racial prejudice gathered momentum during the 1930s, a major setback occurred in the Supreme Court decision *Grovey v. Townsend* (1935), which upheld the Texas Democrats' whites-only primary.

The Scottsboro case

Heywood Patterson (center), one of the defendants in the case, is seen here with his attorney, Samuel Liebowitz (left) in Decatur, Alabama, in 1933.

But the *Grovey* decision held for only nine years and marked the end of the major decisions that for half a century had narrowed application of the civil rights amendments ratified after the Civil War. A reversal had already set in. Two important precedents arose from the celebrated Scottsboro case in 1931, in which nine black youths were convicted of raping two white women while riding a freight train in Alabama. The first verdict failed, the high court ruled in *Powell v. Alabama* (1932), because the judge had not ensured that the accused were provided adequate defense attorneys. In *Norris v. Alabama* (1935), the Court ruled that the systematic exclusion of African Americans from Alabama juries had denied the defendants equal protection of the law—a principle that had widespread impact on state courts.

Like Woodrow Wilson, Franklin Roosevelt did not give a high priority to racial issues. As a consequence many of his New Deal programs failed to help minorities, and in a few instances the new initiatives discriminated against those least able to help themselves. Nevertheless, Roosevelt included in his administration people who did care deeply about racial issues. As his first term drew to a close, Roosevelt found that there was a de facto "black cabinet" of some thirty to forty advisers in government departments and agencies, people who were very concerned about racial issues and the plight of African Americans. Moreover, by 1936 many black voters were fast transferring their political loyalty from the Republicans (the "party of Lincoln") to the Democrats and would vote accordingly in the coming presidential election.

Culture in the Thirties

In view of the celebrated—if exaggerated—alienation of writers, artists, and intellectuals rebelling against the materialism of the 1920s, one might have expected the onset of the Great Depression to have deepened their despair. Instead, it brought a renewed sense of militancy and affirmation, as if society could no longer afford the art-for-art's-sake outlook of the 1920s. Said one writer early in 1932: "I enjoy the period thoroughly. The breakdown of our cult of business success and optimism, the miraculous disappearance of our famous American complacency, all this is having a tonic effect."

In the early 1930s the "tonic effect" of commitment sometimes sparked revolutionary political activities. By the summer of 1932, even the "golden boy" of the lost generation, the writer F. Scott Fitzgerald, had declared that "to bring on the revolution, it may be necessary to work within the Communist party." But few Americans remained Communists for long. Being a notoriously independent lot, most writers rebelled at demands to hew to a shifting party line. And many abandoned communism upon learning that the Soviet leader Joseph Stalin practiced a tyranny more horrible than anything under the czars.

LITERATURE AND THE DEPRESSION   Among the writers who addressed themes of immediate social significance, two novelists deserve special notice: John Steinbeck and Richard Wright. The single piece of fiction that best captured the ordeal of the Depression, Steinbeck's *The Grapes of Wrath* (1939), treats workers as people rather than just a variable in a political formula. Steinbeck had traveled with displaced "Okies" driven from the Oklahoma dust bowl to pursue the illusion of good jobs in the fields of California's Central Valley. This firsthand experience allowed him to create a vivid tale of the Joad family's painful journey west from Oklahoma.

Among the most talented of the young novelists emerging in the 1930s was Richard Wright, an African American born near Natchez, Mississippi. The grandson of former slaves and the son of a Mississippi sharecropper who deserted his family, Wright ended his formal schooling with the ninth grade (as valedictorian of his class). He then worked in Memphis and devoured books he borrowed on a white friend's library card, all the while saving up to go north to escape the racism of the segregated South. In Chicago the Federal Writers' Project gave him a chance to develop his talent. His period as a Communist, from 1934 to 1944, gave him an intellectual framework that did not overpower his fierce independence. *Native Son* (1940), Wright's masterpiece, is the story of Bigger Thomas, a product of the ghetto, a man hemmed in, and finally impelled to murder, by forces beyond his control.

POPULAR CULTURE   While many writers and artists dealt directly with the human suffering and social tensions aroused by the Great Depression, the more popular cultural outlets, such as radio programs and movies, provided patrons with a welcome escape from the decade's grim realities. By the 1930s, radio had become a major source of family entertainment. More than 10 million families owned a radio, and by the end of the decade the number had tripled. "There is radio music in the air, every night, everywhere," reported a San Francisco newspaper. "Anybody can hear it at home on a receiving set which any boy can put up in an hour." Franklin Roosevelt was the first president to take full advantage of the popularity of radio broadcasting. He hosted sixteen "fireside chats" to generate public support for his New Deal initiatives.

In the late 1920s, what had been silent films were transformed by the introduction of sound. The "talkies" made movies by far the most popular form of entertainment during the 1930s—much more popular than they are today. The introduction of double features in 1931 and the construction of outdoor drive-in theaters in 1933 boosted interest and attendance. More than 60 percent of the population—70 million people—saw at least one movie each week.

The movies of the 1930s rarely dealt directly with hard times. Exceptions were the film version of *The Grapes of Wrath* (1940) and the classic documentaries of Pare Lorentz, *The Plow That Broke the Plains* (1936) and *The River* (1937). Much more popular were movies intended for pure entertainment; they transported viewers into the realm of adventure, spectacle, and fantasy. People relished shoot-'em-up gangster films, animated cartoons, spectacular musicals, "screwball" comedies, and horror films such as *Dracula* (1931), *Frankenstein* (1931), *The Mummy* (1932), and *Werewolf of London* (1935).

But the best way to escape the daily troubles of the Depression was to watch one of the zany comedies of the Marx Brothers, former vaudeville performers. As one Hollywood official explained, the movies of the 1930s

The Marx Brothers

In addition to their vaudeville antics, the Marx Brothers satirized social issues such as Prohibition.

were intended to "laugh the big bad wolf of the depression out of the public mind." *The Cocoanuts* (1929), *Animal Crackers* (1930), and *Monkey Business* (1931) introduced Americans to the anarchic antics of Chico, Groucho, Harpo, and Zeppo Marx, who combined slapstick humor with verbal wit to create plotless masterpieces of irreverent satire.

THE SECOND NEW DEAL

During Roosevelt's first year in office, his programs and his personal charms generated massive support. The president's travels and speeches, his twice-weekly press conferences, and his radio-broadcast fireside chats brought vitality and warmth in contrast to the aloof coldness of the Hoover White House. In the congressional elections of 1934, the Democrats increased their strength in both the House and the Senate, an almost unprecedented midterm victory for a party in power. Only seven Republican governors remained in office throughout the country.

ELEANOR ROOSEVELT   One of the reasons for Roosevelt's unprecedented popularity was his wife, Eleanor, who had become an enormous political asset and would prove to be one of the most influential and revered leaders of the time. From an early age, Eleanor Roosevelt had embraced social service and shown ardent concern for the rights of women and blacks. Her compassion resulted in part from the loneliness she had experienced as she was growing up and in part from the sense of betrayal she felt upon learning in 1918 that her husband was engaged in an extramarital affair with Lucy Mercer, her personal secretary. "The bottom dropped out of my own particular world," she recalled. In the face of personal setbacks, Eleanor Roosevelt "lived to be kind." Compassionate without being maudlin, more stoic

The First Lady

An intelligent, principled, and candid woman, Eleanor Roosevelt became a political figure in her own right. Here she is serving as guest host for a radio program, ca. 1935.

than sentimental, she exuded warmth and sincerity, and she challenged the complacency of the comfortable and the affluent. "No woman," observed a friend, "has ever so comforted the distressed or so distressed the comfortable."

Eleanor Roosevelt redefined the role of the presidential spouse. She was the first woman to address a national political convention, to write a nationally syndicated column, and to hold regular press conferences. A tireless advocate and agitator, Eleanor crisscrossed the nation, representing the president and the New Deal, defying local segregation ordinances to meet with African American leaders, supporting women's causes and organized labor, highlighting the plight of unemployed youth, and imploring people to live up to their egalitarian and humanitarian ideals.

Eleanor Roosevelt also became her husband's most visible and effective liaison with many liberal groups, bringing labor leaders, women activists, and African American leaders to the White House after hours and serving to deflect criticism of the president by taking progressive stands and running political risks he himself dared not attempt. He was the politician, she once remarked, and she was the agitator.

CRITICISM   Public criticism of the New Deal during Roosevelt's first year in office was muted, but not for long. The Depression's downward slide had been halted, but unemployment remained high (10 million were still out of work in 1935, more than 20 percent of the workforce), and prosperity remained elusive. "We have been patient and long suffering," said a farm leader in October 1933. "We were promised a New Deal. . . . Instead we have the same old stacked deck." Even more unsettling to some was the dramatic growth of executive power and the emergence of welfare capitalism, whereby workers developed a sense of entitlement to federal support programs. In 1934 a group of conservative businessmen and politicians, including Alfred E. Smith and John W. Davis, two former Democratic presidential candidates, formed the American Liberty League to oppose New Deal measures as violations of personal and property rights.

More potent threats to Roosevelt came from the hucksters of social panaceas. The most flamboyant of the group was Louisiana's "Kingfish," Senator Huey P. Long. A short, strutting man, Long sported pink suits and pastel shirts, red ties, and two-toned shoes. He was a brilliant but unscrupulous reformer driven by a compulsive urge for power and attention. First as Louisiana's governor, then as political boss of the state, Long had delivered tax favors, roads, schools, free textbooks, charity hospitals, and better public services. That he had become a sort of state dictator in the process, using bribery, physical intimidation, and blackmail to achieve his ends, seemed irrelevant to many of his supporters.

In 1933, Long arrived in Washington as a Democratic senator. He initially supported Roosevelt and the New Deal but quickly grew suspicious of the NRA's collusion with big business. He had also grown jealous of Roosevelt's mushrooming popularity, having developed his own presidential aspirations. Promoting himself as a radical egalitarian, a true if self-indulgent friend of the people, Long devised his own plan for dealing with the Great Depression.

"The Kingfish"

Huey Long, governor of Louisiana. Although he often led people to believe he was a country bumpkin, Long was a shrewd lawyer and consummate politician.

Long's Share-the-Wealth program proposed to confiscate large personal fortunes so as to guarantee every poor family a cash grant of $5,000 and every worker an annual income of $2,500, provide pensions to the aged, reduce working hours, pay veterans' bonuses, and ensure a college education for every qualified student. It did not matter to him that his projected budgets failed to add up or that his program offered little to promote an economic recovery. As he told a group of distressed Iowa farmers, "Maybe somebody says I don't understand it. Well, you don't have to. Just shut your damn eyes and believe it. That's all." Whether he had a workable plan or not, by early 1935 the charismatic Long was claiming 7.5 million supporters.

Another popular social scheme was hatched by a gray-haired California doctor, Francis E. Townsend. Outraged by the sight of three elderly women raking through garbage cans for scraps of food, Townsend called for government pensions for the aged. In 1934 he began promoting the Townsend Recovery Plan, which would pay $200 a month to every citizen over sixty who retired from employment and promised to spend the money within each month. The plan had the lure of providing financial security for the aged and stimulating economic growth. Critics noted that the cost of his program, which would serve 9 percent of the population, would be more than half the national income. Yet Townsend, like Long, was indifferent to details and balanced budgets. "I'm not in the least interested in the cost of the plan," he blandly told a House committee.

Promoters of welfare capitalism

Dr. Francis E. Townsend, Rev. Gerald L. K. Smith, and Rev. Charles E. Coughlin (left to right) attended the Townsend Recovery Plan convention in Cleveland, Ohio.

A third huckster of panaceas, Father Charles E. Coughlin, the Roman Catholic "radio priest," founded the National Union for Social Justice in 1935. In broadcasts over the CBS radio network, he promoted schemes for the coinage of more silver to increase the money supply and made attacks on bankers that increasingly hinted at anti-Semitism.

Coughlin, Townsend, and Long drew support largely from desperate lower-middle-class Americans. Of the three, Long had the widest following. A 1935 survey showed that he could draw over 5 million votes as a third-party candidate for president in 1936, perhaps enough to undermine Roosevelt's chances of reelection. Beset by pressures from both ends of the political spectrum, Roosevelt hesitated for months before deciding to "steal the thunder" from the left by instituting an array of new programs. "I'm fighting Communism, Huey Longism, Coughlinism, Townsendism," Roosevelt told a reporter in early 1935. He needed "to save our system, the capitalist system," from such "crackpot ideas." Political pressures impelled Roosevelt to move to the left, but so did the growing influence within the administration of jurists Louis Brandeis and Felix Frankfurter. These powerful advisers urged Roosevelt to be less cozy with big business and to push for restored competition in the marketplace and heavy taxes on large corporations.

OPPOSITION FROM THE COURT A series of Supreme Court decisions finally galvanized the president to act. On May 27, 1935, the Court killed the National Industrial Recovery Act by a unanimous vote. The defendants in *Schechter Poultry Corporation v. United States*, quickly tagged the "sick-chicken" case, had been convicted of selling an "unfit chicken" and violating other NRA code provisions. The high court ruled that Congress had delegated too much power to the executive branch when it granted the code-making authority to the NRA. In addition, Congress had exceeded its power under the commerce clause by regulating intrastate commerce. The poultry in question, the Court decided, had "come to permanent rest within the state," although earlier it had been moved across state lines. In a press conference soon afterward, Roosevelt fumed: "We have been relegated to the horse-and-buggy definition of interstate commerce." The same line of conservative judicial reasoning, he warned, might endanger other New Deal programs—if he did not act swiftly.

LEGISLATIVE ACHIEVEMENTS OF THE SECOND NEW DEAL To rescue his legislative program from such judicial and political challenges, Roosevelt in 1935 launched the second phase of the New Deal. He demanded several pieces of "must" legislation, most of which Congress passed within a few months. The National Labor Relations Act, often called the Wagner Act for its sponsor, New York senator Robert Wagner, gave workers the right to bargain through unions of their own choice and prohibited employers from interfering with union activities. The Wagner Act also created a National Labor Relations Board of five members to supervise plant elections and certify unions as bargaining agents where a majority of the workers approved. The board could also investigate the actions of employers and issue "cease-and-desist" orders against specified unfair practices.

The Social Security Act of 1935, Roosevelt announced, was the New Deal's "cornerstone" and "supreme achievement." Indeed, it has proved to be the most significant and far-reaching of all the New Deal initiatives. The basic concept was by no means new. Progressives during the early 1900s had proposed a federal system of social security for the aged, indigent, disabled, and unemployed. Other nations had already enacted such programs, but the United States

A *monthly check to you —*

FOR THE REST
OF YOUR LIFE
·· BEGINNING
WHEN YOU ARE
65

GET YOUR
SOCIAL SECURITY
ACCOUNT NUMBER
promptly

APPLICATIONS ARE BEING
DISTRIBUTED AT ALL WORK PLACES

WHO IS ELIGIBLE ·· ·EVERYBODY WORKING FOR SALARY OR WAGES
(WITH ONLY A FEW EXCEPTIONS, SUCH AS AGRICULTURE, DOMESTIC SERVICE, AND
GOVERNMENT WORK). APPLICATIONS FOR SOCIAL SECURITY ACCOUNTS ARE AVAIL-
ABLE THROUGH EMPLOYERS. IF YOU DO NOT GET ONE FROM YOUR EMPLOYER, ASK
FOR ONE AT THE POST OFFICE

HOW TO RETURN APPLICATION

— Social Security Board

INFORMATION MAY BE OBTAINED AT ANY POST OFFICE

Social Security

A poster distributed by the government to educate the public about the new Social Security Act.

remained steadfast in its tradition of individual self-reliance. The hardships caused by the Great Depression revived the idea of a social security program, however, and Roosevelt masterfully guided the legislation through Congress.

The Social Security Act included three major provisions. Its centerpiece was a pension fund for retired people over the age of sixty-five and their survivors. Beginning in 1937, workers and employers contributed payroll taxes to establish the fund. Benefit payments started in 1940 and averaged $22 per month, a modest sum even for those depressed times. Roosevelt stressed that the pension program was not intended to guarantee a comfortable retirement; it was designed to supplement other sources of income and protect the elderly from some of the "hazards and vicissitudes of life." Only later did voters and politicians come to view Social Security as the *primary* source of retirement income for most of the aged.

The Social Security Act also set up a shared federal-state unemployment-insurance program, financed by a payroll tax on employers. In addition, the new legislation committed the national government to a broad range of social-welfare activities based upon the assumption that "unemployables"—people who were unable to work—would remain a state responsibility while the national government would provide work relief for the able-bodied. To that end the law inaugurated federal grants-in-aid for three state-administered public-assistance programs—old-age assistance, aid to dependent children, and aid for the blind—and further aid for maternal, child-welfare, and public health services.

When compared with similar programs in Europe, the new Social Security system was quite conservative. It was the only government pension program in the world financed by taxes on the earnings of workers: most other countries funded such programs out of general revenues. The Social Security payroll tax was also a regressive tax: it entailed a single fixed rate for all, regardless of income level. It thus pinched the poor more than the rich, and it also impeded Roosevelt's efforts to revive the economy because it removed from circulation a significant amount of money: the new Social Security tax took money out of workers' pockets and placed it into a retirement trust fund, exacerbating the shrinking money supply that was one of the main causes of the Depression. By taking discretionary income away from workers, the government blunted the sharp increase in consumer spending needed to restore the health of the economy. In addition, the Social Security system initially excluded 9.5 million workers who most needed the new program: farm laborers, domestic workers, and the self-employed, a disproportionate percentage of whom were African Americans.

Roosevelt regretted the limitations of the Social Security Act, but he knew that they were necessary compromises in order to see the legislation through Congress and enable it to withstand court challenges. As he replied to an aide who criticized funding the pension program out of employee contributions:

> I guess you're right on the economics, but those taxes were never a problem of economics. They are politics all the way through. We put those payroll contributions there so as to give the contributors a moral, legal, and political right to collect their pensions and their unemployment benefits. With those taxes in there, no damn politician can ever scrap my Social Security program.

Another major bill making up the second phase of the New Deal was the Revenue Act of 1935, sometimes called the Wealth-Tax Act but popularly known as the soak-the-rich tax. The Revenue Act raised tax rates on annual income above $50,000. Estate and gift taxes also rose, as did the corporate tax on all but small corporations (those with an annual income below $50,000).

Business leaders fumed over Roosevelt's tax and spending policies. They railed against the New Deal and Roosevelt, whom they called a traitor to his own class. By "soaking" the rich, Roosevelt stole much of the thunder from the political left, although the results of his tax policy fell short of the promise. The new soak-the-rich tax failed to increase federal revenue significantly, nor did it result in a significant redistribution of income. Still, the prevailing view among conservatives was that Roosevelt had moved in a dangerously radical direction. The newspaper editor William Randolph Hearst growled that the wealth tax was "essentially communism. This bastard proposal should be ascribed to a composite personality which might be labeled Stalin Delano Roosevelt." Roosevelt countered by stressing his own basic conservatism and asserted that he had no love for socialism: "I am fighting communism. . . . I want to save our system, the capitalistic system." Yet he added that to save it from revolutionary turmoil required a more equal "distribution of wealth."

Roosevelt's Second Term

THE ELECTION OF 1936   On June 27, 1936, Roosevelt accepted the Democratic party's nomination for a second term. He promised a government motivated by "a spirit of charity" rather than a government "frozen in the ice of its own indifference." The popularity of Roosevelt and the New Deal impelled the Republican Convention in 1936 to avoid candidates too closely identified with the "hate-Roosevelt" contingent. The party chose

Campaigning for a second term

Roosevelt campaigning with labor leader John L. Lewis (to the right of Roosevelt) and Marvin McIntyre (far right) in Wilkes-Barre, Pennsylvania.

Governor Alfred M. Landon of Kansas, a former progressive Republican who had endorsed many New Deal programs. He was probably more liberal than most of his backers and clearly more so than the party's platform, which lambasted the New Deal for overextending federal power.

The Republicans hoped that the followers of Long, Coughlin, Townsend, and other dissidents would combine to draw enough Democratic votes away from Roosevelt to throw the election to them. But that possibility faded when an assassin, the son-in-law of a Louisiana judge whom Long had sought to remove, shot and killed the Kingfish in 1935. In the 1936 election, Coughlin, Townsend, and a remnant of the Long movement supported Representative William Lemke of North Dakota on a Union party ticket, but it was a forlorn effort, polling only 882,000 votes.

In 1936, Roosevelt forged a new electoral coalition that would affect national politics for years to come. While holding the support of most traditional Democrats, North and South, the president made strong gains in the West among beneficiaries of New Deal agricultural programs. In the northern cities he held on to the ethnic groups helped by New Deal welfare measures. Many middle-class voters whose property had been saved by New Deal measures flocked to support Roosevelt, as did intellectuals stirred by the ferment of new ideas coming from the government. The revived labor union movement threw its support to Roosevelt. And in the most profound new departure of all, African American voters for the first time cast the majority of their ballots for a Democratic president. "My friends, go home and turn Lincoln's picture to the wall," a Pittsburgh journalist told black Republicans. "That debt has been paid in full." The final tally in the 1936 election revealed that 81 percent of those with an income under $1,000 a year opted for Roosevelt, as did 79 percent of those earning between $1,000 and $2,000. By contrast, only 46 percent of those earning over $5,000 voted for Roosevelt. He later claimed that never before had business leaders been "so united against one candidate." They were "unanimous in their hate for me—and I welcome their hatred." In the 1936 election, Roosevelt wound up carrying every state except Maine and Vermont, with a popular vote of 27.7 million to Landon's 16.7 million. Democrats would also dominate Republicans in the new Congress, by 77 to 19 in the Senate and 328 to 107 in the House.

THE COURT-PACKING PLAN Soon after his landslide reelection, however, Roosevelt found himself deluged in a sea of troubles. His second inaugural address, delivered on January 20, 1937, promised even greater reforms. The challenge to American democracy, he maintained, was that millions of citizens "at this very moment are denied the greater part of what the very lowest standards of today call the necessities of life. . . . I see one-third of a nation ill-housed, ill-clad, ill-nourished." Roosevelt argued that the election of 1936 had been a mandate for even more extensive government action. The overwhelming Democratic majorities in Congress ensured the passage of new legislation to buttress the Second New Deal. But one major roadblock stood in the way: the conservative Supreme Court.

By the end of its 1936 term, the Court had ruled against New Deal programs in seven of the nine major cases it reviewed. Suits against the Social Security and Wagner Acts were pending. Given the tenor of the Court, the Second New Deal seemed in danger of being nullified, just as much of the original New Deal had been.

Court packing

An editorial cartoon commenting on Roosevelt's grandiose plan to enlarge the Supreme Court. He is speaking to Harold Ickes, director of the Public Works Administration (PWA).

For that reason, Roosevelt devised an ill-conceived plan to change the Court's conservative stance by enlarging it, a move for which there was ample precedent and power. Congress, not the Constitution, determines the size of the Supreme Court, which at different times has numbered six, seven, eight, nine, and ten justices and in 1937 numbered nine. On February 5, 1937, Roosevelt sent his plan to Congress, without having consulted congressional leaders. He wanted to create up to fifty new federal judges, including six new Supreme Court justices, and diminish the power of the judges who had served ten or more years or had reached the age of seventy.

But the "Court-packing" maneuver, as opponents quickly tagged the president's scheme, backfired. It was a shade too contrived, much too brazen, and far too political. The normally pro–New Deal *New York World-Telegram* dismissed it as "too clever, too damned clever." By implying that some judges were impaired by senility, Roosevelt affronted the elder statesmen of Congress and the Court, especially Justice Louis D. Brandeis, who was both the oldest and the most liberal of the Supreme Court judges. Roosevelt's Court-packing plan also ran headlong into a deep-rooted public veneration of the courts and aroused fears that a future president might use the precedent for quite different purposes.

As it turned out, unforeseen events blunted Roosevelt's drive to change the Court. A sequence of Court decisions during the spring of 1937 reversed previous judgments in order to uphold the Wagner and Social Security Acts. In addition, a conservative justice resigned, and Roosevelt named to the vacancy one of the most consistent New Dealers, Senator Hugo Black of Alabama.

Roosevelt later claimed he had lost the battle but won the war. The Court had reversed itself on important New Deal legislation, and the president was able to appoint justices in harmony with the New Deal. But the episode fractured the Democratic party and blighted Roosevelt's prestige. For the first time, Democrats in large numbers, especially southerners, opposed the president, and the Republican opposition found a powerful new issue to use against the administration. During the first eight months of 1937, the momentum of Roosevelt's 1936 landslide victory evaporated. As Secretary of Agriculture Henry Wallace later remarked, "The whole New Deal really went up in smoke as a result of the Supreme Court fight."

A NEW DIRECTION FOR UNIONS Rebellions erupted on other fronts even while the Court-packing bill pended. Under the impetus of the New Deal, the dormant labor union movement stirred anew. When the National Industrial Recovery Act demanded that every industry code affirm the workers' right to organize a union, alert unionists quickly translated it to mean "the president wants you to join the union."

John L. Lewis, head of the United Mine Workers (UMW), was among the first to exploit the pro-union spirit of the NIRA. He rebuilt the UMW from 150,000 members to 500,000 within a year. Spurred by Lewis's success, Sidney Hillman of the Amalgamated Clothing Workers and David Dubinsky of the International Ladies Garment Workers organized workers in the clothing industry. As leaders of industrial unions (composed of all types of workers in a particular industry), which were in the minority by far, they found the smaller, more restrictive craft unions (composed of skilled male workers only, with each union serving just one trade) to be obstacles to organizing the country's basic industries.

In 1935, with the passage of the Wagner Act, the industrial unionists formed a Committee for Industrial Organization (CIO), and craft unionists began to fear submergence by the mass unions. Jurisdictional disputes divided them, and in 1936 the AFL expelled the CIO unions, which then formed a permanent structure, called after 1938 the Congress of Industrial Organizations (also known by the initials CIO). The rivalry spurred both groups to greater efforts.

Organized labor

CIO picketers jeer as nonstriking workers enter a mill, 1941.

The CIO's major organizing drives in the automobile and steel industries began in 1936, but until the Supreme Court upheld the Wagner Act in 1937, companies failed to cooperate with its pro-unionist provisions. Employers used blacklisting, private detectives, labor spies, vigilante groups, and other forms of intimidation to fight the infant unions. Early in 1937 automobile workers spontaneously adopted a new technique, the "sit-down strike," in which workers refused to leave a workplace until employers had granted collective-bargaining rights to their union.

Led by the fiery young autoworker and union organizer Walter Reuther, thousands of employees at the General Motors assembly plants in Flint, Michigan, occupied the factories and stopped all production. Female workers supported their male counterparts by picketing at the plant entrances. The wives, daughters, and mothers of the strikers formed a Women's Auxiliary to feed the "sit-down" strikers who slept at the plants. Yet management refused to recognize the union efforts. Company officials called in police to harass the strikers, sent spies to union meetings, and threatened to fire the workers. They also pleaded with President Roosevelt to dispatch federal troops. He refused, while expressing his displeasure with the sit-down strike. The standoff lasted over a month. Then, on February 11, 1937, the company relented and signed a contract recognizing the United Automobile Workers as a legitimate union. Other automobile manufacturers soon followed suit. And the following month, U.S. Steel capitulated to the Steel Workers Organizing Committee (later the United Steelworkers of America), granting the union recognition and its members a 10 percent wage hike and a forty-hour workweek.

The Wagner Act put the power of the federal government behind the principle of unionization. Roosevelt himself, however, had come late to the support of unions and sometimes took exception to their behavior. In the fall of 1937, he became so irritated with the warfare between the mercurial John L. Lewis and the Republic Steel Corporation that he pronounced "a plague on both your houses." The pompous Lewis, who for a year had been trying to organize a union for steelworkers, responded, "It ill behooves one who has supped at labor's table and who has been sheltered in labor's house to curse with equal fervor and fine impartiality both labor and its adversaries when they become locked in a deadly embrace." In 1940 an angry Lewis would back the Republican presidential candidate, but he could not carry the labor vote with him. As more wage workers became organized, they more closely identified with the Democratic party. By August 1937 the CIO claimed over 3.4 million members, more than the AFL. The unions made a difference in the lives of workers and in the political scene. Through their efforts, wages rose and working conditions improved, and Roosevelt and the Democratic party were the beneficiaries of the labor movement. Workers became active voters and reliable Democrats. But unions made little headway in the South, where conservative Democrats and mill owners stubbornly opposed efforts to organize workers.

A SLUMPING ECONOMY   During the years 1935 and 1936 the economy finally showed signs of revival. By the spring of 1937, output had moved above the 1929 level. The prosperity of early 1937 was achieved largely through federal spending. But in 1937, Roosevelt, worried about federal deficits and rising inflation, ordered sharp cuts in government spending. At the same time the Treasury began to diminish disposable income by collecting $2 billion in Social Security payroll taxes. Private spending could not fill the gap left by reductions in government spending, and business leaders still lacked the faith to risk large investments. The result was that the economy suddenly stalled and then slid into a business slump deeper than that of 1929. The Dow Jones stock average fell some 40 percent between August and October of 1937. By the end of the year, 4 million more people had been thrown out of work.

The 1937 recession ignited a fierce debate among Roosevelt's advisers. One group, led by Treasury Secretary Henry Morgenthau Jr., favored less spending and a balanced budget. The slow pace of recovery, Morgenthau thought, resulted from the reluctance of business to invest in new plants and equipment, which resulted in turn from a fear that federal spending would bring inflation and heavy taxes. The other group, which included Harry Hopkins and Harold Ickes, argued for renewed government spending. The recession, they noted, had coincided with cutbacks in federal spending. Their view echoed that of the prominent English economist John Maynard Keynes, who had explored the idea in his book *The General Theory of Employment, Interest, and Money* (1935). Keynesian economics offered a convenient theoretical justification for what New Dealers had already done in pragmatic response to existing conditions.

ECONOMIC POLICY AND LATER REFORMS   Roosevelt waited as the rival theorists sought his approval. When the spring of 1938 failed to bring economic recovery, he asked Congress to adopt a new large-scale federal spending program, and Congress voted almost $3.3 billion in new expenditures. In a short time the increase in spending reversed the economy's decline, but the recession and Roosevelt's reluctance to adopt the truly massive, sustained government spending called for in Keynesian theory forestalled the achievement of full recovery. Only during World War II would employment reach pre-1929 levels.

The Court-packing fight, the sit-down strikes, and the 1937 recession all undercut Roosevelt's prestige and power. When the 1937 congressional session ended, the only major new bills were the Wagner-Steagall National Housing Act and the Bankhead-Jones Farm Tenant Act. In 1938 the Democratic Congress enacted three more major reforms, the last of the New Deal era: the second Agricultural Adjustment Act; the Food, Drug and Cosmetic Act; and the Fair Labor Standards Act.

The Housing Act set up the U.S. Housing Authority in the Department of the Interior, which extended long-term loans to local agencies willing to assume part of the cost of slum clearance and public housing in blighted city neighborhoods. The agency also subsidized rents for poor people. Later, during World War II, it financed housing for workers in new defense plants.

The Farm Tenant Act addressed the epidemic of rural poverty. In some ways the New Deal's larger farm program, the AAA, had aggravated agrarian distress; although tenants were supposed to be kept on farms in spite of government-sponsored cutbacks in production, landlords often evicted workers and pocketed their share of the benefit payments. The Farm Tenant Act was administered by a new agency, the Farm Security Administration (FSA). The program provided rehabilitation loans to shore up marginally profitable farmers and prevent them from sinking into tenancy. It also made loans to tenants for the purchase of their own farms. In the end, however, the FSA proved to be little more than another relief operation that tided a few farmers over during difficult times. Sadly, a more effective answer to the problem awaited national mobilization for war, which landed many struggling tenant farmers in military service or the defense industry, broadened their horizons, and taught them new skills.

The Agricultural Adjustment Act of 1938 addressed problems created by

"A Prop against Human Erosion"

Editorial cartoonist Daniel Fitzpatrick comments on the passing of the Minimum Wage and Hour Law.

the renewed crop surpluses and price declines of the recession. It reenacted the basic devices of the earlier AAA, encouraging farmers to reduce production. The new Food, Drug, and Cosmetic Act broadened the coverage of the 1906 Pure Food and Drug Act and forbade the use of false or misleading advertising. Enforcement of the advertising provision became the responsibility of the Federal Trade Commission. The Fair Labor Standards Act applied only to enterprises engaged in *interstate* commerce. It set a minimum wage of 40¢ an hour and a maximum workweek of forty hours, to be put into effect over several years. The act also prohibited the employment of children under the age of sixteen.

The Legacy of the New Deal

SETBACKS FOR THE PRESIDENT   During the late 1930s the Democratic party fragmented. The conservative southern wing felt threatened when in 1936 the Democratic Convention eliminated the two-thirds rule for nominations, thereby removing the South's veto power, and seated African American delegates. Many southern Democrats balked at the national party's growing dependence on organized labor and northern blacks. Ellison "Cotton Ed" Smith of South Carolina and several other southern delegates walked out of the 1936 convention, with Smith declaring that he would not support any party that views "the Negro as a political and social equal." Other critics believed that Roosevelt was exercising too much power and spending too much money. Some disgruntled southern Democrats drifted toward a coalition with conservative Republicans. By the end of 1937, a bipartisan conservative bloc had coalesced against the New Deal.

In 1938 the conservative opposition stymied an attempt by Roosevelt to reorganize the executive branch, claiming that it would lead to dictatorship. Members of the opposition also secured drastic cuts in the undistributed-profits and capital-gains taxes to help restore business "confidence." That year the House of Representatives set up a Committee on Un-American Activities, chaired by Martin Dies of Texas, who took to the warpath against Communists. Soon he began to brand New Dealers as Communists. "Stalin baited his hook with a 'progressive' worm," Dies wrote in 1940, "and New Deal suckers swallowed the bait, hook, line, and sinker."

As the political season of 1938 advanced, Roosevelt unfolded a new idea as momentous as the Court-packing plan: a proposal to reshape the Democratic party in the image of the New Deal. He announced his plan to intervene in state Democratic primaries as the party leader, "charged with the responsibility of carrying out the definitely liberal declaration of principles set forth in the 1936 Democratic platform." He wanted his own supporters nominated in the state primaries. The effort backfired, however, and broke the spell of Roosevelt's invincibility, or what was left of it. As in the Court-packing fight, the president had risked his prestige while handing his adversaries a combustible issue to use against him. His opponents tagged his intervention in the primaries an attempt to "purge" the Democratic party of its southern conservatives; the word evoked visions of Adolf Hitler and Joseph Stalin, tyrants who had purged their Nazi and Communist parties with blood.

The elections of November 1938 handed the administration another setback, partly a result of the friction among the Democrats. Roosevelt had failed in his efforts to liberalize the party by ousting southern conservatives. The Democratic dominance in the House fell from 229 to 93, in the Senate from 56 to 42. The margins remained large, but the president now headed a divided party. In his State of the Union message in 1939, Roosevelt for the first time proposed no new reforms but spoke of the need "to invigorate the process of [economic] recovery, in order to *preserve* our reforms." In the same year the administration won an expansion of Social Security and finally put through a plan to streamline the federal bureaucracy. Under the Administrative Reorganization Act the president could "reduce, coordinate, consolidate, and reorganize" government agencies. Thereafter, however, Roosevelt lost widespread congressional and popular support. The conservative coalition of Republicans and southern Democrats had stalemated the Roosevelt juggernaut. As one observer noted, the New Deal "has been reduced to a movement with no program, with no effective political organization, with no vast popular party strength behind it."

A HALFWAY REVOLUTION   The New Deal had petered out as war was erupting in Europe and Asia, but it had wrought several enduring changes. By the end of the 1930s, the power of the national government was vastly larger than it had been in 1932, and hope had been restored to people who had grown disconsolate. But the New Deal entailed more than just bigger government and revived public confidence. It also constituted a significant change from the older liberalism embodied in the progressivism of Theodore Roosevelt and Woodrow Wilson. Those reformers, despite their sharp differences, had assumed that the function of progressive government was to use aggressive regulation of industry and business to ensure that the people had an equal opportunity to pursue their notions of happiness.

Franklin Roosevelt and the New Dealers went beyond this concept of regulated capitalism by insisting that the government not simply *respond* to social crises but also take positive steps to *avoid* them. To this end the New Deal's various benefit programs sought to ensure a minimum level of well-being for all Americans. The New Deal had established minimum qualitative standards for labor conditions and public welfare and helped middle-class Americans hold on to their savings, their homes, and their farms. The protection afforded by bank-deposit insurance, unemployment pay, and Social Security pensions would come to be universally accepted as a safeguard against future depressions.

In implementing his domestic program, Roosevelt steered a zigzag course between the extremes of laissez-faire capitalism and socialism. The first New Deal experimented for a time with a managed economy under the NRA but abandoned that experiment for a turn toward enforcing competition and increasing government spending. This tactic finally produced full employment during World War II.

Roosevelt himself, impatient with political theory, was flexible in developing policy: he kept what worked and discarded what did not. The result was,

Meeting of the anti–New Dealers

Senator Ellison D. "Cotton Ed" Smith of South Carolina cringes at the thought of a fourth term for Roosevelt, while meeting with fellow anti–New Dealers at the Mayflower Hotel in Washington.

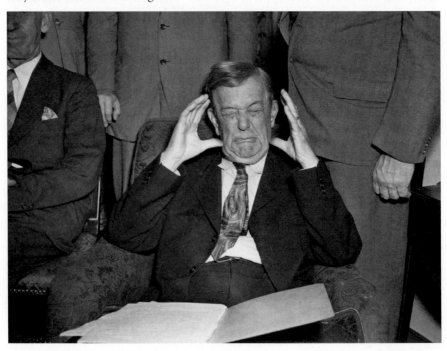

paradoxically, both profoundly revolutionary and profoundly conservative. Roosevelt sharply increased the regulatory functions of the federal government and laid the foundation for what would become an expanding welfare system. Despite what his critics charged, however, his initiatives fell far short of socialism; they left the basic capitalist structure in place. In the process of such bold experimentation and dynamic preservation, the New Deal represented a "halfway revolution" that permanently altered the nation's social and political landscape.

CHAPTER SUMMARY

- **Stabilizing the Economy** In March 1933 the economy, including the farm sector, was shattered, and millions of Americans were without jobs and the most basic necessities of life. FDR and his "brain trust" of advisers set out to restore confidence in the economy by supporting the banking industry and providing short-term emergency relief for the unemployed, promoting industrial recovery, and reducing the size of famers' crops by raising commodity prices.

- **The New Deal** Initially most of the New Deal programs were conceived as temporary relief and recovery efforts. They eased hardships but did not restore prosperity. It was during the Second New Deal that reform measures, such as Social Security and the Wagner Act, reshaped the nation's social structure.

- **New Deal Criticisms** Some conservatives criticized the New Deal for violating personal and property rights and for steering the nation toward socialism. Some liberals believed that the measures did not tax the wealthy enough to provide the aged and disadvantaged with adequate financial security.

- **Federal Expansion** The New Deal expanded the powers of the national government by establishing regulatory bodies and laying the foundation of a social welfare system. The federal government would in the future regulate business to some extent to avoid social and economic problems.

- **Culture of the 1930s** The literature of the 1930s turned away from the alienation from materialism that characterized the literary works of the previous decade's "lost generation." John Steinbeck and Richard Wright, for example, realistically depicted ordinary people living in, and suffering through, extraordinary times. Radio comedies and the new "talking" movies allowed people to escape their daily troubles.

CHRONOLOGY

March 1933	Congress passes the Emergency Banking Relief Act
March 1933	Congress passes the Beer-Wine Revenue Act
March 1933	Congress establishes the Civilian Conservation Corps
May 1933	Congress creates the Tennessee Valley Authority
June 1933	Congress establishes the Federal Deposit Insurance Corporation
November 1933	Congress creates the Civil Works Administration
1935	President Roosevelt creates the Works Progress Administration
1935	Congress passes the Wagner Act
1937	Social Security goes into effect
1939	John Steinbeck's *Grapes of Wrath* is published
1940	Richard Wright's *Native Son* is published

KEY TERMS & NAMES

New Deal p. 1081

Franklin D. Roosevelt
p. 1081

Twenty-first Amendment
p. 1086

Federal Writers' Project
p. 1089

Agricultural Adjustment Act
p. 1091

National Industrial
Recovery Act p. 1092

National Recovery
Administration p. 1092

dust bowl p. 1096

Eleanor Roosevelt p. 1105

Second New Deal p. 1105

Huey Long p. 1106

Share-the-Wealth program
p. 1107

Court-packing plan
p. 1113

Keynesian economics
p. 1118

2 9

FROM ISOLATION
TO GLOBAL WAR

FOCUS QUESTIONS wwnorton.com/studyspace

- What was the effect of isolationism and the peace movement on American politics between the two world wars?
- What events in Europe seemed to herald another international conflict in the 1930s?
- How did the United States respond to German aggression in Europe in the late 1930s?
- How did events in Asia lead to Japan's attack on Pearl Harbor?

I n the late 1930s, as the winds of war swept across Asia and Europe, the focus of American politics moved abruptly from domestic to foreign affairs. Roosevelt, like Woodrow Wilson before him, had to shift attention from social reform to military preparedness and war. And the public again had to wrestle with a painful choice: involve the country in volatile world affairs or remain aloof and officially neutral.

POSTWAR ISOLATIONISM

THE LEAGUE AND THE UNITED STATES Between Woodrow Wilson and Franklin Roosevelt lay two decades of relative isolation from foreign entanglements. The postwar mood of detached indifference to global affairs expressed in the election of 1920 set the pattern. The voters yearned for a restored isolationism, and President-elect Harding lost little time in disposing of the League of Nations. "You just didn't want a surrender of the United States," he stressed in his victory speech. "That's why you didn't care for the League, which is now deceased." The spirit of isolation found other expressions as well: the higher tariff rates on foreign imports, the Red Scare, and the restrictive immigration laws with which the nation all but shut the door to newcomers.

The United States may have felt the urge to insulate itself from a wicked world, but it could hardly ignore its own expanding global interests. American business now had worldwide connections. American investments and loans abroad put in circulation the dollars that enabled foreigners to purchase American exports. Overseas possessions, moreover, directly involved the country in world affairs, especially in the Pacific. Even the League of Nations was too great a fact to ignore. By the end of 1922, the United States sent "unofficial observers" to the League's headquarters in Geneva, and after 1924 U.S. diplomats gradually entered into joint efforts with the League in such matters as the international trade in illegal drugs and arms and the criminal traffic in women and children, and they took part in a variety of economic, cultural, and technical conferences.

WAR DEBTS AND REPARATIONS   Probably nothing did more to heighten American isolationism—or anti-American feeling in Europe—than the war-debt tangle. When in 1917 the Allies had begun to exhaust their ability to pay for American military supplies, the U.S. government had advanced them massive loans, first for the war effort and then for postwar reconstruction.

Most Americans expected the debts to be paid back, but Europeans had a different perception. In the first place, Americans who thought their loan money had flowed to Europe were wrong: most of it went toward purchases of military supplies in the United States, which fueled American prosperity. Then, too, the Allies held off the Germans at great cost while the United States was raising an army. American states, the British noted, had repudiated debts to British investors after the American Revolution; the French pointed out that they had never been repaid for helping the Americans win the Revolution and gain their independence. But most difficult were the practical problems of repayment. To get dollars to use to pay their war-related debts to the United States, European nations had to sell their goods to the United States, but American tariff rates soared in 1921 and 1922 and again in 1930, making European goods more expensive and debts harder to pay.

The French and the British had insisted that they could repay their war-related debts to the United States only as they collected reparations from defeated Germany. Twice during the 1920s the resulting financial strain on Germany brought the structure of international payments to the verge of collapse, and both times the Reparations Commission called in private American bankers to work out rescue plans.

The whole structure finally did collapse during the Great Depression. In 1931, President Hoover negotiated a moratorium on both German reparations and Allied payment of war debts, thereby indirectly accepting the connection between the two. The purpose was in part to shore up American private loans of several billion dollars to Germany, which for a time had kept the international credit structure intact. Once the United States had accepted the connection between reparations and war debt, the Allies virtually canceled German reparations. At the end of 1932, after Hoover's debt moratorium ended, most European countries defaulted on their war debts to the United States. In retaliation, Congress passed the Johnson Debt Default Act of 1934, which prohibited even private loans to any government that had defaulted on its debts to the United States.

ATTEMPTS AT DISARMAMENT   After World War I many Americans decided that excessive armaments had caused the terrible conflict and that arms limitations treaties would bring lasting peace. The United States had no intention of maintaining a large army, but under the shipbuilding program begun in 1916, it constructed a navy second only to that of Britain. Neither the British nor the Americans wanted a naval armaments race, but both were worried about the alarming growth of Japanese power.

As a result of Japan's wartime attempts to expand its presence in China, Japanese-American relations grew increasingly strained during the war and remained so thereafter as the United States objected to continued Japanese encroachments in Asia. In 1915 Japan issued what came to be known as the Twenty-one Demands, which would virtually have brought China under Japanese control. The United States protested, and fortunately the Japanese decided not to force their most rigorous demands. In 1917, after the United States entered the war, Viscount Kikujirō Ishii visited Washington to secure American recognition of Japan's expanding claims in Asia. Secretary of State Robert Lansing signed an ambiguous agreement that recognized Japan's "special interests" (translated by the Japanese as "paramount interests") in China. Americans were unhappy with the Lansing-Ishii Agreement, but it seemed the only way to preserve the appearance of friendship.

After the war ended, Japanese-American relations worsened. To address the problem, President Warren Harding invited eight principal foreign powers to a naval-armaments conference in Washington in 1921. U.S. secretary of state Charles Evans Hughes, in what was expected to be a perfunctory greeting, announced that the only way out of an armaments race "is to end it now." It was one of the most dramatic moments in diplomatic history. In less than fifteen minutes, one electrified reporter said, Hughes had destroyed more warships "than all the admirals of the world have sunk in a cycle of centuries."

Delegates from the United States, Britain, Japan, France, and Italy signed the Five-Power Treaty (1922), which incorporated Hughes's plan for tonnage limits on their navies and a moratorium of ten years during which no battleships would be built. The five major powers also agreed to refrain from further fortification of their Pacific possessions. The agreement in effect partitioned the world: U.S. naval power became supreme in the Western Hemisphere, Japanese power in the western Pacific, and British power from the North Sea to Singapore.

Two other significant agreements emerged from the Washington Naval Conference. With the Four-Power Treaty, the United States, Britain, Japan, and France agreed to respect one another's possessions in the Pacific. The Nine-Power Treaty for the first time pledged the signers to support the principle of the Open Door enunciated by Secretary of State John Hay in 1899. The Open Door enabled all nations to compete for trade and investment opportunities in China on an equal footing rather than allow individual nations to create economic monopolies in particular regions of that country. The signers of the Nine-Power Treaty also promised to respect the territorial integrity of China.

The Washington Conference, 1921

The Big Five at the conference were (from left) Iyesato Tokugawa (Japan), Arthur Balfour (Great Britain), Charles Evans Hughes (United States), Aristide Briand (France), and Carlo Schanzer (Italy).

The nations involved, in addition to those signing the Five-Power Treaty, were China, Belgium, Portugal, and the Netherlands.

With these agreements in hand, President Harding could boast of a brilliant diplomatic stroke that relieved citizens of the need to pay for an enlarged navy and warded off potential conflicts in the Pacific. Yet the agreements were without obligation and without teeth. The signers of the Four-Power Treaty agreed only to consult, not to help one another militarily. The formal endorsement of the Open Door in the Nine-Power Treaty was just as ineffective, for the American people remained unwilling to uphold the principle with anything but pious affirmation. The naval-disarmament treaty set tonnage limits only on capital ships (battleships and aircraft carriers); the race to build cruisers, destroyers, submarines, and other smaller craft continued. Expansionist Japan withdrew from the agreement in 1934. Thus, twelve years after the Washington Conference, the dream of naval disarmament died.

THE KELLOGG-BRIAND PACT   During and after World War I the fanciful ideal of simply abolishing war captured the American imagination. In 1921 a wealthy Chicagoan founded the American Committee for the Outlawry of War. "We can outlaw this war system just as we outlawed slavery and the saloon," said one of the more enthusiastic converts.

The glorious vision of abolishing war at the stroke of a pen culminated in the signing of the Kellogg-Briand Pact in 1928. This unique treaty started with an initiative by the French foreign minister Aristide Briand, who in 1927 proposed to Secretary of State Frank B. Kellogg an agreement whereby the two countries would never go to war against each other. This innocent-seeming proposal was actually a clever ploy to draw the United States into the French security system by the back door. In any future war, for instance, such a pact would inhibit the United States from seeking reprisals in response to any French intrusions on neutral rights. Kellogg gave the idea a cool reception and was outraged to discover that Briand had urged leaders of the American peace movement to put pressure on the government to sign the accord.

Kellogg turned the tables on Briand. He countered with a scheme to have all nations sign the pact. Caught in a trap of his own making, the French foreign minister finally relented. The Pact of Paris (its official name), signed on August 27, 1928, declared that the signatories "condemn recourse to war . . . and renounce it as an instrument of national policy." Eventually sixty-two nations adhered to the pact, but all reserved "self-defense" as an escape hatch. The U.S. Senate included a reservation declaring the preservation of the Monroe Doctrine necessary to self-defense and then ratified the agreement by a vote of 85 to 1. One senator who voted for "this worthless, but perfectly harmless peace treaty" wrote a friend later that he feared it would "confuse the minds of many good people who think that peace may be secured by polite professions of neighborly and brotherly love."

THE "GOOD NEIGHBOR" POLICY   In Latin America the spirit of peace and noninvolvement helped allay long-festering resentments against "Yankee imperialism," which had been freely practiced in the Caribbean during the first two decades of the century. The Harding administration agreed in 1921 to pay the republic of Colombia the $25 million it had once demanded for America's rights to the Panama Canal. In 1924, American troops left the Dominican Republic, occupied since 1916, although U.S. officials continued to collect customs duties there for another twenty-five years.

The marines left Nicaragua in 1925 but returned a year later at the outbreak of disorder and civil war. There, in 1927, the Coolidge administration brought both parties into an agreement for U.S.-supervised elections, but one rebel leader, César Augusto Sandino, held out, and the marines stayed until 1933.

The troubles in Nicaragua increased strains between the United States and Mexico. Relations had already been soured by repeated Mexican threats to expropriate American oil properties in Mexico. In 1928, however, the U.S. ambassador negotiated an agreement protecting American rights acquired before 1917. Expropriation did in fact occur in 1938, but the Mexican government agreed to reimburse American owners.

In 1928, with problems apparently clearing up in Mexico and Nicaragua, President Calvin Coolidge traveled to Havana, Cuba, to open the Pan-American Conference. It was an unusual gesture of friendship, and so was the choice of Charles Evans Hughes, the former secretary of state, to head the American delegation.

César Augusto Sandino

The rebel leader objected to U.S. intervention in Nicaragua.

Hughes announced the United States' intention to withdraw its marines from Nicaragua and Haiti as soon as possible, although he did block a resolution declaring that no nation "has the right to intervene in the affairs of another."

At the end of 1928, President-elect Herbert Hoover toured ten Latin American nations. Once in office he reversed Woodrow Wilson's policy of refusing to recognize "bad" regimes and reverted to the older policy of recognizing governments in power regardless of their actions. In 1930 he generated more goodwill by permitting publication of a memorandum drawn up in 1928 by Undersecretary of State J. Reuben Clark. The Clark Memorandum denied that the Monroe Doctrine justified U.S. military intervention in Latin America. Although Hoover never endorsed the memorandum, he never intervened in the region. Before he left office, steps had been taken to withdraw American forces from Nicaragua and Haiti.

Franklin D. Roosevelt likewise embraced the policy of the "good neighbor" and soon advanced it in practice. In 1933, at the Seventh Pan-American Conference, the United States supported a resolution declaring that no nation "has the right to intervene in the internal or external affairs of another." Under President Franklin Roosevelt the marines completed their withdrawal from Nicaragua and Haiti, and in 1934 the president negotiated with Cuba a treaty that abrogated the Platt Amendment and thus ended the last formal American claim to a right to intervene in Latin America. Roosevelt reinforced hemispheric goodwill in 1936, when he opened the Eighth Pan-American Conference with a speech declaring that outside aggressors "will find a Hemisphere wholly prepared to consult together for our mutual safety and our mutual good."

War Clouds

JAPANESE INCURSIONS INTO CHINA   Improving U.S. relations in the Western Hemisphere during the 1930s proved an exception in an otherwise dismal world scene as war clouds thickened over Europe and Asia. Actual conflict erupted in Asia first, where unsettled conditions in China had invited foreign encroachments since before the beginning of the century. Chinese nationalist aspirations in 1929 and China's subsequent clashes with Russia convinced the Japanese that their own extensive investments in Manchuria, including the South Manchurian Railway, were in danger.

Japanese occupation of Manchuria, a vast contested region in northeast Asia, began with the Mukden incident of 1931, when an explosion destroyed a section of railroad track near that city. The Japanese army based in Manchuria to guard the railway blamed the incident on the Chinese and used it as a pretext to occupy all of Manchuria. In 1932 the Japanese converted much of Manchuria into the puppet empire of Manchukuo.

The Manchuria incident, as the Japanese called their undeclared war, flagrantly violated the Nine-Power Treaty, the Kellogg-Briand Pact, and Japan's pledges as a member of the League of Nations. But when China asked the League and the United States for help, neither responded. President Hoover was unwilling to invoke military or economic sanctions. Secretary of State Henry L. Stimson, who would have preferred to do more, warned in 1932 that the United States refused to recognize any treaty, agreement, or situation that violated American treaty rights, the Open Door agreements, the territorial integrity of China, or any situation brought about by violation of the Kellogg-Briand Pact. This statement, later known as the Stimson Doctrine, had no effect on Japanese action, for soon the Japanese navy attacked and briefly occupied Shanghai, China's great port city.

Japan and China

Japan's seizure of Manchuria in 1931 prompted this American condemnation.

Indiscriminate Japanese bombing of China's civilian population in Shanghai aroused indignation but no further Western action. When the League of Nations condemned Japanese aggression in 1933, Japan withdrew from the League. During the spring of 1933, hostilities in Manchuria gradually subsided and ended with a truce. Then an uneasy peace settled upon east Asia for four years, during which time Japanese military leaders increased their political sway in Tokyo.

ITALY AND GERMANY   The rise of the Japanese militarists paralleled the rise of totalitarian dictators in Italy and Germany. In 1922, Benito Mussolini had seized power in Italy. After returning from World War I as a wounded veteran, he had organized the Fascist movement, a hybrid of nationalism and socialism. The Fascist program, and above all Mussolini's promise to restore order and pride in a country fragmented by dissension, enjoyed a wide appeal. Once in power, Mussolini largely abandoned the socialist part of his platform and gradually suppressed all political opposition. By 1925 he was wielding dictatorial power as "Il Duce" (the Leader).

There was always something ludicrous about the strutting, bombastic Mussolini. Italy, after all, was a declining power. But Germany was another matter, and Americans were not amused, even at the beginning, by Il Duce's German counterpart, Adolf Hitler. Hitler's National Socialist German Workers' (Nazi) party duplicated the major features of Italian fascism, including the ancient Roman salute. The impotence of Germany's democratic Weimar Republic in the face of world depression offered Hitler his opening. Made chancellor on January 30, 1933, he swiftly won dictatorial powers from a subservient Reichstag (parliament). In 1934 he assumed the title "Führer" (national leader), along with absolute powers. The Nazi police state cranked up the engines of tyranny, persecuting socialists and Jews, whom Hitler blamed for Germany's troubles, and re-arming in defiance of the Versailles Treaty. Hitler flouted international agreements, pulled Germany out of the League of Nations in 1933, and threatened to extend control over all German-speaking peoples. Despite Hitler's provocative actions, the European democracies lacked the will to resist his bold grab for power.

THE MOOD IN AMERICA   Most Americans, absorbed by the problems of the Depression, retreated all the more into isolationism during the early 1930s. In the 1932 presidential campaign, Roosevelt renounced his earlier support for the United States' joining the League of Nations. The chief exception to the administration's isolationism was Secretary of State Cordell Hull's grand scheme of reciprocal trade agreements. Hull believed that free

Axis leaders

Mussolini and Hitler in Munich, June 1940.

trade among all nations would advance understanding and preserve peace. In 1934 the administration threw its support behind Hull's pet project. Over the objections of business interests and Republicans, Congress adopted the Trade Agreements Act, which authorized the president to lower tariff rates as much as 50 percent for countries that made similar concessions on American products. The United States had signed such agreements with fourteen countries by the end of 1935 and with a total of twenty-nine by 1945.

Another effort to build foreign markets involved diplomatic recognition of Soviet Russia. By 1933 the reasons for America's refusal to recognize the Bolshevik regime had grown stale. Japanese expansionism in Asia, moreover, gave Russia and the United States a common concern. Given an opening by the shift of opinion, Roosevelt invited Maksim Litvinov, Soviet commissar for foreign affairs, to visit Washington, D.C. After nine days of talks, a formal exchange of notes on November 16, 1933, signaled the renewal of diplomatic relations. Litvinov promised that his country would abstain from promoting Communist propaganda in the United States, extend religious freedom to Americans in the Soviet Union, and reopen the question of unpaid czarist debts to America.

THE EXPANDING AXIS   As the 1930s unfolded, a catastrophic chain of events in Asia and Europe sent the world hurtling toward disaster. In 1934, Japan renounced the Five-Power Treaty. The next year, Mussolini commenced an Italian conquest of Ethiopia. That same year a referendum in Germany's Saar Basin, held in accordance with the Versailles Treaty, delivered the coal-rich region into the hands of Hitler. In 1936, Hitler reoccupied the Rhineland with armed forces, a direct violation of the Versailles Treaty. The French, however, failed to summon the courage to oust the German force. The year

Keeping in mind the terms of the Treaty of Versailles, explain why Hitler began his campaign of expansion by invading the Rhineland and the Sudetenland. Why would Hitler have wanted to retake the Polish Corridor? Why did the attack on Poland begin World War II, whereas Hitler's previous invasions of his European neighbors did not?

1936 also brought the Spanish Civil War, which began with an uprising of the Spanish armed forces in Morocco, led by General Francisco Franco. In three years, Franco had established a fascist dictatorship with help from Hitler and Mussolini while the European democracies stood by and left the Spanish republic to its fate.

On July 7, 1937, Japanese and Chinese troops clashed at the Marco Polo Bridge, west of Peking. The incident quickly developed into a full-scale war. World War II had begun in Asia two years before it would erupt in Europe. That year, Italy joined Germany and Japan in the Anti-Comintern Pact, allegedly directed at the Communist threat, thus establishing the Rome-Berlin-Tokyo "Axis."

By 1938 the peace of Europe trembled in the balance. Having rebuilt German military power, Hitler forced the *Anschluss* (union) of Austria with Germany in March 1938 and six months later took the Sudeten territory from Czechoslovakia after signing an agreement at Munich, according to which Britain and France sought to appease Hitler by abandoning Czechoslovakia, a country that probably had the second-best army in central Europe. The mountainous Sudetenland, largely German in population, was vital to the defense of Czechoslovakia. Having promised that this was his last territorial demand, Hitler brazenly violated his pledge in March 1939: the German army occupied the remainder of Czechoslovakia and seized formerly German territory from Lithuania. In quick succession the Spanish republic collapsed, and Mussolini conquered the kingdom of Albania. During the summer, Hitler heated up a "war of nerves" over control of the free city of Danzig (Gdánsk) and the Polish Corridor, and on September 1, 1939, Germany invaded Poland. A few days before, Hitler had signed a nonaggression pact with Soviet Russia. Having deserted Czechoslovakia, Britain and France now honored their commitment to go to war if Poland was invaded.

DEGREES OF NEUTRALITY   During these years of deepening crisis, the Western democracies seemed paralyzed, hoping in vain that each concession would appease the appetites of fascist dictators. The Americans retreated more deeply into isolation. The prevailing mood was reinforced by a Senate inquiry into the role of bankers and munitions makers in World War I. Under Senator Gerald P. Nye of North Dakota, a progressive Republican, the committee sat from 1934 to 1937 and at last concluded that bankers and munitions makers had made scandalous profits from the war. Although Nye never showed that the armaments industry had impelled Woodrow Wilson to lead the U.S. into war, millions of Americans became convinced that Uncle Sam had been duped by the "merchants of death."

During the 1930s the United States moved toward complete isolation from the quarrels of Europe. In 1935, President Roosevelt signed the first of five neutrality laws intended to keep the United States out of war. The Neutrality Act of 1935 forbade the sale of arms and munitions to any warring nation whenever the president proclaimed that a state of war existed. It also declared that Americans who traveled on belligerents' ships did so at their own risk. Roosevelt would have preferred discretionary authority to levy an embargo only against aggressors but reluctantly accepted the Neutrality Act because it would be in effect for only six months.

Yet on October 3, 1935, just weeks after Roosevelt signed it, Italy invaded Ethiopia and the president invoked the Neutrality Act. One shortcoming became apparent right away: the key problem was neither weapons traffic nor passenger travel but trade in material not covered by the law. While Italy did not need to buy arms, it did need to buy key supplies, such as oil, which the act did not cover. So the sanctions imposed under the Neutrality Act had no deterrent effect on Mussolini or his suppliers. In the summer of 1936, Italy conquered Ethiopia.

When Congress reconvened in 1936, it extended the arms embargo and added a provision forbidding loans to nations at war. It was, in July 1936, while Italian troops were mopping up the last resistance in Ethiopia, that the Spanish army, led by Franco, revolted against the democratic government in Madrid. Roosevelt then became an even greater isolationist than some of the country's most extreme isolationists. Although the Spanish Civil War involved a fascist uprising against a recognized democratic government, Roosevelt accepted the French and British position that only nonintervention would localize the fight. There existed, moreover, a strong bloc of pro-Franco Catholics in America, who worried that the Spanish republic was a threat to the Roman Catholic Church: they feared an atheistic Communist influence in the Spanish government. Intrigues by Spanish Communists did prove divisive, and the Soviet Union did supply aid to the republic, but it was nothing in comparison to the German and Italian assistance to Franco.

The conflict in Spain led Roosevelt to seek another "moral embargo" on the arms trade, and he asked Congress to extend the neutrality laws to instances of civil war. Congress did so in 1937 with only one dissenting vote. The Western democracies then stood by as German and Italian soldiers, planes, and armaments supported Franco's overthrow of Spanish democracy, which was completed in 1939.

In the spring of 1937, isolationist sentiment peaked in the United States. A Gallup poll found that 94 percent of its respondents preferred efforts to keep out of war over efforts to prevent war. That spring, Congress passed another

Neutrality

A 1938 cartoon shows U.S. foreign policy entangled by the serpent of isolationism.

neutrality law. This one maintained restraints on arms sales and loans, forbade Americans to travel on the ships of nations at war, and prohibited the arming of U.S. merchant ships trading with those nations. The president also won discretionary authority to require that goods other than arms or munitions exported to warring nations be sold on a cash-and-carry basis (that is, a purchaser would have to pay cash and then carry the goods away in its own ships). This was an ingenious scheme to preserve a profitable trade without running the risk of war.

The new law faced its first test in July 1937, when Japanese and Chinese forces clashed at the Marco Polo Bridge. Since neither side declared war, Roosevelt was able to use his discretion in invoking the neutrality law. He decided to wait and in fact never invoked it because its net effect would have favored the Japanese. The munitions trade with China flourished as ships carried arms across the Atlantic to England, where they were reloaded on British ships bound for Hong Kong. Roosevelt, by his inaction, had challenged strict isolationism.

Then, on December 12, 1937, Japanese planes bombed and sank the American gunboat *Panay*, which had been lying at anchor in China, on the Yangtze River, prominently flying the American flag; Japan also attacked

July 1937

Japanese troops enter Peking after the clash at the Marco Polo Bridge.

three American oil tankers. Two members of the *Panay* crew and an Italian journalist died; thirty more were injured. Though the Japanese government apologized and paid reparations, the incident heightened American animosity toward Japan. A private boycott of Japanese goods spread, but isolationist sentiment continued strong, as was vividly demonstrated by support for the Ludlow Amendment in Congress. The proposed constitutional amendment would have required a public referendum for a declaration of war except in the case of an attack on U.S. territory. Only by the most severe pressure from the White House, and a vote of 209 to 188, was consideration of the measure tabled in 1938.

After the German occupation of Czechoslovakia in 1939, Roosevelt began to abandon his neutral stance. He could no longer pretend impartiality in the deepening European struggle. Hitler's violation of his Munich pledge convinced Roosevelt that the German ruler was not simply a dictator but an aggressive international gangster who must be stopped. Throughout late 1938 and 1939, Roosevelt struggled to educate the American public about the menace of fascism. He urged Congress to repeal the embargo and permit the United States to sell arms on a cash-and-carry basis to Britain and France, but to no avail. When the Germans attacked Poland on September 1, 1939, Roosevelt proclaimed neutrality but in a radio talk said that he would not, like Woodrow Wilson in 1914, ask Americans to remain neutral in thought because "even a neutral has a right to take account of the facts."

Roosevelt summoned Congress into special session and asked once again for amendments to the Neutrality Act. "I regret the Congress passed the Act," the president said. "I regret equally that I signed the Act." This time he got what he wanted, however. Under the Neutrality Act of 1939, Britain and France could send their own freighters to the United States, buy supplies with cash, and take away arms or anything else they wanted. American ships, on the other hand, were excluded from the ports of warring nations and from specified war zones. Roosevelt then designated as a war zone the Baltic Sea, the waters around Great Britain and Ireland, and the waters from Norway south to the coast of Spain. One unintended effect of this move was to relieve Hitler of any inhibitions about using unrestricted submarine warfare to blockade Britain.

Once the great democracies of western Europe faced war, American public opinion, appalled at Hitler's expansive tyranny, supported measures short of war to help their cause. "What the majority of the American people want," an editor wrote in the *Nation,* "is to be as un-neutral as possible without getting into war." After Hitler overran Poland in less than a month, the war in Europe settled into a stalemate during early 1940 that began to be called the phony war. What lay ahead, it seemed, was a long war of attrition in which Britain and France would have the resources to outlast Hitler. That illusion lasted through the winter.

THE STORM IN EUROPE

BLITZKRIEG   In the spring of 1940, the winter's long *sitzkrieg* (sitting war) suddenly erupted into *blitzkrieg* (lightning war). At dawn on April 9, without warning, Nazi troops occupied Denmark and landed along the Norwegian coast. Denmark fell in a day, Norway within a few weeks. On May 10, Hitler unleashed dive bombers and tank divisions on neutral Belgium and the Netherlands. On May 21, German troops reached the English Channel, cutting off a British force sent to help the Belgians and the French. A desperate evacuation from the beaches at Dunkirk, on the French coast, enlisted every available British boat, from warship to tug. Amid the chaos some 338,000 soldiers, about a third of them French, escaped to England.

Having outflanked the forts on France's eastern perimeter of defense, the Maginot Line, the German forces rushed ahead, cutting the French armies to pieces and spreading panic. On June 14 the German swastika flew over Paris.

The Blitz

In London, St. Paul's Cathedral looms above
the destruction wrought by German bombs
during the Blitz. Winston Churchill's
response: "We shall never surrender."

Eight days later French delegates, in the presence of Hitler, submitted to his surrender terms in the same railroad car in which German delegates had been forced to sign the armistice of 1918.

AMERICA'S GROWING INVOLVEMENT Britain now stood alone, but in Parliament the new prime minister, Winston Churchill, breathed defiance. "We shall go on to the end," he said; "we shall never surrender." Nevertheless, America seemed suddenly vulnerable as Hitler turned his air force against Britain. After World War I the U.S. Army had been reduced to a small force; by 1939 it numbered only 175,000 and ranked sixteenth in the world in size, just behind Romania. It would take time to create a viable military force to stop fascism. President Roosevelt called for a military buildup and the production of 50,000 combat planes a year. By October 1940, Congress had voted more than $17 billion for defense. In response to Churchill's appeal for military supplies, the War and Navy Departments reluctantly followed Roosevelt's orders and began releasing stocks of arms, planes, and munitions to the British.

The world crisis transformed Roosevelt. Having been stalemated for much of his second term by growing congressional opposition, he was revitalized by the war in Europe. Nervous cabinet officers, military leaders, and diplomats now encountered a decisive president willing to exert executive authority on behalf of Britain. In June 1940 the president set up the National Defense Research Committee to coordinate military research, including a top-secret effort to develop an atomic bomb, suggested the previous fall by the physicist Albert Einstein and other scientists. To bolster national unity, Roosevelt named two Republicans to the defense posts in his cabinet: Henry L. Stimson as secretary of war and Frank Knox as secretary of the navy.

The summer of 1940 brought the desperate Battle of Britain, in which the Royal Air Force, with the benefit of radar, a new technology, outfought the numerically superior German Luftwaffe and finally forced the Germans to postpone plans to invade England. German submarine attacks, meanwhile, strained the resources of the battered Royal Navy. To relieve the pressure, Churchill urgently requested the transfer of American warships (destroyers) to the British fleet. Secret negotiations led to an executive agreement under which fifty "overaged" U.S. destroyers went to the British in return for ninety-nine-year American leases on naval and air bases in British territories in the Caribbean. Roosevelt disguised the action as necessary for defense of the hemisphere. On September 16, Roosevelt signed the first peacetime conscription in American history, requiring the registration of all 16 million men aged twenty-one to thirty-five; those chosen in a lottery and found fit were required to fulfill a year's military service within the United States.

"The Only Way We Can Save Her [Democracy]"

Political cartoon suggesting the U.S. not intervene in European wars.

The new state of affairs prompted vigorous debate between "internationalists," who believed national security demanded aid to Britain, and isolationists, who charged that Roosevelt was drawing the United States into a needless war. In 1940, internationalists organized the nonpartisan Committee to Defend America by Aiding the Allies. It drew its strongest support from the East and West Coasts and the South. On the other hand, isolationists formed the America First Committee, which included among its members Herbert Hoover and Charles A. Lindbergh Jr. The isolationists argued that the war involved, in Senator William E. Borah's words, "nothing more than another chapter in the bloody volume of European power politics." Borah and others argued that a Nazi victory over Great Britain, while distasteful, would pose no threat to national security.

FDR'S THIRD TERM   In the midst of these terrible global crises, the quadrennial presidential campaign came due. Isolationist sentiment was strongest in the Republican party. Both leading Republican candidates were noninterventionists, but neither man was of sufficient stature to challenge Roosevelt. Senator Robert A. Taft of Ohio, son of the former president, lacked popular appeal, and New York district attorney Thomas E. Dewey, at thirty-eight seemed young and unseasoned. This left an opening for an in-spired group of political amateurs to promote the dark-horse candidacy of Wendell L. Willkie of Indiana.

Willkie seemed at first an unlikely choice: a former Democrat who had voted for Roosevelt in 1932, but he was also a Hoosier farm boy whose disheveled charm inspired strong loyalty. Unlike the Republican front-runners, he openly supported aid to the Allies, and the Nazi Blitzkrieg had brought many other Republicans to the same viewpoint. When the Republicans met at Philadel-phia on June 28, six days after the French surrender, the convention was overwhelmed by the galleries' cries of "We want Willkie."

The Nazi victory in France also ensured Roosevelt's nomination. Had war not erupted in Europe, Roosevelt would probably have followed custom and retired after his second term. But the crisis led him to run again, for an un-precedented third term. The president cultivated party unity with his foreign policy and kept a sphinxlike silence about his intentions regarding the war. The world crisis reconciled southern conservatives to the man whose foreign policy, at least, they supported. At the July Democratic convention in Chicago, Roosevelt won the nomination for a third term with only token opposition.

Through the summer of 1940, Roosevelt assumed the role of a man above the political fray, busy rather with urgent matters of defense and diplomacy: pan-American agreements for mutual defense, the destroyer-bases deal, and visits to defense facilities that took the place of campaign trips. Willkie was reduced to making attacks on New Deal red tape and promises to run the new federal programs better. In the end, however, he switched to an attack on Roosevelt's conduct of foreign policy. In October he warned: "If you re-elect him you may expect war in April, 1941." To this Roosevelt responded, "I have said this before, but I shall say it again and again and again: Your boys are not going to be sent into any foreign wars." Neither man distinguished himself with such hollow statements, since both knew the risks of all-out aid to Britain, which they both supported.

Roosevelt won the election by a comfortable margin of 27 million votes to Willkie's 22 million and by a wider margin, of 449 to 82, in the Electoral Col-lege. Even so it was Roosevelt's narrowest victory. Willkie polled 5 million more votes than Alf Landon had four years before, a telling indicator of Roosevelt's declining stature. But given the dangerous world situation, a ma-jority of the voters still agreed with the Democrats' slogan: "Don't switch horses in the middle of the stream."

THE "ARSENAL OF DEMOCRACY"   Bolstered by the mandate for an unprecedented third term, Roosevelt moved quickly for greater measures to aid Britain, whose cash was running out. Since direct American loans would arouse memories of earlier war-debt defaults—the Johnson Debt Default Act of 1934 forbade such loans anyway—the president created an ingenious device to bypass that issue and yet supply British needs: the "lend-lease" program. In a fireside radio chat, Roosevelt told the nation that America must become "the great arsenal of democracy" because of the threat of Britain's fall to the Nazis. And to do so it must make new efforts to help the British purchase American supplies. The lend-lease bill, introduced in Congress on January 10, 1941, proposed authorizing the president to sell, transfer, exchange, lend, lease, or otherwise dispose of arms and other equipment and supplies to "any country whose defense the President deems vital to the defense of the United States."

For two months a bitter debate over the lend-lease bill raged in Congress and across the country. Isolationists saw it as the point of no return. "The lend-lease-give program," said Senator Burton K. Wheeler, "is the New Deal's triple A foreign policy; it will plow under every fourth American boy." Roosevelt pronounced this "the rottenest thing that has been said in public life in my generation." Administration supporters denied that lend-lease would lead to war, but they knew that it did increase the risk. Lend-lease became law in March. Almost all of the dissenting votes were Republican senators and congressmen from the staunchly isolationist Midwest.

While the nation debated, the European war expanded. Italy had officially entered the war in June 1940 as Germany's ally. In October 1940, when the American presidential campaign was approaching its climax, Mussolini launched attacks on Greece and, from Italian Libya, on the British in Egypt. But he miscalculated, and his forces had to fall back in both cases. In the spring of 1941, German forces under General Erwin Rommel joined the Italians in Libya, forcing the British to withdraw to Egypt, their resources having been drained to help Greece. In April 1941, Nazi armored divisions overwhelmed Yugoslavia and Greece, and by the end of May German airborne forces had subdued the Greek island of Crete, putting Hitler in a position to menace the entire Middle East.

With Hungary, Romania, and Bulgaria forced into the Axis fold, Hitler controlled nearly all of Europe. But his ambition was unbounded. On June 22, 1941, German armies suddenly fell upon Soviet Russia, their ally. Frustrated in the purpose of subduing Britain, Hitler sought to eliminate the potential threat on his rear with another lightning stroke. The Russian plains offered an ideal theater for Blitzkrieg, or so it seemed. With Romanian and Finnish allies, the Nazis massed 3.6 million troops and thousands of tanks and planes along a 2,000-mile front from the Arctic Ocean to the Black Sea. Then, after

Lend-lease

Members of the "Mother's Crusade," urging defeat of the lend-lease program, kneel in prayer in front of the Capitol. They feared the program would bring the United States into the European war.

four months of grudging retreat, the Russian soldiers rallied in front of Leningrad (formerly St. Petersburg), Moscow, and Sevastopol. During the winter of 1941–1942, Hitler's legions began to learn the bitter lesson the Russians had taught Napoleon and the French army in 1812. Invading armies had to contend with the Russian weather and Russian tenacity. Still, in the summer of 1941 the Nazi juggernaut appeared unstoppable.

Winston Churchill had already decided to offer British support to the Soviet Union in case of such an attack. "If Hitler invaded Hell," he said, "I would make at least a favorable reference to the Devil in the House of Commons." Roosevelt adopted the same pragmatic policy, offering American aid to Russia two days after the German attack. Stalinist Russia, so long as it held out against the Nazis, ensured the survival of Britain. American aid was now indispensable to Europe's defense, and the logic of lend-lease led to deeper American involvement. To deliver aid to Britain, convoys of supply ships had to maneuver through the German submarine "wolf packs" in the North Atlantic. So in April 1941, Roosevelt informed Churchill that the U.S. Navy would extend its patrols in the North Atlantic nearly all the way to Iceland.

In August 1941, Roosevelt and Churchill held a secret meeting off New-foundland, where they drew up a statement of principles known as the Atlantic Charter. Their joint statement called for the self-determination of all peoples, equal access to raw materials, economic cooperation, freedom of the seas, and a new system of international security. In September it was an-nounced that eleven anti-Axis nations, including the Soviet Union, had en-dorsed the charter.

Thus Roosevelt had led the United States into a joint statement of war aims with the anti-Axis powers. It was not long before shooting incidents in-volved Americans in the North Atlantic. The first attack on a U.S. warship occurred on September 4, when a German submarine fired two torpedoes at the destroyer *Greer.* A week later the president issued orders to "shoot on sight" any German or Italian raiders ("rattlesnakes of the Atlantic") that ventured into American waters. Five days later, the U.S. Navy began convoy-ing merchant vessels all the way to Iceland.

Then, on October 17, 1941, while the destroyer *Kearny* was attacking German submarines, it sustained severe damage from a German torpedo, and eleven lives were lost. Two weeks later a German submarine torpedoed and sank the destroyer *Reuben James,* with a loss of 115 seamen, while it was on convoy duty west of Iceland. This action spurred Congress to make addi-tional changes in the 1939 Neutrality Act already requested by the president. On November 17 the legislation was essentially repealed when the bans on arming merchant vessels and allowing them to enter combat zones and the ports of nations at war were removed. Step-by-step the United States had given up neutrality and embarked on naval warfare against Germany. Still the American people hoped to avoid taking the final step into all-out war. The decision to go to war would be made in response to aggression in an un-expected quarter—Hawaii.

THE STORM IN THE PACIFIC

JAPANESE AGGRESSION   After the Nazi victories in the spring of 1940, U.S. relations with Japan took a turn for the worse. Japanese militarists, bogged down in the vastness of China, now eyed new temptations in south Asia: French Indochina (Vietnam, Laos, Cambodia), the Dutch East Indies (Indonesia), British Malaya (Malaysia), and Burma (Myanmar), where they could cut off one of China's last links to the West, the Burma Road. What was more, they could incorporate into their "Greater East Asia Co-Prosperity Sphere" the oil, rubber, and other strategic materials that the crowded Japanese homeland lacked. As it was, Japan depended upon the United States for important supplies, including 80 percent of its fuel.

In 1940, Japan and the United States began a series of moves, each of which aggravated the other and pushed the two nations closer to war. During the summer of 1940, Japan forced the helpless French government, under German control at Vichy, to permit the construction of Japanese airfields in French-controlled northern Indochina and to cut off the railroad into south China. The United States responded with a loan to China and the Export Control Act of July 2, 1940, which authorized the president to restrict the export of American arms and other strategic materials to Japan. Gradually Roosevelt extended embargoes on aviation gas, scrap iron, and other supplies.

On September 27, 1940, the Tokyo government signed a Tripartite Pact with Germany and Italy, by which each pledged to declare war on any nation that attacked any of them. On April 13, 1941, while the Nazis were sweeping through the Balkans, Japan signed a nonaggression pact with the Soviet Union, and once the Nazis invaded Russia in June, the Japanese were freed of any threat from the north.

In July 1941, Japan announced that it was assuming a protectorate over all of French Indochina. Roosevelt took three steps in response: he froze all Japanese assets in the United States, he restricted oil exports to Japan, and he merged the armed forces of the Philippines with the U.S. Army and put their commander, General Douglas MacArthur, in charge of all U.S. forces in east Asia. By September the oil restrictions had tightened into an embargo. The Japanese estimated that their oil reserves would last two years at most. Forced by the American embargo to secure other oil supplies, the Japanese army and navy began planning attacks on the Dutch and British colonies to the south.

Actions by both sides put the United States and Japan on a collision course leading to a war that neither wanted. In his talks with the Japanese ambassador in Washington, Secretary of State Cordell Hull demanded that Japan withdraw from Indochina and China as the price of renewed trade with the United States. A more flexible position might have strengthened the moderates in Japan. The Japanese were not then pursuing a concerted plan of aggression comparable to Hitler's. The Japanese military leadership had stumbled crazily from one act of aggression to another without approval from the government in Tokyo. Prime Minister Fumimaro Konoe, however, while known as a man of liberal principles who preferred peace, caved in to pressures from the militants. Perhaps he had no choice.

The Japanese warlords, for their part, seriously misjudged the United States. The desperate wish of the Americans to stay out of the war might have enabled the Japanese to conquer the British and Dutch colonies in the Pacific. But the warlords decided that they dared not leave the U.S. Navy intact and the Philippines untouched on the flank of their new lifeline to the south.

TRAGEDY AT PEARL HARBOR   Thus a tragedy began to unfold with a fatal certainty—mostly out of sight of the American people, whose attention was focused on the war in the Atlantic and in Europe. Late in August

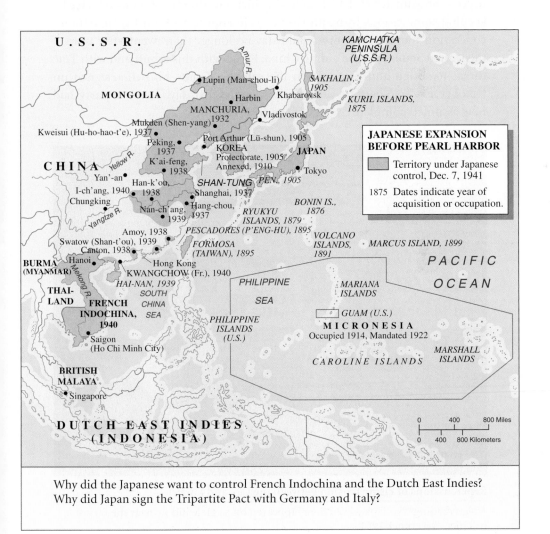

Why did the Japanese want to control French Indochina and the Dutch East Indies? Why did Japan sign the Tripartite Pact with Germany and Italy?

1941, Prime Minister Konoe proposed a meeting with President Roosevelt. Secretary of State Hull urged the president not to meet Konoe unless an agreement on fundamental issues could be reached in advance. Soon afterward, on September 6, a Japanese imperial conference approved preparations for a surprise attack on Hawaii and gave Prime Minister Konoe six weeks in which to reach a settlement.

The Japanese emperor's concern about the risks of an attack afforded the prime minister one last chance to pursue a compromise, but the stumbling block was still the presence of Japanese troops in China. In October, Konoe urged War Minister Hideki Tōjō to consider withdrawal while saving face by keeping some troops in north China. Tōjō countered with his "maximum concession": Japanese troops would stay no longer than twenty-five years if the United States stopped aiding China. Faced with this rebuff and with Tōjō threat to resign and bring down the cabinet, Konoe himself resigned on October 15; Tōjō became prime minister the next day. The war party had now assumed complete control of the government.

Repercussions of rising tension between the U.S. and Japan

A sign reading "No Japs served here" appeared on a cafe window near the Boston fish pier, December 1941.

On the very day that Tōjō became prime minister, a special Japanese envoy conferred with Hull and Roosevelt in Washington. The envoy's arrival was largely a cover for Japan's war plans, although neither he nor the Japanese ambassador knew that. On November 20 they presented Tōjō final proposal: Japan would occupy no more territory in Asia if the United States would cut off aid to China, restore trade, and help Japan get supplies from the Dutch East Indies. Tōjō expected the United States to refuse the demands. On November 26, Hull insisted that Japan withdraw from China altogether. War now seemed inevitable. "The question," Secretary of War Stimson thought, "was how we should maneuver them into the position of firing the first shot without allowing too much danger to ourselves." That same day a Japanese naval force began heading secretly across the North Pacific toward Pearl Harbor, the key American military base in the Pacific.

Officials in Washington knew that war was imminent. Reports of Japanese troop transports moving south from Formosa prompted them to send warnings to U.S. commanders in the Pacific and to the British government. The massive troop movements southward clearly signaled attacks on the British and the Dutch possessions. American leaders had every reason to expect war in the southwest Pacific, but none expected that Japan would commit most of its aircraft carriers to another attack 5,000 miles away, at Hawaii's Pearl Harbor.

In the early morning of December 7, 1941, American servicemen decoded the last part of a fourteen-part Japanese message breaking off the diplomatic negotiations. Japan's ambassador in Washington was instructed to deliver the message at 1 P.M. (7:30 A.M. in Honolulu), about a half hour before the Japanese attack, but delays held up delivery by more than an hour. The War Department sent out an alert at noon that something was about to happen, but the message, which went by commercial telegraph because radio contacts were broken, arrived in Hawaii eight and a half hours later. Even so, the decoded Japanese message had not mentioned Pearl Harbor, and everyone still assumed that any Japanese attack would be in Southeast Asia.

It was still a sleepy Sunday morning in Hawaii when the first Japanese planes roared down the west coast and the central valley of Oahu to begin their assault. For nearly two hours the Japanese planes pummeled an unsuspecting Pacific Fleet. Of the eight battleships in Pearl Harbor, three were sunk, one grounded, one capsized, and the others badly battered. Altogether, nineteen ships were sunk or disabled. At the adjoining Hickam Field and other airfields on the island, the Japanese found planes parked wing to wing and destroyed about 180 of them. The raid killed more than 2,400 American servicemen and civilians and wounded 1,178 more.

The attack on Pearl Harbor

This view from an army airfield shows the destruction brought on by the surprise attack.

The surprise attack fulfilled the dreams of its planners, but it fell short of success in two ways. The Japanese ignored the onshore facilities and oil tanks in Hawaii that supported the U.S. fleet, without which the surviving ships might have been forced back to the West Coast, and they missed the aircraft carriers that had fortuitously left port a few days earlier. In the naval war to come, those aircraft carriers would prove decisive.

Later that day (December 8 in the western Pacific), Japanese forces invaded the Philippines, Guam, Midway, Hong Kong, and the Malay Peninsula. With one stroke the Japanese had silenced America's debate on neutrality—a suddenly unified and vengeful nation prepared for war. The next day, President Roosevelt delivered his war message to Congress: "Yesterday, December 7, 1941—a date which will live in infamy—the United States of America was suddenly and deliberately attacked by naval and air forces of the Empire of Japan." Congress voted for the war resolution with near unanimity, the sole exception being Representative Jeannette Rankin, a Montana pacifist who was unable to vote for war in good conscience in 1917 or 1941. For several days it was uncertain whether war with the other Axis Powers would follow. The Tripartite Pact was ostensibly for defense only, and it carried no obligation for Germany and Italy to take part, but Hitler, impatient with the continuing American aid to Britain, willingly joined his Asian allies. On December 11, Germany and Italy impetuously declared war on the United States. The separate wars that were being waged by armies in Asia and Europe and Africa had become one global conflict—and American isolationism was cast aside.

CHAPTER SUMMARY

- **Isolationism** America distanced itself from global affairs—a stance reflected in the Red Scare, laws limiting immigration, and high tariffs. Yet America could not ignore international events because its business interests were becoming increasingly global. Although the United States never joined the League of Nations, it sent unofficial observers to Geneva. The widespread belief that arms limitations would reduce the chance of future wars led America to participate in the Washington Naval Conference of 1921 and the Kellogg-Briand Pact of 1928.

- **Totalitarianism** Totalitarian dictators came to power in Europe in the 1920s and 1930s. In Italy, Benito Mussolini assumed control by promising law and order. Adolf Hitler's National Socialist German Workers' party succeeded in part by responding to the humiliation many Germans felt after Germany's defeat in the Great War. Hitler rearmed Germany in defiance of the Treaty of Versailles and aimed to unite all German speakers in a new German empire. Civil war in Spain and the growth of the Soviet Union under Joseph Stalin contributed to a precarious balance of power in Europe between the major nations.

- **American Neutrality** By 1938, Hitler had annexed Austria and seized German populated areas of Czechoslovakia. By March 1939, Hitler had seized the rest of Czechoslovakia. He faced no opposition until he sent troops to invade Poland in September of 1939, after signing a nonaggression pact with the Soviet Union. At last, the British and French governments believed that they had no option but to declare war. The United States issued declarations of neutrality, but with the fall of France, President Roosevelt's administration accelerated American aid to France and Britain.

- **Japanese Threat** The bombing of an American gunboat in China by Japanese planes in 1937 alienated Americans. Further Japanese aggression in Asia contributed to the deterioration of U.S.-Japanese relations. After Japan allied itself with Germany and Italy and announced its intention to take control of French Indochina, President Roosevelt froze Japanese assets in the United States and restricted oil exports to Japan. The Japanese leadership, fearing that the U.S. Navy might challenge its conquests in the Pacific, decided to bomb the Pacific Fleet at Pearl Harbor, Hawaii. The attack was a surprise, carried out without a declaration of war.

CHRONOLOGY

1921	Representatives of the United States, Great Britain, France, Italy, and Japan attend the Washington Naval Conference
1922	United States begins sending observers to the League of Nations
1922	Benito Mussolini comes to power in Italy
1928	More than sixty nations sign the Kellogg-Briand Pact pledging not to go to war with one another, except in matters of self-defense
1933	Adolf Hitler becomes chancellor of Germany
1937	In the *Panay* incident, Japanese planes bomb and sink a U.S. gunboat in the Yangtze River
1938	Hitler forces the *Anschluss* (union) of Austria and Germany
1939	Soviet Union agrees to a nonaggression pact with Germany
September 1939	German troops invade Poland
1940	Battle of Britain
September 1940	Germany, Italy, and Japan sign the Tripartite Pact
December 7, 1941	Japanese launch surprise attack on the U.S. military base at Pearl Harbor, Hawaii

KEY TERMS & NAMES

30

THE SECOND WORLD WAR

FOCUS QUESTIONS   wwnorton.com/studyspace

- What effect did World War II have on American society?
- How did the Allied forces win the war in Europe?
- How did the United States gain the upper hand in the Pacific sphere?
- What efforts did the Allies make to shape the postwar world?

The Japanese attack on Pearl Harbor ended a period of tense neutrality for the United States, and it launched the nation into a global conflict that would cost the lives of over 400,000 Americans. The war would also transform the nation's social and economic life, as well as its position in international affairs. The Second World War would become the most destructive and far-reaching conflict in history. It was so terrible in its intensity and obscene in its cruelties that it altered the image of war itself. Devilish new instruments of destruction were invented—plastic explosives, proximity fuses, rockets, jet airplanes, and atomic weapons—and systematic genocide emerged as an explicit war aim of the Nazis. The scorching passions of such an all-out war blanched many moral protocols from the conduct of war. Racist propaganda flourished on both sides, and excited hatred of the enemy caused many military and civilian prisoners to be tortured and executed. Over 50 million deaths resulted from the worldwide war, two thirds of them civilians. The physical destruction was incalculable. Whole cities were leveled, nations dismembered, and societies transformed. The world is still coping with the consequences.

AMERICA'S EARLY BATTLES

At the end of 1941, the United States was woefully unprepared to wage a world war on multiple fronts. The army and navy were understaffed and underequipped. And it would take months for the economy to make the transition to full-scale military production. Yet time was of the essence. Japanese and German forces had seized the initiative and were on the move. Momentum was on their side.

SETBACKS IN THE PACIFIC   For months after the attack on Pearl Harbor, the news from the Pacific was "all bad," as President Roosevelt confessed. In quick sequence the well-armed and well-led Japanese captured numerous Allied outposts before the end of December 1941: Guam, Wake Island, the Gilbert Islands, and Hong Kong. Other British and American territories toppled like dominoes. The fall of Rangoon (present-day Yangon), in Burma, cut off the Burma Road, the main supply route to China. In the Philippines, where General Douglas MacArthur's army abandoned Manila on December 27, the main U.S. forces, outmanned and outgunned, held out on the Bataan Peninsula until April 9 and then retreated to the fortified island of Corregidor. General MacArthur slipped away in March, when he was ordered to Australia to take command of the Allied forces in the southwest Pacific. By May 6, 1942, when the American garrison at Corregidor

Early defeats

U.S. prisoners of war, captured by the Japanese in the Philippines, 1942.

surrendered, Japan controlled a vast new empire, (the "Rising Sun"), which stretched from Burma eastward through the Dutch East Indies and extending to Wake Island and the Gilbert Islands in the western Pacific.

The Japanese might have consolidated an almost impregnable empire with the resources they had seized. But leaders of the Japanese navy succumbed to what one of its admirals later called victory disease: intoxicated with easy victories and lusting for more conquests, they pushed on into the South Pacific, intending to isolate Australia, and strike again at Hawaii. Japanese war planners hoped to destroy the American navy before the productive power of the United States could be brought to bear on the war effort.

A Japanese mistake and a stroke of American luck enabled the U.S. Navy to frustrate the plan, however. Japan's failure to destroy the onshore facilities at Pearl Harbor left the naval base relatively intact, and most of the ships damaged on December 7 would be refitted to fight another day. The aircraft carriers that were luckily at sea during the surprise attack spent several months harassing Japanese outposts. Their most spectacular exploit, an air raid on Tokyo itself, was launched on April 18, 1942. B-25 bombers took off from the carrier *Hornet* and, unable to land on its deck, proceeded to China after dropping their bombs over Tokyo. The raid caused only token damage but did much to lift American morale amid a series of defeats elsewhere.

CORAL SEA AND MIDWAY   During the spring of 1942, U.S. forces finally halted the Japanese advance toward Australia in two key naval battles. The Battle of the Coral Sea (May 7–8, 1942) stopped a fleet convoying Japanese troops toward New Guinea. Planes from the *Lexington* and the *Yorktown* sank one Japanese carrier, damaged another, and destroyed smaller ships. American losses were greater, but the Japanese threat against Australia was repulsed.

Less than a month after the Coral Sea engagement, Admiral Isoroku Yamamoto, the Japanese naval commander, steered his fleet for Midway, the westernmost of Hawaii's inhabited islands, from which he hoped to render Pearl Harbor helpless. This time it was the Japanese who were the victims of surprise. American cryptanalysts had by then broken the Japanese naval code, and Admiral Chester Nimitz, commander of the central Pacific, knew what was up. He reinforced Midway with planes and aircraft carriers.

The first Japanese foray against Midway, on June 4, 1942, severely damaged the island's defenses, but at the cost of about a third of the Japanese planes. American dive bombers struck back before another Japanese attack could be mounted. In the strategic Battle of Midway, the Japanese lost their four best aircraft carriers; the Americans, a carrier and a destroyer. The Japanese navy was forced into retreat less than six months after the attack on Hawaii. The Battle of Midway was the turning point of the Pacific war. It demonstrated that aircraft carriers, not battleships, were the decisive elements of modern naval warfare, and it bought time for the United States to mobilize for a wider war.

SETBACKS IN THE ATLANTIC   Early American setbacks in the Pacific were matched by setbacks in the Atlantic. Since the blitzkrieg of 1940, German submarine "wolf packs" had wreaked havoc in the North Atlantic. In 1942, German submarines appeared off American shores and began to attack coastal shipping. Nearly 400 ships were lost before effective countermeasures brought the problem under control. The naval command accelerated the building of small escort vessels, meanwhile pressing into patrol service all kinds of surface craft and planes, some of them civilian. During the second half of 1942, the losses to Nazi submarines diminished substantially.

MOBILIZATION AT HOME

Roosevelt's declaration of war ended not only the long public debate on isolation and intervention but also the long depression that had ravaged the economy during the 1930s. The war effort would require all of America's immense industrial capacity and full employment of the workforce. Mobilization was in fact already further along than preparedness had been in 1916–1917. The army had grown to more than 1.4 million men by July 1941. With the declaration of war, men between the ages of eighteen and forty-five were drafted. The average soldier or sailor was twenty-six years old, stood five feet eight, and weighed 144 pounds, an inch taller and eight pounds heavier than the typical recruit in World War I. Less than half the soldiers and sailors had finished high school. Altogether, more than 15 million men and women would serve in the armed forces over the course of the conflict.

ECONOMIC CONVERSION   The economy, too, was already partially mobilized for war, by the lend-lease and defense preparedness efforts. The War Powers Act of 1941 had given the president the authority to reshuffle government agencies, and a second War Powers Act empowered the government to allot materials and facilities as needed for defense, with penalties for those companies that failed to comply.

The War Production Board, created in 1942, directed the conversion of industrial manufacturing to war production. Roosevelt established staggering

USE IT UP – WEAR IT OUT–
MAKE IT DO!

OUR LABOR AND OUR GOODS ARE FIGHTING

War-effort advertisement

The Office of War Information created the ad's slogan in 1943.

production goals: 60,000 warplanes in 1942 and twice as many the following year, 55,000 anti-aircraft guns, and tens of thousands of tanks. His purpose was to confront the enemy with a "crushing superiority of equipment."

The war effort required conservation as well as production. "Use it up, wear it out, make do, or do without" became the prevailing slogan encouraging public sacrifice. People collected scrap metal and grew their own food in backyard "victory gardens." Tire and gasoline rationing began in earnest. Through the Office of Scientific Research and Development, Dr. Vannevar Bush mobilized thousands of scientists to create and modify radar, sonar, the proximity fuse, the bazooka, means to isolate blood plasma, and numerous other innovations spurred by the war effort.

The pressure of wartime needs and the stimulus of government spending sent the gross national product soaring from $100 billion in 1940 to $214 billion in 1945. The figure for total government expenditures was twice as great as the total of all previous federal spending, about 10 times what America had spent in World War I and 100 times the expenditures during the Civil War.

FINANCING THE WAR To cover the war's huge cost, the president preferred raising taxes to borrowing. The wartime Congress, however, dominated by conservatives, feared taxes more than deficits and refused to go more than halfway with Roosevelt's fiscal prudence. The Revenue Act of 1942 provided for only about $7 billion in increased revenue, less than half that recommended by the Treasury. It also greatly broadened the tax structure. Whereas in 1939 only about 4 million people filed tax returns, the new act made everyone a taxpayer.

The federal government paid for about 45 percent of its costs from 1939 to 1946 with tax revenues. To cover the rest of its expenses, the government borrowed from the public. War-bond drives induced citizens to invest more than $150 billion in government bonds. Financial institutions picked up most of the rest of the government's debt. In all, by the end of the war the national debt had grown to $260 billion, six times its size at the start of the war.

The basic economic problem was no longer finding jobs but finding workers for the booming shipyards, aircraft factories, and gunpowder mills—many of which operated day and night. Millions of people who had lived on the margins of the economic system, especially women, were now brought fully into the economy. Stubborn pockets of poverty did not disappear, but for most civilians, especially those who had lost their jobs and homes to the depression, the war spelled neither hardship nor suffering but a better life than ever before, despite shortages and the rationing of various consumer items.

ECONOMIC CONTROLS   Increased family income and government spending during the war raised fears of inflation. Some of the available money went into taxes and war bonds, but even so, more was sent chasing after scarce consumer goods just as production was converting to war needs. Consumer durables such as cars, washing machines, and housing in fact ceased to be produced at all. It was apparent that only strict restraints would keep prices from soaring out of sight. In 1942, therefore, Congress authorized the Office of Price Administration to set price ceilings. With prices frozen, goods had to be allocated through rationing, with coupons doled out for sugar, coffee, gasoline, automobile tires, and meat.

Wages and farm prices were not controlled, however, and this complicated things. War prosperity offered farmers a chance to recover from two decades of distress, and farm-state congressmen raised both floors and ceilings on farm prices. Higher food prices reinforced workers' demands for higher wages, and the Stabilization Act of 1942 gave the president the authority to control wages and farm prices.

Businesses and workers chafed at the wage and price controls. On occasion the government seized industries threatened by strikes. Both coal mines and railroads came under government operation for a short time in 1943, and in 1944 the government briefly took over the Montgomery-Ward Company. Soldiers had to carry its chairman out of his office when he stubbornly defied orders of the National War Labor Board. Despite these problems the government effort to stabilize wages and prices succeeded. By the end of the war, consumer prices had risen about 31 percent, a record far better than the World War I rise of 62 percent.

DOMESTIC CONSERVATISM   Despite government efforts to promote patriotic sacrifice among the public, discontent with price controls, labor shortages, rationing, and a hundred other petty vexations spread. In 1942 the congressional elections registered a national swing away from the Democrats. Republicans gained forty-six seats in the House and nine in the Senate, chiefly in the farm areas of the midwestern states. Democratic losses outside the South strengthened the southern delegation's position within the party, and the delegation itself reflected conservative victories in southern primaries. A coalition of conservatives dismantled "nonessential" New Deal agencies. In 1943, Congress abolished the Work Projects Administration (originally the Works Progress Administration), the National Youth Administration, the Civilian Conservation Corps, and the National Resources Planning Board.

Organized labor, despite substantial gains during the war, felt the impact of the conservative trend. In the spring of 1943, when John L. Lewis led the coal miners out on strike, Congress passed the Smith-Connally War Labor Disputes Act, which authorized the government to seize plants and mines useful to the war effort. In 1943 a dozen states adopted laws restricting picketing and other union activities, and in 1944 Arkansas and Florida set in motion a wave of "right-to-work" legislation that outlawed the closed shop (requiring that all employees be union members).

SOCIAL EFFECTS OF THE WAR

MOBILIZATION AND THE DEVELOPMENT OF THE WEST
The dramatic expansion of defense production after 1940 and the mobilization of millions of people in the armed forces accelerated economic development and a population boom in the western states. Nearly 8 million people moved into the states west of the Mississippi River between 1940 and 1950. The Far West experienced the fastest rate of urban growth in the country. Small cities such as Phoenix and Albuquerque mushroomed while Seattle, San Francisco, Los Angeles, and San Diego witnessed dizzying growth. San Diego's population, for example, increased by 147 percent between 1941 and 1945.

The migration of workers to new defense jobs in the West had significant demographic effects. Lured by news of job openings and higher wages, African Americans from Texas, Oklahoma, Arkansas, and Louisiana headed west. During the war years, Seattle's African American population jumped from 4,000 to 40,000, Portland's from 2,000 to 15,000.

Changing focus

With mobilization for war as the nation's priority, many New Deal programs were allowed to expire.

CHANGING ROLES FOR WOMEN   The war marked an important watershed in the status of women. With millions of men going into military service, the demand for labor shook up old prejudices about sex roles in the workplace—and in the military. Nearly 200,000 women served in the Women's Army Corps (WAC) and the navy's equivalent, Women Accepted for Volunteer Emergency Service (WAVES). Lesser numbers joined the Marine Corps, the Coast Guard, and the Army Air Force. Over 6 million women entered the workforce during the war, an increase of more than 50 percent overall and in manufacturing alone an increase of some 110 percent. Old gender barriers fell overnight as women became toolmakers, machinists, crane operators, lumberjacks, stevedores, blacksmiths, and railroad workers.

On the Same Team

Enlist in the WAVES

APPLY TO YOUR NEAREST
NAVY RECRUITING STATION OR OFFICE OF NAVAL OFFICER PROCUREMENT

Women in the military

This navy recruiting poster urged women to join the WAVES (Women Accepted for Volunteer Emergency Service).

The government launched an intense publicity campaign to draw women into traditionally male jobs. "Do your part, free a man for service," one ad pleaded. "Rosie the Riveter," an attractive woman depicted in overalls, became the cover girl for the recruiting campaign. One striking feature of the new labor scene was the proportion of older, married women in the workforce. In 1940 about 15 percent of married women were gainfully employed; by 1945 about 24 percent were.

Many men opposed the trend. One disgruntled male legislator asked what would happen to traditional domestic tasks if women flocked to factories: "Who will do the cooking, the washing, the mending, the humble homey tasks to which every woman has devoted herself; who will rear and nurture the children?" Many women, however, were eager to get away from the grinding routine of domestic life. One female welder remembered that her wartime job "was the first time I had a chance to get out of the kitchen and work in industry and make a few bucks. This was something I had never dreamed would happen." And it was something that many women did not want to relinquish after the war.

AFRICAN AMERICANS IN WORLD WAR II   The most volatile social issue ignited by the war was African American participation in the military. From the start, black leaders demanded equality in the armed forces and defense industries. Eventually about 1 million African Americans served in the armed forces, but usually in segregated units. Every army camp had segregated facilities—and periodic racial "incidents." The most important departure was a 1940 decision to integrate officer-candidate schools, except those for air force cadets. A separate flight school at Tuskegee, Alabama, trained

Tuskegee Airmen, 1942

One of the last segregated military training schools, the flight school at Tuskegee trained African American men for air combat during World War II.

about 600 African American pilots, many of whom distinguished themselves in combat.

War industries were even less hospitable to integration. "We will not employ Negroes," said the president of North American Aviation. But black leaders refused to accept such racist stances. In 1941, A. Philip Randolph, the tall, gentlemanly head of the Brotherhood of Sleeping Car Porters, planned a march on Washington to demand an end to racial discrimination in defense industries. To fend off the march, the Roosevelt administration struck a bargain. The Randolph group called off its demonstration in return for an executive order that forbade discrimination in defense work and training programs and set up the Fair Employment Practices Committee (FEPC). Although it had no power to enforce directives, the FEPC nevertheless offered willing employers the chance to say they were following government policy in giving jobs to black citizens.

During the war, African American leaders challenged all kinds of discrimination, including racial segregation. Membership in the NAACP grew during the war from 50,000 to 450,000. African Americans could look forward to greater political participation after the Supreme Court, in *Smith v. Allwright* (1944), struck down Texas's whites-only primary on the grounds that political primaries were part of the election process and thus subject to the Fifteenth Amendment's requirement that all citizens have the right to vote.

Racial violence in the 1940s did not approach the level of that during World War I, but growing tensions on a hot summer afternoon in Detroit in 1943 sparked incidents at a park. Fighting raged through June 20 and 21, until federal troops arrived on the second evening. By then, twenty-five blacks and nine whites had been killed.

HISPANICS IN THE LABOR FORCE   As rural dwellers moved to the western cities during the war, many farm counties experienced a labor shortage. In an ironic about-face, local and federal government authorities who before the war had striven to force undocumented Mexican laborers back across the border now recruited them to harvest crops. Before it would assist in providing the needed workers, however, the Mexican government insisted that the United States ensure minimum working and living conditions. The result was the creation of the bracero program in 1942, whereby Mexico agreed to provide seasonal farmworkers to the southwestern states in exchange for a promise by the U.S. government not to draft them into military service. The workers were hired on yearlong contracts, and American officials provided transportation from the border to their job sites. Under the bracero program some 200,000 Mexican farmworkers entered the western United States. At least that many more crossed the border as undocumented workers.

The rising tide of Mexican Americans in Los Angeles prompted a growing stream of anti-Mexican editorials and ugly incidents. Even though Mexican Americans fought in the war with great valor, earning seventeen Congressional Medals of Honor, there was constant conflict between servicemen and Mexican American gang members and teenage "zoot-suiters" in southern California. In 1943 several thousand off-duty sailors and soldiers, joined by hundreds of local white civilians, rampaged through downtown Los Angeles streets, assaulting Hispanics, African Americans, and Filipinos. The weeklong violence came to be labeled the zoot-suit riots. (Zoot suits were the flamboyant attire popular in the 1940s and worn by some young Mexican American men.)

NATIVE AMERICANS AND THE WAR EFFORT   Indians supported the war effort more fully than any other group in American society. Almost a third of eligible Native American men, over 25,000 people, served in the armed forces. Another one fourth worked in defense-related industries. Thousands of Indian women volunteered as nurses or joined the WAVES. As was the case with African Americans, Indians benefited from the experiences afforded by the war. Those who left reservations to work in defense plants or to join the military gained new vocational skills as well as a greater awareness of mainstream society and how to succeed within it.

Marine Navajo "code talkers"

The Japanese were never able to break the Native Americans' codes used by signalmen, such as those shown here during the Battle of Bougainville in 1943.

Why did so many Native Americans fight for a nation that had stripped them of their land and decimated their heritage? Some felt that they had no choice. Mobilization for the war effort ended many New Deal programs that had provided Indians with jobs. Reservation Indians thus faced the necessity of finding new jobs elsewhere. Many viewed the Nazis and the Japanese warlords as threats to their own homeland. The most common sentiment, however, seems to have been a genuine sense of patriotism. Whatever the reasons, Indians distinguished themselves in the military. Unlike their African American counterparts, Indian servicemen were integrated into regular units. Perhaps the most distinctive activity performed by Indians was their service as "code talkers": every military branch used Indians to encode and decipher messages using Indian languages.

INTERNMENT OF JAPANESE AMERICANS   The record on civil liberties during World War II was on the whole better than that during World War I, if only because there was virtually no domestic opposition to the war

Internment

This young Japanese American and her parents were forced to relocate from Los Angeles to an internment camp in eastern California in 1942.

effort after the attack on Pearl Harbor. Neither German Americans nor Italian Americans faced the harassments meted out to their counterparts in the previous war; few had much sympathy for Hitler or Mussolini. The shameful exception to an otherwise improved record was the treatment accorded to more than 100,000 Americans of Japanese descent (Nisei), who were forcibly removed from their homes and businesses on the West Coast and transported to "war relocation camps" in the interior. Caught up in the war hysteria and racial prejudice aroused by the attack on Pearl Harbor, President Roosevelt initiated the removal of Japanese Americans when he issued Executive Order 9066 on February 19, 1942. More than 60 percent of the internees were U.S. citizens; a third were under the age of nineteen. Forced to sell their farms and businesses at great losses, the internees lost not only their property but also their liberty. Few if any were disloyal, but all were victims of fear and racial prejudice. Following the attack on Pearl Harbor, Idaho's governor declared, "A good solution to the Jap problem would be to send them all back to Japan, then sink the island." Such vengeful attitudes help explain why the U.S. government sponsored a mass violation of civil liberties. Not until 1983 did the government recognize the injustice of the internment policy. Five years later it authorized granting those Nisei still living $20,000 each in compensation.

THE ALLIED DRIVE TOWARD BERLIN

By mid-1942, the "home front" had begun to get encouraging news from the war fronts. Japanese naval losses at the Battles of Coral Sea and Midway had secured Australia and Hawaii. By midyear a motley fleet of American air and sea subchasers was ending six months of successfully hunting German U-boats off the Atlantic coast. This was all the more important because Allied war plans called for the defeat of Germany first.

WAR AIMS AND STRATEGY There were good reasons for giving top priority to defeating Hitler. Nazi forces in western Europe and the Atlantic posed a more direct threat to the Western Hemisphere than did Japan, and Germany's war potential was greater than Japan's. Yet Japanese attacks involved Americans directly in the Pacific war from the start, and as a consequence during the first year of fighting more American troops went to the Pacific than crossed the Atlantic.

The Pearl Harbor attack brought British prime minister Winston Churchill to Washington, D.C., for lengthy talks about a joint war plan. Thus began a crucial wartime alliance between the United States and Great Britain, a partnership marked almost as much by disagreement and suspicion as by common purpose. As Churchill later remarked, "There is only one thing worse than fighting with allies, and that is fighting without them." Although he and Roosevelt admired each other, they often disagreed about military strategy and the likely makeup of the postwar world.

Initially, at least, such differences of opinion were masked by the need to make basic military decisions. On January 1, 1942, representatives of twenty-six governments then at war with the Axis signed the Declaration of the United Nations, affirming the principles of the Atlantic Charter, pledging their full resources to the war, and promising not to make a separate peace with Germany, Italy, or Japan. The meetings between Churchill and Roosevelt in Washington in 1942 produced several major decisions, including the one to name a supreme allied commander in each major theater of the war. Each commander would be subject to orders from the British-American Combined Chiefs of Staff. Other joint boards allotted munitions, raw material, and ships. Finally, in the course of their talks, the British and American leaders reaffirmed the priority of the war against Germany.

Agreement on war aims did not bring agreement on strategy, however. Roosevelt and Churchill, meeting at the White House again in June 1942, could not agree on the location of their first attack. U.S. military planners wanted to strike directly across the English Channel before the end of 1942, secure a beachhead in German-occupied France, and move against Germany itself in 1943. The British preferred to keep the Germans off balance with hit-and-run raids and air attacks while continuing to build up their forces. With vivid memories of the last war, the British feared a mass bloodletting in trench warfare if they struck prematurely. In eastern Europe two totalitarian regimes—the Germans and the Russians—waged a colossal war while managing horrible death camps. Stalin's henchmen killed more captive people than did Hitler's. The Russians, while quietly victimizing their own, were also bearing the brunt of the massive German attack in the east. Thus they insisted that the Western Allies relieve the pressure. Finally, the Americans accepted Churchill's proposal to invade French North Africa, which had been captured by German and Italian armies.

THE NORTH AFRICA CAMPAIGN   On November 8, 1942, British and American forces commanded by U.S. general Dwight D. Eisenhower landed at Casablanca in Morocco and at Oran and Algiers in Algeria. Completely surprised, French forces under the Vichy government (which collaborated

What was the Atlantic Charter? Compare and contrast the alliances in the First World War with those in the Second World War. How were the Germans able to seize most of the Allied territory so quickly?

with the Germans) had little will to resist. Hitler, in response, occupied the whole of France and sent German forces into Tunisia, a French protectorate.

Farther east, General Bernard Montgomery's British forces were pushing the brilliant German tank commander General Erwin Rommel back across Libya, and untested American forces were confronting seasoned Nazis pouring into Tunisia. Before spring, however, the British forces had taken Libya, and the Germans were caught in a gigantic pair of pincers. Hammered from all sides, unable to retreat across the Mediterranean, an army of over 200,000 Germans and Italians surrendered on May 12, 1943, leaving all of North Africa in Allied hands.

While the Battle of Tunisia unfolded, in January 1943 Roosevelt, Churchill, and the Combined Chiefs of Staff met at Casablanca, Morocco. It was a historic occasion. No U.S. president had ever flown while in office, and none had ever visited Africa. But the absence of precedent did not deter Roosevelt. Stalin declined to leave besieged Russia for the meeting, however, although he continued to press for a second front in western Europe to relieve the pressure on the Soviet Union. Since the German invasion of Russia in 1941, over 90 percent of German military casualties had occurred on the eastern front. The British and American engagements with German forces in North Africa were minuscule in comparison with the scope and fury of the fighting in Russia.

Churchill and Roosevelt spent eight days at Casablanca hammering out key strategic decisions. The Americans wanted to invade German-occupied France as soon as possible, but the British insisted that such a major assault was premature. They convinced the Americans that they should follow up a victory in North Africa with an assault on Sicily and Italy. Roosevelt and Churchill also decided to step up the bombing of Germany and to increase shipments of military supplies to the Soviet Union and the Nationalist Chinese forces fighting the Japanese. The two allied leaders ordered Admiral Chester Nimitz and General Douglas MacArthur to dislodge the Japanese from the Pacific Islands. The top priority, however, went to an anti-submarine campaign in the Atlantic.

Before leaving Casablanca, Roosevelt announced, with Churchill's endorsement, that the war would end only with the "unconditional surrender" of all enemies. This decision was designed to quiet Soviet suspicions that the Western Allies might negotiate separately with the various enemy nations making up the Axis. The announcement also reflected Roosevelt's determination that "every person in Germany should realize that this time Germany is a defeated nation." This dictum was later criticized for having stiffened enemy resistance, but it probably had little effect; in fact, neither the Italian nor

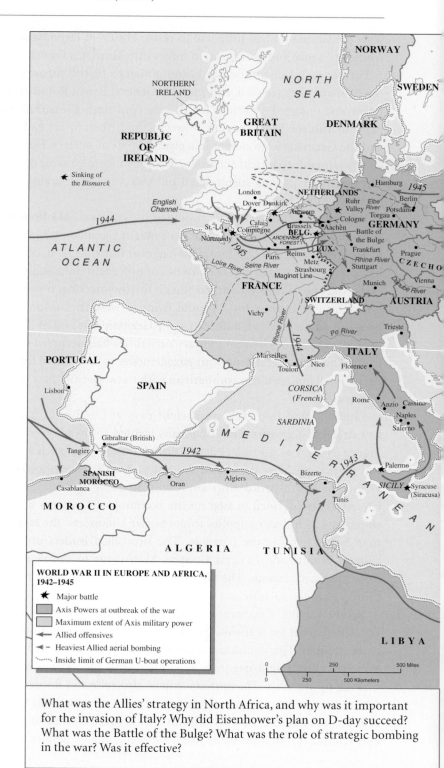

WORLD WAR II IN EUROPE AND AFRICA, 1942–1945

★ Major battle

▨ Axis Powers at outbreak of the war

▢ Maximum extent of Axis military power

◄— Allied offensives

◄- - Heaviest Allied aerial bombing

······· Inside limit of German U-boat operations

What was the Allies' strategy in North Africa, and why was it important for the invasion of Italy? Why did Eisenhower's plan on D-day succeed? What was the Battle of the Bulge? What was the role of strategic bombing in the war? Was it effective?

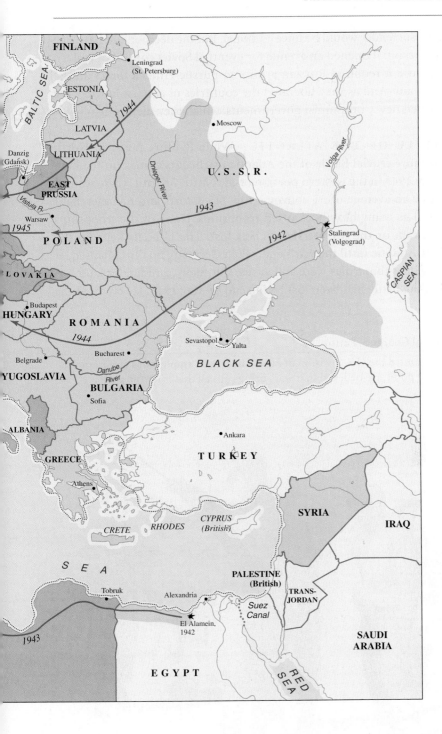

the Japanese surrender would be unconditional. But the decision did have one unexpected result: it opened an avenue for eventual Soviet control of eastern Europe because it required Russian armies to pursue Hitler's forces all the way to Germany. And as they liberated the countries of eastern Europe, the Soviets created new Communist governments, which they then controlled.

THE BATTLE OF THE ATLANTIC   While fighting raged in North Africa, the more crucial Battle of the Atlantic reached its climax on the high seas. By early 1943 in the western portion of the North Atlantic, there were at any one time an average of 31 convoys with 145 escorts and 673 merchant ships, as well as many heavily escorted troopships. None of the troopships going to Britain or the Mediterranean was lost. The U-boats kept up the Battle of the Atlantic until the war's end; when Germany finally collapsed, at least forty-nine submarines were still at sea. But their commander later admitted that the battle had been lost by the end of May 1943. He credited the

Major General George S. Patton

Patton commanded the U.S. invasion of Sicily, the largest amphibious action in the war up to that point. He believed that war "brings out all that is best in men."

difference largely to radar. What he did not know then was that the Allies had a secret weapon: by early 1943 their cryptanalysts were routinely decoding German messages and telling their subchasers where to look for German U-boats.

SICILY AND ITALY   On July 10, 1943, after the Allied victory in North Africa, about 250,000 British and American troops landed on the Italian island of Sicily in the first effort to reclaim territory in Europe since the war began. The entire island was in Allied hands by August 17, although some 40,000 German soldiers escaped to the mainland. Allied success in Sicily ended Mussolini's twenty years of Fascist rule. On July 25, 1943, Italy's King Victor Emmanuel III dismissed Mussolini as prime minister. The new Italian government startled the Allies when it offered not only to surrender but also to switch sides in the war. Unfortunately, mutual suspicions prolonged talks until September 3, during which time the Germans poured reinforcements into Italy. Mussolini, plucked from imprisonment by a daring German airborne raid, became head of a puppet fascist government in northern Italy.

Although American and British troops secured beachheads in Italy and captured Naples, fighting stalled in the Apennine Mountains. The steep terrain favored the German defenders. Allied casualties soared. Finally, on June 4, 1944, the U.S. Fifth Army entered Rome. The capture of Rome received only a brief moment of glory, however, for the long-awaited cross-Channel landing in France came two days later. Italy, always a secondary front, faded from the world's attention.

THE STRATEGIC BOMBING OF EUROPE   Behind the long-postponed landings on the Normandy beaches lay months

"Willie and Joe"

"Joe, yestiddy ya saved my life an' I swore I'd pay ya back. Here's my last pair of dry socks." From a cartoon strip by Bill Mauldin that appeared in the army newspaper *Yank* and featured two infantrymen slogging their way through the Italian campaign.

of preparation. While waiting, the U.S. Army Air Force and the British Royal Air Force (RAF) had attacked the German-controlled areas of Europe. Early in 1943, Americans launched their first air raid on Germany itself. Thereafter, American strategic bombers were full-fledged partners of the RAF in the effort to pound Germany into submission. The RAF confined itself mostly to night raids. The Americans preferred high-level daylight "precision" bombing.

Yet while causing widespread damage, the strategic air offensive had failed to devastate German industrial production; the strikes also, some contend, were unable to break civilian morale. Heavy Allied air losses persisted through 1943. By the end of that year, however, jettisonable gas tanks permitted fighters to escort the long-range bombers all the way to Berlin and back, thus reducing the number of bombers lost to German fighters. Berlin suffered repeated Allied raids. With air supremacy assured, the Allies were free to concentrate on their primary urban and industrial targets and, when the time came, provide cover for the Normandy landings. On April 14, 1944, General Eisenhower assumed control of the strategic air forces for the invasion of German-controlled France. On D-day, June 6, 1944, he told the troops, "If you see fighting aircraft over you, they will be ours."

THE TEHRAN MEETING   Late in the fall of 1943, Churchill and Roosevelt had their first joint meeting with Joseph Stalin, in Tehran, Iran. Prior to the conference, when Britain and America promised a cross-Channel invasion of western Europe, the Soviets pledged to enter the war against Japan after Germany's defeat. On the way to the Tehran meeting with Stalin, Churchill and Roosevelt met in Cairo with China's general Chiang Kai-shek from November 22 to 26. The resultant Declaration of Cairo of December 1, 1943, affirmed that war against Japan would continue until Japan's unconditional surrender, that all Chinese territories taken by Japan would be restored to China, that Japan would lose the Pacific islands acquired after 1941, and that "in due course Korea shall become free and independent."

From November 28 to December 1, the Big Three leaders conferred in Tehran. Their chief subject was the planned invasion of France and a Russian offensive across eastern Europe timed to coincide with it. Stalin repeated his promise to enter the war against Japan at some date in the future, and the three leaders agreed to create an international organization (the United Nations) to maintain peace after the war.

D-DAY AND AFTER   In early 1944, General Dwight D. Eisenhower, smart, efficient, and well organized, arrived in London to take command at the Supreme Headquarters of the Allied Expeditionary Force. Already battle tested in North Africa and the Mediterranean, he now faced the daunting task of planning Operation Overlord, the daring cross-Channel assault on Hitler's "Atlantic Wall," a seemingly impregnable series of fortifications and minefields along the French coastline that German forces had created using captive Europeans for laborers.

The prospect of an amphibious assault against such multilayered defenses in a single huge battle unnerved some Allied planners. As D-day approached, Eisenhower's chief of staff predicted only a fifty-fifty chance of success. Operation Overlord prevailed largely because it was meticulously planned and because it surprised the Germans. The Allies fooled the Nazis into believing that the invasion would come at Pas-de-Calais, on the French-Belgian border, where the English Channel was narrowest. Instead, the landings occurred in Normandy, almost 200 miles south. In April and May 1944, while the vast invasion forces made final preparations, the Allied air forces disrupted the transportation network of northern France, smashing railroads and bridges. By early June all was ready, and D-day fell on June 6, 1944.

Operation Overlord

General Dwight D. Eisenhower instructing paratroopers before they boarded their airplanes to launch the D-day assault.

On the evening of June 5, the chain-smoking Eisenhower visited some of the 16,000 American paratroopers preparing to land behind the German lines in France to create chaos and disrupt communications. The men noticed his look of grave concern and tried to lift his spirits. "Now quit worrying, General," one of them said, "we'll take care of this thing for you." After the planes took off, Eisenhower returned to his car with tears in his eyes. "Well," he said quietly to his driver, "it's on." He knew that many of his troops would die within a few hours.

The night before the assault, airborne forces dropped behind the beaches while planes and battleships pounded the coastal defenses. At dawn the invasion fleet of some 5,300 Allied vessels carrying 370,000 soldiers and sailors filled the horizon off the Normandy coast. Overhead, thousands of Allied planes supported the invasion force. Sleepy German soldiers awoke to see the vast armada arrayed before them. For several hours the local German commanders interpreted the Normandy landings as merely a diversion for the "real" attack at Pas-de-Calais. When Hitler learned of the Allied

The landing at Normandy

D-day, June 6, 1944. Before they could huddle under a seawall and begin to root out the region's Nazi defenders, soldiers on Omaha Beach had to cross a fifty-yard stretch that exposed them to bullets fired from machine guns housed in concrete bunkers.

landings, he boasted that "the news couldn't be better. As long as they were in Britain, we couldn't get at them. Now we have them where we can destroy them." In the United States, word that the long-anticipated invasion had begun captured the attention of the nation. Businesses closed, church bells tolled, and traffic was stopped so that people could pray in the streets.

Despite Eisenhower's intensive planning and the imposing array of Allied troops and firepower, the D-day invasion almost failed. Thick clouds and German anti-aircraft fire caused many of the paratroopers and glider pilots to miss their landing zones. Oceangoing landing craft delivered their troops to the wrong locations. Low clouds led the Allied planes to drop their bombs too far inland. The naval bombardment was equally ineffective. Rough seas caused injuries and nausea and capsized dozens of landing craft. Radios were waterlogged. Over 1,000 men drowned. On Utah Beach the American invaders landed against relatively light opposition, but farther east, on a four-mile segment designated Omaha Beach, bombardment failed to take out the German defenders, and the Americans were caught in heavily mined water. The first units ashore lost over 90 percent of their troops. In one rifle company, 197 of the 205 men were killed or wounded within ten minutes. By nightfall the bodies of some 5,000 killed or wounded Allied soldiers were strewn across the sand and surf of Normandy.

German losses were much higher; entire units were decimated or captured. Operation Overlord was the greatest amphibious invasion in the annals of warfare, but it was small when compared with the offensive launched by the Russians a few weeks after D-day. Between June and August 1944 the Red Army killed, wounded, or captured more German soldiers (350,000) than were stationed in all of Western Europe. Still, the Normandy invasion was a turning point in the war—and a pivotal point in America's rise to global power. With the beachhead secured, the Allied leaders knew that victory was now in their grasp. "What a plan!" Churchill exclaimed to the British Parliament.

Within two weeks the Allies had landed 1 million troops, 556,000 tons of supplies, and 170,000 vehicles in France. They had seized a beachhead sixty miles wide and five to fifteen miles deep. As the weeks passed, they continued to pour men and supplies onto the beaches and to edge inland through the marshes and hedgerows. Hitler issued disastrous orders to contest every inch of land. Field Marshal Rommel, convinced that all was lost, began secret efforts to negotiate a peace agreement with the Allies. Other like-minded German officers, sure that the war was hopeless, tried to kill Hitler at his headquarters on July 20, 1944, but the Führer survived the bomb blast and ordered hundreds of conspirators and suspects tortured to death. Rommel was granted the option of suicide, which he took.

Meanwhile, the Führer's tactics brought calamity to the German forces in western France. On July 25, American units broke out westward into Brittany and eastward toward Paris. On August 15 a joint American-French invasion force landed on the French Mediterranean coast and raced up the Rhone Valley. German resistance in France collapsed. A division of the Free French Resistance, aided by American forces, had the honor of liberating Paris on August 25. Nazi forces retired pell-mell toward the German border, and by mid-September most of France and Belgium had been cleared of enemy troops.

SLOWING MOMENTUM   Events had moved so much faster than expected, in fact, that the Allies were running out of gasoline. Neither their plans nor their supply system could keep up with the rapid movement of tanks and troops. British and Canadian forces under General Bernard Montgomery had moved into Belgium, where they took Antwerp on September 4. From there, Montgomery argued, a quick thrust toward Berlin could end things. On the right flank, General George Patton was just as sure he could take the American Third Army all the way to Berlin. Eisenhower reasoned, however, that a swift, narrow thrust into Germany would be cut off, counterattacked, and defeated. Instead he advocated advancing along a broad front. Prudence demanded getting his supply lines in order first, which required clearing out stubborn German forces and opening a supply channel to Antwerp—a long, hard battle that lasted until the end of November 1944.

LEAPFROGGING TO TOKYO

Even in the Pacific, relegated to a lower priority, Allied forces had brought the war within reach of the enemy's homeland by the end of 1944. The Pacific war's first American offensive, in fact, had been in the southwest Pacific. There the Japanese, stopped at the Battles of Coral Sea and Midway, had captured the southern Solomon Islands and were building an airstrip on Guadalcanal, from which they would be able to attack Allied transportation routes to Australia. On August 7, 1942, two months before the North African landings, the First Marine Division landed on Guadalcanal and seized the airstrip.

MACARTHUR IN NEW GUINEA   Meanwhile, American and Australian forces under General Douglas MacArthur had begun to push the

Japanese out of their positions on the northern coast of New Guinea. These battles, fought through some of the hottest, most humid, and most mosquito-infested swamps in the world, bought advances at a heavy cost, but by the end of January 1943 the eastern tip of New Guinea had been secured.

At this stage, U.S. strategists made a critical decision. The brilliant but egotistical MacArthur, sometimes accused of being a legend in his own mind, wanted to move westward along the northern coast of New Guinea toward the Philippines and ultimately to Tokyo. Admiral Chester Nimitz, from his headquarters at Pearl Harbor, argued for a sweep through the islands of the central Pacific to Formosa and China. In March 1943 the Combined Chiefs of Staff agreed to pursue both plans.

During the Battle of the Bismarck Sea (March 2–3, 1943), American bombers sank eight Japanese troopships and ten warships carrying reinforcements. Thereafter the Japanese dared not risk sending transports to reinforce points under siege, thereby making it possible for the Allies to use the tactic of neutralizing Japanese strongholds with airpower and sea power and moving on, leaving them to die on the vine. Some called it leapfrogging, and Japanese leaders later acknowledged the strategy as a major factor contributing to the Allied victory. Meanwhile, in mid-April, before the offensive got under way, U.S. fighter planes shot down a Japanese plane that code breakers knew was carrying Admiral Yamamoto, Japan's naval commander and the planner of the Pearl Harbor attack. His death shattered Japanese morale—for a time.

NIMITZ IN THE CENTRAL PACIFIC Admiral Nimitz's advance through the central Pacific had as its first target two tiny islands, Makin (Butaritari) and Tarawa. After advance bombing raids, a fleet of 200 ships delivered infantry and marines at dawn on November 20, 1943. Makin, where the Japanese had only a small force, was soon cleared. Tarawa, however, was one of the most heavily protected islands in the Pacific. There, nearly 1,000 American soldiers, sailors, and marines lost their lives rooting out Japanese soldiers who refused to surrender.

Invasion of the Marshall Islands, the next step up the ladder to Tokyo, began on January 31, 1944. American forces took Saipan, in the Marianas, on June 15, bringing the new American B-29 bombers within striking distance of Japan itself. In the Battle of the Philippine Sea, fought mostly in the air on June 19–20, 1944, the Japanese lost 3 more aircraft carriers, 2 submarines, and over 300 planes. The battle secured the Marianas, and soon B-29s were winging their way from Saipan to bomb the Japanese homeland. Defeat in the Marianas convinced General Tōjō that the war was lost. On July 18, 1944, he and his entire cabinet resigned.

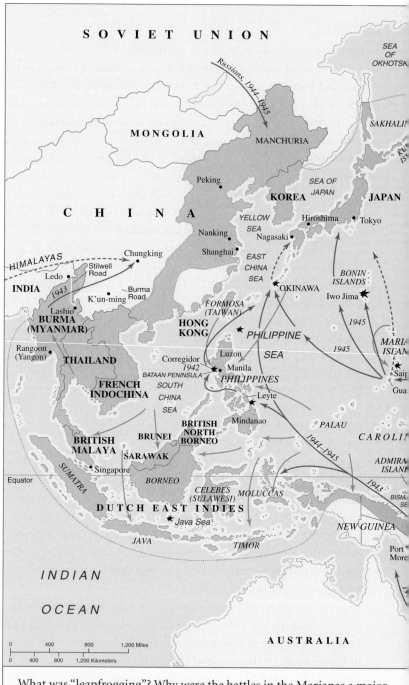

SOVIET UNION

SEA
OF
OKHOTSK

MONGOLIA

MANCHURIA

Russians, 1944–1945

SAKHALIN

KU
ISI

Peking

SEA OF
JAPAN

KOREA

JAPAN

C H I N A

YELLOW
SEA

Hiroshima

Tokyo

Nanking

Nagasaki

Shanghai

EAST
CHINA
SEA

BONIN
ISLANDS

HIMALAYAS

Chungking

Stilwell
Road

Ledo

OKINAWA

Iwo Jima

Burma
Road

1943

INDIA

K'un-ming

1945

FORMOSA
(TAIWAN)

Lashio

BURMA
(MYANMAR)

HONG
KONG

PHILIPPINE

MARI
ISLAN

Rangoon
(Yangon)

THAILAND

Corregidor

Luzon

SEA

1945

1942

Manila

Sai

BATAAN PENINSULA

PHILIPPINES

Gua

FRENCH
INDOCHINA

SOUTH
CHINA
SEA

Leyte

PALAU

CAROLI

Mindanao

BRITISH
NORTH
BORNEO

BRITISH
MALAYA

BRUNEI

1944–1945

ADMIRA
ISLAN

SARAWAK

Singapore

SUMATRA

BORNEO

Equator

1943

CELEBES
(SULAWESI)

MOLUCCAS

BISM
SE

DUTCH EAST INDIES

Java Sea

NEW GUINEA

JAVA

TIMOR

Port
More

INDIAN

OCEAN

AUSTRALIA

| 0 | 400 | 800 | 1,200 Miles |
| 0 | 400 | 800 | 1,200 Kilometers |

What was "leapfrogging"? Why were the battles in the Marianas a major turning point in the war? What was the significance of the Battle of Leyte Gulf? How did the battle at Okinawa affect the way both sides proceeded in the war? Why did President Truman decide to drop atomic bombs on Hiroshima and Nagasaki?

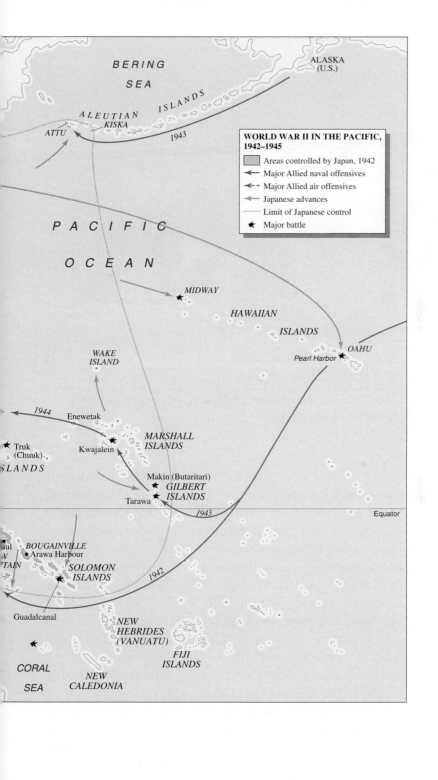

BERING

SEA

ALASKA
(U.S.)

ALEUTIAN
KISKA
ISLANDS

ATTU

1943

WORLD WAR II IN THE PACIFIC,
1942–1945

Areas controlled by Japan, 1942
Major Allied naval offensives
Major Allied air offensives
Japanese advances
Limit of Japanese control
★ Major battle

PACIFIC

OCEAN

MIDWAY

HAWAIIAN

ISLANDS

WAKE
ISLAND

OAHU
Pearl Harbor

1944 Enewetak

Truk
(Chuuk)
SLANDS

MARSHALL
ISLANDS

Kwajalein

Makin (Butaritari)
GILBERT
ISLANDS

Tarawa

1943

Equator

aul
N
TAL

BOUGAINVILLE
Arawa Harbour

SOLOMON
ISLANDS

1942

Guadalcanal

NEW
HEBRIDES
(VANUATU)

FIJI
ISLANDS

CORAL

SEA

NEW
CALEDONIA

MacArthur's triumphant return

General Douglas MacArthur (center) theatrically coming ashore at the island of Leyte in the Philippines, October 1944.

THE BATTLE OF LEYTE GULF   With New Guinea and the Mariana Islands all but conquered, President Roosevelt met with General MacArthur and Admiral Nimitz in Honolulu on July 27–28, 1944. They decided next to liberate the Philippine Islands from Japanese control. MacArthur's forces made their move into the Philippines on October 20, landing first on the island of Leyte. Wading ashore behind the first troops, the pompous general issued an emotional announcement: "People of the Philippines: I have returned. . . . Rally to me. . . . Let no heart be faint."

The Japanese, knowing that the loss of the Philippines would cut them off from the essential raw materials of the East Indies, brought in fleets from three directions. The three encounters that resulted on October 25, 1944, came to be known collectively as the Battle of Leyte Gulf, the largest naval engagement in history. The Japanese lost most of their remaining sea power and the ability to defend the Philippines. The battle also brought the first of the suicide attacks as Japanese pilots crash-dived into American carriers, sinking one and seriously damaging others. The "kamikaze" units, named for the "divine wind" that centuries before was believed to have saved Japan from a Mongol invasion, inflicted considerable damage.

A NEW AGE IS BORN

ROOSEVELT'S FOURTH TERM   In 1944, war or no war, the calendar dictated another presidential election. This time the Republicans turned to former crime fighter and New York governor Thomas E. Dewey as their candidate. No Democrat challenged Roosevelt, but a fight did develop over the second spot on the ticket. Vice President Henry A. Wallace had angered both southern conservatives and northern city bosses, who feared his ties to labor unions. Roosevelt finally fastened on the compromise choice of Missouri senator Harry S. Truman.

Dewey ran under the same handicap as Landon and Willkie had before him. He did not propose to dismantle Roosevelt's programs but argued that it was time for younger men to replace the "tired" old leaders of the New Deal. Roosevelt did show signs of illness and exhaustion, but nevertheless, on November 7, 1944, he was once again elected, this time by a popular vote of 25.6 million to 22 million and an electoral vote of 432 to 99.

CONVERGING MILITARY FRONTS   After their quick sweep eastward across France, the Allied armies lost momentum in the fall of 1944 as they neared Germany. The Germans sprang a surprise in the rugged Ardennes Forest, where the Allied line was thinnest. Attacking on December 16, 1944, the Germans advanced along a fifty-mile bulge in the Allies' lines in Belgium and Luxembourg—hence the Battle of the Bulge. In ten days they penetrated nearly to the Meuse River on their way to Antwerp, but they stalled at Bastogne. Reinforced by the Allies just before it was surrounded, Bastogne held for six days against relentless German attacks. On December 22 the American general Tony McAuliffe gave his memorable answer to the demand for surrender: "Nuts." When a German major asked what the term meant, an American officer said, "It's the same as 'Go to Hell.' And I will tell you something else—if you continue to attack, we will kill every goddamn German that tries to break into this city." The American situation remained desperate until the next day, when the clouds lifted, allowing Allied airpower to hit the Germans and drop in supplies. On December 26, U.S. forces broke through to relieve Bastogne, but it would be mid-January 1945 before the previous lines were restored.

Germany's sudden counterattack upset Eisenhower's timetable, but the devastating outcome shook the Nazis' power and morale. Their desperate effort at Bastogne had weakened their resources on the eastern front, and in January 1945 the Russians began their final offensive westward. The destruction of Hitler's last reserve units at the Battle of the Bulge had also left open the door to Germany's heartland from the west. By early March the Allies had reached the banks of the Rhine River, which runs from Switzerland to Holland. On March 6 they took the historic German city Cologne, and the next day, by remarkable luck, the Allies seized the crucial bridge at Remagen before the Germans could blow it up. Troops poured across the Rhine. The Allies then encircled the Ruhr Valley, center of Germany's heavy industry. By mid-April, resistance there had been overcome. Meanwhile, the Soviet offensive had reached the eastern border of Germany, after taking Warsaw, Poland, on January 17 and Vienna, Austria, on April 13.

With the British and American armies racing across western Germany and the Soviets moving in from the east, the war planners turned their attention to Berlin. Churchill, the British leader, had grown suspicious of the Soviets and worried that if their armies arrived in Berlin first, they would gain dangerous leverage in deciding the postwar map of Europe. He urged Eisenhower to get his troops to Berlin ahead of the Soviets. Eisenhower, however, refused to mix politics with military strategy. He was convinced the Soviets would get to Berlin first. He also knew that the Allied leaders were envisioning separate occupation zones for Germany, and Berlin was in the Soviet zone. Why

The war's end

German prisoners of war being corralled by U.S. soldiers in 1945.

rush to liberate the German capital only to turn it over to the Soviets? Berlin, he decided, was no longer of military significance. His purpose remained the destruction of German ground forces. Churchill disagreed and appealed to Roosevelt, but the American president, now seriously ill, left the decision to the supreme commander. Eisenhower then asked his trusted lieutenant, General Omar Bradley, to estimate what it would take to liberate Berlin before the Soviets. Bradley predicted that it would cost 100,000 Allied casualties, which he described as a "pretty stiff price to pay for a prestige objective." Eisenhower agreed, and they left Berlin to the Soviets.

YALTA AND THE POSTWAR WORLD   As the final offensives against Nazi Germany got under way, the Yalta Conference (February 4–11, 1945) brought the Big Three leaders together again, this time in a czar's palace at a Crimean resort (the only place in Russia both warm enough in February and undamaged enough to be hospitable). While the focus at Tehran in 1943 had been on wartime strategy, the leaders now discussed the shape of the postwar world. Stalin was self-confident, assertive, demanding, and sarcastic. He knew that the Soviet forces' control of key areas would ensure that his

The Yalta Conference

Churchill, Roosevelt, and Stalin confer on the shape of the postwar world in February 1945.

demands were met. Two aims loomed large in Roosevelt's thinking. One was the need to ensure that the Soviet Union would join the war against Japan. The other was based upon the lessons he had drawn from the previous world war. Chief among the mistakes to be remedied this time were the failure of the United States to join the League of Nations and the failure of the Allies to maintain a united front against the German aggressors after the war.

The Yalta meeting began by calling for a conference to create a new world security organization, to be held in the United States beginning on April 25, 1945. Arrangements for the postwar governance of Germany were also made at Yalta. The war map dictated the basic pattern of occupation zones: the Soviets would control eastern Germany, and the Western Allies would control the rich industrial areas of the west. The capital of Berlin, isolated within the Soviet zone, would be subject to joint occupation. Similar arrangements were made for Austria, with Vienna, like Berlin, under joint occupation within the Soviet zone. At the behest of Churchill and Roosevelt, liberated France was granted an occupation zone along its border with Germany and in Berlin. Soviet demands that defeated Germany pay $20 billion in reparations, half of which would go to the Soviet Union, were referred to a reparations commission in Moscow. That commission never reached agreement, however, although the Soviets appropriated massive amounts of German machinery and equipment from their occupation zone.

With respect to Eastern Europe, where Soviet forces were advancing on a broad front, there was little the Western Allies could do to influence events. Roosevelt was inhibited by his wish to win Soviet cooperation in the fight against Japan and in the effort to build the proposed United Nations. Poland became the main focus of Western concern. Britain and France had gone to war in 1939 to defend Poland, and now, six years later, the course of the war had left Poland's fate in the hands of the Soviets.

When Soviet forces reentered Poland in 1944, they placed civil administration under a Polish Committee of National Liberation in Lublin, a puppet Communist regime representing few Poles. As Soviet troops reached the gates of Warsaw, the underground resistance in the city, supporters of the Polish government-in-exile in London, rose up against the Nazi occupiers. The Soviet armies then stopped their offensive for two months while the Nazis killed thousands of defenseless Poles, potential rivals of the Soviets' Lublin puppet government.

The belief that postwar cooperation among the Allies could survive such events was a triumph of hope over experience. The Western Allies could do no more than acquiesce to Soviet demands or stall at Yalta. On the Soviet proposal to expand the Lublin committee into a provisional government together with representatives of the London Poles, Roosevelt and Churchill acquiesced. On the issue of Poland's boundaries, they stalled. The Soviets proposed to keep eastern Poland for themselves, offering land taken from Germany as compensation. Roosevelt and Churchill accepted the proposal but considered the western boundary at the Oder and Neisse Rivers only provisional. The peace conference at which the western boundary of Poland was to be settled never took place, however, because of later disagreements. The presence of the London Poles in the provisional government lent a tone of legitimacy to a Polish regime dominated by Communists, who soon ousted their rivals.

At Yalta the Big Three promised to sponsor free elections, democratic governments, and constitutional safeguards of freedom throughout Europe. The Yalta Declaration of Liberated Europe reaffirmed faith in the principles of the Atlantic Charter, but in the end it made little difference. It may have postponed takeovers in Eastern Europe for a few years, but before long Communist members of coalition governments had ousted the opposition. Russia, twice invaded by Germany in the twentieth century, was determined to create compliant buffer states between it and the Germans.

YALTA'S LEGACY Critics later attacked the Yalta agreements for "giving" Eastern Europe over to Soviet domination. But the course of the war shaped the actions at Yalta. The Soviet army controlled the region. By suppressing opposition in the occupied territories, moreover, the Soviets were acting not under the Yalta accords but in violation of them.

Perhaps the most bitterly criticized of the Yalta accords was a secret agreement on the Far East, not made public until after the war. As the Big Three met, fighting still raged against the Japanese in the Philippines and Burma. The Combined Chiefs of Staff estimated that Japan could hold out for eighteen months after the defeat of Germany. Costly campaigns lay ahead, and the atomic bomb was still an untested gamble. Roosevelt therefore accepted Stalin's demands on postwar arrangements in the Far East, subject technically to agreement later by Chiang Kai-shek. Stalin wanted continued Soviet control of Outer Mongolia through its puppet People's Republic, acquisition of the Kuril Islands from Japan, and recovery of rights and territory lost after the Russo-Japanese War of 1905. Stalin in return promised to enter the war against Japan two or three months after the German defeat, recognize Chinese sovereignty over Manchuria, and conclude a treaty of friendship and alliance with the Chinese Nationalists. Roosevelt's concessions would later appear in a different light, but given their geographic advantages in Asia, as in Eastern Europe, the Soviets were in a position to get what they wanted in any case.

THE COLLAPSE OF NAZI GERMANY   By 1945 the collapse of Nazi resistance was imminent, but President Roosevelt did not live to join the celebrations. Throughout 1944 his health had been declining, and photographs from early 1945, reveal a very sick man. In the spring of 1945, he went to his second home, in Warm Springs, Georgia, to rest up for the charter conference of the United Nations in San Francisco. On April 12, 1945, he died from a cerebral hemorrhage.

Hitler's Germany collapsed less than a month later. The Allied armies rolled up almost unopposed to the Elbe River, where they met advance detachments of Soviets on April 25. Three days later Italian partisans killed Mussolini as he tried to flee. In Berlin, which was under siege by the Soviets, Hitler married his mistress, Eva Braun, in an underground bunker on the last day of April. He then killed her and himself. On May 2, Berlin fell to the Soviets. That same day German forces in Italy surrendered. Finally, on May 7, in the Allied headquarters at Reims, France, General Alfred Jodl, chief of staff of the German armed forces, signed a treaty agreeing to an unconditional surrender. So ended Nazi domination, little more than twelve years after its demonic führer had come to power.

May 8, 1945

The celebration in New York City's Times Square on V-E day.

Massive victory celebrations in Europe on V-E day, May 8, 1945, were tempered by the tragedies that had engulfed the world: mourning for the lost American president and the death and mutilation of untold millions. Most shocking was the realization of the extent of the Holocaust, scarcely believable until the Allied armies came upon the death camps in which the Nazis had sought to apply their "final solution" to the "Jewish problem": the wholesale extermination of some 6 million Jews along with more than 1 million others. During the war, testimony from relief agencies had piled up growing evidence of the Nazis' systematic genocide against the Jews of Europe. Reports appeared in major American newspapers as early as 1942 but were nearly always buried on inside pages. The falsehoods of World War I propaganda had conditioned too many people to doubt all atrocity stories, and rumors of such horror seemed beyond belief.

American government officials, even some Jewish leaders, dragged their feet for fear that relief efforts for Jewish refugees might stir up latent anti-Semitism at home. Under pressure, Roosevelt had set up a War Refugee Board early in 1944. It managed to rescue about 200,000 European Jews and

Holocaust survivors

U.S. troops encounter survivors of the Nazis' Wöbbelin concentration camp in Germany, May 1945.

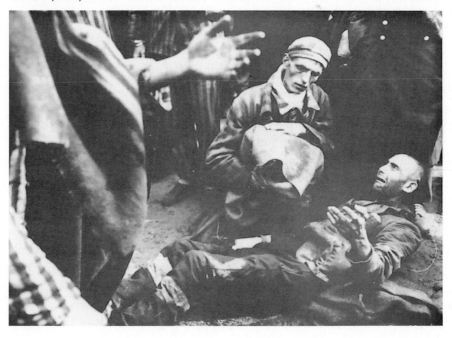

some 20,000 others. More might have been done by broadcasts warning people in Europe that Nazi "labor camps" were in fact death traps. The Allies rejected a plan to bomb the rail lines into Auschwitz, the largest concentration camp, in Poland, although bombers hit industries five miles away. And few refugees were accepted by the United States. The Allied handling of the Holocaust was inept at best and disgraceful at worst.

A GRINDING WAR AGAINST JAPAN   The sobering thought that the defeat of Japan remained to be accomplished cast a further pall over the victory celebrations in Europe in the spring of 1945. American forces continued to assault the Japanese Empire in the early months of 1945, but at a heavy cost. While fighting continued in the Philippines, marines invaded Japanese-controlled Iwo Jima Island on February 19, 1945, a speck of volcanic rock 760 miles from Tokyo that was needed as a base for fighter planes escorting bombers over Japan and as a landing strip for disabled B-29 bombers. Nearly six weeks was required to secure an island five miles square from defenders hiding in underground caves. The cost was more than 20,000 American casualties, including nearly 7,000 deaths.

The fight for Okinawa, beginning on Easter Sunday, April 1, was even bloodier. The largest island in the Ryukyu chain, Okinawa was large enough to afford a staging area for the planned invasion of Japan. Assaulting Okinawa would be the largest amphibious operation of the Pacific war, involving some 300,000 troops. The fight raged until late June. An estimated 140,000 Japanese died. Casualties also included about 42,000 Okinawans. When resistance on Okinawa collapsed, the Japanese emperor instructed his new prime minister to seek peace terms, but with conditions that proved unacceptable to the Allies.

THE ATOMIC BOMB   By that time, however, President Truman had learned of the first successful test explosion of an atomic bomb. It resulted from intensive research and development, begun in 1940, when President Roosevelt set up a committee to study atomic weaponry. The goverment spent over $2 billion on the top-secret Manhattan Project. Gigantic plants sprang up at Oak Ridge, Tennessee, and Hanford, Washington, to provide material for atomic bombs, while a group of physicists under J. Robert Oppenheimer worked out the scientific and technical problems of bomb construction in a laboratory at Los Alamos, New Mexico. On July 16, 1945, the first atomic fireball rose from the desert. Oppenheimer said later that in the observation bunker "a few people laughed, a few people cried, most people were silent."

The American Chemical Society exhibit on atomic energy

J. R. Oppenheimer points to a photograph of the huge column of smoke and flame caused by the bomb upon Hiroshima.

How to use this awful new weapon posed a profound dilemma. Some scientists favored a demonstration explosion in a remote area, but military use was decided upon because only two bombs were available, and even those might misfire. Four Japanese cities were potential targets. Priority went to Hiroshima, a port city of 400,000 people in southern Japan, which was a major assembly point for Japanese naval convoys, a center of war industries, and headquarters of the Second General Army.

On July 25, 1945, President Harry S. Truman, who had been thrust into office after Roosevelt's death in April, ordered the atomic bomb dropped if Japan did not surrender before August 3. Although an intense debate has emerged over the decision to drop the atomic bomb, it is clear that Truman believed that the bomb was "a military weapon and never had any doubt that it should be used." He was convinced that the atomic bomb would save lives by avoiding a costly American invasion of Japan against defenders who would fight like "savages, ruthless, merciless, and fanatic."

The ferocious Japanese defense of Okinawa had convinced military planners that an amphibious invasion of Japan itself, scheduled to begin on November 1, 1945, could cost as many as 250,000 Allied casualties and even more Japanese losses. Moreover, some 100,000 Allied prisoners of war being held in Japan would probably be executed when an invasion began. It is important to remember as well that the bombing of cities and the consequent killing of civilians had become accepted military practice during 1945. Once the Japanese navy was destroyed, American ships had roamed the Japanese coastline, shelling targets onshore. American planes had bombed at will and mined the waters of the Inland Sea. Tokyo, Nagoya, and other major cities had been devastated by firestorms created by incendiary bombs. The fire-bomb raids on Tokyo on a single night in March 1945 killed over 100,000 civilians and left over 1 million people homeless. The use of atomic bombs on Japanese cities was thus seen as a logical next step to end the war without an invasion of Japan. As it turned out, American scientists greatly underestimated the physical effects of the atomic bomb. They predicted that 20,000 people would be killed.

On July 26 the heads of the American, British, and Russian governments issued the Potsdam Declaration, demanding that Japan surrender or face "prompt and utter destruction." The deadline passed, and on August 6, 1945, a B-29 bomber named the *Enola Gay* took off at 2 A.M. from the island of Tinian and headed for Hiroshima. At 8:15 A.M., flying at 31,600 feet, the *Enola Gay* released the five-ton uranium bomb nicknamed Little Boy. Forty-three seconds later, as the *Enola Gay* turned sharply to avoid the blast, the bomb tumbled to an altitude of 1,900 feet, where it exploded as planned with the force of 20,000 tons of TNT. A blinding flash of light was followed by a fireball towering to 40,000 feet. The tail gunner on the *Enola Gay* described the scene: "It's like bubbling molasses down there . . . the mushroom is spreading out . . . fires are springing up everywhere . . . it's like a peep into hell."

The shock wave, firestorm, cyclonic winds, and radioactive rain killed some 80,000 people, including thousands of Japanese soldiers assigned to the Second General Army headquarters and 23 American prisoners of war housed in the city. By the end of the year, the death toll had reached 140,000 as the effects of radiation burns and infection took their toll. In addition, 70,000 buildings were destroyed, and four square miles of the city turned to rubble.

The aftermath of "Little Boy."

This image shows the wasteland that remained after the atomic bomb "Little Boy" decimated Hiroshima in 1945.

In the United States, Americans greeted the news with elation: the bombing promised a quick end to the long nightmare of war. "No tears of sympathy will be shed in America for the Japanese people," the *Omaha World-Herald* predicted. "Had they possessed a comparable weapon at Pearl Harbor, would they have hesitated to use it?" Others were more circumspect. "Yesterday," the journalist Hanson Baldwin wrote in the *New York Times,* "we clinched victory in the Pacific, but we sowed the whirlwind."

Two days after the Hiroshima bombing an opportunistic Soviet Union, eager to share in the spoils of victory, hastened to enter the war in Asia. The Allies had long been urging Stalin to join their fight against the Japanese, but the Soviet dictator had delayed as long as possible so as to conserve economic and human resources. Now, however, with the Japanese on the verge of capitulation, he rushed to engage the Japanese in order to share in the spoils of victory. Truman and his aides, frustrated by the stubborn refusal of Japanese military and political leaders to surrender and fearful that the Soviet Union's entry into the war would complicate negotiations, ordered the second atomic bomb dropped. On August 9, a B-29 aircraft named *Bockscar,* carrying a bomb dubbed Fat Man, flew over its primary target, Kokura. However, the city was so shrouded in haze and smoke from an earlier air raid that the plane turned to its secondary target, Nagasaki, where it dropped its bomb at 11:02 A.M., killing 36,000 people. That night the Japanese emperor urged his cabinet to surrender on the sole condition that he remain as sovereign. The next day the U.S. government announced its willingness to let the emperor keep his throne, but under the authority of an Allied supreme commander. Frantic exchanges ended with Japanese acceptance of the terms on August 14, 1945, when the emperor himself broke with precedent to record a radio message announcing the surrender to the Japanese people.

On September 2, 1945, General Douglas MacArthur and other Allied representatives accepted Japan's formal surrender on board the battleship *Missouri* in Tokyo Bay. MacArthur then settled in at his occupation headquarters across from the imperial palace in Tokyo.

THE FINAL LEDGER

Thus ended the costliest conflict in human history. One estimate has it that 70 million fought in the war, at a cost of 25 million military dead and more than 24 million civilian dead, including Jews and others murdered in Nazi concentration camps. The Soviet Union suffered the greatest losses of all: over 13 million military deaths, over 7 million civilian deaths, and at least 25 million left homeless. World War II was more costly for the United States than any other foreign war: 292,000 battle deaths and 114,000 other deaths. But in proportion to its population, the United States suffered a far smaller loss than that of any of the other major Allies or their enemies, and American territory escaped the devastation visited on so many other parts of the world.

World War II transformed American life. Mobilization for the war stimulated a phenomenal increase in productivity and brought full employment, thus ending the Great Depression and laying the foundation for an era of unprecedented prosperity. New technologies and products developed for military purposes—radar, computers, electronics, plastics and synthetics, jet engines, rockets, atomic energy—began to transform the private sector as well. And new opportunities for African Americans and other minorities as well as for women set in motion changes that would culminate in the civil rights movement of the 1960s and the feminist movement of the 1970s.

The Democratic party benefited from the war effort by solidifying its control of both the White House and Congress. The dramatic expansion of the federal government occasioned by the war continued after 1945. Presidential authority and prestige increased enormously at the expense of congressional and state power. The isolationist sentiment in foreign relations that had been so powerful in the 1920s and 1930s disintegrated as the United States emerged from the war with global responsibilities and interests.

The war opened a new era for the United States in the world arena. It accelerated the growth of American power while devastating all other world powers, leaving the United States economically and militarily the strongest nation on earth. But the Soviet Union, despite its human and material losses, emerged from the war with much new territory and enhanced influence, making it the greatest power on the whole Eurasian landmass. Just a little over a century after the Frenchman Alexis de Tocqueville had predicted that western Europe would be overshadowed by the power of the United States and Russia, his prophecy had come to pass.

End of Chapter Review

CHAPTER SUMMARY

- **WWII and American Society** White and black Americans migrated to states west of the Mississippi, and especially to the Far West, to take jobs in factories; unemployment was soon a thing of the past. Farmers, too, recovered from hard times. Many women took nontraditional jobs, some in the military. About 1 million African Americans served in the military, in segregated units. Among the most famous were some 600 pilots trained in Tuskegee, Alabama. Japanese Americans, however, lost their civil rights; they were interned in "war relocation camps" in the interior, far from the West Coast, where most of them had lived and worked.

- **Road to Allied Victory** The immediate war aim was to defeat Adolf Hitler in Europe. In 1942, British and American troops were engaging German and Italian troops in North Africa; and by 1943, all of North Africa was controlled by the Allies. From there they launched attacks on Sicily and then Italy. Joseph Stalin, meanwhile, demanded a full-scale Allied attack on the Atlantic coast to ease pressure on the eastern front, but D-day was delayed until June 6, 1944. Meanwhile, areas under Axis control were heavily bombed in an unsuccessful attempt to pound Germany into submission.

- **The Pacific War** The Japanese advance was halted as early as June 1942 with the Battle of Midway. Then began the process of regaining territory island by island. The American army fought slow, costly battles in New Guinea, then, in 1943, headed toward the Philippines. Fierce resistance at Iwo Jima and Okinawa and Japan's refusal to surrender after the firebombing of Tokyo led the new president, Harry Truman, to order the use of the newly developed atomic bomb.

- **Postwar World** In January 1942, twenty-six nations at war with the Axis Powers, seeing the need for a permanent peacekeeping force, signed the Declaration of the United Nations. The Big Three—Franklin Roosevelt, Winston Churchill, and Joseph Stalin—meeting in Yalta, on the Crimean Sea, in February 1945, decided that Europe would be divided into occupation zones, in which the Allies would sponsor free elections and democratic governments. It soon became clear, however, that Stalin would not honor that agreement.

CHRONOLOGY

May 1942	Battle of the Coral Sea
June 1942	Battle of Midway
January 1943	Roosevelt, Churchill, and the Combined Chiefs of Staff meet at Casablanca
July 1943	Allied forces land on Sicily
November–December 1943	Roosevelt and Churchill meet Stalin for the first time, in Tehran
June 6, 1944	D-day
February 1945	At the Yalta Conference, Roosevelt, Churchill, and Stalin plan the shape of the postwar world
February 1945	U.S. Marines capture Iwo Jima
April 12, 1945	Franklin Roosevelt dies
April 30, 1945	Hitler commits suicide
May 8, 1945	V-E day
August 6, 1945	Atomic bomb is dropped on Hiroshima
August 9, 1945	Atomic bomb is dropped on Nagasaki
September 2, 1945	Japanese surrender

KEY TERMS & NAMES

Admiral Chester Nimitz p. 1158

Women's Army Corps (WAC) p. 1163

Women Accepted for Volunteer Emergency Services (WAVES) p. 1163

Tuskegee Airmen p. 1164

A. Philip Randolph p. 1165

internment of Japanese Americans p. 1167

Winston Churchill p. 1169

Atlantic Charter p. 1169

Joseph Stalin p. 1170

Dwight D. Eisenhower p. 1170

D-day p. 1176

Operation Overlord p. 1177

Battle of the Bulge p. 1185

Yalta Conference p. 1187

"final solution" p. 1191

J. Robert Oppenheimer p. 1192

Part Seven

THE
AMERICAN
AGE

he United States emerged from World War II the pre-eminent military and economic power in the world. America enjoyed a commanding position in international trade and was the only nation in possession of the atomic bomb. While much of Europe and Asia struggled to recover from the horrific physical devastation of the war, the United States was virtually unscathed, its economic infrastructure intact and operating at peak efficiency. Jobs that had been scarce in the 1930s were now available for the taking. By 1955 the United States, with only 6 percent of the world's population, was producing half of the world's goods. American capitalism not only demonstrated its economic strength but became a dominant cultural force as well. In Europe, Japan, and elsewhere, American products, forms of entertainment, and fashion attracted excited attention.

Yet the specter of a deepening "cold war" cast a pall over the buoyant revival of the American economy. The tense ideological contest with the Soviet Union and Communist China produced numerous foreign crises and sparked a domestic witch hunt for Communists in the United States that far surpassed earlier episodes of political and social repression in the nation's history.

Both major political parties accepted the geopolitical assumptions embedded in the ideological cold war with international communism. Both Republican and Democratic presidents affirmed the need to "contain" the spread of Communist influence around the world. This bedrock assumption eventually embroiled the United States in a costly war in Southeast Asia, which destroyed Lyndon Johnson's presidency and revived isolationist sentiments. The Vietnam War was also the catalyst for a countercultural movement in which young idealists of the "baby boom" generation provided energy for many overdue social reforms, including the reforms that were the focus of the civil rights, gay rights, feminist, and environmental movements. But the youth revolt also contributed to an array of social ills, from street riots to drug abuse to sexual license. The social upheavals of the 1960s and early 1970s also provoked a conservative backlash as well. Richard Nixon's paranoid reaction to his critics led to the Watergate affair and the destruction of his presidency.

Through all of this turmoil, however, the basic premises of welfare-state capitalism that Franklin Roosevelt had instituted with his New Deal programs remained essentially intact. With only a few exceptions, both Republicans and Democrats after 1945 accepted the notion that the federal government must assume greater responsibility for the welfare of individuals than had heretofore been the case. Even Ronald Reagan, a sharp critic of federal social-welfare programs, recognized the need for the government to provide a "safety net" for those who could not help themselves.

Yet this fragile consensus on public policy began to disintegrate in the late 1980s amid stunning international developments and less visible domestic events. The surprising collapse of the Soviet Union and the disintegration of European communism sent policy makers scurrying to respond to a post–cold war world in which the United States remained the only legitimate superpower. After forty-five years, American foreign policy was no longer keyed to a single adversary, and world politics lost its bipolar quality. During the early 1990s the two German nations reunited, apartheid in South Africa ended, and Israel and the Palestinians signed a previously unimaginable treaty ending hostilities—for a while.

At the same time, U.S. foreign policy began to focus less on military power and more on economic competition and technological development. In those arenas, Japan and a reunited Germany challenged the United States for preeminence. By reducing the public's fear of nuclear annihilation, the end of the cold war also reduced American interest in foreign affairs. The presidential election of 1992 was the first since 1936 in which foreign-policy issues played virtually no role. This was an unfortunate development, for post–cold war world affairs remained volatile and dangerous. The implosion of Soviet communism after 1989 unleashed a series of ethnic, nationalist, and separatist conflicts. In the face of inertia among other governments and pleas for assistance, the United States found itself being drawn into crises in faraway lands such as Bosnia, Somalia, Afghanistan, and Iraq.

As the new multipolar world careened toward the end of a century and the start of a new millennium, fault lines began to appear in the American social and economic landscape. A gargantuan federal debt and rising annual deficits threatened to bankrupt a nation that was becoming top-heavy with retirees. Without fully realizing it, much less appreciating its cascading consequences, the American population was becoming disproportionately old. The number of people aged ninety-five to ninety-nine doubled between 1980 and 1990, and the number of centenarians increased 77 percent. The proportion of the population aged sixty-five and older rose steadily during the 1990s. By the year 2010, over half of the elderly population was over seventy-five. This demographic fact harbored profound social and political implications. It exerted increasing stress on health-care costs, nursing-home facilities, and the very survival of the Social Security system.

At the same time that the gap between young and old was increasing, so, too, was the disparity between rich and poor. This trend threatened to stratify a society already experiencing rising levels of racial and ethnic tension. Between 1960 and 1990 the gap between the richest 20 percent of the population and the poorest 20 percent doubled. Over 20 percent of all American children in 1990 lived in poverty, and the infant-mortality rate rose. The infant-death rate in Japan was less than half that in the United States. Despite the much-ballyhooed "war-on-poverty" programs initiated by Lyndon Johnson and continued in one form or another by all of his successors, the chronically poor at the start of the twenty-first century were more numerous and more bereft of hope than in 1964.

31

THE FAIR DEAL AND CONTAINMENT

FOCUS QUESTIONS   wwnorton.com/studyspace

- How did the cold war emerge?
- How did Harry Truman respond to the Soviet occupation of Eastern Europe?
- What was Truman's Fair Deal?
- What was the background of the Korean War, and how did the United States become involved?
- What were the roots of McCarthyism?

o sooner did the Second World War end than a "cold war" began. The uneasy wartime alliance between the United States and the Soviet Union had collapsed by the fall of 1945. The two strongest nations to emerge from the carnage of World War II could not bridge their ideological differences over such basic issues as human rights, individual liberties, economic freedom, and religious beliefs. Mutual suspicion and a race to gain influence and control over the so-called third world countries further polarized the two nations. The defeat of Japan and Germany had created power vacuums that sucked the Soviet Union and the United States into an unrelenting war of words fed by clashing strategic interests. At the same time, the devastation wrought by the war in western Europe and the exhaustion of its peoples led to anti-colonial uprisings in Asia and Africa that threatened to strip Britain and France of their empires.

The postwar world was thus an unstable one in which international tensions shaped the contours of domestic politics and culture as well as foreign relations.

DEMOBILIZATION UNDER TRUMAN

TRUMAN'S UNEASY START   "Who the hell is Harry Truman?" Roosevelt's chief of staff asked the president in the summer of 1944. The question was on more lips when, after less than twelve weeks as vice president, Harry Truman took the presidential oath on April 12, 1945. Clearly he was not Franklin Roosevelt, and that was one of the burdens he would bear.

Roosevelt and Truman came from quite different backgrounds. For Truman there had been no inherited wealth, no early contact with the great and near great, no European travel, no Harvard—indeed, no college at all. Born in 1884 in western Missouri, Truman grew up in Independence, an unglamorous town near Kansas City. Bookish and withdrawn, he moved to his grandmother's farm after high school, spent a few years working in Kansas City banks, and grew into an outgoing young man.

During World War I, Truman served in France as captain of an artillery battery. Afterward he and a partner started a clothing business, but it failed miserably in the recession of 1922, and Truman then became a professional politician under the tutelage of Kansas City's Democratic machine. In 1934, Missouri sent him to the U.S. Senate, where he remained fairly obscure until he became chairman of a committee investigating fraud in the war mobilization effort.

Truman was a plain, decent man who lacked Roosevelt's dash and charm, his brilliance and creativity. He was terribly nearsighted and a clumsy public speaker. Yet he had virtues of his own. Something about Harry Truman evoked the spirit of Andrew Jackson: his decisiveness, his bluntness, his feisty character, his family loyalty. But that was a side of the man the public came to know only as he settled into the presidency. On his first full day as president, he remained awestruck. "Boys, if you ever pray, pray for me now," he told a group of reporters. "I don't know whether you fellows ever had a load of hay fall on you, but when they told me yesterday what had happened, I felt like the moon, the stars and all the planets had fallen on me." But Truman was up to the challenges. Despite his lack of executive experience, he was confident and self-assured—and he needed to be. Managing the transition from war to peace was a monumental task.

Truman favored much of the New Deal and was even prepared to extend its scope, but he was uneasy with many New Dealers. Within ninety days he had replaced much of the Roosevelt cabinet with his own choices. On the whole they were more conservative in outlook and included several mediocrities. Truman suffered the further handicap of seeming to be a caretaker for the remainder of Roosevelt's term. Few, including Truman himself at first, expected him to run in 1948.

Truman gave a significant clue to his domestic policies on September 6, 1945, when he sent Congress a comprehensive peacetime program that proposed to enlarge the New Deal. Its twenty-one points included expansion of unemployment insurance to cover more workers, a higher minimum wage, a permanent Fair Employment Practices Committee, slum clearance and low-rent housing, regional development of the nation's river valleys, and a public-works program. "Not even President Roosevelt asked for so much at one sitting," said the House Republican leader. "It's just a plain case of out-dealing the New Deal." Beset by other problems, Truman soon saw his new domestic proposals mired in disputes over the transition to a peacetime economy.

CONVERTING TO PEACE   The raucous celebrations that greeted Japan's surrender in the summer of 1945 signaled a rapid demobilization of the armed forces and a return to peacetime pursuits. The public demanded

The Eldridge General Store, Fayette County, Illinois

Postwar America quickly demobilized, turning its attention to the pursuit of abundance.

that the president and Congress bring the troops home. By 1947 the total armed forces had shrunk from 12 million to 1.5 million. By early 1950 the army had been reduced to 600,000 troops.

The military veterans eagerly returned to schools, jobs, wives, and babies. Population growth, which had dropped off sharply in the 1930s, now soared. Americans born during this postwar period composed what came to be known as the baby boom generation, and that oversize generation would become a dominant force in the nation's social and cultural life.

The end of the war, with its sudden demobilization and conversion to a peacetime economy, brought sharp dislocations but not the postwar depression that many had feared. Several shock absorbers cushioned the economic impact of demobilization: unemployment insurance and other Social Security benefits; the Servicemen's Readjustment Act of 1944, known as the GI Bill of Rights, under which the federal government spent $13 billion on military veterans for education, vocational training, medical treatment, unemployment insurance, and loans for building houses and going into business; and most important, the pent-up postwar demand for consumer goods that was fueled by wartime deprivation. The gross national product first exceeded the 1929 level in 1940, when it reached $101 billion; by annual increases (except in 1946) it had grown to $347 billion by 1952, Truman's last full year in office.

CONTROLLING INFLATION   The most acute economic problem Truman faced was not depression but inflation. During the war, America was essentially fully employed. The government also froze wages and prices—and prohibited labor strikes. When wartime controls were removed, prices shot up. Prices of farm commodities soared 14 percent in one month and by the end of 1945 were 30 percent higher then they had been in August. As prices rose, so, too, did corporate profits. Labor unions increasingly demanded that they receive their share of the postwar bounty.

Within six weeks of the war's end, corporations had confronted a wave of union demands for higher wages and better benefits. A series of strikes followed. By January 1946 more workers were on strike than ever before in U.S. history. A strike in the steel industry generalized a formula for settling most of the disputes. President Truman suggested a pay raise of 18.5¢ per hour, which the United Steelworkers accepted but management refused. To break the logjam, the administration in 1946 agreed to let the company increase its prices in order to raise wages. That sequence of events became the pattern for settlements in other industries and set a dangerous precedent of price-wage spirals that would plague consumers in the postwar world.

Major disputes soon developed in the coal and railroad industries. John L. Lewis, head of the United Mine Workers, wanted more than the 18.5¢-per-hour wage increase. He also demanded improved safety regulations and a health and welfare fund for union members. Mine owners refused the demands, and a strike followed. The government used its wartime powers to seize the mines; Truman's interior secretary then accepted nearly all of the union's demands. Truman also seized control of the railroads and won a five-day postponement of a strike. But when the union leaders refused to budge further, the president lashed out against their "obstinate arrogance" and threatened to draft strikers into the armed forces. The strike ended a few weeks later.

Into 1946 the wartime Office of Price Administration maintained some restraint on price increases while gradually ending the rationing of most consumer goods. After the congressional elections of 1946, however, Truman gave up the battle to control prices.

PARTISAN COOPERATION AND CONFLICT   The legislative history of 1946 was not all deadlock and frustration, however. In 1946 the administration backed an employment bill proposing that the government calibrate federal spending to ensure full employment. Conservatives objected to what they denounced as carte blanche for deficit spending and proposed a nonpartisan commission to advise the president on the economy. Compromise resulted in the Employment Act of 1946, which dropped the commitment to full employment and set up a three-member Council of Economic Advisers to make appraisals of the economy and advise the president in an annual economic report. A new congressional Joint Committee on the Economic Report would propose legislation.

As congressional elections approached in the fall of 1946, public discontent ran high, with most of it focusing on the administration. Both sides held Truman responsible for labor problems. A speaker at the national convention of the Congress of Industrial Organizations had tagged Truman "the No. 1 strikebreaker," while much of the public, angry at the striking unions, also blamed the strikes on the White House. Earlier in the year, Truman had fired ultraliberal Henry A. Wallace as secretary of commerce in a disagreement over foreign policy, thus offending the Democratic left. At the same time, Republicans charged that Communists had infiltrated the government. Republicans had a field day coining partisan slogans. In the elections, Republicans shouted "To err is Truman," and they won majorities in both houses of Congress for the first time since 1928. "The New Deal is kaput," one newspaper editor crowed—prematurely, as it turned out. Truman launched a ferocious defense of his administration and its policies.

Taft-Hartley Act cartoons

Organized labor is pulled under by the Taft-Hartley Act (left); while in the other cartoon, Taft and Hartley look for John Lewis, the head of the Mine Workers Union.

The new Republican Congress, in a effort to curb the power of the unions, passed the Taft-Hartley Labor Act of 1947, which banned the closed shop (in which nonunion workers could not be hired) but permitted a union shop (in which workers newly hired were required to join the union) unless banned by state law. It included provisions forbidding "unfair" union prac-tices such as staging secondary boycotts or jurisdictional strikes (by one union to exclude another from a given company or field), "featherbedding" (paying for work not done), refusing to bargain in good faith, and contribut-ing to political campaigns. Furthermore, union leaders had to take oaths declaring that they were not members of the Communist party. The act also forbade strikes by federal employees and imposed a "cooling-off" period of eighty days on any strike that the president found to be dangerous to the na-tional health or safety.

Truman's veto of the "shocking" Taft-Hartley bill, which unions called "the slave-labor act," restored his credit with organized labor, and many unionists who had gone over to the Republicans in 1946 returned to the Democrats. The bill passed over Truman's veto, however. By 1954 fifteen states, mainly in the South, had used the Taft-Hartley Act's authority to enact "right-to-work" laws forbidding union shops.

Truman clashed with the Republicans on other domestic issues. He vetoed a tax cut on the principle that in times of high production and high employment the federal debt should be reduced. Yet the conflicts between Truman and Congress obscured the high degree of bipartisan cooperation in matters of government reorganization and foreign policy. In 1947, Congress passed the National Security Act, which created a National Military Establishment, headed by the secretary of defense with subcabinet Departments of the Army, the Navy, and the Air Force, and the National Security Council, which included the president, the secretary of defense and the new subcabinet Departments, and the secretary of state, among others. The act made permanent the Joint Chiefs of Staff, a wartime innovation, and established the Central Intelligence Agency (CIA) to coordinate global intelligence-gathering activities.

THE COLD WAR

BUILDING THE UNITED NATIONS   The wartime military alliance against Nazism disintegrated after 1945. The pragmatic Roosevelt had expected that the great powers in the postwar world would have separate spheres of influence around the world but thought he had to support the creation of an organization "which would satisfy widespread demand in the United States for new idealistic or universalist arrangements for assuring the peace."

On April 25, 1945, two weeks after Roosevelt's death and two weeks before the German surrender, delegates from fifty nations at war with the Axis met in San Francisco to draw up the Charter of the United Nations. Additional members would be admitted by a two-thirds vote of the General Assembly. This body, one of the two major agencies set up by the charter, included delegates from all member nations and was to meet annually to approve the budget, receive annual reports from UN agencies, and choose members of the Security Council and other bodies. The Security Council, the other major agency called for in the charter, would remain in permanent session and would have "primary responsibility for the maintenance of international peace and security." Its eleven members (fifteen after 1965) included six (later ten) members elected for two-year terms and five permanent members: the United States, the Soviet Union (replaced by the Russian Federation in 1991), Britain, France, and the Republic of China (replaced by the People's Republic of China in 1971). Each permanent member has a veto on any question of substance. The Security Council might investigate any dispute, recommend settlement or reference to an International Court at The Hague, in the Netherlands, and take measures, including a resort to military force. The U.S. Senate ratified the UN charter by a vote of 98 to 2. The organization held its first meeting in London in 1946, pending completion of its permanent home in New York City.

TRYING WAR CRIMINALS   The Allies agreed that those responsible for the atrocities of World War II should face trial and punishment. Both German and Japanese officials were tried for crimes against peace, humanity, and the established rules of war. At Nuremberg, site of the annual Nazi party rallies, twenty-one major German offenders faced an international military tribunal. After a ten-month trial marked by massive documentation of Nazi atrocities, the court acquitted three and sentenced eleven to death, three to life imprisonment, and four to shorter terms. In Tokyo a similar tribunal put twenty-five Japanese leaders on trial in 1946 and sentenced seven to death, sixteen to life imprisonment, and two to lesser prison terms. Other international tribunals tried thousands of others.

DIFFERENCES WITH THE SOVIETS   Since the end of World War II, historians have debated which side held greater responsibility for the onset of the cold war. The conventional, or "orthodox," view argues that the Soviets, led by Josef Stalin, a paranoid dictator, tried to dominate the globe. The United States had no choice but to stand firm in defense of democratic capitalist values. By contrast, scholars known as revisionists argue that Truman and American economic imperialists were the culprits. Instead of continuing Roosevelt's efforts to collaborate with Stalin and the Soviets, revisionists assert, Truman adopted an aggressive foreign policy that sought to create American spheres of influence around the world. Truman's provocative policies thus crystallized the tensions between the two countries. Yet such an interpretation fails to recognize that Truman inherited a deteriorating relationship with the Soviets. Events of 1945 made compromise and conciliation more difficult, whether for Roosevelt or for Truman.

There were signs of trouble in the Grand Alliance of Britain, the Soviet Union, and the United States as early as the spring of 1945 as the Soviet Union installed compliant governments in Eastern Europe, violating the Yalta promises of democratic elections. On February 1 the Polish Committee of National Liberation, a puppet group already claiming the status of provisional government, moved from Lublin to Warsaw. In March the Soviets installed a puppet prime minister in Romania. Protests against such actions led to Soviet counterprotests that the British and Americans were negotiating a German surrender in Italy "behind the back of the Soviet Union" and that German forces were being concentrated against the Soviet Union.

Nazi leaders

Hermann Goering (far left, leaning forward) and Rudolf Hess (second from left, covering his eyes) in 1945 at Nuremberg, where they were on trial for war crimes.

Such was the atmosphere when Truman entered the White House. A few days before the San Francisco conference to organize the United Nations, Truman gave Soviet foreign minister Vyacheslav Molotov a tongue-lashing in Washington on the Polish situation. "I have never been talked to like that in my life," Molotov said. "Carry out your agreements," Truman snapped, "and you won't get talked to like that."

On May 12, 1945, four days after victory in Europe, Winston Churchill sent a telegram to Truman: "What is to happen about Europe? An iron curtain is drawn down upon [the Russian] front. We do not know what is going on behind [it]. . . . Surely it is vital now to come to an understanding with Russia, or see where we are with her, before we weaken our armies mortally." Nevertheless, as a gesture of goodwill, and over Churchill's protest, U.S. forces withdrew from the German occupation zone that had been assigned to the Soviet Union at Yalta. American diplomats still hoped that the Yalta agreements would be carried out, at least after a fashion, and that the Soviet Union would help defeat Japan.

Although the Soviets admitted British and American observers to their sectors of occupied Eastern Europe, there was little the Western powers could have done to prevent Soviet control of the region even if they had not let their military forces dwindle. The presence of Soviet armed forces frustrated the efforts of non-Communists to gain political influence in Eastern European countries. The leaders of those opposed to Soviet influence were exiled, silenced, executed, or imprisoned.

Secretary of State James F. Byrnes, who took office in 1945, struggled through 1946 with the problems of postwar treaties. In early 1947 the Council of Foreign Ministers finally produced treaties for Italy, Hungary, Romania, Bulgaria, and Finland. In effect these treaties confirmed Soviet control over Eastern Europe, which in Russian eyes seemed but a parallel to American control over Japan and Western control over most of Germany and all of Italy. The Yalta guarantees of democracy in Eastern Europe had turned out much like the Open Door policy in China, little more than pious rhetoric sugarcoating the realities of raw power and national interest. The Soviets controlled Eastern Europe and refused to budge.

Byrnes's impulse to pressure Soviet diplomats by brandishing the atomic bomb only added to the irritations, intimidating no one. As early as April 1945, he had suggested to Truman that possession of the new weapon "might well put us in position to dictate our own terms at the end of the war." After becoming secretary of state, he had threatened Soviet diplomats with America's growing arsenal of nuclear weapons. But they paid little notice.

CONTAINMENT   By the beginning of 1947, relations with the Soviet Union had become even more troubled. A year before, Stalin had pronounced international peace impossible "under the present capitalist development of the world economy." His statement impelled George F. Kennan, counselor of the American embassy in Moscow, to send the secretary of state an 8,000-word dispatch in which he sketched the roots of Soviet policy and warned that Stalinists were "committed fanatically to the belief that . . . it is desirable and necessary that the internal harmony of our society be disrupted, our traditional way of life be destroyed, the international authority of our state be broken, if Soviet power is to be secure."

More than a year later, Kennan, now back at the State Department in Washington, spelled out his ideas for a proper response to the Soviets in a 1947 article published anonymously in *Foreign Affairs*. Kennan provided a brilliant psychological analysis of Soviet insecurity and intentions. He predicted that the Soviets would try to fill "every nook and cranny available . . . in the basin of world power." Yet their insecurity also meant that they would usually act

cautiously to reduce their risks. Therefore, he insisted, "the main element of
any United States policy toward the
Soviet Union must be that of a long-
term, patient but firm and vigilant *containment* of Russian expansive tendencies . . . by the adroit application of
counterforce as a series of constantly
shifting geopolitical and political points,
corresponding to the shifts and maneuvers of Soviet policy." Kennan predicted
"that Soviet power, like the capitalist
world of its conception, bears within
it the seeds of its own decay, and that
the sprouting of those seeds is well
advanced."

George F. Kennan

Kennan's 1947 *Foreign Affairs* article
spelled out the doctrine of containment.

Kennan's containment concept dove-
tailed with the outlook of Truman and his advisers. They all harbored a
growing fear that the Soviet lust for power reached beyond Eastern Europe,
posing dangers in the eastern Mediterranean, the Middle East, and western
Europe itself. Indeed, the Soviet Union sought to gain access to the Mediterranean, long important to Russia for purposes of trade and defense. After
the war the Soviet Union pressed Turkey for territorial concessions and the
right to build naval bases on the Bosporus, an important gateway between
the Black Sea and the Mediterranean. In 1946, civil war broke out in Greece
between a government backed by the British and a Communist-led faction
that held the northern part of the country and drew supplies from Soviet-
dominated Yugoslavia, Bulgaria, and Albania. In 1947 the British ambassador informed the U.S. government that the British could no longer bear
the economic and military burden of aiding Greece. When Truman conferred with congressional leaders, the chairman of the Senate Foreign
Relations Committee recommended a strong presidential appeal to the
American people.

THE TRUMAN DOCTRINE AND THE MARSHALL PLAN   On March 12,
1947, President Truman asked Congress for $400 million in economic aid to
Greece and Turkey. In his speech the president enunciated what quickly
came to be known as the Truman Doctrine. It justified aid to Greece and
Turkey in terms more provocative than George Kennan's ambiguous idea of
containment and more general than this specific case warranted. "I believe,"

Truman declared, "that it must be the policy of the United States to support free peoples who are resisting attempted subjugation by armed minorities or by outside pressures." George Kennan blanched at Truman's indiscriminate commitment to "contain" communism everywhere.

In 1947, Congress passed the Greek-Turkish aid bill and by 1950 had spent $659 million on the program. Turkey achieved economic stability, and Greece defeated a Communist insurrection in 1949. But the principles embedded in the Truman Doctrine committed the United States to intervene throughout the world in order to "contain" the spread of communism, a global commitment that would produce failures as well as successes in the years to come.

The Truman Doctrine marked the beginning, or at least the open acknowledgment, of a contest that the former government official Bernard Baruch named in a 1947 speech to the legislature of South Carolina: "Let us not be deceived—today we are in the midst of a cold war." Greece and Turkey were but the front lines in an ideological struggle that was spreading to western Europe. There, wartime damage and dislocation had devastated factory production, and a severe drought in 1947, followed by a harsh winter, had destroyed crops. Coal shortages in London left only enough fuel to heat and light homes for a few hours each day. In Berlin, people were freezing or starving to death. The transportation system in Europe was in shambles: bridges were out, canals clogged, and rail networks destroyed. Amid the chaos the Communist parties of France and Italy were flourishing. Aid from the United Nations had staved off mass starvation but provided little basis for economic recovery.

In the spring of 1947, former general George C. Marshall, who had replaced James Byrnes as secretary of state, called for massive aid to rescue western Europe from disaster. The retired chairman of the Joint Chiefs of Staff and orchestrator of the Allied victories over Germany and Japan, Marshall had been the highest-ranking general during World War II. "He is the great one of the age," said Truman. Marshall used the occasion of the 1947 Harvard graduation ceremonies to outline his plan for the reconstruction of Europe. "Our policy," he said, "is directed not against country or doctrine, but against hunger, poverty, desperation, and chaos." Marshall offered aid to all European countries, including the Soviet Union, and called upon them to take the lead in judging their own needs. On June 27 the foreign ministers of France, Britain, and the Soviet Union met in London to discuss Marshall's overture. Soviet foreign minister Molotov arrived with eighty advisers but during the talks got word from Moscow to withdraw from the "imperialist" scheme.

In December 1947, Truman submitted his proposal for the European Recovery Program to Congress. Two months later a Communist-led coup in

Czechoslovakia ended the last remaining coalition government in Eastern Europe. The Communist seizure of power in Prague ensured congressional passage of the Marshall Plan. From 1948 until 1951, the Economic Cooperation Administration, which managed the Marshall Plan, poured $13 billion into European economic recovery.

DIVIDING GERMANY   The Marshall Plan drew the nations of western Europe closer together, but the breakdown of the wartime alliance between the United States and the Soviet Union left the problem of postwar Germany unsettled. The German economy had stagnated, requiring the U.S. Army to support a staggering burden of civilian relief. Slowly zones of occupation evolved into functioning governments. In 1948 the British, French, and Americans united their zones. The "West Germans" then organized state governments and elected delegates to a federal constitutional convention.

Soviet leaders resented the Marshall Plan and the political unification of West Germany. In April 1948 the Soviets began to restrict road and rail traffic into West Berlin; on June 23 they stopped all traffic. The next day, Stalin cut electricity to the western sector of the city. The Soviets hoped the blockade would force the Allies to give up either Berlin or the plan to unify West Germany. It was war by starvation and intimidation. But the American commander in Germany proposed to stand firm. "When Berlin falls, Western Germany will be next," he declared. "If we mean . . . to hold Europe against communism, we must not budge."

Truman agreed, saying, "We are going to stay—period." After considering the use of armed

"It's the Same Thing"

The Marshall Plan, which distributed aid throughout Europe, is represented in this 1949 cartoon as a modern tractor driven by a prosperous farmer. In the foreground a poor, overworked man is yoked to an old-fashioned "Soviet" plow, forced to go over the ground of the "Marshal Stalin Plan," while Stalin himself tries to persuade others that "it's the same thing without mechanical problems."

convoys to supply West Berlin, he opted for a massive airlift. At the time it seemed like an impossible task. But the Allied air forces quickly brought in planes from around the world and by October 1948 were flying in up to 13,000 tons of food, medicine, coal, and equipment a day. The massive Berlin airlift went on for months. Finally, on May 12, 1949, after extended talks, the Soviets lifted the blockade. Before the end of the year, the Federal Republic of Germany had a government functioning under Chancellor Konrad Adenauer. At the end of May 1949, an independent German Democratic Republic arose in the Soviet-controlled eastern zone, formalizing the division of Germany. West Germany gradually acquired more authority, until the Western powers recognized its full sovereignty in 1955.

BUILDING ALLIANCES   As relations between the Soviets and western Europe chilled, transatlantic unity ripened into a formal military alliance. On April 4, 1949, the North Atlantic Treaty was signed by representatives of twelve nations: the United States, Britain, France, Belgium, the Netherlands, Luxembourg, Canada, Denmark, Iceland, Italy, Norway, and Portugal. Greece and Turkey joined the alliance in 1952, Germany in 1955, Spain in 1982. Senate ratification of the North Atlantic Treaty by a vote of 82 to 13 demonstrated that the isolationism of the prewar period had disappeared in the face of Soviet communism. The treaty pledged that an attack against any one of the members would be considered an attack against all and provided for a council of the North Atlantic Treaty Organization (NATO).

The eventful year of 1948 produced another foreign-policy decision with long-term consequences. Palestine, as the biblical Holy Land had come to be known, had been under Turkish rule until the League of Nations made it a British protectorate after World War I. During the early years of the twentieth century, many Zionists, who advocated a Jewish nation in the region, had migrated there. More arrived after the British gained control, and many more arrived during the Nazi persecution of European Jews and just after the Second World War ended. The British having offered the promise of a national homeland, the Jews of Palestine demanded their own

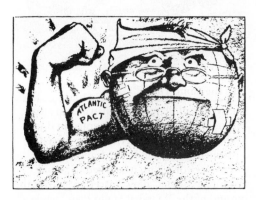

NATO

NATO is depicted as a symbol of renewed strength for a battered Europe.

How did the Allies divide Germany and Austria at the Yalta Conference? What was the "iron curtain"? Why did the Allies airlift supplies to Berlin?

state. Efforts to create a Jewish nation in Palestine benefited from the earnest support of American Jews and worldwide Jewish organizations.

Late in 1947, the UN General Assembly voted to partition Palestine into Jewish and Arab states, but this plan met fierce Arab opposition. No action was taken until the British mandate expired on May 14, 1948, at which time Jewish leaders in Palestine proclaimed the independence of Israel. President Truman, who had been in close touch with American Jewish leaders, ordered recognition of Israel within minutes; the United States became the first nation to act. The neighboring Arab states thereupon attacked Israel, which held its own. UN mediators gradually worked out truce agreements with Israel's Arab neighbors, and an uneasy peace was restored by May 11, 1949, when Israel joined the United Nations. But the hard feelings and intermittent warfare between Israel and the Arab states have festered ever since, complicating U.S. foreign policy, which has tried to maintain friendship with both sides but has tilted toward Israel.

CIVIL RIGHTS DURING THE 1940S

The social tremors triggered by World War II and the onset of the cold war transformed America's racial landscape. The government-sponsored racism of the German Nazis, the Italian Fascists, and the Japanese imperialists focused attention on the need for the United States to improve its own race relations and to provide for equal rights under the law. As a *New York Times* editorial explained in early 1946, "This is a particularly good time to campaign against the evils of bigotry, prejudice, and race hatred because we have witnessed the defeat of enemies who tried to found a mastery of the world upon such cruel and fallacious policy." The postwar confrontation with the Soviet Union gave American leaders an added incentive to improve race relations at home. In the ideological contest with communism for influence in Africa, American diplomats were at a disadvantage as long as racial segregation continued in the United States; the Soviets often compared racial segregation in the American South to the Nazis' treatment of the Jews.

For most of his political career, Harry Truman had shown little concern for the plight of African Americans. He had grown up in western Missouri assuming that blacks and whites preferred to be segregated from one another. As president, however, he began to reassess his convictions. In the fall of 1946, Truman hosted a delegation of civil rights activists, who urged him to issue a public statement condemning the resurgence of the Ku Klux Klan and the lynching of African Americans. The delegation graphically described incidents of torture and intimidation against blacks in the South. Truman was aghast. He soon appointed a Committee on Civil Rights to investigate violence against African Americans and to recommend preventive measures. In its recommendations the committee urged the renewal of the Fair Employment Practices Committee and the creation of a permanent civil rights commission to investigate abuses. It also argued that federal aid be denied to any state that mandated segregated schools and public facilities.

On July 26, 1948, Truman banned racial discrimination in the hiring of federal employees. Four days later he issued an executive order ending racial segregation in the armed forces. The air force and navy quickly complied, but the army dragged its feet until the early 1950s. By 1960 the armed forces were the most racially integrated of all national organizations. Desegregating the military was, Truman claimed, "the greatest thing that ever happened to America."

Jackie Robinson

Racial discrimination remained widespread throughout the postwar period. In 1947, Jackie Robinson of the Brooklyn Dodgers became the first black player in major league baseball.

JACKIE ROBINSON Meanwhile, racial segregation was being confronted in a much more public field of endeavor: professional baseball. In April 1947, as the baseball season opened, the National League's Brooklyn Dodgers included on its roster the first African American player to cross the color line in major league baseball: Jackie Robinson. Born in Georgia and raised in California, Robinson was an army veteran and a baseball player in the Negro leagues. During his first season with the Dodgers, teammates and opposing players viciously baited Robinson, pitchers threw at him, base runners spiked him, and spectators booed him in every city. Hotels refused him rooms, and restaurants denied him service. Hate mail arrived by the bucket load. On the other hand, black spectators were electrified by Robinson's courageous example; they turned out in droves to watch him play. As time passed, Robinson won over many fans and players with his quiet courage, self-deprecating wit, and determined performance. Soon other teams signed black players. Baseball's pathbreaking efforts stimulated the integration of other professional sports teams. Jackie Robinson vividly demonstrated that racism, not inferiority, impeded African American advancement in the postwar era and that segregation need not be a permanent condition of American life.

SHAPING THE FAIR DEAL The determination Truman projected in foreign affairs did not alter his weak image on the domestic front. By early 1948, after three years in the White House, he had yet to shake the impression that he was not up to the job. The Democratic party seemed about to fragment:

southern conservatives resented Truman's outspoken support of civil rights, while the left had flared up in 1946 over his firing of Secretary of Commerce Henry Wallace after a speech critical of the administration's policy. "Getting tough [with the Soviet Union]," Wallace had argued, "never brought anything real and lasting—whether for schoolyard bullies or world powers. The tougher we get, the tougher the Russians will get." The left itself was splitting between the Progressive Citizens of America, formed in 1946, which supported Wallace, and the Americans for Democratic Action, formed in 1947, which also criticized Truman but endorsed his firm anti-Communist stance.

By 1948 most political analysts presumed that Truman would lose the November election. Such gloomy predictions did not faze the combative president, however. He resolved to mount a furious reelection compaign. His first step was to shore up the major elements of the New Deal coalition. He needed strong support among farmers. In metropolitan areas he needed to carry the labor union and African American vote, which he wooed by working closely with unions and liberals and pressing the cause of civil rights.

Like other presidents, Truman used his State of the Union message to set the agenda for an election year. The 1948 speech offered something to nearly every group the Democrats hoped to attract. The first goal, Truman said, was "to secure fully the essential human rights of our citizens," and he promised a special message later on civil rights. "To protect human resources," he proposed federal aid to education, increased and extended unemployment and retirement benefits, a comprehensive system of health insurance, more federal support for housing, and the extension of rent controls. He continued to pile on the demands: for more rural electrification, for a higher minimum wage, for the admission of thousands

"I Stand Pat!"

Truman's support of civil rights for African Americans had its political costs, as this 1948 cartoon suggests.

of international refugees to the United States, for money for the Marshall Plan, and for a "cost-of-living" tax credit.

THE ELECTION OF 1948   The Republican-controlled Congress for the most part spurned the Truman program, an action it would later regret. At the Republican Convention, New York governor Thomas E. Dewey won the presidential nomination on the third ballot. The platform endorsed most of the New Deal reforms and approved the administration's bipartisan foreign policy; Dewey promised to run things more efficiently, however.

In July a glum Democratic Convention gathered in Philadelphia expecting to do little more than go through the motions but found itself doubly surprised: first by the battle over the civil rights plank and then by Truman's acceptance speech. To keep from stirring southern hostility, the administration sought a platform plank that opposed racial discrimination only in general terms. Liberal Democrats, however, sponsored a plank that called on Congress to take specific action and commended Truman "for his courageous stand on the issue of civil rights." Thirty-seven-year-old Minneapolis mayor Hubert H. Humphrey electrified the delegates and set off a ten-minute demonstration when he declared, "The time has arrived for the Democratic party to get out of the shadow of states' rights and walk forthrightly into the

Picketing in Philadelphia

The opening of the 1948 Democratic National Convention was marked by demonstrations against racial segregation, led by A. Philip Randolph (left).

bright sunshine of human rights." Segregationist delegates from Alabama and Mississippi instead walked out of the convention. The solid Democratic South had fractured for the first time since Reconstruction.

After the Democratic Convention had nominated Truman, the feisty president pledged to "win this election and make the Republicans like it" and added, "Don't you forget it!" He also vowed to call Congress back into session "to get the laws the people need," many of which the Republican platform had endorsed.

On July 17 a group of rebellious southern Democrats met in Birmingham, Alabama. While waving Confederate flags and singing "Dixie," the dissident Democrats nominated South Carolina governor Strom Thurmond on a States' Rights Democratic ticket, quickly dubbed the Dixiecrat party. The Dixiecrats denounced Truman's "infamous" civil rights initiatives and championed states' rights. They hoped to draw enough electoral votes to preclude a majority for either major party, throwing the election into the House of Representatives, where they might strike a sectional bargain. A few days later, on July 23, the left wing of the Democratic party gathered in Philadelphia to nominate Henry A. Wallace on a Progressive party ticket. These splits in the Democratic ranks seemed to spell the final blow to Truman. The special session of Congress petered out in futility.

The Dixiecrats

The Dixiecrats nominated South Carolina governor Strom Thurmond (center) to lead their ticket in the 1948 election.

"Dewey Defeats Truman"

Truman's victory in 1948 was a huge upset, so much so that even the early edition of the *Chicago Daily Tribune* was caught off guard, running this presumptuous headline.

But Truman, undaunted, set out on a 31,000-mile "whistle-stop" train tour, during which he castigated the "do-nothing" Eightieth Congress. Friendly audiences shouted, "Pour it on, Harry!" and "Give 'em hell, Harry." Truman responded: "I don't give 'em hell. I just tell the truth and they think it's hell." Dewey, in contrast, ran a restrained campaign designed to avoid rocking the boat. By so doing, he may have snatched defeat from the jaws of victory.

The polls and the pundits predicted a sure win for Dewey, but on election day Truman chalked up the biggest upset in history, taking 24.2 million votes (49.5 percent) to Dewey's 22 million (45.1 percent) and winning a thumping margin of 303 to 189 in the Electoral College. Thurmond and Wallace each got more than 1 million votes, but the revolt of right and left had worked to Truman's advantage. The Dixiecrat rebellion backfired by angering black voters, who turned out in droves to support Truman, while the Progressive party's radicalism made it hard to tag Truman as soft on communism. Thurmond carried four Deep South states (South Carolina, Mississippi, Alabama, and Louisiana) with 39 electoral votes, including one from a Tennessee elector who repudiated his state's decision for Truman. Thurmond's success hastened a momentous disruption of the Democratic Solid South. But Truman's victory carried Democratic majorities into Congress, where the new group of senators included Hubert Humphrey and, by eighty-seven disputed votes, "Landslide Lyndon" Johnson of Texas.

Truman viewed his victory as a vindication for the New Deal and a mandate for moderate liberalism. "We have rejected the discredited theory that the fortunes of the nation should be in the hands of a privileged few," he said. His State of the Union message repeated the agenda he had set forth the year before. "Every segment of our population and every individual," he declared, "has a right to expect from his government a fair deal." Whether deliberately or not, he had invented a tag, the Fair Deal, to distinguish his program from the New Deal.

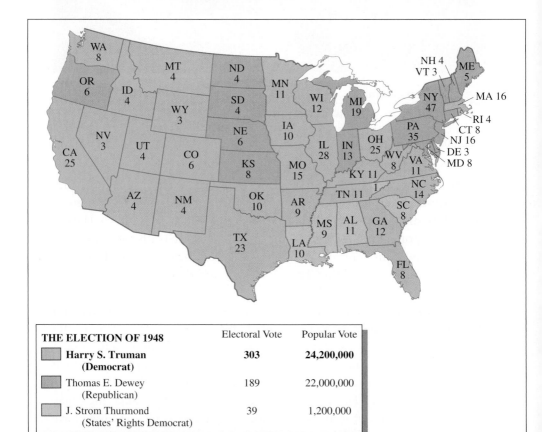

THE ELECTION OF 1948	Electoral Vote	Popular Vote
Harry S. Truman (Democrat)	303	24,200,000
Thomas E. Dewey (Republican)	189	22,000,000
J. Strom Thurmond (States' Rights Democrat)	39	1,200,000

Why did the political pundits predict a Dewey victory? Why was civil rights a divisive issue at the Democratic Convention? How did the candidacies of Thurmond and Wallace help Truman?

Most of Truman's Fair Deal proposals were extensions or enlargements of New Deal programs already in place: a higher minimum wage, expansion of Social Security coverage to workers not included in the original bill, extension of rent controls, increased farm subsidies, and a sizable slum-clearance and public-housing program. Despite Democratic majorities, however, the conservative coalition of southern Democrats and Republicans thwarted any drastic new departures in domestic policy. Congress rejected civil rights bills, national health insurance, federal aid to education, and a plan to provide subsidies that would have raised farm income rather than farm prices. Congress also turned down Truman's demand for repeal of the Taft-Hartley Act.

THE COLD WAR HEATS UP

Global concerns, never far from center stage in the postwar world, plagued Truman's second term, as they had his first. Now some Americans began to fear that Communists were infiltrating their society. In his inaugural address, Truman called for a vigilant anti-Communist foreign policy to rest on four pillars: the United Nations, the Marshall Plan, NATO, and a "bold new plan" for technical assistance to underdeveloped parts of the world, a global economic-assistance program that came to be known simply as Point Four. But other issues kept the Point Four program from ever reaching its potential.

"LOSING" CHINA AND THE BOMB   One of the most intractable problems, the China tangle, was fast unraveling in 1949. The Chinese Nationalists, led by Chiang Kai-shek, had been fighting Mao Tse-tung* and the Communists since the 1920s. The outbreak of war with Japan in 1937 had halted this civil war, and both Roosevelt and Stalin believed that the Nationalists would control China after the war. But the commanders of U.S. forces in China during World War II concluded that Chiang's government was hopelessly corrupt, tyrannical, and inefficient. After the war, American forces nevertheless ferried Nationalist Chinese armies back into the eastern and northern provinces of China as the Japanese withdrew. U.S. policy during

---

*The traditional (Wade-Giles) spelling is used here. In 1958 the Chinese government adopted the pinyin transliteration system, which became more widely used after Mao's death in 1976, so that, for example, Mao Tse-tung became Mao Zedong, and Peking became Beijing.

and immediately after the war promoted peace between the factions in China, but sporadic civil war broke out late in 1945.

It soon became a losing fight for the Nationalists as the Communists won over the land-hungry peasantry. By the end of 1949, the Nationalist government had fled to the island of Formosa, which it renamed Taiwan. Truman's critics now asked bitterly, "Who lost China?" A State Department study blamed Chiang for his failure to hold on to the support of the Chinese people. In fact it is hard to imagine how the U.S. government could have prevented a Communist victory short of getting involved in a massive military intervention, which would have been risky and unpopular. The United States continued to recognize the Nationalist government on Taiwan as the rightful government of China, delaying formal relations with Communist China for thirty years. Seeking to shore up friendly regimes in Asia, in 1950 the United States recognized the French-supported government of Emperor Bao Dai in Vietnam and shortly afterward extended aid to the French in their battle against Ho Chi Minh's guerrillas there.

As Mao and the Communists were gaining control of China, U.S. intelligence found an unusual level of radioactivity in the air, evidence that the Soviets had successfully tested an atomic bomb. The American nuclear monopoly had lasted just four years. The discovery of the Soviet bomb in 1949 triggered an intense reappraisal of the strategic balance of power in the world, causing Truman in 1950 to order the construction of a hydrogen bomb, a weapon far more powerful than the atomic bombs dropped on Japan, lest the Soviets make one first.

The discovery that the Soviets had atomic weapons led the National Security Council to produce a top-secret document, known as NSC-68, that called for rebuilding America's conventional military forces to provide options other than nuclear war. Such a plan represented a major departure from the nation's time-honored aversion to keeping large standing armies in peacetime. It was also an expensive proposition. But the public was growing more receptive to the nation's new role as world leader, and an invasion of South Korea in 1950 by Communist forces from the north clinched the issue for most Americans.

WAR IN KOREA   The Japanese had occupied Korea since 1910, and after their defeat and withdrawal in 1945 the victorious Allies faced the difficult task of creating a new Korean nation. Complicating that task was the fact that Soviet troops had advanced into northern Korea and accepted the surrender of Japanese forces above the 38th parallel, while U.S. forces had done the same south of that line. The Soviets quickly organized a Korean government in the north along Stalinist lines, while the Americans set up a Western-style regime in the south.

The division of Korea at the end of World War II, like the division of Germany, was a temporary expedient that became permanent. In the hectic days of August 1945, the Soviets accepted an American proposal to divide Korea at the 38th parallel until steps could be taken to unify the war-torn country. With the onset of the cold war, however, it became clear that agreement on unification was no more likely in Korea than in Germany. By the end of 1948, separate regimes had appeared in the two sectors and occupation forces had withdrawn. The weakened state of the U.S. military contributed to the impression that South Korea was vulnerable to a Communist assault. Evidence later gleaned from Soviet archives reveals that Stalin encouraged the North Koreans to unify their country and oust the Americans from the peninsula. The Soviet-designed war plan called for North Korean forces to seize South Korea within a week. Stalin apparently assumed that the United States would not intervene.

On June 25, 1950, over 80,000 North Korean soldiers crossed the boundary into South Korea and swept down the peninsula. President Truman responded decisively. He and his advisers assumed that the North Korean attack was directed by Moscow and was a brazen indication of the aggressive designs of Soviet communism. "The attack upon Korea makes it plain beyond all doubt," Truman told Congress, "that communism has passed beyond the use of subversion to conquer independent nations and will now use armed invasion and war." Truman then made two critical decisions. First, he decided to wage war under the auspices of the United Nations rather than unilaterally. Second, he decided to engage the armed forces without asking Congress for a formal declaration of war.

An emergency meeting of the UN Security Council quickly censured the North Korean "breach of peace." The Soviet delegate, who held a veto power, was at the time boycotting the council because it would not seat Communist China in place of Nationalist China. On June 27, its first resolution having been ignored, the Security Council called on UN members to "furnish such assistance to the Republic of Korea as may be necessary to repel the armed attack and to restore international peace and security in the area." Truman ordered American air, naval, and ground forces into action. In all, some fourteen other nations contributed token military units. General Douglas MacArthur was put in command. The American defense of South Korea set a precedent of profound consequence: war by order of a president rather than by vote of Congress. Yet it had the sanction of the UN Security Council and could technically be considered a "police action," not a war. To be sure, other presidents had ordered U.S. troops into action without a declaration of war, but never on such a scale.

Truman's conviction that Stalin and the Soviets were behind the invasion of South Korea prompted two other decisions that had far-reaching consequences. First, Truman viewed the Korean conflict as actually a diversion for a Soviet invasion of western Europe, so he ordered a major expansion of American forces in Europe. Second, he increased assistance to French troops in Indochina, creating the Military Assistance Advisory

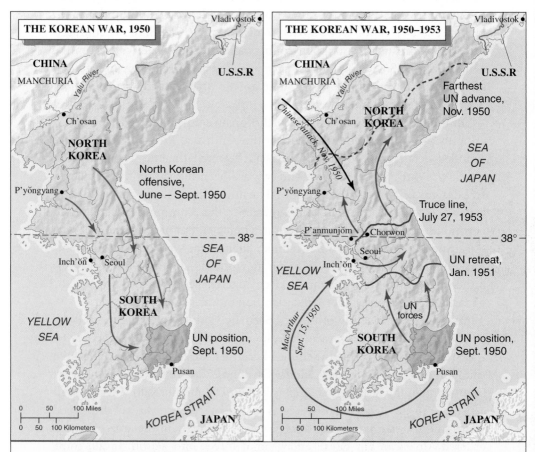

How did the surrender of the Japanese in Korea set up the conflict between Soviet-influenced North Korea and U.S.-influenced South Korea? What was General MacArthur's strategy for retaking Korea? Why did President Truman remove MacArthur from command?

Group for Indochina—the start of America's deepening military involvement in Vietnam.

For three months the fighting in Korea went badly for the Republic of Korea and the UN forces. By September they were barely hanging on to the Pusan perimeter in the southeast corner of Korea. Then, in a brilliant maneuver on September 15, 1950, MacArthur landed a new force to the North Korean rear at Inch'ŏn, the port city for Seoul. Synchronized with a breakout from Pusan, the sudden blow stampeded the North Korean forces back across the border. At that point, MacArthur persuaded Truman to allow him to push north and seek to reunify Korea. By now the Soviet delegate was back in the Security Council, wielding his veto. So on October 7 the United States won approval for this course from the UN General Assembly, where the veto did not apply. U.S. forces had crossed the North Korean boundary by October 1 and were continuing northward. President Truman, concerned about intervention by Communist China, flew 7,000 miles to Wake Island for a conference with General MacArthur on October 15. There the general discounted chances that the Chinese Red Army would act, but if it did, he predicted, "there would be the greatest slaughter."

September 1950

American soldiers engaged in the recapture of Seoul from the North Koreans.

That same day, the Communist government in Peking announced that China "cannot stand idly by." On October 20, UN forces had entered P'yŏng-yang, the North Korean capital, and on October 26 advance units had reached Ch'osan, on the Yalu River, Korea's northern border with China. MacArthur predicted total victory by Christmas. On the night of November 25, however, some 260,000 Chinese "volunteers" counterattacked, and massive "human-wave" attacks, with the support of tanks and planes, turned the tables on the UN troops, sending them into a desperate retreat just at the onset of winter. It had become "an entirely new war," MacArthur said. He criticized Truman for requiring that he conduct a limited war. He asked for thirty-four atomic bombs and proposed air raids on China's "privileged sanctuary" in Manchuria, a naval blockade of China, and an invasion of the Chinese mainland by the Taiwan Nationalists.

Truman opposed leading the United States into the "gigantic booby trap" of war with China, and the UN forces soon rallied. By January 1951 over 900,000 UN troops under General Matthew Ridgway finally secured their lines below Seoul and then launched a counterattack that in some places carried them back across the 38th parallel in March. When Truman seized the chance and offered negotiations to restore the prewar boundary, General MacArthur undermined the move by issuing an ultimatum for China to make peace or suffer an attack. Truman then decided that MacArthur, whom he called Mr. Prima Donna, would have to go. On April 5, on the floor of Congress, the Republican minority leader read a letter in which MacArthur criticized the president and said that "there is no substitute for victory." Such an act of open insubordination left the commander in chief no choice but to accept MacArthur's demands or fire him. Civilian control of the military was at stake, Truman later said, and he acted swiftly. On April 11, 1951, the president removed the popular MacArthur from all his commands and replaced him with Ridgway.

Truman's action ignited an uproar across the country, and a tumultuous reception greeted MacArthur upon his first return home since 1937. MacArthur's emotional speech to a joint session of Congress provided the climactic event. He recalled a barracks ballad of his youth "which proclaimed most proudly that old soldiers never die, they just fade away." And like the old soldiers of that ballad, he said, "I now close my military career and just fade away, an old soldier who tried to do his duty as God gave him the light to see that duty." A Senate investigation brought out the administration's arguments, best summarized by General Omar Bradley, chairman of the Joint Chiefs of Staff. "Taking on Red China," he explained, would lead only "to a larger deadlock at greater expense." The MacArthur strategy "would involve us in the wrong war at the wrong place at the wrong time and with the wrong enemy." Most Americans found General Bradley's logic persuasive.

On June 24, 1951, the Soviet representative at the United Nations proposed a cease-fire in Korea along the 38th parallel; Secretary of State Dean Acheson accepted the cease-fire a few days later with the consent of the United Nations. China and North Korea responded favorably—at the time, General Ridgway's "meat-grinder" offensive was inflicting severe losses—and truce talks started on July 10, 1951, at P'anmunjŏm, only to drag on for two years while the fighting continued. The chief snags were exchanges of prisoners and the South Korean president's insistence on unification. By the time a truce was reached, on July 27, 1953, Truman had relinquished the White House to Dwight D. Eisenhower. The truce line followed the war front at that time, mostly a little north of the 38th parallel, with a demilitarized zone of two and a half miles separating the forces; repatriation of prisoners would be voluntary, supervised by a neutral commission. No peace conference ever took place, and Korea, like Germany, remained divided. The war had cost the United States more than 33,000 battle deaths and 103,000 wounded or missing. South Korean casualties, all told, were about 1 million, and North Korean and Chinese casualties an estimated 1.5 million.

ANOTHER RED SCARE   The Korean War excited a second Red Scare, which had grown since 1945 as the domestic counterpart to the cold war abroad and reached a climax during the Korean conflict. Since 1938 the House Un-American Activities Committee (HUAC) had kept up a drumbeat of accusations about supposed Communist subversives in the federal government. On March 21, 1947, just nine days after he announced the Truman Doctrine, the president signed an executive order setting up procedures for an employee loyalty program in the federal government. Every person entering federal service would be subject to a background investigation. By early 1951 the Civil Service Commission had cleared over 3 million people, while over 2,000 had resigned and 212 had been dismissed for doubtful loyalty.

Perhaps the case most damaging to the administration involved Alger Hiss, president of the Carnegie Endowment for International Peace, who had served in several government departments. Whittaker Chambers, a former Soviet agent and later an editor of *Time* magazine, told the HUAC in 1948 that Hiss had given him secret documents ten years earlier, when Chambers was spying for the Soviets and Hiss was working in the State Department.

Alger Hiss

Accused of leading a Soviet spy ring, Hiss testifies before the House Un-American Activities Committee in August 1948.

Hiss sued for libel, and Chambers produced microfilms of the State Department documents that he said Hiss had passed to him. Hiss denied the accusation, whereupon he was indicted and, after one mistrial, convicted in 1950. The charge was perjury, but he was convicted of lying about espionage, for which he could not be tried because the statute of limitations on that crime had expired.

Most damaging to the administration was that President Truman, taking at face value the many testimonials to Hiss's integrity, had called the charges against him a "red herring." The Hiss affair had another political consequence: it raised to national prominence a young California congressman, Richard M. Nixon, who doggedly insisted on pursuing the case and then exploited his anti-Communist rhetoric to win election to the Senate in 1950.

More cases of Communist infiltration surfaced. In 1949 eleven top leaders of the Communist party in the United States were convicted under the Smith Act of 1940, which outlawed any conspiracy to advocate the overthrow of the government. The Supreme Court upheld the law under the doctrine of a "clear and present danger," which overrode the right to free speech. What was more, in 1950 the government unearthed the existence of a British-American spy network that had fed information about the development of the atomic bomb to the Soviet Union. These disclosures led to the arrest of, among others, Klaus Fuchs in Britain and Julius and Ethel Rosenberg in the United States.

McCARTHY'S ANTI-COMMUNIST WITCH HUNT Revelations of Soviet spying encouraged politicians to exploit the public's fears. If a man of such respectability as Hiss was guilty, many wondered, who could be trusted? The United States, which bestrode the world like a colossus in 1945, had since "lost" Eastern Europe and Asia to communism and its atomic secrets to Russia. Early in 1950 a little-known Republican senator,

Joseph McCarthy

Senator McCarthy (left) and his aide Roy Cohn (right) exchange comments during testimony.

Joseph R. McCarthy of Wisconsin, suddenly surfaced as the most ruthless exploiter of the nation's anxieties. He took up the cause of anti-communism with an incendiary speech at Wheeling, West Virginia, on February 9, 1950, in which he claimed that the State Department was infested with Communists—and he had their names. Later there was confusion as to whether he had said there were 205, 81, 57, or "a lot" of names on the list and even whether the sheet of paper he brandished contained any such list.

Despite his outlandish claims, McCarthy never uncovered a single Communist agent in the government. But with the United States at war with Korean Communists in mid-1950, it was easy for him to arouse public fears. By 1951 he had outrageously called General George Marshall a traitor. His smear campaign went unchallenged until the end of the Korean War.

Fears of Communist espionage led Congress in 1950 to pass the McCarran Internal Security Act over President Truman's veto, making it unlawful "to combine, conspire, or agree with any other person to perform any act which would substantially contribute to . . . the establishment of a totalitarian dictatorship." Communist and Communist-front organizations had to register with the attorney general. Aliens who had belonged to totalitarian parties were barred from admission to the United States. The McCarran

Internal Security Act, Truman said in his veto message, would "put the Government into the business of thought control." He might in fact have said as much about the Smith Act of 1940 or even his own program of loyalty investigations. Yet documents recently uncovered in Russian archives and U.S. security agencies reveal that the Soviets did indeed operate an extensive espionage ring in the United States. Russian agents recruited several hundred American spies to ferret out secrets regarding atomic weapons, defense systems, and military intelligence.

ASSESSING THE COLD WAR   In retrospect the onset of the cold war after the end of World War II takes on an appearance of terrible inevitability. American and Soviet misunderstanding of each other's motives was virtually unavoidable. America's preference for international principles such as self-determination, free trade, and democracy conflicted with the Soviet Union's preference for international spheres of influence and totalitarianism. Russia, after all, had been invaded by Germany twice in the first half of the twentieth century, and Soviet leaders wanted tame buffer states on their borders for protection. The people of Eastern Europe were again caught in the middle. But the Communists themselves held to a universal principle: world revolution.

If international conditions set the stage for the cold war, the actions of political leaders and thinkers set events in motion. President Truman may have erred in seeming to include all the world in his 1947 doctrine of Communist containment. The government loyalty program, following on the heels of the Truman Doctrine, may have incited the anti-Communist hysteria. Containment itself proved hard to contain, its author, George Kennan, later confessed, in part because he failed at the outset to spell out its limits.

The years after World War II were unlike any other postwar period in American history. Having taken on global burdens, the nation had become committed to a permanent national military establishment, along with the attendant National Security Council and Central Intelligence Agency. In 1952 the president created the enormous National Security Agency, entrusted with monitoring all media and communications for foreign intelligence.

The policy initiatives of the Truman years led the country to abandon its long-standing aversion to peacetime alliances. It was a far cry from the world of 1796, when George Washington in his farewell address warned his countrymen against "those overgrown military establishments which . . . are inauspicious to liberty" and advised his country "to steer clear of permanent alliances with any portion of the foreign world." But then Washington had warned only against participation in the "ordinary" combinations and collusions of Europe, and surely the postwar years had seen extraordinary events and unprecedented new alliances.

CHAPTER SUMMARY

- **The Cold War** The cold war was an ideological contest between the democracies of the Western Hemisphere (especially the United States) and the Communist countries of the Eastern Hemisphere (especially the Soviet Union and China) that emerged after World War II. Immediately after the war, the Soviet Union established satelite governments in Eastern Europe, violating promises made at the Yalta Conference. The United States and the Soviet Union, former allies, differed on issues of human rights, individual liberties, and self-determination.

- **Containment** President Truman responded to the Soviet occupation of Eastern Europe with the policy of containment, the aim of which was to halt the spread of communism. Truman proposed giving economic aid to countries in danger of Communist control, such as Greece and Turkey; and with the Marshall Plan, he offered such aid to all European nations. In a defensive move, the United States in 1949 became a founding member of the North Atlantic Treaty Organization (NATO), a military alliance of Western democracies.

- **Truman's Fair Deal** Truman proposed not only to preserve the New Deal but also to expand it. He vetoed a Republican attempt to curb unions. He oversaw the expansion of Social Security and through executive orders ended segregation in the military and banned racial discrimination in the hiring of federal employees.

- **The Korean War** After a Communist government came to power in China in 1949, Korea became a "hot spot." The peninsula had been divided at the 38th parallel after World War II, with a Communist regime in the north and a Western-style regime in the south. After North Koreans crossed the dividing line in June 1950, Truman decided to go to war under the auspices of the United Nations and without asking Congress to declare war. The war was thus waged by the United States with the participation of more than a dozen member nations of the United Nations. A truce, concluded in July 1953, established a demilitarized zone on either side of the 38th parallel.

- **McCarthyism** The onset of the cold war inflamed another Red Scare. During the Korean War, investigations by the House Committee on Un-American Activities (known as HUAC) sought to find "subversives" within the federal government. Senator Joseph R. McCarthy of Wisconsin exploited Americans' fears of Soviet spies' infiltrating the highest levels of the U.S. government. McCarthy was successful in the short term because, with most Eastern European nations being held as buffer states by the Soviet Union and the war in Korea being indirectly fought against Communist China, the threat of a world dominated by Communist governments seemed real to many Americans.

32

THROUGH THE PICTURE WINDOW: SOCIETY AND CULTURE, 1945–1960

FOCUS QUESTIONS wwnorton.com/studyspace

- Why did the U.S. economy grow rapidly in the postwar period?
- To what extent was conformity the main characteristic of society in the 1950s?
- What was the image of the family in this period, and what was the reality?
- What were the characteristics of the Beat generation?

Americans emerged from World War II elated, proud of their military strength and industrial might, and eager to pursue peacetime prosperity. As the editors of *Fortune* magazine proclaimed in 1946, "This is a dream era, this is what everyone was waiting through the blackouts for. The Great American Boom is on." So it was, from babies to Buicks to Admiral television sets. A society that had known mostly deprivation and sacrifice for a decade and a half began to enjoy unprecedented economic growth, access to a cornucopia of new consumer products, and seeming social contentment. Divorce and homicide rates fell, the birthrate soared, and the prevailing mood seemed aggressively upbeat—at least on the surface. By 1957 the editors of *U.S. News and World Report* had proclaimed that "never have so many people, anywhere, been so well off."

Amid the rising affluence and comfortable domesticity, however, many social critics, writers, and artists expressed a growing sense of unease with what they deemed the vulgarity and superficiality of middle-class culture. Was postwar society becoming too complacent, too conformist, too materialistic? Such questions reflected the perennial tension in American life between idealism and materialism, a tension that arrived with the first settlers and remains with us today. Americans have always struggled to accumulate goods and cultivate goodness. During the postwar era the nation again tried to do both. For a while, at least, it appeared to succeed.

PEOPLE OF PLENTY

The dominant feature of post–World War II society was its remarkable prosperity. After a surprisingly brief postwar recession, businesses shifted from wartime production to the peacetime manufacture of an array of consumer goods. The economy soared to record heights. The gross national product nearly doubled between 1945 and 1960, and the 1960s witnessed an even more spectacular expansion of the economy. By 1970 the gap between the living standard in the United States and that in the rest of the world had become a chasm: with 6 percent of the world's population, America produced and consumed two thirds of its goods. Poverty remained a chronic condition for many among the rural poor and for the minorities in urban ghettos, but their plight was largely ignored amid the wave of boosterism and consumerism.

During the 1950s government officials assured the citizenry that they should not fear another economic collapse. "Never again shall we allow a depression in the United States," President Eisenhower promised. Several factors contributed to the prolonged economic surge that fueled his optimism. The massive federal expenditures to meet military needs during the war had catapulted the economy out of the Great Depression. High government spending continued in the postwar era, thanks to the tensions generated by the cold war. The military budget after 1945 represented the single most important stimulant to the postwar economic boom. Military research also helped spawn the new glamour industries of the postwar era: chemicals, electronics, and aviation.

Most of the other major industrial nations of the world—England, France, Germany, Japan, the Soviet Union—had been physically devastated during the war, leaving American manufacturers with a virtual monopoly on international trade. In addition, technological innovations contributed to the "automation" of the workplace and thereby created spectacular increases in productivity.

The widespread use of new and more efficient machinery and computers led to a 35 percent jump in worker productivity between 1945 and 1955.

The major catalyst in promoting economic expansion after 1945 was the unleashing of pent-up consumer demand. During the war, Americans had postponed purchases of such major items as cars and houses and in the process had saved over $150 billion. Now they were eager to buy. The United States after World War II experienced a purchasing frenzy.

THE GI BILL OF RIGHTS   Part of that frenzy was indirectly financed by the federal government. Fears that a sharp drop in military spending and the sudden influx of veterans into the workforce would send the economy into a downward spiral and produce widespread unemployment led Congress to pass the Servicemen's Readjustment Act of 1944. Popularly known as the GI Bill of Rights (*GI* meaning "government issue," a phrase that was stamped on military uniforms and became slang for "serviceman"), it led to the creation of a new government agency, the Veterans Administration, and included provisions for mustering-out pay, unemployment pay for veterans for one year, preference for government jobs, loans for home construction, access to government hospitals, and generous subsidies for postsecondary education.

Between 1944 and 1956 almost 8 million veterans took advantage of $14.5 billion in GI Bill subsidies to attend college or job-training programs. Some 5 million veterans bought new homes with GI Bill mortgage loans, which required no down payment and provided up to twenty years for repayment. Before World War II approximately 160,000 Americans graduated from college each year. By 1950 the figure had risen to 500,000. In 1949, veterans accounted for 40 percent of all college enrollments, and the United States could boast the world's best-educated workforce.

For the first time in the nation's history, a significant number of working-

THE
G. I. BILL OF RIGHTS

SUPPLEMENT TO

Answers to Servicemen's *Questions*

about Life Insurance and Government Benefits . . . Prepared to Serve our Policyholders in the Armed Forces

THE PENN MUTUAL LIFE INSURANCE COMPANY

GI Bill of Rights supplement

This booklet informed servicemen about the new legislation.

class men had the opportunity to earn a college degree. In turn, a college education or vocational training served as a lever into the middle class. But while the GI Bill helped erode class barriers, it was less successful in dismantling racial barriers. Many African American veterans could not take equal advantage of the education benefits. Most colleges and universities after the war remained racially segregated, either by regulation or by practice. Of the 9,000 students enrolled at the University of Pennsylvania in 1946, for example, only 46 were African Americans. Those blacks who did manage to gain admission to white colleges or universities were barred from playing on athletic teams, attending dances and other social events, and joining fraternities or sororities. In 1946 only a fifth of the 100,000 African Americans who had applied for education benefits had enrolled in a program.

THE BABY BOOM   The return of some 12 million veterans to private life also helped generate the postwar baby boom, which peaked in 1957. Many young married couples who had delayed having children during the Depression

The baby boom

Much of America's social history since the 1940s has been the story of the baby boom generation.

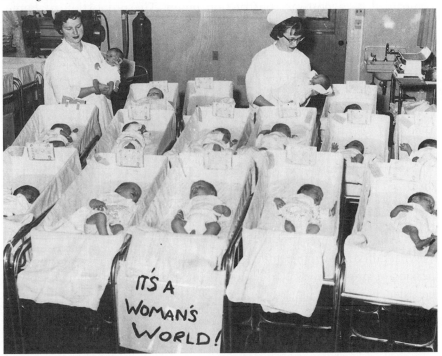

or the war were intent on making up for lost time. Between 1946 and 1964, 76 million Americans were born, reversing a century-long decline in the nation's birthrate and creating a massive demographic upheaval whose repercussions are still being felt. Much of America's social history since the 1940s has been the story of this unusually large baby boom generation and its progress through the stages of life. The postwar baby boom created a massive demand for diapers, baby food, toys, medicine, schools, books, teachers, furniture, and housing. The baby boomers were raised during the 1950s and 1960s, a period of unprecedented prosperity and American omnipotence abroad, but they entered adulthood during the 1970s, a period of energy crises, inflationary pressures, and diminished national prestige. They inherited a nation flush with affluence and will bequeath a nation mired in debt. During their childhood the baby boomers lived amid a child-obsessed culture; in their youth the nation was youth obsessed. The iconoclastic Columbia University historian Richard Hofstadter worried that America was being overrun by the "overvalued child." The baby boomer novelist Benjamin Cheever confessed that "we were spoiled. No denying that. And we have spoiled our children."

AN EXPANDING CONSUMER CULTURE   The baby boom was accompanied by a postwar construction boom. The proportion of homeowners in the population increased by 50 percent between 1945 and 1960. And those new homes featured the latest appliances: refrigerators, washing machines, sewing machines, vacuum cleaners, freezers, electric mixers, electric carving knives, electric shoe polishers.

By far the most popular new household product was the television set. In 1946 there were 7,000 primitive black-and-white TV sets in the country; by 1960 there were 50 million high-quality sets. Nine out of ten homes had one, and by 1970, 38 percent of homes had one of the new color sets. *TV Guide* was the fastest-growing new periodical of the 1950s. Watching television displaced listening to the radio as an essential daily activity for millions of people. As a media executive predicted in 1945, the new television industry would make the United States "a more democratic, more progressive, more closely knit community."

What differentiated the affluence of the post–World War II era from earlier periods of prosperity was its ever-widening dispersion. Although poverty persisted, few commentators noticed such exceptions to the prevailing affluence during the 1950s. When George Meany was sworn in as head of the American Federation of Labor–Congress of Industrial Organizations (AFL-CIO) in 1955, he proclaimed that "American labor never had it so good."

On the surface many African Americans were also beneficiaries of the wave of prosperity that swept over postwar society. By 1950, blacks were earning on average more than four times their 1940 wages. But while gains had been made, African Americans and members of other minority groups lagged behind whites in their rate of improvement. The gap between the average yearly income of whites and blacks widened during the decade of the 1950s. Yet such trends were rarely noticed amid the boosterism of the day. The need to present a united front against communism led commentators to ignore issues of racial and economic injustice. Such

Black cotillion dance

Presentation of the debutantes of 1954.

corrosive neglect would fester and explode during the 1960s, but for now the emphasis was on consensus, conformity, and economic growth.

To perpetuate the postwar prosperity, marketing specialists targeted consumers' desires and social envy. Expenditures for TV advertising increased 1,000 percent during the 1950s. Such startling growth rates led the president of NBC to claim in 1956 that the primary reason for the postwar prosperity was that "advertising has created an American frame of mind that makes people want more things, better things, and newer things."

Paying for such "things" was no problem. Between 1945 and 1957 consumer credit soared 800 percent. Whereas families in other industrialized nations were typically saving 10 to 20 percent of their income, American families by the 1960s were saving only 5 percent. "Never before have so many owed so much to so many," *Newsweek* announced in 1953. "Time has swept away the Puritan conception of immorality in debt and godliness in thrift." This consumer revolution had far-reaching cultural effects. Shopping became a major recreational activity. In 1945 there were only 8 "shopping centers" in the entire country; by 1960 there were 3,840. Much as life in a medieval town revolved around the cathedral, life in postwar America centered on the new giant shopping centers.

THE SUBURBAN FRONTIER The postwar era witnessed a mass migration to a new frontier—the suburbs. The burgeoning population created

A mink coat for father

An advertisement for a Ford Thunderbird claims that "what a mink coat does to perk up a lady, a Thunderbird does for a male."

new communities and required an array of new services. Almost the entire population increase of the 1950s and 1960s (97 percent) was an urban or suburban phenomenon. Dramatic new technological advances in agricultural production reduced the need for manual laborers. Almost 20 million people left farms and villages for the city between 1940 and 1970.

Much of the urban population growth occurred in the South, the Southwest, and the West, in an arc that stretched from the Carolinas to California, a region that by the 1970s was being labeled the sunbelt. Air-conditioning, developed by Willis Haviland Carrier in the first decade of the century, became a common household fixture in the 1950s and enhanced the appeal of living in warm climates. But the Northeast remained the most densely populated area; by the early 1960s, 20 percent of the nation's population lived in the corridor that stretched from Boston to Norfolk, Virginia.

While more people concentrated in cities, post–World War II Americans were spreading out within the metropolitan areas. During the 1950s, suburbs grew six times faster than cities. By 1970 more people lived in suburbs (76 million) than in central cities (64 million). "Suburbia," proclaimed the *Christian Century* in 1955, "is now a dominant social group in American life." Suburban development required cars, highways, and government-guaranteed mortgages. It also required visionary entrepreneurs.

William Levitt, a brassy New York developer, led the suburban revolution. In 1947, on 1,200 acres of Long Island farmland, he built 10,600 houses, to be inhabited by more than 40,000 people, mostly adults under thirty-five and their children. Other developers soon mimicked Levitt's efforts across the country. This suburban revolution benefited greatly from government assistance. By insuring loans for up to 95 percent of the value of a house, the Federal Housing Administration made it easy for a builder to construct low-cost homes. Veterans got added benefits: a veteran could buy a Levitt house with no down payment and monthly mortgage installments of $56.

Expanded automobile ownership and highway construction also facilitated the rush to the suburbs as people were able to commute longer distances to work. Car production soared, and a "car culture" soon transformed social behavior. As one commentator observed, the proliferation of automobiles "changed our dress, manners, social customs, vacation habits, the shape of our cities, consumer purchasing patterns, [and] common tastes." Widespread car ownership also necessitated an improved road network. Local

Levittown

Identical mass-produced houses in Levittown, New York, and other suburbs across the country provided veterans and their families with affordable homes.

and state governments built many new roads, but the guiding force was the federal government. In 1947, Congress authorized the construction of 37,000 miles of highways, and nine years later it funded over 42,000 additional miles in a new national system of interstate expressways.

New cars and roads provided easy access to the suburbs, and Americans—mostly middle-class white Americans—rushed to take advantage of the new living spaces. The motives for moving to the suburbs were numerous. The availability of more spacious homes and yards, greater security, and better educational opportunities for children played a role. Racial considerations were also a factor. After World War II, African Americans from the South migrated to the cities of the North and the Midwest. As they moved in, many white residents moved out. Those engaged in "white flight" were usually eager to maintain residential segregation in their new suburban communities. As William Levitt explained, "We can solve a housing problem or we can try to solve a racial problem. But we can't combine the two." Contracts for houses in Levittown, Long Island, specifically excluded "members of other than the Caucasian race." Such discrimination, whether explicit or implicit, was widespread; the nation's suburban population in 1970 was 95 percent white.

THE GREAT BLACK MIGRATION The mass migration of rural southern blacks to the urban North and Midwest after World War II was much larger than that after World War I, and its social consequences were more dramatic. After 1945 more than 5 million southern blacks, mostly farm folk, left their native region in search of better jobs, higher wages, decent housing, and greater social equality. During the 1950s, for example, the African American population of Chicago more than doubled. The South Side of Chicago soon became known as the capital of black America. It remains the neighborhood with the largest concentration of African Americans in the nation.

Many southern blacks streamed northward in search of a new promised land only to see their dreams dashed. The writer Richard Wright, himself a migrant from the Mississippi Delta to Chicago, observed that "never in history has a more utterly unprepared folk wanted to go to the city." In northern cities such as Chicago, Philadelphia, Newark, Detroit, New York, Boston, and Washington, D.C., rural African Americans from the South confronted harsh new realities. Slumlords gouged them for rent, employers refused to hire them, and union bosses denied them membership. Soon the promised land had become an ugly nightmare of slum housing, joblessness, illiteracy, dysfunctional families, welfare dependency, street gangs, pervasive crime, and racism.

Family on relief

Many black families who migrated from the South
became a part of a marginalized population in Chicago,
dependent on public housing.

The unexpected tidal wave of African American migrants severely taxed
the resources of northern urban governments and the patience of white
racists. For several nights during 1951, a white mob in a Chicago suburb
assaulted a building into which a black family had moved. The National
Guard had to quell the disturbance and disperse the crowd. Like other
northern cities, Chicago sought to deal with the migrants and alleviate racial
stress by constructing massive public-housing projects to accommodate the
newcomers. These overcrowded all-black enclaves soon became segregated
prisons. To be sure, many black migrants and their children did manage
through extraordinary determination and ingenuity to "clear"—to climb
out of the teeming ghettos and into the middle class. But most did not. As a
consequence the great black migration produced a web of complex social
problems in northern cities that in the 1960s would erupt into a crisis.

A CONFORMING CULTURE

In the 1950s, social commentators mostly ignored people and cultures
outside the middle-class mainstream. As evidenced in many of the new look-
alike suburbs sprouting up across the land, much of middle-class social life

during the two decades after the end of World War II exhibited an increasingly homogenized character. Suburban life encouraged uniformity. In new communities of strangers, people felt a need for companionship and a sense of belonging. Changes in corporate life as well as the influence of the consumer culture also played an important socializing role. "Conformity," predicted a journalist in 1954, "may very well become the central social problem of this age."

CORPORATE LIFE   The composition of the workforce and the very nature of work itself were dramatically changing during the postwar era. Fewer people were self-employed, and manual labor was rapidly giving way to mental labor. By the mid-1950s white-collar (salaried) workers outnumbered blue-collar (hourly wage) workers for the first time in history. During World War II, big business had grown bigger. The government relaxed its anti-trust activity, and huge defense contracts promoted corporate concentration and consolidation. In 1940, for example, the 100 largest companies were responsible for 30 percent of all manufacturing output; three years later they were providing 70 percent. After the war a wave of mergers occurred, and dominant

Office in a Small City

Edward Hopper's 1953 painting suggests the alienation associated with white-collar work and the corporate atmosphere of the 1950s.

corporate giants appeared in every major industry, providing the primary source of new jobs. By 1960, 38 percent of the workforce was employed by organizations with more than 500 employees. In such huge companies, as well as similarly large government agencies and universities, the working atmosphere promoted conformity rather than individualism.

WOMEN'S "PLACE"   Increasing conformity in the middle-class workplace was mirrored in the middle-class home. A special issue of *Life* magazine in 1956 featured the "ideal" middle-class woman, a thirty-two-year-old "pretty and popular" white suburban housewife, mother of four, who had married at age sixteen. She was described as an excellent wife, mother, volunteer, and "home manager" who made her own clothes, hosted dozens of dinner parties each year, sang in her church choir, worked with the parent-teacher association and the Campfire Girls, and was devoted to her husband. "In her daily round," *Life* reported, "she attends club or charity meetings, drives the children to school, does the weekly grocery shopping, makes ceramics, and is planning to study French."

Life's description of the middle-class woman was symptomatic of a cult of feminine domesticity that witnessed a dramatic revival in the postwar era. The soaring birthrate reinforced the deeply embedded notion that a

The new household

A Tupperware party in a middle-class suburban home.

woman's place was in the home. "Of all the accomplishments of the American woman," the *Life* cover story proclaimed, "the one she brings off with the most spectacular success is having babies."

Even though millions of women had responded to wartime appeals and joined the traditionally male workforce, afterward they were encouraged—and even forced—to turn their jobs over to the returning male veterans and resume their full-time commitment to home and family. A 1945 article in *House Beautiful* lectured women on their postwar responsibilities. The returning veteran, it said, was "head man again . . . Your part in the remaking of this man is to fit his home to him, understanding why he wants it this way, forgetting your own preferences." Women were also to dismiss wartime-generated thoughts of their own career in the workplace. "Women must boldly announce," a Barnard College trustee asserted in 1950, "that no job is more exacting, more necessary, or more rewarding than that of housewife and mother."

THE SEARCH FOR COMMUNITY   Americans were on the move after World War II. Not only were they moving from the central cities to the suburbs and from the rural South to the North, but they were also moving from farm to city, suburb to suburb, state to state. Some 20 percent of the population changed their place of residence each year. The major cause of the mobility was the largest corporations' standard policy of relocating their sales and managerial employees. Executives of International Business Machines (IBM) Corporation told friends that the company initials actually stood for "I've Been Moved." Such flux led people to search for a sense of community and rootedness. Hence middle-class Americans, even more than usual, tended to be joiners: they joined civic clubs, garden clubs, bridge clubs, carpools, and babysitting groups.

A RELIGIOUS NATION   Americans also joined churches and synagogues in record numbers. The postwar era witnessed a massive renewal of religious participation. In 1940 less than half the adult population belonged to a church; by 1960 over 65 percent were official communicants. Sales of Bibles soared during the postwar era, and books, movies, and songs with religious themes were pervasive.

Conservative Protestants found willing allies among Republican leaders in their effort to reaffirm America's Christian commitment. President Eisenhower repeatedly promoted a patriotic crusade to bring Americans back to God. "Recognition of the Supreme Being," he declared, "is the first, the most basic, expression of Americanism. Without God, there could be no American form of government, nor an American way of life." The president had himself

Billy Graham preaches to thousands, 1955

The Baptist evangelist used radio and television to promote his huge crusades, as droves of Americans, encouraged by the president, Congress, and billboard advertising, joined churches and attended revival meetings.

joined a church only in 1953, but he characterized himself as the "most intensely religious man I know." Not to be outdone, Congress in 1954 added the phrase "under God" to the Pledge of Allegiance and in 1956 made the statement "In God We Trust" mandatory on all coins and currency. In 1956, Congress made "In God We Trust" the national motto. A godly nation, it was widely assumed, would better withstand the march of godless communism.

The prevailing tone of the popular religious revival of the 1950s was upbeat and soothing. Many ministers assumed that people were not interested in fire-and-brimstone harangues from the pulpit; congregants did not want their conscience overburdened with a sense of personal sin or social guilt about such issues as racial segregation and inner-city poverty. Instead, they wanted to be reassured that their comfortable way of life was indeed God's will. As the Protestant Council of New York City explained to its corps of radio and television speakers, their addresses "should project love, joy, courage, hope, faith, trust in God, goodwill. Generally avoid condemnation, criticism, controversy. In a very real sense we are 'selling' religion, the good news of the Gospel."

The best salesman of this gospel of reassuring "good news" was the Reverend Norman Vincent Peale, champion of feel-good theology. No speaker was more in demand during the 1950s, and no writer was more widely read. Peale's book *The Power of Positive Thinking* (1952) was a phenomenal best-seller throughout the decade—and for good reason. It offered a simple how-to course in personal happiness. "Flush out all depressing, negative, and tired thoughts," Peale advised. "Start thinking faith, enthusiasm, and joy." By following this simple formula for success, he pledged, the reader could become "a more popular, esteemed, and well-liked individual."

NEO-ORTHODOXY   "Stop worrying and start living" was Peale's simple credo. But was it too simplistic? The "peace-of-mind" and "positive-thinking" psychology struck some members of the religious community as shallow and misleading. They argued that the gospel of good news was primarily a way of promoting sociability or a sense of "belonging." These advocates of "neo-orthodoxy" criticized those who identified the United States as the only truly providential society and who used faith as a sanction for the social status quo.

The most significant spokesman for such neo-orthodoxy was Reinhold Niebuhr. A brilliant preacher-professor at New York's Union Theological Seminary, Niebuhr lambasted the "undue complacency and conformity" that had settled over postwar life. He disdained the popular religion of self-assurance and material success. Spiritual peace, Niebuhr insisted, involves not the cheap comfort and sedating reassurance offered by Peale and other popular evangelists but the reality of pain, a pain "caused by love and responsibility" for the well-being of the entire human race.

CRACKS IN THE PICTURE WINDOW

Reinhold Niebuhr was one of many social critics who challenged the moral complacency and conformity of American life during the 1950s and early 1960s. One of the most striking aspects of postwar culture was the sharp contrast between the buoyant public mood and the increasingly bitter social criticism coming from intellectuals, theologians, novelists, playwrights, poets, and artists.

THE LONELY CROWD   The critics of postwar life and values shared a common fear: America was becalmed in a sea of conformity, content to succumb to the soul-denying demands of the corporate "rat race" and eager to wallow in the consumer culture. In *The Affluent Society* (1958), for example, the economist John Kenneth Galbraith attacked the prevailing notion that sustained economic growth would solve chronic social problems. The public

Suburban life

A woman vaccums her living room in Queens, New York, 1953, illustrating the 1950s ideal of domestic perfection.

sector was starved for funds, Galbraith argued, and public enterprises were everywhere deteriorating. He reminded readers that for all of America's vaunted postwar prosperity, the nation had yet to eradicate poverty.

Postwar cultural critics also questioned the supposed bliss of middle-class life. John Keats, in *The Crack in the Picture Window* (1956), launched the most savage assault on life in the huge new suburban developments. He ridiculed Levittown and other mass-produced communities as having been "conceived in error, nurtured in greed, corroding everything they touch." Locked into a monotonous routine, hounded by financial insecurity, and engulfed by mass mediocrity, suburbanites, he concluded, were living in a "homogeneous, postwar Hell."

Mass-produced suburban developments did exhibit a startling sameness. Levittown, for example, encouraged and even enforced uniformity. The houses all sold for the same price—$7,990—and featured the same floor plan and accessories. Each had a picture window, a living room, bathroom, kitchen, and two bedrooms. A tree was planted every twenty-eight feet. Homeowners were required to cut their grass once a week, fences were prohibited, and laundry could not be hung out on weekends. However, Levittown was in many ways distinctive rather than representative. There were thousands of suburbs by the mid-1950s, and few were as regimented or as unvarying as Keats and other critics implied. Keats also failed to recognize the benefits that the suburbs offered those who otherwise would have remained in crowded urban apartments.

Critics also lambasted the huge modern corporations. The most comprehensive analysis of the new corporate character was David Riesman's *The Lonely Crowd* (1950). Riesman and his research associates detected a fundamental shift in the dominant American personality from what they called the "inner-directed" type to the "other-directed" type. Inner-directed people possess a deeply internalized set of basic values implanted by strong-minded parents or other elders. These values act as a built-in stabilizer that keeps them on course. Such an assured, self-reliant personality, Riesman argued, had prevailed throughout the nineteenth century. But during the mid–twentieth century an other-directed personality had displaced it. The new corporate culture demanded employees who could win friends and influence people rather than rugged individualists indifferent to personal popularity. Other-directed people were concerned more with being well liked than with being independent. In the workplace they were always smiling, always glad-handing, always trying to please the boss.

By the mid-1950s social commentators were growing increasingly concerned about the negative effects of such a managerial personality. In his influential study *White Collar Society* (1951), the sociologist C. Wright Mills attacked the attributes and influence of modern corporate life. "When white-collar people get jobs," Mills explained, "they sell not only their time and energy, but their personalities as well. They sell by the week or month their smiles and their kindly gestures, and they must practice the prompt repression of resentment and aggression."

ALIENATION AND LIBERATION

THE STAGE   Many of the best theatrical productions of the postwar period reinforced David Riesman's image of modern American society as a "lonely crowd" of individuals without internal values, hollow at the core, groping for a sense of belonging and affection. Arthur Miller's play *Death of a Salesman* (1949), for example, was a powerful exploration of the theme. The play's protagonist, Willy Loman, an aging, confused salesman in decline, has centered his life and that of his family on the notion that material success is secured through personal popularity, only to be abruptly told by his boss that he is in fact a failure. Loman insists that it is "not what you say, it's how you say it—because personality always wins the day." Yet Willy, for all his puffery about being well liked, admits in a fit of candor that he is "terribly lonely." He has no real friends; even his relations with his family are neither honest nor intimate. When Willy finally realizes that he has been leading a counterfeit existence, he is so dumbfounded that he decides he can endow his life with meaning only by ending it.

***Death of a Salesman* (1949)**

In Arthur Miller's play, Willy Loman (center, played by Lee J. Cobb) destroys his life and his family with the credo "be liked and you will never want."

THE NOVEL The most enduring novels of the postwar period display a preoccupation with the individual's struggle for survival amid the smothering and disorienting forces of mass society. The characters in novels such as James Jones's *From Here to Eternity* (1951), Saul Bellow's *Dangling Man* (1944) and *Seize the Day* (1956), William Styron's *Lie Down in Darkness* (1951), and John Updike's *Rabbit, Run* (1961), among many others, tend to be like Willy Loman—restless, tormented, and often socially impotent individuals who can find neither contentment nor respect in an overpowering or uninterested world.

Ralph Ellison

Ellison is best remembered for his 1952 novel *Invisible Man*.

The immensely talented African American writer Ralph Ellison explored the theme of the lonely individual imprisoned in privacy in his kaleidoscopic novel *Invisible Man* (1952). By using a black narrator struggling to find and liberate himself in the midst of an oppressive white society, Ellison forcefully accentuated the problem of alienation. The narrator opens by confessing: "All my life I had been looking for something, and everywhere I turned someone tried to tell me what it was. I accepted their answers too, though they were often in contradiction and even self-contradictory. I was naive. I was looking for myself and asking everyone except myself questions which I, and only I, could answer."

PAINTING   The powerful artist Edward Hopper also explored the theme of desolate loneliness in postwar urban-industrial American life. Virtually all of his paintings of the period depict isolated individuals, melancholy, anonymous, motionless. The silence of his scenes is deafening, the monotony striking, the alienation absorbing. (For an example of Hopper's work, see p. 1250.)

A group of younger painters in New York City decided that postwar society was so repulsive that it precluded any attempt at literal representation. As the artist Jackson Pollock maintained, "the modern painter cannot express this age—the airplane, the atomic bomb, the radio—in the old form of the Renaissance or of any past culture. Each age finds its own technique." The anarchic technique Pollock adopted came to be called abstract expressionism, and during the late 1940s and 1950s it dominated not only the American art scene but the international field as well. In addition to Pollock, its adherents included Robert Motherwell, Willem de Kooning, and Mark Rothko. "Abstract art," Motherwell explained, "is an effort to close the void that modern men feel." In practice this meant that the *act* of painting was as important as the result.

THE BEATS   In Saul Bellow's novel *Dangling Man,* a character concludes that the essence of life is the "desire for pure freedom." The desire to liberate self-expression, to surmount organizational constraints and discard traditional conventions, was an abiding goal of the abstract expressionists. It was also the central concern of a small but highly visible and controversial group of young writers, poets, painters, and musicians known as the Beats. These angry young men—Jack Kerouac, Allen Ginsberg, Gary Snyder, William Burroughs, and Gregory Corso, among others—rebelled against the regimented horrors of war and the mundane horrors of middle-class life.

The self-described Beats grew out of the bohemian underground in New York's Greenwich Village. There they began their quest for a visionary sensibility and a spontaneous way of life. Essentially apolitical throughout the 1950s, they were more interested in transforming themselves than in reforming the world. They sought personal rather than social solutions to their anxieties. As Kerouac insisted, his friends were not beat in the sense of

Allen Ginsberg

Ginsberg, considered the poet laureate of the Beat generation, reads his uncensored poetry to a crowd in Washington Square Park in New York City.

beaten; they were "mad to live, mad to talk, mad to be saved." Their road to salvation lay in hallucinogenic drugs and alcohol, sex, a penchant for jazz and the street life of urban ghettos, an affinity for Buddhism, and a restless, vagabond spirit that took them speeding back and forth across the country between San Francisco and New York during the 1950s.

This existential mania for intense experience and frantic motion provided the subject matter for the Beats' writing. Ginsberg's long prose poem *Howl*, published in 1956, features an explicit sensuality as well as an impressionistic attempt to catch the color, movement, and dynamism of modern life. Kerouac issued his autobiographical novel *On the Road* a year later. In frenzied prose and plotless ramblings, it portrays the Beats' life of "bursting ecstasies" and maniacal traveling.

Howl and *On the Road* elicited sarcasm and anger from many reviewers, but the books enjoyed brisk sales, especially among young people. *On the Road* made the best-seller list, and soon the terms *Beat generation* and *beatnik* referred to almost any young rebel who openly dissented from middle-class life. Defiant, unruly actors such as James Dean and Marlon Brando were added to the pantheon of Beat "anti-heroes." The anarchic gaiety of the Beats played an important role in preparing for the more widespread youth revolt of the 1960s.

YOUTH CULTURE AND DELINQUENCY   Young people occupied a distinctive place in postwar life. The children of the baby boom were becoming adolescents during the 1950s, and in the process a distinctive teen subculture began to emerge. Living amid such a prosperous era, teenagers had more money and more free time than any previous generation. A vast new teen market arose for goods ranging from transistor radios, Hula-Hoops, and rock-and-roll records to cameras, surfboards, *Seventeen* magazine, and Pat Boone movies. Teenagers in the postwar era knew nothing of economic depressions or wartime rationing; immersed in abundance from an early age, the children of prospering parents took the notion of carefree consumption for granted.

Most young people during the 1950s embraced the values of their parents and the capitalist system. One critic labeled the college students of the postwar era "the silent generation," content to cavort at fraternity parties and "sock hops" before landing a job with a large corporation, marrying, and settling down to the routine of middle-class suburban life.

Yet such general descriptions masked a great deal of turbulence. During the 1950s a wave of juvenile delinquency swept across middle-class society. By 1956 over 1 million teens were being arrested each year. Car theft was the

Suburban pastimes

A suburban family enjoys playing with Hula-hoops in their backyard.

Youth culture

A drugstore soda fountain, a popular outlet for teenagers' consumerism in the 1950s.

leading offense, but larceny, rape, beatings, and even murder were not uncommon. What was causing the delinquency? J. Edgar Hoover, head of the Federal Bureau of Investigation, insisted that the root of the problem was a lack of religious training. Others pointed to the growing number of urban slums. Such "bad" and "brutish" environments almost ensured that children would become criminals. The problem with those explanations was that they failed to explain why so many middle-class kids from God-fearing families were becoming delinquents. One contributing factor may have been the unprecedented mobility of young people. Access to automobiles enabled teens to escape parental control, and in the words of one journalist, cars provided "a private lounge for drinking and for petting or sex episodes."

ROCK AND ROLL   Many concerned observers blamed teen delinquency on a new form of music that emerged during the postwar era: rock and roll. In 1955, *Life* magazine published a long article about a mysterious new "frenzied teenage music craze" that was creating "a big fuss." Alan Freed, a Cleveland disc jockey, had coined the term *rock and roll* in 1951. At a record store he had noticed white teenagers buying rhythm and blues (R&B)

records that had heretofore been purchased only by African Americans and Hispanic Americans. Freed began playing R&B records but labeled the music "rock and roll" (a phrase used in African American communities to refer to dancing and sex) to surmount the racial barrier. Freed's radio program was an immediate success, and its popularity helped bridge the gap between "white" and "black" music. African American singers such as Chuck Berry, Little Richard, and Ray Charles and Hispanic American performers such as Ritchie Valens (Richard Valenzuela) were suddenly the rage among young white middle-class audiences eager to claim their own cultural style and message.

Elvis Presley, 1956

The teenage children of middle-class America made rock and roll a thriving industry in the 1950s and Elvis its first star. The strong beat of the music combined with the electric guitar, its signature instrument, produced a distinctive new sound.

At the same time, Elvis Presley, a young white truck driver and aspiring singer from Memphis, Tennessee, began experimenting with "rockabilly" music, his unique blend of gospel, country-and-western, and R&B rhythms and lyrics. In 1956 the twenty-one-year-old Presley released his smash hit "Heartbreak Hotel" and over the next two years emerged as the most popular musician in American history. Presley's long hair and sideburns, his swiveling hips and smirking self-confidence, his leather jacket and tight blue jeans—all shouted defiance of adult conventions. His sexually suggestive stage performances drove teenagers wild.

Such hysterics prompted cultural conservatives to urge parents to destroy Presley's records because they promoted "a pagan concept of life." A Catholic cardinal denounced Presley as a vile symptom of a teenage "creed of dishonesty, violence, lust and degeneration." Patriotic groups claimed that rock-and-roll music was a tool of Communist insurgents designed to corrupt youth. Yet rock and roll survived the assaults, and in the process it gave adolescents a self-conscious sense of belonging to a unique social group with distinctive characteristics. It also represented an unprecedented intermingling of racial, ethnic, and class identities.

A PARADOXICAL ERA

Rock and roll would become one of the major vehicles of the youth revolt of the 1960s. In the 1950s, however, it had little impact on the prevailing patterns of social and cultural life. The same held true for most of the critics who attacked the smug conformity and excessive materialism they saw pervading their society. The public had become weary of larger social or political concerns in the aftermath of the Depression and the war. Instead, Americans eagerly focused on personal and family goals and material achievements.

Yet those achievements, considerable as they were, eventually created a new set of problems. The benefits of abundance were by no means equally distributed during the 1950s, and millions of people still lived in poverty. For those more fortunate, unprecedented affluence and security fostered greater leisure and independence, which in turn provided opportunities for pursuing more varied notions of what the good life entailed. Yet the conformist mentality of the cold war era discouraged experimentation. By the mid-1960s, tensions between innovation and convention would erupt into open conflict. Members of the baby boom generation would become the leaders of the 1960s rebellion against corporate conformity and consumerism. Ironically, the person who would warn Americans of the 1960s of the mounting dangers of the burgeoning "military-industrial complex" was the president who had long symbolized its growth: Dwight D. Eisenhower.

End of Chapter Review

- **Growth of U.S. Economy** High levels of government spending, begun before the war, continued during the postwar period. The GI Bill of Rights gave a boost to home buying and helped many veterans attend college and thereby enter the middle class. Unemployment was virtually nonexistent, and consumer demand for homes, cars, and household goods that had been unavailable during the war fueled the economy, as did buying on credit.

- **Conformity in American Society** After World War II, with the growth of suburbs, corporations, and advertising, society appeared highly uniform, yet pockets of poverty persisted, and minorities did not prosper to the extent that white Americans did. Most white mothers did not work outside the home and were expected to find pleasure in housework. Attendance at worship services soared. The semblance of uniformity was perhaps a reaction to a feeling that society was threatened by an atheistic communism. Although popular culture reflected the affluence of the white middle class, the art and literature of the period hinted at an underlying alienation.

- **The American Family** Conformity extended to the image of the family as depicted on television and in magazines. Typically a family consisted of a father who worked in a city and a mother who stayed at home in the suburbs, devoting herself to home, husband, and children. This image did not reflect everyone's reality, however. A wave of juvenile delinquency swept middle-class society, and millions of Americans, especially minorities, lived in poverty during this era of affluence. The great black migration allowed some black families to climb into the middle class, but left many stuck in the teeming ghettos in northern cities.

- **The Beat Generation** Dissatisfaction with conformity was reflected in the literature and art of the Beat generation. Artists such as Edward Hopper dwelled on the desolate loneliness of urban settings, and a group of younger painters turned from realism to abstract expressionism in the belief that modern society was too chaotic to be represented in a literal manner. The Beats were a small yet highly visible group of writers and artists who rebelled against the regimented horrors of war and the mundane horrors of middle-class life. They sought to transform themselves, more than the world, and they sought their salvation through the use of hallucinogenic drugs, alcohol, sex, and music in their attempts to capture the vitality of modern life.

CHRONOLOGY

1944	Congress passes the Servicemen's Readjustment Act (GI Bill of Rights)
1949	Arthur Miller's *Death of a Salesman* is produced
1950	David Riesman's *The Lonely Crowd* is published
1952	Ralph Ellison's *Invisible Man* is published
1956	Elvis Presley's "Heartbreak Hotel" is released
1956	Allen Ginsberg's *Howl* is published
1957	Jack Kerouac's *On the Road* is published
1957	Baby boom peaks
1958	John Kenneth Galbraith's *The Affluent Society* is published

KEY TERMS & NAMES

33

CONFLICT AND DEADLOCK: THE EISENHOWER YEARS

FOCUS QUESTIONS

wwnorton.com/studyspace

- What were the main characteristics of Dwight Eisenhower's "dynamic conservatism"?
- What shaped American foreign policy in the 1950s?
- What events in Southeast Asia led to America's involvement in Vietnam?
- How did the civil rights movement come to emerge in the 1950s?

The New Deal political coalition established by Franklin Roosevelt and sustained by Harry Truman posed a formidable challenge to Republicans after World War II. To counter the potent combination of Solid South white Democrats, African Americans, members of other minority groups, and organized labor, the Grand Old Party in 1952 turned to General Dwight David Eisenhower, a military hero with an infectious grin, a widely respected candidate capable of attracting independent voters as well as some Democrats. Eisenhower's commitment to a "moderate Republicanism" promised to slow the rate of government expansion while retaining many of the coveted social programs established by Roosevelt and Truman. Eisenhower promised to restore the authority of state and local governments and restrain the federal government from political and social "engineering." In the process, the former general sought to renew traditional virtues and inspire Americans with a vision of a brighter future amid a continuing "cold war."

"TIME FOR A CHANGE"

By 1952 the Truman administration had piled up a heavy burden of political liabilities. Its bold stand in Korea had brought a bloody stalemate in the war, renewed wage and price controls at home, partisan charges of Communist subversion and disloyalty, and the embarrassing exposure of corrupt lobbyists and influence peddlers who rigged favors in Washington. The disclosure of corruption led Truman to fire nearly 250 employees of the Internal Revenue Service. Doubts lingered that the president would ever finish the housecleaning.

THE POLITICAL RISE OF EISENHOWER   It was, Republicans claimed, "time for a change," and they saw public sentiment turning their way as the 1952 election approached. Republican leaders recruited General Dwight D. Eisenhower to be their candidate. Eisenhower, then the commander of NATO, affirmed that he was a Republican, left his NATO post, and permitted his name to be entered in party primaries. An outpouring of public enthusiasm greeted his candidacy. Bumper stickers announced simply, "I Like Ike." Eisenhower won the presidential nomination on the first ballot. He balanced the ticket with a youthful Californian, the thirty-nine-year-old senator Richard M. Nixon, who had built a career on opposition to left-wing "subversives" holding government posts in the Truman administration.

THE ELECTION OF 1952   The Twenty-second Amendment, ratified in 1951, forbade any president from serving more than two terms. The amendment exempted the current incumbent, Harry Truman. But he had no desire to run again. Weary of the war in Korea and harassed by charges of subversion and corruption in his administration, Truman withdrew and endorsed Governor Adlai E. Stevenson of Illinois, who roused the Democratic delegates at the presidential nominating convention with an eloquent speech welcoming them to Chicago.

The 1952 campaign matched two contrasting personalities. Eisenhower, though a political novice, was a world military hero who had been in the public eye for a decade. Stevenson was hardly known outside Illinois and was never able to escape the burden of Truman's liabilities. The genial Eisenhower, who had led the Allied crusade against Hitler, now opened a domestic crusade to clean up "the mess in Washington." To this he added a promise, late in the campaign, that as president-elect he would secure "an early and honorable" peace in Korea. Stevenson possessed a lofty eloquence spiced with a quick wit, but he came across as a tad too aloof, a shade too intellectual. The

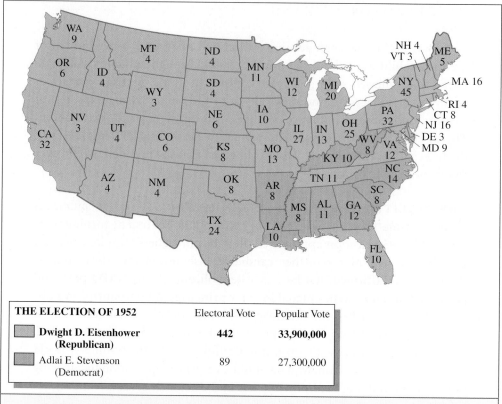

THE ELECTION OF 1952	Electoral Vote	Popular Vote
Dwight D. Eisenhower (Republican)	442	33,900,000
Adlai E. Stevenson (Democrat)	89	27,300,000

Why was the contest between Adlai Stevenson and Dwight Eisenhower lopsided? Why was Eisenhower's victory in the South remarkable? Did Eisenhower's broad appeal help congressional Republicans win more seats?

Republicans labeled him an egghead in contrast to Eisenhower, the man of the people, the general of decisive action.

In the end, Stevenson's humor and intellect were no match for Eisenhower's popularity. The war hero triumphed in a landslide of nearly 34 million votes to Stevenson's slightly more than 27 million and 442 electoral votes to Stevenson's 89. The election marked a turning point in Republican fortunes in the South: for the first time since the 1850s, the South was moving toward a two-party system. Stevenson carried only eight southern states plus West Virginia. He also failed to win his home state of Illinois. Eisenhower picked up five states on the periphery of the Deep South: Florida, Oklahoma, Tennessee, Texas, and Virginia. The "nonpolitical" Eisenhower had made it respectable, even fashionable, to vote Republican in the South. Elsewhere, too, the former general made inroads into the Democrats' New Deal coalition, attracting supporters among the ethnic and religious minorities in the major cities who had long identified with the Democratic party.

The voters, it turned out, liked Eisenhower better than they liked his party. In the 1952 election, Democrats retained most of the governorships, lost control of the House by only eight seats, and broke even in the Senate, where only the vote of the vice president ensured Republican control. The congressional elections two years later would weaken the Republican grip on Congress, and Eisenhower would have to work with a Democratic Congress throughout his term in office.

Good first impression

In the 1952 election the Republican party won significant support in the South for the first time.

EISENHOWER'S "HIDDEN-HAND" PRESIDENCY

IKE   Born in Denison, Texas, on October 14, 1890, Dwight David Eisenhower grew up in Abilene, Kansas, and attended the U.S. Military Academy at West Point, New York. During World War II he commanded American forces in the European theater and directed the invasion of North Africa in 1942. Two years later he assumed the post of supreme commander of Allied forces in preparation for the invasion of Nazi-controlled Europe. After the war, by then a five-star general of the army, he assumed command of NATO forces, with a brief interlude as president of Columbia University in New York City.

Far from being a "do-nothing" president, as some have charged, Eisenhower was an effective leader. The art of leadership, he once explained, required "persuasion—and conciliation—and education—and patience. That's the only kind of leadership I know—or believe in—or will practice." Ike was a midwestern middle-of-the-road patriot, a common man with a winning smile who read little, was uninformed about trends in intellectual and artistic life, and was prone to giving folksy advice. A diplomat labeled him "the nation's number one Boy Scout." But those who were closer to Ike have presented another side. When provoked, the genial general could unleash a fiery temper and release a stream of scalding profanity. One student of Eisenhower's leadership techniques has spoken of a "hidden-hand" presidency, in which Ike deliberately cultivated a public image of passivity to cloak his active involvement in policy decisions.

"DYNAMIC CONSERVATISM" AT HOME Like Ulysses Grant, Eisenhower enjoyed hobnobbing with rich men. In the Eisenhower cabinet, the president of General Motors became secretary of defense, one auto distributor became secretary of the interior, and another became postmaster general. The New Dealers, Adlai Stevenson wryly remarked, "have all left Washington to make way for the car dealers."

Eisenhower called his domestic program dynamic conservatism, which meant being "conservative when it comes to money and liberal when it comes to human beings." The new administration set out to slash both New Deal programs and national defense spending. Eisenhower warned repeatedly against the dangers of "creeping socialism," "huge bureaucracies," and perennial budget deficits. He abolished the Reconstruction Finance Corporation, ended wage and price controls, and reduced farm-price subsidies.

In 1954 the Eisenhower administration formulated tax reductions that resembled the Republican programs of the 1920s in providing benefits mainly to corporations and wealthy individuals. The new budget slashed expenditures by nearly 10 percent. But a business slump followed, which reduced government revenues, making it harder to balance the budget. Eisenhower's fiscal and monetary policies thereafter became more flexible. The government accepted easier credit and deficits as necessary "countercyclical" methods to avoid a recession.

Although Eisenhower chipped away at several Democratic programs, his presidency in the end kept the basic structure and premises of the New Deal. He was a pragmatist. In a letter to his brother in 1954, Eisenhower observed, "Should any political party attempt to abolish Social Security and eliminate labor laws and farm programs, you would not hear of that party again in our political history." In some ways the Eisenhower administration expanded the New Deal, especially after 1954, when it had the help of Democratic Congresses. Amendments to the Social Security Act in 1954 and 1956 brought coverage to millions of workers formerly excluded: white-collar professionals, domestic and clerical workers, farmworkers, and members of the armed forces. In 1959 the program's expenses went up 7 percent. Federal expenditures for public health rose steadily in the Eisenhower years, and the president went so far as to endorse federal participation in health insurance, but Congress twice refused to act on such a plan. Low-income housing continued to be built with federal funds, although on a much reduced scale.

Some agriculture aid programs were expanded during the Eisenhower years as well. The president also continued to support federal construction projects that served national needs. Two such programs left major monuments to his presidency: the St. Lawrence Seaway and the interstate highway system. The St. Lawrence Seaway opened the Great Lakes to oceangoing ships by means of locks and dredging. Even more important, in 1956 the Federal-Aid Highway Act authorized the federal government to pay 90 percent of the cost of building a national network of interstate superhighways to serve the needs of commerce and defense, as well as the convenience of private citizens. The states put up the remaining 10 percent. Eisenhower viewed such highways as crucial to national defense. They would enable the rapid movement of military convoys and the evacuation of cities after a nuclear attack. It was only afterward that Americans realized that the huge national commitment to the automobile might have come at the expense of the nation's railroad system, already in a state of advanced decay.

CONCLUDING AN ARMISTICE   America's new global responsibilities absorbed much of Eisenhower's attention. The most pressing problem when he entered office was the painful deadlock in the Korean peace talks. UN negotiators refused to return prisoners of war who did not want to go back to Communist North Korea. North Korean and Chinese negotiators insisted that all prisoners be returned regardless of their wishes. To break the stalemate, Eisenhower took a bold step. In mid-May 1953 he intensified aerial bombardment of North Korea, then had Secretary of State John Foster Dulles threaten to use atomic warfare. Whether for that reason or others, negotiations moved quickly toward an armistice along the established border just above the 38th parallel and toward a complicated arrangement for an exchange of prisoners that allowed captives to accept or refuse repatriation.

On July 26, 1953, President Eisenhower announced the end of fighting in Korea. Whether he had pulled a masterful bluff in getting the agreement has never become clear; no one knows whether he would have used atomic weapons. Perhaps the more decisive factors in bringing about a settlement were rising Chinese losses, which China's leaders increasingly found unacceptable, and the spirit of uncertainty and caution felt by the Soviet Communists after the death of Joseph Stalin on March 5, 1953, six weeks after Ike's inauguration.

CONCLUDING A WITCH HUNT   The Korean armistice helped to end the meteoric career of Senator Joseph McCarthy. The Wisconsin senator had launched a one-man crusade to root out Communists and spies on American soil. Eventually McCarthy's unscrupulous tactics led to his self-destruction, but not before he had left still more careers and reputations in ruins. The Republicans thought their victory in 1952 would curb his reck-lessness, but McCarthy grew more outlandish in both his charges and his investigative methods.

The freewheeling McCarthy finally overreached himself when he made the absurd charge that the U.S. Army itself was "soft" on communism. From April 22 to June 17, 1954, televised Senate hearings displayed McCarthy at his capricious worst, bullying witnesses, dragging out lengthy irrele-vances, repeatedly calling "point of order." He became the perfect foil for the army's gentle but unflappable legal counsel, Joseph Welch of Boston, whose rapier wit repeatedly drew blood. When McCarthy tried to smear one of Welch's young associates, Welch was outraged: "Until this moment, Senator, I think I never really gauged your cruelty or your recklessness. . . . Have you no sense of decency, sir, at long last?" When the audience burst into applause, the confused, skulking senator was reduced to whispering, "What did I do?"

On December 2, 1954, the Senate voted 67 to 22 to "condemn" McCarthy for contempt of the Senate. McCarthy's political career collapsed, and he began drinking heavily. Three years later, at the age of forty-eight, he was dead. To the end, Eisenhower refused to "get down in the gutter with that

The Army-McCarthy hearings, June 1954

The attorney Joseph Welch (hand on head) listening incredulously to Senator McCarthy's claims of Communist infiltration of the U.S. Army.

guy" and sully the dignity of the presidency, but he did work resolutely against McCarthy behind the scenes. At the same time, however, Eisenhower believed that Communist espionage posed a real danger to national security. He denied clemency to Julius and Ethel Rosenberg, who were convicted of transmitting atomic secrets to the Russians, on the grounds that they "may have condemned to death tens of millions of innocent people." Despite passionate pleas for clemency, the Rosenbergs were electrocuted on June 19, 1953.

INTERNAL SECURITY   The anti-Communist crusade survived the downfall of McCarthy. Eisenhower stiffened the government security program that Truman had set up in 1947. In 1953 an executive order broadened the basis for firing subversive government workers by replacing Truman's criterion of "disloyalty" with the new category of "security risk." Under the new edict, federal workers could lose their jobs because of dubious political associations or personal behavior that might make them careless or vulnerable to blackmail. The Supreme Court, however, modified some of the more extreme expressions of the Red Scare.

In 1953, Eisenhower appointed former Republican governor Earl Warren of California as chief justice, a decision he later pronounced the "biggest damnfool mistake I ever made." Warren, who had seemed safely conservative while active in politics, proved to have a social conscience and a streak of libertarianism that was shared by another Eisenhower Court appointee,

William J. Brennan Jr. The Warren Court (1953–1969), under the chief justice's influence, became an important force for social and political change through the 1960s. In connection with security programs and loyalty requirements, the Court upheld individual rights. A 1957 opinion narrowly construed the Smith Act of 1940, aimed at anti-government conspirators, to apply only to those advocating "revolutionary" action. Merely teaching a revolutionary doctrine in the abstract could not be construed as a crime under the act. This, along with decisions setting rigid standards for admissible evidence, rendered the Smith Act a dead letter.

Chief Justice Earl Warren

One of the most influential Supreme Court justices of the twentieth century.

FOREIGN INTERVENTION

DULLES AND FOREIGN POLICY   The Eisenhower administration promised new departures in foreign policy under the direction of Secretary of State John Foster Dulles. Grandson of one former secretary of state and nephew of another, Dulles had pursued a lifetime career as an international lawyer and sometime diplomat. As counselor to the Truman State Department, he had negotiated the Japanese peace treaty at the end of World War II. Son of a minister and himself an active Presbyterian layman, Dulles, in the words of the British ambassador, resembled those old zealots of the wars of religion who "saw the world as an arena in which the forces of good and evil were continuously at war." Dulles displayed dour sternness and Calvinist righteousness, but he was also a man of immense energy, intelligence, and experience.

The foreign-policy planks of the 1952 Republican platform, which Dulles wrote, showed both the moralist and the tactician at work. The Democratic policy of "containing" communism was needlessly defensive, Dulles thought. Americans should instead work toward the "liberation" of Eastern Europe from Soviet domination. Eisenhower was quick to explain, however, that liberating Eastern Europe from Soviet control would not involve military force. He would promote independence "by every peaceful means, but only by peaceful means."

Yet for all his bold talk of liberating Eastern Europe, Dulles made no significant departure from the strategy of containment created under Truman. Instead, he institutionalized containment in the rigid mold of his cold war rhetoric and extended it to the military strategy of deterrence. His endorsement of "massive retaliation" was an effort to get, in the slogan soon current, "more bang for the buck." Budgetary considerations lay at the root of any military plans, for Eisenhower and his cabinet feared that in the effort to build superior war power the country could spend itself into bankruptcy. During 1953, members of the Joint Chiefs of Staff began planning a new military posture. The heart of their so-called New Look was the assumption that nuclear weapons could be used in limited-war situations, allowing reductions in conventional forces and thus budgetary savings. Dulles, who announced the policy in early 1954, explained that savings in the Defense budget would come "by placing more reliance on deterrent power, and less dependence on local defensive power."

By this time both the United States and the Soviet Union had developed hydrogen bombs. With the new policy of deterrence, what Winston Churchill called a "balance of terror" had replaced the old balance of power. The threat of nuclear holocaust was terrifying, but the notion that the United States would risk such a disaster in response to local wars had little credibility.

Dulles's policy of "brinkmanship" depended for its strategic effect upon those very fears of nuclear disaster. Dulles argued in 1956 that in following a tough policy of confronting communism, a nation sometimes had to "go to the brink" of nuclear war. Such a firm stand, he believed, had halted further aggression in Korea in 1953 when America threatened to break the stalemate by removing restraints from the armed forces. Dulles had also employed brinkmanship in 1954 in Indochina,

"Don't Be Afraid—I Can Always Pull You Back."

Secretary of State John Foster Dulles pushes a reluctant America to the brink of war.

when the United States sent aircraft carriers into the South China Sea "both to deter any Red Chinese attack against Indochina and to provide weapons for instant retaliation."

INDOCHINA: THE BACKGROUND TO WAR   Dulles's use of brinkmanship in Indochina neglected the complexity of the situation there, which presented a special case of the nationalism that swept through the old colonial world of Asia and Africa after World War II. By the early 1950s most of British Asia was independent or on its way to independence: India, Pakistan, Ceylon (later Sri Lanka), Burma (later Myanmar), and the Malay States (later the Federation of Malaysia). The Dutch and the French, however, were less ready than the British to give up their colonies, a situation that created a dilemma for U.S. policy makers. Americans sympathized with the colonial nationalists but wanted Dutch and French help fending off incursions of communism. The Dutch and the French concentrated on maintaining control of their colonial possessions, which meant that they had to reconquer areas that had passed from Japanese occupation into the hands of local patriots. The Truman administration had felt obliged to answer the colonials' pleas for aid.

In the Dutch East Indies the Japanese had created a puppet Indonesian republic, which emerged from World War II virtually independent. The Dutch effort to regain control of their colony met with resistance that exploded into open warfare. American pressure persuaded the Dutch to accept Indonesian self-government under a Dutch-Indonesian alliance in 1949, but that lasted only until 1954, when the Republic of Indonesia became independent.

In 1955 the Bandung Conference in Indonesia, attended by delegates from twenty-nine countries of Asia and Africa, signaled the emergence of a "third world" of underdeveloped countries, unaligned with either the United States or the Soviet bloc. Among other actions, the conference denounced "colonialism in all its manifestations," a statement that implicitly condemned the Soviet Union, the United States, and Europe.

French Indochina, created in the nineteenth century out of the old kingdoms of Cambodia, Laos, and Vietnam, offered a variation on colonial nationalism. During World War II, when the Japanese controlled the region, they continued to use French civil servants and opposed the local nationalists. Chief among the latter were members of the Viet Minh (League for the Independence of Vietnam), which fell under the influence of Communists led by Ho Chi Minh, a seasoned revolutionary and passionate Vietnamese nationalist obsessed by a single goal: independence for his country. At the end of the war, Ho's followers controlled part of northern Vietnam, and on September 2, 1945, Ho Chi Minh proclaimed a Democratic Republic of Vietnam, with its capital in Hanoi.

Ho Chi Minh

A seasoned revolutionary, Ho Chi Minh cultivated a humble, proletarian image of himself as Uncle Ho, a man of the people.

Ho's declaration of Vietnamese independence borrowed from Thomas Jefferson, opening with the words "We hold these truths to be self-evident. That all men are created equal." Ho had secretly received American help against the Japanese during the war, but his bids for additional aid after the war went unanswered. Vietnam was a low priority in U.S. diplomatic concerns at the time, and Truman could not stomach aiding a professed Communist.

In 1946 the French recognized Ho's new government as a "free state" within the French-Indochinese union. Before the year was out, however, Ho's forces had challenged French efforts to restore their colonial regime in the southern provinces, and this clash soon expanded into the First Indochina War. In 1949, having set up puppet rulers in Laos and Cambodia, the French reinstated former emperor Bao Dai as head of Vietnam. The victory of the Communists in China later in 1949 was followed by China's diplomatic recognition of the Viet Minh government in Hanoi and then recognition of Bao Dai by the United States and Britain.

The Viet Minh movement thereafter became more dependent upon the Soviet Union and Communist China for help. In 1950, with the outbreak of fighting in Korea, the struggle in Vietnam became a major battleground in the cold war. When the Korean War ended, the United States continued its efforts to bolster French control of Vietnam, begun by the Truman administration. By the end of 1953, the Eisenhower administration was paying about two thirds of the cost of the French military effort in Indochina, and the United States had found itself at the "brink" of the kind of intervention to

Dien Bien Phu

Captured French soldiers march through the battlefield after their surrender.

which Dulles later referred. A major French force had been sent to Dien Bien Phu, near the Laotian border, in the hope of luring Viet Minh guerrillas into the open and overwhelming them with superior firepower. The French instead found themselves trapped by a Viet Minh force that threatened to overrun their stronghold.

In March 1954 the French government requested an American air strike to relieve the pressure on Dien Bien Phu. Eisenhower seemed to endorse forceful action, but when congressional leaders expressed reservations, he opposed U.S. intervention unless the British joined the effort. When they refused, he backed away from unilateral military action in Vietnam.

On May 7, 1954, the Communist Viet Minh overwhelmed the last French resistance at Dien Bien Phu. The action occurred on the very eve of the day on which an international conference at Geneva took up the question of Indochina. Six weeks later, as French forces continued to suffer defeats in Vietnam, a new French government promised to get an early settlement. On July 20, representatives of France, Britain, the Soviet Union, the People's Republic of China, and the Viet Minh signed the Geneva Accords. The agreement proposed to make Laos and Cambodia independent and divide Vietnam at the 17th parallel. The Viet Minh would take power in the north, and the French would remain south of the line until elections in 1956 would reunify Vietnam. American and South Vietnamese representatives refused to join in the accords leading the Soviet Union and China to back away from earlier hints that they would guarantee the Geneva settlement.

Dulles responded to the growing Communist influence in Vietnam by organizing mutual defense agreements for Southeast Asia. On September 8, 1954, at a meeting in Manila, the United States joined seven other countries in forming the Southeast Asia Treaty Organization (SEATO). The impression that it paralleled NATO was false, for SEATO was neither a common defense organization like NATO, nor was it primarily Asian. The signers agreed that in case of attack on one, the others would act according to their "constitutional practices," and in case of threats or subversion they would "consult immediately." The members included only three Asian countries—the Philippines, Thailand, and Pakistan—together with Britain, France, Australia, New Zealand, and the United States. India and Indonesia, the two most populous countries in the region, refused to join. A special protocol added to the treaty extended coverage to Indochina. The treaty reflected what Dulles's critics called pactomania, which by the end of the Eisenhower administration contracted the United States to defend forty-three foreign countries.

Eisenhower announced that though the United States "had not itself been party to or bound by the decision taken at the [Geneva] Conference," any

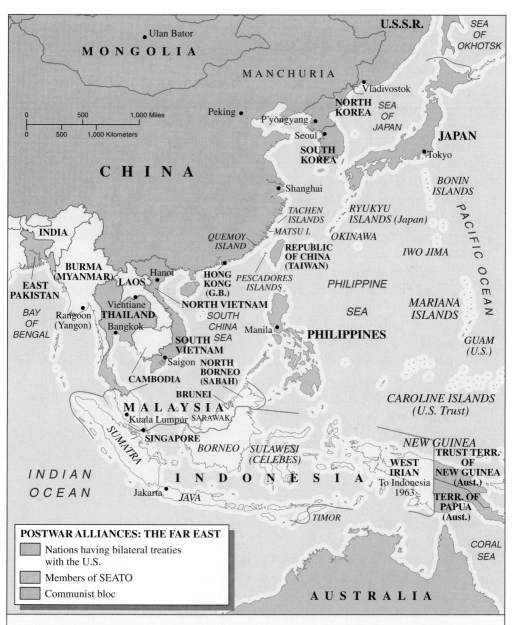

POSTWAR ALLIANCES: THE FAR EAST

- Nations having bilateral treaties with the U.S.
- Members of SEATO
- Communist bloc

How did the United States become increasingly involved in Vietnam? Why did the installation of Ngo Dinh Diem by the French and the Americans backfire and generate more conflict in Vietnam? Why was the protection of Taiwan important to the United States?

renewal of Communist aggression in Southeast Asia "would be viewed by us as a matter of grave concern." (He failed to note that the United States had agreed at Geneva to "refrain from the threat or use of force to disturb" the agreements that the U.S. refused to sign.) In Vietnam, when Ho Chi Minh took over the north, those who wished to leave for South Vietnam, mostly Catholics, did so with American aid. Power in the south gravitated to a new premier imposed on Emperor Bao Dai by the French at American urging: Ngo Dinh Diem, a Catholic who had opposed both the French and the Viet Minh. In 1954, Eisenhower offered to assist Diem "in developing and maintaining a strong, viable state, capable of resisting attempted subversion or aggression through military means." In return the United States expected Diem to enact democratic reforms and distribute land to the peasants. U.S. aid took the form of training Diem's armed forces and police. Eisenhower remained opposed to the use of U.S. combat troops. He was convinced that such military intervention would bog down into a costly stalemate—as it eventually did.

Instead of instituting political and economic reforms, however, Diem suppressed his political opponents on both the right and the left, offering little or no land distribution and permitting widespread corruption. In 1956 he refused to join in the elections to reunify Vietnam. After the French withdrawal from the country, Diem ousted Bao Dai and declared himself president. His efforts to eliminate all opposition played into the hands of the Communists, who found eager recruits among the discontented. By 1957 guerrilla forces known as the Viet Cong had begun attacks on the Diem government, and in 1960 the resistance groups coalesced as the National Liberation Front. As guerrilla warfare was disrupting South Vietnam, the Eisenhower administration was helpless to do anything but "sink or swim with Ngo Dinh Diem."

PROTECTING TAIWAN   Just before the Manila conference in 1954, Chinese artillery began shelling the offshore islands of Quemoy and Matsu, in Taiwan Strait, held by Chiang Kai-shek's Nationalists. On his way back from Manila, Secretary of State Dulles stopped in Taipei, Taiwan's capital, and worked out a mutual defense treaty that bound the United States to defend Taiwan and the nearby Pescadores Islands. In 1955 Eisenhower secured a congressional resolution giving him full power to defend Taiwan and the Pescadores and authorizing him to secure and protect "related positions of that area now in friendly hands" in order to defend Taiwan. Congress's endorsement was overwhelming—the resolution drew only three negative votes in each house—for so sweeping a grant of power to wage war if deemed necessary.

The Communist Chinese kept up their provocative activity nonetheless, and the security of the islands Quemoy and Matsu became a symbol of the American will to protect Taiwan. The U.S. chief of naval operations leaked word to journalists that the administration was considering a plan "to destroy Red China's military potential and thus end its expansionist tendencies." Soon afterward the Chinese backed away from the brink. At the Bandung Conference in April 1955, with diplomatic encouragement from other Asian nations, the Chinese premier, Chou En-lai, declared that the People's Republic of China was ready to discuss the Taiwan Strait issue directly with the United States. In 1955, representatives of the two governments began meetings in Geneva, and the guns fell silent.

REELECTION AND FOREIGN CRISES

As the United States continued to forge cold war alliances and bring pressure to bear on foreign governments by practicing brinkmanship, a new presidential campaign unfolded. Despite having suffered heart problems in the fall of 1955 and undergoing an operation for ileitis (an intestinal inflammation) in early 1956, Eisenhower decided to run for reelection. He retained widespread public support although the Democrats controlled Congress. Meanwhile, new crises in foreign and domestic affairs required him to take decisive action.

A LANDSLIDE FOR IKE   In 1956 the Republican Convention renominated Eisenhower by acclamation and again named Richard Nixon the vice-presidential candidate. The party platform endorsed Eisenhower's "modern Republicanism." The Democrats turned again to Adlai Stevenson. The platform revived old Democratic issues: less "favoritism" to big business, repeal of the Taft-Hartley Act, and tax relief for those in low-income brackets.

Neither candidate generated much excitement. During the last week of the campaign, however, fighting erupted along the Suez Canal in Egypt and in the streets of Budapest, Hungary. These two unrelated events caused a profound international crisis. The attack on Egypt by Britain, France, and Israel disrupted the Western alliance and damaged any claim to moral outrage at the Soviet Union's repressive actions in Hungary. For the Soviets, the Suez War afforded both a smoke screen for the subjugation of rebellious Hungary and a chance to enlarge their influence in the Middle East, an increasingly important source of oil.

The two crises led Adlai Stevenson to declare the administration's foreign policy "bankrupt." Most voters, however, reasoned that the foreign turmoil spelled a poor time to switch leaders, and they handed Eisenhower another landslide victory. In carrying Louisiana, Eisenhower became the first Republican to win a Deep South state since Reconstruction; nationally he carried all but seven states. The decision was unmistakably clear: Eisenhower won more than 35.5 million popular votes to a little over 26 million for Stevenson and 457 electoral votes to the Democrat's 73.

A delighted Eisenhower declared on election night "that modern Republicanism has now proved itself. And America has approved of modern Republicanism." Eisenhower Republicans, it seemed clear, had assimilated the New Deal as an accomplished fact. But Eisenhower's decisive win failed to swing a congressional majority for his party in either house, the first time events had worked out that way since the election of Zachary Taylor in 1848.

CRISIS IN THE MIDDLE EAST   To forestall Soviet penetration in the Middle East, Dulles in 1955 completed his series of alliances across the northern tier of the region. Under American sponsorship, Britain had joined the Middle Eastern states of Turkey, Iraq, Iran, and Pakistan in the Middle East Treaty Organization (METO), or Baghdad Pact Organization, as the treaty was commonly called. By linking the easternmost NATO state (Turkey) to the westernmost SEATO state (Pakistan), METO had a certain superficial logic, but after Iraq, the only Arab member, withdrew in 1959, the alliance lost its cohesion and its credibility. The neighboring Arab states remained aloof from the organization. These were the states of the Arab League (Egypt, Jordan, Lebanon, Syria, Iraq, Saudi Arabia, and Yemen), which had warred on Israel in 1948–1949 and remained committed to its destruction.

The most fateful developments in the Middle East turned on the rise of the Egyptian general Gamal Abdel Nasser after the overthrow of King Farouk in 1952. The bone of contention was the Suez Canal, which had opened in 1869 as a joint French-Egyptian venture. But in 1875 the British government had acquired the largest block of shares, and from 1882 on British troops were posted along the canal to protect the British Empire's maritime "lifeline" to India and other colonies. When Nasser's nationalist regime pressed for the withdrawal of British forces from the canal zone, Eisenhower and Dulles supported the demand, and in 1954 an Anglo-Egyptian treaty provided for British withdrawal within twenty months. Nasser, like other leaders of the third world, remained unaligned in the cold

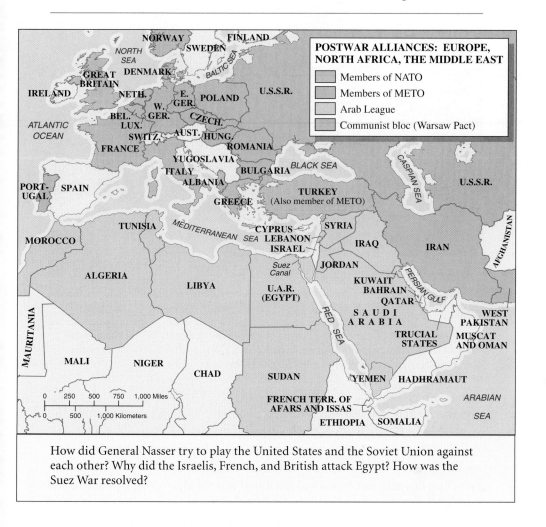

POSTWAR ALLIANCES: EUROPE, NORTH AFRICA, THE MIDDLE EAST

- Members of NATO
- Members of METO
- Arab League
- Communist bloc (Warsaw Pact)

How did General Nasser try to play the United States and the Soviet Union against each other? Why did the Israelis, French, and British attack Egypt? How was the Suez War resolved?

war and sought to play both sides off against each other. The United States, meanwhile, courted Egyptian support by offering a loan to build a huge hydroelectric plant at Aswān on the Nile River.

From the outset the administration's proposal was opposed by Jewish constituencies concerned with Egyptian threats to Israel and by southern congressmen who feared the competition from Egyptian cotton. In 1956, when Nasser increased trade with the Soviet bloc and recognized the People's Republic of China, Dulles abruptly canceled the loan offer. The outcome was far from a triumph of American diplomacy. The chief victims, it turned out, were Anglo-French interests in the Suez. Unable to retaliate against the United States, Nasser took control of the Suez Canal Company. The British

General Moshe Dayan

Commander of the Israeli forces during the Sinai campaign in 1956, Dayan (with eye patch) receives bread on the noon chow line, along with soldiers who volunteered to strengthen Israel's defenses on the Gaza Strip.

and the French were furious. Fruitless negotiations dragged on through the summer, and finally, on October 29, Israeli forces invaded the Gaza Strip and the Sinai Peninsula. The Israelis attacked ostensibly to root out Arab guerrillas but actually to synchronize with the British and the French, who began bombing Egyptian air bases and occupied Port Said, at the northern end of the canal.

The Suez War put the United States in a quandary. Either the administration could support its European allies and see the troublesome Nasser crushed, or it could defend the UN Charter and champion Arab nationalism against imperialist aggression. Eisenhower opted for the latter course, with the unusual result that the Soviet Union sided with the United States. Once American pressure had forced the Anglo-French-Israeli capitulation, the Soviets capitalized on the situation by threatening to use missiles against the Western aggressors. This belated bravado won for the Soviet Union in the Arab world some of the credit actually owed the United States.

REPRESSION IN HUNGARY   In the Soviet Union, Premier Nikita Khrushchev had come out on top in the post-Stalin power struggles. Khrushchev in 1956 had delivered a "secret" speech on the crimes of the

Stalin era before a Communist party congress and had hinted at relaxed policies and "different roads to socialism" that countries might take. This new policy of "de-Stalinization" put Stalinist leaders in the satellite countries of Eastern Europe on the defensive and emboldened the more independent leaders to take action. Riots in the Polish city of Poznań led to the rise of Władysław Gomułka, a Polish nationalist, as leader of the Polish Communist party. Gomułka managed to win a degree of independence by avoiding an open break with the Soviets.

In Hungary, however, a similar movement got out of hand. On October 23, 1956, fighting broke out in Budapest, after which Imre Nagy, a moderate Communist, was installed as head of the government. Again the Soviets seemed content to let de-Stalinization follow its course, and on October 28 they withdrew their forces from Budapest. But Nagy's announcement three days later that Hungary would withdraw from the Warsaw Pact (a military alliance linking the Eastern European countries under Soviet control) brought Soviet troops back into Budapest. Although Khrushchev was willing to relax relations with the Eastern European satellites, he refused to allow them to break with the Soviet Union or abandon their mutual defense obligations. The Soviets installed a more compliant leader in Hungary, János Kádár, and hauled Nagy off to Moscow, where a firing squad executed him in 1958. It was a tragic ending to an independence movement that at the outset promised the sort of moderation that might have vindicated George Kennan's policy of containment, if not Dulles's notion of liberation.

REACTIONS TO SPUTNIK   On October 4, 1957, the Soviets launched the first satellite, called *Sputnik 1*. Americans, until then complacent about their technical superiority, panicked. If the Soviets were so advanced in rocketry, then perhaps they could hit American cities with armed missiles. A Democratic senator demanded that Eisenhower call a special session of Congress to address the Sputnik crisis. The president refused, not wanting to heighten anxieties. All along, Eisenhower had known that the "missile gap" was more illusory than real, but he could not reveal the fact that high-altitude spy planes were gathering that information. Even so, American missile development was in a state of disarray, with a tangle of agencies and committees creating waste and duplication.

Soviet success with its Sputnik program prompted the United States to increase defense spending, offer NATO allies intermediate-range ballistic missiles pending development of long-range intercontinental ballistic missiles (ICBMs), set up a new agency to coordinate space efforts, and establish a crash program in science education and military research. The "Sputnik syndrome,"

By the rocket's red glare

The Soviet success in space shocked Americans and created concerns about a "missile gap."

compounded by a sharp recession through the winter of 1957–1958, loosened the purse strings of frugal legislators, who added to the new budget more than Eisenhower wanted for both defense and domestic programs. During 1958, Britain, Italy, and Turkey accepted U.S. missiles on their territory. Also in 1958, Congress created the National Aeronautics and Space Administration (NASA) to coordinate research and development in the field. Before the end of the year, NASA had unveiled a program to put people in orbit, but the first manned flight, by Commander Alan B. Shepard Jr., did not take place until May 5, 1961. Finally, in 1958, Congress enacted the National Defense Education Act, which authorized federal grants for training in mathematics, science, and modern languages, as well as for student loans and fellowships.

Festering Problems Abroad

Once the Suez and Hungary crises had faded from the front pages, Eisenhower enjoyed eighteen months of smooth sailing in foreign affairs. Nonetheless, a brief flurry of media attention occurred in 1958 when hostile demonstrations were held in Peru and Venezuela against Vice President Richard Nixon, who was on a goodwill tour of eight Latin American countries. Meanwhile, tensions in the Middle East and Europe continued to simmer, only to boil over in 1958.

CRISIS IN THE MIDDLE EAST In 1958, Congress approved what came to be called the Eisenhower Doctrine, a resolution that promised to extend economic and military aid to Middle East nations and to use armed force if necessary to assist any such nation against armed aggression by any Communist country.

President Gamal Abdel Nasser of Egypt, meanwhile, had emerged from the Suez crisis with heightened prestige, and in 1958 he created the United Arab Republic by a (short-lived) merger with Syria. Then, on July 14, a leftist coup in Iraq, supposedly inspired by Nasser and the Soviets, threw out the pro-Western government and killed the king, the crown prince, and the premier. In Lebanon, already unsettled by internal conflict, the government appealed to the United States for support to fend off a similar fate. Eisenhower immediately ordered 5,000 marines into Lebanon. British forces meanwhile went into Jordan at the request of King Hussein. In October 1958, once the situation had stabilized and the Lebanese factions had reached a compromise, U.S. forces (up to 15,000 at one point) withdrew.

CRISIS IN EAST ASIA   East Asia heated up again in 1958 when, on August 23, the People's Republic of China renewed its shelling of the Chinese Nationalists on the islands of Quemoy and Matsu. In September the U.S. Seventh Fleet began to escort Nationalist convoys but stopped short of entering Chinese territorial waters. On October 1, Eisenhower suggested that a cease-fire would provide "an opportunity to negotiate in good faith." China ordered such a cease-fire on October 6 and on October 25 said that it would reserve the right to bombard the islands on alternate days. With that strange stipulation the worst of the crisis passed, but the tensions between Communist China and Taiwan continued to fester.

CRISIS IN BERLIN   The problem of Berlin, an urban island of Western capitalism deep in Soviet-controlled East Germany, festered too: Soviet premier Nikita Khrushchev called Berlin a "bone in his throat." After World War II, West Berlin served as a "showplace" of Western democracy and prosperity, a listening post for Western intelligence gathering, and a funnel through which news and propaganda from the West penetrated what British leader Winston Churchill had labeled the iron curtain. Although East Germany had sealed its western frontiers,

Nikita Khrushchev

The Soviet premier speaks on the problem of Berlin, 1959.

refugees could still pass from East to West Berlin. On November 10, 1958, however, Khrushchev threatened to give East Germany control of East Berlin and the air lanes into West Berlin. After the deadline he set, May 27, 1959, Western occupation authorities would have to deal with the East German government, in effect recognizing it, or face the possibility of another blockade.

Eisenhower refused to budge from his position on Berlin but sought a settlement. Khrushchev, it turned out, was no more eager for confrontation than Eisenhower. In talks with British prime minister Harold Macmillan, Khrushchev suggested that the main thing was to begin discussions of the Berlin issue, postponing for the moment talks about the May 27 deadline. Macmillan in turn won Eisenhower's consent to a meeting of the Big Four foreign ministers representing the United States, Great Britain, France, and the Soviet Union.

There was little hope of resolving the conflicting views on Berlin and German reunification, but the talks distracted attention from Khrushchev's deadline of May 27: it passed almost unnoticed. In September 1959, after the Big Four talks had adjourned, Premier Khrushchev visited the United States, stopping in New York, Washington, D.C., Los Angeles, San Francisco, and Iowa. In talks with Eisenhower, Khrushchev endorsed "peaceful coexistence," and Eisenhower admitted that the Berlin situation was "abnormal." They agreed that the time was ripe for a summit meeting in the spring.

THE U-2 SUMMIT The planned summit meeting blew up in Eisenhower's face, however. On May 1, 1960, a Soviet rocket brought down an American spy plane. Such planes had been flying secret missions over the Soviet Union for three and a half years, and now Khrushchev set out to entrap Eisenhower—and he succeeded. At first the Soviets announced only that the plane had been shot down. When the State Department insisted that there had been no attempt to violate Soviet airspace, Khrushchev disclosed that the Soviets had American pilot Francis Gary Powers "alive and kicking" and also had his plane's photographs of Soviet military installations. On May 11, Eisenhower abandoned his efforts to cover up the incident and finally took personal responsibility—an unprecedented action for a head of state—justifying the aerial spying on grounds of national security. In Paris five days later Khrushchev withdrew an invitation for Eisenhower to visit the Soviet Union and called upon the president to repudiate the spy flights. When Eisenhower refused, Khrushchev cut off discussion. (Later, in 1962, Powers was exchanged for a captured Soviet spy.)

CASTRO'S CUBA   Yet for all of Eisenhower's crises in foreign affairs, the greatest thorn in his side was the new Communist regime of Fidel Castro, which came to power in Cuba on January 1, 1959, after two years of guerrilla warfare against the dictator Fulgencio Batista. In their struggle against Batista, Castro's forces had the support of many Americans who hoped for a democratic government in Cuba. When American television covered unfair political trials and summary executions of political enemies conducted by the victorious Castro, however, those hopes were dashed. Castro's programs of land redistribution and nationalization of foreign-owned property worsened relations with the United States. Some observers believed, however, that by rejecting Castro's requests for loans and other help, the U.S. government lost a chance to influence the direction of the Cuban revolution, and by acting on the assumption that Communists already had the upper hand in his movement, the administration may have ensured that fact.

Castro, on the other hand, readily embraced Soviet support. In 1960 he entered a trade agreement to swap Cuban sugar for Soviet oil and machinery.

Fidel Castro

Castro (center) became Cuba's Communist premier in 1959, following three years of guerrilla warfare against the Batista regime. He planned a social and agrarian revolution and opposed foreign control of the Cuban economy.

Then, after Cuba had seized three British-American oil refineries that refused to process Soviet oil, Eisenhower ordered strict limits on imports of Cuban sugar. Premier Khrushchev warned in response that any American military intervention in Cuba would trigger a Soviet response. The United States next suspended imports of Cuban sugar and embargoed most trade between the United States and Cuba. One of Eisenhower's last acts as president, on January 3, 1961, was to suspend diplomatic relations with Cuba. The president also authorized the CIA to begin secretly training a force of Cuban refugees to oust Castro. But the final decision on the use of that force would rest with the next president, John F. Kennedy.

THE EARLY YEARS OF THE CIVIL RIGHTS MOVEMENT

While the cold war had produced a tense stalemate by the mid-1950s, race relations in the United States threatened to explode the domestic tranquility masking years of injustice. Eisenhower entered office committed to civil rights in principle, and he pushed the issue in areas of federal authority. During his first three years, public facilities in Washington, D.C., were

Civil rights stirrings

In the late 1930s the NAACP began to test the constitutionality of racial segregation.

desegregated. Beyond that, however, two aspects of the president's philosophy limited progress in civil rights: his preference for state or local action over federal involvement and his doubt that laws could change racial attitudes. "I don't believe you can change the hearts of men with laws or decisions," he said. Eisenhower's stance meant that government leadership in the civil rights field would come from the judiciary more than from the executive or legislative branch of the government.

In the mid-1930s the NAACP had resolved to test the separate-but-equal doctrine that had upheld racial segregation since the *Plessy* decision in 1896. Charles H. Houston, vice dean of the Howard University Law School, laid the plans, and his former student Thurgood Marshall served as chief NAACP lawyer. They decided to begin their efforts to integrate society by focusing on higher education. But it took almost fifteen years to convince the courts that segregation must end. In *Sweatt v. Painter* (1950), the Supreme Court ruled that a separate black law school in Texas was not equal in quality to the state's whites-only schools. The Court ordered the state to remedy the situation.

THE *BROWN* DECISION   By the early 1950s, challenges to state laws mandating segregation in the public schools were rising through the appellate courts. Five such cases, from Kansas, Delaware, South Carolina, Virginia, and the District of Columbia—usually cited by reference to the first, *Brown v. Board of Education of Topeka, Kansas*—came to the Supreme Court for joint argument by NAACP attorneys in 1952. Chief Justice Earl Warren wrote the opinion, handed down on May 17, 1954, in which a unanimous Court declared that "in the field of public education the doctrine of 'separate but equal' has no place." In support of its opinion, the Court cited sociological and psychological findings demonstrating that even if separate facilities were equal in quality, the mere fact of separating students by race engendered feelings of inferiority. A year later, after further argument, the Court directed that the process of racial integration should move "with all deliberate speed."

Eisenhower refused to force states to comply with the Court's decisions, however. Privately he maintained "that the Supreme Court decision *set back* progress in the South *at least fifteen years*. The fellow who tries to tell me you can do these things by *force* is just plain *nuts*." While token integration began as early as 1954 in the border states of Kentucky and Missouri, hostility mounted in the Deep South and Virginia, led by the newly formed Citizens' Councils. The Citizens' Councils were middle- and upper-class versions of the Ku Klux Klan that spread quickly across the region and eventually enrolled 250,000 members. Instead of physical violence, the Councils used economic coercion against blacks who crossed racial boundaries. African Americans who defied white supremacy would lose their jobs, have their insurance policies canceled, or be denied personal loans or home mortgages. The Citizens' Councils grew so powerful in many communities that membership became almost a prerequisite for an aspiring white politician.

Before the end of 1955, opponents of court-ordered integration grew dangerously belligerent. Virginia senator Harry F. Byrd supplied a rallying cry: "Massive Resistance." In 1956, 101 members of Congress signed a "Southern Manifesto" denouncing the Supreme Court's decision in the *Brown* case as "a clear abuse of judicial power." At the end of 1956 in six southern states, not a single black child attended school with whites.

THE MONTGOMERY BUS BOYCOTT   The essential role played by the NAACP and the courts in providing a legal lever for the civil rights movement often overshadows the courageous contributions of individual African Americans who took great personal risks to challenge segregation. In Montgomery, Alabama, for example, on December 1, 1955, Mrs. Rosa Parks, a black seamstress who was an officer in the local NAACP chapter, boldly refused to give up her seat on a city bus to a white man. (As was the case in many southern communities, Montgomery had a local ordinance that required blacks to give up their bus or train seat to a white when asked.) She was "tired of giving in" to the system of white racism. When the bus driver told Parks he would have her arrested, she replied, "You may do that." Police thereupon arrested her, an event that changed the course of history, for the next night, black community leaders met in the Dexter Avenue Baptist Church to organize a massive bus boycott.

In Dexter Avenue's twenty-six-year-old pastor, Martin Luther King Jr., the boycott movement found a charismatic leader. Born in Atlanta, the grandson of a slave and the son of a minister, King was endowed with intelligence, courage, and eloquence. After graduating from Morehouse College in Atlanta, he attended divinity school, earned a doctorate in philosophy from Boston University, and accepted a call to preach in Montgomery. He inspired the civil rights movement with a compelling plea for nonviolent disobedience based upon the Gospels, the writings of Henry David Thoreau, and the example of Mahatma Gandhi in India. "We must use the weapon of love," King told his supporters. "We must realize so many people are taught to hate us that they are not totally responsible for their hate." To his antagonists he said, "We will soon wear you down by our capacity to suffer, and in winning

Montgomery, Alabama

Martin Luther King Jr., here facing arrest for leading a civil rights march, advocated nonviolent resistance to racial segregation.

our freedom we will so appeal to your heart and conscience that we will win you in the process."

The Montgomery bus boycott achieved a remarkable solidarity. For 381 days, African Americans used car pools, hitchhiked, or simply walked. But the white civic leaders held out against the boycott and against the pleas of a bus company tired of losing money. The boycotters finally won a federal case they had initiated against bus segregation, and in 1956 the Supreme Court affirmed that "the separate but equal doctrine can no longer be safely followed as a correct statement of the law." The next day, King and other African Americans boarded the buses.

To keep alive the spirit of the boycott and spread the civil rights movement beyond Alabama, King and a group of associates in 1957 organized the Southern Christian Leadership Conference. Several days later King found an unexploded dynamite bomb on his front porch. Two hours afterward he addressed his congregation:

I'm not afraid of anybody this morning. Tell Montgomery they can keep shooting and I'm going to stand up to them; tell Montgomery they can keep bombing and I'm going to stand up to them. If I had to die tomorrow morning I would die happy because I've been to the mountain top and I've seen the promised land and it's going to be here in Montgomery.

THE ROLE OF RELIGION   The African American leaders of the civil rights movement were animated by powerful religious beliefs. Ministers were in the vanguard of the movement for racial equality and social justice. As the Reverend Andrew Young, one of King's lieutenants, said, "Ours was an evangelical freedom movement that identified salvation with not just one's personal relationship with God, but a new relationship between people black and white." African American congregations were the seedbed for civil rights protesters and volunteers. A deep religious faith bolstered those who risked life and freedom by marching, picketing, and protesting racial injustice. Numerous black churches were bombed by white racists who viewed them as the primary locus of African American activism. The evangelical tradition in the African American community also provided many of the gospel "freedom" songs that enlivened civil rights marches and protests and gave solace and encouragement to those arrested. "We Shall Overcome,"

"Freedom" songs

Church congregation singing during the early civil rights movement.

derived from an old gospel hymn, became the anthem of the civil rights movement.

An Atlanta newspaper reporter highlighted the courageous role of black churches in the movement when he asked, "Have they not provided the meeting-places, theme-song, and leaders for the center of non-violent protest?" The contrast with the indifferent attitude of southern white churches was vivid. White churches were "doing nothing at all," said the editor of the *Atlanta Constitution*. He explained that it was "strikingly clear that Christianity and the [black] churches have never been more relevant (taken as a whole)—or less on the sidelines."

THE CIVIL RIGHTS ACT   Despite President Eisenhower's reluctance to take the lead in desegregating schools, he supported the right of African Americans to vote. In 1956, hoping to exploit divisions between northern and southern Democrats and to reclaim some of the black vote for the Republicans, Eisenhower proposed legislation that became the Civil Rights Act of 1957. The first civil rights law passed since Reconstruction, it finally got through the Senate, after a year's delay, with the help of majority leader Lyndon B. Johnson, a Texas Democrat who won southern acceptance by watering it down. The Civil Rights Act established the Civil Rights Commission, which was later extended indefinitely, and a new Civil Rights Division in the Justice Department, which could seek injunctions to prevent interference with the right to vote. Yet by 1959 the Civil Rights Act had not added a single southern black to the voting rolls. Neither did the Civil Rights Act of 1960, which provided for federal court referees to register African Americans to vote in districts where a court found a "pattern and practice" of discrimination, and made it a federal crime to interfere with any court order. This bill, too, lacked teeth and depended upon vigorous presidential enforcement to achieve any tangible results.

DESEGREGATION IN LITTLE ROCK   A few weeks after the Civil Rights Act of 1957 was passed, Arkansas governor Orval Faubus called out the National Guard to prevent nine black students from entering Little Rock's Central High School under a federal court order. A conference between the president and the governor proved fruitless, but on court order Governor Faubus withdrew the National Guard. When the African American students tried to enter the school, a hysterical white mob forced local authorities to remove the students. At that point, Eisenhower, who had said two months before that he could not "imagine any set of circumstances that would ever induce me to send federal troops," ordered 1,000 federal paratroopers to Little Rock to protect the black students, and he placed local National Guard units on federal service. The soldiers stayed through the school year.

In the summer of 1958, Faubus decided to close the Little Rock high schools rather than allow integration, and court proceedings dragged on into 1959 before the schools could be reopened. In that year, massive resistance to integration in Virginia collapsed when both state and federal courts struck down state laws that had cut off funds to integrated schools. Thereafter, massive resistance for the most part was confined to the Deep South, where five states—from South Carolina west through Louisiana—still opposed even token integration.

ASSESSING THE EISENHOWER PRESIDENCY

During President Eisenhower's second term the country added Alaska and Hawaii as states (1959), experienced an economic slump, a drop in tax revenues, and a large federal deficit. The country also suffered the embarrassments of the U-2 spy-plane incident and Cuba's embrace of communism. Emotional issues such as civil rights, defense policy, and corrupt aides compounded Eisenhower's troubles. The president's reluctance to enforce civil rights rulings and his unwillingness to speak out on behalf of racial equality undermined his efforts to promote the general welfare. One observer called the Eisenhower years "the time of the great postponement," during which the president left domestic and foreign policies "about where he found them in 1953."

Yet opinion of Eisenhower's presidency has improved with time. Even critics now grant that Eisenhower succeeded in ending the war in Korea and muzzling Joseph McCarthy. If Eisenhower failed to end the cold war and in fact institutionalized global confrontation, he did sense the limits of American global power and kept its application to low-risk situations. He also tried to restrain the arms race. If he took few initiatives in addressing social and racial problems, he did sustain the major innovations of the New Deal. If he tolerated unemployment of as much as 7 percent, he saw to it that inflation remained minimal during his two terms.

Eisenhower's January 17, 1961, farewell address to the American people showed his remarkable foresight in his own area of expertise, the military. Like George Washington, Eisenhower couched his wisdom largely in the form of warnings: that America faced in communism "a hostile ideology, global in scope, atheistic in character, ruthless in purpose, and insidious in method"; that America's "leadership and prestige depend, not merely upon our unmatched material strength, but on how we use our power in the interests of world peace and human betterment"; that the temptation to find easy answers should take into account "the need to maintain balance in and among national problems"; and above all that Americans "must avoid the impulse to live only for today, plundering, for our own ease and convenience, the precious resources of tomorrow."

As a former soldier, Eisenhower highlighted, perhaps better than anyone else could have, the dangers of a large military establishment in a time of peace: "In the councils of government we must guard against the acquisition of unwarranted influence, whether sought or unsought, by the military-industrial complex. The potential for the disastrous rise of misplaced power exists and will persist." Eisenhower confessed that his great disappointment was that he could affirm only that "war has been avoided," not that "a lasting peace is in sight."

CHAPTER SUMMARY

- **Eisenhower's Dynamic Conservatism** As president, Eisenhower accepted most of the New Deal's social legislation. He expanded Social Security coverage and launched ambitious public works programs, such as the construction of the interstate highway system and the St. Lawrence Seaway. He opposed massive government spending and large budget deficits, however, so he cut spending on an array of domestic programs and on national defense.

- **American Foreign Policy in the 1950s** Eisenhower continued the policy of containment to stem the spread of communism. His first major foreign-policy accomplishment in this respect was to end the fighting in Korea. To confront Soviet aggression, Eisenhower relied on nuclear deterrence, which allowed for reductions in conventional military forces and thus led to budgetary savings.

- **Communism in S.E. Asia** After World War II, Truman and then Eisenhower believed that the French should regain control of Indochina so that the country could serve as a barrier against the spread of communism in Southeast Asia. Ho Chi Minh, a nationalist and a Communist, led the Viet Minh movement, which in 1954 defeated the French at the Battle of Dien Bien Phu. The Geneva Accords, adopted in 1954 temporarily divided the country in half, with the Viet Minh ruling in the north and the dictator Ngo Dinh Diem ruling in the south. Communist guerrilla forces, known as the Viet Cong, found recruits among discontented South Vietnamese and attacked the Diem government. By 1957 the Eisenhower administration had no option but to "sink or swim with Ngo Dinh Diem."

- **Civil Rights Movement** In the 1930s the National Association for the Advancement of Colored People began laying the foundation for challenging the "separate but equal" doctrine, through a series of test cases in federal courts. By the early 1950s, the NAACP was targeting state-mandated segregation in public schools. In the most significant case, *Brown v. Board of Education*, the Court nullified the "separate but equal" doctrine. Whereas white southerners defended their old way of life, rallying to a call for "massive resistance," African Americans and other proponents of desegregation sought to achieve integration through nonviolent means. The Montgomery, Alabama, bus boycott was significant because it was the first large-scale—and ultimately successful—instance of nonviolent resistance and because it galvanized the civil rights movement under the leadership of Dr. Martin Luther King Jr. The desegregation of a public high school in Little Rock, Arkansas, marked another turning point when President Eisenhower reluctantly threw the support of the federal government behind the integrationists.

CHRONOLOGY

March 1953	Joseph Stalin dies
June 1953	Ethel and Julius Rosenberg are executed
July 1953	Armistice is reached in Korea
April–June 1954	Army-McCarthy hearings are televised
1954	Supreme Court issues ruling in *Brown v. Board of Education of Topeka, Kansas*
July 1954	Geneva Accords propose a settlement to the war in Indochina
December 1955	Montgomery, Alabama, bus boycott begins
1956	In Suez War, Israel, Britain, and France attack Egypt
1956	Hungarian revolt against the Warsaw Pact is quickly suppressed
1957	Federal troops are ordered to guarantee the safety of students attempting to integrate Central High School in Little Rock, Arkansas
1957	Soviet Union launches *Sputnik 1*
1960	U-2 incident reveals that the United States is flying spy planes over the Soviet Union

KEY TERMS & NAMES

34

NEW FRONTIERS: POLITICS AND SOCIAL CHANGE IN THE 1960s

FOCUS QUESTIONS wwnorton.com/studyspace

- What were the goals of John F. Kennedy's New Frontier program, and how successful was it?
- What was the aim of Lyndon Johnson's Great Society program, and how successful was it?
- What were the achievements of the civil rights movement by 1968?
- Why did the United States become increasingly involved in Vietnam?
- Why and how did Kennedy attempt to combat communism in Cuba?

For those pundits who considered the social and political climate of the 1950s dull, the following decade would provide a striking contrast. The 1960s were years of extraordinary social turbulence and innovation in public affairs—as well as sudden tragedy and prolonged trauma. Many social ills that had been festering for decades suddenly forced their way onto the national agenda. At the same time, the deeply entrenched assumptions of the cold war ideology directed against communism led the country into the longest, most controversial, and least successful war in its history.

THE NEW FRONTIER

KENNEDY VERSUS NIXON In 1960 there was little awareness of such dramatic change on the horizon. The presidential election of that year pitted against each other two candidates—Richard M. Nixon and John F. Kennedy—with very different personalities and backgrounds. Though better known than Kennedy because of his eight years as Eisenhower's vice president, Nixon had developed the reputation of a cunning chameleon, the "Tricky Dick" who concealed his duplicity behind a series of masks. "Nixon doesn't know who he is," Kennedy told an aide, "and so each time he makes a speech he has to decide which Nixon he is, and that will be very exhausting."

But Nixon could not be so easily dismissed. He possessed a shrewd intelligence and a compulsive love for combative politics. Born in suburban Los Angeles in 1913, he grew up in a working-class Quaker family that struggled to make ends meet. In 1946, having completed law school and a wartime stint in the navy, Nixon jumped into the political arena as a Republican and won election to Congress. Four years later he became a senator.

Nixon arrived in Washington eager to reverse the tide of New Deal liberalism. As a campaigner he unleashed scurrilous personal attacks on his opponents, employing half-truths, lies, and rumors, and he shrewdly manipulated the growing anti-Communist hysteria. Yet Nixon became both a respected and an effective member of Congress, and by 1950 he was the most requested Republican speaker in the country. The reward for his rapid rise to political stardom was the vice-presidential nomination in 1952, which led to successive terms as the partner of the popular Eisenhower and ensured his nomination for president in 1960.

In comparison to his Republican opponent, John F. Kennedy was inexperienced. He boasted an abundance of assets, however, including a record of heroism in World War II, a glamorous wife, a bright, agile mind and a Harvard education, a rich, powerful Roman Catholic family, a handsome face, movie-star charisma, and a robust outlook. Yet the forty-three-year-old candidate had not distinguished himself in the House or the Senate. His political rise owed not so much to his abilities or his accomplishments as to the effective public relations campaign engineered by his ambitious father, Joseph Kennedy, a self-made tycoon.

During his campaign for the 1960 Democratic presidential nomination, Kennedy had shown that he had the energy and wit to match his grace and ambition, even though he suffered from serious spinal problems, Addison's disease (a debilitating disorder of the adrenal glands), recurrent blood disorders, venereal disease, and fierce fevers. He took medicine daily, sometimes hourly. Like Franklin Roosevelt, he and his aides and family members masked his physical ailments from the public.

By the time of the Democratic Convention in 1960, the relentless Kennedy had traveled over 65,000 miles, visited twenty-five states, and made over 350 speeches. In his acceptance speech he featured the stirring, muscular rhetoric that would stamp the rest of his campaign and his presidency: "We stand today on the edge of a New Frontier—the frontier of unknown opportunities and perils—a frontier of unfulfilled hopes and threats." Kennedy and his staff fastened upon the frontier metaphor as the label for their domestic program because Americans had always been adventurers, eager to conquer and exploit new frontiers. Kennedy promised to use his administration to get the country "moving again."

Three events shaped the presidential campaign that fall. First, as the only Catholic to run for the presidency since Al Smith in 1928, Kennedy strove to dispel the impression that his religion was a major political liability. In a speech before the Greater Houston Ministerial Association in 1960, he stressed that "the separation of church and state is absolute" and "no Catholic prelate would tell the President—should he be a Catholic—how to act and no Protestant minister should tell his parishioners for whom to vote." The religious question thereafter drew little public attention; Kennedy's candor had neutralized it.

Second, Richard Nixon violated one of the cardinal rules of politics when he agreed to debate his less prominent opponent on television. During the first of four debates, few significant policy differences surfaced, allowing viewers to shape their opinions more on matters of appearance and style. Some 70 million people watched this first-ever televised debate. They saw an obviously uncomfortable Nixon, still weak from a recent illness, perspiring heavily and looking haggard, uneasy, and even sinister before the camera. Kennedy, on the other hand, projected a cool poise and offered crisp answers that made him seem equal, if not superior, in his fitness for the office. Kennedy's popularity immediately shot up in the polls. In the words of a bemused southern senator, Kennedy combined "the best qualities of Elvis Presley and Franklin D. Roosevelt."

Still, the momentum created by the first debate was not enough to ensure a Kennedy victory. The third key event in the campaign involved the deepening controversy over civil rights. Democratic strategists knew that in order to offset the loss of conservative southern Democrats suspicious of Kennedy's Catholicism and strong civil rights positions, they had to increase the registration of minority voters and generate a high turnout among African Americans.

Perhaps the most crucial incident of the campaign occurred when Martin Luther King Jr. and some fifty demonstrators were arrested in Atlanta for "trespassing" in an all-white restaurant. Although the other demonstrators were soon released, King was sentenced to four months in prison, ostensibly because of an earlier traffic violation. Robert Kennedy, the candidate's

Kennedy-Nixon debates

John Kennedy's poise and precision in the debates with Richard Nixon impressed viewers and voters.

younger brother and campaign manager, phoned the judge handling King's case, imploring him with the argument "that if he was a decent American, he would let King out of jail by sundown." King was soon released on bail, and the Kennedy campaign seized full advantage of the outcome, distributing some 2 million pamphlets in African American neighborhoods extolling Kennedy's efforts on behalf of Dr. King.

When the votes were counted, Kennedy and his running mate, Lyndon B. Johnson of Texas, had won the closest presidential election since 1888. The winning margin was only 118,574 votes out of more than 68 million cast. Kennedy's wide lead in the electoral vote, 303 to 219, belied the paper-thin margin in several key states. Nixon had in fact carried more states than Kennedy, sweeping most of the West and holding four of the six southern states that Eisenhower had carried in 1956. Kennedy's majority was built on victories in southern New England, the populous middle Atlantic states, and key states in the South where African American voters provided the critical margin of victory. Yet ominous rumblings of discontent appeared in the once-solid Democratic South, as all eight of Mississippi's electors and six of Alabama's eleven (as well as one elector from Oklahoma) defied the national ticket and voted for Virginia senator Harry Byrd, the arch segregationist.

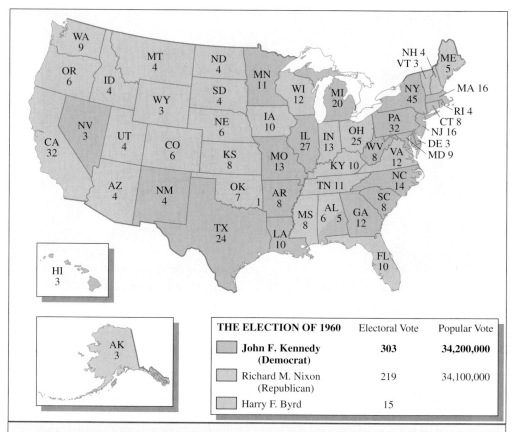

THE ELECTION OF 1960	Electoral Vote	Popular Vote
John F. Kennedy (Democrat)	**303**	**34,200,000**
Richard M. Nixon (Republican)	219	34,100,000
Harry F. Byrd	15	

How did the election of 1960 represent a sea change in American presidential politics? What three events shaped the campaign? How did John F. Kennedy win the election in spite of winning fewer states than Richard M. Nixon?

THE NEW ADMINISTRATION   John F. Kennedy was the youngest person ever elected president, and he was determined to surround himself with the "best and the brightest" minds, individuals who would provide new ideas and fresh thinking—and inject a tough, pragmatic, and vigorous outlook into government affairs. Adlai Stevenson was favored by liberal Democrats for the post of secretary of state, but Kennedy chose Dean Rusk, a career diplomat. Stevenson received the post of ambassador to the United Nations. Robert McNamara, one of the whiz kids who had reorganized the Ford Motor Company, was asked to bring his managerial magic to bear on the Department of Defense. C. Douglas Dillon, a Republican banker, was made secretary of the Treasury in an effort to reassure conservative business executives. When critics attacked the appointment of Kennedy's thirty-five-year-old brother Robert as attorney general, the president quipped, "I don't see what's wrong with giving Bobby a little experience before he goes into law practice." Harvard professor McGeorge Bundy, whom Kennedy called "the second smartest man I know," was made special assistant for national security affairs, lending additional credence to the impression that foreign policy would remain under tight White House control.

The inaugural ceremonies set the tone of elegance and youthful vigor that would come to be called the Kennedy style. Kennedy dazzled listeners with uplifting rhetoric. "Let the word go forth from this time and place," he proclaimed. "Let every nation know, whether it wishes us well or ill, that we shall pay any price, bear any burden, meet any hardship, support any friend, oppose any foe, to assure the survival and success of liberty. And so, my fellow Americans: ask not what your country can do for you—ask what you can do for your country." Spines tingled at the time; the glittering atmosphere and inspiring language of the inauguration seemed to herald an era of fresh promise and youthful energy.

THE KENNEDY RECORD Despite his idealistic rhetoric, however, Kennedy called himself a realist or "an idealist without illusions," and he had a difficult time launching his New Frontier domestic program. Elected by a razor-thin margin, he did not enjoy a popular mandate. "Great innovations," Kennedy said, quoting Thomas Jefferson, "should not be forced on slender majorities." The new president did not show much skill in shepherding legislation through a Congress controlled by a conservative southern coalition, which blocked his efforts to increase federal aid to education, provide health insurance for the aged, and create a department of urban affairs. The Senate blocked his initiatives on behalf of unemployed youths, migrant workers, and mass transit. When Kennedy finally followed the advice of his advisers in 1963 and submitted a drastic tax cut, Congress blocked that as well.

Administration proposals did nevertheless win some notable victories in Congress. Legislators readily approved broad Alliance for Progress programs to help Latin America and the celebrated Peace Corps, created in 1961 to supply volunteers who would provide educational and technical services abroad. Kennedy's greatest legislative accomplishment, however, may have been the Trade Expansion Act of 1962, which eventually led to tariff cuts averaging 35 percent on goods traded between the United States and the European Economic Community (the Common Market).

In the field of domestic social legislation, the Kennedy administration persuaded Congress to pass a Housing Act that earmarked nearly $5 billion for urban renewal over four years; an increase in the minimum wage and its application to more than 3 million additional workers; the Area Redevelopment Act of 1961, which provided nearly $400 million in loans and grants to "distressed areas"; an increase in Social Security benefits; and additional funds for sewage-treatment plants. Kennedy also won support for an accelerated outer-space exploration program with the goal of landing astronauts on the moon before the end of the decade.

THE WARREN COURT   Under Chief Justice Earl Warren the Supreme Court continued to be a decisive influence on domestic life during the 1960s. In 1962 the Court ruled that a school prayer adopted by the New York State Board of Regents violated the constitutional prohibition against an established religion. In *Gideon v. Wainwright* (1963), the Court required that every felony defendant be provided a lawyer regardless of the defendant's ability to pay. In 1964 the Court ruled in *Escobedo v. Illinois* that a person accused of a crime must also be allowed to consult a lawyer before being interrogated by police. Two years later, in *Miranda v. Arizona,* the Court issued perhaps its most bitterly criticized ruling when it ordered that an accused person in police custody be informed of certain basic rights: the right to remain silent; the right to know that anything said can be used against the individual in court; and the right to have a defense attorney present during interrogation. In addition, the Court established rules for police to follow in informing suspects of their legal rights before questioning could begin.

EXPANSION OF THE CIVIL RIGHTS MOVEMENT

The most important development in domestic life during the 1960s occurred in civil rights. John F. Kennedy entered the White House reluctant to challenge conservative southern Democrats on the race issue. He was never as personally committed to the cause of civil rights as his younger brother Robert, the attorney general. Despite a few dramatic gestures of support toward African American leaders, President Kennedy only belatedly grasped the moral and emotional significance of the most widespread reform movement of the decade. Like Franklin Roosevelt, he celebrated racial equality but did little to promote it. Eventually, however, his conscience was pricked by the grassroots civil rights movement led by Martin Luther King Jr.

SIT-INS AND FREEDOM RIDES   After the Montgomery bus boycott of 1955–1956, King's philosophy of "militant nonviolence" inspired others to challenge the deeply entrenched patterns of racial segregation in the South. At the same time, lawsuits to desegregate the public schools got thousands of parents and young people involved. The momentum generated the first genuine mass movement in African American history when four black college students sat down and demanded service at a "whites-only" Woolworth's lunch counter in Greensboro, North Carolina, on February 1, 1960. Within a week the "sit-in" movement had spread to six more towns in the state, and within two months demonstrations had occurred in fifty-four cities in nine states.

In 1960, student activists, black and white, formed the Student Nonviolent Coordinating Committee (SNCC), which worked with King's Southern Christian Leadership Conference (SCLC) to broaden the civil rights movement. The

Sit-in at Woolworth's lunch counter, Greensboro, North Carolina

Four of the protesters, students at North Carolina A&T College, were (from left) Joseph McNeil, Franklin McCain, Billy Smith, and Clarence Henderson.

sit-ins became "kneel-ins" at churches and "wade-ins" at segregated public swimming pools.

Most of the activists practiced King's concept of nonviolent protest. They refused to retaliate, even when struck with clubs, poked with cattle prods, or subjected to vicious verbal abuse. The conservative white editor of the *Richmond News Leader* conceded his admiration for their courage:

> Here were the colored students, in coats, white shirts, ties, and one of them was reading Goethe, and one was taking notes from a biology text. And here, on the sidewalk, was a gang of white boys come to heckle, a ragtail rabble, slack-jawed, black-jacketed, grinning fit to kill, and some of them, God save the mark, were waving the proud and honored flag of the Southern States in the last war fought by gentlemen.

During the year after the Greensboro sit-ins, over 3,600 black and white activists spent time in jail. In many communities they were pelted with rocks, burned with cigarettes, and subjected to unending verbal abuse.

In May 1961 the Congress of Racial Equality (CORE) sent a group of black and white "freedom riders" on buses to test a federal court ruling that had banned segregation on buses and trains and in terminals. In Alabama, mobs attacked the travelers with fists and pipes, burned one of the buses, and assaulted Justice Department observers, but the demonstrators persisted and drew national attention, generating new respect and support for their cause. Yet President Kennedy was not inspired by the courageous freedom riders. Preoccupied with a crisis in Berlin, he ordered an aide to tell them to "call it off." Former president Harry Truman dismissed the bus activists northern "busybodies." It fell to Attorney General Robert Kennedy to use federal marshals to protect the freedom riders during the summer of 1961.

FEDERAL INTERVENTION   In 1962, the racist governor Ross Barnett of Mississippi, who believed that God made "the Negro different to punish him," defied a court order by refusing to allow James Meredith, an African American student whose grandfather had been a slave, to enroll at the University of Mississippi. Attorney General Robert Kennedy dispatched federal marshals to enforce the law. When the marshals were assaulted by a white mob, federal troops intervened, but only after two deaths and many injuries. Meredith was registered at Ole Miss a few days later.

In 1963, Martin Luther King launched a series of demonstrations in Birmingham, Alabama, where Police Commissioner Eugene "Bull" Connor

Birmingham, Alabama, May 1963

Eugene "Bull" Connor's police unleash dogs on civil rights demonstrators.

served as the perfect foil for King's tactic of nonviolent civil disobedience. Connor's police used dogs, tear gas, electric cattle prods, and fire hoses on the protesters while millions of outraged Americans watched the confrontations on television.

King, who was arrested and jailed during the demonstrations, wrote his now-famous Letter from Birmingham City Jail, a stirring defense of the nonviolent strategy that became a classic document of the civil rights movement. "One who breaks an unjust law," he stressed, "must do so openly, lovingly, and with a willingness to accept the penalty." In his letter, King signaled a shift in his strategy for social change. Heretofore he had emphasized the need to educate southern whites about the injustice of segregation and other patterns of discrimination. Now he focused more on gaining federal enforcement of the law and new legislation by provoking racists to display their violent hatred in public. As King admitted in his letter, he sought through organized nonviolent protest to "create such a crisis and foster such a tension that a community which has constantly refused to negotiate is forced to confront the issue." This concept of confrontational civil disobedience outraged J. Edgar Hoover, the powerful head of the FBI, who labeled King "the most dangerous Negro of the future in this nation." He ordered agents to follow King, bugged his telephones and motel rooms, and circulated scandalous rumors to discredit him.

The sublime courage that King and many other protesters displayed helped mobilize national support for their integrationist objectives. (In 1964, King would be awarded the Nobel Peace Prize.) Nudged by his brother Robert, a man of greater conviction, compassion, and vision, President Kennedy finally decided that enforcement of existing statutes was not enough; new legislation was needed to deal with the race question. In 1963 he told the nation that racial discrimination "has no place in American life or law." He then endorsed an ambitious civil rights bill intended to end discrimination in public facilities, desegregate public schools, and protect African American voters. But the bill was quickly blocked in Congress by southern conservatives, who had become increasingly resistant to social change since mobilizing to thwart Roosevelt's New Deal in the late 1930s. As Kennedy told Martin Luther King: "This is a very serious fight. We're in this up to the neck. The worst trouble would be to lose the fight in Congress. . . . A good many programs I care about may go down the drain as a result of this [bill]—We may all go down the drain . . . so we are putting a lot on the line."

Throughout the Deep South, white traditionalists defied efforts at racial integration. In the fall of 1963, the confrontational Alabama governor George Wallace dramatically stood in the doorway of a building at the University of Alabama to block the enrollment of African American students, but he stepped aside in the face of insistent federal marshals. That night, President Kennedy for the first time highlighted the *moral* issue facing the nation: "If an American, because his skin is black, cannot enjoy the full and free life which all of us want, then who among us would be content to have the color of his skin changed and stand in his place? Who among us would be content with the counsels of patience and delay?" Later the same night, NAACP official Medgar Evers was shot to death as he returned to his home in Jackson, Mississippi.

The high point of the integrationist phase of the civil rights movement occurred on August 28, 1963, when over 200,000 blacks and whites marched down the Mall in Washington, D.C., toward the Lincoln Memorial, singing "We Shall Overcome." The March on Washington for Jobs and Freedom was the largest civil rights demonstration in history. Standing in front of Lincoln's famous statue, Martin Luther King Jr. delivered one of the century's most memorable speeches:

"I Have a Dream," August 28, 1963

Protesters in the March on Washington make their way to the Lincoln Memorial, where Martin Luther King Jr. delivered his now-famous speech.

I say to you today, my friends, that in spite of the difficulties and frustrations of the moment I still have a dream. It is a dream deeply rooted in the American dream.

I have a dream that one day this nation will rise up and live out the true meaning of its creed: "We hold these truths to be self-evident; that all men are created equal."

I have a dream that one day . . . the sons of former slaves and the sons of former slaveowners will be able to sit together at the table of brotherhood.

Such racial harmony had not yet arrived, however. Two weeks later a bomb exploded in a Birmingham, Alabama, church, killing four black girls. Yet King's dream—shared and promoted by thousands of other activists—survived. The intransigence and violence that civil rights workers encountered won converts to their cause all across the country. Moreover, corporate and civic leaders in large southern cities promoted civil rights advances in large part because the continuing protests threatened economic development. Atlanta, for example, described itself as "the city too busy to hate."

FOREIGN FRONTIERS

EARLY SETBACKS   John Kennedy's record in foreign relations, like that in domestic affairs, was mixed, but more spectacularly so. Upon taking office, he learned that a secret CIA operation was training 1,500 anti-Castro Cubans for an invasion of their homeland. The Joint Chiefs of Staff assured the inexperienced Kennedy that the plan was feasible in theory; CIA analysts predicted that the invasion would inspire Cubans to rebel against Castro and his Communist regime.

But the scheme, poorly planned and poorly executed, had little chance of succeeding. When the ragtag invasion force landed at the Bay of Pigs in Cuba on April 17, 1961, it was brutally subdued in two days; more than 1,100 men were captured. A *New York Times* columnist lamented that the United States "looked like fools to our friends, rascals to our enemies, and incompetents to the rest." Kennedy called the bungled Bay of Pigs invasion a "colossal mistake." The planners had underestimated Castro's popularity and his ability to react to the surprise attack. The invasion also suffered from poor communication,

The Berlin Wall

Two West Berliners communicate with family members (visible in the open window on the upper right side of the apartment building) on the East Berlin side of the newly constructed Berlin Wall. The wall physically divided the city and served as a wedge between the United States and the Soviet Union.

inaccurate maps, faulty equipment, and ineffective leadership. Former president Eisenhower characterized Kennedy's role in the clumsy invasion as a "Profile in Timidity and Indecision," a sarcastic reference to Kennedy's book *Profiles in Courage* (1956). Kennedy responded to the Bay of Pigs fiasco by firing the CIA director and the CIA officer who coordinated the invasion.

Two months after the Bay of Pigs debacle, Kennedy met Soviet premier Nikita Khrushchev in Vienna. The volatile Khrushchev bullied and browbeat Kennedy and threatened to limit Western access to Berlin, the divided city located 100 miles within Communist East Germany. Khrushchev decided that Kennedy was "a youngster who had a great deal to learn and not much to offer." Kennedy, in turn, was stunned by the Soviet leader's aggressive demeanor. Upon his return home, he demonstrated his resolve by calling up Army Reserve and National Guard units. The Soviets responded by erecting the Berlin Wall, isolating West Berlin and preventing all movement between the two parts of the city. The Berlin Wall plugged the most accessible escape hatch for East Germans, demonstrated the Soviets' willingness to challenge American resolve in Europe, and became another intractable barrier to improved relations between East and West.

THE CUBAN MISSILE CRISIS   A year later, in the fall of 1962, Khrushchev and the Soviets posed another challenge, this time ninety miles off the coast of Florida. Kennedy's unwillingness to commit the forces necessary to overthrow Fidel Castro at the Bay of Pigs suggested a failure of will, and the Soviets reasoned that they could install ballistic missiles in Cuba without U.S. opposition. Their motives were to protect Cuba from another American-backed invasion, which Castro believed to be imminent, and to redress the strategic imbalance caused by the presence of U.S. missiles in Turkey aimed at the Soviet Union. Khrushchev relished the idea of throwing "a hedgehog at Uncle Sam's pants."

U.S. officials decided that Soviet missiles in Cuba represented a real threat to American security. Kennedy also worried that acquiescence to a Soviet military presence in Cuba would weaken the credibility of the American nuclear deterrent among Europeans and demoralize anti-Castro elements in Latin America. At the same time, the installation of Soviet missiles served Khrushchev's purpose of demonstrating his toughness to Chinese and Soviet critics of his earlier advocacy of peaceful coexistence. But he misjudged the American response.

On October 14, 1962, U.S. intelligence analysts discovered Soviet missile sites under construction in Cuba. From the beginning, even though the Soviet actions violated no law or treaty, the administration decided that the

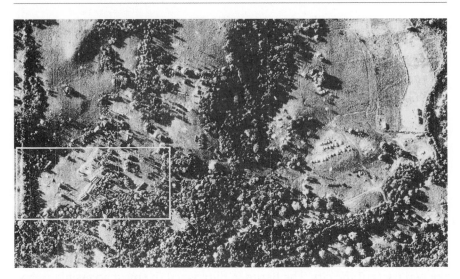

The Cuban missile crisis

Photographs taken from a U.S. surveillance plane on October 14, 1962, revealed both missile launchers and missile shelters near San Cristóbal, Cuba.

weapons had to be removed; the only question was how. As the air force chief of staff told Kennedy, "You're in a pretty bad fix, Mr. President." In a grueling series of secret meetings, the Executive Committee of the National Security Council narrowed the options to a choice between a "surgical" air strike and a naval blockade of Cuba. President Kennedy wisely opted for a blockade, which was carefully disguised by the euphemism *quarantine,* since a blockade was technically an act of war. A blockade offered the advantage of forcing the Soviets to shoot first, if matters came to that, and left open the options of stronger action. Thus, Monday, October 22, began the most perilous week in world history. On that day the president announced the discovery of the missile sites in Cuba and the naval quarantine of the island nation. The United States and the Soviet Union now headed toward their closest encounter with nuclear war.

Tensions grew as Khrushchev blustered that Kennedy had pushed humankind "toward the abyss of a world nuclear-missile war." Soviet ships, he declared, would ignore the quarantine. But on Wednesday, October 24, five Soviet ships, presumably with missiles aboard, stopped short of the quarantine line. Two days later the Soviets offered to withdraw the missiles in return for a public pledge by the United States not to invade Cuba. Secretary of State Dean Rusk replied that the administration was interested but stressed to a newscaster, "Remember, when you report this, that eyeball to eyeball, they [the Soviets] blinked first."

That evening, Kennedy received two messages from Khrushchev, the first repeating the original offer and the second demanding the removal of American missiles from Turkey. The two messages probably reflected divided counsels in the Kremlin. Ironically, Kennedy had already ordered removal of the outmoded missiles from Turkey, but he refused now to act under the gun. Instead, he followed Robert Kennedy's suggestion that he respond favorably to the first letter and ignore the second. On Sunday, October 28, Khrushchev agreed to remove the Soviet missiles from Cuba.

In the aftermath of the crisis, tensions between the United States and the Soviet Union subsided, relaxed in part by several symbolic steps: an agreement to sell the Soviet Union surplus American wheat, the installation of a "hot-line" telephone between Washington and Moscow to provide instant contact between the heads of government, and the removal of obsolete American missiles from Turkey, Italy, and Britain. On June 10, 1963, President Kennedy revealed that direct discussions with the Soviets would soon begin, and he called upon Americans to reexamine their attitudes toward peace, the Soviet Union, and the cold war. Those discussions resulted in a treaty with the Soviet Union and Britain to end nuclear testing in the atmosphere, oceans, and outer space. The treaty, ratified in September 1963, was an important symbolic and substantive move toward détente. As Kennedy put it, "A journey of a thousand miles begins with one step."

KENNEDY AND VIETNAM   As tensions with the Soviet Union were easing, a crisis was growing in Southeast Asia. Events there were moving toward what would become the greatest American foreign-policy calamity of the century. During John Kennedy's "Thousand Days" in office, the turmoil of Indochina never preoccupied public attention for any extended period, but it dominated international diplomatic debates from the time the administration entered office.

The landlocked kingdom of Laos, along with neighboring Cambodia to the south, had been declared neutral in the Geneva Accords of 1954, but thereafter Laos had fallen into a complex struggle for power between the Communist Pathet Lao insurgents and the inept Royal Laotian Army. There matters stood when Eisenhower left office, and he told Kennedy that "you might have to go in there and fight it out." After a lengthy consideration of alternatives, Kennedy and his advisers decided to promote a neutral coalition government in Laos that would include Pathet Lao representatives yet prevent a Pathet Lao victory and would avoid U.S. military involvement. The Soviets, who were extending aid to the Pathet Lao, indicated a readiness to negotiate, and in 1961 talks began in Geneva. After more than a year of tangled negotiations, all parties agreed to a neutral coalition government. American and Soviet aid to the opposing Laotian factions was supposed to end, but both countries in fact continued covert operations while North Vietnam kept open the Ho Chi Minh Trail through eastern Laos, which it used to supply its Viet Cong allies in South Vietnam.

The situation in South Vietnam worsened thereafter under the leadership of Premier Ngo Dinh Diem. At the time the problem was less the scattered Communist guerrilla attacks than Diem's failure to deliver promised social and economic reforms and his inability to rally popular support. His repressive tactics, directed not only against Communists but also against the Buddhist majority and other critics, played into the hands of his enemies. In 1961, White House assistant Walt Rostow and General Maxwell Taylor, the first in a long train of presidential emissaries to South Vietnam's capital, proposed a major increase in the U.S. military presence. Kennedy rejected the proposal but continued to dispatch more military "advisers" in the hope of stabilizing the situation: when he took office, there had been 2,000 U.S. troops in Vietnam; by the end of 1963, there were 16,000, none of whom had been officially committed to battle.

By 1963, Kennedy was receiving sharply divergent reports from the South Vietnamese countryside. American military advisers expressed confidence in the Army of the Republic of Vietnam. On-site political reporters, however, watching the reactions of the Vietnamese people, predicted civil turmoil as long as Diem remained in power. By midyear, growing Buddhist demonstrations against Diem ignited the discontent in the south. The spectacle of

Ngo Dinh Diem

The Vietnamese premier in 1962, celebrating the anniversary of Vietnam's independence from colonial rule.

Buddhist monks setting themselves on fire in protest against government tyranny stunned Americans. By the fall of 1963, the Kennedy administration had decided that the autocratic Diem had to go. When dissident generals proposed a coup d'état, the U.S. ambassador assured them that America would not stand in the way. On November 1 they seized the South Vietnamese government and murdered Diem. But the rebel generals provided no more stability than had earlier regimes, and successive coups set the fragile country spinning from one military leader to another.

KENNEDY'S ASSASSINATION   By the fall of 1963, President Kennedy had acknowledged the intractability of the situation in Vietnam. In September 1963 he declared of the South Vietnamese: "In the final analysis it's their war. They're the ones who have to win it or lose it. We can help them as advisers but they have to win it." The following month he announced the administration's intention to withdraw U.S. forces from South Vietnam by the end of 1965. What Kennedy would have done thereafter has remained a matter of endless controversy, endless because it is unanswerable, and unanswerable because on November 22, 1963, while visiting Dallas, Texas, Kennedy was shot in the neck and head by Lee Harvey Oswald, a twenty-four-year-old ex-marine drifter who worked in the Texas School Book Depository, from which the shots were fired at Kennedy.

Oswald's motives remain unknown. Although a federal commission appointed by President Lyndon Johnson and headed by Chief Justice Earl Warren concluded that Oswald acted alone, debate still swirls around various conspiracy theories. Footage of Kennedy's assassination and then the murder of Oswald two days later by Jack Ruby, a Dallas nightclub owner, was shown over and over again on television, the medium that had so helped Kennedy's rise to the presidency and now captured his death and the moving funeral at Arlington National Cemetery. Kennedy's assassination enshrined the young president in the public imagination as a martyred leader cut down in the prime of his life.

LYNDON JOHNSON AND THE GREAT SOCIETY

Lyndon Johnson took the presidential oath of office on board the plane that brought John Kennedy's body back to Washington from Dallas. Fifty-five years old, he had spent twenty-six years on the Washington scene and had served nearly a decade as Democratic leader in the Senate, where he had displayed the greatest gift for compromise since Henry Clay.

Presidential assassination

John F. Kennedy's vice president, Lyndon B. Johnson, takes the presidential oath aboard Air Force One before its return from Dallas with Jacqueline Kennedy (right), the presidential party, and the body of the assassinated president.

Johnson brought to the White House a marked change of style from Kennedy. A self-made and self-centered man who had worked his way out of a hardscrabble rural Texas environment to become one of Washington's most powerful figures, Johnson had none of the Kennedy elegance. He was a bundle of conflicting elements: earthy, idealistic, domineering, insecure, gregarious, suspicious, affectionate, manipulative, ruthless, and compassionate. Johnson's ego was as huge as his ambition. Like another southern president, Andrew Johnson, he harbored a sense of being the perpetual outsider despite his long experience with legislative power. And indeed he was so regarded by Kennedy insiders. He, in turn, "detested" the way Kennedy and his aides had ignored him as vice president.

Those who viewed Johnson as a stereotypical southern conservative failed to appreciate his long-standing admiration for Franklin Roosevelt, the depth of his concern for the poor, and his commitment to the cause of civil rights. "I'm going to be the best friend the Negro ever had," he told a member of the White House staff. In foreign affairs, however, he was, like Woodrow Wilson, a novice. Johnson wanted to be the greatest American president, the one who did the most good for the most people. And he would let nothing stand in his way. In the end, however, the grandiose Johnson promised far more than he could accomplish, raising false hopes and stoking fiery resentments.

POLITICS AND POVERTY
Domestic policy was Johnson's
first priority. Amid the national
grief after the assassination, he
declared that Kennedy's legislative program, stymied in congressional committees, would
be passed. Johnson loved the
political infighting and legislative detail that Kennedy had
loathed. The logjam in Congress
that had blocked Kennedy's legislative efforts broke under Johnson's forceful leadership, and a
torrent of legislation poured
through.

Before 1963 was out, Con-
gress had approved a pending
foreign-aid bill and a plan to
sell wheat to the Soviet Union.
This commitment to foreign

The Johnson treatment

Lyndon Johnson used powerful body language to intimidate and manipulate anyone
who dared disagree with him.

aid then drew attention to America's own people's needs. In 1964 the Council of Economic Advisers reported that 9.3 million American families, about
20 percent of the population, were living below the "poverty line." "Unfortunately, many Americans live on the outskirts of hope," Johnson told Congress in his first State of the Union message, "some because of their poverty
and some because of their color, and all too many because of both." At the
top of his agenda, he put Kennedy's stalled measures for tax reductions and
civil rights. In 1962, Kennedy had announced a then-unusual plan to jump-
start the sluggish economy: a tax cut to stimulate consumer spending. Congressional Republicans opposed the idea because it would increase the federal
budget deficit. And polls showed that public opinion was also skeptical. So
Kennedy had postponed the proposed tax cut for a year. It was still bogged
down in Congress when the president was assassinated, but Lyndon Johnson
was able to break the logjam. The Revenue Act of 1964 did provide a needed
boost to the economy.

Likewise, the Civil Rights Act that Kennedy had presented to Congress in
1963 became law in 1964 through Johnson's forceful leadership. It prohibited racial segregation in public facilities such as bus terminals, restaurants,
theaters, and hotels. And it outlawed long-standing racial discrimination in

The Civil Rights Act of 1964

President Johnson reaches to shake hands with Dr. Martin Luther King Jr. after presenting the civil rights leader with one of the pens used to sign the Civil Rights Act of 1964.

the registration of voters and the hiring of employees. The civil rights bill passed the House in February 1964. In the Senate, however, southern legislators launched a filibuster that lasted two months. Johnson finally prevailed, and the bill became law on July 2. But the new president knew that it had come at a political price. On the night after signing the bill, Johnson told an aide that "we have just delivered the South to the Republican Party for a long time to come."

In addition to fulfilling Kennedy's major promises, Johnson launched an ambitious legislative program of his own. In his 1964 State of the Union address, he added to his must-do list a bold new idea that bore the Johnson brand: "This Administration today, here and now, declares unconditional war on poverty in America." The particulars of this "war on poverty" were to come later, the product of a task force that was at work before Johnson took office.

Americans had "rediscovered" poverty in 1962 when the social critic Michael Harrington published a powerful exposé titled *The Other America*. Harrington argued that more than 40 million people were mired in a "culture of poverty." Unlike the upwardly mobile immigrant poor at the beginning of the century, the modern poor lacked hope. "To be impoverished," Harrington asserted, "is to be an internal alien, to grow up in a culture that is radically different from the one that dominates the society." President Kennedy had asked his advisers to investigate the poverty problem and suggest solutions. Upon taking office as president, Lyndon Johnson announced that he wanted an anti-poverty package that was "big and bold, that would hit the nation with real impact." Money for the program would come from the tax revenues generated by corporate profits made possible by the tax reduction of 1964, which had led to one of the longest sustained economic booms in history.

The administration's war on poverty was embodied in an economic-opportunity bill that incorporated a wide range of programs: a Job Corps for inner-city youths aged sixteen to twenty-one, a Head Start program for disadvantaged preschoolers, work-study programs for college students, grants to farmers and rural businesses, loans to employers willing to hire the chronically unemployed, the Volunteers in Service to America (a domestic Peace Corps), and the Community Action Program, which would allow the poor "maximum feasible participation" in directing neighborhood programs designed for their benefit. Speaking at Ann Arbor, Michigan, in 1964, Johnson called for a "Great Society" resting on "abundance and liberty for all. The Great Society demands an end to poverty and racial injustice, to which we are fully committed in our time."

THE ELECTION OF 1964   Johnson's well-intentioned but hastily conceived "war on poverty" and Great Society social program provoked a Republican counterattack. Over the years, Republicans had come to fear that the Republican party had fallen into the hands of an "eastern establishment" that had given in to the same internationalism and big-government policies that liberal Democrats promoted. Ever since 1940, so the theory went, the party had nominated "me-too" candidates who merely promised to run more efficiently the programs that Democrats designed. Offer the Republican voters "a choice, not an echo," they reasoned, and a true conservative majority would assert itself.

By 1960, Arizona senator Barry Goldwater, a millionaire department-store magnate, had emerged as the leader of the Republican right. In his book *The Conscience of a Conservative* (1960), Goldwater proposed the abolition of the income tax, sale of the Tennessee Valley Authority, and a drastic overhaul of Social Security. Almost from the time of Kennedy's victory in 1960, a movement to draft Goldwater had begun, mobilizing right-wing activists to capture party caucuses and contest primaries. In 1964 they took an early lead, and they swept the all-important California primary. Thus Goldwater's forces controlled the Republican Convention when it gathered in San Francisco. "I would remind you," Goldwater told the delegates, "that extremism in the defense of liberty is no vice."

During the 1964 campaign, Goldwater displayed a gift for frightening voters. He urged wholesale bombing of North Vietnam and left the impression of being trigger-happy. He savaged Johnson's war on poverty and the entire New Deal tradition. At times he was foolishly candid. In Tennessee he proposed the sale of the Tennessee Valley Authority; in St. Petersburg, Florida, a major retirement community, he questioned the value of Social Security. He also opposed the nuclear test ban and the 1964 Civil Rights Act. To Republican campaign buttons that claimed "In your heart, you know he's right," Democrats responded, "In your guts, you know he's nuts."

Barry Goldwater

Many voters feared that the Republican presidential candidate in 1964, Senator Barry Goldwater, was trigger-happy. In this cartoon, Goldwater wields in one hand his book *The Conscience of a Conservative* and in the other a hydrogen bomb.

Johnson, on the other hand, portrayed himself as a responsible centrist. He chose as his running mate Hubert Humphrey of Minnesota, a prominent liberal senator who had long promoted civil rights. In contrast to Goldwater's bellicose rhetoric on Vietnam, Johnson pledged, "We are not about to send American boys nine or ten thousand miles from home to do what Asian boys ought to be doing for themselves."

The result was a landslide. Johnson polled 61 percent of the total vote; Goldwater carried only Arizona and five states in the Deep South, where race remained the salient issue. Vermont went Democratic for the first time ever in a presidential election. Johnson won the electoral vote by a whopping 486 to 52. In the Senate the Democrats increased their majority by two (68 to 32) and in the House by thirty-seven (295 to 140), but Goldwater's success in the Deep South continued that traditionally Democratic region's shift to the Republican party. Johnson knew that his mandate could quickly erode; he shrewdly told his aides, "Every day I'm in office, I'm going to lose votes. I'm going to alienate somebody. . . . We've got to get this legislation fast. You've got to get it during my honeymoon."

LANDMARK LEGISLATION   In 1965, Johnson flooded the new Congress with Great Society legislation that, he promised, would end poverty, revitalize decaying central cities, provide every young American with the chance to attend college, protect the health of the elderly, enhance the nation's cultural life, clean up the air and water, and make the highways safer and prettier. The scope of Johnson's legislative program was unparalleled since Franklin Roosevelt's Hundred Days.

Priority went to federal health insurance and aid to education, proposals that had languished since President Truman had proposed them in 1945. For twenty years a comprehensive medical-insurance program had been stalled by the steadfast opposition of the physicians making up the American Medical Association. But now that Johnson had the votes, the AMA joined Republicans in supporting a bill serving those over age sixty-five. The act that finally emerged went well beyond the original proposal. It created not just a Medicare program for the aged but also a program of federal grants to states to help cover medical payments for the indigent. President Johnson signed the bill on July 30, 1965, in Independence, Missouri, with eighty-one-year-old Harry Truman looking on.

Five days after he submitted his Medicare program, Johnson sent to Congress a massive program of federal aid to elementary and secondary schools. Such proposals had been ignored since the 1940s, blocked alternately by issues of segregation and issues of separation of church and state. The first issue had been laid to rest, legally at least, by the Civil Rights Act of 1964. Now Congress devised a means of extending aid to "poverty-impacted" school districts regardless of their public or religious character.

The momentum generated by these measures had already begun to carry others along, and that process continued through the following year. Before the Eighty-ninth Congress adjourned, it had established a record in the passage of landmark legislation unequaled since the time of the New Deal. Altogether, the tide of Great Society legislation had carried 435 bills through the Congress. Among them was the Appalachian Regional Development Act of 1966, which allocated $1 billion for programs in remote mountain areas that had long been pockets of desperate poverty. The Housing and Urban Development Act of 1965 provided for construction of 240,000 public-housing units and $3 billion for urban renewal. Funds for rent supplements for low-income families followed in 1966, and in that year a new Department of Housing and Urban Development appeared, headed by Robert C. Weaver, the first African American cabinet member. Lyndon Johnson had, in the words of one Washington reporter, "brought to harvest a generation's backlog of ideas and social legislation."

THE IMMIGRATION ACT   Little noticed in the stream of legislation flowing from Congress was a major new immigration bill that had originated in the Kennedy White House. President Johnson signed the Immigration and Nationality Services Act of 1965 in a ceremony held on Liberty Island in New York Harbor. In his speech he stressed that the new law would redress the wrong done to those "from southern and eastern Europe" and the "developing continents" of Asia, Africa, and Latin America. It would do so by abolishing the discriminatory quotas based upon national origin that had governed immigration policy since the 1920s. The new law treated all nationalities and races equally. In place of national quotas, it created hemispheric ceilings on visas issued: 170,000 for persons from outside the Western Hemisphere, 120,000 for persons from within. It also stipulated that no more than 20,000 people could come from any one country each year. The new act allowed the entry of immediate family members of American residents without limit. During the 1960s, Asians and Latin Americans became the largest contingent of new Americans.

ASSESSING THE GREAT SOCIETY   The Great Society programs included several successes. The Highway Safety Act and the National Traffic and Motor Vehicle Safety Act (both 1966) established safety standards for highway design and automobile manufacturers, and the scholarships provided

Great Society initiatives

President Johnson listens to Tom Fletcher, a father of eight children, describe some of the economic problems in his hometown.

for college students under the Higher Education Act (1965) were quite popular. Many of the Great Society initiatives aimed at improving the health, nutrition, and education of poor Americans, young and old, made some headway. So, too, did federal efforts to clean up air and water pollution. Several of Johnson's most ambitious programs, however, were ill conceived, others were vastly underfunded, and many were mismanaged. Medicare, for example, removed incentives for hospitals to control costs, so medical bills skyrocketed. The Great Society helped reduce the number of people living in poverty, but it did so largely by providing federal welfare payments, not by finding people productive jobs. The war on poverty ended up being as disappointing as the war in Vietnam. Often funds appropriated for a program never made it through the tangled bureaucracy to the needy. Widely publicized cases of welfare fraud became a powerful weapon in the hands of those who were opposed to liberal social programs. By 1966 middle-class resentment over the cost and waste of the Great Society programs had generated a conservative backlash that fueled a Republican resurgence at the polls.

FROM CIVIL RIGHTS TO BLACK POWER

CIVIL RIGHTS LEGISLATION   Early in 1965, Martin Luther King Jr. organized an effort to enroll the 3 million African Americans in the South who had not registered to vote. In Selma, Alabama, civil rights protesters began a march to Montgomery, about forty miles away, only to be violently dispersed by state troopers. A federal judge agreed to allow the march, and President Johnson provided troops for protection. By March 25, when the demonstrators reached Montgomery, some 35,000 people were with them, and King delivered a rousing address from the steps of the state capitol.

Several days earlier, President Johnson had gone before Congress with a moving plea that reached its climax when he slowly intoned the words of the civil rights movement's hymn: "And we shall overcome." The resulting Voting Rights Act of 1965 ensured all citizens the right to vote. It authorized the attorney general to dispatch federal examiners to register voters. In states or counties where fewer than half the adults had voted in 1964, the act suspended literacy tests and other devices commonly used to defraud citizens of the vote. By the end of the year, some 250,000 African Americans were newly registered.

BLACK POWER   Amid this success, however, the civil rights movement began to fragment. On August 11, 1965, less than a week after the passage of the Voting Rights Act, Watts, a predominantly black and poor community in Los Angeles, exploded in a frenzy of rioting and looting. When the uprising ended, 34 were dead, almost 4,000 rioters were in jail, and property damage exceeded $35 million. Chicago and Cleveland, along with forty other American cities, experienced similar race riots in the summer of 1966. The following summer, Newark and Detroit burst into flames.

In retrospect, it was predictable that the civil rights movement would shift its focus from the rural South to the plight of urban blacks nationwide. By the middle 1960s about 70 percent of the nation's African Americans were living in metropolitan areas, most in central-city ghettos that the postwar prosperity had bypassed. And again it seemed clear, in retrospect, that the nonviolent tactics that had worked in the South would not work as readily in large cities across the nation. "It may be," wrote a contributor to *Esquire* magazine, "that looting, rioting and burning . . . are really nothing more than radical forms of urban renewal, a response not only to the frustrations of the ghetto but the collapse of all ordinary modes of change, as if a body despairing of the indifference of doctors sought to rip a cancer out of itself." A special Commission on Civil Disorders noted that the urban upheavals of the middle 1960s were initiated by blacks themselves; whites, by contrast, had started earlier riots, which had then prompted black counterattacks. Now blacks visited violence and destruction upon themselves in an effort to destroy what they could not stomach and what civil rights legislation seemed unable to change.

By 1966, "black power" had become an imprecise but riveting rallying cry for young militants. When Stokely Carmichael, a twenty-five-year-old graduate of Howard University, became head of the Student Nonviolent Coordinating Committee (SNCC) in 1966, he made the separatist philosophy of black power the official objective of the organization and ousted whites from the organization. H. Rap Brown, who succeeded Carmichael as head of SNCC in 1967, was even more outspoken and incendiary. He urged blacks to "get you some guns" and "kill the honkies." Carmichael, meanwhile, had moved on to the Black Panther party, a group of urban revolutionaries founded in Oakland, California, in 1966. Headed by Huey P. Newton, Bobby Seale, and Eldridge Cleaver, the provocative, armed Black Panthers initially terrified the public but eventually fragmented in spasms of violence.

The most articulate spokesman for black power was Malcolm X (formerly Malcolm Little, the X denoting his lost African surname). Malcolm had risen from a ghetto childhood involving narcotics dealing and other crimes to become the chief disciple of Elijah Muhammad, the Black Muslim leader in the United States. "Yes, I'm an extremist," Malcolm acknowledged in 1964. "The black race in the United States is in extremely bad shape. You show me a black man who isn't an extremist and I'll show you one who needs psychiatric attention." By 1964, Malcolm had broken with Elijah Muhammad and founded an organization committed to the establishment of alliances between African Americans and the nonwhite peoples of the world. But shortly after the publication of his *Autobiography* in 1964, Malcolm was gunned down in Harlem by assassins representing a rival faction of Black Muslims. With him went the most effective voice for urban black militancy since Marcus Garvey in the 1920s. What made the assassination of

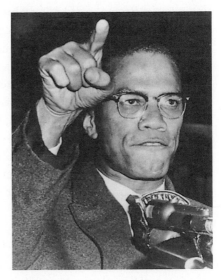

Malcolm X

Malcolm X was the black power movement's most influential spokesman.

Malcolm X especially tragic was that he had just months before begun to abandon his strident anti-white rhetoric and preach a biracial message of social change.

Although widely publicized and highly visible, the black power movement never attracted more than a small minority of mostly young African Americans. Only about 15 percent of American blacks labeled themselves separatists. The preponderant majority continued to identify with the philosophy of nonviolent, Christian-centered integration promoted by Martin Luther King Jr. and with organizations such as the NAACP. King dismissed black separatism and the promotion of violent social change. He reminded his followers that "we can't win violently."

Despite its hyperbole, violence, and few adherents, the black power philosophy had two positive effects upon the civil rights movement. First, it motivated African Americans to take greater pride in their racial heritage. As Malcolm X often pointed out, prolonged slavery and institutionalized racism had eroded the self-esteem of many blacks. "The worst crime the white man has committed," he declared, "has been to teach us to hate ourselves." He and others helped blacks appreciate their African roots and their American accomplishments. In fact, it was Malcolm X who insisted that blacks call themselves African Americans as a symbol of pride in their roots and as a spur to learn more about their history as a people. As the popular singer James Brown urged, "Say it loud—I'm black and I'm proud."

Second, the assertiveness of black power advocates forced King and other mainstream black leaders and organizations to focus attention on the plight of poor inner-city blacks. Legal access to restaurants, schools, and other public accommodations, King pointed out, meant little to people mired in a culture of urban poverty. They needed jobs and decent housing as much as they needed legal rights. To this end, King began to emphasize the economic plight of the black urban underclass. The time had come for radical measures "to provide jobs and income for the poor." Yet as King and others sought to heighten the war on poverty at home, the escalating war in Vietnam was consuming more and more of America's resources and energies.

THE TRAGEDY OF VIETNAM

As racial violence erupted in America's cities, the war in Vietnam reached new levels of intensity and destruction. In November 1963, when John Kennedy was assassinated, there were 16,000 U.S. military "advisers" in South Vietnam. Lyndon Johnson inherited from Kennedy and Eisenhower a long-standing commitment to prevent a Communist takeover in Indochina as well as a reluctance on the part of American presidents to assume primary responsibility for fighting the Viet Cong (the Communist-led guerrillas in South Vietnam) and their North Vietnamese allies. Beginning with Harry Truman, one president after another had done just enough to avoid being charged with having "lost" Vietnam to communism. Johnson initially sought to do the same, fearing that any other course of action would undermine his political influence and jeopardize his Great Society programs in Congress. But this path took the United States deeper into an expanding military commitment in Southeast Asia. Early on, Johnson doubted that the poverty-stricken, peasant-based Vietnam was worth military involvement. In May 1964 he told his national security adviser, McGeorge Bundy, that he had spent a sleepless night worrying about Vietnam: "It looks to me like we are getting into another Korea. . . . I don't think we can fight them 10,000 miles away from home. . . . I don't think it's worth fighting for. And I don't think we can get out. It's just the biggest damned mess that I ever saw."

Yet Johnson's fear of appearing weak abroad was stronger than his misgivings and forebodings. By the end of 1965, there were 184,000 U.S. troops in Vietnam; in 1966 there were 385,000; and by 1969, at the height of the American presence, 542,000. By the time the last troops left, in March 1973, some 58,000 Americans had died and another 300,000 had been wounded. The massive, prolonged war had cost taxpayers $150 billion, siphoned funding from many Great Society programs; it had produced 570,000 draft offenders and 563,000 less-than-honorable military discharges, toppled Johnson's administration, and divided the country as no event in history had since the Civil War.

"How Deep Do You Figure We'll Get Involved, Sir?"

Although U.S. soldiers were first sent to Vietnam as noncombatant advisers, they soon found themselves involved in a quagmire of fighting.

ESCALATION The official sanction for military "escalation" in Southeast Asia—a

Defense Department term favored in the Vietnam era—was the Tonkin Gulf resolution, voted by Congress on August 7, 1964, after merely thirty minutes of discussion. On that day, Johnson told a national television audience that two destroyers, the U.S.S. *Maddox* and the U.S.S. *C. Turner Joy,* had been

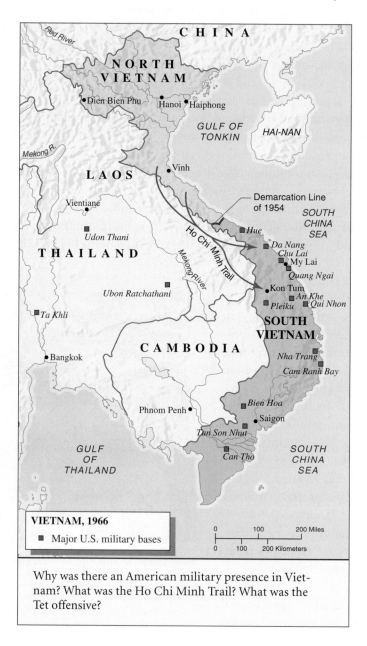

VIETNAM, 1966

■ Major U.S. military bases

| 0 | 100 | 200 Miles |
| 0 | 100 | 200 Kilometers |

Why was there an American military presence in Vietnam? What was the Ho Chi Minh Trail? What was the Tet offensive?

attacked by North Vietnamese vessels on August 2 and 4 in the Gulf of Tonkin, off the coast of North Vietnam. Johnson described the attack, called the Gulf of Tonkin incident, as unprovoked. In truth the destroyers had been monitoring South Vietnamese attacks against two North Vietnamese islands—attacks planned by American advisers. The Tonkin Gulf resolution authorized the president to "take all necessary measures to repel any armed attack against the forces of the United States and to prevent further aggression." Only Senator Wayne Morse of Oregon and Senator Ernest Gruening of Alaska voted against the resolution, which Johnson thereafter interpreted as equivalent to a congressional declaration of war.

Soon after his landslide victory over Goldwater in November 1964, Johnson, while still plagued by private doubts, made the crucial decisions that committed the United States to a full-scale war in Vietnam for the next four years. On February 5, 1965, Viet Cong guerrillas killed 8 and wounded 126 Americans at Pleiku, in South Vietnam. Further attacks later that week led Johnson to order Operation Rolling Thunder, the first sustained bombing of North Vietnam, which was intended to stop the flow of soldiers and supplies into the south. Six months later an extensive study concluded that the bombing had not slowed the supplies pouring down the Ho Chi Minh Trail from North Vietnam through Laos and into South Vietnam.

In March 1965 the new U.S. commander in Vietnam, General William C. Westmoreland, greeted the first installment of combat troops. By the summer, American forces were engaged in "search-and-destroy" operations throughout South Vietnam. As combat operations increased, so did casualties, announced each week on the nightly television news, along with the "body count" of alleged Viet Cong dead. "Westy's war," although fought with helicopter gunships, chemical defoliants, and napalm, became like the trench warfare of World War I—a war of attrition.

THE CONTEXT FOR POLICY   Lyndon Johnson's decision to "Americanize" the Vietnam War, so ill-starred in retrospect, was consistent with the foreign-policy principles pursued by all presidents after World War II. The version of the theory intended to "contain" communism articulated in the Truman Doctrine, endorsed by Eisenhower throughout the 1950s and reaffirmed by Kennedy, pledged U.S. opposition to the advance of communism anywhere in the world. "Why are we in Vietnam?" Johnson asked rhetorically at Johns Hopkins University in 1965. "We are there because we have a promise to keep. . . . To leave Vietnam to its fate would shake the confidence of all these people in the value of American commitment." Secretary of State Dean Rusk frequently repeated this rationale, warning that the rest of Southeast Asia would fall "like dominoes" to communism if American forces withdrew from Vietnam. Military intervention was thus a logical culmination of the assumptions that were widely shared by the foreign-policy establishment and the leaders of both political parties since the early days of the cold war.

At the same time, Johnson and his advisers presumed that military involvement in Vietnam must not reach levels that would cause the Chinese or Soviets to intervene directly. And that meant, in effect, that a complete military victory was never possible. The goal of the United States was not to win the war in any traditional sense but to prevent the North Vietnamese and the Viet Cong from winning and, eventually, to force a negotiated settlement with the North Vietnamese. This meant that the United States would have to maintain a military presence as long as the enemy retained the will to fight.

As it turned out, American support for the war eroded faster than the will of the North Vietnamese leaders to tolerate devastating casualties and destruction. Systematic opposition to the war on college campuses began in 1965 with "teach-ins" at the University of Michigan. The following year, Senator J. William Fulbright of Arkansas, chairman of the Senate Foreign Relations Committee, began congressional investigations into American policy in Vietnam. George Kennan, the author of the containment doctrine, told Senator Fulbright's committee that the doctrine was appropriate for Europe but not for Southeast Asia. And a respected general testified that General Westmoreland's military strategy had no chance of achieving victory. By 1967 anti-war demonstrations were attracting massive support. Nightly television accounts of the fighting—Vietnam was the first war to receive extended television coverage and hence was dubbed the living-room war—called into question the official optimism. By May 1967 even Secretary of Defense Robert McNamara was wavering: "The picture of the world's greatest superpower killing or injuring 1,000 noncombatants a week, while trying to pound a tiny backward nation into submission on an issue whose merits are hotly disputed, is not a pretty one."

In a war of political will, North Vietnam had the advantage. Johnson and his advisers grievously underestimated the tenacity of the North Vietnamese commitment to unify Vietnam and expel American forces. While the United States fought a limited war for limited objectives, the Vietnamese Communists fought an all-out war for their very survival. Just as General Westmoreland was assuring Johnson and the public that the war effort in early 1968 was on the verge of gaining the upper hand, the Communists organized widespread assaults that jolted American confidence and resolve.

THE TURNING POINT   On January 31, 1968, the first day of the Vietnamese New Year (Tet), the Viet Cong defied a holiday truce to launch ferocious assaults on American and South Vietnamese forces throughout South Vietnam. The old capital city of Hue fell to the Communists, and Viet Cong units temporarily occupied the grounds of the U.S. embassy in Saigon, the capital of South Vietnam. General Westmoreland proclaimed the Tet offensive a major defeat for the Viet Cong, and most students of military strategy later agreed with him. While Viet Cong casualties were enormous, however, the impact of the surprise attacks on the American public was more telling. The scope and intensity of the offensive contradicted upbeat claims by U.S. commanders that the war was going well. *Time* and *Newsweek* magazines soon ran anti-war editorials urging withdrawal. Polls showed that Lyndon Johnson's popularity had declined to 35 percent. Civil rights leaders and social activists felt betrayed as they saw federal funds earmarked for the war on poverty gobbled up by the expanding war. In 1968 the United States was spending

The Tet offensive

Many Vietnamese were driven from their homes during the bloody street battles of the 1968 Tet offensive. Here, following a lull in the fighting, civilians carrying a white flag approach U.S. Marines.

Johnson and Vietnam

The Vietnam War sapped the spirit of Lyndon Johnson, who decided not to run for reelection in 1968.

$322,000 on every Communist killed in Vietnam; the poverty programs at home received only $53 per person.

During 1968 a despondent Lyndon Johnson grew increasingly embittered and isolated. He suffered from depression and bouts of paranoia. It had become painfully evident that the Vietnam War was a never-ending stalemate that was fragmenting the nation and undermining the Great Society programs. Clark Clifford, Johnson's new secretary of defense, reported to the president that a task force of prominent soldiers and civilians saw no prospect for a military victory. Robert Kennedy, now a senator from New York, was considering a run for the presidency in order to challenge Johnson's Vietnam policy. Senator Eugene McCarthy of Minnesota, a devout Catholic and a poet, had already decided to oppose Johnson in the Democratic primaries. With anti-war students rallying to his "Dump Johnson" candidacy, McCarthy polled a stunning 42 percent of the vote to Johnson's 48 percent in New Hampshire's March primary. It was a remarkable showing for a little-known senator. Each presidential primary now promised to become a referendum on Johnson's Vietnam policy. The war in Vietnam had become Lyndon Johnson's war; as more and more voters soured on the fighting, he saw his public support evaporate. In Wisconsin, scene of the next Democratic primary, the president's political advisers forecast a humiliating defeat.

On March 31, Johnson made a dramatic decision. He appeared on national television to announce a limited halt to the bombing of North Vietnam and fresh initiatives for a negotiated cease-fire. Then he added a stunning postscript: "I shall not seek, and I will not accept, the nomination of my party for another term as your President." Although U.S. troops would remain in Vietnam for five more years and the casualties would continue, the quest for military victory had ended. Now the question was how the most powerful nation in the world could extricate itself from Vietnam with a minimum of damage to its prestige and its South Vietnamese allies.

Sixties Crescendo

A TRAUMATIC YEAR   Change moved at a fearful pace throughout the 1960s, but 1968 was the most turbulent and the most traumatic year of all. On April 4, only four days after Johnson's withdrawal from the presidential race, Martin Luther King Jr. was gunned down in Memphis, Tennessee, by a white racist, James Earl Ray. King's death set off an outpouring of grief among whites and blacks. It also ignited riots in over sixty cities.

Two months later, on June 5, Senator Robert Kennedy was shot in the head by a young Palestinian, Sirhan Sirhan, who resented Kennedy's strong support of Israel. Kennedy's death occurred at the end of the day on which he had convincingly defeated Eugene McCarthy in the California Democratic primary, thereby momentarily assuming leadership of the anti-war forces in the race for the presidential nomination. Political reporter David Halberstam of the *New York Times* thought back to the assassinations of John Kennedy and Malcolm X, then to the violent end of King, the most influential African American leader of the twentieth century, and then to Robert Kennedy, the heir to leadership of the Kennedy clan. "We could make a calendar of the decade," Halberstam wrote, "by marking where we were at the hours of those violent deaths."

CHICAGO AND MIAMI   In August 1968, Democratic delegates gathered inside a Chicago convention hall to nominate for president Johnson's faithful vice president, Hubert Humphrey, while almost 20,000 police officers and national guardsmen and a small army of television reporters stood watch over a gathering of eclectic protesters herded together miles away in a public park. Chicago mayor Richard J. Daley, who had given "shoot-to-kill" orders to police during the April riots protesting King's assassination, warned that he would not tolerate disruptions. Nonetheless, riots broke out and were televised nationwide. As police tear gas and billy clubs struck down demonstrators, others chanted "The whole world is watching." (See pages 1345–1346 for further details.)

The Democratic party's liberal tradition was clearly in disarray, a fact that gave heart to the Republicans, who gathered in Miami Beach to nominate Richard Nixon. Only six years earlier, after he lost the California gubernatorial race, Nixon had vowed never again to run for public office. But by 1968 he had changed his mind and had become a spokesman for the values of "middle America." Nixon and the Republicans offered a vision of stability and order that appealed to a majority of Americans—soon to be called the silent majority.

George Wallace, the Democratic governor of Alabama who had made his reputation as an outspoken defender of segregation, ran on the American Independent party ticket. Wallace moderated his position on the race issue

The 1968 election

Richard Nixon (left) and running mate Spiro Agnew (right).

but appealed even more candidly than Nixon to voters' concerns about riot-ing anti-war protesters, the mushrooming welfare system, and the growth of the federal government. Wallace's reactionary candidacy generated consid-erable appeal outside his native South, especially among white working-class communities, where resentment of Lyndon Johnson's Great Society liberal-ism flourished. Although never a possible winner, Wallace did pose the pos-sibility of denying Humphrey or Nixon an electoral majority and thereby throwing the choice into the House of Representatives, which would have provided an appropriate climax to a chaotic year.

NIXON AGAIN   It did not happen that way. Richard Nixon enjoyed an enormous lead in the polls, which narrowed as the election approached. Wallace's campaign was hurt by his outspoken running mate, retired air force general Curtis LeMay, who favored expanding the war in Vietnam and using nuclear weapons. In October 1968, Hubert Humphrey infuriated Johnson when he announced that, if elected, he would stop bombing North Vietnam "as an acceptable risk for peace."

Nixon and Governor Spiro Agnew of Maryland, his running mate, eked out a narrow victory of about 500,000 votes, a margin of about 1 percentage point. The electoral vote was more decisive, 301 to 191. George Wallace received

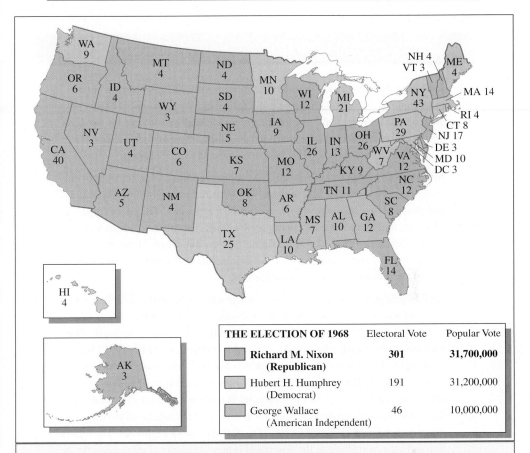

THE ELECTION OF 1968

		Electoral Vote	Popular Vote
	Richard M. Nixon **(Republican)**	**301**	**31,700,000**
	Hubert H. Humphrey (Democrat)	191	31,200,000
	George Wallace (American Independent)	46	10,000,000

How did the riots at the Chicago Democratic Convention affect the 1968 presidential campaign? What does the electoral map reveal about the support base for each of the three major candidates? How was Nixon able to win enough electoral votes in such a close, three-way presidential race? What was Wallace's appeal to 10 million voters?

10 million votes, 13.5 percent of the total. It was the best showing by a third-party candidate since Robert La Follette ran on the Progressive Party ticket in 1924. All but one of Wallace's 46 electoral votes were from the Deep South. Nixon swept all but four of the states west of the Mississippi. Humphrey's support came almost exclusively from the Northeast.

So at the end of a turbulent year, near the end of a traumatic decade, a nation on the verge of violent chaos looked to Richard Nixon to provide what he had promised in the campaign: "peace with honor" in Vietnam and a middle ground on which a majority of Americans, silent or otherwise, could come together.

CHAPTER SUMMARY

- **Kennedy's New Frontier** President Kennedy promised "new frontiers" in domestic policy, but without a clear Democratic majority in Congress he was unable to increase federal aid to education, provide health insurance for the aged, create a cabinet-level department of urban affairs, or expand civil rights. He championed tariff cuts, however, and an expanded space program.

- **Johnson's Great Society** President Johnson was committed to social reform, including civil rights. He forced the Civil Rights Act through Congress in 1964 and declared "a war" on poverty. Under the Great Society, welfare was expanded, Medicare and Medicaid were created, more grants for college students were established, and racial quotas for immigration were abolished. These programs were expensive and, coupled with the soaring costs of the war in Vietnam, necessitated tax increases, which were unpopular.

- **Civil Rights' Achievements** By the 1960s significant numbers of African Americans and whites were staging nonviolent sit-ins. In 1961, "freedom riders" attempted to integrate buses, trains, and bus and train stations in the South. The high point of the early phase of the civil rights movement was the 1963 March on Washington for Jobs and Freedom, at which Martin Luther King Jr. delivered his famous "I Have a Dream" speech. In 1964, President Johnson signed the far-reaching Civil Rights Act. In 1965, King set in motion a massive drive to enroll the 3 million southern African Americans who were not registered to vote. Later that year, Johnson persuaded Congress to pass the Voting Rights Act. The legislation did little to ameliorate the poverty of inner-city blacks or stem the violence that swept northern cities in the hot summers of the late 1960s. By 1968, nonviolent resistance had given way to the more militant black power movement.

- **Escalation in Vietnam** The United States supported the government of South Vietnam even though it failed to deliver promised reforms, win the support of its citizens, or defeat the Communist insurgents, the Viet Cong. Kennedy increased America's commitment by sending advisers, and Johnson went further, deploying combat troops. A turning point in the war was the Viet Cong's Tet offensive, which served to rally anti-war sentiment.

- **Communist Cuba** In early 1961, Kennedy inherited a CIA plot to topple the regime of Fidel Castro, the premier of Cuba. Kennedy naïvely agreed to the plot, whereby some 1,500 anti-Castro Cubans landed at Cuba's Bay of Pigs. The plotters failed to inspire a revolution, and most were quickly captured. Kennedy's seeming weakness in the face of Soviet aggression led the Russian premier, Nikita Khrushchev, to believe that the Soviets could install ballistic missiles in Cuba without American opposition. In October 1962 in a tense standoff, Kennedy ordered a blockade of Cuba and succeeded in forcing Khrushchev to withdraw the missiles.

CHRONOLOGY

1961	Bay of Pigs fiasco
1961	Soviets erect the Berlin Wall
October 1962	Cuban missile crisis
August 1963	March on Washington for Jobs and Freedom
November 1963	John F. Kennedy is assassinated in Dallas, Texas
1964	Congress passes the Civil Rights Act
August 1964	Congress passes the Tonkin Gulf resolution
1965	Malcolm X is assassinated by a rival group of black Muslims
1965	Riots break out in the African American community of Watts, California
January 1968	Viet Cong stage the Tet offensive
April 1968	Martin Luther King Jr. is assassinated
June 1968	Robert Kennedy is assassinated

KEY TERMS & NAMES

35

REBELLION AND REACTION IN THE 1960s AND 1970s

FOCUS QUESTIONS wwnorton.com/studyspace

- What characterized the social rebellion and struggles for civil rights in the 1960s and 1970s?
- How did the war in Vietnam end?
- What was Watergate, and why did it lead to Nixon's resignation?
- Why had the Middle East become an area of concern by the 1970s, and how did the Carter administration deal with crises in the area?

As Richard Nixon entered the White House in early 1969, he faced a nation whose social fabric was in tatters. Everywhere, it seemed, traditional institutions and notions of authority were under attack. The traumatic events of 1968 revealed how deeply divided society had become and how difficult a task Nixon faced in carrying out his pledge to restore social harmony. The stability he promised proved elusive. His policies and his combative temperament heightened rather than reduced societal tensions. Those tensions reflected profound fissures in the post–World War II consensus promoted by Eisenhower and inherited by Kennedy and Johnson. Ironically, many of the same forces that had enabled the flush times of the Eisenhower years—the baby boom, the containment doctrine of anti-communism, and the burgeoning consumer culture—helped generate the social upheaval of the 1960s and 1970s.

THE ROOTS OF REBELLION

YOUTH REVOLT   By the early 1960s the baby boomers were maturing. Now young adults, they differed from their elders in that they had experienced neither economic depression nor a major war. In record numbers they were attending colleges and universities: enrollment quadrupled between 1945 and 1970. Many universities had become gigantic institutions dependent upon research contracts from corporations and the federal government. As these "multiversities" grew more bureaucratic and hierarchical, they unwittingly invited resistance from a generation of students wary of involvement in what President Eisenhower had labeled the military-industrial complex.

The Greensboro sit-ins in 1960 not only precipitated a decade of civil rights activism but also signaled an end to the supposed apathy that had enveloped college campuses and social life during the 1950s. Although most immediately concerned with the rights and status of African Americans, the sit-ins, marches, protests, ideals, and sacrifices associated with the civil rights movement provided the model and inspiration for other groups that demanded justice, freedom, and equality as well: women, Native Americans, Hispanics, and homosexuals.

During 1960–1961 a small but significant number of white students joined African Americans in the sit-in movement. They and many others were also inspired by President Kennedy's direct appeals to their youthful idealism. Thousands enrolled in the Peace Corps and VISTA (Volunteers in Service to America), and others continued to participate in civil rights demonstrations. But as it became clear that politics was mixed with principle in the president's position on civil rights and later, as criticism of escalating military involvement in Vietnam mounted, more and more young people grew disillusioned with the government. Cynicism bred activism. By the mid-1960s a full-fledged youth revolt had erupted across the country. Rebellious youths flowed into two distinct yet frequently overlapping movements: the New Left and the counterculture.

THE NEW LEFT   The explicitly political strain of the youth revolt originated when Tom Hayden and Al Haber, two University of Michigan students, formed Students for a Democratic Society (SDS) in 1960. In 1962, Hayden and Haber convened a meeting of sixty activists at Port Huron, Michigan, where Hayden drafted what became known as the Port Huron Statement. It begins: "We are the people of this generation, bred in at least moderate comfort, housed in universities, looking uncomfortably to the world we inherit."

Hayden's manifesto focused on the absence of individual freedom in modern life. The country, he insisted, was dominated by huge organizational structures—governments, corporations, unions, universities—all of which conspired to oppress and alienate the individual. Inspired by the example of African American activism in the South, Hayden declared that students had the power to restore "participatory democracy" by wresting "control of the educational process from the administrative bureaucracy" and then forging links with other dissident movements. He and others adopted the term New Left to distinguish their efforts at grassroots democracy from those of the Old Left of the 1930s, which had espoused an orthodox Marxism.

In the fall of 1964, students at the University of California at Berkeley took Hayden's program to heart. Several of them had returned to the campus after spending the summer working with the SNCC voter-registration project in Mississippi, where three volunteers had been killed, dozens shot, and nearly 1,000 arrested. When UC Berkeley chancellor Clark Kerr announced that political demonstrations would no longer be allowed, several hundred students staged a sit-in. Soon thereafter over 2,000 more joined in. After a tense thirty-two-hour standoff the administration relented. Student groups then formed the free-speech movement.

The free-speech movement

Mario Savio, a founder of the free-speech movement, speaks at a rally at the University of California at Berkeley.

Led by Mario Savio, a philosophy major and compelling public speaker, the free-speech movement initially protested on behalf of students' rights. But it quickly grew into a more general criticism of the modern university and what Savio called the "depersonalized, unresponsive bureaucracy" infecting American life. In 1964, Savio led hundreds of students into UC Berkeley's administration building and organized a sit-in. In the early-morning hours, 600 policemen, dispatched by the governor, arrested the protesters.

The goals and tactics of the free-speech movement and SDS spread to colleges across the country. Issues large and small became the subject of student protest: unpopular faculty tenure decisions, mandatory ROTC (Reserve Officers' Training Corps) programs, dress codes, curfews, dormitory regulations.

Escalating U.S. involvement in Vietnam soon changed the students' agenda. With the dramatic expansion of the war after 1965, millions of young men faced the grim prospect of being drafted to fight in an increasingly unpopular war. In fact, however, the Vietnam conflict, like virtually every other war, was primarily a poor man's fight. Deferments enabled college students to postpone military service until they received their degree or reached the age of twenty-four; in 1965–1966, college students made up only 2 percent of all military inductees. In 1966, however, the Selective Service System modified the provisions so that even undergraduates were eligible for the draft.

As the war dragged on and opposition mounted, 200,000 young men simply refused to obey their draft notices, and some 4,000 of them served prison sentences. Another 56,000 men qualified for conscientious objector status during the Vietnam War, compared with only 7,600 during the Korean conflict. Still others left the country altogether—several thousand fled to Canada or Sweden—to avoid military service. The most popular way to avoid the draft was to flunk the physical examination. Whatever the preferred method, many students succeeded in avoiding military service. Of the 1,200 men in the Harvard senior class of 1970, only 56 served in the military, and just 2 of those went to Vietnam.

In the spring of 1967, 500,000 war protesters of all ages converged on Manhattan's Central Park, where the most popular chant was "Hey, hey, LBJ, how many kids did you kill today?" Dozens of young men ceremoniously burned their draft cards, igniting the so-called resistance phase of the antiwar movement. Thereafter a coalition of resistance groups around the country sponsored draft-card-burning rallies and sit-ins that led to numerous arrests. Meanwhile, some SDS leaders were growing even more militant. Inspired by the rhetoric and violence of black power spokesmen such as Stokely Carmichael, H. Rap Brown, and Huey Newton, Tom Hayden abandoned his earlier commitment to passive civil disobedience. Rap Brown told the white radicals to remember the heritage of John Brown: "Take up a gun and go shoot the enemy." As the SDS became more militant, it grew more centralized and authoritarian. Capitalist imperialism replaced university bureaucracy as the primary foe.

Throughout 1967 and 1968, the anti-war movement grew more volatile as inner-city ghettos were exploding in flames of racial violence. Frustration over patterns of discrimination in employment and housing and staggering rates of joblessness among inner-city African American youths provoked chaotic violence. "There was a sense everywhere, in 1968," the journalist Garry Wills wrote, "that things were giving way. That man had not only lost control of his history, but might never regain it."

During the eventful spring of 1968—when Lyndon Johnson announced that he would not run for reelection and Martin Luther King Jr. was assassinated—campus unrest enveloped the country. Over 200 major demonstrations took place. The turmoil reached a climax with the disruption of Columbia University. There Mark Rudd, an SDS leader, and a cadre of radicals occupied the president's office and classroom buildings. They also kidnapped a dean—all in protest of the university's decision to displace a near by African American

Students for a Democratic Society take over Columbia University

Mark Rudd, leader of SDS at Columbia University, talking to representatives of the media during student protests of university policies, April 1968.

neighborhood in order to build a new gymnasium. During the next week, more buildings were occupied, faculty and administrative offices were ransacked, and classes were canceled. University officials finally called in the New York City police. In the process of arresting the protesters, officers injured innocent bystanders. Such excessive force outraged many unaligned students, who then staged a strike that shut down the university for the remainder of the semester. The riotous events at Columbia buoyed militants across the nation. Similar clashes among students, administrators, and police occurred at Harvard, Cornell, and San Francisco State.

At the 1968 Democratic Convention in Chicago, the polarization of society reached a bizarre climax. Inside the tightly guarded convention hall, Democrats nominated Hubert Humphrey while on Chicago's streets the whole spectrum of anti-war dissenters gathered, from the earnest supporters of Senator Eugene McCarthy to the nihilistic Yippies, members of the new Youth International party. The Yippies were determined to create anarchy in the streets of Chicago. Abbie Hoffman, one of their leaders, explained that their "conception of revolution is that it's fun." The Yippies distributed a leaflet at the convention calling for the immediate legalization of marijuana and all psychedelic drugs, student-run schools, promiscuous sex, and the abolition of money.

The outlandish behavior of the Yippies and the other demonstrators provoked an equally outlandish response by Mayor Richard J. Daley and his army of city police. As a horrified television audience watched, many police officers went berserk, clubbing and gassing demonstrators as well as bystanders caught up in the melee. The spectacle lasted three days and seriously damaged Humphrey's presidential candidacy. The Chicago riots also angered many middle-class Americans, creating a backlash that Richard Nixon and the Republicans exploited at their nominating convention in Miami Beach. At the same time, the

Upheaval in Chicago

The violence that accompanied the 1968 Democratic National Convention in Chicago seared the nation.

riots fragmented the anti-war movement. Those groups committed to non-violent protest, while castigating the reactionary policies of Mayor Daley and the police, felt betrayed by the actions of the Yippies and other anarchist militants.

In 1968 the SDS fractured into rival factions, the most extreme of which called itself the Weathermen, a name derived from a lyric by the songwriter Bob Dylan: "You don't need a weather man to know which way the wind blows." These hardened young activists embarked on a campaign of violence and disruption, firebombing university buildings and killing innocent people—as well as several of their own. Government forces arrested most of the Weathermen, and the rest went underground. By 1971 the New Left was dead as a political movement. In large measure it had committed suicide by abandoning the pacifist principles that had originally inspired participants and given the movement moral legitimacy. The larger anti-war movement also began to fade. There would be a wave of student protests against the Nixon administration in 1970–1971, but thereafter campus unrest virtually disappeared as Nixon's initiatives related to the draft and the war defused the resistance movement.

If the social mood was changing during the early 1970s, a large segment of the public continued the quest for social justice. The burgeoning environmental movement attested to the continuity of sixties idealism. A *New York Times* survey of college campuses in 1969 revealed that many students were refocusing their attention on the environment. This new ecological awareness would blossom in the 1970s into one of the most compelling items on the nation's social agenda.

THE COUNTERCULTURE   The numbing events of 1968 led other disaffected activists away from radical politics altogether, toward another manifestation of the sixties youth revolt: the counterculture. Long hair on men and women, blue jeans, tie-dyed shirts, sandals, mind-altering drugs, rock music, and experimental living arrangements were more important than revolutionary ideology to the hippies, the direct descendants of the Beats of the 1950s. Advocates of the counterculture were, like their New Left peers, primarily well-educated middle-class young whites alienated by the Vietnam War, racism, political and parental demands, runaway technology, and a crass corporate mentality that equated the good life with material goods. In their view a complacent materialism had settled over urban and suburban life. But they were not attracted to organized political action. Instead, they eagerly embraced the credo outlined by the zany Harvard professor Timothy Leary: "Tune in, turn on, drop out."

For some the counterculture entailed the embrace of Asian mysticism. For many it meant the daily use of hallucinogenic drugs. Collective living in urban enclaves such as San Francisco's Haight-Ashbury district, New York's East Village, and Atlanta's Fourteenth Street was the rage for a time among hippies, until conditions grew so crowded, violent, and depressing that residents migrated elsewhere. Rural communes also attracted bourgeois rebels. During the 1960s and early 1970s, thousands of inexperienced romantics flocked to the countryside, eager to liberate themselves from parental and institutional restraints, live in harmony with nature, and coexist in an atmosphere of love and openness.

But only a handful of their utopian homesteads survived more than a few months. Rooted in the pleasure principle, rustic hippies were more self-indulgent than self-sufficient; they often produced more babies than bread. They fled conventional society, only to find themselves utterly dependent upon it, and they were soon panhandling on street corners or lined up at government offices, collecting welfare, unemployment compensation, and food stamps to help them survive the rigors of natural living.

Huge outdoor rock concerts were a popular source of community. The largest of these was the Woodstock Music and Art Fair. In August 1969 some 500,000 young people converged on a 600-acre farm near the tiny rural town of Bethel, New York. For three days the assembled flower children reveled in good music, cheap marijuana, and casual sex. "Everyone swam nude in the lake," a journalist reported. The country had never "seen a society so free of repression."

But the carefree spirit of the Woodstock festival was short-lived. When other concert promoters tried to replicate the scene four months later, this time at Altamont Speedway forty miles east of San Francisco, the counterculture encountered the criminal culture. The Rolling Stones rock band hired the Hells Angels motorcycle gang to provide "security" for their show. During the band's performance of "Under My Thumb," drunken white motorcyclists beat to death an eighteen-year-old African American man wielding a gun in front of the stage. Three other spectators were accidentally killed that night; much of the vitality and innocence of the counterculture died with them.

After 1969 the hippie phenomenon began to wane. The counterculture had become counterproductive and had developed both faddish and fashionable overtones. Entrepreneurs were quick to see profits in protest. Retailers developed a banner business in faded blue jeans, surplus army jackets, beads, incense, and sandals. Health-food stores and "head" shops appeared in shopping malls alongside Neiman Marcus and Sears. Rock-music groups,

Woodstock

The Woodstock music festival drew nearly half a million people to a farm in Bethel, New York. The concert was billed as three days of "peace, music, . . . and love."

for all their lyrical protests against the capitalist system, made millions from it. The search on the part of alienated youth for a better society and a good life was strewn with irony, hypocrisy, disillusionment, and tragedy.

FEMINISM   The seductive ideal of liberation spawned during the sixties helped accelerate a powerful women's rights crusade. Like the New Left, the new feminism drew much of its inspiration and many of its tactics from the civil rights movement. Its aim was to challenge the conventional cult of female domesticity that had prevailed since the 1950s.

The mainstream of the women's movement was led by Betty Friedan. Her influential book, *The Feminine Mystique* (1963), launched the new phase of female protest on a national level. During the 1950s, Friedan, a Smith College graduate, raised three children in a New York suburb. Still politically active but now socially domestic, she mothered her children, pampered her husband, "read *Vogue* under the hair dryer" in the beauty salon, and occasionally did some freelance writing. In 1957 she conducted a poll of her fellow Smith alumnae and discovered that despite the prevailing rhetoric about the happy suburban housewife, many well-educated women were in fact miserable. This revelation led to more research, which culminated in the publication of *The Feminine Mystique.*

Women, Friedan wrote, had actually lost ground during the years after World War II, when many left wartime employment and settled down in suburbia. A propaganda campaign engineered by advertisers and women's magazines encouraged them to do so by creating the "feminine mystique" of blissful domesticity. This notion that women were "gaily content in a world of bedroom, kitchen, sex, babies, and home" in fact served to imprison them.

Betty Friedan

Author of *The Feminine Mystique.*

In Friedan's view the middle-class home had become "a comfortable concentration camp" where women suffocated and stagnated in an atmosphere of mindless materialism, daytime television, and neighborhood gossip.

The Feminine Mystique, an immediate best seller, inspired many women who felt trapped in their domestic doldrums. Moreover, Friedan discovered that there were far more women working outside the home than the pervasive "feminine mystique" suggested. Many of these working women were frustrated by the demands of holding "two full-time jobs instead of just one—underpaid clerical worker and unpaid housekeeper."

In 1966, Friedan and other activists founded the National Organization for Women (NOW). NOW initially sought to end discrimination in the workplace on the basis of gender and went on to spearhead efforts to legalize abortion and obtain federal and state support for child-care centers.

In the early 1970s, members of Congress, the Supreme Court, and NOW advanced the cause of gender equality. Under Title IX of the Education Amendments of 1972, colleges were required to institute "affirmative-action" programs to ensure equal opportunities for women. Also in 1972, Congress overwhelmingly approved an equal-rights amendment to the federal constitution, which had been bottled up in a House committee for almost half a century. In 1973 the Supreme Court, in *Roe v. Wade*, struck down state laws

Feminist awakenings

In 1967, Syracuse University student Kathy Switzer challenged the Boston Marathon's tradition of excluding women. Officials tried to pull Switzer from the course, but with the aid of fellow runners she completed the race. Women did not become official entrants until 1971.

forbidding abortions during the first three months of pregnancy. Meanwhile, the all-male educational bastions, including Yale and Princeton, led a movement for coeducation that swept the country. "If the 1960s belonged to blacks," said one feminist, "the next ten years are ours."

By the end of the 1970s, however, sharp disputes between moderate and radical feminists had fragmented the women's movement. The movement's failure to broaden its appeal much beyond the confines of the middle class also caused reform efforts to stagnate. The equal-rights amendment, which had once seemed a straightforward assertion of equal opportunity ("Equality of rights under the law shall not be denied or abridged by the United States or by any State on account of sex") and assured of ratification, was stymied in several state legislatures. By 1982 it had died, several states short of passage. And the very success of NOW's efforts to liberalize local and state abortion laws generated a powerful backlash, especially among Catholics and fundamentalist Protestants, who mounted a potent "right-to-life" crusade that helped ignite the conservative political resurgence in the 1970s and thereafter.

Yet the success of the women's movement endured long after the militant rhetoric had evaporated. A growing presence in the labor force brought women a greater share of economic and political influence. By 1976 over half the married women and nine out of ten female college graduates were employed outside the home, a development that one economist called "the single most outstanding phenomenon of this century." Most career women, however, did not regard themselves as feminists; they took jobs because they and their families needed the money to achieve higher levels of material comfort. Whatever their motives, women were changing traditional gender roles and child-bearing practices to accommodate the two-career family and the sexual revolution.

THE SEXUAL REVOLUTION AND THE PILL   The feminist movement coincided with the so-called sexual revolution, a much-discussed loosening of traditional restrictions on social behavior. Young people opposed to the conflict in Vietnam chanted "Make Love, Not War." Other members of the counterculture promoted "free love" as an alternative to a repressive, materialistic capitalist society. Activists promoting more permissive sexual attitudes staged rallies, formed organizations, engaged in civil disobedience, filed suits against prevailing laws, and flouted social norms.

The publicity given to the sexual revolution exaggerated its scope and depth, but the movement did help generate two major cultural changes: society became more tolerant of premarital sex, and women became more sexually active. Between 1960 and 1975 the number of college women engaging in sexual intercourse doubled, from 27 percent to 50 percent. What facilitated this change was a scientific breakthrough in contraception: the birth-control pill.

Approved by the Food and Drug Administration in 1960, the pill, as it came to be known, blocks ovulation by releasing synthetic hormones into a

Birth control

In an effort to spread the word about birth-control options, Planned Parenthood in 1967 displayed posters like this one in New York City buses.

woman's body. Initially, birth-control pills were available only to married couples, but that restriction soon ended. Widespread access to the pill gave women a greater sense of sexual freedom than had any previous contraceptive device. It also contibuted to a rise in sexually transmitted diseases. Yet many women viewed the birth-control pill as a godsend. "When the pill came out, it was a savior," recalled Eleanor Smeal, president of the Feminist Majority Foundation. "The whole country was waiting for it. I can't even describe to you how excited people were."

The pill quickly became the most popular birth-control method. In 1960 the U.S. birth rate was 3.6 children per woman. By 1970 it had plummeted to 2.5 children, and since 1980 it has remained slightly below 2. Eight out of ten women have taken birth-control pills at some time in their lives. Clare Boothe Luce, a congresswoman, ambassador, journalist, and playwright, viewed the advent of the pill as a key element in the broader women's movement: "Modern woman is at last free as a man is free, to dispose of her own body, to earn her living, to pursue the improvement of her mind, to try a successful career."

HISPANIC RIGHTS   The activism that animated the student revolt, the civil rights movement, and the crusade for women's rights soon spread to various ethnic minority groups. *Hispanic*, a term used in the United States to refer to people who are from, or trace their ancestry to, Spanish-speaking Latin America or Spain, came into increasing use after 1945 in conjunction with growing efforts to promote economic and social justice for such people. (Although frequently used as a synonym for Hispanic, the term *Latino* technically refers only to people of Latin American descent.) The labor shortages during World War II had led defense industries to offer Hispanic Americans their first significant access to skilled-labor jobs. And as was the case with African Americans, service in the military during the war years helped to heighten an American identity among Hispanic Americans and excite their desire for equal rights and social opportunities.

But equality was elusive. After World War II, Hispanic Americans still faced widespread discrimination in hiring, housing, and education. Poverty was widespread. In 1960, for example, the median income of a Mexican American family was only 62 percent of the median income of a family in the general population. Hispanic American activists during the 1950s and 1960s mirrored the efforts of black civil rights leaders. They, too, denounced segregation, promoted efforts to improve the quality of public education, and struggled to increase Hispanic American political influence and economic opportunities.

One of the most popular initiatives was the use of the term *Chicano* as an inclusive label for all Mexican immigrants, Spanish Americans in New Mexico as well as old Californios (descendants of the inhabitants of California before it was seized by the United States, most of whom were Indians or of mixed ancestry) and Tejanos (descendants of the inhabitants of Texas before it became independent). The word *Chicano* was originally Mexican slang for a clumsy person. Over the years, Anglo Americans had fastened upon the term as a pejorative reference. Now it took on a positive connotation. In southern California, members of Young Citizens for Community Action re-formed as Young Chicanos for Community Action, or the Brown Berets, a social-service group designed to promote greater self-reliance and local involvement within Mexican American neighborhoods. Members protested the disproportionate number of Hispanics being killed in the Vietnam War and demanded improvements in their neighborhood schools.

Unlike their African American counterparts, however, Chicano leaders faced an awkward dilemma: what should they do about the continuing stream of undocumented Mexicans flowing across the border? Many Mexican Americans argued that their hopes for economic advancement and social equality were put at risk by the daily influx of undocumented Mexican laborers willing to accept low-paying jobs. Mexican American leaders thus helped end the bracero program in 1964 (which trucked in contract day laborers from Mexico at harvesttime) and in 1962 formed the United Farm Workers (UFW), originally the National Farm Workers Association, to represent Mexican American migrant workers.

The founder of the UFW was the charismatic Cesar Chavez. Born in Yuma, Arizona, in 1927 to Mexican immigrants, Chavez moved with his family to California in 1939. There they joined thousands of other migrant farmworkers, moving from job to job, living in tents, cars, or ramshackle cabins. In 1944, at age seventeen, Chavez joined the navy. After the war he married and found work, first as a sharecropper tending strawberries and then as a migrant laborer in apricot orchards. In 1952, Chavez joined the Community Service Organization (CSO), a social-service group that sought to educate and organize the migrant poor so that they could become self-reliant. He founded new CSO chapters and was named general director in 1958.

Chavez left the organization in 1962 when it refused to back his proposal to establish a union for farmworkers. Other CSO leaders believed that it was impossible to organize migrant workers into an effective union. They thought migrants were too mobile, too poor, too illiterate, too ethnically diverse, and too easily replaced by braceros. Moreover, farmworkers did not

United Farm Workers

Cesar Chavez (center) with organizers of the grape boycott. In 1968, Chavez ended a three-week fast by taking Communion and breaking bread with Senator Robert Kennedy.

enjoy protected status under the National Labor Relations Act of 1935 (the Wagner Act). Unlike industrial laborers they were not guaranteed the right to organize or the right to receive a minimum wage. Nor did federal regulations govern the safety of their workplace.

Despite such obstacles, Chavez resolved to organize migrant farmworkers. His fledgling National Farm Workers Association gained national attention in 1965 when it joined a strike by Filipino farmworkers against the corporate grape growers in California's San Joaquin Valley. Chavez's energy and Catholic piety, his insistence upon nonviolent tactics and his reliance upon college-student volunteers, his skillful alliance with organized labor and religious groups—all combined to attract media interest and popular support. Soon the UFW began organizing migrant workers in the fields of the Salinas Valley.

Still, the grape strike itself brought no tangible gains. So Chavez organized a nationwide consumer boycott of grapes. In 1970 the grape strike and the consumer boycott brought twenty-six grape growers to the bargaining table. They signed formal contracts recognizing the UFW, and soon migrant workers throughout the West were benefiting from Chavez's strenuous efforts on their behalf. Wages increased, and working conditions improved. In 1975 the California state legislature passed a bill that required growers to bargain collectively with the elected representatives of the farmworkers.

The chief strength of the Hispanic rights movement lay less in the duplication of civil rights strategies than in the rapid growth of the Hispanic population. In 1960, Hispanics in the United States numbered slightly more than 3 million; by 1970 their numbers had increased to 9 million; and by 2006 they numbered over 40 million, making them the country's largest minority. By 1980 aspiring presidential candidates were openly courting the

Hispanic vote. The voting power of Hispanics and their concentration in states with key electoral votes has helped give the Hispanic point of view significant political clout.

NATIVE AMERICAN RIGHTS   American Indians—many of whom had begun calling themselves Native Americans—also emerged as a political force in the late 1960s. Two conditions combined to make Indian rights a priority: first, whites felt a persistent sense of guilt for the destructive policies of their ancestors toward a people who had, after all, been here first; second, the plight of the Native American minority was more desperate than that of any other group in the country. Indian unemployment was 10 times the national rate, life expectancy was 20 years lower than the national average, and the suicide rate was a whopping 100 times higher than the rate for whites.

Although President Lyndon Johnson recognized the poverty of the Native Americans and attempted to funnel federal anti-poverty-program funds into reservations, militants within the Indian community grew impatient with the pace of change. They organized protests and demonstrations against local, state, and federal agencies. In 1963 two Chippewas (or Ojibwas) living in Minneapolis, George Mitchell and Dennis Banks, founded the American Indian Movement (AIM) to promote "red power." The leaders of AIM occupied Alcatraz Island in San Francisco Bay in 1969, claiming the site "by right of discovery." And in 1972 a sit-in at the Department of the Interior's Bureau of Indian Affairs (BIA) in Washington attracted national attention. The BIA was then—and still is—widely viewed as the worst-managed federal agency. Instead of finding creative ways to promote tribal autonomy and economic self-sufficiency, the BIA has served as a classic example of government inefficiency and paternalism gone awry.

In 1973, AIM led 200 Sioux in the occupation of the tiny village of Wounded Knee, South Dakota, where the Seventh Cavalry massacred a Sioux village in 1890. Outraged by the light sentences given a group of local whites who had killed a Sioux in 1972, the organizers also sought to draw attention to the plight of the Indians living on the reservation there. Half of the families were dependent upon government welfare checks, alcoholism was rampant, and over 80 percent of the children had dropped out of school. After the militants took eleven hostages, federal marshals and FBI agents surrounded the encampment. For ten weeks the two sides engaged in a tense standoff. When AIM leaders tried to bring in food and supplies, a shoot-out resulted, with one Indian killed and another wounded. Soon thereafter the tense confrontation ended with a government promise to reexamine Indian treaty rights.

Wounded Knee

Instigating a standoff with the FBI, members of AIM and local Oglala Sioux occupied the town of Wounded Knee, South Dakota, in March 1973 in an effort to focus attention on poverty and rampant alcoholism among Indians on reservations.

Indian protesters subsequently discovered a more effective tactic than direct action and sit-ins: they went into federal courts armed with copies of old treaties and demanded that those documents become the basis for restitution. In Alaska, Maine, South Carolina, and Massachusetts they won significant settlements that provided legal recognition of their tribal rights and financial compensation at levels that upgraded the standard of living on several reservations.

GAY RIGHTS   The liberationist impulses of the 1960s also encouraged homosexuals to organize and assert their right to equal treatment. On June 27, 1969, New York City police raided the Stonewall Inn, a male gay bar in Greenwich Village. The patrons fought back, and the struggle spilled into the streets. Hundreds of other gays and their supporters joined the fracas against the police. Rioting lasted throughout the weekend. When it ended, homosexuals had forged a new sense of solidarity and a new organization, the Gay Liberation Front. "Gay is good for all of us," proclaimed one of its members. "The artificial categories 'heterosexual' and 'homosexual' have been laid on us by a sexist society."

As news of the Stonewall riots spread across the country, the gay rights movement assumed national proportions. One of its main tactics was to encourage people to "come out," to make public their homosexuality. This was by no means an easy decision, for professing gays faced social ostracism, physical assault, exclusion from the military and civil service, and discrimination in the workplace. Yet despite the risks, thousands of homosexuals did come out. By 1973 almost 800 gay organizations had been formed across the country, and every major city had a visible gay community and cultural life.

As was the case with the civil rights crusade and the women's movement, however, the campaign for gay rights soon suffered from internal divisions and a conservative backlash. Gay activists engaged in fractious disputes over tactics and objectives, and conservative moralists and Christian fundamentalists launched a nationwide counterattack. By the end of the 1970s, the gay movement had lost its initial momentum and was struggling to salvage many of its hard-won gains.

NIXON AND VIETNAM

The numerous liberation movements of the 1960s transformed the tone and texture of social life. By the early 1970s, however, the national mood was swinging back toward conservatism. The election of Richard Nixon in 1968 and the rise of George Wallace as a national political force reflected the emergence of the "silent majority," those predominantly white working-class and middle-class citizens who were determined to regain control of a society they feared was awash in permissiveness, anarchy, and tyranny by the minority. Many among the "silent majority" also believed that Lyndon Johnson's Great Society programs were ineffective and inefficient. Such attitudes were highlighted in one of the period's most popular television shows, *All in the Family*, whose central character, Archie Bunker, was a reactionary lower-middle-class husband outraged by the permissiveness of modern society and the radicalism of young people. Large as the gap was between the "silent majority" and the forces of dissent, both sides agreed that the Vietnam War remained the dominant event of the time. Until the war ended and all troops had returned home, the nation would find it difficult to achieve the equilibrium that the new president had promised.

GRADUAL WITHDRAWAL   Looking back on the Vietnam War, former secretary of state and national security adviser Henry Kissinger called it a "nightmare": "We should have never been there at all." But when Richard

Nixon was inaugurated as president in January 1969, he inherited the nightmare; there were 530,000 U.S. troops in Vietnam. Nixon believed that "there's no way to win the war. But we can't say that of course" because the United States needed to "keep some bargaining leverage" at the negotiating table. During the 1968 presidential campaign, he had claimed to have a secret plan that would bring "peace with honor" in Vietnam. He insisted that the United States could not simply "cut and run," leaving the 17 million South Vietnamese to a cruel fate under Communist tyranny. Yet he assured an aide that "I'm not going to end up like LBJ, holed up in the White House afraid to show my face on the street. I'm going to stop that war. Fast."

Peace, however, was long in coming and not very honorable. Nixon and Kissinger overestimated the ability of the Soviets to exert pressure on the North Vietnamese to sign a negotiated settlement, just as they misread their own ability to manipulate the South Vietnamese government. By the time a settlement was reached, in 1973, another 20,000 Americans had died, the morale of the U.S. military had been shattered, millions of Asians had been killed or wounded, and fighting continued in Southeast Asia. In the end, Nixon's policy gained nothing the president could not have accomplished in 1969.

The trauma of Vietnam

Even as the Nixon administration began a phased withdrawal of U.S. troops from Vietnam, the war took a heavy toll on Vietnamese and Americans alike.

The new Vietnam policy implemented by Nixon and Kissinger moved along three fronts. First, U.S. negotiators in Paris demanded the withdrawal of Communist forces from South Vietnam and the preservation of the U.S.-backed regime of President Nguyen Van Thieu. The North Vietnamese and Viet Cong negotiators insisted on retaining a Communist military presence in the south and reunifying the Vietnamese people under a government dominated by the Communists. There was no common ground on which to come together. Hidden from public awareness and from America's South Vietnamese allies were secret meetings between Henry Kissinger, then Nixon's national security adviser, and the North Vietnamese.

On the second front, Nixon tried to quell domestic unrest stemming from the war. He labeled the anti-war movement a "brotherhood of the misguided, the mistaken, the well-meaning, and the malevolent." He sought to defuse the anti-war movement by reducing the number of U.S. troops in Vietnam, justifying the reduction as the natural result of "Vietnamization"—the equipping and training of the South Vietnamese to assume the burden of ground combat in place of Americans. From a peak of 560,000 in 1969, U.S. combat troops were withdrawn at a steady pace that matched almost precisely the pace of the buildup from 1965 to 1969. By 1973 only 50,000 troops remained in Vietnam. In 1969, Nixon also established a draft lottery system that eliminated many inequities and clarified the likelihood of being drafted: only nineteen-year-olds with low lottery numbers would have to go—and in 1973 the president did away with the draft altogether by creating an all-volunteer military. Nixon was more successful in reducing anti-war activity than in forcing concessions from the North Vietnamese negotiators in Paris.

On the third front, while reducing the number of U.S. combat troops, Nixon and Kissinger expanded the air war over Vietnam to persuade the enemy to come to terms. Heavy bombing of North Vietnam was part of what Nixon called his "madman theory." He wanted the North Vietnamese leaders to believe that he "might do *anything* to stop the war." In March 1969 the United States began a fourteen-month-long bombing campaign aimed at Communist forces in Cambodia. Congress did not learn of those secret raids until 1970, although the total tonnage of bombs dropped was four times that dropped on Japan during World War II. Still Hanoi's leaders did not flinch. Then, on April 30, 1970, Nixon announced what he called an "incursion" into "neutral" Cambodia by U.S. troops to "clean out" North Vietnamese military staging areas. The head of Cambodia's government for two decades, Prince Norodom Sihanouk, had previously objected to raids into his country, but a coup by General Lon Nol had replaced Sihanouk earlier in the spring, clearing the way for the American invasion. Nixon knew that sending troops into Cambodia would ignite ferocious criticism. Secretary of State William Rogers predicted that "this will make the [anti-war] students puke." Nixon told Kissinger, who strongly endorsed the decision to extend the fighting into Cambodia, "If this doesn't work, it'll be your ass, Henry."

DIVISIONS AT HOME   Nixon's slow withdrawal of combat forces from Vietnam had a devastating effect on the military's morale and reputation. "No one wants to be the last grunt to die in this lousy war," said one soldier. Between 1969 and 1971 there were 730 reported fragging incidents, efforts by troops to kill or injure their own officers, usually with fragmentation grenades. Drug abuse became a major problem in the armed forces. In 1971 four times as many troops were hospitalized for drug overdoses as for combat-related wounds.

Back on the home front, revelations of suppressed reports of atrocities in Vietnam caused even the staunchest supporters of the war to wince. Late in 1969 the story of the My Lai Massacre broke in the press, plunging the country into two years of exposure to the gruesome tale of Lieutenant William Calley, who ordered the murder of 347 civilians in the village of My Lai in 1968. Twenty-five army officers were charged with complicity in the massacre and subsequent cover-up, but only Calley was convicted; Nixon later granted him parole.

The loudest public outcry against Nixon's Indochina policy occurred in the wake of the Cambodian "incursion." In the spring of 1970, campuses across the country exploded in what the president of Columbia University called "the most disastrous month of May in the history of American higher education." Student protests led to the closing of hundreds of colleges and universities. At Kent State University, the Ohio National Guard was called in to quell rioting, during which the building housing the campus ROTC (Reserve

Kent State University

National guardsmen shot and killed four bystanders during anti-war demonstrations on the campus of Kent State University in Ohio.

Officers' Training Corps) was burned down by anti-war protesters. The poorly trained guardsmen panicked and opened fire on the rock-throwing demonstrators, killing four student bystanders. Nixon was visibly shaken by what one aide called the "absolute public hysteria" unleashed by the Cambodian invasion. Although an official investigation of the Kent State episode condemned the "casual and indiscriminate shooting," polls indicated that the public supported the National Guard; students had "got what they were asking for." Eleven days after the Kent State tragedy, on May 15, Mississippi highway patrolmen riddled a dormitory at Jackson State College with bullets, killing two students. In New York City, anti-war demonstrators who gathered to protest the deaths at Kent State and the invasion of Cambodia were attacked by "hard-hat" construction workers, who forced the protesters to disperse and then marched on City Hall to raise the flag, which had been lowered to half staff in mourning for the Kent State victims.

The following year in June, the *New York Times* began publishing excerpts from *The History of the U.S. Decision-Making Process of Vietnam Policy*, a secret Defense Department study commissioned by Robert McNamara before his resignation as Lyndon Johnson's secretary of defense in 1968. The so-called Pentagon Papers, leaked to the press by a former Defense Department official, Daniel Ellsberg, confirmed what many critics of the war had long suspected: Congress and the public had not received the full story on the Gulf of Tonkin incident of 1964, and contingency plans for American entry into the war were being drawn up while President Johnson was promising that combat troops would never be sent to Vietnam. Moreover, there was no plan for bringing the war to an end so long as the North Vietnamese persisted. Although the Pentagon Papers dealt with events only up to 1965, the Nixon administration blocked their publication, arguing that they endangered national security and that their publication would prolong the war. By a vote of 6 to 3, the Supreme Court ruled against the government. Newspapers throughout the country began publication of the controversial documents the next day.

WAR WITHOUT END   The mounting social divisions at home and the approach of the 1972 presidential election influenced the negotiations in Paris between the United States and representatives of North Vietnam. In the summer of 1972, Henry Kissinger again began meeting privately with Le Duc Tho, the North Vietnamese negotiator, and he now dropped his insistence upon the removal of all North Vietnamese troops from the south before the withdrawal of the remaining U.S. troops. On October 26, only a week before the U.S. presidential election, Kissinger announced, "Peace is at hand." But this was a cynical ploy to win votes. Several days earlier the Thieu regime in South Vietnam had rejected the Kissinger plan for a cease-fire, fearful that the presence of North Vietnamese troops in the south would virtually guarantee a Communist victory. The Paris peace talks broke off on December 16, and two days later the newly reelected Nixon ordered massive bombing of Hanoi and Haiphong, the two largest cities in North Vietnam. These so-called Christmas bombings and the simultaneous mining of North Vietnamese harbors aroused worldwide protest.

But the bombings also made the North Vietnamese more flexible at the negotiating table. The "Christmas bombings" stopped on December 29, and the talks in Paris soon resumed. On January 27, 1973, the United States, North and South Vietnam, and the Viet Cong signed an "agreement on ending the war and restoring peace in Vietnam." While Nixon and Kissinger claimed that the bombing had brought North Vietnam to its senses, in truth the North Vietnamese never altered their basic stance; they kept 150,000 troops in the south and remained committed to the reunification of Vietnam under one government. What had changed since the previous fall was the willingness of the South Vietnamese, who were never allowed to participate in the negotiations, to accept these terms, albeit reluctantly, on the basis of Nixon's promise that the United States would respond "with full force" to any Communist violation of the agreement. Kissinger had little confidence that the treaty provisions would enable South Vietnam to survive on its own. He told a White House staffer, "If they're lucky, they can hold out for a year and a half."

On March 29, 1973, the last U.S. combat troops left Vietnam. On that same day almost 600 American prisoners of war, most of them downed pilots, were released from Hanoi. Within months, however, the cease-fire in Vietnam collapsed, the war between north and south resumed, and the Communist forces gained the upper hand. In Cambodia (renamed the Khmer Republic after it fell to the Communists and now called Kampuchea) and Laos, where fighting had been more sporadic, a Communist victory also seemed inevitable. In 1975 the North Vietnamese launched a full-scale armored invasion, and South Vietnamese president Thieu appealed to Washington for the promised U.S. assistance. Congress refused. The much-mentioned "peace with honor" had proved to be, in the words of one CIA official, only a "decent interval"—enough time for the United States to extricate itself from Vietnam before the collapse of the South Vietnamese government. On April 30, 1975, Americans watched on television as North Vietnamese tanks rolled into Saigon, soon to be renamed Ho Chi Minh City, and helicopters lifted

Panic amid the withdrawal from Saigon

Soldiers block people from climbing over the walls of the U.S. embassy in Saigon, South Vietnam, in 1975. South Vietnamese were seeking to flee before the Communist forces seized the city.

the U.S. embassy officials to ships waiting offshore. In those desperate, chaotic final moments, terrified South Vietnamese fought to get on board the departing helicopters, for they knew that the Communists would be merciless victors.

The longest war in American history was finally over, leaving in its wake a bitter legacy. During the period of U.S. involvement in the fighting, almost 2 million combatants and civilians were killed on both sides. North Vietnam absorbed incredible losses—some 600,000 soldiers and countless civilians killed. More than 58,000 Americans died in Vietnam, 300,000 were wounded, 2,500 were declared missing, almost 100,000 returned missing one or more limbs, and over 150,000 combat veterans suffered drug or alcohol addiction or severe psychological disorders. Most of the Vietnam veterans readjusted well to civilian life, but even they carried for years the stigma of a lost war.

The "loss" of the war and revelations of American atrocities such as those at My Lai eroded respect for the military so thoroughly that many young people came to regard military service as corrupting and ignoble. The Vietnam War, initially described as a crusade on behalf of democratic ideals, instead suggested that democracy was not easily transferable to third world regions that lacked any historical experience with representative government. Fought to show the world that the United States would be steadfast in containing the spread of communism, instead the war sapped the national will and fragmented the national consensus that had governed foreign affairs since 1947. It also changed the balance of power in domestic politics. Not only did the war undermine Lyndon Johnson's presidency; it also created enduring fissures in the Democratic party. Said anti-war senator and 1972 Democratic presidential candidate George McGovern, "The Vietnam tragedy is at the root of the confusion and division of the Democratic party. It tore up our souls."

Most people at war's end wanted to put Vietnam behind them and forget. Although subsequent debates over foreign policy in the Middle East, Africa, and Latin America frequently referred to "the lessons of Vietnam," the phrase was used by different factions for diametrically opposed purposes, ranging from refusal to commit any American troops and resources in El Salvador and Nicaragua to an insistence on massive military commitments unfettered by any presidential restrictions that might preclude outright victory. "In the end, then," one journalist wrote concerning the Vietnam era, "there was no end at all."

NIXON AND MIDDLE AMERICA

Richard Nixon had been elected in 1968 as the representative of middle America, those middle-class citizens fed up with the liberal politics and radical culture of the 1960s. Nixon selected men for his cabinet and White House staff who would restore conservative values and carry out his orders with blind obedience. John Mitchell, the gruff attorney general who had been a senior partner in Nixon's New York law firm, was the new president's closest confidant. H. R. (Bob) Haldeman, an imperious former advertising executive, served as Nixon's chief of staff. As Haldeman explained, "Every President needs a son of a bitch, and I'm Nixon's. I'm his buffer, I'm his bastard." He was succeeded in 1973 by General Alexander Haig, whom Nixon described as "the meanest, toughest, most ambitious son of a bitch I ever knew." John Ehrlichman, a Seattle attorney and college schoolmate of Haldeman's, served as chief domestic-policy adviser. As secretary of state, Nixon tapped his old friend William Rogers, who had served as attorney general under Eisenhower. Rogers's control over foreign policy was quickly pre-empted by Henry Kissinger, a distinguished Harvard political scientist who served as national security adviser before becoming secretary of state in 1973. Kissinger came to dominate the Nixon administration's diplomatic planning and emerged as one of the most respected and internationally famous members of the staff. Nixon often had to mediate the tensions between Rogers and Kissinger, noting that Rogers considered the German-born Kissinger "Machiavellian, deceitful, egotistical, arrogant, and insulting," while Kissinger viewed Rogers as "vain, emotional, unable to keep a secret, and hopelessly dominated by the State Department bureaucracy."

DOMESTIC AFFAIRS   A major reason for Richard Nixon's election in 1968 was the effective "southern strategy" fashioned by his campaign staffers. To garner support among Republican delegates from the South and then win over southern voters in the election, Nixon had assured conservatives that he would slow federal enforcement of civil rights laws and appoint pro-southern justices to the Supreme Court. Once in office, Nixon followed through on his pledges. He appointed no African Americans to his cabinet and refused to meet with the Congressional Black Caucus. In 1970 he launched a concerted effort to block congressional renewal of the Voting Rights Act of 1965 and delay implementation of court orders requiring the desegregation of school districts in Mississippi. Sixty-five lawyers in the Justice Department signed a letter of protest against the administration's stance. The Democratic Congress then extended the Voting Rights Act over Nixon's veto. The Supreme Court, in the first decision made under the new chief justice, Warren Burger—a Nixon appointee—mandated the integration of the Mississippi public schools. In *Alexander v. Holmes County Board of Education* (1969), a unanimous Court ordered a quick end to segregation. During Nixon's first term and despite his wishes, more schools were desegregated than in all the Kennedy-Johnson years combined.

Critics of integration

Demonstrators at the Boston State House protest forced integration of the school system, May 1973.

Nixon also failed in his attempts to block desegregation efforts in urban areas. The Burger Court ruled unanimously in *Swann v. Charlotte-Mecklenburg Board of Education* (1971) that school systems must bus students out of their neighborhoods if necessary to achieve racial integration. Protest over desegregation now began to erupt more in the North, the Midwest, and the Southwest than in the South as white families in Boston, Denver, and other cities denounced the destruction of "the neighborhood school." Angry parents in Pontiac, Michigan, firebombed school buses.

Nixon asked Congress to impose a moratorium on all busing orders by the federal courts. The House of Representatives, equally attuned to voter outrage at busing to achieve racial integration, went along. But a Senate filibuster blocked the president's anti-busing bill. Busing opponents won a limited victory when the Supreme Court ruled, in *Milliken v. Bradley* (1974), that desegregation plans in Detroit requiring the transfer of students from the inner city to the suburbs were unconstitutional. This landmark case, along with the *Regents of the University of California v. Bakke* (1978) decision, which restricted the use of college-admissions quotas to achieve racial balance, marked the transition of desegregation from an issue of simple justice to a more tangled thicket of conflicting group and individual rights.

President Nixon invented several names for his domestic program. At one point it was called the New Federalism and promised to "start resources and power flowing back from Washington to the states and to the people." To that end in 1972 he pushed through Congress a five-year revenue-sharing plan that would distribute $30 billion of federal revenues to the states for use as they saw fit. At another point, Nixon called for a "new American Revolution" to revive traditional values. These catchphrases never caught on as the New Frontier or the Great Society had, most likely because Nixon's domestic program was a hodgepodge of reactionary and progressive initiatives. His speechwriter William Safire explained that although Nixon's "heart was on the right, his head was, with FDR, slightly left of center." Nixon was a shrewd—and often devious—pragmatist who juggled opposing positions in an effort to maintain public support. He was, said the journalist Tom Wicker, "at once liberal and conservative, generous and begrudging, cynical and idealistic, choleric and calm, resentful and forgiving." Nixon also had to deal with a stern political fact: the Democrats controlled both houses of Congress during his first term.

The Democratic Congress moved forward with new legislation: the right of eighteen-year-olds to vote in national elections (1970), and in all elections under the Twenty-sixth Amendment (1971); increases in Social Security benefits indexed to the inflation rate and a rise in food-stamp funding; the

Occupational Safety and Health Act (1970); the Clean Air Act (1970); new bills to control water pollution (1970 and 1972); and the Federal Election Campaign Act (1971), which modified the rules of campaign finance. These measures accounted for a more rapid rise in spending on social programs than President Lyndon Johnson's Great Society programs had.

ECONOMIC MALAISE The major domestic development during the Nixon years was a floundering economy. Overheated by the expense of the Vietnam War, the annual inflation rate began to rise in 1967, when it was at 3 percent. By 1973 it was at 9 percent; a year later it was at 12 percent, and it remained in double digits for most of the 1970s. The Dow Jones average of major industrial stocks fell by 36 percent between 1968 and 1970, its steepest decline in more than thirty years. Meanwhile unemployment, at a low of 3.3 percent when Nixon took office, climbed to 6 percent by the end of 1970 and threatened to keep rising. Somehow the economy was undergoing a recession and an inflation at the same time. Economists coined the term *stagflation* to describe the syndrome that defied the orthodox laws of economics.

The economic malaise had at least three deep-rooted causes. First, the Johnson administration had attempted to pay for both the Great Society

Oil crisis, 1973

The scarcity of oil was dealt with by the rationing of gasoline. Gas stations, such as this one in Colorado, closed on Sundays to conserve supplies.

social-welfare programs and the war in Vietnam without a major tax increase, thereby generating larger federal deficits, a major expansion of the money supply, and price inflation. Second and more important, by the late 1960s U.S. goods faced stiff competition in international markets from West Germany, Japan, and other emerging industrial powers. American technological and economic superiority was no longer unchallenged. Third, the economy had depended heavily upon cheap sources of energy; no other nation was more dependent upon the automobile and the automobile industry, and no other nation was more careless in its use of fossil fuels in factories and homes.

Just as domestic petroleum reserves began to dwindle and dependence upon foreign sources increased, the Organization of Petroleum Exporting Countries (OPEC) resolved to use its huge oil supplies as a political and economic weapon. In 1973, after the United States sent massive aid to Israel after a devastating Syrian-Egyptian attack on Yom Kippur, the holiest day on the Jewish calendar, OPEC announced that it would not sell oil to nations supporting Israel and that it was raising its prices by 400 percent. American motorists thereafter faced long lines at gas stations, and factories cut production.

Another condition leading to stagflation was the flood of new workers—mainly baby boomers and women—entering the labor market. From 1965 to 1980, the workforce grew by 40 percent, almost 30 million workers, a number greater than the total labor force of France or West Germany. The number of new jobs could not keep up, leaving many unemployed. At the same time, worker productivity declined, further increasing inflation in the face of rising demand.

Stagflation posed a new set of economic problems, but Nixon responded erratically and ineffectively, trying old remedies for a new problem. First he tried to reduce the federal deficit by raising taxes and cutting the budget. When the Democratic Congress refused to cooperate with that approach, he encouraged the Federal Reserve Board to reduce the money supply by raising interest rates. The stock market immediately collapsed, and the economy plunged into the "Nixon recession."

A sense of desperation seized the White House. In 1969, when asked about government restrictions on wages and prices, Nixon had been unequivocal: "Controls. Oh, my God, no! . . . We'll never go to controls." But in 1971 he reversed himself. He froze all wages and prices for ninety days and announced that the United States would no longer convert dollars into gold for foreign banks. The dollar, its link to gold severed, now drifted lower on world currency exchanges. After ninety days, Nixon established mandatory guidelines for subsequent wage and price increases under the supervision of a federal agency. Still the economy floundered. By 1973 the wage and price guidelines were made voluntary and were therefore almost entirely ineffective.

ENVIRONMENTAL PROTECTION   The OPEC oil boycott and price increase fueled an energy crisis in the United States. People began to realize that natural resources were not infinitely expendable. "Although it's positively un-American to think so," said one sociologist, "the environmental movement and energy shortage have forced us all to accept a sense of our limits, to lower our expectations, to seek prosperity through conservation rather than growth."

The widespread recognition that America faced limits to economic growth fueled broad support for environmental protection in the early 1970s. The realization that cities and industrial development were damaging the environment and altering the earth's ecology was not new: Rachel Carson's pathbreaking book *Silent Spring* (1962) had sounded the warning years earlier. But in Nixon's first term the Democratic-controlled Congress took concerted action, passing several acts to protect and clean up the environment. Bowing to pressure from both parties, Nixon told an aide to "keep me out of trouble on environmental issues." Ever the pragmatic politician, the president recognized that the public mood was shifting toward greater environmental protections. So he reluctantly signed the amended Endangered Species Preservation Act in late 1969 and the National Environmental Policy Act in early 1970. The latter legislation created a Council on Environmental Quality in the White House that reported annually to Congress and required environmental-impact studies prior to any federal construction project. In 1970, Nixon also signed legislation creating a federal Environmental Protection Agency and a National Oceanic and Atmospheric Administration.

As stagflation persisted into the middle and late 1970s, corporate criticism that environmental regulations were cutting into jobs and profit margins

Environmental awareness

An Earth Day demonstration dramatizing the dangers of air pollution, April 1972.

grew more persuasive, especially when the staggering cost of cleaning up accumulated toxic waste sites became known. "Why worry about the long run," said one unemployed steelworker in 1976, "when you're out of work right now." Polls showed that protection of the environment remained a high priority among a majority of Americans but few were willing to suffer a cutback in their standard of living to achieve that goal. People still lived for the moment. "It was," bemoaned one journalist, "as if passengers knew they were boarding the *Titanic*, but preferred to jostle with one another for first class accommodations so they might enjoy as much of the voyage as possible."

NIXON TRIUMPHANT

Richard Nixon was the first president since Eisenhower in 1957 to confront a Congress under the control of the opposition party. It followed that he focused his energies on foreign policy, where presidential initiatives were less encumbered. In tandem with Henry Kissinger, he achieved several major breakthroughs. He also continued to support the Apollo space program to beat the Soviets to the moon. In July 1969 the astronaut Neil Armstrong became the first person to walk on the moon.

This extraordinary technological achievement boosted American spirits at a time when troops were mired in Vietnam, cities were boiling over in

Race to the moon

In July 1969 the Apollo space program begun by President Kennedy reached its goal: putting a man on the moon.

racial unrest, and the economy was languishing. Similarly, Nixon's foreign-policy successes gave Americans some measure of confidence in their government. His administration managed to improve relations with the major powers of the Communist world—China and the Soviet Union—and to shift fundamentally the pattern of the cold war.

By 1969, Nixon had perceived that a new multipolar world order was emerging to replace the conventional cold war confrontation between the United States and the Soviet Union. Since 1945 the United States had lost its monopoly on nuclear weapons and its overwhelming economic dominance and geopolitical influence. The rapid rise of competing power centers in Europe, China, and Japan complicated international relations—China had replaced the United States as the Soviet Union's most threatening competitor—but also provided strategic opportunities, which Nixon and Kissinger seized.

In early 1970, Nixon announced a significant alteration in foreign policy. The United States could no longer be the world's policeman guarding against communism; the long-standing and unlimited containment policy developed by President Truman must be revised: "America cannot—and will not—conceive *all* the plans, design *all* the programs, execute *all* the decisions, and undertake *all* the defense of the free nations of the world." In explaining what became known as the Nixon Doctrine, the president declared that "our interests must shape our commitments, rather than the other way around." The United States, he and Kissinger stressed, must become more strategic and more realistic in its commitments, and it would begin to establish selected partnerships with Communist countries in areas of mutual interest.

CHINA   In 1971, Henry Kissinger made a secret trip to Peking to explore the possibility of U.S. recognition of Communist China. Since 1949, when Mao Tse-tung's revolutionary movement established control in China, the United States had refused to recognize Communist China, preferring to regard Chiang Kai-shek's exiled regime on the island of Taiwan as the legitimate Chinese government. In one simple but stunning stroke, Nixon and Kissinger ended two decades of diplomatic isolation of the People's Republic of China. In 1972, Americans watched on television as Nixon visited famous Chinese landmarks and drank toasts with Premier Chou En-lai and Mao Tse-tung. The United States and China agreed to scientific and cultural exchanges, steps toward the resumption of trade, and the eventual reunification of Taiwan with the mainland. A year after the Nixon visit, "liaison offices" were established in Washington and Peking that served as unofficial embassies, and in 1979 diplomatic recognition was formalized. Richard Nixon, the former anti-Communist crusader who had condemned the State Department for "losing" China in

The United States and China

With President Richard Nixon's visit to China in 1972, the United States formally recognized China's Communist government. Here Nixon and Chinese premier Chou En-lai drink a toast.

1949, had accomplished a diplomatic feat that his Democratic predecessors could not.

DÉTENTE In truth, China welcomed the breakthrough in relations with the United States because its festering rivalry with the Soviet Union, with which it shares a long border, had become more threatening than its rivalry with the West. The Soviet leaders, troubled by the Sino-American agreements, were also eager to ease tensions with the United States. This was especially true now that they had, as a result of a huge arms buildup following the Cuban missile crisis, achieved virtual parity with the United States in nuclear weapons. Once again President Nixon surprised the world, announcing that he would visit Moscow in 1972 for discussions with Leonid Brezhnev, the Soviet premier. The high theater of the China visit was repeated in Moscow, with toasts and elegant dinners attended by world leaders who had previously regarded each other as incarnations of evil.

What became known as détente with the Soviets offered the promise of a more orderly and restrained competition between the two superpowers. Nixon and Brezhnev signed agreements reached at the Strategic Arms Limitation Talks (SALT), which negotiators had been working on since 1969. The SALT agreement did not end the arms race, but it did limit both the number of ICBMs each nation could possess and prohibited the construction of antiballistic missile systems. In effect the Soviets were allowed to retain a greater number of missiles with greater destructive power while the United States retained a lead in the total number of warheads. No limitations were placed on new weapons systems, though each side agreed to work toward a permanent freeze on all nuclear weapons. The Moscow summit also produced new trade agreements, including an arrangement whereby the United States sold almost a quarter of its wheat crop to the Soviets at a favorable price. American farmers rejoiced, since the wheat deal raised prices for their

crop. Critics, however, grumbled that the deal would raise food prices in the United States, serving mainly to rescue the Soviets from troublesome economic problems. In sum, the Moscow summit revealed the dramatic easing of tensions between the two cold war superpowers. For Nixon and Kissinger the agreements with China and the Soviet Union represented monumental changes in the global order.

SHUTTLE DIPLOMACY   The Nixon-Kissinger initiatives in the Middle East were less dramatic and less conclusive than the agreements with China and the Soviet Union, but they did show that the United States recognized Arab power in the region and its own dependence upon Middle Eastern oil, even though the Arab nations were fundamentally opposed to the existence of Israel. In the Six-Day War of 1967, Israeli forces routed the armies of Egypt, Syria, and Jordan and seized territory from all three nations. Moreover, the number of Palestinian refugees, many of them homeless since the creation of Israel in 1948, increased after the 1967 Israeli victory. When Israel recovered from the initial shock of the surprise Yom Kippur War of 1973, Henry Kissinger now secretary of state, negotiated a cease-fire and

Henry Kissinger's "shuttle diplomacy"

President Sadat of Egypt and Secretary of State Henry Kissinger, during one of Kissinger's many visits to the Middle East, talk with reporters in an effort to bring peace.

exerted pressure to prevent Israel from taking additional Arab territory. He also promoted closer ties with Egypt and its president, Anwar el-Sadat, and more restrained support for Israel. In an attempt to broker a lasting settlement, Kissinger made numerous flights among the capitals of the Middle East. This "shuttle diplomacy" won acclaim from all sides, but Kissinger failed to find a comprehensive formula for peace in the troubled region and ignored the Palestinian problem. He did, however, lay groundwork for the accord between Israel and Egypt in 1977.

THE ELECTION OF 1972   Nixon's foreign-policy achievements allowed him to stage the presidential campaign of 1972 as a triumphal procession. The main threat to his reelection came from Alabama's Democratic governor George Wallace, who had the potential as a third-party candidate to deprive the Republicans of conservative votes and thereby throw the election to the Democrats or to the Democratic-controlled Congress. That threat dissipated, however, on May 15, 1972, when Wallace was shot and left paralyzed below the waist by a man eager to achieve a grisly brand of notoriety. Wallace was forced to withdraw from the campaign.

Meanwhile, the Democrats were further ensuring Nixon's victory by nominating Senator George S. McGovern of South Dakota, a steadfast liberal who embodied anti-war principles and embraced progressive social-welfare policies. At the Democratic Convention in Miami Beach, McGovern benefited from party reforms that increased the representation of women, African Americans and other minorities. But those changes alienated party regulars. Mayor Richard Daley of Chicago was actually ousted from the convention, and the AFL-CIO refused to endorse the liberal Democratic candidate.

The 1972 campaign was an exercise in futility for McGovern. Nixon won the greatest victory of any Republican presidential candidate in history, capturing 520 electoral votes to only 17 for McGovern. The popular vote was equally decisive: 46 million to 28 million, a proportion of the total vote (60.8 percent) that was second only to Lyndon Johnson's victory over Barry Goldwater in 1964.

Nonetheless, Nixon's easy victory did not ensure an easy—or complete—second term. During the course of the presidential campaign, George McGovern had complained about the numerous "dirty tricks" orchestrated by members of the Nixon administration. On several occasions, Nixon sought to coerce the Internal Revenue Service to investigate and intimidate his opponents. McGovern was especially disturbed by a curious incident on June 17, when five burglars were caught breaking into the Democratic campaign committee headquarters in the Watergate apartment complex outside

Washington, D.C. The burglars were former CIA agents, one of whom, James W. McCord, worked for the Nixon campaign. At the time, McGovern's shrill Watergate accusations seemed the lamentations of a candidate running far behind in the polls. Nixon and his staff ignored the news of the burglary. The president said that no one cares "when somebody bugs somebody else." Privately, however, he and his aides Bob Haldeman, John Dean, and John Ehrlichman began feverish efforts to cover up the Watergate break-in so as not to endanger his reelection campaign. The White House offered legal assistance to the burglars in an effort to buy their silence and tried to keep the FBI out of the investigation. Nixon and his closest aides also discussed using the CIA to derail the Justice Department investigation of the Watergate break-in.

WATERGATE

During the trial of the accused Watergate burglars in January 1973, the relentless prodding of Judge John J. Sirica led one of the accused to tell the full story of the Nixon administration's complicity in the Watergate episode. James McCord, security chief of the Committee to Re-elect the President (CREEP), was the first in a long line of informers in a melodrama that unfolded over two years. It ended in the first resignation of a president in American history, the conviction and imprisonment of twenty-five officials of the Nixon administration, including four cabinet members, and the most serious constitutional crisis since the impeachment trial of President Andrew Johnson in 1868.

UNCOVERING THE COVER-UP   The trail of evidence pursued first by Judge John Sirica, then by a grand jury, and then by a Senate committee headed by Democrat Samuel J. Ervin Jr. of North Carolina led directly to the White House. No evidence surfaced linking Nixon to the order to commit the break-in or suggesting that he was aware of plans to burglarize the Democratic National Committee. From the start, however, Nixon was personally involved in the cover-up of the incident. He used his presidential powers to discredit and block the investigation. And most alarming, the Watergate burglary was merely one small part of a larger pattern of corruption and criminality sanctioned by the Nixon White House.

In 1970, after the *New York Times* had disclosed that the secret American bombings in Cambodia had been going on for years, a furious Nixon ordered illegal telephone taps on several journalists and government employees

suspected of leaking the story. The covert activity against the press and critics of Nixon's Vietnam policies increased in 1971, during the crisis generated by the publication of the Pentagon Papers, when a team of burglars under the direction of White House adviser John Ehrlichman broke into Daniel Ellsberg's psychiatrist's office in an effort to obtain damaging information on Ellsberg, the man who had given the Pentagon Papers to the press. By the spring of 1972, Ehrlichman was overseeing a team of "dirty tricksters" who performed various acts of sabotage against prospective Democratic candidates—for example, falsely accusing Senators Hubert Humphrey and Henry Jackson of sexual improprieties, forging press releases, setting off stink bombs at Democratic rallies, and associating the opposition candidates with racist remarks. By the time of the Watergate break-in, the money to finance these pranks was being illegally collected through CREEP and had been placed under the control of the White House staff.

The Watergate cover-up unraveled as various people, including John Dean, legal counsel to the president, began to cooperate with prosecutors. It unraveled further in 1973 when L. Patrick Gray, acting director of the FBI, resigned after confessing that he had confiscated and destroyed several incriminating documents. On April 30, Ehrlichman and Haldeman resigned, together with Attorney General Richard Kleindienst. A few days later the president nervously assured the public in a television address, "I am not a crook." Then John Dean, whom Nixon had dismissed because of his cooperation with prosecutors, testified to the Ervin committee that there had been a White House-orchestrated cover-up and Nixon had approved it. Nixon, meanwhile, refused to provide the Ervin committee with documents it requested, citing "executive privilege" to protect national security. In another bombshell disclosure, a White House aide told the committee that Nixon had

The unraveling

Fired Deputy Attorney General Ruckelshaus discusses Watergate during an interview.

installed a taping system in the White House and that many of the conversations about the Watergate burglary and cover-up had been recorded.

A yearlong legal battle for the "Nixon tapes" began. Harvard law professor Archibald Cox, whom Nixon's new attorney general, Elliot Richardson, had appointed as special prosecutor to investigate the Watergate case, took the president to court in October 1973 to obtain the tapes. Nixon refused to release the recordings and ordered Cox fired. In what became known as the Saturday Night Massacre, on October 20 Attorney General Elliot Richardson and Deputy Attorney General William Ruckelshaus resigned rather than fire the special prosecutor. Solicitor General Robert Bork finally fired Cox. Nixon's dismissal of Cox produced a firestorm of public indignation. Numerous newspaper and magazine editorials, as well as a growing chorus of legislators, called for the president to be impeached for obstructing justice. A Gallup poll revealed that Nixon's approval rating had plunged to 17 percent, its lowest level ever. And the firing of Cox failed to end Nixon's legal troubles. Cox's replacement as special prosecutor, Leon Jaworski, also took the president to court. In March 1974 the Watergate grand jury indicted John Ehrlichman, H. R. Haldeman, and John Mitchell for obstruction of justice and named Nixon as an "unindicted co-conspirator." By the summer of 1974, Nixon was in full retreat, besieged on all fronts and morosely combative, melancholy, or petty, at times talking of resignation and on other occasions expressing determination to fight impeachment efforts. In December 1973, Senator Barry Goldwater reported that the president "jabbered incessantly, often incoherently." He seemed "to be cracking."

On July 24, 1974, the Supreme Court ruled unanimously, in *United States v. Richard M. Nixon*, that the president must surrender all of the tape recordings. A few days later the House Judiciary Committee voted to recommend three articles of impeachment: obstruction of justice through the payment

Nixon's resignation

Having resigned his office, Richard Nixon waves farewell outside the White House on August 9, 1974.

of "hush money" to witnesses and the withholding of evidence, abuse of power through the use of federal agencies to deprive citizens of their constitutional rights, and defiance of Congress by withholding the tapes. But before the House of Representatives could meet to vote on impeachment, Nixon handed over the complete set of White House tapes. Investigators then learned that sections of certain recordings were missing, including eighteen minutes of a key conversation in June 1972 during which Nixon first mentioned the Watergate burglary. The president's loyal secretary tried to accept blame for the erasure, claiming that she had accidentally pushed the wrong button, but experts later concluded that the missing segments had been intentionally deleted. On August 9, 1974, fully aware that the evidence on the tapes implicated him in the cover-up, Richard Nixon resigned from office, the only president ever to do so. Nixon had begun his presidency hoping to heal America. He left the presidency having deeply wounded the nation. The credibility gap between the presidency and the public that had developed under Lyndon Johnson had become a chasm under Nixon.

THE EFFECTS OF WATERGATE   Vice President Spiro Agnew did not succeed Nixon because he had been forced to resign in October 1973 for having accepted bribes from contractors before and during his term as vice president. The vice president at the time of Nixon's resignation was Gerald Ford, the former Michigan congressman and House minority leader whom Nixon had appointed, with the approval of Congress, under the provisions of the Twenty-fifth Amendment. Ratified in 1967, the amendment provided for the appointment of a vice president when the office became vacant.

President Ford initially insisted that he had no intention of pardoning Nixon, who was still liable for criminal prosecution. "I do not think the public would stand for it," he said. But a month after Nixon's resignation, on September 8, the new president did issue the pardon, explaining that it was necessary to end the national obsession with the Watergate scandal. Many Americans, however, were not in a forgiving mood. After the pardon was announced, Ford's approval rating plummeted from 71 percent to 49 percent in one day, the steepest drop ever recorded. Even the president's press secretary resigned in protest. Ford was devastated by the "hostile reaction" to the pardon, and the new president never recovered the public's confidence. Many Americans suspected that Nixon and Ford had made a deal, though there was no evidence to confirm the speculation. President Ford testified personally to a congressional committee: "There was no deal, period."

If there was a silver lining in the dark cloud of Watergate, it was the vigor and resilience of the institutions that had brought a rogue president to

justice—the press, Congress, the courts, and an aroused public opinion. Congress responded to the Watergate revelations with several pieces of legislation designed to curb executive power. Already nervous about possible efforts to renew American military assistance to South Vietnam, the Democratic-led Congress passed the War Powers Act (1973), which requires a president to inform Congress within forty-eight hours if U.S. troops are deployed in combat abroad and to withdraw troops after sixty days unless Congress specifically approves their stay. In an effort to correct abuses in the use of campaign funds, Congress enacted legislation in 1974 that set new ceilings on political contributions and expenditures. And in reaction to the Nixon claim of "executive privilege" as a means of withholding evidence, Congress strengthened the 1966 Freedom of Information Act to require prompt responses to requests for information from government files and to place on government agencies the burden of proof for classifying information as secret.

With Nixon's resignation, the nation had weathered a profound constitutional crisis, but the aftershock of the Watergate episode produced a deep sense of disillusionment with the so-called imperial presidency. Apart from Nixon's illegal actions, the vulgar language used in the White House and made public on the tapes stripped away the veils of mystery and majesty surrounding national leaders and left even the die-hard defenders of presidential authority shocked at the crudity and duplicity of Nixon and his subordinates. Coming on the heels of the erosion of public confidence generated by the Vietnam War, the Watergate affair renewed public cynicism toward a government that had systematically lied to the people and violated their civil liberties.

AN UNELECTED PRESIDENT

During Richard Nixon's last year in office, the Watergate crisis so dominated national politics that major domestic and foreign problems received little executive attention. The perplexing combination of inflation and recession worsened, as did the oil crisis. At the same time, Secretary of State Henry Kissinger, who assumed control of foreign policy, watched helplessly as the South Vietnamese forces crumbled before North Vietnamese attacks, attempted with limited success to establish a framework for peace in the Middle East, and supported a CIA role in the overthrow of Salvador Allende Gossens, the popularly elected Marxist president of Chile. Allende was subsequently murdered and replaced by General Augusto Pinochet Ugarte, a military dictator supposedly friendly to the United States.

THE FORD YEARS   Gerald Ford inherited those simmering problems when he assumed office after Nixon's resignation. An amiable, honest man, Ford candidly admitted upon becoming vice president, "I am a Ford, not a Lincoln." "Jerry Ford," explained the *Washington Post*, "is the most normal, sane, down-to-earth individual to work in the Oval Office since Harry Truman left." As president, Gerald Ford soon adopted the posture he had developed as a conservative minority leader in the House: nay-saying leader of the opposition who believed that the federal government exercised too much power over domestic affairs. In his fifteen months as president, Ford vetoed thirty-nine bills, thereby outstripping Herbert Hoover's veto record in less than half the time. By resisting congressional pressure to reduce taxes and increase federal spending, he succeeded in plummeting the economy into the deepest recession since the Great Depression. Unemployment jumped to 9 percent in 1975, and the federal deficit hit a record the next year. Ford rejected wage and price controls to curb inflation, preferring voluntary restraints that he tried to bolster by passing out WIN buttons,

Meeting at Vladivostok, in Siberia

President Gerald Ford shakes hands with Soviet Communist Party Chief Leonid Brezhnev.

symbolizing his campaign to "Whip Inflation Now." The WIN buttons instead became a national joke and a popular symbol of Ford's ineffectiveness in the fight against stagflation.

In foreign policy, Ford retained Henry Kissinger as secretary of state and attempted to continue Nixon's goals of stability in the Middle East, rapprochement with China, and détente with the Soviet Union. Late in 1974, Ford met with Soviet leader Leonid Brezhnev at Vladivostok, in Siberia, and accepted the framework for another arms-control accord that was to serve as the basis for SALT II. Meanwhile, Kissinger's tireless shuttling between Cairo and Tel Aviv produced an important agreement: Israel promised to return to Egypt most of the Sinai territory captured in the 1967 War, and the two nations agreed to rely upon negotiations rather than force to settle future disagreements. These limited but significant achievements should have enhanced Ford's image, but they were drowned in the sea of criticism and carping that followed the collapse of South Vietnam to the Communists in May 1975.

Not only had a decade of American effort in Vietnam proved futile, but the Khmer Rouge, the Cambodian Communist movement, had also won a resounding victory, plunging that country into a colossal bloodbath. The Khmer Rouge organized a genocidal campaign to destroy their opponents, killing almost a third of the population. Meanwhile, the OPEC oil cartel was threatening another worldwide boycott, and various third world nations denounced the United States as a depraved and declining imperialist power. Ford lost his patience when he sent marines to rescue the crew of the American merchant ship *Mayaguez*, which had been captured by the Cambodian Communists. This vigorous move won popular acclaim until it was disclosed that the Cambodians had already agreed to release the captured Americans: the forty-one Americans killed in the operation had died for no purpose.

THE ELECTION OF 1976   Amid such turmoil the Democrats could hardly wait for the 1976 election. At the Republican Convention, Ford fended off a powerful challenge for the nomination from Ronald Reagan, a former California governor and Hollywood actor. The Democrats chose an obscure former naval officer and engineer turned peanut farmer who had served one term as governor of Georgia. Jimmy Carter campaigned harder than any of the other Democratic hopefuls; he capitalized on the post-Watergate cynicism by promising "I will never tell a lie to the American people" and by citing his inexperience in the byways of Washington politics as an asset. Facing the prospect of the first president from the Deep South since 1849, reporters marveled at a Baptist candidate who claimed to be "born again."

To the surprise of many pundits, the little-known Carter revived the New Deal coalition of southern whites, blacks, urban labor, and ethnic groups to win 41 million votes to Ford's 39 million and a narrow electoral-vote majority of 297 to 240. A heavy turnout of African Americans in the South enabled Carter to sweep every state in the region except Virginia. Carter also benefited from the appeal of Walter F. Mondale, his liberal running mate and a favorite among blue-collar workers and the urban poor. Carter lost most of the trans-Mississippi West, but no Democratic candidate had made much headway there since Harry Truman in 1948. The big story of the election was the low voter turnout. "Neither Ford nor Carter won as many votes as Mr. Nobody," said one reporter, commenting on the fact that almost half the eligible voters, apparently alienated by Watergate and the lackluster candidates, chose to sit out the election.

THE CARTER INTERREGNUM

POLICY STALEMATE   Once in office, Jimmy Carter suffered the fate of all presidents since John Kennedy: after an initial honeymoon, during which he displayed folksy charm by, for example, walking down Pennsylvania Avenue after his inauguration rather than riding in a limousine and wearing cardigan sweaters during televised "fireside chats," his popularity and political effectiveness waned. Like Ford before him, Carter faced an almost insurmountable set of domestic and international problems. He was expected to cure the economic recession and reduce inflation at a time when all industrial economies were shaken by a shortage of energy and confidence. He was expected to reassert America's global power at a time of waning respect for America's international authority. And he was expected to do that, as well as buoy the national spirit, through a set of political institutions in which many Americans had lost faith.

Yet during the first two years of his term, Carter enjoyed several successes. His administration included more African Americans and women than ever before. Carter created a federal task force to study the problem of Vietnam-era draft evaders and eventually offered amnesty to the thousands of young men who had fled the country rather than serve in Vietnam. He reformed the civil service to provide rewards for merit, and he created new cabinet-level Departments of Energy and Education. He also pushed through Congress several significant environmental initiatives, including a bill to establish controls over strip mining, a "superfund" of $1.6 billion to clean up chemical waste sites, and a proposal to protect over 100 million acres of Alaskan land from development.

But success was short-lived. Carter's political predicament surfaced in the protracted debate over energy policy. Carter disliked stroking legislators or wheeling and dealing to get legislation passed. As a result, the energy bill that he signed in 1978 was a gutted version of the original legislation proposed by the administration, reflecting the power of special-interest lobbies. One Carter aide said that the bill looked like it had been "nibbled to death by ducks." The clumsy political maneuvers that plagued Carter and his inexperienced aides repeatedly frustrated efforts to remedy the energy crisis.

The Carter administration

President Jimmy Carter and his wife, Rosalynn, forgo the traditional limousine and walk down Pennsylvania Avenue after the inauguration, January 20, 1977.

In the summer of 1979, when renewed violence in the Middle East produced a second fuel shortage in the United States, motorists were again forced to wait in long lines for limited supplies of gas, which they regarded as excessively expensive. Opinion polls showed Carter with an approval rating of only 26 percent.

Several of Carter's early foreign-policy initiatives also got caught in political crossfires. Soon after his inauguration, Carter vowed that "the soul of our foreign policy" should be the defense of human rights abroad. This human rights campaign aroused opposition from two sides, however: those who feared it sacrificed a detached appraisal of national interest for high-level moralizing and those who believed that human rights were important but that the administration was applying the standard inconsistently.

Similarly, Carter's successful negotiation of treaties to turn over control of the Panama Canal to the government of Panama generated intense criticism. Republican Ronald Reagan claimed that the Canal Zone was sovereign American soil purchased "fair and square" in Theodore Roosevelt's administration. (In the congressional debate one senator quipped, "We stole it fair and square, so why can't we keep it?") Carter argued that the limitations on U.S. influence in Latin America and the deep resentment of American colonialism in Panama left the United States with no other choice but to transfer the canal to Panama. The Canal Zone would revert to Panama in stages, with completion of the process in 1999. The Senate ratified the treaties by a paper-thin margin (68 to 32, two votes more than the required two thirds), but conservatives lambasted Carter for surrendering American authority in a strategically critical part of the world.

THE CAMP DAVID ACCORDS   Carter's crowning foreign-policy achievement, which even his most bitter critics applauded, was his brokering of a peace agreement between Israel and Egypt. In 1977, Egyptian president Anwar el-Sadat flew to Tel Aviv at the invitation of Israeli prime minister Menachem Begin. Sadat's bold act, and his accompanying announcement that Egypt was willing to recognize the legitimacy of the Israeli state, opened up diplomatic opportunities that Carter and Secretary of State Cyrus Vance quickly pursued.

In 1978, Carter invited Sadat and Begin to the presidential retreat at Camp David, in Maryland, for two weeks of difficult negotiations. The first

The Camp David Accords

Egyptian president Anwar el-Sadat (left), Jimmy Carter (center), and Israeli prime minister Menachem Begin (right) at the announcement of the Camp David Accords, September 1978.

part of the eventual agreement called for Israel to return all land in the Sinai in exchange for Egyptian recognition of Israel's sovereignty. This agreement was successfully implemented in 1982, when the last Israeli settler vacated the peninsula. But the second part of the agreement, calling for Israel to negotiate with Sadat to resolve the Palestinian refugee dilemma, began to unravel soon after the Camp David summit.

By March 26, 1979, when Begin and Sadat returned to Washington to sign the formal treaty, Begin had already refused to block new Israeli settlements on the West Bank of the Jordan River, which Sadat had regarded as a prospective homeland for the Palestinians. In the wake of the Camp David Accords, most of the Arab nations condemned Sadat as a traitor. Islamic extremists assassinated him in 1981. Still, Carter and Vance's high-level diplomacy made an all-out war between Israel and the Arab world less likely.

MOUNTING TROUBLES   Carter's crowning failure, which even his most avid supporters acknowledged, was his mismanagement of the economy. In effect he inherited a bad situation and made it worse. Carter employed the same economic policies as Nixon and Ford to fight stagflation, but he reversed the order of the federal "cure," preferring first to fight unemployment with a tax cut and increased public spending. Unemployment declined slightly, from 8 to 7 percent in 1977, but the annual inflation rate soared; at 5 percent when he took office, it reached 10 percent in 1978 and kept going. During one month in 1980, it measured 18 percent. Like previous presidents, Carter then reversed himself to fight the other side of the economic malaise: budget deficits caused by the sagging economy. By midterm he was delaying tax reductions and vetoing government spending programs that he had proposed in his first year. The result was the worst of both possible worlds: a deepened recession and inflation averaging between 12 and 13 percent per year.

The signing of a controversial new Strategic Arms Limitation Talks treaty with the Soviets (SALT II) put Carter's leadership to the test just as the mounting economic problems made him the subject of biting editorial cartoons nationwide. The new agreement placed a ceiling of 2,250 bombers and missiles on each side and set limits on the number of warheads and new weapons systems each power could assemble. But the proposed SALT II treaty became moot in 1979 when the Soviet army invaded Afghanistan to prop up the faltering Communist government there, which was being challenged by Muslim rebels. To protest the Soviet action, Carter immediately shelved SALT II, suspended grain shipments to the Soviet Union, and called for an international boycott of the 1980 Olympics, which were to be held that summer in Moscow.

IRAN   Then came the Iranian crisis, a yearlong cascade of unwelcome events that epitomized the inability of the United States to control world affairs and heightened public perceptions of Carter's weak leadership. The crisis began with the fall of the shah of Iran in 1979. The revolutionaries who toppled the shah's government rallied around Ayatollah Ruhollah Khomeini, a fundamentalist Muslim religious leader who symbolized the orthodox Islamic values the shah had tried to replace with Western ways. Khomeini's hatred of the United States dated back to the CIA-sponsored overthrow of the government of Mohammed Mossadegh in 1953. Nor did it help the American image that the CIA had trained SAVAK, the shah's ruthless secret-police force. Late in 1979 the exiled shah was allowed to enter the United States to undergo treatment for cancer. A few days later, on November 4, a frenzied Iranian mob stormed the U.S. embassy in Tehran and seized the diplomats and staff. Khomeini endorsed the mob action and demanded the return of the shah along with all his wealth in exchange for the release of the fifty-two hostages still held captive.

Indignant Americans demanded a military response, but Carter's range of options was limited. He appealed to the United Nations, but Khomeini

Tehran, 1979

Iranian militants stormed the U.S. embassy in Tehran and held fifty-two Americans hostage for over a year. Here one of the hostages (face covered) is paraded before a camera.

scoffed at UN requests for the release of the hostages. Carter then froze all Iranian assets in the United States and appealed to American allies for a trade embargo of Iran. The trade restrictions were only partially effective—even America's most loyal European allies did not want to lose their access to Iranian oil—so a frustrated and besieged Carter authorized a risky rescue attempt by commandos in 1980. Secretary of State Cyrus Vance resigned in protest against the rescue attempt and Carter's sharp turn toward a more hawkish foreign policy. The commando raid was aborted because of helicopter failures and ended on April 25, 1980, with eight fatalities when a helicopter collided with a transport plane in the desert. Nightly television coverage of the taunting Iranian rebels generated a near obsession with the falling fortunes of the United States and the fate of the hostages. The end came after 444 days, on January 20, 1981, when Carter released several billion dollars of Iranian assets to ransom the kidnapped hostages. By then however, Ronald Reagan had been elected president, and Carter was headed into retirement.

The turbulent and often tragic events of the 1970s—the Communist conquest of South Vietnam, the Watergate scandal and Nixon's resignation, the energy shortage and stagflation, the Iranian hostage episode—generated what Carter labeled a "crisis of confidence" in America's outlook. By 1980, U.S. power and prestige seemed to be on the decline, the economy remained in a shambles, and the social revolution launched in the 1960s, with the questions it raised for the family and other basic social and political institutions, had sparked a backlash of resentment among middle America. With theatrical timing, Ronald Reagan emerged to tap the growing reservoir of public frustration and transform his political career into a crusade to make America "stand tall again." He told his supporters that there was "a hunger in this land for a spiritual revival, a return to a belief in moral absolutes." The United States, he declared, remained the "greatest country in the world. We have the talent, we have the drive, we have the imagination. Now all we need is the leadership."

CHAPTER SUMMARY

- **Rebellion and Reaction** Civil rights activism was the catalyst for a heightened interest in social causes, especially among the young. Students for a Democratic Society launched the New Left. Other prominent causes of the era included the anti-war movement, the women's liberation movement, Native American rights, Hispanic rights, and gay rights. By 1970 a counterculture had emerged, featuring young people who used mind-altering drugs, lived on communes, and in other ways "dropped out" of the conventional world, which they viewed as corrupt.

- **End of the Vietnam War** Richard Nixon campaigned for the presidency pledging to secure a "peace with honor" in Vietnam, but years would pass before the war ended. His delays prompted an acceleratation of anti-war protests. After the Kent State University shootings, the divisions between supporters and opponents of the war became especially contentious. The publication of the Pentagon Papers in 1971 and the heavy bombing of North Vietnam by the United States in December 1972 aroused intense worldwide protests. A month later North and South Vietnam agreed to end the war. The last U.S. troops left Vietnam in March 1973; two years later the government of South Vietnam collapsed, and the country was reunited under a Communist government.

- **Watergate** In an incident in 1972, burglars were caught breaking into the Democratic campaign headquarters at the Watergate complex in Washington, D.C. Eventually the Committee to Re-elect the President (CREEP) was implicated, and investigators began to probe the question of President Nixon's involvement. Nixon tried to block the judicial process which led the public to call for the president to be impeached for obstruction of justice. In 1974, in *United States v. Richard M. Nixon*, the Supreme Court ruled that the president had to surrender the so-called Watergate tapes. Nixon resigned to avoid being impeached.

- **Middle East Crisis** After the 1973 Yom Kippur War in the Middle East, the Organization of Petroleum Exporting Countries (OPEC) declined to sell oil to states supporting Israel until a cease-fire was reached. President Carter brokered the Camp David Accords of 1978, which laid the groundwork for a peace treaty between Israel and Egypt. The next year an Islamic revolution took place in Iran. Enraged militants stormed the U.S. embassy in Tehran and seized American diplomats and staff members. In retaliation, President Carter froze all Iranian assets in the United States. Carter at last released several billion dollars in Iranian assets to ransom the hostages. The Iranians released the hostages—but not until Ronald Reagan was in office.

CHRONOLOGY

1960	Students in Greensboro, North Carolina, stage a sit-in to demand service at a "whites-only" lunch counter
1960	Food and Drug Administration approves the birth-control pill
1963	Betty Friedan's *The Feminine Mystique* is published
March 1969	U.S. planes begin a fourteen-month-long bombing campaign aimed at Communist sanctuaries in Cambodia
July 1969	Neil Armstrong becomes the first person to walk on the moon
1971	Ratification of the Twenty-sixth Amendment gives eighteen-year-olds the right to vote in all elections
January 1973	In Paris, the United States, North and South Vietnam, and the Viet Cong agree to restore peace in Vietnam
1973	Congress passes the War Powers Act
April 1975	Saigon falls to the North Vietnamese
1978	Jimmy Carter brokers the Camp David Accords, an agreement between Israel and Egypt
1978	Supreme Court issues the *Bakke* decision
November 1979	Islamic militants storm the U.S. embassy in Tehran and take more than fifty Americans hostage

KEY TERMS & NAMES

36

A CONSERVATIVE INSURGENCY

FOCUS QUESTIONS wwnorton.com/studyspace

- What explains the rise of Ronald Reagan and Republican conservatism?

- What was the Iran-Contra affair, and what did it show about the nature of the executive branch of government, even after Watergate?

- What factors led to the end of the cold war?

- What characterized the economy and society in the 1980s?

- What were the causes of the Gulf War?

President Jimmy Carter and his embattled Democratic administration hobbled through 1979 and the onset of another presidential campaign season. The economy remained sluggish, double-digit annual inflation rates stymied spending, long waits angered drivers lined up at gas stations, and failed efforts to free the U.S. hostages in Iran combined to sour voters on the administration. Carter's inability to persuade the nation to embrace his energy-conservation program revealed mortal flaws in his reading of the public mood and his understanding of legislative politics. That Democratic senator Edward Kennedy of Massachusetts, youngest brother of President John Kennedy, chose to challenge Carter for the presidential nomination revealed how frustrated many Democrats were with their president.

While the lackluster Carter administration was foundering, Republican conservatives were forging an aggressive plan to win the White House in

1980 and assault "liberalism" in Washington. Those plans centered on the popularity and charisma of Ronald Reagan, the Hollywood actor turned California governor and prominent political commentator. Reagan was not a deep thinker, but he was a superb analyst of the public mood, an unabashed patriot, and a committed champion of conservative principles. He was also charming and cheerful, a likable politician renowned for his folksy anecdotes and optimistic outlook. Where the dour Carter denounced the evils of free-enterprise capitalism and scolded Americans to revive long-forgotten virtues of frugality, a sunny Reagan promised a "revolution of ideas" designed to unleash the capitalist spirit, restore national pride, and regain international respect.

Reagan promised to increase military spending, dismantle the "bloated" federal bureaucracy, reduce taxes and regulations, and in general shrink the role of the federal government. He also wanted to affirm old-time religious values by banning abortions and reinstituting prayer in public schools. Reagan's appeal derived from his remarkable skill as a public speaker and his dogmatic commitment to a few overarching ideas and simple themes. As a true believer and an able compromiser, he combined the fervor of a revolutionary with the pragmatism of a diplomat.

Such attributes won Reagan two presidential terms, in 1980 and 1984, and ensured the election of his successor, George H. W. Bush, in 1988. Just how revolutionary the Reagan era was remains a subject of intense debate. What cannot be denied, however, is that Reagan's actions and beliefs set the tone for the decade's political and economic life.

THE REAGAN REVOLUTION

THE MAKING OF A PRESIDENT Born in Tampico, Illinois, in 1911, Ronald Reagan graduated from Eureka College and then worked as a radio announcer and sportscaster before starting a movie career in Hollywood in 1937. As president of the Screen Actors Guild, Reagan was at first a liberal unionist who supported Franklin Roosevelt's New Deal programs. But he bounced to the far right on the political spectrum during the 1950s. He campaigned for both Eisenhower (in 1952 and 1956) and Nixon (in 1960), switched his party affiliation to Republican in 1962, then achieved political stardom in 1964 when he delivered a rousing speech on national television on behalf of Barry Goldwater's presidential candidacy.

Republican conservatives found in Ronald Reagan a new idol, whose appeal survived the defeat of Goldwater. Those who dismissed Reagan as a

"The Great Communicator"

Ronald Reagan in 1980, shortly before his election.

minor actor and a mental midget underrated his many virtues, including the importance of his years in front of a camera. Politics is a performing art, all the more so in an age of television, and few if any others in public life had Reagan's stage presence or extraordinary charm. Drawn by wealthy admirers into the campaign for governor of California in 1966, Reagan won the governorship by a landslide.

By the eve of the 1980 election, Reagan had become the beneficiary of a development that made his conservative vision of America more than a harmless flirtation with nostalgia. The 1980 census revealed that the elderly proportion of the population was soaring and moving to the sunbelt states of the South and the West. This dual development—an increase in the number of senior citizens and the steady relocation of a significant portion of the population to conservative regions of the country, where hostility to "big government" was deeply rooted—meant that demographics were carrying the United States toward Reagan's conservative political philosophy.

THE MORAL MAJORITY   Reagan's political aspirations also benefited from a massive revival of evangelical religion. No longer a local or provincial phenomenon, Catholic conservatives and Protestant evangelicals now owned television and radio stations and operated schools and universities. A survey in 1977 revealed that more than 70 million Americans described themselves as born-again Christians. And religious conservatives formed the strongest grassroots movement of the late twentieth century.

The Reverend Jerry Falwell's Moral Majority (later renamed the Liberty Alliance) expressed the major political and social goals of the religious right wing: the economy should operate without "interference" by the government, which should be reduced in size; the Supreme Court decision in *Roe v. Wade* (1973) legalizing abortion should be reversed; Darwinian evolution should be replaced in schoolbooks by the biblical story of creation; prayer should be allowed back in public schools; women should submit to their husbands; and Soviet communism should be opposed as a form of pagan totalitarianism. The moralistic zeal and financial resources of the religious right made its adherents formidable opponents of liberal political candidates and programs. By 1980, Falwell's Moral Majority claimed over 4 million members. Its base of support was in the South and was strongest among Baptists, but its appeal extended across the country. As Falwell declared, the Moral Majority was "pro-life, pro-family, pro-morality, and pro-American."

A curiosity of the 1980 presidential campaign was that the religious right opposed Jimmy Carter, a self-professed born-again Baptist, and supported Ronald Reagan, a man who was neither conspicuously pious nor even often in church. His divorce and remarriage, once an almost automatic disqualification for the presidency, raised little notice. Nor did the fact that as governor he had signed one of the most permissive abortion laws in the country. That Ronald Reagan became the messiah of the religious right was a tribute both to the force of social issues and to the candidate's political skills. Although famous for his personal piety, Carter lost the support of religious conservatives because he failed to promote their key social issues. He was not willing to ban abortions or restore daily prayers in public schools. His endorsement of the equal-rights constitutional amendment (ERA) for women and civil rights protections for gays also lost him votes from the religious right.

FEMINIST BACKLASH Another factor contributing to the conservative resurgence was a well-organized and well-financed backlash against the feminist movement. During the 1970s, women who opposed the social goals of feminism formed counterorganizations with names like Women Who Want to Be Women and Females Opposed to Equality. Spearheading those efforts was Phyllis Schlafly, a right-wing Republican activist from Illinois. She orchestrated the campaign to defeat the ERA and thereafter served as the galvanizing force behind a growing anti-feminist movement. Schlafly characterized feminists as a "bunch of bitter women seeking a constitutional cure for their personal problems," and she urged women to embrace their "God-given" roles as wives and mothers. Feminists, she charged, were "anti-family, anti-children, and pro-abortion."

Many of Schlafly's supporters in the anti-ERA campaign also participated in the mushrooming anti-abortion, or "pro-life," movement. By 1980 the National Right to Life Committee, supported by the National Conference of Catholic Bishops, boasted 11 million members representing most religious denominations. The intensity of its members' commitment made it a

Anti-abortion movement

Anti-abortion demonstrators pass the Washington Monument on their way to the Capitol.

powerful political force in its own right, and the Reagan campaign was quick to highlight its own support for traditional "family values," gender roles, and the "rights" of the unborn. Such cultural issues helped persuade many northern Democrats—mostly working-class Catholics—to support Reagan. Whites alienated by the increasingly liberal social agenda of the Democratic party became a crucial element in Reagan's electoral strategy.

THE ELECTION OF 1980   By 1980, voters were applauding Reagan's cheery promises of less government, lower taxes, renewed prosperity, waning inflation, and revived military strength and national pride. His "supply-side" economics proposals, soon dubbed Reaganomics by supporters and voodoo economics by critics, suggested that the stagflation of the 1970s had resulted from excessive taxes, which weakened incentives to work, save, and reinvest. The solution was to slash tax rates so as to boost economic growth. For a long-suffering nation it was, in theory, an alluring economic panacea.

Reagan was a colorful campaigner who used jokes to punctuate his themes. At one campaign stop, for instance, he quipped: "A recession is when your neighbor loses his job. A depression is when you lose yours. A recovery is when Jimmy Carter loses his." On election day, Reagan swept to a decisive

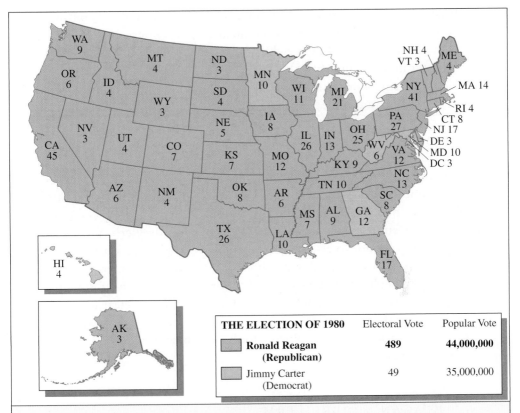

THE ELECTION OF 1980	Electoral Vote	Popular Vote
■ Ronald Reagan (Republican)	**489**	**44,000,000**
□ Jimmy Carter (Democrat)	49	35,000,000

Why was Ronald Reagan an appealing candidate in 1980? What was the impact of "nonvoting"? Why was there so much voter apathy?

victory, with 489 electoral votes to 49 for Carter, who carried only six states. The popular vote was 44 million (51 percent) for Reagan to Carter's 35 million (41 percent), with 7 percent going to John Anderson, a moderate Republican who bolted the party after Reagan's nomination and ran on an independent ticket. Carter was the first incumbent president since Herbert Hoover to lose a bid for reelection.

More than a victory for the "new conservatism," the 1980 election reflected the triumph of what one political scientist called the "largest mass movement of our time": nonvoting. Almost as striking as Reagan's one-sided victory was the fact that his total votes represented only 28 percent of the potential electorate. Only 53 percent of eligible voters cast ballots in the 1980 election; in western European countries such as France and Germany, voter participation hovered at 85 percent in national elections during the 1970s.

Where had all the voters gone? Analysts noted that most of the nonvoters were working-class Democrats in the major urban centers. Voter turnout was lowest in poor inner-city neighborhoods. Turnout was highest, by contrast, in the affluent suburbs of large cities, areas where the Republican party was experiencing a dramatic surge in popularity. Explanations for the high level of voter apathy among working-class Americans vary. Some argue that it reflected a sense of disillusionment with government itself that grew out of the Watergate affair. Others point to the widespread perception that the Democratic party had turned its back on its traditional blocs of support. Democratic leaders no longer spoke eloquently on behalf of those at the bottom of America's social scale. By embracing a fiscal conservatism indistinguishable from that of the Republicans, as Carter had done, Democrats lost their appeal among blue-collar workers and ghetto dwellers. And so the largest group of nonvoters in the 1980 election was made up of former Democrats who had decided that neither party served their interests. When viewed in this light, Ronald Reagan's victory represented both a resounding victory for conservative Republicans and a self-inflicted defeat by a fractured Democratic party. Flush with a sense of power and destiny, President-elect Reagan headed toward Washington with a blueprint for dismantling the welfare state.

REAGAN'S FIRST TERM

REAGANOMICS   Ronald Reagan brought to Washington a cheerful conservative philosophy embodied in a simple message. "Government is not the solution to our problem," he insisted; "government is the problem." He credited Calvin Coolidge and Coolidge's Treasury secretary, Andrew Mellon, with demonstrating that by reducing taxes and easing government regulation of business, free-market capitalism would revive the economy. By cutting taxes and domestic federal spending, he claimed, a surging economy would produce *more* government revenues, which in turn would help reduce the budget deficit.

Early on, Reagan focused on implementing his major campaign promises: increased defense spending, reduced social spending, and passage of a sweeping tax-reduction plan. On August 1, 1981, the president signed the Economic Recovery Tax Act, which cut personal income taxes by 25 percent, lowered the maximum rate from 70 to 50 percent for 1982, cut the capital gains tax by a third, and offered a broad array of other tax concessions.

The new legislation embodied an idea that went back to Alexander Hamilton, George Washington's Treasury secretary: more money in the hands of the affluent would benefit society at large, since the wealthy would engage in productive investment. A closer parallel, as Reagan had pointed out, was Treasury Secretary Andrew Mellon's tax-reduction program of the 1920s. The difference was that the Reagan tax cuts were accompanied by modest reductions in domestic spending and massive increases in defense spending, which generated ever-mounting federal deficits. Reagan's advisers insisted that the unbalanced budgets were only temporary; the new tax plan would eventually fuel economic growth and thereby boost tax revenues as personal income and corporate profits skyrocketed. But it did not work out that way. By the summer of 1983, a major economic recovery was under way, but the federal deficits had grown ever larger, so much so that the president, who in 1980 had pledged to balance the federal budget by 1983, had in fact run up debts larger than those of all his predecessors combined. Yet Congress was in part responsible for the deficits. Legislators consistently approved budgets that were higher than those the president requested.

Reaganomics

Demonstrators in Ohio rail against the effects of Reaganomics, protesting an economics package that sacrificed funding in areas such as Social Security.

BUDGET CUTS   David Stockman, Reagan's budget director, pushed through $35 billion in budget cuts in education and cultural programs, housing, food stamps, and school lunches. Reagan assured critics that despite these cuts he was committed to maintaining the "safety net" of government services for the "truly needy." This meant that aid would remain available only to those who could not work because of either disability or child-care responsibilities. Cuts in programs for the disadvantaged, when added to the sluggish economy, helped raise the percentage of people living under the poverty level from 11.7 in 1979 to 15.3 in 1983.

David Stockman realized that the cuts in domestic spending had fallen far short of what would be needed to balance the budget in four years, as Reagan had promised. The result was a soaring budget deficit and the worst economic recession since the 1930s. The deficit, said one reporter, was Reagan's "greatest failure." Aides finally convinced the president that to reassure the public about deficits and the threat of inflation, the government needed "revenue enhancements," a euphemism for tax increases. With Reagan's support, Congress passed a new tax bill in 1982 that would raise almost $100 billion. During the midterm elections of 1982, Reagan urged voters to "stay the course" and appealed for more time to let his economic program take effect. Meanwhile, the economic slump persisted through that year, with unemployment standing at 10.4 percent, and the Republicans experienced moderate losses in the elections.

CONFLICTS OF INTEREST   The Reagan administration paralleled the Harding administration in that it found itself embroiled in charges of conflict of interest, ethical misconduct, and actual criminal behavior. Public outcry forced the administrator of the Environmental Protection Agency to resign for granting favors to industrial polluters. Although some 200 Reagan appointees were accused of unethical or illegal activities, the president himself remained untouched by any hint of impropriety. His personal charisma and aloof managerial style shielded him from the political fallout associated with the growing scandals and conflicts of interest involving his aides and cronies.

CONFLICTS OF REAGAN'S ANTI-LIBERALISM   Also during the Reagan years, organized labor suffered severe setbacks. Presidential appointments to the National Labor Relations Board tended to favor management, and in 1981 Reagan fired members of the Professional Air Traffic Controllers Organization who had participated in an illegal strike. Even more important, Reagan's smashing electoral victories in 1980 and 1984 broke the political power of the AFL-CIO, the powerful confederation of national labor unions. His criticism of unions reflected a general trend in public opinion. Although record numbers of new jobs were created during the 1980s, union membership steadily dropped. By 1987, unions represented only 17 percent of the nation's full-time workers, down from 24 percent in 1979.

Reagan also went on the offensive against feminism. He opposed the ERA, abortion on demand, and the legal guarantee of equal pay for jobs of comparable worth. He did name Sandra Day O'Connor as the first woman Supreme Court justice, but critics labeled it a token gesture rather than a reflection of any genuine commitment to gender equality. Reagan also cut funds for civil rights enforcement and the Equal Employment Opportunity Commission, and he initially opposed renewal of the Voting Rights Act of 1965 but was overruled by Congress.

THE DEFENSE BUILDUP   Reagan's conduct of foreign policy reflected his belief that trouble in the world stemmed mainly from Moscow, the capital of what he called the "evil empire." He charged that the Soviets were "prepared to commit any crime, to lie, to cheat" and do anything necessary to promote world communism. To thwart the advance of Soviet communism,

Strategic Defense Initiative

President Reagan addresses the nation on March 23, 1983, about the development of a space-age shield to intercept Soviet missiles.

Reagan and Secretary of Defense Caspar Weinberger embarked upon a major buildup of nuclear and conventional weapons. In 1983, Reagan escalated the nuclear arms race by authorizing the Defense Department to develop a Strategic Defense Initiative, which involved a complex anti-missile defense system in outer space. Despite skepticism among the media and many scientists that such a "Star Wars" defense system could be built, the new program forced the Soviets to launch an expensive research and development effort of their own to keep pace.

Reagan borrowed the rhetoric of Harry Truman, John Foster Dulles, and John F. Kennedy's inaugural to express American resolve in the face of "Communist aggression anywhere in the world." Détente deteriorated even further when the Soviets imposed martial law in Poland during the winter of 1981. The crackdown came after Polish workers, united under the banner of an independent union called Solidarity, challenged the Communist monopoly of power. As with the Soviet interventions in Hungary in 1956 and Czechoslovakia in 1968, the United States could not force the Soviets to loosen their grip on Eastern Europe. But Reagan did protest the crackdown in Poland and imposed economic sanctions against Poland's Communist government. He also worked behind the scenes to support the Solidarity movement.

THE AMERICAS   Reagan's foremost international concern, however, was in Central America, where he detected the most serious Communist threat. The tiny nation of El Salvador, caught up since 1980 in a brutal struggle between Communist-supported revolutionaries and right-wing militants, received U.S. economic and military assistance. Reagan stopped short of sending troops, but he did increase the number of military advisers and the amount of financial aid sent to the Salvadoran government. He also abandoned Jimmy Carter's strident criticism of right-wing Salvadoran militants, whose "death squads" engaged in systematic terror and murder. Critics argued that U.S. involvement ensured that the revolutionary forces would emerge as the victorious representatives of Salvadoran nationalism by capitalizing on "anti-Yankee" sentiment. Supporters countered by warning that the failure of the United States to act would allow for a repeat of the Communist victory in Nicaragua and that Honduras, Guatemala, and then all of Central America would enter the Communist camp. By 1984, however, the U.S.-backed government of President José Napoleón Duarte had brought a modicum of stability to El Salvador.

Even more troubling was the situation in Nicaragua. The State Department claimed that the Cuban-sponsored Sandinista government, which had only recently taken control of the country after ousting a corrupt dictator,

"Shhhh. It's Top Secret."

A comment on the Reagan administration's covert operations in Nicaragua.

was funneling Soviet and Cuban arms to leftist Salvadoran rebels. In response, the Reagan administration ordered the CIA to train and supply guerrilla bands of anti-Communist Nicaraguans, tagged Contras, who staged attacks on Sandinista bases and officials from sanctuaries in Honduras. In supporting these "freedom fighters," Reagan sought not only to impede the traffic in arms to Salvadoran rebels but also to replace the Sandinistas with a democratic government.

Critics of Reagan's anti-Sandinista policy accused the Contras of being mostly right-wing fanatics who indiscriminately killed civilians as well as Sandinista soldiers. They also feared that the United States might eventually commit its own combat forces, thereby precipitating a Vietnam-like intervention. Reagan warned that if the Communists prevailed in Central America, "our credibility would collapse, our alliances would crumble, and the safety of our homeland would be jeopardized."

THE MIDDLE EAST   The Middle East remained a tinderbox of conflict during the 1980s. No peaceable end seemed possible in the prolonged bloody Iran-Iraq War, entangled as it was with the passions of Islamic fundamentalism. In 1984 both sides began to attack tankers in the Persian Gulf, a major source of the world's oil. (The main international response was the sale of arms to both sides.) Nor was any settlement in sight in Afghanistan, where the Soviet occupation forces had bogged down as badly as the Americans had in Vietnam.

American administrations continued to see Israel as the strongest and most reliable ally in the volatile region, all the while seeking to encourage moderate Arab groups. But the forces of moderation were dealt a blow during the mid-1970s when Lebanon, long an enclave of peace despite its ethnic complexity, collapsed into an anarchy of warring groups. The capital, Beirut, became a battleground for Sunni and Shiite Muslims, the Druze, the Palestine Liberation Organization (PLO), Arab Christians, Syrian invaders cast as peacekeepers, and Israelis responding to PLO attacks across the border.

In 1982, Israeli forces pushed the PLO from southern Lebanon all the way north to Beirut and then began shelling PLO strongholds in Beirut. The United States sent a special ambassador to negotiate a settlement. Israeli troops moved into Beirut and looked the other way when Christian militiamen slaughtered Muslim women and children in Palestinian refugee camps. French, Italian, and U.S. forces then moved into Lebanon as "peacekeepers," but in such small numbers as to become targets themselves. Angry Muslims kept them constantly harassed. American warships and planes responded by shelling and bombing Muslim positions in the highlands behind Beirut, thereby increasing Muslim resentment. On October 23, 1983, an Islamic suicide bomber drove a truck laden with explosives into the U.S. Marine headquarters at the Beirut airport; the explosion left 241 Americans dead. In early 1984, Reagan announced that the marines would be "redeployed" to warships offshore. The Israeli forces pulled back to southern Lebanon, while the Syrians remained in eastern Lebanon. Bloody anarchy remained a way of life in a formerly peaceful country.

GRENADA   Fortune, as it happened, presented Reagan the chance for an easy triumph closer to home, a "rescue mission" that eclipsed news of the debacle in Lebanon. On the tiny Caribbean island of Grenada, the smallest independent country in the Western Hemisphere, a leftist government had admitted Cuban workers to build a new airfield and signed military agreements with Communist countries. In 1983 an even more radical military council seized power.

Appeals from the governments of neighboring islands led Reagan to order 1,900 marines to invade the island, depose the new government, and evacuate a small group of American students at Grenada's medical school. The UN General Assembly condemned the action, but it was popular among Grenadans and their neighbors and immensely popular in the United States. Although a lopsided affair, the decisive action served as notice to Latin American revolutionaries that Reagan might use military force elsewhere in the region.

REAGAN'S SECOND TERM

By 1983, prosperity had returned, and Reagan's "supply-side" economic program was at last working as touted. The gradual unraveling of the OPEC cartel and Reagan's decision to remove government controls on oil and natural gas produced a decline in oil prices that helped fuel economic growth.

THE ELECTION OF 1984   By 1984, Reagan had restored strength and vitality to the White House and the nation. Reporters began to tout the "Reagan Revolution." The economy surged with new energy. The slogan at the Republican Convention was "America is back." By contrast, the nominee of the Democrats, former vice president Walter Mondale, never quite got his act together. Endorsed by the AFL-CIO, the National Organization for Women, and many prominent African Americans, Mondale was viewed as the candidate of the special interests. He set a precedent by choosing as his running mate New York representative Geraldine Ferraro, who was quickly placed on the defensive by the need to explain her spouse's complicated business dealings.

A fit of frankness in his acceptance speech further complicated Mondale's campaign. "Mr. Reagan will raise taxes, and so will I," he told the convention. "He won't tell you. I just did." Reagan responded by vowing never to approve a tax increase and by chiding Mondale for his commitment to tax increases. Mondale never caught up. In the end, Reagan took 59 percent of the popular vote and lost only Minnesota and the District of Columbia.

DOMESTIC CHALLENGES   Buoyed by his overwhelming victory, Reagan called for "a Second American Revolution of hope and opportunity." He dared Congress to raise taxes. His veto pen was ready: "Go ahead and make my day," he said in an echo of a popular line from a movie. Through much of 1985, the president drummed up support for a tax-simplification plan. After vigorous debate that ran nearly two years, Congress passed, and in 1986 the president signed, a comprehensive Tax Reform Act. The new measure reduced the number of federal tax brackets from fourteen to two and reduced rates from the maximum of 50 percent to 15 and 28 percent— the lowest since Calvin Coolidge was president.

THE IRAN-CONTRA AFFAIR   During the fall of 1986, the Reagan administration suffered a double blow. In the midterm elections, Democrats regained control of the Senate by 55 to 45. The Democrats picked up only 6 seats in the House, but they increased their already comfortable margin to 259 to 176. For his last two years as president, Reagan would face an opposition Congress.

What was worse, on election day reports surfaced that the United States had been secretly selling arms to Iran in the hope of securing the release of American hostages held in Lebanon by extremist groups sympathetic to Iran. Such action contradicted Reagan's repeated insistence that his administration would never negotiate with terrorists. The disclosures angered America's allies as well as many Americans who vividly remembered the 1979 Iranian takeover of their country's embassy in Tehran.

There was even more to the sordid story. Over the next several months, revelations reminiscent of the Watergate affair disclosed a complicated series of covert activities carried out by administration officials. At the center of what came to be called the Iran-Contra affair was the much-decorated marine lieutenant colonel Oliver North. A swashbuckling aide to the National Security Council who specialized in counterterrorism, North, from the basement of the White House, had been running secret operations involving many government, private, and foreign individuals. His most far-fetched scheme sought to use the profits from the secret sale of military supplies to Iran to subsidize the Contra rebels fighting in Nicaragua at a time when Congress had voted to ban such aid.

Oliver North's activities, it turned out, had been approved by national security adviser Robert McFarlane; McFarlane's successor, Admiral John Poindexter; and CIA director William Casey. Both Secretary of State George Shultz and Secretary of Defense Caspar Weinberger criticized the arms sale to Iran, but their objections were ignored, and they were thereafter kept in the dark about what was going on. Later, on three occasions, Shultz threatened to resign over the continuing operation of the "pathetic" scheme. After information about the secret (and illegal) dealings surfaced in the press, McFarlane attempted suicide, Poindexter resigned, and North was fired. Casey, who denied any connection, left the CIA for health reasons and died shortly thereafter from a brain tumor.

The Iran-Contra affair

National security adviser Robert McFarlane (left) tells reporters about his resignation. Vice Admiral John Poindexter (far right) succeeds him in the post.

Under increasing criticism, Reagan appointed both an independent counsel and a three-man commission, led by former Republican senator John Tower, to investigate the scandal. The Tower Commission issued a devastating report early in 1987 that placed much of the responsibility for the bungled Iran-Contra affair on Reagan's loose management style. During the spring and summer of 1987, a joint House-Senate investigating committee began holding hearings into the Iran-Contra affair. The sessions, which were televised, revealed a tangled web of inept financial and diplomatic transactions, the shredding of incriminating government documents, crass profiteering, and misguided patriotism.

The investigations of the independent counsel led to six indictments in 1988. A Washington jury found Oliver North guilty of three relatively minor charges but innocent of nine more serious counts, apparently reflecting the jury's reasoning that he acted as an agent of higher-ups. His conviction was later overturned on appeal. Of those involved in the affair, only John Poindexter got a jail sentence—six months for his conviction on five felony counts of obstructing justice and lying to Congress.

TURMOIL IN CENTRAL AMERICA The Iran-Contra affair showed the lengths to which members of the Reagan administration would go to support the rebels fighting the ruling Sandinistas in Nicaragua. Fearing heightened Soviet and U.S. involvement in Central America, neighboring countries during the mid-1980s pressed for a negotiated settlement to the unrest in Nicaragua. In 1988, Daniel Ortega, the Nicaraguan president, pledged to negotiate directly with the Contra rebels. In the spring of 1988, those negotiations produced a cease-fire agreement, ending nearly seven years of fighting in Nicaragua. Secretary of State George Shultz called the pact an "important step forward," but the settlement surprised and disappointed hard-liners within the Reagan administration, who saw in it a Contra surrender. The Contra leaders themselves, aware of the eroding support for their cause in the U.S. Congress, saw the truce as their only chance for tangible concessions such as amnesty for political prisoners, the return of the Contras from exile, and "unrestricted freedom of expression."

In neighboring El Salvador, meanwhile, the Reagan administration's attempt to shore up the centrist government of José Napoleón Duarte through economic and military aid suffered a setback when the far-right ARENA party scored an upset victory at the polls during the spring of 1988.

DEBT AND THE STOCK MARKET PLUNGE   During the 1980s, all kinds of debt—personal, corporate, and government—increased dramatically.

Black Monday

A frenzied trader calls for attention in the pit of the Chicago Board Options Exchange as the Dow Jones stock average loses over 500 points.

Whereas Americans in the 1960s saved on average 10 percent of their income, in 1987 the figure was less than 4 percent. The federal debt more than tripled, from $908 billion in 1980 to $2.9 trillion at the end of the 1989 fiscal year. Then, on October 19, 1987, the bill collector suddenly arrived at the nation's doorstep. On that "Black Monday," the stock market experienced a tidal wave of selling reminiscent of the 1929 crash. The Dow Jones industrial average plummeted 508 points, or an astounding 22.6 percent. The market plunge nearly doubled the record 12.8 percent fall on October 28, 1929. Wall Street's selling frenzy reverberated throughout the capitalist world, sending stock prices plummeting in Tokyo, London, Paris, and Toronto.

In the aftermath of the calamitous selling spree on Black Monday, few observers actually feared a depression of the magnitude of the 1930s; there were too many safeguards built into the system to allow that. But there was real concern of an impending recession, and this fear led business leaders and economists to attack the president for glossing over such a profound warning signal. Within a few weeks, Reagan had agreed to work with Congress to develop a deficit-reduction package and for the first time indicated a willingness to include increased taxes in such a package. But the eventual compromise plan was so modest that it did little to restore investor confidence. As one Republican senator lamented, "There is a total lack of courage among those of us in the Congress to do what we all know has to be done."

THE POOR, THE HOMELESS, AND THE VICTIMS OF AIDS

The 1980s were years of vivid contrast. Despite unprecedented prosperity among the wealthiest Americans, there were beggars in the streets and homeless people sleeping in doorways, in cardboard boxes, and on ventilation grates. A variety of causes had led to a shortage of low-cost housing: the government had given up on building public housing; urban-renewal programs had demolished blighted areas but provided no housing for those they displaced; and owners had abandoned unprofitable buildings in poor neighborhoods or converted them into expensive condominiums, a process called gentrification. In addition, after new medications allowed for the deinstitutionalization of many mentally ill patients, many of them ended up on the streets because the promised community mental-health services failed to materialize. By the summer of 1988, the New York Times estimated, more than 45 percent of New York's adults constituted an underclass totally outside the labor force, because of a lack of skills, lack of motivation, drug use, and other problems.

Still another group of outcasts was composed of people suffering from a newly identified malady that had been named AIDS (acquired immunodeficiency syndrome). At the beginning of the 1980s, public health officials had

The AIDS crisis

A quilt commemorating the deaths of many thousands of Americans from AIDS was displayed in front of the White House in October 1988 so that friends and family could walk amid its panels.

reported that gay men and intravenous drug users were especially at risk for developing AIDS. Those infected with the virus that causes AIDS showed signs of fatigue, developed a strange combination of infections, and soon died; people contracted the virus, HIV, by coming into contact with the blood or body fluids of an infected person.

The Reagan administration showed little interest in AIDS in part because it initially was viewed as a "gay" disease. Patrick Buchanan, the conservative spokesman who served as Reagan's director of communications, said that homosexuals had "declared war on nature, and now nature is extracting an awful retribution."

By 2000, AIDS had claimed almost 300,000 American lives and was spreading among a larger segment of the population. Nearly 1 million Americans were carrying the deadly virus, and it had become the leading cause of death among men aged twenty-five to forty-four. The potential for the spread of HIV prompted the surgeon general to launch a controversial public-education program, which included encouraging "safe sex" through the use of condoms. With no prospect for a simple cure and with skyrocketing treatment costs, AIDS emerged as one of the nation's most intractable problems.

A HISTORIC TREATY The main prospect for positive achievement before the end of Reagan's second term seemed to lie in an arms-reduction agreement with the Soviet government. Under Mikhail Gorbachev the Soviets pursued renewed détente so that they could focus their energies and financial resources on pressing domestic problems. The logjam that had impeded arms negotiations suddenly broke in 1987, when Gorbachev announced that he

Foreign relations

A light moment at a meeting between U.S. president Ronald Reagan (left) and Soviet premier Mikhail Gorbachev (right).

was willing to consider a medium-range missile treaty. After nine months of strenuous negotiations, Reagan and Gorbachev met amid much fanfare in Washington, D.C., on December 9, 1987, and signed a treaty to eliminate intermediate-range (300- to 3,000-mile) nuclear missiles.

It was an epochal event, not only because it marked the first time that the two nations had agreed to destroy a whole class of weapons systems but also because it represented a key first step toward the eventual end of the arms race altogether. Under the terms of the treaty, the United States would destroy 859 missiles, and the Soviets would eliminate 1,752. Still, the reductions represented only 4 percent of the total nuclear-missile count on both sides. Arms-control advocates thus looked toward a second and more comprehensive treaty dealing with long-range strategic missiles.

Gorbachev's successful efforts to liberalize Soviet domestic life and improve East-West foreign relations cheered Americans. The Soviets suddenly began stressing cooperation with the West in dealing with hot spots around the world. They urged the PLO to recognize Israel's right to exist and advocated a greater role for the United Nations in the volatile Persian Gulf. Perhaps the most dramatic symbol of a thawing cold war was the phased withdrawal of 115,000 Soviet troops from Afghanistan, which began in 1988.

THE REAGAN LEGACY   Although Ronald Reagan had declared in 1981 his intention to "curb the size and influence of the federal establishment," the welfare state remained intact when he left office in early 1989. Neither the Social Security system nor Medicare had been dismantled or overhauled, nor had any other major welfare programs. And the federal agencies that Reagan had threatened to abolish, such as the Department of Education, not only remained in place in 1989 but had seen their budgets grow. The federal budget as a percentage of the gross domestic product was higher when Reagan left office than when he had entered. Moreover, he did not try to push through Congress the incendiary social issues championed by the religious right, such as school prayer and a ban on abortions.

What Ronald Reagan did accomplish was to redefine the national political agenda and accelerate the conservative insurgency that had been developing for over twenty years. He excelled as a leader because he was relentlessly optimistic about America's potential and unflinchingly committed to a philosophy of free enterprise, limited government, and strenuous anti-communism. His greatest successes were in renewing America's soaring sense of possibilities, bringing inflation under control, stimulating the longest sustained period of peacetime prosperity in history, negotiating the nuclear disarmament treaty, and helping to light the fuse of democratic freedom in Eastern Europe. In 1987, Reagan visited the Berlin Wall and in a key speech called upon the Soviet Union to allow greater freedom within the Warsaw Pact countries. "General Secretary Gorbachev, if you seek peace, if you seek prosperity for the Soviet Union and Eastern Europe, if you seek liberalization: Come here to this gate! Mr. Gorbachev, open this gate! Mr. Gorbachev, tear down this wall!" By redirecting the thrust of both domestic and foreign policy during the 1980s, Reagan put the fragmented Democratic party on the defensive and forced conventional New Deal "liberalism" into a panicked retreat.

THE ELECTION OF 1988   In 1988 eight Democratic presidential candidates engaged in a wild scramble for their party's nomination. As the primary season progressed, however, it soon became a two-man race between Massachusetts governor Michael Dukakis and Jesse Jackson, a charismatic African American civil rights activist who had been one of Martin Luther King Jr.'s chief lieutenants. Dukakis eventually won out and managed a difficult reconciliation with the Jackson forces that left the Democrats unified and confident as the fall campaign began.

The Republicans nominated Reagan's two-term vice president, George H. W. Bush, who after a bumpy start had easily cast aside his rivals in the primaries. A veteran government official, having served as a Texas congressman, an envoy to China, an ambassador to the UN, and head of the CIA, Bush projected none of Reagan's charisma or rhetorical skills. One Democrat described him as a man born "with a silver foot in his mouth." Early polls showed Dukakis with a wide lead.

Yet Bush delivered a forceful address at the nominating convention that sharply enhanced his stature. Although pledging to continue the Reagan agenda, he also recognized that "things aren't perfect" in America. Bush promised to use the White House to fight bigotry, illiteracy, and homelessness. Humane sympathies, he insisted, would guide his conservatism. "I want a kinder, gentler nation," Bush said softly in his acceptance speech. But the most memorable line was a defiant statement on taxes: "The Congress will push me to raise taxes, and I'll say no, and they'll push, and I'll say no, and they'll push again. And I'll say to them: Read my lips. No new taxes."

In a not-so gentle campaign given over to mudslinging, Bush and his aides attacked Dukakis as a camouflaged liberal in the mold of George McGovern, Jimmy Carter, and Walter Mondale. The Republican onslaught took its toll against the less organized, less focused Dukakis campaign. In the end, Dukakis took only ten states plus the District of Columbia, with clusters of support in the Northeast, Midwest, and Northwest. Bush carried the rest, with a margin of about 54 percent to 46 percent in the popular vote and 426 to 111 in the Electoral College.

The 1988 election

George H. W. Bush (right) at the 1988 Republican National Convention with his newly chosen running mate, Dan Quayle, a senator from Indiana.

Generally speaking, the more affluent and better-educated voters preferred the Republican ticket. While Dukakis won the inner-city vote, garnering 86 percent of the African American vote, Bush scored big in the suburbs and in rural areas, especially in the once-Democratic South, where his margin of support by white voters ranged from a low of 63 percent in

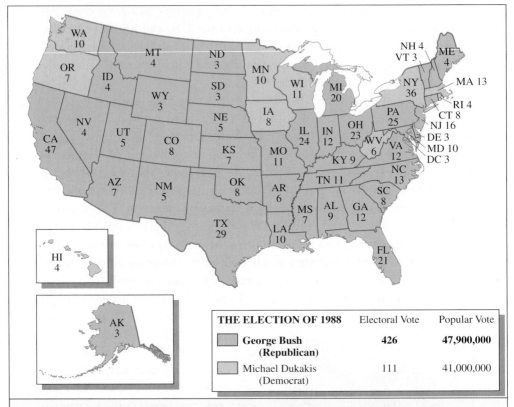

THE ELECTION OF 1988	Electoral Vote	Popular Vote
▨ **George Bush** **(Republican)**	**426**	**47,900,000**
▨ Michael Dukakis (Democrat)	111	41,000,000

How did George H. W. Bush overtake Michael Dukakis's lead in the polls? What was the role of race and class in the election results?

Florida to a high of 80 percent in Mississippi. More significant was Bush's success among blue-collar workers: he captured 46 percent of these typically Democratic voters.

THE BUSH ADMINISTRATION

George Bush viewed himself as a guardian president rather than an activist. He lacked Reagan's visionary outlook. Bush was a pragmatist caretaker eager to avoid "stupid mistakes" and find a way to get along with the Democratic majority in Congress. "We don't need to remake society," he announced. Bush therefore sought to consolidate and nurture the initiatives that Reagan had put in place rather than launch his own array of programs and policies.

DOMESTIC INITIATIVES   The biggest problem facing the Bush administration was the national debt, which stood at $2.6 trillion in 1989, nearly three times its 1980 level. Bush's taboo on tax increases (meaning mainly income taxes) and his insistence upon lowering capital-gains taxes—on profits from the sale of stocks and other property—made it more difficult to reduce the annual deficit or trim the long-term debt. By 1990 the country faced "a fiscal mess." Eventually Bush decided "that both the size of the deficit problem and the need for a package that can be enacted" required budget cuts and "tax revenue increases," which he had sworn to avoid.

Another domestic initiative was President Bush's war on illegal drugs. During the 1980s cocaine addiction spread through sizable segments of society, luring not only those with money to spend but also those with little money to spare, who used the drug in its smokable form, known as crack. Bush vowed to make drug abuse his number-one domestic priority and appointed William J. Bennett, former education secretary, as "drug czar," or head of a new Office of National Drug Control Policy, with cabinet status but no department. Yet federal spending on programs intended to curb drug abuse rose only modestly. The message, on this and on education, housing, and other social problems, was that more of the burden should fall on state and local authorities.

THE DEMOCRACY MOVEMENT ABROAD   George Bush entered the White House with more foreign-policy experience than most presidents, and he found the spotlight of the world stage more congenial than wrestling with the intractable problems of the inner cities, drug abuse, and the deficit. Within two years of his inauguration, Bush would lead the United States into two wars. Throughout most of 1989, however, he merely had to sit back and observe the dissolution of one totalitarian or authoritarian regime after another. For the first time in years, democracy was on the march in a sequence of mostly bloodless revolutions that surprised the world.

Although a grassroots democracy movement in China came to a tragic end in 1989 when government forces mounted a deadly assault on demonstrators in Beijing's Tiananmen Square, Eastern Europe had an entirely different experience. With a rigid economic system failing to deliver the goods to the Soviet people, Mikhail Gorbachev responded with policies of perestroika (restructuring) and glasnost (openness), a loosening of centralized economic planning and censorship. His foreign policy sought rapprochement and trade with the West, and he aimed to relieve the Soviet economy of burdensome military costs.

Gorbachev also backed off from Soviet imperial ambitions. Early in 1989, Soviet troops left Afghanistan after spending nine years bogged down in civil

Dissolution of the Soviet Empire

West Germans hacking away at the Berlin Wall on November 11, 1989, two days after all crossings between East Germany and West Germany were opened.

war there. Gorbachev then repudiated the Brezhnev Doctrine, which asserted the right of the Soviet Union to intervene in the internal affairs of other Communist countries. The days when Soviet tanks rolled through Warsaw and Prague were over, and hard-line leaders in the Eastern-bloc countries found themselves beset by demands for reform from their own people. With opposition strength building, the old regimes fell with surprisingly little bloodshed. Communist party rule ended first in Poland and Hungary, then in Czechoslovakia and Bulgaria. In Romania the year of peaceful revolution ended in a bloodbath when the people joined the army in a bloody uprising against the brutal dictator Nicolae Ceaușescu. He and his wife were captured, tried, and then executed on Christmas Day.

The most spectacular event in the collapse of the Soviet Empire came on November 9, 1989, when the chief symbol of the cold war—the Berlin Wall—was torn down by Germans using small tools and even their hands. With the borders to the West now fully open, the Communist government of East Germany collapsed, a freely elected government came to power, and on October 3, 1990, the five states of East Germany were united with West

Action against Gorbachev

In August 1991, one day after Mikhail Gorbachev was placed under house arrest by Communists planning a coup, Russian president Boris Yeltsin (holding papers) makes a speech criticizing the plotters.

Germany. The unified German nation remained in NATO, and the Communist Warsaw Pact alliance was dissolved.

The reform impulse that Gorbachev helped unleash in the Eastern-bloc countries careened out of control within the Soviet Union, however. Gorbachev proved unusually adept at political restructuring, yielding the Communist monopoly of government but building a new presidential system that gave him, if anything, increased powers. His skills in the Byzantine politics of the Kremlin, though, did not extend to an antiquated economy that resisted change. The revival of ethnic allegiances added to the instability. Although Russia proper included slightly more than half the Soviet Union's population, it was only one of fifteen constituent republics, most of which began to seek autonomy, if not independence.

Gorbachev's popularity shrank in the Soviet Union as it grew abroad. It especially eroded among the Communist hard-liners, who saw in his reforms the unraveling of their bureaucratic and political empire. Once the genie of freedom was released from the Communist lamp, however, it took on a momentum of its own. On August 18, 1991, a cabal of political and military leaders tried to seize the reins of power in Russia. They accosted Gorbachev at his vacation retreat in the Crimea and demanded that he sign a decree proclaiming a state of emergency and transferring his powers to them. He replied, "Go to hell," whereupon he was placed under house arrest.

The coup was doomed from the start, however. Poorly planned and clumsily implemented, it lacked effective coordination. The plotters failed to arrest popular leaders such as Boris Yeltsin, the president of the Russian republic; they neglected to close the airports or cut off telephone and television communications; and they were opposed by key elements of the military and KGB (the secret police). But most important, the plotters failed to recognize the strength of the democratic idealism unleashed by Gorbachev's reforms.

As the political drama unfolded in the Soviet Union, foreign leaders denounced the coup. On August 20, President Bush responded favorably to Yeltsin's request for support and persuaded other leaders to join him in refusing to recognize the legitimacy of the new Soviet government. The next day, word began to seep out that the plotters had given up and were fleeing. Several committed suicide, and a newly released Gorbachev ordered the others arrested. Yet things did not go back to the way they had been. Although Gorbachev reclaimed the title of president of the Soviet Union, he was forced to resign as head of the Communist party and admit that he had made a grave mistake in appointing the men who had turned against him. Boris Yeltsin emerged as the most popular political figure in the country.

So what had begun as a reactionary coup turned into a powerful accelerant for stunning changes in the Soviet Union, or the Soviet Disunion, as one wag termed it. Most of the fifteen republics proclaimed their independence, with the Baltic republics of Latvia, Lithuania, and Estonia regaining the status of independent nations. The Communist party apparatus was dismantled, prompting celebrating crowds to topple statues of Lenin and other Communist heroes.

A chastened Gorbachev could only acquiesce in the breakup of the Soviet Empire, whereas the systemic problems burdening the Soviet Union before the coup remained intractable. The economy was stagnant, food and coal shortages loomed on the horizon, and consumer goods remained scarce. The reformers had won, but they had yet to establish deep roots in a country with no democratic tradition. Leaping into the unknown, they faced years of hardship and uncertainty.

The aborted coup also accelerated Soviet and American efforts to reduce their stockpiles of nuclear weapons. In late 1991, President Bush stunned the world by announcing that the United States would destroy all its tactical nuclear weapons on land and at sea in Europe and Asia, take its long-range bombers off twenty-four-hour-alert status, and initiate discussions with the Soviet Union for the purpose of instituting sharp cuts in ICBMs with multiple warheads. Bush explained that the prospect of a Soviet invasion of western Europe was "no longer a realistic threat," and this transformation provided an unprecedented opportunity for reducing the threat of nuclear holocaust. President Gorbachev responded by announcing reciprocal Soviet cutbacks.

PANAMA   The end of the cold war did not spell the end of international tensions and conflict, however. Indeed, before the end of 1989, U.S. troops were engaged in battle in Panama, where a petty tyrant provoked the first of America's military engagements under George H. W. Bush. In 1983, General Manuel Noriega had maneuvered himself into the position of leader of the Panamanian Defense Forces, which made him the de facto head of the government in fact if not in title. Earlier, when Bush headed the CIA, Noriega, as chief of military intelligence, had developed a profitable business of supplying information on the region to the CIA. At the same time, he developed avenues in the region for drug smuggling and gunrunning, laundering the money from those activities through Panamanian banks. For a time, American intelligence analysts looked the other way, regarding Noriega as a useful contact, but eventually he became an embarrassment. In 1987 a rejected associate published charges of Noriega's drug activities and accused him further of rigged elections and political assassination.

In 1988 federal grand juries in Miami and Tampa indicted Noriega and fifteen others on drug charges. The next year the Panamanian president tried to fire Noriega, but the National Assembly ousted the president and named Noriega "maximum leader." The legislators then declared Panama "in a state of war" with the United States. The next day, December 16, 1989, a U.S. marine in Panama was killed. President Bush thereupon ordered an invasion of Panama with the purpose of capturing Noriega so that he might stand trial in the United States and installing a government headed by President Guillermo Endara.

The 12,000 U.S. military personnel already in Panama were quickly joined by 12,000 more, and in the early morning of December 20 five military task forces struck at strategic targets in the country. Within hours, Noriega had surrendered. Twenty-three U.S. servicemen were killed in the action, and estimates of Panamanian casualties, including many civilians, were as high as 4,000. In April 1992, Noriega was convicted in the United States on eight counts of racketeering and drug distribution.

THE GULF WAR   Months after Panama had moved to the background of public attention, Saddam Hussein, dictator of Iraq, focused attention on the Middle East when his army suddenly invaded tiny Kuwait on August 2,

1990. Kuwait had raised its production of oil, contrary to agreements with OPEC. The resulting drop in global oil prices offended the Iraqi regime, deep in debt and heavily dependent upon oil revenues. Saddam Hussein was surprised by the backlash his invasion of Kuwait caused. The UN Security Council unanimously condemned the invasion and demanded withdrawal. U.S. Secretary of State James A. Baker III and the Soviet foreign minister issued a joint statement of condemnation. On August 6 the Security Council endorsed Resolution 661, an embargo on trade with Iraq.

Bush condemned Iraq's "naked aggression" and dispatched planes and troops to Saudi Arabia on a "wholly defensive" mission: to protect Saudi Arabia. British forces soon joined in, as did Arab units from Egypt, Morocco, Syria, Oman, the United Arab Emirates, and Qatar. On August 22, Bush ordered the mobilization of American reserve forces for the operation, now dubbed Desert Shield.

A flurry of peace efforts sent diplomats scurrying, but without result. Iraq refused to yield. On January 12, Congress authorized the use of U.S. armed forces. By January 1991 over thirty nations were committed to Operation Desert Shield. Some nations sent only planes, ships, or support forces, but

The Gulf War

U.S. soldiers adapt to desert conditions during Operation Desert Shield, December 1990.

sixteen, including ten Islamic countries, committed ground forces. Desert Shield became Operation Desert Storm when the first allied cruise missiles began to hit Iraq on January 16.

Saddam Hussein, expecting a landing on the Kuwaiti coast and an allied attack northward into Kuwait, concentrated his forces in that country. The Iraqis were outflanked when 200,000 allied troops, largely American, British, and French, turned up on the undefended Iraqi border with Saudi Arabia 100 to 200 miles to the west. The swift-moving allied ground assault began on February 24 and lasted only four days. Iraqi soldiers surrendered by the thousands.

On February 28, six weeks after the fighting began, President Bush called for a cease-fire, the Iraqis accepted, and the shooting ended. There were 137 American fatalities. The lowest estimate of Iraqi deaths, civilian and military, was 100,000. The coalition forces occupied about a fifth of Iraq. The consequences of the brief but intense Persian Gulf War, the "mother of all battles" in Saddam Hussein's words, would be played out in the future.

End of Chapter Review

CHAPTER SUMMARY

- **Rise of Conservatism** Ronald Reagan's charm, coupled with disillusionment over Jimmy Carter's presidency and the Republicans' call for a return to traditional values, won Reagan the presidency in 1980. The Republican insurgency was characterized by a cultural backlash against the feminist movement, and it was supported by Christian evangelicals and people who wanted lower taxes and a smaller, less intrusive federal government.

- **Iran-Contra Scandal** Members of Reagan's administration secretly sold arms to Iran in the hopes of securing the release of American hostages held in Lebanon by extremists sympathetic to Iran. The deal contradicted the president's public claims that he would never deal with terrorists. Furthermore, profits from the arms sales were used to fund right-wing rebels in Nicaragua, known as Contras, despite Congress's having voted to ban any aid to the Contras. An independent commission appointed by the president determined that Reagan's loose management style was responsible for the illegal activities, and Reagan admitted that he had lied to the American people.

- **End of the Cold War** Toward the end of the century, democratic movements exploded in China, where they failed, and in Eastern Europe, where they largely succeeded. In the Soviet Union, Mikhail Gorbachev's steps to restructure the economy and promote more open policies led to demands for further reform. Communist party rule collapsed in the Soviet satellite states. In November 1989 the Berlin Wall was torn down, and a year later Germany was reunified. Russia itself survived a coup by hard-liners, and by 1991 the cold war had ended.

- **Reaganomics** Americans in the 1980s experienced unprecedented prosperity, yet beggars and homeless people were visible in most cities. The prevailing mood was conservative, and AIDS was condemned as a "gay" disease. "Reaganomics" failed to reduce public spending, but the president nevertheless championed tax cuts for the rich. The result was massive public debt and the stock market collapse of 1987.

- **The Gulf War** Saddam Hussein of Iraq invaded Kuwait in 1990. The United Nations condemned Hussein's action and authorized the use of force to dislodge Iraq from Kuwait. Over thirty nations committed themselves to Operation Desert Shield. When Hussein did not withdraw, the allied forces launched Operation Desert Storm, and the Iraqis surrendered within six weeks.

37

TRIUMPH AND TRAGEDY: AMERICA AT THE TURN OF THE CENTURY

FOCUS QUESTIONS wwnorton.com/studyspace

- How did the demographics of the United States change between 1980 and 2009?
- What led to the Democratic resurgence of the early 1990s and the surprising Republican landslide of 1994?
- What caused the surge and decline of the financial markets in the 1990s and the early twenty-first century?
- What were the consequences of the rise of global terrorism in the early twenty-first century?
- In what ways was the 2008 presidential election historic?

The United States entered the final decade of the twentieth century triumphant. American vigilance in the cold war had fueled the shocking collapse of the Soviet Union and the birth of democratic capitalism in eastern Europe. The United States was now the world's only superpower. Not since ancient Rome had one nation exercised such influence in world affairs, for good and for ill. By the mid-1990s the American economy would become the marvel of the world as remarkable gains in productivity afforded by new technologies created the greatest period of prosperity in modern history. Yet no sooner did the century come to an end than America's comfortable sense of physical and material security was shattered by a horrifying terrorist assault that killed thousands, plummeted the economy into a steep recession, and called into question conventional notions of national security and personal safety.

AMERICA'S CHANGING MOSAIC

DEMOGRAPHIC SHIFTS   The nation's population had grown to over 306 million by 2010. During the last quarter of the twentieth century, the sunbelt states of the South and the West continued to lure residents from the Midwest and the Northeast. Fully 90 percent of the nation's total population growth during the 1980s occurred in southern or western states. These population shifts forced a massive redistricting of the House of Representatives, with Florida, California, and Texas gaining seats and northern states such as New York losing them. The sunbelt states were attractive not only because of their mild climate; they also had the lowest tax rates in the nation, the highest rates of economic growth, and growing numbers of evangelical Christians and retirees. Such attributes also made the sunbelt states fertile ground for the Republican party.

Women continued to enter the workforce in large numbers. In 1970, 38 percent of the workforce was female; in 2000 the figure was almost 50 percent. Women made up over a third of the new doctors (up from 4 percent in 1970), 40 percent of the new lawyers (up from 8 percent in 1970), and 23 percent of the new dentists (up from less than 1 percent in 1970).

The decline of the traditional family unit continued. In 2005 less than 65 percent of children lived with two parents, down from 85 percent in 1970. And more people were living alone than ever before, largely as a result of high divorce rates or a growing practice among young people of delaying marriage until well into their twenties. The number of single mothers increased 35 percent during the decade. The rate was much higher for African Americans: in 2000 fewer than 32 percent of black children lived with both parents, down from 67 percent in 1960.

Young African Americans in particular faced shrinking economic opportunities at the start of the twenty-first century. The urban poor more than others were victimized by high rates of crime and violence, with young black men suffering the most. In 2000 the leading cause of death among African American men between the ages of fifteen and twenty-four was homicide. Over 25 percent of African American men aged twenty to twenty-nine were in prison, on parole, or on probation, while only 4 percent were enrolled in college. And nearly 40 percent of African American men were functionally illiterate.

THE NEW IMMIGRANTS   The racial and ethnic composition of the country also changed rapidly in the early twenty-first century. During the

1990s the foreign-born population increased by 57 percent, to 31 million, the largest ever. By 2010 the United States had more foreign-born and first-generation residents than ever before, and each year 1 million more immigrants arrived. Over 30 percent of Americans claimed African, Asian, Latino, or American Indian ancestry. Hispanics represented 16 percent of the total population, African Americans 11 percent, Asians about 4 percent, and American Indians almost 1 percent. The rate of increase among those four groups was twice as fast as it had been during the 1970s. In 2005, Hispanics became the nation's largest minority group.

The primary cause of this dramatic change in the nation's ethnic mix was a surge of immigration. In 2000 the United States welcomed more than twice as many immigrants as all other countries in the world combined. For the first time in the nation's history, the majority of immigrants came not from Europe but from other parts of the world: Asia, Latin America, and Africa. Among the legal immigrants, Mexicans made up the largest share,

Illegal immigration

Increasing numbers of Chinese risked their savings and their lives to gain entry to the United States. These illegal immigrants are trying to keep warm after being forced to swim ashore when the freighter carrying them to the United States ran aground near Rockaway Beach in New York City in June 1993.

averaging over 100,000 a year. Many new immigrants compiled an astonishing record of achievement, yet their very success contributed to the resentment they encountered from other groups.

THE COMPUTER REVOLUTION   Not only demographic shifts and immigration but also technological changes were transforming the nation at the end of the twentieth century. The computer age had arrived. The idea of a programmable machine that would rapidly perform mental tasks had been around since the eighteenth century, but it took the crisis of World War II to gather the intellectual and financial resources needed to create such a "computer." In 1946 a team of engineers at the University of Pennsylvania created ENIAC (electronic numerical integrator and computer), the first all-purpose, all-electronic digital computer.

The next major breakthrough was the invention in 1971 of the microprocessor—a tiny computer on a silicon chip. The functions that had once been performed by computers taking up an entire room could be performed by a microchip circuit the size of a postage stamp. The microchip made

The computer age

Beginning with the cumbersome electronic numerical integrator and computer (ENIAC), pictured here in 1946, computer technology flourished, leading to the development of personal computers in the 1980s and the popularization of the Internet in the 1990s.

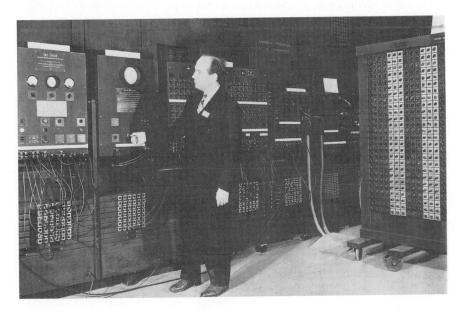

possible the personal computer. In 1975 an engineer named Ed Roberts developed the prototype of the so-called personal computer. The Altair 8800 was imperfect and cumbersome, with no display, no keyboard, and not enough memory to do anything useful. But its potential excited a Harvard sophomore named Bill Gates. He improved the software of the Altair 8800, dropped out of college, and formed a company called Microsoft to sell the new system. By 1977, Gates and others had helped transform the personal computer from a machine for hobbyists into a mass consumer product.

During the 1990s the development of the Internet and electronic mail allowed for instantaneous communication, thereby accelerating what came to be called the globalization of the economy and dramatically increasing productivity in the workplace.

CULTURAL CONSERVATISM

Cultural conservatives helped elect Ronald Reagan and George Bush in the 1980s, but they were disappointed with the results. Once in office, neither president had, in the eyes of those conservatives, adequately addressed their moral agenda, including a complete ban on abortions and the restoration of prayer in public schools. By the 1990s a new generation of young conservative activists, mostly political independents or Republicans and largely from the sunbelt states, had emerged as a major force in national affairs. They were more ideological, more libertarian, more partisan, and more impatient than their predecessors. The new breed of cultural conservatives abhorred the excesses of social liberalism. They lamented the disappearance of basic forms of decency and propriety, and they attacked affirmative-action programs designed to redress historic injustices committed against women and minorities. During the 1990s powerful groups inside and outside the Republican party mobilized to roll back government programs that gave preference to certain social groups. Prominent African American conservatives supported such efforts, arguing that racially based preferences were demeaning and condescending remedies for historical injustices.

THE RELIGIOUS RIGHT Although quite diverse, cultural conservatives tended to be evangelical Christians or orthodox Catholics, and they joined together to exert increasing religious pressure on the political process. In 1989 the Virginia-based television evangelist Pat Robertson organized the Christian Coalition to replace Jerry Falwell's Moral Majority as the flagship organization of the resurgent religious right. The Christian Coalition chose the Republican party as the best vehicle for promoting its pro–school prayer, anti-abortion, anti–gay rights positions. In addition to celebrating "traditional family values," it urged politicians to "radically downsize and delimit government." In many respects the religious right took control of the political and social agendas in the nineties. As one journalist acknowledged in 1995, "the religious right is moving toward center stage in American secular life."

BUSH TO CLINTON

For months after the Persian Gulf War in 1991, George H. W. Bush seemed unbeatable; his approval rating rose to 91 percent. But the aftermath of Desert Storm was mixed, with Saddam Hussein's despotic grip on Iraq still intact. Despite his image of strength abroad, Bush began to look weak even on foreign policy. The Soviet Union meanwhile stumbled on to its surprising end. On December 25, 1991, the Soviet flag over the Kremlin was replaced by

The Persian Gulf War

Iraqi soldiers surrender to the Allied forces in Kuwait.

the flag of the Russian Federation. The cold war had ended with the dismemberment of the Soviet Union and its fifteen constituent republics. As a result, the United States had become the world's only superpower.

"Containment" of the Soviet Union, the bedrock of U.S. foreign policy for more than four decades, had lost its reason for being. Bush, the ultimate cold war careerist—formerly ambassador to the United Nations, envoy to China, head of the CIA, and vice president under Reagan—struggled to interpret the fluid new international scene. He spoke of a "new world order" but never defined it. By his own admission he had trouble with "the vision thing." By the end of 1991, a listless Bush faced a challenge in the Republican primary from the feisty television commentator and former White House aide Patrick Buchanan, who adopted the slogan "America First" and called on Bush to "bring home the boys." As the euphoria of the Gulf War victory wore off, a popular bumper sticker reflected the growing public frustration with the Bush administration: "Saddam Hussein still has his job. What about you?"

RECESSION AND DOWNSIZING   For the Bush administration and for the nation, the most devastating development in the early nineties was a prolonged economic recession. The first major economic setback in more than eight years, it grew into the longest, if not the deepest, since the Great Depression. During 1991, 25 million workers—about 20 percent of the labor force—were unemployed at some point. The euphoria over the allied victory in the Gulf War quickly gave way to surly anxiety generated by the depressed economy. At the end of 1991, *Time* magazine declared that "no one, not even George Bush" could deny "that the economy was sputtering." With his domestic policies in disarray and his foreign policy abandoned, George Bush tried a clumsy balancing act in addressing the recession, on the one hand acknowledging that "people are hurting" while on the other telling Americans that "this is a good time to buy a car."

REPUBLICAN TURMOIL   President Bush had already set a political trap for himself when he declared at the 1988 Republican Convention: "Read my lips. No new taxes." Fourteen months into his presidency, he decided that the federal budget deficit was a greater risk than violation of his no-new-taxes pledge. After intense negotiations with congressional Democrats, Bush announced that reducing the federal deficit required "tax revenue increases." His backsliding set off a revolt among House Republicans, but a bipartisan majority (with most Republicans still opposed) finally approved a tax-increase measure, raising the top personal rate from 28 to 31 percent, disallowing certain deductions in the upper brackets, and raising various special taxes. Such actions increased federal revenue and eroded Bush's political support. Conservative Republicans would not let George Bush forget his abandoned pledge not to raise taxes.

At the 1992 Republican Convention, Patrick Buchanan, who had won about a third of the votes in the party's primaries, lambasted Bush for breaking his pledge not to raise taxes and for becoming the "biggest spender in American history." Buchanan claimed to be a crusader "for a Middle American revolution" that would halt illegal immigration and liberal permissiveness. As the 1992 election unfolded, Bush's real problem was not Pat Buchanan and the conservative wing of the Republican party, however. What threatened his reelection was his own listless effort to jump-start the economy.

DEMOCRATIC RESURGENCE   In contrast to divisions among Republicans, the Democrats at their 1992 convention presented an image of centrist forces in control. For several years the Democratic Leadership Council, in which Arkansas governor William Jefferson Clinton figured prominently, had been pushing the party from the liberal left to the center of the political spectrum. Clinton strove to move the Democrats closer to the mainstream of political opinion. A graduate of Georgetown University, he had won a Rhodes scholarship to Oxford University and then earned a law degree from Yale, where he met his future wife, Hillary Rodham. By 1979, at age thirty-two, Bill Clinton was back in his native Arkansas, having been elected the youngest governor in the country. He served three more terms as governor and in the process emerged as a dynamic young leader committed to winning back the middle-class whites who had voted Republican during the 1980s. Democrats had grown so liberal, he argued, that they had alienated their key constituency, the "vital center."

A self-described moderate seeking the Democratic presidential nomination, Clinton promised to cut the defense budget, provide tax relief for the middle class, and create a massive economic aid package for the former republics of the Soviet Union to help them forge democratic societies. Witty, intelligent, and a compelling speaker, Clinton projected energy, youth, and optimism, reminding many political observers of John F. Kennedy.

But underneath the veneer of Clinton's charisma were several flaws. He often seemed so determined to become president that he was willing to sacrifice consistency and principle. He made extensive use of polls to shape his stance on issues, pandered to special-interest groups, and flip-flopped on

The 1992 presidential campaign

Presidential candidate Bill Clinton and his running mate, Al Gore, brought youthful enthusiasm to the campaign trail.

controversial subjects, leading critics to label him Slick Willie. Said one former opponent in Arkansas: "He'll be what people want him to be. He'll do or say what it will take to get elected." Even more enticing to the media and more embarrassing to Clinton were charges that he was a chronic adulterer and that he had manipulated the ROTC program during the Vietnam War to avoid the draft. Clinton's evasive denials of both allegations could not dispel a lingering distrust of his character.

Yet after a series of bruising party primaries, Clinton emerged as the front-runner at the Democratic nominating convention in the summer of 1992. Once nominated, Clinton chose Senator Albert Gore Jr. of Tennessee as his running mate. So the candidates were two Southern Baptists from adjoining states. Flushed with their convention victory and sporting a ten-point lead over Bush in the polls, the Clinton-Gore team stressed economic issues to win over working-class white and black voters. Clinton won the election with 370 electoral votes and about 43 percent of the vote; Bush received 168 electoral votes and 39 percent of the vote; and off-and-on independent candidate H. Ross Perot of Texas garnered 18 percent of the popular vote but no electoral votes. A puckish billionaire, Perot found a large audience for his simplified explanations of public problems and his offers to just "get under the hood and fix them."

DOMESTIC POLICY IN CLINTON'S FIRST TERM

Clinton's inexperience in international affairs and congressional maneuvering led to several missteps in his first year as president. Like George Bush before him, he reneged on several campaign promises. He abandoned his proposed middle-class tax cut in order to keep down the federal deficit. When his attempt to allow professed homosexuals to serve in the armed forces aroused strong opposition among military commanders and in Congress, he backed down nine days into office and later announced an ambiguous new policy concerning gays in the military that came to be known as "don't ask, don't tell." In Clinton's first two weeks in office, his approval rating dropped 20 percent.

THE ECONOMY   As a candidate, Clinton had pledged to reduce the federal deficit without damaging the economy. To this end, on February 17 he proposed higher taxes for corporations and for individuals in higher tax brackets and called for an economic stimulus package for "investment" in public works (transportation, utilities, and the like) and "human capital" (education, skills, health, and welfare). The hotly contested bill finally passed by 218 to 216 in the House and 51 to 50 in the Senate, with Vice President Gore breaking the tie.

Equally contested was the North American Free Trade Agreement (NAFTA), which the Bush administration had negotiated with Canada and Mexico. The debate over its congressional approval revived old arguments on the tariff. Clinton stuck with his party's tradition of low tariffs and urged approval of NAFTA, which would make North America the largest free-trade area in the world. He and

NAFTA protesters

Protesters going to a rally where House Majority Leader Richard Gephardt spoke to hundreds of opponents.

his supporters argued that tariff reductions would open up foreign markets to American industries. Opponents of the bill, such as gadfly Ross Perot and organized labor, favored barriers that would discourage cheaper foreign products and believed that with NAFTA the country would hear the "giant sucking sound" of American jobs being drawn to Mexico. Yet Clinton prevailed with solid Republican support while losing a sizable minority of Democrats, mostly from the South, where people feared that textile mills would lose business to "cheap-labor" countries, as they did.

HEALTH-CARE REFORM   Clinton's major public-policy initiative was a federal health-care plan. Government-subsidized health insurance was not a new idea. Other industrial countries had long ago started national health-insurance programs, Germany as early as 1883, Britain in 1911. Off and on throughout the twentieth century the idea had been a subject of political discussion in the United States. Medicare, initiated in 1965, provided insurance for people sixty-five and older, and Medicaid supported state medical assistance for the indigent. Those programs had grown enormously, as had business spending on private health insurance.

Sentiment for health-care reform spread as annual medical costs skyrocketed and some 39 million Americans went without insurance either by choice or out of necessity. The Clinton administration argued that universal medical insurance would reduce the overall costs of health care. Medicare covered older people, the most vulnerable to medical expenses, and its costs were soaring. Many of the working poor could not afford insurance, and many younger, healthier people took a chance on doing without.

Clinton's federal health-care plan

President Bill Clinton holds up a proposed health security I.D. card while outlining his plan for health-care reform to Congress.

Universal medical coverage as proposed by Clinton would entitle every citizen and legal immigrant to health insurance. Government would subsidize all or part of the payments for small businesses and the poor, the latter from funds that formerly went to Medicaid, and would collect a "sin tax" on tobacco and perhaps alcoholic beverages to pay for the program. Throughout 1994 a comprehensive health-insurance plan remained the centerpiece of the Clinton agenda. The bill aroused opposition from vested interests, however, especially the pharmaceutical and insurance industries. By the summer of 1994, Clinton's health-insurance plan was pretty well doomed. Lacking the votes to stop a filibuster by Senate Republicans, the Democrats acknowledged defeat and gave up the fight for universal medical coverage.

REPUBLICAN INSURGENCY

During 1994, Bill Clinton began to see his coveted presidency unravel. Unable to get either health-care reform or welfare-reform bills through the Democratic Congress and having failed to carry out his campaign pledge for middle-class tax relief, he and his party found themselves on the defensive. In the midterm elections of 1994, the Democrats suffered a humbling defeat. It was the first election since 1952 in which Republicans captured both houses of Congress at the same time. Not a single Republican incumbent was defeated. Republicans also won a net gain of eleven governorships and fifteen state legislatures.

The election returns signaled a repudiation of Clinton and the Democratic Congress. Clinton's waffling on major issues convinced many in his own party that he was a politician rather than a leader, someone who thrived as a campaigner but was bereft of genuine convictions. When Clinton joined the chorus of conservatives calling for a scaling back of affirmative-action plans designed to remedy historic patterns of racial discrimination in hiring and the awarding of government contracts, liberal Democrats felt betrayed.

THE CONTRACT WITH AMERICA   A Georgian named Newton Leroy Gingrich led the Republican insurgency in Congress during the mid-1990s. Gingrich, a brilliant former history professor with an oversize ego, had helped mobilize religious and social conservatives associated with the Christian Coalition. In early 1995 he became the first Republican Speaker of the House in forty-two years. Gingrich announced that "we are at the end of an era." Liberalism, he claimed, was dead, and the Democratic party was dying. Gingrich pledged to start a new reign of congressional Republican dominance that would dismantle the "corrupt liberal welfare state." He was aided by freshman Republicans who promoted what Gingrich called the Contract with America. The ten-point contract outlined an anti-big-government program with less regulation, less environmental conservation, term limits for members of Congress, a line-item veto for the president, welfare reform, and a balanced-budget amendment.

Yet the much-ballyhooed GOP revolution and the Contract with America quickly fizzled out. The revolution that the imperious Gingrich touted was far too ambitious to be carried out in so limited a time with so slim a majority and so little sense of crisis. What is more, many of the Republican freshman representatives were scornful of compromise and were amateurs at legislative procedure; they limited Gingrich's ability to maneuver. The Senate, whose members were less spellbound by Gingrich and not party to the Contract with America anyway, rejected many of the bills that had been passed in the House. The "Republican revolution" of 1994 fizzled out, too, because Newt Gingrich became such an unpopular figure, both in Congress and among the electorate. He was too ambitious, too slick, too aggressive, too rambunctious. "No political figure in modern time," a journalist declared in 1996, "has done more to undermine the power of his message with the defects of his personality than the disastrously voluble Speaker of the House."

LEGISLATIVE BREAKTHROUGH   In the late summer of 1996, as lawmakers were preparing to adjourn and participate in the presidential nominating conventions, the 104th Congress broke through its partisan gridlock and passed a flurry of important legislation that President Clinton quickly signed, including bills increasing the minimum wage and broadening public access to health insurance. Even more significant was a comprehensive welfare-reform measure that ended the federal government's open-ended guarantee of aid to the poor, a guarantee that had been in place since 1935. The Personal Responsibility and Work Opportunity Act of 1996 turned over the major federal welfare programs to the states, which would receive federal grants to fund them. The bill also limited the amount of time during which a person could receive welfare benefits funded by federal money and required that at least half of a state's welfare recipients have jobs or be enrolled in job-training programs by 2002. States failing to meet the deadline would have their federal funds cut.

The Republican-sponsored welfare-reform legislation passed the Senate by a vote of 74 to 24, and the president eagerly signed it into law. Liberals charged that Clinton was abdicating Democratic social principles in order to gain reelection amid the conservative climate. Said one corporate executive, "Clinton is the most Republican Democrat in a long time."

THE 1996 CAMPAIGN
After clinching the Republican
presidential nomination in 1996,
Senate majority leader Bob
Dole resigned his seat in order
to devote his attention to defeating Bill Clinton. As the 1996
presidential campaign unfolded,
however, Clinton maintained
a large lead in the polls. With
an improving economy and no
major foreign-policy crises to
confront, cultural and personal issues surged into prominence. Concern about Dole's age

Bob Dole

The Republican presidential candidate
and former Senate majority leader on the
campaign trail.

(seventy-three) and his acerbic personality, as well as rifts in the Republican
party between economic conservatives and social conservatives over issues
such as abortion and gun control, hampered Dole's efforts to generate widespread support.

On November 5, 1996, Clinton won again, with an electoral vote of 379 to
159 and 49 percent of the popular vote. Clinton was the first Democratic
presidential candidate to win an election while the Republicans controlled
Congress. And he was the first Democratic president to win a second term
since Franklin Roosevelt in 1936. Dole received only 41 percent of the popular vote, and third-party candidate Ross Perot got 8 percent. The Republicans lost eight seats in the House but retained an edge, 227 to 207, over the
Democrats in the House; in the Senate, Republicans gained two seats for a
55–45 majority.

THE CLINTON YEARS AT HOME

As the twentieth century came to a close, the United States benefited
from a prolonged period of unprecedented prosperity. Buoyed by low inflation, high employment, declining federal budget deficits, dramatic improvements in productivity, the rapid globalization of economic life, and the
leadership of Federal Reserve Board chairman Alan Greenspan, business and
industry witnessed record profits.

THE "NEW ECONOMY"   During the late 1990s the stock market soared. In 1993 the Dow Jones Industrial Average hit 3,500. By 1996 it had topped 6,000. During 1998 it reached 9,000, defying the predictions of experts that the economy could not sustain such performance. The "new economy" was centered on high-flying computer, software, telecommunications, and Internet firms. By early 2000 these dot-com enterprises had come to represent almost a third of stock-market values even though many of them were hollow-shelled companies fueled by the speculative mania. The result was a financial bubble that soon burst, but during the run-up in the 1990s investors gave little thought to a possible collapse. In 1998, unemployment was only 4.3 percent, the lowest since 1970. People began to claim that the new economy defied the boom-and-bust cycles of the previous hundred years. "It is possible," Greenspan suggested, "that we have moved 'beyond history.'"

One major factor producing the economic boom of the 1990s was the "peace dividend." The end of the cold war enabled the U.S. government to reduce the proportion of the annual budget devoted to defense spending. Another major factor was the Clinton administration's 1993 initiative cutting taxes and reducing overall federal spending. But perhaps the single most important reason for the surge in prosperity was dramatic growth in per-worker productivity. New technologies and new production processes allowed for greater efficiency. Whatever the reasons, the robust economy set records in every area: low inflation, low unemployment, federal budget surpluses for the first time in modern history, and dizzying corporate profits.

RACE INITIATIVES   After the triumphs of the civil rights movement in the 1960s, the momentum for minority advancement had run out—except for gains in college admissions and employment under the rubric of affirmative action. The conservative mood during the mid-1990s manifested itself in the Supreme Court. In 1995 the Court ruled against election districts redrawn to create African American or Latino majorities and narrowed federal affirmative-action programs.

In one of those cases, *Adarand Constructors v. Peña* (1995), the Court assessed a program that gave some advantages to businesses owned by "disadvantaged" minorities. A Hispanic-owned firm had won a highway guardrail contract over a lower bid by a white-owned company. The white-owned company sued on the grounds of "reverse discrimination." Writing for the majority, Justice Sandra Day O'Connor said that such affirmative-action programs had to be "narrowly tailored" to serve a "compelling national interest." O'Connor did not define what the Court meant by a "compelling national interest," but the implication of her language was clear: the Court had come to embrace the growing public suspicion of the value and legality of such race-based programs.

In 1996 two major steps were taken against affirmative action in college admissions. In *Hopwood v. Texas*, the U.S. Court of Appeals for the Fifth Circuit ruled that considering race to achieve a diverse student body at the University of Texas was "not a compelling interest under the Fourteenth Amendment." Later that year the state of California passed Proposition 209, an initiative that ruled out race, sex, ethnicity, and national origin as criteria for preferring any group. These rulings eviscerated affirmative-action programs and drastically reduced African American college enrollments, prompting second thoughts. In addition, the nation still had not addressed intractable problems that lay beyond civil rights—that is, problems of dependency: illiteracy, poverty, unemployment, urban decay, and slums.

THE SCANDAL MACHINE   During his first term, President Clinton was dogged by allegations of improper involvement in the Whitewater Development Corporation. In 1978, as governor of Arkansas, he had invested in a resort to be built in northern Arkansas. The project turned out to be a fraud and a failure, and the Clintons took a loss on their investment. In 1994, Kenneth Starr, a Republican, was appointed to serve as independent counsel in an investigation of the Whitewater case. Starr's extensive investigation did not uncover evidence that the Clintons were directly involved in the fraud, although several of their close associates had been caught in the web and convicted of various charges, some related to Whitewater and some not.

In the course of another investigation, a salacious scandal erupted when it was revealed that Bill Clinton had engaged in a sexual affair with a White House intern, Monica Lewinsky, and had pressed her to lie about their relationship under oath. Clinton initially denied the charges, but the scandal would not disappear. In August 1998 he agreed to appear before a grand jury convened to investigate the sexual allegations, thus becoming the first president in history to testify before a grand jury. On August 17, Clinton recanted his earlier denials and acknowledged having had "inappropriate intimate physical contact" with Monica Lewinsky. That evening the president delivered a four-minute nationally televised address in which he admitted to having had an improper relationship with Lewinsky but insisted that he had done nothing illegal.

Public reaction to Clinton's remarkable about-face was mixed. A majority of Americans expressed sympathy for the president because of his public

The Whitewater scandal

The ongoing Whitewater investigation threatened to derail important initiatives as it occupied the attention of the president and Congress.

humiliation and wanted the entire matter dropped. But Clinton's credibility had suffered a serious blow on account of his reckless lack of self-discipline and his efforts to deny and then cover up the scandal.

Then, on September 9, 1998, Kenneth Starr submitted to Congress a 445-page report and eighteen boxes of supporting material. The Starr Report found "substantial and creditable" evidence of presidential wrongdoing. On October 8 the House of Representatives voted 258 to 176 to begin a wide-ranging impeachment inquiry of the president. Thirty-one Democrats joined the Republicans in supporting the investigation. On December 19, 1998, William Jefferson Clinton became the second president to be impeached by the House of Representatives. The House officially approved two articles of impeachment, charging Clinton with lying under oath to a federal grand jury and obstructing justice.

The Senate trial of President Clinton began on January 7, 1999. Five weeks later, on February 12, the Senate acquitted Clinton. Rejecting the first charge of perjury, 10 Republicans and all 45 Democrats voted "not guilty." On the

Impeachment

Representative Edward Pease, a member of the House Judiciary Committee, covers his face during the vote on the third of four articles of impeachment charging President Clinton with "high crimes and misdemeanors," December 1998.

charge of obstruction of justice, the Senate split 50–50 (which meant acquittal, since 67 votes were needed for conviction). In both instances, senators had a hard time interpreting Clinton's philandering as instances of "high crimes and misdemeanors," the constitutional requirement for removal of a president from office. Clinton's supporters portrayed him as the victim of a puritanical special prosecutor and a partisan conspiracy run amok. His critics lambasted him as a lecherous man without honor or integrity. Both characterizations were incomplete. Politically astute, charismatic, and well-informed, Clinton had as much ability and potential as any president. Yet he was also shamelessly self-indulgent. The result was a scandalous presidency punctuated by dramatic achievements in welfare reform, economic growth, and foreign policy.

FOREIGN-POLICY CHALLENGES

Like Woodrow Wilson, Lyndon Johnson, and Jimmy Carter before him, Bill Clinton was a Democratic president who came into office determined to focus on the nation's domestic problems only to find himself mired in foreign entanglements. Clinton continued the Bush administration's military intervention in Somalia, on the northeastern horn of Africa, where collapse of the government early in 1991 had left the country in anarchy, prey to tribal marauders. President Bush in 1992 had gained UN sanction for a military force led by American troops to relieve hunger and restore peace. The Somalian operation proved successful at its primary mission, but it never solved the political problems that lay at the root of the population's starvation.

HAITI   The most successful departure in foreign policy for the Clinton administration during its first term came in Haiti. The Caribbean island nation had emerged suddenly from a cycle of coups with a democratic election in 1990, which brought to the presidency a popular priest, Jean-Bertrand Aristide. When a Haitian army general ousted Aristide, the United States announced its intention to bring him back and welcomed the United Nations to the process. With drawn-out negotiations leading nowhere, Clinton moved in July 1994 to get a UN resolution authorizing force as a last resort. At that juncture, former president Jimmy Carter asked permission to negotiate. In Port-au-Prince he convinced the military leaders to quit by October 15. Aristide returned to Haiti and on March 31, 1995, the occupation was turned over to a UN force commanded by an American general.

THE MIDDLE EAST   Clinton also continued George Bush's policy of sponsoring patient negotiations between the Arabs and the Israelis. A new development was the inclusion of the PLO in the negotiations. In 1993 secret talks between Israeli and Palestinian representatives in Oslo, Norway, resulted in a draft agreement between Israel and the PLO. This agreement provided for the restoration of Palestinian self-rule in the occupied Gaza Strip and in Jericho, on the West Bank, in an exchange of land for peace as provided in UN Security Council resolutions. A formal signing occurred at the White House on September 13, 1993. With President Clinton presiding, Israeli prime minister Yitzhak Rabin and PLO leader Yasir Arafat exchanged handshakes, and their foreign ministers signed the agreement.

The Middle East peace process suffered a terrible blow in early November 1995, however, when Prime Minister Rabin was assassinated at a peace rally in Tel Aviv by a Jewish Israeli zealot who resented Rabin's efforts to negotiate with the Palestinians. Some observers feared that the assassin had killed the peace process as well when seven months later conservative hard-liner Benjamin Netanyahu narrowly defeated the U.S.-backed Shimon Peres in the Israeli national elections. Yet in October 1998, Clinton brought Arafat,

Clinton and the Middle East

President Clinton presides as Israeli prime minister Yitzhak Rabin (left) and PLO leader Yasir Arafat (right) agree to a peace accord between Israel and the Palestinians, September 1993.

Netanyahu, and King Hussein of Jordan together at a conference center in Wye Mills, Maryland, where they reached an agreement. Under the Wye River Memorandum, Israel agreed to surrender land in return for security guarantees by the Palestinians.

THE BALKANS   Clinton's foreign policy also addressed the chaotic transition in eastern Europe from Soviet domination to independence. When Yugoslavia imploded in 1991, fanatics and tyrants triggered ethnic conflict as four of its six republics seceded. Serb minorities, backed by the new republic of Serbia, stirred up civil wars in Croatia and Bosnia. In Bosnia especially, the war involved "ethnic cleansing"—driving Muslims from their homes and towns. Clinton sent food and medical supplies to besieged Bosnians and dispatched planes to retaliate for attacks on places designated "safe havens" by the United Nations.

In 1995, American negotiators finally persuaded the foreign ministers of Croatia, Bosnia, and the Federal Republic of Yugoslavia to agree to a comprehensive peace plan. Bosnia would remain a single nation but would be divided into two states: a Muslim-Croat federation controlling 51 percent of the territory and a Bosnian-Serb republic controlling the remaining 49 percent. Basic human rights would be restored and free elections would be held to appoint a parliament and joint president. To enforce the agreement,

60,000 NATO peacekeeping troops would be dispatched to Bosnia. A cease-fire went into effect in October 1995.

In 1998 the Balkan tinderbox flared up again, this time in the Yugoslav province of Kosovo, which has long been considered sacred ground by Christian Serbs. By 1989, however, over 90 percent of the 2 million Kosovars were ethnic Albanian Muslims. In that year, Yugoslav president Slobodan Milošević decided to reassert Serbian control over the province. He stripped Kosovo of its autonomy and established de facto martial law. When the Albanian Kosovars resisted and large numbers of Muslim men began to join the Kosovo Liberation Army, Serbian soldiers and state police ruthlessly suppressed them and launched another program of "ethnic cleansing," burning Albanian villages, murdering men, raping women, and displacing hundreds of thousands of Muslim Albanian Kosovars.

On March 24, 1999, NATO, relying heavily upon U.S. military resources and leadership, launched air strikes against Yugoslavia. "Ending this tragedy is a moral imperative," explained President Clinton. After seventy-two days of unrelenting bombardment, Milošević sued for peace on NATO's terms. An agreement was reached on June 3, 1999. It was an unprecedented victory for airpower and for NATO, which was celebrating its fiftieth birthday. Not a single allied pilot was killed in combat. As the Albanian Kosovars began to return to Kosovo, however, large numbers of Serbs, fearful of Muslim retribution, began to leave the province, and some of them were killed. Members of the Kosovo Liberation Army stepped into the vacuum left by the departing Serbs and began to take control of the province.

GLOBALIZATION   The deepening involvement of the United States in the complex affairs of eastern Europe symbolized the broadening scope of globalization. As the proliferation of globe-spanning information and communications technologies shrank time and distance, a cornucopia of consumer goods was produced, distributed, marketed, and sold by multinational companies all over the world, not just in the United States. As more nations entered the world economy and experienced prosperity, they benefited corporations in the United States by buying more American products and sending more and better goods to the United States. U.S. exports rose dramatically in the last twenty years of the twentieth century. By the end of the twentieth century, the U.S. economy had become dependent on the global economy; foreign trade had become central to American prosperity—and to American politics. By 2000 over a third of the production of American multinational companies was occurring abroad, compared with only 9 percent in

1980. By the end of the twentieth century, the U.S. economy had become internationalized to such a profound extent that global concerns exercised an overwhelming influence on domestic and foreign policies.

THE ELECTION OF 2000

The election of 2000 revealed that voters were split evenly along partisan lines. The two major-party candidates for president, Vice President Al Gore, the Democrat, and Texas governor George W. Bush, the Republican and son of the former president, presented sharply contrasting views on the role of the federal government, tax cuts, environmental policies, and the best way to preserve Social Security and Medicare. Gore, a Tennessee native and Harvard graduate whose father had been a senator, favored an active federal government that would preserve Social Security, subsidize prescription-medicine expenses for the elderly, and protect the environment.

Bush, on the other hand, proposed a transfer of power from the federal government to the states, particularly in regard to environmental and educational policies. He promoted exploration for oil on federal land, and he endorsed the use of vouchers (cash grants) to enable parents to send their children to private schools. In international affairs, Bush questioned the need to maintain U.S. peacekeeping forces in Bosnia and the continuing expense of other global military commitments. He urged a more "humble" foreign policy, one that would end efforts at "nation building" around the world.

Two independent candidates added zest to the 2000 presidential campaign: conservative columnist Patrick Buchanan and liberal activist Ralph Nader. Buchanan focused his campaign on criticism of NAFTA, while Nader concentrated on the corrupting effects of campaign finances and the need for more robust efforts to protect the environment.

In the end the election was the one of the closest—and most controversial—in history. The television networks initially reported that Gore had narrowly won the state of Florida and its decisive twenty-five electoral votes. Later in the evening, however, the networks reversed themselves, saying that Florida was too close to call. In the chaotic early-morning hours the networks declared Bush the overall winner. Gore called Bush to concede, only to issue a retraction a short time later when it appeared that Florida remained a toss-up. The final tally in Florida showed Bush with a razor-thin lead, and state law required a recount. For the first time in 125 years, the results of a presidential election remained in doubt for weeks after the voting.

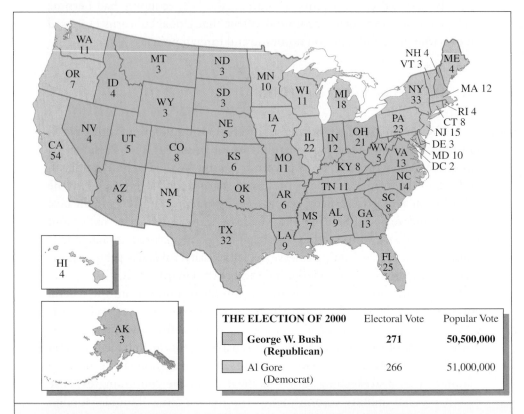

THE ELECTION OF 2000	Electoral Vote	Popular Vote
George W. Bush (Republican)	271	50,500,000
Al Gore (Democrat)	266	51,000,000

Why was the 2000 presidential election so close? How was the conflict over the election results resolved? How were differences between urban and rural voters key to the outcome of the election?

As a painstaking hand count of presidential ballots proceeded in Florida, supporters of Bush and Gore pursued victory through legal maneuvers in the Florida courts and the U.S. Supreme Court; each side accused the other of trying to steal the election. The political drama remained stalemated for five weeks. At last, on December 12, 2000, a harshly divided Supreme Court halted the statewide manual recounts in Florida. In the case known as *Bush v. Gore,* a bare 5–4 majority ruled that any new recount would clash with existing Florida law.

Bush was deemed the winner in Florida by the slimmest of margins: 537 votes. Although Gore had amassed a 540,000-vote lead nationwide, he lost in the Electoral College by two votes when he lost Florida. Although Al Gore

The Florida recount

A rally in Florida protesting the counting of ballots in the disputed 2000 presidential election.

"strongly disagreed" with the Supreme Court's decision, he asked voters to rally around President-elect Bush and move forward: "Partisan rancor must be put aside."

The 2000 election revealed the remarkable balance that had emerged in American politics. Not since the 1880s had the two major parties been so evenly divided. Republicans retained a slim lead in the House, 49.2 percent to 47.9 percent. The number of senators was split down the middle, fifty-fifty. For all of the strident rhetoric in the campaign, both Bush and Gore represented the moderate center of their parties when compared with the more ideological candidacies of Buchanan and Nader. Bush talked frequently about his commitment to "compassionate conservatism." Gore ran on a platform dedicated to "fiscal responsibility." Analysts stressed that cultural issues such as abortion and gun control, as well as the Clinton scandals, had become more important to many voters than economic concerns over taxes or defense spending. Some 71 percent of city residents voted for Gore while only 26 percent chose Bush. Conversely, 59 percent of rural voters cast ballots for Bush while only 37 percent opted for Gore. Gore won fewer than one third of the votes in the South and his home state of Tennessee. Bush won the mountain West and the South while Gore dominated the Northeast, the West Coast, and the industrial Midwest. Women favored Gore over Bush by 11 percentage points, exactly the reverse of the male voters.

COMPASSIONATE CONSERVATISM

THE SECOND BUSH PRESIDENCY   George W. Bush arrived in the White House amid the controversy of a disputed election to confront a sputtering economy and a falling stock market. By the spring of 2000, the high-tech companies that had led the dizzying run-up on Wall Street during the 1990s had collapsed. Many of the dazzling new dot-com businesses declared bankruptcy. Greed fed by record profits and speculative excesses had led businesses, investors, and consumers to take dangerous risks and engage in self-indulgent behavior. Consumer confidence and capital investment plummeted with the stock market. By March 2001 the economy was in recession for the first time in over a decade.

Yet neither the plummeting stock market and floundering economy nor the close political balance in Congress prevented President Bush from launching an ambitious legislative agenda. Confident that he could win over Democrats, he promised to provide "an explosion of legislation" promoting his goal of "compassionate conservatism" within a few months of his inauguration. The top item on Bush's wish list was a tax cut intended to stimulate the sagging economy. Bush signed it into law on June 7, 2001. White House celebrations of the tax-cut victory were quickly deflated by the defection of Vermont senator James Jeffords, however, who changed his party affiliation from Republican to independent—a major blow for the president since it resulted in the Democrats' gaining narrow control of the Senate, 50–49.

NO CHILD LEFT BEHIND   In addition to tax reduction, one of President Bush's top priorities was education reform. In late 2001, Congress passed a comprehensive education-improvement plan called No Child Left Behind, and the president signed the bill in early 2002. It required states to set new learning standards and ensure that all students were "proficient" at reading and math by 2014. It also mandated that all teachers be "highly qualified" in their subject area by 2005, allowed children in low-performing schools to transfer to other schools, and required states to submit annual reports of students' scores on standardized tests. Schools and school districts that fell short of the new standards were eligible for financial and technical assistance, but if progress did not occur, the federal government would issue a series of sanctions; ultimately a chronically failing school district would be taken over by the state. States soon criticized the program, claiming that it provided insufficient funds for remedial programs and that poor school districts, many of them in blighted inner cities or rural areas, would be especially hard-pressed to meet the guidelines.

EXPLOITING THE ENVIRONMENT   The Bush administration's environmental policies ignited a firestorm of controversy. The president sought to roll back restrictions on economic development imposed by long-standing environmental regulations. In addition, he allowed more logging in national forests and opened up more federal land, including wildlife sanctuaries, to exploration for oil and natural gas.

GLOBAL TERRORISM

With the collapse of the Soviet Union and the end of the cold war, world politics had grown more unstable during the 1990s. Where ideologies such as capitalism and communism had earlier been the cause of conflict and tension in foreign relations, issues of religion, ethnicity, and clashing cultural values now divided peoples. Islamic militants around the world especially resented what they viewed as the "imperial" globalization of American culture and power. Nebulous multinational groups inspired by religious fanaticism and anti-American rage were using high-tech terrorism to gain notoriety and exact vengeance. Well-financed and well-armed terrorists flourished in the cracks of fractured nations such as Sudan, Somalia, Pakistan, Yemen, and Afghanistan. Throughout the 1990s the United States fought a losing secret war against organized terrorism. The ineffectiveness of Western intelligence agencies in tracking the movements and intentions of militant extremists became tragically evident in the late summer of 2001.

SEPTEMBER 11, 2001: A DAY OF INFAMY   At 8:45 A.M. on September 11, 2001, a commercial airliner hijacked by Islamic terrorists slammed into the north tower of the World Trade Center in New York City. A second hijacked jumbo jet, traveling at 500 miles per hour, hit the south tower eighteen minutes later. The fuel-laden planes turned the majestic buildings into infernos. The iconic twin towers, both 110 stories tall and occupied by thousands of employees, collapsed from the intense heat. Surrounding buildings also collapsed. The entire southern end of Manhattan—ground zero—became a hellish scene of twisted steel, suffocating smoke, and wailing sirens.

September 11, 2001

Smoke pours out of the north tower of the World Trade Center as the south tower bursts into flames after being struck by a second hijacked airplane. Both towers collapsed about an hour later.

While the catastrophic drama in New York was unfolding, a third hijacked plane crashed into the Pentagon in Washington, D.C. A fourth airliner, probably headed for the White House, missed its mark when passengers—who had heard reports of the earlier hijackings via cell phones—assaulted the hijackers to prevent the plane from being used as a weapon. During the struggle in the cockpit, the plane went out of control and plummeted into the Pennsylvania countryside, killing all aboard.

The hijackings represented the costliest terrorist assault in the nation's history. There were 266 passengers and crew members aboard the crashed jets. More than 100 civilians and military personnel were killed at the Pentagon. The death toll at the World Trade Center was nearly 2,600, with many firefighters, police officers, and rescue workers among the dead. Hundreds of those killed were foreign nationals working in the financial district; some eighty nations lost citizens in the attacks. The terrorists also destroyed a powerful symbol of America: the World Trade Center towers were the central offices of global capitalism.

The terrorist attacks of September 11 created shock and chaos, grief and anger. They also prompted an unprecedented display of national unity and patriotism. People rushed to donate blood, food, and money. Volunteers clogged military-recruiting centers. American flags were in evidence everywhere. Citizens around the world held vigils at U.S. embassies. World leaders offered condolences and support. For the first time in its history, NATO invoked Article 5 of its charter, which states that an attack on any member will be considered an attack on all members.

Within hours of the hijackings, officials had identified the nineteen dead terrorists as members of al Qaeda (the Base), a well-financed worldwide network of Islamic extremists led by a wealthy Saudi renegade, Osama bin Laden. Years before, bin Laden had declared jihad (holy war) on the United States, Israel, and the Saudi monarchy. For several years he had been using remote bases in war-torn Afghanistan as terrorist training centers. Collaborating with bin Laden's terrorist network was Afghanistan's ruling Taliban, a coalition of ultraconservative Islamists that had emerged in the mid-1990s following the forced withdrawal of Soviet troops from Afghanistan. Taliban leaders provided bin Laden with a safe haven in exchange for his financial and military support against the Northern Alliance, a coalition of rebel groups opposed to Taliban rule. Bin Laden recruited Muslim militants energized by local causes and sought to mobilize them into a global army. As many as 20,000 recruits from twenty different countries circulated through his Afghan training camps. Most of the terrorists received religious indoctrination and basic infantry training to prepare them to fight for the Taliban. A smaller group was selected by al Qaeda for elite training to organize secret cells around the world and engage in urban warfare, assassination, demolition, and sabotage, with the United States and Europe as the primary targets.

WAR ON TERRORISM The September 11 assault on the United States changed the course of the Bush presidency, the nation, and even the world. The economy, already in decline, went into free fall. President Bush, who had never professed to know much about international relations or world affairs and had shown only disdain for Bill Clinton's "multilateralism," was thrust onto center stage as commander in chief of a wounded nation eager for vengeance. The inexperienced new president, elected by the slimmest electoral margin since 1876, responded with unexpected poise, grit, and courage. He told the nation that the "deliberate and deadly attacks . . . were more than acts of terror. They were acts of war." The crisis gave the untested, happy-go-lucky

Bush a profound sense of purpose. "I will not yield. I will not rest. I will not relent in waging this struggle for freedom and security."

The Bush administration immediately forged an international coalition to strike at terrorism worldwide. The coalition demanded that Afghanistan's Taliban government surrender the terrorists or risk military attack. In a televised address on September 20, Bush warned Americans that the war against terrorism would be a lengthy campaign involving covert action as well as conventional military forces and would target not only terrorists but also the groups and governments that abet them. "Every nation in every region," he said, "now has a decision to make: either you are with us or you are with the terrorists."

On October 7, after the Taliban defiantly refused to turn over bin Laden, the United States and its allies launched a ferocious military campaign—Operation Enduring Freedom—to punish terrorists or "those harboring terrorists." American and British cruise missiles and bombers destroyed Afghan military installations and al Qaeda training camps. The coalition found key allies in neighboring Pakistan and in Afghanistan's Northern Alliance. On

Operation Enduring Freedom

Smoke rises from the Taliban village of Khanaqa, fifty-five miles from the Afghan capital Kabul, after a U.S. aircraft released bombs.

The Taliban

A young woman shows her face in public for the first time in five years after Northern Alliance troops capture Kabul, the capital of Afghanistan, in November 2001. The strict sharia law enforced by the Taliban required that women be covered from head to foot.

December 9, only two months after the U.S.-led military campaign in Afghanistan had begun, the Taliban regime collapsed. The war in Afghanistan then devolved into a high-stakes manhunt for the elusive Osama bin Laden and an international network of terrorists operating in sixty countries.

TERRORISM AT HOME   While the military campaign continued in Afghanistan, officials in Washington worried that terrorists might launch additional attacks in the United States with biological, chemical, or even nuclear weapons. To address the threat and to help restore public confidence, President Bush created a new federal agency, the Office of Homeland Security. Another new federal agency, the Transportation Security Administration, assumed responsibility for screening airline passengers. At the same time, President Bush and a supportive Congress created new legislation, known as the USA Patriot Act, which gave government agencies the right to eavesdrop on confidential conversations between prison inmates and their lawyers and permitted suspected terrorists to be tried in secret military courts. Civil liberties groups voiced grave concerns that the measures jeopardized constitutional rights and protections. But the crisis atmosphere after September 11 caused most people to support these extraordinary steps.

THE BUSH DOCTRINE In the fall of 2002, President Bush unveiled a new national security doctrine that marked a distinct shift from that of previous administrations. Containment and deterrence had been the guiding strategic concepts of the cold war years. Beginning with Harry Truman in 1947, American presidents had helped organize multilateral international groups such as the United Nations and NATO to "contain" communism and keep it from spreading. Likewise, U.S. administrations had sought to "deter" the Soviets and Chinese Communists from overt military action by promising "massive retaliation." Thus the threat of nuclear war and mutual destruction kept the major nations in check during the cold war era. In the new unconventional war against terrorism, however, the cold war policies were outdated. Fanatics willing to act as suicide bombers would not be deterred or contained. The growing menace posed by "shadowy networks" of terrorist groups and unstable rogue nations with "weapons of mass destruction," President Bush declared, required a new doctrine of preemptive military action. "If we wait for threats to fully materialize," he explained, "we will have waited too long. In the world we have entered, the only path to safety is the path of action. And this nation will act."

Bush's defense policy

President George W. Bush addresses soldiers in July 2002 as part of an appeal to Congress to speed approval of increased defense spending after the September 11 terrorist attacks.

A SECOND PERSIAN GULF WAR   During 2002 and 2003, Iraq emerged as the focus of the Bush administration's decisive new policy of "preemptive" military action to prevent terrorism and destroy presumed weapons of mass destruction. In September 2002, President Bush urged the United Nations to confront the "grave and gathering danger" posed by Saddam Hussein's dictatorial regime in Iraq. He warned that the United States would act alone if the UN did not respond. In October, Congress approved a resolution proposed by Bush authorizing him to use "all means that he determines to be appropriate, including force," to defend the United States against the threat posed by Iraq's supposed possession of biological and chemical weapons. On November 8 the UN Security Council passed Resolution 1441 ordering Iraq to disarm immediately or face "serious consequences."

On March 17, 2003, President Bush issued an ultimatum to Saddam Hussein: he and his sons must leave Iraq within forty-eight hours or face a U.S.-led invasion. Hussein refused. Two days later, on March 19, American and British forces, supported by what George Bush called the "coalition of the willing," attacked Iraq. Operation Iraqi Freedom involved a massive bombing campaign followed closely by a fast-moving invasion across the Iraqi desert from bases in Kuwait. Some 250,000 American soldiers, sailors, and marines were joined by 50,000 British troops as well as small contingents from other countries, including Australia and Poland. On April 9, after three weeks of intense fighting amid sweltering heat and blinding sandstorms, allied forces occupied Baghdad, the capital of Iraq. Hussein's regime and his inept army collapsed and fled a week later. On May 1, 2003, an exuberant President Bush landed on the aircraft carrier U.S.S. *Abraham Lincoln* and proudly declared that the war was essentially over. "The battle of Iraq," he said, "is one victory in a war on terror that began on September 11, 2001, and still goes on."

The complicated Iraqi military campaign was a brilliantly orchestrated demonstration of intense firepower, daring maneuver, and complex logistical support. No one had predicted such a quick and decisive victory—or so few casualties among the allied forces. The six-week war came at a cost of fewer than 200 combat deaths among the 300,000 coalition troops. Over 2,000 Iraqi soldiers were killed; civilian casualties numbered in the tens of thousands.

REBUILDING IRAQ   It proved easier to win the war than to rebuild Iraq, however. Secretary of Defense Donald Rumsfeld saw the Iraq War as an opportunity to showcase America's new military strategy, with its focus on airpower, precision weaponry, sophisticated communications, and mobile ground forces adept at stealth and speed. Yet no sooner had Saddam Hussein's tyranny been destroyed than the allies faced the daunting task of restoring order and installing a democratic government in a chaotic Iraq torn by age-old religious feuds and ethnic tensions. Violence engulfed the war-torn country. Vengeful Islamic jihadists (holy warriors) from around the world streamed in to wage a merciless campaign of terror and sabotage against the coalition forces and their Iraqi allies.

Defense Department analysts had greatly underestimated the difficulty of pacifying and reconstructing postwar Iraq. By the fall of 2003, President Bush admitted that substantial numbers of American troops (around 150,000) would remain in Iraq much longer than originally anticipated and that rebuilding the fractured nation would take years. Victory on the battlefields of Iraq did not bring peace to the Middle East. Militant Islamic groups seething with hatred for the United States remained a constant global threat. In addition, the dispute over the war strained relations between the Anglo-American alliance and France, Germany, and Russia, all of which opposed the Iraq War.

A continued presence in Iraq

U.S. military police patrol the market in Abu Ghraib, on the outskirts of Baghdad.

Throughout 2003 and 2004, the Iraqi insurgency and its campaign of terror grew in scope and savagery. Near-daily suicide car bombings and roadside ambushes of U.S. military convoys wreaked havoc among Iraqi civilians and allied troops. Terrorists kidnapped foreign civilians and beheaded several of them in grisly rituals videotaped for the world to see. In the United States the euphoria of battlefield victory turned to dismay as the number of casualties and the expense of the occupation soared. In the face of mounting criticism, President Bush urged Americans to "stay the course," insisting that a democratic Iraq would bring stability to the volatile Middle East and thereby blunt the momentum of Islamic terrorism.

But the president's credibility suffered a sharp blow in January 2004 when administration officials admitted that no weapons of mass destruction—the primary reason for launching the invasion—had been found in Iraq. The chief arms inspector told Congress that the intelligence reports about Hussein's supposed secret weapons were "almost all wrong." Furthermore, shocking photographs that surfaced in April 2004 showing American soldiers torturing and abusing Iraqi prisoners further eroded public confidence in Bush's handling of the war and its aftermath.

By September 2004, U.S. military deaths in Iraq had reached 1,000, and by the end of 2006 the number was nearly 3,000. Although Saddam Hussein had been captured in December 2003 and a new Iraqi government would hold its first democratic elections in January 2005, Iraq seemed less secure than ever to an anxious American public worried about the rising cost of an unending commitment in Iraq. The continuing guerrilla wars in Iraq and Afghanistan strained U.S. military resources and the federal budget.

THE ELECTION OF 2004 Growing public concern about the turmoil in Iraq complicated George Bush's campaign for a second presidential term. Throughout 2004 his approval rating plummeted. And in the new century the electorate had become deeply polarized. A ferocious partisanship dominated political discourse and media commentary in the early years of the century. Democrats still fumed over the contested election results of 2000. When asked about the intensity of his critics, a combative George Bush declared the furor "a compliment. It means I'm willing to take a stand." One of his advisers explained it more bluntly: "He likes being hated. It lets him know he's doing the right thing."

The 2004 presidential campaign was punctuated by negative attacks on each candidate as the two parties sought to galvanize their loyalists. The Democratic nominee, Senator John Kerry of Massachusetts, lambasted the Bush administration for misleading the nation on the issue of weapons of

The 2004 election

President George W. Bush (center) and Democratic candidate Senator John Kerry (left) participate in the second presidential debate, a town-hall-style exchange held at Washington University in St. Louis, Missouri.

mass destruction in Iraq and for its inept handling of the postwar Iraq occupation. Kerry also highlighted the record budget deficits occurring under the Republican leadership. Bush countered that the tortuous efforts to create a democratic government in Iraq would enhance America's long-term security.

On election day, November 2, 2004, the exit polls suggested a Kerry victory, but in the end the election hinged on the crucial swing state of Ohio. No Republican had ever lost Ohio and still won the presidency. After an anxious night viewing returns from Ohio, Kerry conceded the election. "The outcome," he stressed, "should be decided by voters, not a protracted legal battle." By narrowly winning Ohio, Bush garnered 286 electoral votes to Kerry's 251. The 2004 election was remarkable for its high voter turnout. Almost 120 million people voted, some 15 million more than in the disputed 2000 election.

Bush won the popular vote by 50.73 to 48.27 percent, the narrowest margin won by any incumbent president. Yet in some respects the close election was not so close. Bush received 3.5 million more votes nationwide than Kerry, and Republicans increased their control of both the House and the Senate. Trumpeting "the will of the people at my back," Bush pledged after his reelection to bring democracy and stability to Iraq, overhaul the tax code

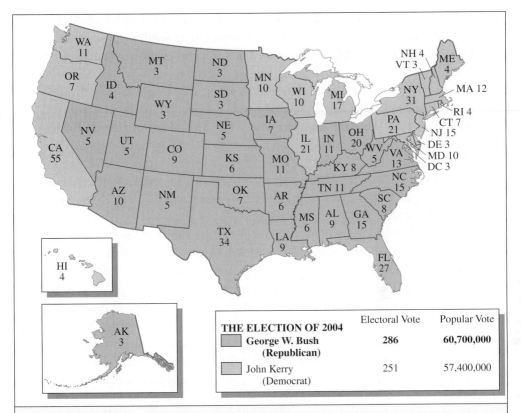

THE ELECTION OF 2004	Electoral Vote	Popular Vote
George W. Bush (Republican)	286	60,700,000
John Kerry (Democrat)	251	57,400,000

How did the war in Iraq polarize the electorate? In what ways did the election of 2004 give Republicans a mandate?

and eliminate the estate tax, revamp Social Security, trim the federal budget deficit, limit financial awards for medical malpractice lawsuits, pass a major energy bill, and create many more jobs. "I earned capital in the campaign, political capital, and now I intend to spend it," he told reporters.

SECOND-TERM BLUES

Yet like many modern presidents, George Bush floundered in his second term. In 2005 he pushed through Congress an energy bill and a Central American Free Trade Act. But his effort to privatize Social Security retirement accounts, enabling individuals to invest their accumulated pension dollars themselves, went nowhere, and soaring budget deficits made many fiscal conservatives feel betrayed.

Developments within the Supreme Court commanded much of Bush's attention early in his second term. The retirement of Sandra Day O'Connor from the Court in July 2005 ignited a ferocious national debate over vexing cultural issues such as abortion, gay marriage, and affirmative action. Because O'Connor had been a moderate swing vote on the closely divided Court, the battle over her replacement was especially intense. Militants on the left and on the right pressured the White House to ensure that Bush's choice to succeed O'Connor fit their agenda's demands, but Bush's shrewd decision to nominate John G. Roberts Jr., a socially conservative circuit court judge, stalemated critics because Roberts's legal credentials were impeccable. The Senate overwhelmingly confirmed Roberts (78 to 22) on September 29, 2005.

Yet the fractious debates over the future of the Court did not subside. In early September, Chief Justice William Rehnquist died. Bush then named Roberts the new chief justice and nominated Harriet E. Miers, a longtime friend and his former personal lawyer turned White House legal counsel, to replace O'Connor. Critics, many of them Republican conservatives, denounced Miers as a legal mediocrity and a presidential crony. The furor led Miers to withdraw her nomination in late October, a humiliating development for President Bush that further hobbled his stalled legislative efforts. To heal the ruptures within the Republican coalition, at the end of October Bush nominated Samuel Alito Jr., a federal judge and a favorite of conservatives, to fill O'Connor's seat on the Supreme Court. The Senate confirmed Alito on January 31, 2006.

HURRICANE KATRINA   In 2005, President Bush's eroding public support suffered another blow, this time when a natural disaster turned into a political crisis. In late August a killer hurricane named Katrina slammed into the Gulf coast, devastating large areas of Alabama, Mississippi, and Louisiana. The sultry metropolis of New Orleans was virtually destroyed as levees and flood walls holding back the Mississippi River and Lake Pontchartrain burst, inundating three quarters of the city, most of which is below sea level and below the levees channeling the Mississippi River.

New Orleans had always been at war with its environment. Since its founding in the early eighteenth century, the sodden city surrounded by mosquito-infested swamps and regularly visited by floods had placed its faith in engineering to keep back the surrounding water. This time nature won. After Katrina roared through the city, whole neighborhoods were under water, often up to the roofline. Nearly 500,000 New Orleans residents

Hurricane Katrina

Cars and buildings are partially submerged on Canal Street, a central thoroughfare in New Orleans, September 3, 2005.

were displaced, most of them poor and many of them African American. Looting was so widespread that officials declared martial law; the streets were awash with soldiers and police. Katrina's awful wake left over 1,000 people dead in three states and millions homeless and hopeless.

Local political officials and the Federal Emergency Management Agency (FEMA) were caught unprepared as the catastrophe unfolded. Disaster plans were incomplete; confusion and incompetence abounded. A wave of public outrage crashed against the Bush administration. In the face of blistering criticism, President Bush accepted responsibility for the balky federal response to the disaster and accepted the resignation of the FEMA director. Rebuilding the Gulf coast would take a long time and a lot of money.

The havoc wreaked by Katrina was only partly the result of natural forces run amok, however. Environmental calamities usually expose human failings. And in washing away property and lives, Katrina revealed all the elements of a disaster waiting to happen: poor planning, social inequalities, embedded corruption, and racial injustice. The destruction of New Orleans could have been mitigated or avoided altogether if, for example, warnings about the integrity of the aging levees had been heeded. The failure of the levees revealed scandalous breaches in public policy and political leadership. New Orleans had come to depend upon the Army Corps of Engineers for its lifeline of levees and pumps designed to keep the Mississippi River and Lake Pontchartrain at bay. Yet the city's flood-control funding had been reduced by 44 percent since 2001. At the same time, corruption and incompetence had been rife within the levee boards responsible for administering public funds. The weakening of wetlands protections to favor developers had also made the city far more vulnerable to the flood surge generated by hurricanes. Marshes absorb storm water, but much of the wetland surrounding New Orleans had disappeared as a result of strenuous efforts to reroute the Mississippi River in order to facilitate the passage of ships and, ironically, provide better flood control. Realigning the river had prevented silt from building up in the delta and nourishing the wetlands. So the natural calamity was made much worse by human action—and inaction.

A STALLED PRESIDENCY George Bush bore the brunt of public indignation over the bungled federal response to the Katrina disaster. Thereafter, his second presidential term was beset by political problems, a sputtering economy, and growing public dissatisfaction with his performance and the continuing war in Iraq. Even his support among Republicans crumbled, and many social conservatives felt betrayed by his sporadic attention to their ideological concerns. The editors of the *Economist*, an influential conservative newsmagazine, declared that Bush had become "the least popular re-elected president since Richard Nixon became embroiled in the Watergate fiasco."

Soaring gasoline prices and the federal budget deficit fueled public frustration with the Bush administration. The president's efforts to reform the tax code, Social Security, and immigration laws languished during his second term, and the turmoil and violence in Iraq showed no signs of abating. Senator Chuck Hagel, a Nebraska Republican, declared in 2005 that "we're losing in Iraq."

VOTER REBELLION In the November 2006 congressional elections the Democrats capitalized on the public disapproval of the Bush administration to win control of the House of Representatives, the Senate, and a majority of governorships and state legislatures. The election results were so lopsided that for the first time in history the victorious party (the Democrats) did not lose a single incumbent or open congressional seat or governorship. Former Republican congressman Dick Armey said that "the Republican Revolution of 1994 officially ended" with the 2006 election. "It was a rout." George Bush admitted that the voters had given him and his party a "thumpin'" that would require a "new era of cooperation" with the victorious Democrats. As it turned out, however, the Bush White House and the Democratic Congress became mired in partisan gridlock. Stalemate trumped bipartisanship.

House Speaker Nancy Pelosi

At a news conference on Capitol Hill.

The transformational election also included a significant milestone: Californian Nancy Pelosi, the leader of the Democrats in the House of Representatives, became the highest-ranking woman in the history of the U.S. Congress upon her election as House Speaker in January 2007.

THE "SURGE" IN IRAQ   The 2006 election was largely a referendum on the lack of progress in the Iraq War. Throughout the fall the violence and casualties in Iraq had spiked. The newly elected Iraqi government remained unstable, and fighting among the various religious and ethnic factions grew more chaotic. Bush remained stubbornly "committed to victory" in Iraq. But he responded to declining public and political support by replacing Donald Rumsfeld, the combative secretary of defense, with Robert Gates, a former head of the CIA. The president also created the Iraq Study Group, a nonpartisan task force co-chaired by Lee H. Hamilton, a former Democratic congressman, and James A. Baker III, secretary of state under the first President Bush. The group's report recommended that the United States step up the training of Iraqi troops and withdraw virtually all U.S. combat forces from a "grave and deteriorating Iraq" by the spring of 2008.

President Bush disagreed with the findings of the Iraq Study Group and others, including key military leaders, who urged a phased withdrawal. On January 10, 2007, he announced that he was sending a "surge" of 20,000 (eventually 30,000) additional American troops to Iraq, bringing the ultimate total to almost 170,000. Most Democrats opposed the escalation and

General David Petraeus

General Petraeus salutes U.S. soldiers during his visit at the village of Jadihah northeast of Baghdad, Iraq.

instead called for an exit strategy. Senate majority leader Harry Reid, a Nevada Democrat, proclaimed in April 2007 that the United States had "lost" the war in Iraq and should beat a hasty retreat. During the summer of 2007, congressional Democrats tried to force the withdrawal of U.S. forces from Iraq, but Bush held firm. The "surge" of additional soldiers, he explained, would involve a change in strategy as well as additional soldiers. The U.S. troops would shift their focus from offensive operations to the protection of Iraqi civilians from attacks by terrorist insurgents and sectarian militias. Bush hoped that the additional security would enable Iraqi leaders to promote political reconciliation among the war-torn country's major factions, the Shiites, Sunnis, and Kurds.

From a military perspective, the "surge" strategy succeeded. By the fall of 2008, the convulsive violence in Iraq had declined dramatically, and the U.S.-supported Iraqi government had grown in stature and confidence. But the financial expenses and human casualties of American involvement in Iraq continued to generate widespread criticism, and the "surge" failed to

The "surge"

An Iraqi reads a pamphlet asking for information on insurgents, handed to him by U.S. troops brought to Baghdad in an attempt to bring security to the city.

attain its political objectives. Iraqi political leaders had yet to build a stable, self-sustaining democracy. The U.S. general who masterminded the "surge" strategy admitted that the gains remained "fragile and reversible." In 2008, as the number of U.S. combat deaths in Iraq passed 4,000, President Bush acknowledged that the conflict was "longer and harder and more costly than we anticipated." During 2008 over 60 percent of Americans said that going to war in Iraq had been a mistake.

ECONOMIC WOES   After the intense but brief 2001 recession, the American economy had begun a period of prolonged expansion. Prosperity was fueled primarily by a prolonged housing boom, ultra-low interest and mortgage rates, easy credit, and reckless consumer spending. Home values across the nation had risen at rates that were unprecedented—and, as it turned out, unsustainable. Between 1997 and 2006, home prices in the United States, especially in the Sunbelt states, rose 85 percent, leading to a frenzy of irresponsible lending and building—and a debt-fueled consumer spending spree. Tens of millions of people bought houses that were more expensive than they could afford, refinanced their mortgages, or tapped home-equity loans to make discretionary purchases. The irrational confidence in soaring housing prices also led government regulatory agencies and mortgage lenders to ease credit restrictions so that more people could buy homes. Predatory lenders offered an array of so-called subprime loans with low initial "teaser" rates to home buyers with weak credit ratings and a low annual income. Investment banks and brokerage firms exacerbated the housing bubble by buying and selling bundles of home mortgages and other complex financial instruments, which they marketed as safe forms of "securitized" investments.

Such mortgage-backed securities were viable assets as long as home prices kept rising faster than personal income. In 2007, however, home values and housing sales began a precipitous decline. By the fall of 2007, the housing bubble had burst. Sales of new homes plummeted—as did asking prices. During 2008 the loss of trillions of dollars in home-equity value set off a seismic shock across the economy. Record numbers of mortgage borrowers defaulted on their payments. Foreclosures soared, adding to the glut of homes for sale and further reducing home prices. Banks lost billions, first on shaky subprime mortgages, then on most other categories of debt: credit cards, car loans, student loans, and an array of commercial mortgage-backed securities.

Capitalism depends on access to capital; short-term credit is the lifeblood of the economy. In 2008, however, the nation's credit supply froze up. Concerned about their own insolvency as well as their ability to gauge credit risks, banks essentially stopped lending—to the public and to each other. So people stopped buying; businesses stopped selling; industries slashed production and postponed investment. The sudden contraction of consumer credit, corporate spending, and consumer purchases pushed the economy into a deepening recession in 2008. The scale and suddenness of the slump caught economic experts and business leaders by surprise. Some of the nation's most prestigious banks, investment firms, and insurance companies went belly-up. The price of food and gasoline spiked. Unemployment soared. "Almost all businesses are in a survival mode," said one economist, "and they're slashing payrolls and investments. We're in store for some big job losses." Indeed, some two million jobs disappeared in 2008.

The high-flying stock market, itself fed by artificially low interest rates, began to tremble in September 2008; during October the bottom fell out. The Dow Jones Industrial Average lost a third of its value. Panic set in amid the turmoil. By late fall 2008 the United States was facing its greatest financial crisis since the Great Depression of the 1930s. What had begun as a decline in home prices had become a global economic meltdown—fed by the paralyzing fright of insecurity. No investment seemed safe. As people saw their retirement savings accounts gutted, they were left confused, anxious, and angry. A Missouri couple expressed a common concern: "We were always optimistic when we

The financial bailout

President Bush (left) and Treasury Secretary Henry Paulson speak to reporters from the steps of the Treasury Department after the House passed the $700 billion financial bailout bill (TARP).

were young. We thought that every year, things would get better." Now the bubble had burst. Even Alan Greenspan, the former chairman of the Federal Reserve Board, found himself in a state of "shocked disbelief."

Amid what quickly became a global financial crisis, policy makers faced the challenge of shoring up the financial system and dealing with the social effects (panic) of a deepening recession. The crisis demanded decisive action. On October 3, 2008, after two weeks of contentious and often emotional congressional debate, President Bush signed into law a far-reaching historic bank bailout fund called the Troubled Asset Relief Program (TARP). The TARP called for the Treasury Department to spend $700 billion to keep banks and other financial institutions from collapsing. "By coming together on this legislation, we have acted boldly to prevent the crisis on Wall Street from becoming a crisis in communities across our country," Bush said after the House voted 263 to 171 to pass the TARP bill. Despite such unprecedented government investment in the private financial sector, the economy still sputtered. In early October, stock markets around the world began to crash. Economists warned that the world was at risk of careening into a depression.

A HISTORIC ELECTION

The economic crisis had potent political effects. As two preeminent economists noted, "In the eight years since George W. Bush took office, nearly every component of the U.S. economy has deteriorated." Budget deficits, trade deficits, and consumer debt had reached record levels, and the total expense of the American war in Iraq was projected to top $3 trillion. During the president's last year in office, just 29 percent of the voters "approved" of his leadership. And more than 80 percent said that the nation was headed in the "wrong direction." Even a prominent Republican strategist, Kevin Phillips, deemed Bush "perhaps the least competent president in modern history."

Bush's vulnerability excited Democrats about the possibility of regaining the White House in the 2008 election. As a journalist predicted in November 2007, "It looks highly likely that this will be the Democrats' year." Not only was the Bush presidency floundering, but the once-indomitable Republican party was in disarray, plagued by scandals, riven by factions, and lacking effective leadership. In 2004 the American electorate had been evenly divided by party identification: 43 percent for both the Democratic and

The Clinton campaign

Democratic presidential hopeful Senator Hillary Clinton speaks at the Fort Worth Stockyards.

the Republican parties. By 2008 the Democrats were leading the Republicans 50 percent to 35 percent.

The early front-runner for the Democratic nomination was New York senator Hillary Clinton, the highly visible spouse of ex-president Bill Clinton. Like her husband, she displayed an impressive command of policy issues and mobilized a well-funded campaign team. And as the first woman with a serious chance of gaining the presidency, she garnered widespread support among voters eager for female leadership. But in the end an overconfident Clinton was upset in the Democratic primaries and caucuses by little-known first-term senator Barack Obama of Illinois, an inspiring speaker who attracted huge crowds by promising a "politics of hope" and bolstering their de-

The Obama campaign

Democratic presidential hopeful, Senator Barack Obama waves to supporters at Waterfront Park in Portland, Oregon.

sire for "change." While the Clinton campaign courted the powerful members of the party establishment, Obama mounted an innovative Internet-based campaign directed at grassroots voters, donors, and volunteers. Obama was especially popular among young people. In early June 2008, Obama gained enough delegates to secure the Democratic nomination.

Obama was the first African American presidential nominee of either party, the gifted biracial son of a white mother from Kansas and a black Kenyan father who left the household and returned to Africa when Barack was a toddler. The forty-seven-year-old Harvard Law School graduate and former professor, community organizer, and state legislator presented himself as a conciliator who could inspire and unite a diverse people and forge bipartisan collaborations.

Obama exuded poise, confidence, and energy. By contrast, his Republican opponent, seventy-two-year-old Arizona senator John McCain, was the oldest

The 2008 presidential debates

Republican presidential candidate John McCain (left) and Democratic presidential candidate Barack Obama (right) focused on foreign policy, national security, and the financial crisis at the first of three presidential debates.

presidential candidate in history. The son and grandson of distinguished Navy admirals, McCain had graduated from the U.S. Naval Academy before serving as a pilot in the Vietnam War. Captured after his plane was shot down, he spent over five years as a prisoner of war in Hanoi, suffering frequent torture. As a twenty-five-year veteran of Congress, a leading Republican senator, and a 2004 candidate for the Republican presidential nomination, he had developed a reputation as a bipartisan maverick willing to work with Democrats to achieve key legislative goals. McCain had voted against President Bush's tax cuts for the wealthy in 2001 and 2003, and he criticized the religious right for being "agents of intolerance."

Concerns about McCain's support among Republican conservatives led him to select Alaska governor Sarah Palin as his running mate, the first woman on a Republican ticket. Although hardly known outside party circles, Palin held the promise of winning over religious conservatives nervous about McCain's ideological purity. She opposed abortion, gay marriage (Obama opposed it too), and stem-cell research, and she endorsed the teaching of creationism in public schools. For his part, Barack Obama rejected calls to choose Hillary Clinton as his running mate. Instead, he selected veteran Delaware senator Joseph Biden.

THE 2008 ELECTION The presidential campaign started in August 2008 with polls suggesting a very tight race. But the dramatic economic downturn in September and October gave Obama and the Democrats a powerful partisan weapon. Obama shrewdly capitalized on widespread dissatisfaction with the Republicans and centered his campaign on the echoing promise of "change." He repeatedly linked McCain with the unpopular George W. Bush. His pledge to avoid politics as usual and adopt a "post-partisan" approach resonated with voters tired of attack politics. Obama denounced the prevailing Republican "economic philosophy that says we should give more and more to those with the most and hope that prosperity trickles down to everyone else." He described the 2008 financial meltdown as the "final verdict on this failed philosophy."

While Obama's campaign projected a youthful, vibrant, energetic, disciplined, and consistent tone, John McCain struggled to define himself and his

Election night rally

President-elect Barack Obama, his wife Michelle, and two daughters, Sasha and Malia wave to the crowd of supporters in Chicago's Grant Park.

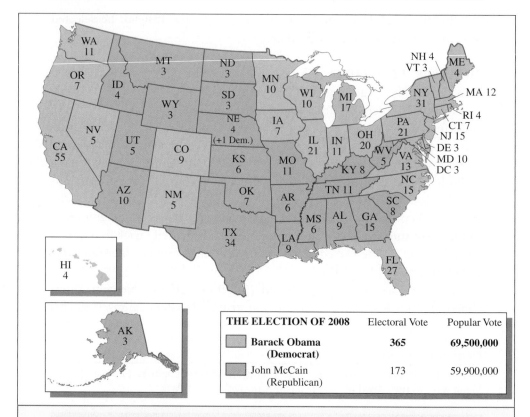

THE ELECTION OF 2008	Electoral Vote	Popular Vote
Barack Obama (Democrat)	**365**	**69,500,000**
John McCain (Republican)	173	59,900,000

How did the economic crisis affect the outcome of the election? What are the similarities and differences between the map of the 2004 election and the map of the 2008 election?

message. With each successive televised debate, the calm and confident Obama widened his lead. Meanwhile, as the editors of *Newsweek* magazine noted, the "U.S. economy went from being *an* issue in the presidential election to the *only* issue." With the country's finances in a tailspin, McCain made a clumsy statement in September–"the fundamentals of our economy are strong"—that would come back to haunt him. Within ten days, McCain reversed himself, announcing that the economic crisis was so serious that he needed to suspend his campaign in order to return to the Senate. Still floundering, he tried to refocus the campaign debate on his support for the Iraq War and the success of the "surge" strategy. Obama parried by promising a phased withdrawal of American forces. The Obama campaign also pledged to broaden health-insurance coverage, promote renewable energy, raise taxes on the wealthy, and get the economy growing again.

On November 4, 2008, Barack Obama made history by becoming the nation's first person of color elected president. "Change has come to America," he announced in his victory speech. His triumph was decisive and sweeping. The inspirational Obama won the popular vote by seven points: 53 percent to 46 percent. His margin in the electoral vote was even more impressive: 365 to 173. The president-elect won big among his core supporters—voters under age thirty, women, minorities, the very poor, and first-time voters. He collected 95 percent of the African American vote and 66 percent of voters aged eighteen to twenty-nine, and he won the Hispanic vote. Obama also helped the Democrats win solid majorities in the House and Senate races.

Within days of his electoral victory, Barack Obama had adopted a bipartisan approach in selecting his new cabinet members. He appointed Hillary Clinton secretary of state, renewed Republican Robert Gates as secretary of defense, selected retired general James Jones, who had campaigned for McCain, as his national security adviser, and appointed Eric Holder as the nation's first African American attorney general.

THE FIRST ONE HUNDRED DAYS

On January 20, 2009, President Obama delivered a sobering inaugural address in frigid weather amid daunting challenges. The United States was embroiled in two wars, in Iraq and Afghanistan. The economy was in shambles, unemployment was soaring, and the national debt was hemorrhaging. Yet it was Obama's inspiring promise of hope and change that led millions of spectators to crowd into Washington, D.C., to witness the historic swearing-in ceremony.

The Oath of Office

Barack Obama takes the oath as the forty-fourth President of the United States.

Like Franklin Roosevelt, a supremely self-confident Obama acted quickly—some said too quickly—to fulfill his campaign pledges. With a boldness and scope reminiscent of Ronald Reagan, Obama launched an audacious agenda. He would overhaul government regulations, reform education, energy, environmental, and health-care policies, restructure the tax code, invigorate the economy, and recast U.S. foreign policy. On his second day in office, he issued an executive order to begin a case-by-case review of all suspected terrorists being held at the U.S. detention center at the Guantánamo Bay Naval Base in Cuba. The prisoners were to be released or transferred to other prisons, and the detention center would be closed within a year. In March, Obama eased restrictions on the federal funding of human embryonic stem-cell research. His doing so outraged abortion opponents but pleased those who believe that stem-cell research can lead to medical cures for many diseases. Obama also lifted restrictions on American travel to Cuba that had been in place for nearly fifty years. And he offered to talk with the totalitarian leaders of Iran and North Korea, something his predecessors had refused to do.

REVIVING THE ECONOMY The new Obama administration's main challenge was to keep the deepening recession from becoming a prolonged depression. Unemployment in early 2009 had passed 8 percent and was still rising. More than 5 million people had lost their jobs since 2007. The financial sector remained paralyzed. At the same time, U.S. military forces remained embroiled in the conflicts in Iraq and Afghanistan. Like Franklin Roosevelt, Obama wanted to be a "transformative" president. To do so, he needed to move swiftly to enact his ambitious agenda while still enjoying widespread public support. Like Roosevelt in 1933, the new president sought to restore public confidence during these "difficult and uncertain times" by acting "boldly and wisely" to fulfill his campaign pledges and stimulate the stagnant economy. He assured the nation that "we will rebuild, we will recover."

In mid-February, after a prolonged and often strident debate, Congress passed, and Obama signed, a $787-billion economic stimulus bill—the largest in history—called the American Recovery and Reinvestment Act. The gargantuan bill (over 1,000 pages long) included cash distributions to the states, funds for food stamps, unemployment benefits, construction projects to renew the nation's infrastructure (roads, bridges, levees, government buildings, and the electricity grid), funds for renewable-energy systems, and tax reductions. But the passage of the stimulus bill showed no evidence that Obama was successful in implementing a "bipartisan" presidency. Only three Senate Republicans voted for the bill. Not a single House Republican voted for it, and eleven House Democrats opposed it as well. In February, Obama continued his calibrated boldness by ordering the Treasury Department to implement tax cuts for 95 percent of Americans (all but the most wealthy), and he announced plans to let the tax cuts for the rich implemented by George W. Bush expire in 2010. During the summer of 2009, Democratic Congressional leaders began working with the White House to develop the two largest and most controversial of Obama's proposals: health-care reform and climate-change legislation.

LEAVING IRAQ?   President Obama announced on February 27, 2009, that all U.S. combat troops would be withdrawn from Iraq by the end of 2011. A "transitional force" of 35,000 to 50,000 troops would assist Iraqi security forces, protect Americans and fight terrorism, Obama said. "The drawdown of our military should send a clear signal that Iraq's future is now its own responsibility. The long-term success of the Iraqi nation will depend on decisions made by Iraq's leaders and the fortitude of the Iraqi people," Obama said. At the same time that he was reducing U.S. military involvement in Iraq, Obama dispatched 21,000 additional troops to Afghanistan, which he called "ground zero" in the battle against terrorism. Obama's Iraqi withdrawal plan prompted many hard questions: Did his timetable provide enough time for Iraqis to forge a self-reliant government and economy? Could the U.S. withdrawal trigger a civil war between Sunnis and Shiites? Only time would tell.

End of Chapter Review

CHAPTER SUMMARY

- **Changing Demographics** From 1980 to 2009 the population of the United States grew by 20 percent to 290 million. The South and the West lured residents from the Midwest and the Northeast. The number of traditional family units continued to decline; the poverty rate was especially high among African Americans. A wave of immigrants caused Latinos to surpass African Americans as the nation's largest minority.

- **Divided Government** The popularity of President George H. W. Bush waned after the Gulf War, an economic recession, and his decision to raise taxes. The election of William Jefferson Clinton and the Democratic victory was short-lived, however. Speaker Newt Gingrich mobilized the Christian Coalition against "liberalism" with his Contract with America to achieve the Republican landslide of 1994.

- **Economic Prosperity and Crises** The United States benefited from a period of unprecedented prosperity during the 1990s, fueled by the dramatic effect of the new computer-based industries on the economy. The collapse of high-tech companies in 2000 betrayed the underlying insecurity of the market. Economic growth soon surged again primarily because of consumers' ability to borrow against the skyrocketing value of their home mortgages. In 2007 the country experienced an unparalleled crisis when the global financial markets collapsed under the weight of "toxic" financial securities.

- **Global Terrorism** The September 11 attacks led President George W. Bush to declare a war on terrorism and enunciate the Bush Doctrine. In 2002 the Bush administration shifted its focus to Saddam Hussein. The American-led Operation Iraqi Freedom succeeded in removing Hussein from power but was fully unprepared to establish order in a country that was soon driven by sectarian violence. The American public became bitterly divided over the Iraq War.

- **2008 Presidential Election** The 2008 presidential campaigns, included the first major female candidate, Senator Hillary Clinton; an African American, Senator Barack Obama; and Senator John McCain, the oldest candidate in history. Obama won the popular vote and a landslide victory in the Electoral College, becoming the nation's first African American president. His victory was fueled by the collapse of the economy, an unprecedented Internet- and grassroots-based campaign, and voters' weariness with President Bush and the Republican policies of the preceding eight years.

GLOSSARY

36°30′ According to the Missouri Compromise, any part of the Louisiana Purchase north of this line (Missouri's southern border) was to be excluded from slavery.

54th Massachusetts Regiment After President Abraham Lincoln's Emancipation Proclamation, the Union army organized all black military units, which white officers led. The 54th Massachusetts Regiment was one of the first of such units to be organized.

Abigail Adams (1744–1818) As the wife of John Adams, she endured long periods of separation from him while he served in many political roles. During these times apart, she wrote often to her husband; and their correspondence has provided a detailed portrait of life during the Revolutionary War.

abolition In the early 1830s, the anti-slavery movement shifted its goal from the gradual end of slavery to the immediate end or abolition of slavery.

John Adams (1735–1826) He was a signer of the Declaration of Independence and a delegate to the First and Second Continental Congress. During the Revolutionary War, he worked as a diplomat in France and Holland and negotiated the peace treaty with Britain. After the Revolutionary War, he served as the minister to Britain as well as the vice president and the second president of the United States. As president, he passed the Alien and Sedition Acts and endured a stormy relationship with France, which included the XYZ affair.

John Quincy Adams (1767–1848) As secretary of state under President Monroe, he negotiated agreements to define the boundaries of the Oregon country and the Transcontinental Treaty. He urged President Monroe to issue the Monroe Doctrine, which incorporated Adams's views. As president, Adams envisioned an expanded federal government and a broader use of federal powers. Adams's nationalism and praise of European leaders caused a split in his party. Some Republicans suspected him of being a closet monarchist and left to form the Democrat party. In the presidential election 1828, Andrew Jackson claimed that Adams had gained the presidency through a "corrupt bargain" with Henry Clay, which helped Jackson win the election.

Samuel Adams (1722–1803) A genius of revolutionary agitation, he believed that English Parliament had no right to legislate for the colonies. He organized the Sons of Liberty as well as protests in Boston against the British.

Jane Addams (1860–1935) As the leader of one of the best known settlement houses, she rejected the "do-goodism" spirit of religious reformers. Instead, she focused on solving the practical problems of the poor and tried to avoid the assumption that she and other social workers knew what was best for poor immigrants. She established child care for working mothers, health clinics, job training, and other social programs. She was also active in the peace movement and was awarded the Noble Peace Prize in 1931 for her work on its behalf.

Agricultural Adjustment Act (1933) New Deal legislation that established the Agricultural Adjustment Administration (AAA) to improve agricultural prices by limiting market supplies; declared unconstitutional in *United States v. Butler* (1936).

Emilio Aguinaldo (1869?–1964) He was a leader in Filipino struggle for independence. During the war of 1898, Commodore George Dewey brought Aguinaldo back to the Philippines from exile to help fight the Spanish. However, after the Spanish surrendered to Americans, America annexed the Philippines and Aguinaldo fought against the American military until he was captured in 1901.

Alamo, Battle of the Siege in the Texas War for Independence of 1836, in which the San Antonio mission fell to the Mexicans. Davy Crockett and Jim Bowie were among the courageous defenders.

Alien and Sedition Acts (1798) Four measures passed during the undeclared war with France that limited the freedoms of speech and press and restricted the liberty of noncitizens.

American Federation of Labor Founded in 1881 as a federation of trade unions made up of skilled workers, the AFL under president Samuel Gompers successfully pushed for the eight-hour workday.

American Indian Movement Fed up with the poor conditions on Indian reservations and the federal government's unwillingness to help, Native Americans founded the American Indian Movement (AIM) in 1963. In 1973, AIM led 200 Sioux in the occupation of Wounded Knee. After a ten-week standoff with the federal authorities, the government agreed to reexamine Indian treaty rights and the occupation ended.

American Protective Association Nativist, anti-Catholic secret society founded in Iowa in 1887 and active until the end of the century.

American Recovery and Reinvestment Act Hoping to restart the weak economy, President Obama signed this $787-billion economic stimulus bill in February of 2009. The bill included cash distributions to states, funds for food stamps, unemployment benefits, construction projects to renew the nation's infrastructure, funds for renewable-energy systems, and tax reductions.

American System Program of internal improvements and protective tariffs promoted by Speaker of the House Henry Clay in his presidential campaign of 1824; his proposals formed the core of Whig ideology in the 1830s and 1840s.

anaconda strategy Union General Winfield Scott developed this three-pronged strategy to defeat the Confederacy. Like a snake strangling its prey, the Union army would crush its enemy through exerting pressure on Richmond, blockading Confederate ports, and dividing the South by invading its major waterways.

Annapolis Convention In 1786, all thirteen colonies were invited to a convention in Annapolis to discuss commercial problems, but only representatives from five states attended. However, the convention was not a complete failure because the delegates decided to have another convention in order to write the constitution.

anti-Federalists Forerunners of Thomas Jefferson's Democratic-Republican party; opposed the Constitution as a limitation on individual and states' rights, which led to the addition of a Bill of Rights to the document.

Anti-Masonic party This party grew out of popular hostility toward the Masonic fraternal order and entered the presidential election of 1832 as a third party. It was the first party to run as a third party in a presidential election as well as the first to hold a nomination convention and announce a party platform.

Benedict Arnold (1741–1801) A traitorous American commander who planned to sell out the American garrison at West Point to the British, but his plot was discovered before it could be executed and he joined the British army.

Atlanta Compromise Speech to the Cotton States and International Exposition in 1895 by educator Booker T. Washington, the leading black spokesman of the day; black scholar W. E. B. Du Bois gave the speech its derisive name and criticized Washington for encouraging blacks to accommodate segregation and disenfranchisement.

Atlantic Charter Issued August 12, 1941, following meetings in Newfoundland between President Franklin D. Roosevelt and British Prime Minister Winston Churchill, the charter signaled the allies' cooperation and stated their war aims.

Crispus Attucks (1723–1770) During the Boston Massacre, he was supposedly at the head of the crowd of hecklers who baited the British troops. He was killed when the British troops fired on the crowd.

Stephen F. Austin (1793–1836) He established the first colony of Americans in Texas, which eventually attracted 2,000 people.

Axis powers In World War II, the nations of Germany, Italy, and Japan.

Aztec Empire Mesoamerican people who were conquered by the Spanish under Hernando Cortés, 1519–1528.

baby boom Markedly higher birth rate in the years following World War II; led to the biggest demographic "bubble" in American history.

Bacon's Rebellion Unsuccessful 1676 revolt led by planter Nathaniel Bacon against Virginia governor William Berkeley's administration, because it had failed to protect settlers from Indian raids.

Bank of the United States Proposed by the first Secretary of the Treasury Alexander Hamilton, the bank opened in 1791 and operated until 1811 to issue a uniform currency, make business loans, and collect tax monies. The second Bank of the United States was chartered in 1816 but was not renewed by President Andrew Jackson twenty years later.

barbary pirates Plundering pirates off the Mediterranean coast of Africa; President Thomas Jefferson's refusal to pay them tribute to protect

American ships sparked an undeclared naval war with North African nations, 1801–1805.

Battle of the Bulge On December 16, 1944, the German army launched a counter attack against the Allied forces, which pushed them back. However, the Allies were eventually able to recover and breakthrough the German lines. This defeat was a great blow to the Nazi's morale and their army's strength. The battle used up the last of Hitler's reserve units and opened a route into Germany's heartland.

Bear Flag Republic On June 14, 1846, a group of Americans in California captured Sonoma from the Mexican army and declared it the Republic of California whose flag featured a grizzly bear. In July, the commodore of the U.S. Pacific Fleet landed troops on California's shores and declared it part of the United States.

Beats A group of writers, artists, and musicians whose central concern was the discarding of organizational constraints and traditional conventions in favor of liberated forms of self expression. They came out of the bohemian underground in New York's Greenwich Village in the 1950s and included the writers Jack Kerouac, Allen Ginsberg, and William Burroughs. Their attitudes and lifestyles had a major influence on the youth of the 1960s.

beatnik A name referring to almost any young rebel who openly dissented from the middle-class life. The name itself stems from the Beats.

Nicholas Biddle (1786–1844) He was the president of the second Bank of the United States. In response to President Andrew Jackson's attacks on the bank, Biddle curtailed the bank's loans and exchanged its paper currency for gold and silver. He was hoping to provoke an economic crisis to prove the bank's importance. In response, state banks began printing paper without restraint and lent it to speculators, causing a binge in speculating and an enormous increase in debt.

Bill of Rights First ten amendments to the U.S. Constitution, adopted in 1791 to guarantee individual rights and to help secure ratification of the Constitution by the states.

Osama bin Laden (1957–) He is the leader of al Qaeda whose members attacked America on September 11, 2001. Years before the attack, he had declared *jihad* (holy war) on the United States, Israel, and the Saudi monarchy. In Afghanistan, the Taliban leaders gave Osama bin Laden a safe haven in exchange for aid in fighting the Northern Alliance, who were rebels opposed to the Taliban. After the 9/11 terrorist attacks, the United States asked the Taliban to turn over bin Laden. Following their refusal, America and multinational coalition invaded Afghanistan and overthrew the Taliban, but they did not capture bin Laden.

black codes Laws passed in southern states to restrict the rights of former slaves; to combat the codes, Congress passed the Civil Rights Act of 1866 and the Fourteenth Amendment and set up military governments in southern states that refused to ratify the amendment.

black power A more militant form of protest for civil rights that originated in urban communities, where nonviolent tactics were less effective than in the South. Black power encouraged African Americans to take pride in their racial heritage and forced black leaders and organizations to focus attention on the plight of poor inner-city blacks.

James Gillepsie Blaine (1830–1893) As a Republican congressman from Maine, he developed close ties with business leaders, which contributed to him losing the presidential election of 1884. He later opposed President Cleveland's efforts to reduce tariffs, which became a significant issue in the 1888 presidential election. Blaine served as secretary of state under President Benjamin Harrison and his flamboyant style often overshadowed the president.

"bleeding" Kansas Violence between pro- and antislavery settlers in the Kansas Territory, 1856.

blitzkrieg The German "lightening war" strategy used during World War II; the Germans invaded Poland, France, Russia, and other countries with fast-moving, well-coordinated attacks using aircraft, tanks, and other armored vehicles, followed by infantry.

Bolsheviks Under the leadership of Vladimir Lenin, this Marxist party led the November 1917 revolution against the newly formed provisional government in Russia. After seizing control, the Bolsheviks negotiated a peace treaty with Germany, the Treaty of Brest-Litovsk, and ended their participation in World War I.

Bonus Expeditionary Force Thousands of World War I veterans, who insisted on immediate payment of their bonus certificates, marched on Washington in 1932; violence ensued when President Herbert Hoover ordered their tent villages cleared.

Daniel Boone (1734–1820) He found and expanded a trail into Kentucky, which pioneers used to reach and settle the area.

John Wilkes Booth (1838?–1865) He assassinated President Abraham Lincoln at the Ford's Theater on April 14, 1865. He was pursued to Virginia and killed.

Bourbons In post–Civil War southern politics, the opponents of the Redeemers were called Bourbons. They were known for having forgotten nothing and learned nothing from the ordeal of the Civil War.

Joseph Brant (1742?–1807) He was the Mohawk leader who led the Iroquois against the Americans in the Revolutionary War.

brinkmanship Secretary of State John Foster Dulles believed that communism could be contained by bringing America to the brink of war with an aggressive communist nation. He believed that the aggressor would back down when confronted with the prospect of receiving a mass retaliation from a country with nuclear weapons.

John Brown (1800–1859) He was willing to use violence to further his antislavery beliefs. In 1856, a pro-slavery mob sacked the free-state town of Lawrence, Kansas. In response, John Brown went to the pro-slavery settlement of Pottawatomie, Kansas and hacked to death several people, which led to a guerrilla war in the Kansas territory. In 1859, he attempted to raid the federal arsenal at Harpers Ferry. He had hoped to use the stolen weapons to arm slaves, but he was captured and executed. His failed raid instilled panic throughout the South, and his execution turned him into a martyr for his cause.

***Brown v. Board of Education of Topeka* (1954)** U.S. Supreme Court decision that struck down racial segregation in public education and declared "separate but equal" unconstitutional.

William Jennings Bryan (1860–1925) He delivered the pro-silver "cross of gold" speech at the 1896 Democratic Convention and won his party's nomination for president. Disappointed pro-gold Democrats chose to walk out of the convention and nominate their own candidate, which split the Democratic party and cost them the White House. Bryan's loss also crippled the Populist movement that had endorsed him.

"Bull Moose" Progressive party In the 1912 election, Theodore Roosevelt was unable to secure the Republican nomination for president. He left the Republican party and formed his own party of progressive Republicans, called the "Bull Moose" party. Roosevelt and Taft split the Republican vote, which allowed Democrat Woodrow Wilson to win.

Bull Run, Battles of (First and Second Manassas) First land engagement of the Civil War took place on July 21, 1861, at Manassas Junction, Virginia, at which surprised Union troops quickly retreated; one year later, on August 29–30, Confederates captured the federal supply depot and forced Union troops back to Washington.

Martin Van Buren (1782–1862) During President Jackson's first term, he served as secretary of state and minister to London. He often politically fought Vice President John C. Calhoun for the position of Jackson's successor. A rift between Jackson and Calhoun led to Van Buren becoming vice president during Jackson's second term. In 1836, Van Buren was elected president, and he inherited a financial crisis. He believed that the government should not continue to keep its deposits in state banks and set up an independent Treasury, which was approved by Congress after several years of political maneuvering.

General John Burgoyne (1722–1792) He was the commander of Britain's northern forces during the Revolutionary War. He and most of his troops surrendered to the Americans at the Battle of Saratoga.

burned-over district Area of western New York strongly influenced by the revivalist fervor of the Second Great Awakening; Disciples of Christ and Mormons are among the many sects that trace their roots to the phenomenon.

Aaron Burr (1756–1836) Even though he was Thomas Jefferson's vice president, he lost favor with Jefferson's supporters who were Republicans. He sought to work with the Federalists and run as their candidate for the governor of New York. Alexander Hamilton opposed Burr's candidacy and his stinging remarks on the subject led to Burr challenging him to duel in which Hamilton was killed.

George H. W. Bush (1924–) He had served as vice president during the Reagan administration and then won the presidential election of 1988. During his presidential campaign, Bush promised not to raise taxes. However, the federal deficit had become so big that he had to raise taxes. Bush chose to make fighting illegal drugs a priority. He created the Office of National Drug Control Policy, but it was only moderately successful in stopping drug use. In 1989, Bush ordered the invasion of Panama and the capture of Panamanian leader Manuel Noriega, who was wanted in America on drug charges. He was captured, tried, and convicted. In 1990, Saddam Hussein invaded Kuwait; and Bush sent the American military to Saudi Arabia on a defensive mission. He assembled a multinational force and launched Operation Desert Storm, which took Kuwait back from Saddam in 1991. The euphoria over the victory in Kuwait was short lived as the country slid into a recession. He lost the 1992 presidential election to Bill Clinton.

George W. Bush (1946-) In the 2000 presidential election, Texas governor George W. Bush ran as the Republican nominee against Democratic nominee Vice President Al Gore. The election ended in controversy over the final vote tally in Florida. Bush had slightly more votes, but a recount was required by state law. However, it was stopped by Supreme Court and Bush was declared president. After the September 11 terrorist attacks, he launched his "war on terrorism." President George W. Bush adapted the Bush Doctrine, which claimed the right to launch preemptive military attacks against enemies. The United States invaded Afghanistan and Iraq with unclear outcomes leaving the countries divided. In the summer of 2006, Hurricane Katrina struck the Gulf Coast and left destruction across several states and three-quarters of New Orleans flooded. Bush was attacked for the unpreparedness of the federal government to handle the disaster as well as his own slowness to react. In September 2008, the nation's economy nosedived as a credit crunch spiraled into a global economic meltdown. Bush signed into law the bank bailout fund called Troubled Asset Relief Program (TARP), but the economy did not improve.

***Bush v. Gore* (2000)** The close 2000 presidential election came down to Florida's decisive twenty-five electoral votes. The final tally in Florida gave Bush a slight lead, but it was so small that a recount was required by state law. While the votes were being recounted, a legal battle was being waged to stop the recount. Finally, the case, *Bush v. Gore*, was present to the Supreme Court who ruled 5–4 to stop the recount and Bush was declared the winner.

Bush Doctrine Believing that America's enemies were now terrorist groups and unstable rogue nations, President George W. Bush adapted a foreign policy that claimed the right to launch preemptive military attacks against enemies.

buying (stock) on margin The investment practice of making a small down payment (the "margin") on a stock and borrowing the rest of money need for the purchase from a broker who held the stock as security against a down market. If the stock's value declined and the buyer failed to meet a margin call for more funds, the broker could sell the stock to cover his loan.

John C. Calhoun (1782–1850) He served in both the House of Representatives and the Senate for South Carolina before becoming secretary of war under President Monroe and then John Quincy Adams's vice president. He introduced the bill for the second national bank to Congress and led the minority of southerners who voted for the Tariff of 1816. However, he later chose to oppose tariffs. During his time as secretary of war under President Monroe, he authorized the use of federal troops against the Seminoles who were attacking settlers. As John Quincy Adams's vice president, he supported a new tariffs bill to win presidential candidate Andrew Jackson additional support. Jackson won the election, but the new tariffs bill passed and Calhoun had to explain why he had changed his opinion on tariffs.

Camp David Accords Peace agreement between Israeli Prime Minister Menachem Begin and Egyptian President Anwar Sadat, brokered by President Jimmy Carter in 1978.

"Scarface" Al Capone (1899–1947) He was the most successful gangster of the Prohibition era whose Chicago-based criminal empire included bootlegging, prostitution, and gambling.

Andrew Carnegie (1835–1919) He was a steel magnate who believed that the general public benefited from big business even if these companies employed harsh business practices. This philosophy became deeply ingrained in the conventional wisdom of some Americans. After retiring, he devoted himself to philanthropy in hopes of promoting social welfare and world peace.

carpetbaggers Northern emigrants who participated in the Republican governments of the reconstructed South.

Jimmy Carter (1924–) Jimmy Carter, an outsider to Washington, capitalized on the post-Watergate cynicism and won the 1976 presidential election. He created departments of Energy and Education and signed into law several environmental initiatives. However, his efforts to support the Panama Canal Treaties and his unwillingness to make deals with legislators caused other bills to be either gutted or stalled in Congress. Despite his efforts to improve the economy, the recession continued and inflation increased. In 1978, he successfully brokered a peace agreement between Israel and Egypt called the Camp David Accords. Then his administration was plagued with a series of crises. Fighting in the Middle East produced a fuel shortage in the United States. The Soviets invaded Afghanistan and Carter responded with the suspension of an arms-control treaty with the Soviets, the halting of grain shipments to the Soviet Union, and a call for a boycott of the Olympic Games in Moscow. In Iran, revolutionaries toppled the shah's government and seized the American embassy, taking hostage those inside. Carter struggled to get the hostages released and was unable to do so until after he lost the 1980 election to Ronald Reagan. He was awarded the Nobel Peace Prize in 2002 for his efforts to further peace and democratic elections around the world.

Jacques Cartier (1491–1557) He led the first French effort to colonize North America and explored the Gulf of St. Lawrence and reached as far as present day Montreal on the St. Lawrence River.

Bartolomé de Las Casas (1484–1566) A Catholic missionary who renounced the Spanish practice of coercively converting Indians and advocated the better treatment for them. In 1552, he wrote *A Brief Relation of the Destruction of the Indies*, which described the Spanish's cruel treatment of the Indians.

Fidel Castro (1926–) In 1959, his Communist regime came to power in Cuba after two years of guerrilla warfare against the dictator Fulgenico Batista. He enacted land redistribution programs and nationalized all foreign-owned property. The latter action as well as his political trials and summary executions damaged relations between Cuba and America. Castro was turned down when he asked for loans from the United States. However, he did receive aid from the Soviet Union.

Carrie Chapman Catt (1859–1947) She was a leader of a new generation of activists in the women's suffrage movement who carried on the work started by Elizabeth Cady Stanton and Susan B. Anthony.

Cesar Chavez (1927–1993) He founded the United Farm Workers (UFW) in 1962 and worked to organize migrant farm workers. In 1965, the UFW joined Filipino farm workers striking against corporate grape farmers in California's San Joaquin Valley. In 1970, the strike and a consumer boycott on grapes compelled the farmers to formally recognize the UFW. As the result of Chavez's efforts, wages and working conditions improved for migrant workers. In 1975, the California state legislature passed a bill that required growers to bargain collectively with representatives of the farm workers.

Chinese Exclusion Act (1882) The first federal law to restrict immigration on the basis of race and class. Passed in 1882, the act halted Chinese immigration for ten years, but it was periodically renewed and then indefinitely extended in 1902. Not until 1943 were the barriers to Chinese immigration finally removed.

Church of Jesus Christ of Latter-day Saints / Mormons Founded in 1830 by Joseph Smith, the sect was a product of the intense revivalism of the burned-over district of New York; Smith's successor Brigham Young led 15,000 followers to Utah in 1847 to escape persecution.

Winston Churchill (1874–1965) The British prime minister who led the country during World War II. Along with Roosevelt and Stalin, he helped shape the post-war world at the Yalta Conference. He also coined the term "iron curtain," which he used in his famous "The Sinews of Peace" speech.

"city machines" Local political party officials used these organizations to dispense patronage and favoritism amongst voters and businesses to ensure their loyal support to the political party.

Civil Rights Act of 1957 First federal civil rights law since Reconstruction; established the Civil Rights Commission and the Civil Rights Division of the Department of Justice.

Civil Rights Act of 1964 Outlawed discrimination in public accommodations and employment.

Henry Clay (1777–1852) In the first half of the nineteenth century, he was the foremost spokesman for the American system. As speaker of the House in the 1820s, he promoted economic nationalism, "market revolution," and the rapid development of western states and territories. He formulated the "second" Missouri Compromise, which denied the Missouri state legislature the power to exclude the rights of free blacks and mulattos. In the deadlocked presidential election of 1824, the House of Representatives decided the election. Clay supported John Quincy Adams, who won the presidency and appointed Clay to secretary of state. Andrew Jackson claimed that Clay had entered into a "corrupt bargain" with Adams for his own selfish gains.

Hillary Rodham Clinton (1947–) In the 2008 presidential election, Senator Hillary Clinton, the spouse of former President Bill Clinton, initially was the front-runner for the Democratic nomination, which made her the first woman with a serious chance to win the presidency. However,

Senator Barack Obama's Internet-based and grassroots-orientated campaign garnered him enough delegates to win the nomination. After Obama became president, she was appointed secretary of state.

William Jefferson Clinton (1946–) The governor of Arkansas won the 1992 presidential election against President George H. W. Bush. In his first term, he pushed through Congress a tax increase, an economic stimulus package, the adoption of the North America Free Trade Agreement, welfare reform, a raise in the minimum wage, and improved public access to health insurance. However, he failed to institute major health-care reform, which had been one of his major goals. In 1996, Clinton defeated Republican presidential candidate Bob Dole. Clinton was scrutinized for his investment in the fraudulent Whitewater Development Corporation, but no evidence was found of him being involved in any wrongdoing. In 1998, he was revealed to have had a sexual affair with a White House intern. Clinton had initially lied about the affair and tried to cover up it, which led to a vote in Congress on whether or not to begin an impeachment inquiry. The House of Representatives voted to impeach Clinton, but the Senate found him not guilty. Clinton's presidency faced several foreign policy challenges. In 1994, he used U.S. forces to restore Haiti's democratically elected president to power after he had been ousted during a coup. In 1995, the Clinton Administration negotiated the Dayton Accords, which stopped the ethnic strife in the former Yugoslavia and the Balkan region. Clinton sponsored peace talks between Arabs and Israelis, which culminated in Israeli Prime Minister Yitzhak Rabin and the Palestine Liberation Organization leader Yasir Arafat signing the Oslo Accords in 1993. This agreement provided for the restoration of Palestinian self-rule in specific areas in exchange for peace as provided in UN Security Council resolutions.

Coercive Acts / Intolerable Acts (1774) Four parliamentary measures in reaction to the Boston Tea Party that forced payment for the tea, disallowed colonial trials of British soldiers, forced their quartering in private homes, and set up a military government.

coffin ships Irish immigrants fleeing the potato famine had to endure a six-week journey across the Atlantic to reach America. During these voyages, thousands of passengers died of disease and starvation, which led to the ships being called "coffin ships."

Christopher Columbus (1451–1506) The Italian sailor who persuaded King Ferdinand and Queen Isabella of Spain to fund his expedition across the Atlantic to discover a new trade route to Asia. Instead of arriving at China or Japan, he reached the Bahamas in 1492.

Committee on Public Information During World War I, this committee produced war propaganda that conveyed the Allies' war aims to Americans as well as attempted to weaken the enemy's morale.

Committee to Re-elect the President (CREEP) During Nixon's presidency, his administration engaged in a number of immoral acts, such as attempting to steal information and falsely accusing political appointments of sexual improprieties. These acts were funded by money illegally collected through CREEP.

Thomas Paine's *Common Sense* This pamphlet refocused the blame for the colonies' problems on King George III rather than on Parliament and advocated a declaration of independence, which few colonialists had considered prior to its appearance.

Compromise of 1850 Complex compromise mediated by Senator Henry Clay that headed off southern secession over California statehood; to appease the South it included a stronger fugitive slave law and delayed determination of the slave status of the New Mexico and Utah territories.

Compromise of 1877 Deal made by a special congressional commission on March 2, 1877, to resolve the disputed presidential election of 1876; Republican Rutherford B. Hayes, who had lost the popular vote, was declared the winner in exchange for the withdrawal of federal troops from the South, marking the end of Reconstruction.

Conestoga wagons These large horse-drawn wagons were used to carry people or heavy freight long distances, including from the East to the western frontier settlements.

conquistadores Spanish term for "conqueror," applied to European leaders of campaigns against indigenous peoples in central and southern America.

consumer culture In the post-World War II era, affluence seemed to be forever increasing in America. At the same time, there was a boom in construction as well as products and appliances for Americans to buy. As a result, shopping became a major recreational activity. Americans started spending more, saving less, and building more shopping centers.

containment U.S. strategy in the cold war that called for containing Soviet expansion; originally devised in 1947 by U.S. diplomat George F. Kennan.

Continental army Army authorized by the Continental Congress, 1775–1784, to fight the British; commanded by General George Washington.

Contras The Reagan administration ordered the CIA to train and supply guerrilla bands of anti-Communist Nicaraguans called Contras. They were fighting the Sandinista government that had recently come to power in Nicaragua. The State Department believed that the Sandinista government was supplying the leftist Salvadoran rebels with Soviet and Cuban arms. A cease-fire agreement between the Contras and Sandinistas was signed in 1988.

Calvin Coolidge "Silent Cal" (1872–1933) After President Harding's death, his vice president, Calvin Coolidge, assumed the presidency. Coolidge believed that the nation's welfare was tied to the success of big business, and he worked to end government regulation of business and industry as well as reduce taxes. In particular, he focused on the nation's industrial development.

Hernán Cortés (1485–1547) The Spanish conquistador who conquered the Aztec Empire and set the precedent for other plundering conquistadores.

General Charles Cornwallis (1738–1805) He was in charge of British troops in the South during the Revolutionary War. His surrendering to George Washington at the Battle of Yorktown ended the Revolutionary War.

Corps of Discovery Meriwether Lewis and William Clark led this group of men on an expedition of the newly purchased Louisiana territory, which took them from Missouri to Oregon. As they traveled, they kept detailed journals and drew maps of the previously unexplored territory. Their reports attracted traders and trappers to the region and gave the United States a claim to the Oregon country by right of discovery and exploration.

"corrupt bargain" A vote in the House of Representatives decided the deadlocked presidential election of 1824 in favor of John Quincy Adams, who Speaker of the House Henry Clay had supported. Afterward, Adams appointed Clay secretary of state. Andrew Jackson charged Clay with having made a "corrupt bargain" with Adams that gave Adams the presidency and Clay a place in his administration. There was no evidence of such a deal, but it was widely believed.

the counterculture "Hippie" youth culture of the 1960s, which rejected the values of the dominant culture in favor of illicit drugs, communes, free sex, and rock music.

court-packing plan President Franklin D. Roosevelt's failed 1937 attempt to increase the number of U.S. Supreme Court justices from nine to fifteen in order to save his Second New Deal programs from constitutional challenges.

covenant theory A Puritan concept that believed true Christians could enter a voluntary union for the common worship of God. Taking the idea one step further, the union could also be used for the purposes of establishing governments.

Coxey's Army Jacob S. Coxey, a Populist, led this protest group that demanded the federal government provide the unemployed with meaningful employment. In 1894, Coxey's Army joined other protests groups in a march on Washington D.C. The combination of the march and the growing support of Populism scared many Americans.

Credit Mobilier scandal Construction company guilt of massive overcharges for building the Union Pacific Railroad were exposed; high officials of the Ulysses S. Grant administration were implicated but never charged.

George Creel (1876–1953) He convinced President Woodrow Wilson that the best approach to influencing public opinion was through propaganda rather than censorship. As the executive head of the Committee on Public Information, he produced propaganda that conveyed the Allies' war aims.

"Cross of Gold" Speech In the 1896 election, the Democratic party split over the issue of whether to use gold or silver to back American currency. Significant to this division was the "Cross of Gold" speech that William Jennings Bryan delivered at the Democratic convention. This pro-silver speech was so well received that Bryan won the nomination to be their presidential candidate. Disappointed pro-gold Democrats chose to walk out of the convention and nominate their own candidate.

Cuban missile crisis Caused when the United States discovered Soviet offensive missile sites in Cuba in October 1962; the U.S.–Soviet confrontation was the cold war's closest brush with nuclear war.

cult of domesticity The belief that women should stay at home to manage the household, educate their children with strong moral values, and please their husbands.

George A. Custer (1839–1876) He was a reckless and glory-seeking Lieutenant Colonel of the U.S. Army who fought the Sioux Indians in the Great Sioux War. In 1876, he and his detachment of soldiers were entirely wiped out in the Battle of Little Bighorn.

D-day June 6, 1944, when an Allied amphibious assault landed on the Normandy coast and established a foothold in Europe from which Hitler's defenses could not recover.

Jefferson Davis (1808–1889) He was the president of the Confederacy during the Civil War. When the Confederacy's defeat seemed invitable in early 1865, he refused to surrender. Union forces captured him in May of that year.

Eugene V. Debs (1855–1926) He founded the American Railway Union, which he organized against the Pullman Palace Car Company during the Pullman strike. Later he organized the Social Democratic party, which eventually became the Socialist Party of America. In the 1912 presidential election, he ran as the Socialist party's candidate and received more than 900,000 votes.

Declaratory Act Following the repeal of the Stamp Act in 1766, Parliament passed this act which asserted Parliament's full power to make laws binding the colonies "in all cases whatsoever."

deism Enlightenment thought applied to religion; emphasized reason, morality, and natural law.

détente In the 1970s, the United States and Soviet Union began working together to achieve a more orderly and restrained competition between each other. Both countries signed an agreement to limit the number of Intercontinental Long Range Ballistic Missiles (ICBMs) that each country could possess and to not construct antiballistic missiles systems. They also signed new trade agreements.

George Dewey (1837–1917) On April 30, 1898, Commodore George Dewey's small U.S. naval squadron defeated the Spanish warships in Manila Bay in the Philippines. This quick victory aroused expansionist fever in the United States.

John Dewey (1859–1952) He is an important philosopher of pragmatism. However, he preferred to use the term *instrumentalism*, because he saw ideas as instruments of action.

Ngo Dinh Diem (1901–1963) Following the Geneva Accords, the French, with the support of America, forced the Vietnamese emperor to accept Dinh Diem as the new premier of South Vietnam. President Eisenhower sent advisors to train Diem's police and army. In return, the United States expected Diem to enact democratic reforms and distribute land to the peasants. Instead, he suppressed his political opponents, did little or no land distribution, and let corruption grow. In 1956, he refused to participate in elections to reunify Vietnam. Eventually, he ousted the emperor and declared himself president.

Dorothea Dix (1802–1887) She was an important figure in increasing the public's awareness of the plight of the mentally ill. After a two-year investigation of the treatment of the mentally ill in Massachusetts, she presented her findings and won the support of leading reformers. She eventually convinced twenty states to reform their treatment of the mentally ill.

Dixiecrats Deep South delegates who walked out of the 1948 Democratic National Convention in protest of the party's support for civil rights legislation and later formed the States' Rights (Dixiecrat) party, which nominated Strom Thurmond of South Carolina for president.

dollar diplomacy The Taft administration's policy of encouraging American bankers to aid debt-plagued governments in Haiti, Guatemala, Honduras, and Nicaragua.

Donner party Forty-seven surviving members of a group of migrants to California were forced to resort to cannibalism to survive a brutal winter trapped in the Sierra Nevadas, 1846–1847; highest death toll of any group traveling the Overland Trail.

Stephen A. Douglas (1812–1861) As a senator from Illinois, he authored the Kansas-Nebraska Act. Once passed, the act led to violence in Kansas between pro- and antislavery factions and damaged the Whig party. These damages prevented Senator Douglas from being chosen as the presidential candidate of his party. Running for senatorial reelection in 1858, he engaged Abraham Lincoln in a series of public debates about slavery in the territories. Even though Douglas won the election, the debates gave Lincoln a national reputation.

Frederick Douglass (1818–1895) He escaped from slavery and become an eloquent speaker and writer against slavery. In 1845, he published his autobiography entitled *Narrative of the Life of Frederick Douglass* and two years later he founded an abolitionist newspaper for blacks called the *North Star*.

dot-coms In the late 1990s, the stock market soared to new heights and defied the predictions of experts that the economy could not sustain such a performance. Much of the economic success was based on dot-com enterprises, which were firms specializing in computers, software, telecommunications, and the internet. However, many of the companies' stock market values were driven higher and higher by speculation instead of financial success. Eventually the stock market bubble burst.

***Dred Scott v. Sandford* (1857)** U.S. Supreme Court decision in which Chief Justice Roger B. Taney ruled that slaves could not sue for freedom and that Congress could not prohibit slavery in the territories, on the grounds that such a prohibition would violate the Fifth Amendment rights of slaveholders.

W. E. B. Du Bois (1868–1963) He criticized Booker T. Washington's views on civil rights as being accommodationist. He advocated "ceaseless agitation" for civil rights and the immediate end to segregation and an enforcement of laws to protect civil rights and equality. He promoted an education for African Americans that would nurture bold leaders who were willing to challenge discrimination in politics.

John Foster Dulles (1888–1959) As President Eisenhower's secretary of state, he institutionalized the policy of containment and introduced the strategy of deterrence. He believed in using brinkmanship to halt the spread of communism. He attempted to employ it in Indochina, which led to the United States' involvement in Vietnam.

"Dust Bowl" Great Plains counties where millions of tons of topsoil were blown away from parched farmland in the 1930s; massive migration of farm families followed.

Peggy Eaton (1796–1879) The wife of John Eaton, President Jackson's secretary of war, was the daughter of a tavern owner with an unsavory past. Supposedly her first husband had committed suicide after learning that she was having an affair with John Eaton. The wives of members of Jackson's cabinet snubbed her because of her lowly origins and past. The scandal that resulted was called the Eaton Affair.

Jonathan Edwards (1703–1758) New England Congregationalist minister, who began a religious revival in his Northampton church and was an important figure in the Great Awakening.

Election of 1912 The presidential election of 1912 featured four candidates: Wilson, Taft, Roosevelt, and Debs. Each candidate believed in the basic assumptions of progressive politics, but each had a different view on how progressive ideals should be implemented through policy. In the end, Taft and Roosevelt split the Republican party votes and Wilson emerged as the winner.

Queen Elizabeth I of England (1533–1603) The protestant daughter of Henry VIII, she was Queen of England from 1558-1603 and played a major role in the Protestant Reformation. During her long reign, the doctrines and services of the Church of England were defined and the Spanish Armada was defeated.

General Dwight D. Eisenhower (1890–1969) During World War II, he commanded the Allied Forces landing in Africa and was the supreme Allied commander as well as planner for Operation Overlord. In 1952, he was elected president on his popularity as a war hero and his promises to clean up Washington and find an honorable peace in the Korean War. His administration sought to cut the nation's domestic programs and budget, but he left the basic structure of the New Deal intact. In July of 1953, he announced the end of fighting in Korea. He appointed Earl Warren to the Supreme Court whose influence helped the court become an important force for social and political change. His secretary of state, John Foster Dulles, institutionalized the policies of containment and deterrence. Eisenhower supported the withdrawal of British forces from the Suez Canal and established the Eisenhower doctrine, which promised to aid any nation against aggression by a communist nation. Eisenhower preferred that state and local institutions to handle civil rights issues, and he refused to force states to comply with the Supreme Court's civil rights decisions. However, he did propose the legislation that became the Civil Rights Act of 1957.

Ellis Island Reception center in New York Harbor through which most European immigrants to America were processed from 1892 to 1954.

Emancipation Proclamation (1863) President Abraham Lincoln issued a preliminary proclamation on September 22, 1862, freeing the slaves in the Confederate states as of January 1, 1863, the date of the final proclamation.

Ralph Waldo Emerson (1803–1882) As a leader of the transcendentalist movement, he wrote poems, essays, and speeches that discussed the sacredness of nature, optimism, self-reliance, and the unlimited potential of the individual. He wanted to transcend the limitations of inherited conventions and rationalism to reach the inner recesses of the self.

encomienda System under which officers of the Spanish conquistadores gained ownership of Indian land.

Enlightenment Revolution in thought begun in the seventeenth century that emphasized reason and science over the authority of traditional religion.

enumerated goods According to the Navigation Act, these particular goods, like tobacco or cotton, could only be shipped to England or other English colonies.

Erie Canal Most important and profitable of the barge canals of the 1820s and 1830s; stretched from Buffalo to Albany, New York, connecting the Great Lakes to the East Coast and making New York City the nation's largest port.

ethnic cleansing The act of killing an entire group of people in a region or country because of its ethnic background. After the collapse of the former Yugoslavia in 1991, Serbs in Bosnia attacked communities of Muslims, which led to intervention by the United Nations. In 1998, fighting broke out again in the Balkans between Serbia and Kosovo. Serbian police and military attacked, killed, raped, or forced Muslim Albanian Kosovars to leave their homes.

Fair Employment Practices Commission Created in 1941 by executive order, the FEPC sought to eliminate racial discrimination in jobs; it possessed little power but represented a step toward civil rights for African Americans.

Farmers' Alliance Two separate organizations (Northwestern and Southern) of the 1880s and 1890s that took the place of the Grange, worked for similar causes, and attracted landless, as well as landed, farmers to their membership.

Federal Writers' Project During the Great Depression, this project provided writers, such as Ralph Ellison, Richard Wright, and Saul Bellow, with work, which gave them a chance to develop as artists and be employed.

The Federalist Collection of eighty-five essays that appeared in the New York press in 1787–1788 in support of the Constitution; written by Alexander Hamilton, James Madison, and John Jay but published under the pseudonym "Publius."

Geraldine Ferraro (1935–) In the 1984 presidential election, Democratic nominee, Walter Mondale, chose her as his running mate. As a member of the U.S. House of Representatives from New York, she was the first woman to be a vice-presidential nominee for a major political party. However, she was placed on the defensive because of her husband's complicated business dealings.

Fifteenth Amendment This amendment forbids states to deny any person the right to vote on grounds of "race, color or pervious condition of servitude." Former Confederate states were required to ratify this amendment before they could be readmitted to the Union.

the "final solution" The Nazi party's systematic murder of some 6 million Jews along with more than a million other people including, but not limited to, gypsies, homosexuals, and handicap individuals.

Food Administration After America's entry into World War I, the economy of the home front needed to be reorganized to provide the most efficient means of conducting the war. The Food Administration was a part of this effort. Under the leadership of Herbert Hoover, the organization sought to increase agricultural production while reducing civilian consumption of foodstuffs.

force bill During the nullification crisis between President Andrew Jackson and South Carolina, Jackson asked Congress to pass this bill, which authorized him to use the army to force South Carolina to comply with federal law.

Gerald Ford (1913–2006) He was President Nixon's vice president and assumed the presidency after Nixon resigned. President Ford issued Nixon a pardon for any crimes related to the Watergate scandal. The American public's reaction was largely negative; and Ford never regained the public's confidence. He resisted congressional pressure to both reduce taxes and increase federal spending, which sent the American economy into the deepest recession since the Great Depression. Ford retained Kissinger as his secretary of state and continued Nixon's foreign policy goals, which included the signing of another arms-control agreement with the Soviet Union. He was heavily criticized following the collapse of South Vietnam.

Fort Laramie Treaty (1851) Restricted the Plains Indians from using the Overland Trail and permitted the building of government forts.

Fort Necessity After attacking a group of French soldiers, George Washington constructed and took shelter in this fort from vengeful French troops. Washington eventually surrendered to them after a day-long battle. This conflict was a significant event in igniting the French and Indian War.

Fort Sumter First battle of the Civil War, in which the federal fort in Charleston (South Carolina) Harbor was captured by the Confederates on April 14, 1861, after two days of shelling.

"forty-niners" Speculators who went to northern California following the discovery of gold in 1848; the first of several years of large-scale migration was 1849.

Fourteen Points President Woodrow Wilson's 1918 plan for peace after World War I; at the Versailles peace conference, however, he failed to incorporate all of the points into the treaty.

Fourteenth Amendment (1868) Guaranteed rights of citizenship to former slaves, in words similar to those of the Civil Rights Act of 1866.

Franciscan Missions In 1769, Franciscan missioners accompanied Spanish soldiers to California and over the next fifty years established a chain of missions from San Diego to San Francisco. At these missions, friars sought to convert Indians to Catholicism and make them members of the Spanish empire. The friars stripped the Indians of their native heritage and used soldiers to enforce their will.

Benjamin Franklin (1706–1790) A Boston-born American, who epitomized the Enlightenment for many Americans and Europeans, Franklin's wide range of interests led him to become a publisher, inventor, and statesman. As the latter, he contributed to the writing of the Declaration of Independence, served as the minister to France during the Revolutionary War, and was a delegate to the Constitutional Convention.

Free-Soil party Formed in 1848 to oppose slavery in the territory acquired in the Mexican War; nominated Martin Van Buren for president in 1848, but by 1854, most of the party's members had joined the Republican party.

Freedmen's Bureau Reconstruction agency established in 1865 to protect the legal rights of former slaves and to assist with their education, jobs, health care, and landowning.

freedom riders In 1961, the Congress of Racial Equality had this group of black and white demonstrators ride buses to test the federal court ruling that had banned segregation on buses and trains and in terminals. Despite being attacked, they never gave up. Their actions drew national attention and generated respect and support for their cause.

John C. Frémont "the Pathfinder" (1813–1890) He was an explorer and surveyor who helped inspire Americans living in California to rebel against the Mexican government and declare independence.

French and Indian War Known in Europe as the Seven Years' War, the last (1755–1763) of four colonial wars fought between England and France for control of North America east of the Mississippi River.

Sigmund Freud (1865–1939) He was the founder of psychoanalysis, which suggested that human behavior was motivated by unconscious and irrational forces. By the 1920s, his ideas were being discussed more openly in America.

Fugitive Slave Act of 1850 Gave federal government authority in cases involving runaway slaves; so much more punitive and prejudiced in favor of slaveholders than the 1793 Fugitive Slave Act had been that Harriet Beecher Stowe was inspired to write *Uncle Tom's Cabin* in protest; the new law was part of the Compromise of 1850, included to appease the South over the admission of California as a free state.

fundamentalism Anti-modernist Protestant movement started in the early twentieth century that proclaimed the literal truth of the Bible; the name came from *The Fundamentals*, published by conservative leaders.

"gag rule" In 1831, the House of Representatives adopted this rule, which prevented the discussion and presentation of any petitions for the abolition of slavery to the House. John Quincy Adams, who was elected to the House after his presidency ended, fought the rule on the grounds that it violated the First Amendment. In 1844, he succeeded in having it repealed.

William Lloyd Garrison (1805–1879) In 1831, he started the anti-slavery newspaper *Liberator* and helped start the New England Anti-Slavery Society. Two years later, he assisted Arthur and Lewis Tappan in the founding of the American Anti-Slavery Society. He and his followers believed that America had been thoroughly corrupted and needed a wide range of reforms. He embraced every major reform movement of the day: abolition, temperance, pacifism, and women's rights. He wanted to go beyond just freeing slaves and grant them equal social and legal rights.

Marcus Garvey (1887–1940) He was the leading spokesman for Negro Nationalism, which exalted blackness, black cultural expression, and black exclusiveness. He called upon African Americans to liberate themselves from the surrounding white culture and create their own businesses, cultural centers, and newspapers. He was also the founder of the Universal Negro Improvement Association.

Citizen Genêt (1763–1834) As the ambassador to the United States from the new French Republic, he engaged American privateers to attack British ships and conspired with frontiersmen and land speculators to organize an attack on Spanish Florida and Louisiana. His actions and the French radicals excessive actions against their enemies in the new French Republic caused the French Revolution to lose support among Americans.

Geneva Accords In 1954, the Geneva Accords were signed, which ended French colonial rule in Indochina. The agreement created the independent nations of Laos and Cambodia and divided Vietnam along the 17th parallel until an election in 1956 would reunify the country.

German U-boat German submarines, or U-boats, were used to attack enemy merchant ships in the waters around the British Isles during World War I. The sinking of the ocean liner *Lusitania* by a German submarine caused a public outcry in America, which contributed to the demands to expand the United States' military.

Gettysburg, Battle of Fought in southern Pennsylvania, July 1–3, 1863; the Confederate defeat and the simultaneous loss at Vicksburg spelled the end of the South's chances in the Civil War.

Ghost Dance movement This spiritual and political movement came from a Paiute Indian named Wovoka (or Jack Wilson). He believed that a messiah would come and rescue the Indians and restore their lands. To hasten the arrival of the messiah, the Indians needed to take up a ceremonial dance at each new moon.

Newt Gingrich (1943–) He led the Republican insurgency in Congress in the mid 1990s through mobilizing religious and social conservatives. Along with other Republican congressmen, he created the Contract with America, which was a ten-point anti-big government program. However, the program fizzled out after many of its bills were not passed by Congress.

The Gilded Age Mark Twain and Charles Dudley Warner's 1873 novel, the title of which became the popular name for the period from the end of the Civil War to the turn of the century.

glasnost Soviet leader Mikhail Gorbachev instituted this reform, which brought about a loosening of censorship.

Glorious Revolution In 1688, the Protestant Queen Mary and her husband, William of Orange, took the British throne from King James II in a bloodless coup. Afterward, Parliament greatly expanded its power and passed the Bill of Rights and the Act of Toleration, both of which would influence attitudes and events in the colonies.

Barry Goldwater (1909–1998) He was a leader of the Republican right whose book, *The Conscience of a Conservative*, was highly influential to that segment of the party. He proposed eliminating the income tax and overhauling Social Security. In 1964, he ran as the Republican presidential candidate and lost to President Johnson. He campaigned against Johnson's war on poverty, the tradition of New Deal, the nuclear test ban and the Civil Rights Act of 1964. He advocated the wholesale bombing of North Vietnam.

Samuel Gompers (1850–1924) He served as the president of the American Federation of Labor from its inception until his death. He focused on achieving concrete economic gains such as higher wages, shorter hours, and better working conditions.

"good neighbor" policy Proclaimed by President Franklin D. Roosevelt in his first inaugural address in 1933, it sought improved diplomatic relations between the United States and its Latin American neighbors.

Mikhail Gorbachev (1931–) In the late 1980s, Soviet leader Mikhail Gorbachev attempted to reform the Soviet Union through his programs of *perestroika* and *glasnost*. He pursued a renewal of détente with America and signed new arms-control agreements with President Reagan. Gorbachev chose not to involve the Soviet Union in the internal affairs of other Communist countries, which removed the threat of armed Soviet crackdowns on reformers and protesters in Eastern Europe. Gorbachev's decision allowed the velvet revolutions of Eastern Europe to occur without outside interference. Eventually the political, social, and economic upheaval he had unleashed would lead to the break-up of the Soviet Union.

Al Gore (1948–) He served as a senator of Tennessee and then as President Clinton's vice president. In the 2000 presidential election, he was the Democratic candidate and campaigned on preserving Social Security, subsidizing prescription-medicine expenses for the elderly, and protecting the environment. His opponent was Governor George W. Bush, who promoted compassionate conservatism and the transferring of power from the federal government to the states. The election ended in controversy. The close election came down to Florida's electoral votes. The final tally in Florida gave Bush a slight lead, but it was so small that a recount was required by state law. While the votes were being recounted, a legal battle was being waged to stop the recount. Finally, the case, *Bush v. Gore*, was presented to the Supreme Court who ruled 5–4 to stop the recount and Bush was declared the winner.

Jay Gould (1836–1892) As one of the biggest railroad robber barons, he was infamous for buying rundown railroads, making cosmetic improvements and then reselling them for a profit. He used corporate funds for personal investments and to bribe politicians and judges.

gradualism This strategy for ending slavery involved promoting the banning of slavery in the new western territories and encouraging the release of slaves from slavery. Supporters of this method believed that it would bring about the gradual end of slavery.

Granger movement Political movement that grew out of the Patrons of Husbandry, an educational and social organization for farmers founded in 1867; the Grange had its greatest success in the Midwest of the 1870s, lobbying for government control of railroad and grain elevator rates and establishing farmers' cooperatives.

Ulysses S. Grant (1822–1885) After distinguishing himself in the western theater of the Civil War, he was appointed general in chief of the Union army in 1864. Afterward, he defeated General Robert E. Lee through a policy of aggressive attrition. He constantly attacked Lee's army until it was grind down. Lee surrendered to Grant on April 9th, 1865 at the Appomattox Court House. In 1868, he was elected President and his tenure suffered from scandals and fiscal problems including the debate on whether or not greenbacks, paper money, should be removed from circulation.

Great Awakening Fervent religious revival movement in the 1720s through the 1740s that was spread throughout the colonies by ministers like

New England Congregationalist Jonathan Edwards and English revivalist George Whitefield.

great black migration After World War II, rural southern blacks began moving to the urban North and Midwest in large numbers in search of better jobs, housing, and greater social equality. The massive influx of African American migrants overwhelmed the resources of urban governments and sparked racial conflicts. In order to cope with the new migrants and alleviate racial tension, cities constructed massive public-housing projects that segregated African Americans into overcrowded and poor neighborhoods.

Great Compromise (Connecticut Compromise) Mediated the differences between the New Jersey and Virginia delegations to the Constitutional Convention by providing for a bicameral legislature, the upper house of which would have equal representation and the lower house of which would be apportioned by population.

Great Depression Worst economic depression in American history; it was spurred by the stock market crash of 1929 and lasted until World War II.

Great Sioux War In 1874, Lieutenant Colonel Custard led an exploratory expedition into the Black Hills, which the United States government had promised to the Sioux Indians. Miners soon followed and the army did nothing to keep them out. Eventually, the army attacked the Sioux Indians and the fight against them lasted for fifteen months before the Sioux Indians were forced to give up their land and move onto a reservation.

Great Society Term coined by President Lyndon B. Johnson in his 1965 State of the Union address, in which he proposed legislation to address problems of voting rights, poverty, diseases, education, immigration, and the environment.

Horace Greeley (1811–1872) In reaction to Radical Reconstruction and corruption in President Ulysses S. Grant's administration, a group of Republicans broke from the party to form the Liberal Republicans. In 1872, the Liberal Republicans chose Horace Greeley as their presidential candidate who ran on a platform of favoring civil service reform and condemning the Republican's Reconstruction policy.

greenbacks Paper money issued during the Civil War. After the war ended, a debate emerged on whether or not to remove the paper currency from circulation and revert back to hard-money currency (gold coins).

Opponents of hard-money feared that eliminating the greenbacks would shrink the money supply, which would lower crop prices and make it more difficult to repay long-term debts. President Ulysses S. Grant, as well as hard-currency advocates, believed that gold coins were morally preferable to paper currency.

Greenback party Formed in 1876 in reaction to economic depression, the party favored issuance of unsecured paper money to help farmers repay debts; the movement for free coinage of silver took the place of the greenback movement by the 1880s.

Nathanael Greene (1742–1786) He was appointed by Congress to command the American army fighting in the South during the Revolutionary War. Using his patience and his skills of managing men, saving supplies, and avoiding needless risks, he waged a successful war of attrition against the British.

Sarah Grimké (1792–1873) and **Angelina Grimké (1805–1879)** These two sisters gave anti-slavery speeches to crowds of mixed gender that caused some people to condemn them for engaging in unfeminine activities. The sisters rejected this opinion and made the role of women in the anti-slavery movement a prominent issue. In 1840, William Lloyd Garrison convinced the Anti-Slavery Society to allow women equal participation in the organization. A group of members that did not agree with this decision left the Anti-Slavery Society to form the American and Foreign Anti-Slavery Society.

Half-Way Covenant Allowed baptized children of church members to be admitted to a "halfway" membership in the church and secure baptism for their own children in turn, but allowed them neither a vote in the church, nor communion.

Alexander Hamilton (1755–1804) His belief in a strong federal government led him to become a contributor to *The Federalist* and leader of the Federalists. As the first secretary of the Treasury, he laid the foundation for American capitalism through his creation of a federal budget, funded debt, a federal tax system, a national bank, a customs service, and a coast guard. His "Reports on Public Credit" and "Reports on Manufactures" outlined his vision for economic development and government finances in America. He died in a duel against Aaron Burr.

Warren Harding (1865–1923) In the 1920 presidential election, he was the Republican nominee who promised Americans a "return to normalcy," which would mean a return to conservative values and a turning away from President Wilson's internationalism. His message resonated with voters' conservative postwar mood; and he won the election. Once in office, Harding's administration dismantled many of the social and economic components of progressivism and pursued a pro-business agenda. Harding appointed four pro-business Supreme Court Justices and his administration cut taxes, increased tariffs and promoted a lenient attitude towards government regulation of corporations. However, he did speak out against racism and ended the exclusion of African Americans from federal positions. His administration did suffer from a series of scandals as the result of him appointing members of the Ohio gang to government positions.

Harlem Renaissance African American literary and artistic movement of the 1920s and 1930s centered in New York City's Harlem district; writers Langston Hughes, Jean Toomer, Zora Neale Hurston, and Countee Cullen were among those active in the movement.

Hartford Convention Meeting of New England Federalists on December 15, 1814, to protest the War of 1812; proposed seven constitutional amendments (limiting embargoes and changing requirements for officeholding, declaration of war, and admission of new states), but the war ended before Congress could respond.

Patrick Henry (1736–1799) He inspired the Virginia Resolves, which declared that Englishmen could only be taxed by their elected representatives. In March of 1775, he met with other colonial leaders to discuss the goals of the upcoming Continental Congress and famously declared "Give me liberty or give me death." During the ratification process of the U.S. Constitution, he became one of the leaders of the anti-federalists.

Hideki Tōjō (1884–1948) He was Japan's war minister and later prime minister during World War II.

Alger Hiss (1904–1996) During the second Red Scare, Alger Hiss, who had served in several government departments, was accused of being a spy for the Soviet Union and was convicted of lying about espionage. The case was politically damaging to the Truman administration because the president called the charges against Hiss a "red herring." Richard

Nixon, then a California congressman, used his persistent pursuit of the case and his anti-Communist rhetoric to raise his national profile and to win election to the Senate.

Adolph Hitler "*Führer*" (1889–1945) The leader of the Nazis who advocated a violent anti-Semitic, anti-Marxist, pan-German ideology. He started World War II in Europe and orchestrated the systematic murder of some 6 million Jews along with more than a million others.

HIV/AIDS Human Immunodeficiency Virus (HIV) is a virus that attacks the body's T-cells, which are necessary to help the immune system fight off infection and disease. Acquired Immunodeficiency Syndrome (AIDS) occurs after the HIV virus has destroyed the body's immune system. HIV is transferred when body fluids, such as blood or semen, which carry the virus, enter the body of an uninfected person. The virus appeared in America in the early 1980s. The Reagan administration was slow to respond to the "AIDS Epidemic," because effects of the virus were not fully understood and they deemed the spread of the disease as the result of immoral behavior.

Homestead Act (1862) Authorized Congress to grant 160 acres of public land to a western settler, who had only to live on the land for five years to establish title.

Herbert Hoover (1874–1964) Prior to becoming president, Hoover served as the secretary of commerce in both the Harding and Coolidge administrations. During his tenure at the Commerce Department, he pursued new markets for business and encouraged business leaders to share information as part of the trade-association movement. The Great Depression hit while he was president. Hoover believed that the nation's business structure was sound and sought to revive the economy through boosting the nation's confidence. He also tried to restart the economy with government constructions projects, lower taxes and new federal loan programs, but nothing worked.

House Un-American Activities Committee (HUAC) Formed in 1938 to investigate subversives in the government; best-known investigations were of Hollywood notables and of former State Department official Alger Hiss, who was accused in 1948 of espionage and Communist party membership.

Sam Houston (1793–1863) During Texas's fight for independence from Mexico, Sam Houston was the commander in chief of the Texas forces, and he led the attack that captured General Antonio López de Santa Anna. After Texas gained its independence, he was name its first president.

Jacob Riis' *How the Other Half Lives* Jacob Riis was an early muckraking journalist who exposed the slum conditions in New York City in his book *How the Other Half Lives.*

General William Howe (1729–1814) As the commander of the British army in the Revolutionary War, he seized New York City from Washington's army, but failed to capture it. He missed several more opportunities to quickly end the rebellion, and he resigned his command after the British defeat at Saratoga.

Saddam Hussein (1937–2006) The former dictator of Iraq who became the head of state in 1979. In 1980, he invaded Iran and started the eight-year-long Iran-Iraq War. In 1990, he invaded Kuwait, which caused the Gulf War of 1991. In 2003, he was overthrown and captured when the United States invaded. He was sentenced to death by hanging in 2006.

Anne Hutchinson (1591–1643) The articulate, strong-willed, and intelligent wife of a prominent Boston merchant, who espoused her belief in direct divine revelation. She quarreled with Puritan leaders over her beliefs; and they banished her from the colony.

impressment The British navy used press-gangs to kidnap men in British and colonial ports who were then forced to serve in the British navy.

"Indian New Deal" This phrase refers to the reforms implemented for Native Americans during the New Deal era. John Collier, the commissioner of the Bureau of Indian Affairs (BIA), increased the access Native Americans had to relief programs and employed more Native Americans at the BIA. He worked to pass the Indian Reorganization Act. However, the version of the act passed by Congress was a much-diluted version of Collier's original proposal and did not greatly improve the lives of Native Americans.

indentured servant Settler who signed on for a temporary period of servitude to a master in exchange for passage to the New World; Virginia and Pennsylvania were largely peopled in the seventeenth and eighteenth centuries by English indentured servants.

Indian Removal Act (1830) Signed by President Andrew Jackson, the law permitted the negotiation of treaties to obtain the Indians' lands in exchange for their relocation to what became Oklahoma.

Indochina This area of Southeast Asian consists of Laos, Cambodia, became and Vietnam and was once controlled by France as a colony. After the Viet Minh defeated the French, the Geneva Accords were signed, which ended French colonial rule. The agreement created the independent nations of Laos and Cambodia and divided Vietnam along the 17th parallel until an election would reunify the country. Fearing a communist take over, the United States government began intervening in the region during the Truman administration, which led to President Johnson's full-scale military involvement in Vietnam.

Industrial Workers of the World A radical union organized in Chicago in 1905, nicknamed the Wobblies; its opposition to World War I led to its destruction by the federal government under the Espionage Act.

internationalists Prior to the United States' entry in World War II, internationalists believed that America's national security depended on aiding Britain in its struggle against Germany.

internment of Japanese Americans In 1942, President Roosevelt issued an executive order to have all Japanese Americans forcibly relocated to relocation camps. More than 60 percent of the more than 100,000 internees were American citizens.

interstate highway system In the late 1950s, construction began on a national network of interstate superhighways for the purpose of commerce and defense. The interstate highways would enable the rapid movement of military convoys and the evacuation of cities after a nuclear attack.

Iranian Hostage Crisis In 1979, a revolution in Iran placed the Ayatollah Ruhollah Khomeini, a fundamental religious leader, in power. In November 1979, revolutionaries seized the American embassy in Tehran and held those inside hostage. President Carter struggled to get the hostages. He tried pressuring Iran through appeals to the United Nations, freezing Iranian assets in the United States and imposing a trade embargo. During an aborted rescue operation, a helicopter collided with a transport plane and killed eight U.S. soldiers. Finally, Carter unfroze several billion dollars in Iranian assets, and the hostages were released after being held for 444 days; but not until Ronald Reagan had become president of the United States.

Iran-Contra affair Scandal of the second Reagan administration involving sale of arms to Iran in partial exchange for release of hostages in Lebanon and use of the arms money to aid the Contras in Nicaragua, which had been expressly forbidden by Congress.

Irish Potato Famine In 1845, an epidemic of potato rot brought a famine to rural Ireland that killed over 1 million peasants and instigated a huge increase in the number or Irish immigrating to America. By 1850, the Irish made up 43 percent of the foreign-born population in the United States; and in the 1850s, they made up over half the population of New York City and Boston.

iron curtain Term coined by Winston Churchill to describe the cold war divide between western Europe and the Soviet Union's Eastern European satellites.

Iroquois League An alliance of the Iroquois tribes that used their strength to force Europeans to work with them in the fur trade and to wage war across what is today eastern North America.

Andrew Jackson (1767–1837) As a major general in the Tennessee militia, he defeated the Creek Indians, invaded the panhandle of Spanish Florida and won the Battle of New Orleans. In 1818, his successful campaign against Spanish forces in Florida gave the United States the upper hand in negotiating for Florida with Spain. As president, he vetoed bills for the federal funding of internal improvements and the re-chartering of the Second National Bank. When South Carolina nullified the Tariffs of 1828 and 1832, Jackson requested that Congress pass a "force bill" that would authorize him to use the army to compel the state to comply with the tariffs. He forced eastern Indians to move west of the Mississippi River so their lands could be used by white settlers. Groups of those who opposed Jackson come together to form a new political part called the Whigs.

Jesse Jackson (1941–) An African American civil rights activist who had been one of Martin Luther King Jr.'s chief lieutenants. He is most famous for founding the social justice organization the Rainbow

Coalition. In 1988, he ran for the Democratic presidential nomination, which became a race primarily between him and Michael Dukakis. Dukakis won the nomination, but lost the election to Republican nominee Vice President George H. W. Bush.

Thomas "Stonewall" Jackson (1824–1863) He was a Confederate general who was known for his fearlessness in leading rapid marches, bold flanking movements, and furious assaults. He earned his nickname at the Battle of the First Bull Run for standing courageously against Union fire. During the battle of Chancellorsville, his own men accidently mortally wounded him.

William James (1842–1910) He was the founder of Pragmatism and one of the fathers of modern psychology. He believed that ideas gained their validity not from their inherent truth, but from their social consequences and practical application.

Jay's Treaty Treaty with Britain negotiated in 1794 by Chief Justice John Jay; Britain agreed to vacate forts in the Northwest Territories, and festering disagreements (border with Canada, prewar debts, shipping claims) would be settled by commission.

Thomas Jefferson (1743–1826) He was a plantation owner, author, the drafter of the Declaration Independence, ambassador to France, leader of the Republican party, secretary of state, and the third president of the United States. As president, he purchased the Louisiana territory from France, withheld appointments made by President Adams leading to *Marybury v. Madison,* outlawed foreign slave trade, and was committed to a "wise and frugal" government.

Jesuits A religious order founded in 1540 by Ignatius Loyola. They sought to counter the spread of Protestantism during the Protestant Reformation and spread the Catholic faith through work as missionaries. Roughly 3,500 served in New Spain and New France.

"Jim Crow" laws In the New South, these laws mandated the separation of races in various public places that served as a way for the ruling whites to impose their will on all areas of black life.

Andrew Johnson (1808–1875) As President Abraham Lincoln's vice president, he was elevated to the presidency after Lincoln's assassination. In order to restore the Union after the Civil War, he issued an amnesty proclamation and required former Confederate states to ratify the Thirteenth Amendment. He fought Radical Republicans in Congress over whether he or Congress had the authority to restore states rights to the former Confederate states. This fight weakened both his political and public support. In 1868, the Radical Republicans attempted to impeach Johnson but fell short on the required number of votes needed to remove him from office.

Lyndon B. Johnson (1908–1973) Former member of the United States House of Representatives and the former Majority Leader of the United States Senate, Vice President Lyndon Johnson, assumed the presidency after President Kennedy's assassination. He was able to push through Congress several pieces of Kennedy's legislation that had been stalled including the Civil Rights Act of 1964. He declared "war on poverty" and promoted his own social program called the Great Society, which sought to end poverty and racial injustice. In 1965, he signed the Immigration and Nationality Service Act, which abolished the discriminatory quotas system that had been the immigration policy since the 1920s. Johnson greatly increased America's role in Vietnam. By 1969, there were 542,000 U.S. troops fighting in Vietnam and a massive anti-war movement had developed in America. In 1968, Johnson announced that he would not run for re-election.

Kansas-Nebraska Act (1854) Law sponsored by Illinois senator Stephen A. Douglas to allow settlers in newly organized territories north of the Missouri border to decide the slavery issue for themselves; fury over the resulting nullification of the Missouri Compromise of 1820 led to violence in Kansas and to the formation of the Republican party.

Florence Kelley (1859–1932) As the head of the National Consumer's League, she led the crusade to promote state laws to regulate the number of working hours imposed on women who were wives and mothers.

George F. Kennan (1904–2005) While working as an American diplomat, he devised the strategy of containment, which called for the halting of Soviet expansion. It became America's choice strategy throughout the cold war.

John F. Kennedy (1917–1963) Elected president in 1960, he was interested in bringing new ideas to the White House. Despite the difficulties he had in getting his legislation through Congress, he did establish the Alliance for Progress programs to help Latin America, the Peace Corps, the Trade

Expansion Act of 1962, and funding for urban renewal projects and the space program. He mistakenly proceeded with the Bay of Pigs invasion, but he successfully handled the Cuban missile crisis. In Indochina, his administration became increasingly involved in supporting local governments through aid, advisors, and covert operations. In 1963, he was assassinated by Lee Harvey Oswald in Dallas, Texas.

Kent State During the spring of 1970, students on college campuses across the country protested the expansion of the Vietnam War into Cambodia. At Kent State University, the National Guard attempted to quell the rioting students. The guardsmen panicked and shot at rock-throwing demonstrators. Four student bystanders were killed.

Kentucky and Virginia Resolutions (1798–1799) Passed in response to the Alien and Sedition Acts, the resolutions advanced the state-compact theory that held states could nullify an act of Congress if they deemed it unconstitutional.

Francis Scott Key (1779–1843) During the War of 1812, he watched British forces bombard Fort McHenry, but fail to take it. Seeing the American flag still flying over the fort at dawn inspired him to write "The Star-Spangled Banner," which became the American national anthem.

Keynesian economics A theory of economics developed by John Maynard Keynes. He argued that increased government spending, even if it increased the nation's deficit, during an economic downturn was necessary to reinvigorate a nation's economy. This view was held by Harry Hopkins and Harold Ickes who advised President Franklin Roosevelt during the Great Depression.

Martin Luther King Jr. (1929–1968) As an important leader of the civil rights movement, he urged people to use nonviolent civil disobedience to demand their rights and bring about change. He successfully led the Montgomery bus boycott. While in jail for his role in demonstrations, he wrote his famous "Letter from Birmingham City Jail," in which he defended his strategy of nonviolent protest. In 1963, he delivered his famous "I Have a Dream Speech" from the steps of the Lincoln Memorial as a part of the March on Washington. A year later, he was awarded the Nobel Peace Prize. In 1968, he was assassinated.

King William's War (War of the League of Augsburg) First (1689–1697) of four colonial wars between England and France.

King Philip (?–1676) or Metacomet The chief of the Wampanoages, who the colonists called King Philip. He resented English efforts to convert Indians to Christianity and waged a war against the English colonists in which he was killed.

Henry Kissinger (1923–) He served as the secretary of state and national security advisor in the Nixon administration. He negotiated with North Vietnam for an end to the Vietnam War. In 1973, an agreement was signed between America, North and South Vietnam, and the Viet Cong to end the war. The cease-fire did not last; and South Vietnam fell to North Vietnam. He helped organize Nixon's historic trips to China and the Soviet Union. In the Middle East, he negotiated a cease-fire between Israel and its neighbors following the Yom Kippur War and solidified Israel's promise to return to Egypt most of the land it had taken during the 1967 war.

Knights of Labor Founded in 1869, the first national union picked up many members after the disastrous 1877 railroad strike, but lasted under the leadership of Terence V. Powderly, only into the 1890s; supplanted by the American Federation of Labor.

Know-Nothing party Nativist, anti-Catholic third party organized in 1854 in reaction to large-scale German and Irish immigration; the party's only presidential candidate was Millard Fillmore in 1856.

Ku Klux Klan Organized in Pulaski, Tennessee, in 1866 to terrorize former slaves who voted and held political offices during Reconstruction; a revived organization in the 1910s and 1920s stressed white, Anglo-Saxon, fundamentalist Protestant supremacy; the Klan revived a third time to fight the civil rights movement of the 1950s and 1960s in the South.

Marquis de Lafayette (1757–1834) A wealthy French idealist excited by the American cause, he offered to serve in Washington's army for free in exchange for being named a major general. He overcame Washington's initial skepticism to become one of his most trusted aides.

Land Ordinance of 1785 Directed surveying of the Northwest Territory into townships of thirty-six sections (square miles) each, the sale of the sixteenth section of which was to be used to finance public education.

Bartolomé de Las Casas (1484–1566) A Catholic missionary who renounced the Spanish practice of coercively converting Indians and advocated the better treatment for them. In 1552, he wrote *A Brief Relation of the Destruction of the Indies*, which described the Spanish's cruel treatment of the Indians.

League of Nations Organization of nations to mediate disputes and avoid war established after World War I as part of the Treaty of Versailles; President Woodrow Wilson's "Fourteen Points" speech to Congress in 1918 proposed the formation of the league.

Mary Elizabeth Lease (1850–1933) She was a leader of the farm protest movement who advocated violence if change could not be obtained at the ballot box. She believed that the urban-industrial East was the enemy of the working class.

Robert E. Lee (1807–1870) Even though he had served in the United States Army for thirty years, he chose to fight on the side of the Confederacy and took command of the Army of North Virginia. Lee was excellent at using his field commanders; and his soldiers respected him. However, General Ulysses S. Grant eventually wore down his army, and Lee surrendered to Grant at the Appomattox Court House on April 9, 1865.

Lend-Lease Act (1941) Permitted the United States to lend or lease arms and other supplies to the Allies, signifying increasing likelihood of American involvement in World War II.

John Dickinson's "Letters from a Farmer in Pennsylvania" These twelve letters appeared in the *Pennsylvania Chronicle* and argued that Parliament could regulate colonial commerce and collect duties that related to that purpose, but it did not have the right to levy taxes for revenue.

Levittown First low-cost, mass-produced development of suburban tract housing built by William Levitt on Long Island, New York, in 1947.

Lexington and Concord, Battle of The first shots fired in the Revolutionary War, on April 19, 1775, near Boston; approximately 100 Minutemen and 250 British soldiers were killed.

Liberator William Lloyd Garrison started this anti-slavery newspaper in 1831 in which he renounced gradualism and called for abolition.

Queen Liliuokalani (1838–1917) In 1891, she ascended to the throne of the Hawaiian royal family and tried to eliminate white control of the Hawaiian government. Two years later, Hawaii's white population revolted and seized power with the support of American marines.

Abraham Lincoln (1809–1865) His participation in the Lincoln-Douglas debates gave him a national reputation and he was nominated as the Republican party candidate for president in 1860. Shortly after he was elected president, southern states began succeeding from the Union and in April of 1861 he declared war on the succeeding states. On January 1, 1863, Lincoln signed the Emancipation Proclamation, which freed all slaves. At the end of the war, he favored a reconstruction strategy for the former Confederate states that did not radically alter southern social and economic life. However, before his plans could be finalized, John Wilkes Booth assassinated Lincoln at Ford's Theater on April 14, 1865.

Lincoln-Douglas debates Series of senatorial campaign debates in 1858 focusing on the issue of slavery in the territories; held in Illinois between Republican Abraham Lincoln, who made a national reputation for himself, and incumbent Democratic senator Stephen A. Douglas, who managed to hold onto his seat.

John Locke (1632–1704) An English philosopher whose ideas were influential during the Enlightenment. He argued in his *Essay on Human Understanding* (1690) that humanity is largely the product of the environment, the mind being a blank tablet, *tabula rasa*, on which experience is written.

Henry Cabot Lodge (1850–1924) He was the chairman of the Senate Foreign Relations Committee who favored limiting America's involvement in the League of Nations' covenant and sought to amend the Treaty of Versailles.

de Lôme letter Spanish ambassador Depuy de Lôme wrote a letter to a friend in Havana in which he described President McKinley as "weak" and a seeker of public admiration. This letter was stolen and published in the *New York Journal*, which increased the American public's dislike of Spain and moved the two countries closer to war.

Lone Star Republic After winning independence from Mexico, Texas became its own nation that was called the Lone Star Republic. In 1836, Texans drafted themselves a constitution, legalized slavery, banned free blacks, named Sam Houston president, and voted for the annexation to the United States. However, quarrels over adding a slave state and fears of instigating a war with Mexico delayed Texas's entrance into the Union until December 29, 1845.

Huey Long (1893–1935) He began his political career in Louisiana where he developed a reputation for being an unscrupulous reformer. As a U.S. senator, he became a critic of President Roosevelt's New Deal Plan and offered his alternative called the Share-the-Wealth program. He was assassinated in 1935.

Lords Commissioners of Trade and Plantations (the Board of Trade) William III created this organization in 1696 to investigate the enforcement of the Navigations Act, recommend ways to limit colonial manufactures, and encourage the production of raw materials in the colonies that were needed in Britain.

Louisiana Purchase President Thomas Jefferson's 1803 purchase from France of the important port of New Orleans and 828,000 square miles west of the Mississippi River to the Rocky Mountains; it more than doubled the territory of the United States at a cost of only $15 million.

Lowell System Lowell mills were the first to bring all the processes of spinning and weaving cloth together under one roof and have every aspect of the production mechanized. In addition, the Lowell mills were designed to be model factory communities that provided the young women employees with meals, a boardinghouse, moral discipline, and educational and cultural opportunities.

Martin Luther (1483–1546) A German monk who founded the Lutheran church. He protested abuses in the Catholic Church by posting his Ninety-five Theses, which began the Protestant Reformation.

General Douglas MacArthur (1880–1964) During World War II, he and Admiral Chester Nimitz dislodged the Japanese military from the Pacific Islands they had occupied. Following the war, he was in charge of the occupation of Japan. After North Korea invaded South Korea, Truman sent the U.S. military to defend South Korea under the command of MacArthur. Later in the war, Truman expressed his willingness to negotiate the restoration of prewar boundaries which MacArthur attempted to undermine. Truman fired MacArthur for his open insubordination.

James Madison (1751–1836) He participated in the Constitutional Convention during which he proposed the Virginia Plan. He believed in a strong federal government and was a leader of the Federalists and a contributor to *The Federalist*. However, he also presented to Congress the Bill of Rights and drafted the Virginia Resolutions. As the secretary of state, he withheld a commission for William Marbury, which led to the landmark *Marbury v. Madison* decision. During his presidency, he declared war on Britain in response to violations of American shipping rights, which started the War of 1812.

Alfred Thayer Mahan's ***The Influence of Sea Power Upon History, 1660–1783*** Alfred Thayer Mahan was an advocate for sea power and Western imperialism. In 1890, he published *The Influence of Sea Power Upon History*, 1660–1783 in which he argued that a nation's greatness and prosperity comes from maritime power. He believed that America's "destiny" was to control the Caribbean, build the Panama Canal, and spread Western civilization across the Pacific.

Malcolm X (1925–1964) The most articulate spokesman for black power. Originally, the chief disciple of Elijah Muhammad, the black Muslim leader in the United States, Malcolm X broke away from him and founded his own organization committed to establishing relations between African Americans and the nonwhite peoples of the world. Near the end of his life, he began to preach a biracial message of social change. In 1964, he was assassinated by members of a rival group of black Muslims.

Manchuria incident The northeast region of Manchuria was an area contested between China and Russia. In 1931, the Japanese claimed that they needed to protect their extensive investments in the area and moved their army into Manchuria. They quickly conquered the region and set up their own puppet empire. China asked both the United States and the League of Nations for help and neither responded.

Manifest Destiny Imperialist phrase first used in 1845 to urge annexation of Texas; used thereafter to encourage American settlement of European colonial and Indian lands in the Great Plains and Far West.

Horace Mann (1796–1859) He believed the public school system was the best way to achieve social stability and equal opportunity. As a reformer of education, he sponsored a state board of education, the first state-supported "normal" school for training teachers, a state association for teachers, the minimum school year of six months, and led the drive for a statewide school system.

Marbury v. Madison **(1803)** First U.S. Supreme Court decision to declare a federal law—the Judiciary Act of 1801—unconstitutional; President John Adams's "midnight appointment" of Federalist judges prompted the suit.

March on Washington Civil rights demonstration on August 28, 1963, where the Reverend Martin Luther King Jr. gave his "I Have a Dream" speech on the steps of the Lincoln Memorial.

George C. Marshall (1880–1959) As the chairman of the Joint Chiefs of Staff, he orchestrated the Allied victories over Germany and Japan in World War II. In 1947, he became President Truman's secretary of state and proposed the massive reconstruction program for western Europe called the Marshall Plan.

Chief Justice John Marshall (1755–1835) During his long tenure as chief justice of the supreme court (1801–1835), he established the foundations for American jurisprudence, the authority of the Supreme Court, and the constitutional supremacy of the national government over states.

Marshall Plan U.S. program for the reconstruction of post–World War II Europe through massive aid to former enemy nations as well as allies; proposed by General George C. Marshall in 1947.

massive resistance In reaction to the *Brown v. Board of Education* decision of 1954, U.S. Senator Harry Byrd encouraged southern states to defy federally mandated school integration.

Senator Joseph R. McCarthy (1908–1957) In 1950, this senator became the shrewdest and most ruthless exploiter of America's anxiety of communism. He claimed that the United States government was full of Communists and led a witch hunt to find them, but he was never able to uncover a single communist agent.

George B. McClellan (1826–1885) In 1861, President Abraham Lincoln appointed him head of the Army of the Potomac and, later, general in chief of the U.S. Army. He built his army into well trained and powerful force. However, he often delayed taking action against the enemy even though Lincoln wanted him to attack. After failing to achieve a decisive victory against the Confederacy, Lincoln removed McClellan from command in 1862.

Cyrus Hall McCormick (1809–1884) In 1831, he invented a mechanical reaper to harvest wheat, which transformed the scale of agriculture. By hand a farmer could only harvest a half an acre a day, while the McCormick reaper allowed two people to harvest twelve acres of wheat a day.

William McKinley (1843–1901) As a congressman, he was responsible for the McKinley Tariff of 1890, which raised the duties on manufactured products to their highest level ever. Voters disliked the tariff and McKinley, as well as other Republicans, lost their seats in Congress the next election. However, he won the presidential election of 1896 and raised the tariffs again. In 1898, he annexed Hawaii and declared war on Spain. The war concluded with the Treaty of Paris, which gave America control over Puerto Rico, Guam, and the Philippines. Soon America was fighting Filipinos, who were seeking independence for their country. In 1901, McKinley was assassinated.

Robert McNamara (1916–) He was the secretary of defense for both President Kennedy and President Johnson and a supporter of America's involvement in Vietnam.

McNary-Haugen Bill Vetoed by President Calvin Coolidge in 1927 and 1928, the bill to aid farmers would have artificially raised agricultural prices by selling surpluses overseas for low prices and selling the reduced supply in the United States for higher prices.

Andrew Mellon (1855–1937) As President Harding's secretary of the Treasury, he sought to generate economic growth through reducing government spending and lowering taxes. However, he insisted that the tax reductions mainly go to the rich because he believed the wealthy would reinvest their money and spur economic growth. In order to bring greater efficiency and nonpartisanship to the government's budget process, he persuaded Congress to pass the Budget and Accounting Act of 1921, which created a new Bureau of the Budget and a General Accounting Office.

mercantile system A nationalistic program that assumed that the total amount of the world's gold and silver remained essentially fixed with only a nation's share of that wealth subject to change.

James Meredith (1933–) In 1962, the governor of Mississippi defied a Supreme Court ruling and refused to allow James Meredith, an African American, to enroll at the University of Mississippi. Federal marshals were sent to enforce the law which led to clashes between a white mob and the marshals. Federal troops intervened and two people were killed and many others were injured. A few days later, Meredith was able to register at the university.

Merrimack* (ship renamed the *Virginia*) and the *Monitor First engagement between ironclad ships; fought at Hampton Roads, Virginia, on March 9, 1862.

Metacomet (?–1676) or King Philip The chief of the Wampanoages, who the colonists called King Philip. He resented English efforts to convert Indians to Christianity and waged a war against the English colonists in which he was killed.

militant nonviolence After the success of the Montgomery bus boycott, people were inspired by Martin Luther King Jr.'s use of this nonviolent form of protest. Throughout the civil rights movement, demonstrators used this method of protest to challenge racial segregation in the South.

Ho Chi Minh (1890–1969) He was the Vietnamese communist resistance leader who drove the French and the United States out of Vietnam. After the Geneva Accords divided the region into four countries, he controlled North Vietnam, and ultimately became the leader of all of Vietnam at the conclusion of the Vietnam War.

minstrelsy A form of entertainment that was popular from the 1830s to the 1870s. The performances featured white performers who were made up as African Americans or blackface. They performed banjo and fiddle music, "shuffle" dances and lowbrow humor that reinforced racial stereotypes.

Minutemen Special units organized by the militia to be ready for quick mobilization.

Miranda v. Arizona **(1966)** U.S. Supreme Court decision required police to advise persons in custody of their rights to legal counsel and against self-incrimination.

Mississippi Plan In 1890, Mississippi instituted policies that led to a near-total loss of voting rights for blacks and many poor whites. In order to vote, the state required that citizens pay all their taxes first, be literate, and have been residents of the state for two years and one year in an electoral district. Convicts were banned from voting. Seven other states followed this strategy of disenfranchisement.

Missouri Compromise Deal proposed by Kentucky senator Henry Clay to resolve the slave/free imbalance in Congress that would result from Missouri's admission as a slave state; in the compromise of March 20, 1820, Maine's admission as a free state offset Missouri, and slavery was prohibited in the remainder of the Louisiana Territory north of the southern border of Missouri.

Model T Ford Henry Ford developed this model of car so that it was affordable for everyone. Its success led to an increase in the production of automobiles which stimulated other related industries such steel, oil, and rubber. The mass use of automobiles increased the speed goods could be transported, encouraged urban sprawl, and sparked real estate booms in California and Florida.

modernism As both a mood and movement, modernism recognized that Western civilization had entered an era of change. Traditional ways of thinking and creating art were being rejected and replaced with new understandings and forms of expression.

Molly Maguires Secret organization of Irish coal miners that used violence to intimidate mine officials in the 1870s.

Monroe Doctrine President James Monroe's declaration to Congress on December 2, 1823, that the American continents would be thenceforth closed to colonization but that the United States would honor existing colonies of European nations.

Montgomery bus boycott Sparked by Rosa Parks's arrest on December 1, 1955, a successful year-long boycott protesting segregation on city buses; led by the Reverend Martin Luther King Jr.

moral majority Televangelist Jerry Falwell's political lobbying organization, the name of which became synonymous with the religious right—conservative evangelical Protestants who helped ensure President Ronald Reagan's 1980 victory.

J. Pierpont Morgan (1837–1913) As a powerful investment banker, he would acquire, reorganize, and consolidate companies into giant trusts. His biggest achievement was the consolidation of the steel industry into the United States Steel Corporation, which was the first billion-dollar corporation.

James Monroe (1758–1831) He served as secretary of state and war under President Madison and was elected president. As the latter, he signed the Transcontinental Treaty with Spain which gave the United States Florida and expanded the Louisiana territory's western border to the Pacific coast. In 1823, he established the Monroe Doctrine. This foreign policy proclaimed the American continents were no longer open to colonization and America would be neutral in European affairs.

Robert Morris (1734–1806) He was the superintendent of finance for the Congress of the Confederation during the final years of the Revolutionary War. He envisioned a national finance plan of taxation and debt management, but the states did not approve the necessary amendments to the Articles of Confederation need to implement the plan.

Samuel B. Morse (1791–1872) In 1832, he invented the telegraph and revolutionized the speed of communication.

mountain men Inspired by the fur trade, these men left civilization to work as trappers and reverted to a primitive existence in the wilderness. They were the first whites to find routes through the Rocky Mountains, and they pioneered trails that settlers later used to reach the Oregon country and California in the 1840s.

muckrakers Writers who exposed corruption and abuses in politics, business, meat-packing, child labor, and more, primarily in the first decade of the twentieth century; their popular books and magazine articles spurred public interest in progressive reform.

Mugwumps Reform wing of the Republican party that supported Democrat Grover Cleveland for president in 1884 over Republican James G. Blaine, whose influence peddling had been revealed in the Mulligan letters of 1876.

Benito Mussolini "*Il Duce*" (1883–1945) The Italian founder of the Fascist party who came to power in Italy in 1922 and allied himself with Adolf Hitler and the Axis powers during World War II.

My Lai Massacre In 1968, Lieutenant William Calley and his soldiers massacred 347 Vietnamese civilians in the village of My Lai. Twenty-five army officers were charged with complicity in the massacre and its cover-up but only Calley was convicted. Later, President Nixon granted him parole.

NAFTA Approved in 1993, the North American Free Trade Agreement with Canada and Mexico allowed goods to travel across their borders free of tariffs; critics argued that American workers would lose their jobs to cheaper Mexican labor.

National Industrial Recovery Act (1933) Passed on the last of the Hundred Days; it created public-works jobs through the Federal Emergency Relief Administration and established a system of self-regulation for industry through the National Recovery Administration, which was ruled unconstitutional in 1935.

National Recovery Administration This organization's two goals were to stabilize business and generate purchasing power for consumers. The first goal was to be achieved through the implementation industry-wide codes that set wages and prices, which would reduce the chaotic competition. To provide consumers with purchasing power, the administration would provide jobs, define workplace standards, and raise wages.

National Socialist German Workers' Party (Nazi) Founded in the 1920s, this party gained control over Germany under the leadership of Adolf Hitler in 1933 and continued in power until Germany's defeat at the end of World War II. It advocated a violent anti-Semitic, anti-Marxist, pan-German ideology. The Nazi party systematically murdered some 6 million Jews along with more than a million others.

nativism Anti-immigrant and anti-Catholic feeling in the 1830s through the 1850s; the largest group was New York's Order of the Star-Spangled Banner, which expanded into the American, or Know-Nothing party in 1854. In the 1920, there was a surge in nativism as Americans grew to fear immigrants who might be political radicals. In response, new strict immigration regulations were established.

nativist A native-born American who saw immigrants as a threat to his way of life and employment. During the 1880s, nativist groups worked to stop the flow of immigrates into the United States. Of these groups, the most successful was the American Protective Association who promoted government restrictions on immigration, tougher naturalization requirements, the teaching of English in schools and workplaces that refused to employ foreigners or Catholics.

Navigation Acts Passed by the English Parliament to control colonial trade and bolster the mercantile system, 1650–1775; enforcement of the acts led to growing resentment by colonists.

new conservatism The political philosophy of those who led the conservative insurgency of the early 1980s. This brand of conservatism was personified in Ronald Reagan who believed in less government, supply-side economics, and "family values."

New Deal Franklin D. Roosevelt's campaign promise, in his speech to the Democratic National Convention of 1932, to combat the Great Depression with a "new deal for the American people;" the phrase became a catchword for his ambitious plan of economic programs.

New France The name used for the area of North America that was colonized by the French. Unlike Spanish or English colonies, New France had a small number of colonists, which forced them to initially seek good relations with the indigenous people they encountered.

New Freedom Democrat Woodrow Wilson's political slogan in the presidential campaign of 1912; Wilson wanted to improve the banking system, lower tariffs, and, by breaking up monopolies, give small businesses freedom to compete.

New Frontier John F. Kennedy's program, stymied by a Republican Congress and his abbreviated term; his successor Lyndon B. Johnson had greater success with many of the same concepts.

New Jersey Plan The delegations to the Constitutional Convention were divided between two plans on how to structure the government: New Jersey wanted one legislative body with equal representation for each state.

New Nationalism Platform of the Progressive party and slogan of former President Theodore Roosevelt in the presidential campaign of 1912; stressed government activism, including regulation of trusts, conservation, and recall of state court decisions that had nullified progressive programs.

"new Negro" In the 1920s, a slow and steady growth of black political influence occurred in northern cities where African Americans were freer to speak and act. This political activity created a spirit of protest that expressed itself culturally in the Harlem Renaissance and politically in "new Negro" nationalism.

New Netherlands Dutch colony conquered by the English to become four new colonies New York, New Jersey, Pennsylvania, and Delaware.

New South *Atlanta Constitution* editor Henry W. Grady's 1886 term for the prosperous post–Civil War South: democratic, industrial, urban, and free of nostalgia for the defeated plantation South.

William Randolph Hearst's *New York Journal* In the late 1890s, the *New York Journal* and its rival, the *New York World*, printed sensationalism on the Cuban revolution as part of their heated competition for readership. The *New York Journal* printed a negative letter from the Spanish ambassador about President McKinley and inflammatory coverage of the sinking of the *Maine* in Havana Harbor. These two events roused the American public's outcry against Spain.

Joseph Pulitzer's *New York World* In the late 1890s, the *New York World* and its rival, *New York Journal*, printed sensationalism on the Cuban revolution as part of their heated competition for readership.

Admiral Chester Nimitz (1885–1966) During World War II, he was the commander of central Pacific. Along with General Douglas MacArthur, he dislodged the Japanese military from the Pacific Islands they had occupied.

Nineteenth Amendment (1920) Granted women the right to vote.

Richard Nixon (1913–1994) He first came to national prominence as a congressman involved in the investigation of Alger Hiss. Later he served as vice president during the Eisenhower administration. In 1960, he ran as the Republican nominee for president and lost to John Kennedy. In 1968, he ran and won the presidency against Democratic nominee Hubert Humphrey. During his campaign, he promised to bring about "peace with honor" in Vietnam. He told southern conservatives that he would slow the federal enforcement of civil rights laws and appoint pro-southern justices to the Supreme Court. After being elected, he fulfilled the latter promise attempted to keep the former. He opened talks with the North Vietnamese and began a program of Vietnamization of the war. He also bombed Cambodia. In 1973, America, North and South Vietnam, and the Viet Cong agreed to end the war and the United States withdrew. However, the cease-fire was broken, and the South Vietnam fell to North Vietnam. In 1970, Nixon changed U.S. foreign policy. He declared that the America was no longer the world's policemen and he would seek some partnerships with Communist countries. With his historic visit to China, he ended twenty years of diplomatically isolating China and he began taking steps towards cultural exchanges and trade. In 1972, Nixon travelled to Moscow and signed agreements with the Soviet Union on arms control and trade. That same year, Nixon was reelected, but the Watergate scandal erupted shortly after his victory. When his knowledge of the break-in and subsequent cover-up was revealed, Nixon resigned the presidency under threat of impeachment.

No Child Left Behind President George W. Bush's education reform plan that required states to set and meet learning standards for students and make sure that all students were "proficient" in reading and writing by 2014. States had to submit annual reports of students' standardized test scores. Teachers were required to be "proficient" in their subject area.

Schools who failed to show progress would face sanctions. States criticized the lack of funding for remedial programs and noted that poor school districts would find it very difficult to meet the new guidelines.

Lord North (1732–1792) The first minister of King George III's cabinet whose efforts to subdue the colonies only brought them closer to revolution. He helped bring about the Tea Act of 1773, which led to the Boston Tea Party. In an effort to discipline Boston, he wrote, and Parliament passed, four acts that galvanized colonial resistance.

North Atlantic Treaty Organization (NATO) Defensive alliance founded in 1949 by ten western European nations, the United States, and Canada to deter Soviet expansion in Europe.

Northwest Ordinance Created the Northwest Territory (area north of the Ohio River and west of Pennsylvania), established conditions for self-government and statehood, included a Bill of Rights, and permanently prohibited slavery.

nullification Concept of invalidation of a federal law within the borders of a state; first expounded in the Kentucky and Virginia Resolutions (1798), cited by South Carolina in its Ordinance of Nullification (1832) of the Tariff of Abominations, used by southern states to explain their secession from the Union (1861), and cited again by southern states to oppose the *Brown v. Board of Education* decision (1954).

Nuremberg trials At the site of the annual Nazi party rallies, twenty-one major German offenders faced an international military tribunal for Nazi atrocities. After a ten-month trial, the court acquitted three and sentenced eleven to death, three to life imprisonment, and four to shorter terms.

Barack Obama (1961–) In the 2008 presidential election, Senator Barack Obama mounted an innovative Internet based and grassroots orientated campaign that garnered him enough delegates to win the Democratic nomination. As the nation's economy nosedived in the fall of 2008, Obama linked the Republican economic philosophy with the country's dismal financial state and promoted a message of "change" and "politics of hope," which resonated with voters. He decisively won the presidency and became America's first person of colored to be elected president.

Sandra Day O'Connor (1930–) She was the first woman to serve on the Supreme Court of the United States and was appointed by President Reagan. Reagan's critics charged that her appointment was a token gesture and not a sign of any real commitment to gender equality.

Ohio gang In order to escape the pressures of the White House, President Harding met with a group of people, called the "Ohio gang," in a house on K Street in Washington D.C. Members of this gang were given low-level positions in the American government and they used their White House connection to "line their pockets" by granting government contracts without bidding, which led to a series of scandals, most notably the Teapot Dome Scandal.

Frederick Law Olmsted (1822–1903) In 1858, he constructed New York's Central Park, which led to a growth in the movement to create urban parks. He went on to design parks for Boston, Brooklyn, Chicago, Philadelphia, San Francisco, and many other cities.

Opechancanough (?–1644) The brother and successor of Powhatan who led his tribe in an attempt to repel the English settlers in Virginia in 1622.

Open Door Policy In hopes of protecting the Chinese market for U.S. exports, Secretary of State John Hay unilaterally announced in 1899 that Chinese trade would be open to all nations.

Operation Desert Shield After Saddam Hussein invaded Kuwait in 1990, President George H. W. Bush sent American military forces to Saudi Arabia on a strictly defensive mission. They were soon joined by a multinational coalition. When the coalition's mission changed to the retaking of Kuwait, the operation was renamed Desert Storm.

Operation Desert Storm Multinational allied force that defeated Iraq in the Gulf War of January 1991.

Operation Overlord The Allies' assault on Hitler's "Atlantic Wall," a seemingly impregnable series of fortifications and minefields along the French coastline that German forces had created using captive Europeans for laborers.

J. Robert Oppenheimer (1904–1967) He led the group of physicists at the laboratory in Los Alamos, New Mexico, who constructed the first atomic bomb.

Oregon Country The Convention of 1818 between Britain and the United States established the Oregon Country as being west of the crest of the

Rocky Mountains and the two countries were to jointly occupy it. In 1824, the United States and Russia signed a treaty that established the line of 54°40′ as the southern boundary of Russia's territorial claim in North America. A similar agreement between Britain and Russia finally gave the Oregon Country clearly defined boarders, but it remained under joint British and American control.

Oregon fever Enthusiasm for emigration to the Oregon Country in the late 1830s and early 1840s.

Osceola (1804?–1838) He was the leader of the Seminole nation who resisted the federal Indian removal policy through a protracted guerilla war. In 1837, he was treacherously seized under a flag of truce and imprisoned at Fort Moultrie, where he was left to die.

Overland (Oregon) Trail Route of wagon trains bearing settlers from Independence, Missouri, to the Oregon Country in the 1840s to 1860s.

A. Mitchell Palmer (1872–1936) As the attorney general, he played an active role in government's response to the Red Scare. After several bombings across America, including one at Palmer's home, he and other Americans became convinced that there was a well-organized Communist terror campaign at work. The federal government launched a campaign of raids, deportations, and collecting files on radical individuals.

Panic of 1819 Financial collapse brought on by sharply falling cotton prices, declining demand for American exports, and reckless western land speculation.

panning A method of mining that used a large metal pan to sift gold dust and nuggets from riverbeds during the California gold rush of 1849.

Rosa Parks (1913–2005) In 1955, she refused to give up her seat to a white man on a city bus in Montgomery, Alabama, which a local ordinance required of blacks. She was arrested for disobeying the ordinance. In response, black community leaders organized the Montgomery bus boycott.

Alice Paul (1885–1977) She was a leader of the women's suffrage movement and head of the Congressional Committee of National Women Suffrage Association. She instructed female suffrage activists to use more militant tactics, such as picketing state legislatures, chaining themselves to public buildings, inciting police to arrest them, and undertaking hunger strikes.

Norman Vincent Peale (1898–1993) He was a champion of the upbeat and feel-good theology that was popular in the 1950s religious revival. He advocated getting rid of any depressing or negative thoughts and replacing them with "faith, enthusiasm and joy," which would make an individual popular and well liked.

"peculiar institution" This term was used to describe slavery in America because slavery so fragrantly violated the principle of individual freedom that served as the basis for the Declaration of Independence.

Pentagon papers Informal name for the Defense Department's secret history of the Vietnam conflict; leaked to the press by former official Daniel Ellsberg and published in the *New York Times* in 1971.

Pequot War Massacre in 1637 and subsequent dissolution of the Pequot Nation by Puritan settlers, who seized the Indians' lands.

perestroika Soviet leader Mikhail Gorbachev introduced these political and economic reforms, which included reconstructing the state bureaucracy, reducing the privileges of the political elite, and shifting from a centrally planned economy to a mixed economy.

Commodore Matthew Perry (1794–1858) In 1854, he negotiated the Treaty of Kanagawa, which was the first step in starting a political and commercial relationship between the United States and Japan.

John J. Pershing (1860–1948) After Pancho Villa had conducted several raids into Texas and New Mexico, President Woodrow Wilson sent troops under the command of General John J. Pershing into Mexico to stop Villa. However, after a year of chasing Villa and not being able to catch him, they returned to the United States. During World War I, Pershing commanded the first contingent of U.S. soldiers sent to Europe and advised the War Department to send additional American forces.

"pet banks" During President Andrew Jackson's fight with the national bank, Jackson resolved to remove all federal deposits from it. To comply with Jackson's demands, Secretary of Treasury Taney continued to draw on government's accounts in the national bank, but deposit all new federal receipts in state banks. The state banks that received these deposits were called "pet banks."

Pilgrims Puritan Separatists who broke completely with the Church of England and sailed to the New World aboard the *Mayflower*, founding Plymouth Colony on Cape Cod in 1620.

Dien Bien Phu The defining battle in the war between French colonialists and the Viet Minh. The Viet Minh's victory secured North Vietnam for Ho Chi Minh and was crucial in compelling the French to give up Indochina as a colony.

Gifford Pinchot (1865–1946) As the head of the Division of Forestry, he implemented a conservation policy that entailed the scientific management of natural resources to serve the public interest. His work helped start the conservation movement. In 1910, he exposed to the public the decision of Richard A. Ballinger's, President Taft's secretary of the interior, to open up previously protected land for commercial use. Pinchot was fired, but the damage to Taft's public image resulted in the loss of many pro-Taft candidates in 1910 congressional election.

Elizabeth Lucas Pinckney (1722? –1793) One of the most enterprising horticulturists in colonial America, she began managing her family's three plantations in South Carolina at the age of sixteen. She had tremendous success growing indigo, which led to many other plantations growing the crop as well.

Pinckney's Treaty Treaty with Spain negotiated by Thomas Pinckney in 1795; established United States boundaries at the Mississippi River and the 31st parallel and allowed open transportation on the Mississippi.

Francisco Pizarro (1478?–1541) In 1531, he lead his Spanish soldiers to Peru and conquered the Inca Empire.

planters In the antebellum South, the owner of a large farm worked by twenty or more slaves.

James Knox Polk "Young Hickory" (1795–1849) As President, his chief concern was the expansion of the United States. In 1846, his administration resolved the dispute with Britain over the Oregon Country border. Shortly, after taking office, Mexico broke off relations with the United States over the annexation of Texas. Polk declared war on Mexico and sought to subvert Mexican authority in California. The United States defeated Mexico; and the two nations signed the Treaty of Guadalupe Hidalgo in which Mexico gave up any claims on Texas north of the Rio Grande River and ceded New Mexico and California to the United States.

Pontiac's Rebellion The Peace Treaty of 1763 gave the British all French land east of the Mississippi River. This area included the territory of

France's Indian allies who were not consulted about the transfer of their lands to British control. In an effort to recover their autonomy, Indians captured British forts around the Great Lakes and in the Ohio Valley as well as attacked settlements in Pennsylvania, Maryland, and Virginia.

popular sovereignty Allowed settlers in a disputed territory to decide the slavery issue for themselves.

Populist / the People's party Political success of Farmers' Alliance candidates encouraged the formation in 1892 of the People's party (later renamed the Populist party); active until 1912, it advocated a variety of reform issues, including free coinage of silver, income tax, postal savings, regulation of railroads, and direct election of U.S. senators.

Chief Powhatan Wahunsonacock He was called Powhatan by the English after the name of his tribe, and was the powerful, charismatic chief of numerous Algonquian-speaking towns in eastern Virginia representing over 10,000 Indians.

pragmatism William James founded this philosophy in the early 1900s. Pragmatists believed that ideas gained their validity not from their inherent truth, but from their social consequences and practical application.

Proclamation of 1763 Royal directive issued after the French and Indian War prohibiting settlement, surveys, and land grants west of the Appalachian Mountains; although it was soon over-ridden by treaties, colonists continued to harbor resentment.

proprietary colonies A colony owned by an individual, rather than a joint-stock company.

pueblos The Spanish term for the adobe cliff dwellings of the indigenous people of the southwestern United States.

Pullman Strike Strike against the Pullman Palace Car Company in the company town of Pullman, Illinois, on May 11, 1894, by the American Railway Union under Eugene V. Debs; the strike was crushed by court injunctions and federal troops two months later.

Puritans English religious group that sought to purify the Church of England; founded the Massachusetts Bay Colony under John Winthrop in 1630.

Quakers George Fox founded the Quaker religion in 1647. They rejected the use of formal sacraments and ministry, refused to take oaths and embraced pacifism. Fleeing persecution, they settled and established the colony of Pennsylvania.

Radical Republicans Senators and congressmen who, strictly identifying the Civil War with the abolitionist cause, sought swift emancipation of the slaves, punishment of the rebels, and tight controls over the former Confederate states after the war.

Raleigh's Roanoke Island Colony English expedition of 117 settlers, including Virginia Dare, the first English child born in the New World; colony disappeared from Roanoke Island in the Outer Banks sometime between 1587 and 1590.

A. Philip Randolph (1889–1979) He was the head of the Brotherhood of Sleeping Car Porters who planned a march on Washington D.C. to demand an end to racial discrimination in the defense industries. To stop the march, Roosevelt administration negotiated an agreement with the Randolph group. The demonstration would be called off and an executive order would be issued that forbid discrimination in defense work and training programs and set up the Fair Employment Practices Committee.

range wars In the late 1800s, conflicting claims over land and water rights triggered violent disputes between farmers and ranchers in parts of the western United States.

Ronald Reagan (1911–2004) In 1980, the former actor and governor of California was elected president. In office, he reduced social spending, cut taxes, and increased defense spending. He was criticized for cutting important programs, such as housing and school lunches and increasing the federal deficit. By 1983, prosperity had returned to America and Reagan's economic reforms appeared to be working, but in October of 1987 the stock market crashed. Some blamed the federal debt, which had tripled in size since Reagan had taken office. In the early 1980s, HIV/AIDS cases were beginning to be reported in America, but the Reagan administration chose to do little about the growing epidemic. Reagan believed that most of the world's problems came from the Soviet Union, which he called the "evil empire." In response, he conducted a major arms build up. Then in 1987, he signed an arms-control treaty with the Soviet Union. He authorized covert CIA operations in Central America. In 1986, the Iran-Contra scandal came to light which revealed arms sales were being conducted with Iran in a partial exchange for the release of hostages in Lebanon. The arms money was being used to aid the Contras.

Reaganomics Popular name for President Ronald Reagan's philosophy of "supply side" economics, which combined tax cuts, less government spending, and a balanced budget with an unregulated marketplace.

Reconstruction Finance Corporation Federal program established in 1932 under President Herbert Hoover to loan money to banks and other institutions to help them avert bankruptcy.

Red Scare Fear among many Americans after World War I of Communists in particular and noncitizens in general, a reaction to the Russian Revolution, mail bombs, strikes, and riots.

Redeemers In post–Civil War southern politics, redeemers were supporters of postwar Democratic leaders who supposedly saved the South from Yankee domination and the constraints of a purely rural economy.

Dr. Walter Reed (1851–1902) His work on yellow fever in Cuba led to the discovery that the fever was carried by mosquitoes. This understanding helped develop more effective controls of the worldwide disease.

Reformation European religious movement that challenged the Catholic Church and resulted in the beginnings of Protestant Christianity. During this period, Catholics and Protestants persecuted, imprisoned, tortured, and killed each other in large numbers.

reparations As a part of the Treaty of Versailles, Germany was required to confess its responsibility for World War I and make payments to the victors for the entire expense of the war. These two requirements created a deep bitterness among Germans.

Alexander Hamilton's Report on Manufactures First Secretary of the Treasury Alexander Hamilton's 1791 analysis that accurately foretold the future of American industry and proposed tariffs and subsidies to promote it.

"return to normalcy" In the 1920 presidential election, Republican nominee Warren G. Harding campaigned on the promise of a "return to normalcy," which would mean a return to conservative values and a turning away from President Wilson's internationalism.

Paul Revere (1735–1818) On the night of April 18, 1775, British soldiers marched towards Concord to arrest American Revolutionary leaders and seize their depot of supplies. Paul Revere famously rode through the night and raised the alarm about the approaching British troops.

Roaring Twenties In 1920s, urban America experienced an era of social and intellectual revolution. Young people experimented with new forms of recreation and sexuality as well as embraced jazz music. Leading young urban intellectuals expressed a disdain for old-fashioned rural and small-town values. The Eastern, urban cultural shift clashed with conservative and insular midwestern America, which increased the tensions between the two regions.

Jackie Robinson (1919–1972) In 1947, he became the first African American to play major league baseball. He won over fans and players and stimulated the integration of other professional sports.

rock-and-roll music Alan Freed, a disc jockey, noticed white teenagers were buying rhythm and blues records that had been only purchased by African Americans and Hispanic Americans. Freed began playing these records, but called them rock-and-roll records as a way to overcome the racial barrier. As the popularity of the music genre increased, it helped bridge the gap between "white" and "black" music.

John D. Rockefeller (1839–1937) In 1870, he founded the Standard Oil Company of Ohio, which was his first step in creating his vast oil empire. Eventually, he perfected the idea of a holding company: a company that controlled other companies by holding all or at least a majority of their stock. During his lifetime, he donated over $500 million in charitable contributions.

Romanticism Philosophical, literary, and artistic movement of the nineteenth century that was largely a reaction to the rationalism of the previous century; Romantics valued emotion, mysticism, and individualism.

Eleanor Roosevelt (1884–1962) She redefined the role of the presidential spouse and was the first woman to address a national political convention, write a nationally syndicated column and hold regular press conferences. She travelled throughout the nation to promote the New Deal, women's causes, organized labor, and meet with African American leaders. She was her husband's liaison to liberal groups and brought women activists and African American and labor leaders to the White House.

Franklin D. Roosevelt (1882–1945) Elected during the Great Depression, Roosevelt sought to help struggling Americans through his New Deal programs that created employment and social programs, such as Social Security. Prior to American's entry into World War II, he supported Britain's fight against Germany through the lend-lease program. After the bombing of Pearl Harbor, he declared war on Japan and Germany and led the country through most of World War II before dying of cerebral hemorrhage. In 1945, he met with Winston Churchill and Joseph Stalin at the Yalta Conference to determine the shape of the post-War world.

Theodore Roosevelt (1858–1919) As the assistant secretary of the navy, he supported expansionism, American imperialism and war with Spain. He led the First Volunteer Cavalry, or Rough Riders, in Cuba during the war of 1898 and used the notoriety of this military campaign for political gain. As President McKinley's vice president, he succeeded McKinley after his assassination. His forceful foreign policy became known as "big stick diplomacy." Domestically, his policies on natural resources helped start the conversation movement. Unable to win the Republican nomination for president in 1912, he formed his own party of progressive Republicans called the "Bull Moose" party.

Roosevelt Corollary to the Monroe Doctrine (1904) President Theodore Roosevelt announced in what was essentially a corollary to the Monroe Doctrine that the United States could intervene militarily to prevent interference from European powers in the Western Hemisphere.

Rough Riders The First U.S. Volunteer Cavalry, led in battle in the Spanish-American War by Theodore Roosevelt; they were victorious in their only battle near Santiago, Cuba; and Roosevelt used the notoriety to aid his political career.

Nicola Sacco (1891–1927) In 1920, he and Bartolomeo Vanzetti were Italian immigrants who were arrested for stealing $16,000 and killing a paymaster and his guard. Their trial took place during a time of numerous bombings by anarchists and their judge was openly prejudicial. Many liberals and radicals believe that the conviction of Sacco and Vanzetti was based on their political ideas and ethnic origin rather than the evidence against them.

"salutary neglect" Edward Burke's description of Robert Walpole's relaxed policy towards the American colonies, which gave them greater independence in pursuing both their economic and political interests.

Sandinista Cuban-sponsored government that came to power in Nicaragua after toppling a corrupt dictator. The State Department believed that the Sandinistas were supplying the leftist Salvadoran rebels with Cuban and Soviet arms. In response, the Reagan administration ordered the CIA to train and supply guerrilla bands of anti-Communist Nicaraguans called Contras. A cease-fire agreement between the Contras and Sandinistas was signed in 1988.

Margaret Sanger (1883–1966) As a birth-control activist, she worked to distribute birth control information to working-class women and opened the nation's first family-planning clinic in 1916. She organized the American Birth Control League, which eventually changed its name to Planned Parenthood.

General Antonio López de Santa Anna (1794–1876) In 1834, he seized political power in Mexico and became a dictator. In 1835, Texans rebelled against him and he led his army to Texas to crush their rebellion. He captured the missionary called the Alamo and killed all of its defenders, which inspired Texans to continue to resistance and Americans to volunteer to fight for Texas. The Texans captured Santa Anna during a surprise attack and he bought his freedom by signing a treaty recognizing Texas's independence.

Saratoga, Battle of Major defeat of British general John Burgoyne and more than 5,000 British troops at Saratoga, New York, on October 17, 1777.

scalawags White southern Republicans—some former Unionists—who served in Reconstruction governments.

Phyllis Schlafly (1924–) She was a right-wing Republican activist who spearheaded the anti-feminism movement. She believed feminist were "anti-family, anti-children, and pro-abortion." She worked against the equal-rights amendment for women and civil rights protection for gays.

Winfield Scott (1786–1866) During the Mexican War, he was the American general who captured Mexico City, which ended the war. Using his popularity from his military success, he ran as a Whig party candidate for President.

Sears Roebuck and Company By the end of the nineteenth century, this company dominated the mail-order industry and helped create a truly national market. Its mail-order catalog and low prices allowed people living in rural areas and small towns to buy products that were previously too expensive or available only to city dwellers.

secession Shortly after President Abraham Lincoln was elected, southern states began dissolving their ties with the United States because they believed Lincoln and the Republican party were a threat to slavery.

second Bank of the United States In 1816, the second Bank of the United States was established in order to bring stability to the national economy, serve as the depository for national funds, and provide the government with the means of floating loans and transferring money across the country.

Second Great Awakening Religious revival movement of the early decades of the nineteenth century, in reaction to the growth of secularism and rationalist religion; began the predominance of the Baptist and Methodist churches.

Second New Deal To rescue his New Deal program form judicial and political challenges, President Roosevelt launched a second phase of the New Deal in 1935. He was able to convince Congress to pass key pieces of legislation including the National Labor Relations act and Social Security Act. Roosevelt called the latter the New Deal's "supreme achievement" and pensioners started receiving monthly checks in 1940.

Seneca Falls Convention First women's rights meeting and the genesis of the women's suffrage movement; held in July 1848 in a church in Seneca Falls, New York, by Elizabeth Cady Stanton and Lucretia Coffin Mott.

"separate but equal" Principle underlying legal racial segregation, which was upheld in *Plessy v. Ferguson* (1896) and struck down in *Brown v. Board of Education* (1954).

separation of powers The powers of government are split between three separate branches (executive, legislative, and judicial) who check and balance each other.

September 11 On September 11, 2001, Islamic terrorists, who were members of al Qaeda terrorist organization, hijacked four commercial airliners. Two were flown into the World Trade Center and a third into the Pentagon. A fourth plane was brought down in Shanksville, Pennsylvania, when its passengers attacked the cockpit. In response, President George W. Bush launched his "war on terrorism." His administration assembled an international coalition to fight terrorism, and they invaded Afghanistan after the country's government would not turn over al Qaeda's leader, Osama bin Laden. However, bin Laden evaded capture. Fearful of new attacks, Bush created the Office of Homeland Security and the Transportation Security Administration.

Bush and Congress passed the U.S.A. Patriot Act, which allowed government agencies to try suspected terrorists in secret military courts and eavesdrop on confidential conversations.

settlement houses Product of the late nineteenth-century movement to offer a broad array of social services in urban immigrant neighborhoods; Chicago's Hull House was one of hundreds of settlement houses that operated by the early twentieth century.

Shakers Founded by Mother Ann Lee Stanley in England, the United Society of Believers in Christ's Second Appearing settled in Watervliet, New York, in 1774 and subsequently established eighteen additional communes in the Northeast, Indiana, and Kentucky.

sharecropping Type of farm tenancy that developed after the Civil War in which landless workers—often former slaves—farmed land in exchange for farm supplies and a share of the crop; differed from tenancy in that the terms were generally less favorable.

Share-the-Wealth program Huey Long, a critic of President Roosevelt, offered this program as an alternative to the New Deal. The program proposed to confiscate large personal fortunes, which would be used to guarantee every poor family a cash grant of $5,000 and every worker an annual income of $2,500. Under this program, Long promised to provide pensions, reduce working hours, pay veterans' bonuses, and ensures a college education to every qualified student.

Shays's Rebellion Massachusetts farmer Daniel Shays and 1,200 compatriots, seeking debt relief through issuance of paper currency and lower taxes, stormed the federal arsenal at Springfield in the winter of 1787 but were quickly repulsed.

William T. Sherman's March through Georgia Union General William T. Sherman believed that there was a connection between the South's economy, morale, and ability to wage war. During his March through Georgia, he wanted to demoralize the civilian populace and destroy the resources they needed to fight. His army seized food and livestock that the Confederate Army might have used as well as wrecked railroads and mills and burned plantations.

Sixteenth Amendment (1913) Legalized the federal income tax.

Alfred E. Smith (1873–1944) In the 1928 presidential election, he won the Democratic nomination, but failed to win the presidency. Rural voters distrusted him for being Catholic and the son of Irish immigrants as well as his anti-Prohibition stance.

Captain John Smith (1580–1631) A swashbuckling soldier of fortune with rare powers of leadership and self-promotion, he was appointed to the resident council to manage Jamestown.

Joseph Smith (1805–1844) In 1823, he claimed that the Angel Moroni showed him the location of several gold tablets on which the Book of Mormon was written. Using the Book of Mormon as his gospel, he founded the Church of Jesus Christ of Latter-day Saints, or Mormons. Joseph and his followers upset non-Mormons living near them so they began looking for a refuge from persecution. In 1839, they settled in Commerce, Illinois, which they renamed Nauvoo. In 1844, Joseph and his brother were arrested and jailed for ordering the destruction of a newspaper that opposed them. While in jail, an anti-Mormon mob stormed the jail and killed both of them.

social Darwinism Application of Charles Darwin's theory of natural selection to society; used the concept of the "survival of the fittest" to justify class distinctions and to explain poverty.

social gospel Preached by liberal Protestant clergymen in the late nineteenth and early twentieth centuries; advocated the application of Christian principles to social problems generated by industrialization.

social justice An important part of the Progressive's agenda, social justice sought to solve social problems through reform and regulation. Methods used to bring about social justice ranged from the founding of charities to the legislation of a ban on child labor.

Sons of Liberty Organized by Samuel Adams, they were colonialists with a militant view against the British government's control of the colonies.

Hernando de Soto (1500?–1542) A conquistador who explored the west coast of Florida, western North Carolina and along the Arkansas river from 1539 till his death in 1542.

Southern Christian Leadership Conference (SCLC) Civil rights organization founded in 1957 by the Reverend Martin Luther King Jr., and other civil rights leaders.

"southern strategy" This strategy was a major reason for Richard Nixon's victory in the 1968 presidential election. To gain support in the South, Nixon assured southern conservatives that he would slow the federal enforcement of civil rights laws and appoint pro-southern justices to the Supreme Court. As president, Nixon fulfilled these promises.

Spanish flu Unprecedentedly lethal influenza epidemic of 1918 that killed more than 22 million people worldwide.

Herbert Spencer (1820–1903) As the first major proponent of social Darwinism, he argued that human society and institutions are subject to the process of natural selection and that society naturally evolves for the better. Therefore, he was against any form of government interference with the evolution of society, like business regulations, because it would help the "unfit" to survive.

spoils system The term—meaning the filling of federal government jobs with persons loyal to the party of the president—originated in Andrew Jackson's first term; the system was replaced in the Progressive Era by civil service.

stagflation During the Nixon administration, the economy experienced inflation and a recession at the same time, which is syndrome that defies the orthodox laws of economics. Economists named this phenomenon "stagflation."

Joseph Stalin (1879–1953) The Bolshevik leader who succeeded Lenin as the leader of the Soviet Union in 1924 and ruled the country until his death. During his totalitarian rule of the Soviet Union, he used purges and a system of forced labor camps to maintain control over the country. During the Yalta Conference, he claimed vast areas of Eastern Europe for Soviet domination. After the end of World War II, the alliance between the Soviet Union and the Western powers altered into the tension of the cold war and Stalin erected the "iron curtain" between Eastern and Western Europe.

Stalwarts Conservative Republican party faction during the presidency of Rutherford B. Hayes, 1877–1881; led by Senator Roscoe B. Conkling of New York, Stalwarts opposed civil service reform and favored a third term for President Ulysses S. Grant.

Stamp Act Congress Twenty-seven delegates from nine of the colonies met from October 7 to 25, 1765 and wrote a Declaration of the Rights and Grievances of the Colonies, a petition to the King and a petition to Parliament for the repeal of the Stamp Act.

Standard Oil Company of Ohio John D. Rockefeller found this company in 1870, which grew to monopolize 90 to 95 percent of all the oil refineries in the country. It was also a "vertical monopoly" in that the company controlled all aspects of production and the services it needed to conduct business. For example, Standard Oil produced their own oil barrels and cans as well as owned their own pipelines, railroad tank cars, and oil-storage facilities.

Elizabeth Cady Stanton (1815–1902) She was a prominent reformer and advocate for the rights of women, and she helped organize the Seneca Falls Convention to discuss women's rights. The convention was the first of its kind and produced the Declaration of Sentiments, which proclaimed the equality of men and women.

staple crop, or cash crop A profitable market crop, such as cotton or tobacco.

Thaddeus Stevens (1792–1868) As one of the leaders of the Radical Republicans, he argued that the former Confederate states should be viewed as conquered provinces, which were subject to the demands of the conquerors. He believed that all of southern society needed to be changed, and he supported the abolition of slavery and racial equality.

Adlai E. Stevenson (1900–1965) In the 1952 and 1956 presidential elections, he was the Democratic nominee who lost to Dwight Eisenhower. He was also the U.S. Ambassador to the United Nations and is remembered for his famous speech in 1962 before the UN Security Council that unequivocally demonstrated that the Soviet Union had built nuclear missile bases in Cuba.

Strategic Defense Initiative ("Star Wars") Defense Department's plan during the Reagan administration to build a system to destroy incoming missiles in space.

Levi Strauss (1829–1902) A Jewish tailor who followed miners to California during the gold rush and began making durable work pants that were later dubbed blue jeans or Levi's.

Students for a Democratic Society (SDS) Major organization of the New Left, founded at the University of Michigan in 1960 by Tom Hayden and Al Haber.

suburbia The postwar era witnessed a mass migration to the suburbs. As the population in cities areas grew, people began to spread further out within the urban areas, which created new suburban communities. By 1970 more people lived in the suburbs (76 million) than in central cities (64 million).

Sunbelt The label for an arc that stretched from the Carolinas to California. During the postwar era, much of the urban population growth occurred in this area.

the "surge" In early 2007, President Bush decided he would send a "surge" of new troops to Iraq and implement a new strategy. U.S. forces would shift their focus from offensive operations to the protection of Iraqi civilians from attacks by terrorist insurgents and sectarian militias. While the "surge" reduced the violence in Iraq, Iraqi leaders were still unable to develop a self-sustaining democracy.

Taliban A coalition of ultraconservative Islamists who rose to power in Afghanistan after the Soviets withdrew. The Taliban leaders gave Osama bin Laden a safe haven in their country in exchange for aid in fighting the Northern Alliance, who were rebels opposed to the Taliban. After September 11 terrorist attacks, the United States asked the Taliban to turn over bin Laden. After they refused, America invaded Afghanistan, but bin Laden evaded capture.

Tammany Hall The "city machine" used by "Boss" Tweed to dominate politics in New York City until his arrest in 1871.

Tariff of 1816 First true protective tariff, intended strictly to protect American goods against foreign competition.

Tariff of 1832 This tariff act reduced the duties on many items, but the tariffs on cloth and iron remained high. South Carolina nullified it along with the tariff of 1828. President Andrew Jackson sent federal troops to the state and asked Congress to grant him the authority to enforce the tariffs. Henry Clay presented a plan of gradually reducing the tariffs until 1842, which Congress passed and ended the crisis.

TARP In 2008 President George W. Bush signed into law the bank bailout fund called Troubled Asset Relief Program (TARP), which required the Treasury Department to spend $700 billion to keep banks and other financial institutions from collapsing.

Zachary Taylor (1784–1850) During the Mexican War, he scored two quick victories against Mexico, which made him very popular in America. President Polk chose him as the commander in charge of the war. However, after he was not put in charge of the campaign to capture Mexico City, he chose to return home. Later he used his popularity from his military victories to be elected the president as a member of the Whig party.

Taylorism In his book *The Principles of Scientific Management*, Frederick W. Taylor explained a management system that claimed to be able to reduce waste through the scientific analysis of the labor process. This system called Taylorism, promised to find the optimum technique for the average worker and establish detailed performance standards for each job classification.

Teapot Dome Harding administration scandal in which Secretary of the Interior Albert B. Fall profited from secret leasing to private oil companies of government oil reserves at Teapot Dome, Wyoming, and Elk Hills, California.

Tecumseh (1768–1813) He was a leader of the Shawnee tribe who tried to unite all Indians into a confederation that could defend their hunting grounds. He believed that no land cessions could be made without the consent of all the tribes since they held the land in common. His beliefs and leadership made him seem dangerous to the American government and they waged war on him and his tribe. He was killed at the Battle of the Thames.

Tejanos Texas settlers of Spanish or Mexican descent.

Teller Amendment On April 20, 1898, a joint resolution of Congress declared Cuba independent and demanded the withdrawal of Spanish forces. The Teller amendment was added to this resolution, and it declaimed any designs the United States had on Cuban territory.

Tenochtitlán The capital city of the Aztec Empire. The city was built on marshy islands on the western side of Lake Tetzcoco, which is the site of present-day Mexico City.

Tet offensive Surprise attack by the Viet Cong and North Vietnamese during the Vietnamese New Year of 1968; turned American public opinion strongly against the war in Vietnam.

Thirteenth Amendment This amendment to the U.S. Constitution freed all slaves in the United States. After the Civil War ended, the former confederate states were required to ratify this amendment before they could be readmitted to the Union.

Gulf of Tonkin incident On August 2 and 4 of 1964, North Vietnamese vessels attacked two American destroyers in Gulf of Tonkin off the coast of North Vietnam. President Johnson described the attacks as unprovoked. In reality, the U.S. ships were monitoring South Vietnamese attacks on North Vietnamese islands that America advisors had planned. The incident spurred the Tonkin Gulf resolution.

Tonkin Gulf resolution (1964) Passed by Congress in reaction to supposedly unprovoked attacks on American warships off the coast of North Vietnam; it gave the president unlimited authority to defend U.S. forces and members of SEATO.

Tories Term used by Patriots to refer to Loyalists, or colonists who supported the Crown after the Declaration of Independence.

Trail of Tears Cherokees' own term for their forced march, 1838–1839, from the southern Appalachians to Indian lands (later Oklahoma); of 15,000 forced to march, 4,000 died on the way.

Transcendentalism Philosophy of a small group of mid-nineteenth-century New England writers and thinkers, including Ralph Waldo Emerson, Henry David Thoreau, and Margaret Fuller; they stressed "plain living and high thinking."

Transcontinental railroad First line across the continent from Omaha, Nebraska, to Sacramento, California, established in 1869 with the linkage of the Union Pacific and Central Pacific railroads at Promontory, Utah.

triangular trade Means by which exports to one country or colony provided the means for imports from another country or colony. For example, merchants from colonial New England shipped rum to West Africa and used it to barter for slaves who were then taken to the West Indies. The slaves were sold or traded for materials that the ships brought back to New England including molasses which is need to make rum.

Treaty of Ghent The signing of this treaty in 1814 ended the War of 1812 without solving any of the disputes between Britain and the United States.

Harry S. Truman (1884–1972) As President Roosevelt's vice president, he succeeded him after his death near the end of World War II. After the war, Truman wrestled with the inflation of both prices and wages, and his attempts to bring them both under control led to clashes with organized labor and Republicans. He did work with Congress to pass the National Security Act, which made the Joint Chiefs of Staff a permanent position and created the National Military Establishment and the Central Intelligence Agency. He banned racial discrimination in the hiring of federal employees and ended racial segregation in the armed forces. In foreign affairs, he established the Truman Doctrine to contain communism and the Marshall Plan to rebuild Europe. After North Korea invaded South Korea, Truman sent the U.S. military to defend

South Korea under the command of General Douglas MacArthur. Later in the war, Truman expressed his willingness to negotiate the restoration of prewar boundaries which MacArthur attempted to undermine. Truman fired MacArthur for his open insubordination.

Truman Doctrine President Harry S. Truman's program of post–World War II aid to European countries—particularly Greece and Turkey—in danger of being undermined by communism.

Sojourner Truth (1797? –1883) She was born into slavery, but New York State freed her in 1827. She spent the 1840s and 1850s travelling across the country and speaking to audiences about her experiences as slave and asking them to support abolition and women's rights.

Harriet Tubman (1820–1913) She was born a slave, but escaped to the North. Then she returned to the South nineteen times and guided 300 slaves to freedom.

Nat Turner (1800–1831) He was the leader of the only slave revolt to get past the planning stages. In August of 1831, the revolt began with the slaves killing the members of Turner's master's household. Then they attacked other neighboring farmhouses and recruited more slaves until the militia crushed the revolt. At least fifty-five whites were killed during the uprising and seventeen slaves were hanged afterwards.

Tuskegee Airmen During World War II, African Americans in the armed forces usually served in segregated units. African American pilots were trained at a separate flight school in Tuskegee, Alabama, and were known as Tuskegee Airmen.

Mark Twain (1835–1910) Born Samuel Langhorne Clemens in Missouri, he became a popular humorous writer and lecturer and established himself as one of the great American authors. Like other authors of the local-color movement, his stories expressed the nostalgia people had for rural culture and old folkways as America became increasingly urban. His two greatest books, *The Adventures of Tom Sawyer* and *The Adventures of Huckleberry Finn*, drew heavily on his childhood in Missouri.

"Boss" Tweed (1823–1878) An infamous political boss in New York City, Tweed used his "city machine," the Tammany Hall ring, to rule, plunder and sometimes improve the city's government. His political domination of New York City ended with his arrest in 1871 and conviction in 1873.

Twenty-first Amendment (1933) Repealed prohibition on the manufacture, sale, and transportation of alcoholic beverages, effectively nullifying the Eighteenth Amendment.

Underground Railroad Operating in the decades before the Civil War, the "railroad" was a clandestine system of routes and safehouses through which slaves were led to freedom in the North.

Unitarianism Late eighteenth-century liberal offshoot of the New England Congregationalist church; Unitarianism professed the oneness of God and the goodness of rational man.

United Nations Security Council A major agency within the United Nations which remains in permanent session and has the responsibility of maintaining international peace and security. Originally, it consisted of five permanent members, (United States, Soviet Union, Britain, France, and the Republic of China), and six members elected to two-year terms. After 1965, the number of rotating members was increased to ten. In 1971, the Republic of China was replaced with the People's Republic of China and the Soviet Union was replaced by the Russian Federation in 1991.

Utopian communities These communities flourished during the Jacksonian era and were attempts to create the ideal community. They were social experiments conducted in relative isolation, so they had little impact on the world outside of their communities. In most cases, the communities quickly ran out of steam and ended.

Cornelius Vanderbilt (1794–1877) In the 1860s, he consolidated several separate railroad companies into one vast entity, New York Central Railroad.

Bartolomeo Vanzetti (1888–1927) In 1920, he and Nicola Sacco were Italian immigrants who were arrested for stealing $16,000 and killing a paymaster and his guard. Their trial took place during a time of numerous bombings by anarchists and their judge was openly prejudicial. Many liberals and radicals believe that the conviction of Sacco and Vanzetti was based on their political ideas and ethnic origin rather than the evidence against them.

Amerigo Vespucci (1455–1512) Italian explorer who reached the New World in 1499 and was the first to suggest that South America was a new continent. Afterward, European mapmakers used a variant of his first name, America, to label the New World.

Viet Cong In 1956, these guerrilla forces began attacking South Vietnam's government and in 1960 the resistance groups coalesced as the National Liberation Front.

Vietnamization President Nixon's policy of equipping and training the South Vietnamese so that they could assume ground combat operations in the place of American soldiers. Nixon hoped that a reduction in U.S. forces in Vietnam would defuse the anti-war movement.

Vikings Norse people from Scandinavia who sailed to Newfoundland about A.D. 1001.

Pancho Villa (1877–1923) While the leader of one of the competing factions in the Mexican civil war, he provoked the United States into intervening. He hoped attacking the United States would help him build a reputation as an opponent of the United States, which would increase his popularity and discredit Mexican President Carranza.

Virginia Company A joint stock enterprise that King James I chartered in 1606. The company was to spread Christianity in the New World as well as find ways to make a profit in it.

Virginia Plan The delegations to the Constitutional Convention were divided between two plans on how to structure the government: Virginia called for a strong central government and a two-house legislature apportioned by population.

George Wallace (1919–1998) An outspoken defender of segregation. As the governor of Alabama, he once attempted to block African American students from enrolling at the University of Alabama. He ran as the presidential candidate for the American Independent party in 1968. He appealed to voters who were concerned about rioting anti-war protestors, the welfare system, and the growth of the federal government.

War Hawks In 1811, congressional members from the southern and western districts who clamored for a war to seize Canada and Florida were dubbed "war hawks."

Warren Court The U.S. Supreme Court under Chief Justice Earl Warren, 1953–1969, decided such landmark cases as *Brown v. Board of Education* (school desegregation), *Baker v. Carr* (legislative redistricting), and *Gideon v. Wainwright* and *Miranda v. Arizona* (rights of criminal defendants).

Booker T. Washington (1856–1915) He founded a leading college for African Americans in Tuskegee, Alabama, and become the foremost black educator in America by the 1890s. He believed that the African American community should establish an economic base for its advancement before striving for social equality. His critics charged that his philosophy sacrificed educational and civil rights for dubious social acceptance and economic opportunities.

George Washington (1732–1799) In 1775, the Continental Congress named him the commander in chief of the Continental Army. He had previously served as an officer in the French and Indian War, but had never commanded a large unit. Initially, his army was poorly supplied and inexperienced, which led to repeated defeats. Washington realized that he could only defeat the British through wearing them down, and he implemented a strategy of evasion and selective confrontations. Gradually, the army developed into an effective force and, with the aid of the French, defeated the British. In 1787, he was the presiding officer over the Constitutional Convention, but participated little in the debates. In 1789, the Electoral College chose Washington to be the nation's first president. He assembled a cabinet of brilliant minds, which included Thomas Jefferson, James Madison, and Alexander Hamilton. Together, they would lay the foundations of American government and capitalism. Washington faced the nation's first foreign and domestic crises. In 1793, the British and French were at war. Washington chose to keep America neutral in the conflict even though France and the United States had signed a treaty of alliance. A year later, the Whiskey Rebellion erupted in Pennsylvania, and Washington sent militiamen to suppress the rebels. After two terms in office, Washington chose to step down; and the power of the presidency was peacefully passed to John Adams.

Watergate Washington office and apartment complex that lent its name to the 1972–1974 scandal of the Nixon administration; when his knowledge of the break-in at the Watergate and subsequent cover-up was revealed, Nixon resigned the presidency under threat of impeachment.

Daniel Webster (1782–1852) As a representative from New Hampshire, he led the New Federalists in opposition to the moving of the second national bank from Boston to Philadelphia. Later, he served as representative and a senator for Massachusetts and emerged as a champion of a stronger national government. He also switched from opposing to supporting tariffs because New England had built up its manufactures with the understanding tariffs would protect them from foreign competitors.

Webster-Ashburton Treaty Settlement in 1842 of U.S.–Canadian border disputes in Maine, New York, Vermont, and in the Wisconsin Territory (now northern Minnesota).

Webster-Hayne debate U.S. Senate debate of January 1830 between Daniel Webster of Massachusetts and Robert Hayne of South Carolina over nullification and states' rights.

Ida B. Wells (1862–1931) After being denied a seat on a railroad car because she was black, she became the first African American to file a suit against such discrimination. As a journalist, she criticized Jim Crow laws, demanded that blacks have their voting rights restored and crusaded against lynching. In 1909, she helped found the National Association for the Advancement of Colored People (NAACP).

western front The military front that stretched from the English Channel through Belgium and France to the Alps during World War I.

Whig party Founded in 1834 to unite factions opposed to President Andrew Jackson, the party favored federal responsibility for internal improvements; the party ceased to exist by the late 1850s, when party members divided over the slavery issue.

Whigs Another name for revolutionary Patriots.

Whiskey Rebellion Violent protest by western Pennsylvania farmers against the federal excise tax on corn whiskey, 1794.

Eli Whitney (1765–1825) He invented the cotton gin which could separate cotton from its seeds. One machine operator could separate fifty times more cotton than worker could by hand, which led to an increase in cotton production and prices. These increases gave planters a new profitable use for slavery and a lucrative slave trade emerged from the coastal South to the Southwest.

George Whitefield (1714–1770) A true catalyst of the Great Awakening, he sought to reignite religious fervor in the American congregations. During his tour of the American Colonies in 1739, he gave spellbinding sermons and preached the notion of "new birth"—a sudden, emotional moment of conversion and salvation.

Wilderness Road Originally an Indian path through the Cumberland Gap, it was used by over 300,000 settlers who migrated westward to Kentucky in the last quarter of the eighteenth century.

Roger Williams (1603–1683) Puritan who believed that the purity of the church required a complete separation between church and state and freedom from coercion in matters of faith. In 1636, he established the town of Providence, the first permanent settlement in Rhode Island and the first to allow religious freedom in America.

Wendell L. Willkie (1892–1944) In the 1940 presidential election, he was the Republican nominee who ran against President Roosevelt. He supported aid to the Allies and criticized the New Deal programs. Voters looked at the increasingly dangerous world situation and chose to keep President Roosevelt in office for a third term.

Wilmot Proviso Proposal to prohibit slavery in any land acquired in the Mexican War, but southern senators, led by John C. Calhoun of South Carolina, defeated the measure in 1846 and 1847.

Woodrow Wilson (1856–1924) In the 1912 presidential election, Woodrow Wilson ran under the slogan of New Freedom, which promised to improve of the banking system, lower tariffs, and break up monopolies. He sought to deliver on these promises through passage of the Underwood-Simmons Tariff, the Federal Reserve Act of 1913, and new antitrust laws. Though he was weak on implementing social change and showed a little interest in the plight of African Americans, he did eventually support some labor reform. At the beginning of World War I, Wilson kept America neutral, but provided the Allies with credit for purchases of supplies. However, the sinking of U.S. merchant ships and the news of Germany encouraging Mexico to attack America caused Wilson to ask Congress to declare war on Germany. Following the war, Wilson supported the entry of America into the League of Nations and the ratification of the Treaty of Versailles; but Congress would not approve the entry or ratification.

John Winthrop Puritan leader and Governor of the Massachusetts Bay Colony who resolved to use the colony as a refuge for persecuted Puritans and as an instrument of building a "wilderness Zion" in America.

Women Accepted for Voluntary Emergency Services (WAVES) During World War II, the increased demand for labor shook up old prejudices about gender roles in workplace and in the military. Nearly 200,000 women served in the Women's Army Corps or its naval equivalent, Women Accepted for Volunteer Emergency Service (WAVES).

Women's Army Corps (WAC) During World War II, the increased demand for labor shook up old prejudices about gender roles in workplace and in the military. Nearly 200,000 women served in the Women's Army

Corps or its naval equivalent, Women Accepted for Volunteer Emergency Service (WAVES).

Woodstock In 1969, roughly a half a million young people converged on a farm near Bethel, New York, for a three-day music festival that was an expression of the flower children's free spirit.

Wounded Knee, Battle of Last incident of the Indians Wars took place in 1890 in the Dakota Territory, where the U.S. Cavalry killed over 200 Sioux men, women, and children who were in the process of surrender.

XYZ affair French foreign minister Tallyrand's three anonymous agents demanded payments to stop French plundering of American ships in 1797; refusal to pay the bribe led to two years of sea war with France (1798–1800).

Yalta Conference Meeting of Franklin D. Roosevelt, Winston Churchill, and Joseph Stalin at a Crimean resort to discuss the postwar world on February 4–11, 1945; Soviet leader Joseph Stalin claimed large areas in eastern Europe for Soviet domination.

yeomen Small landowners (the majority of white families in the South) who farmed their own land and usually did not own slaves.

surrender at Yorktown Last battle of the Revolutionary War; General Lord Charles Cornwallis along with over 7,000 British troops surrendered at Yorktown, Virginia, on October 17, 1781.

Brigham Young (1801–1877) Following Joseph Smith's death, he became the leader of the Mormons and promised Illinois officials that the Mormons would leave the state. In 1846, he led the Mormons to Utah and settled near the Salt Lake. After the United States gained Utah as part of the Treaty of Guadalupe Hidalgo, he became the governor of the territory and kept the Mormons virtually independent of federal authority.

youth culture The youth of the 1950s had more money and free time than any previous generation which allowed a distinct youth culture to emerge. A market emerged for products and activities that were specifically for young people such as transistor radios, rock records, *Seventeen* magazine, and Pat Boone movies.

APPENDIX

APPENDIX

THE DECLARATION OF INDEPENDENCE (1776)

WHEN IN THE COURSE OF HUMAN EVENTS, it becomes necessary for one people to dissolve the political bands which have connected them with another, and to assume the Powers of the earth, the separate and equal station to which the Laws of Nature and of Nature's God entitle them, a decent respect to the opinions of mankind requires that they should declare the causes which impel them to the separation.

We hold these truths to be self-evident, that all men are created equal, that they are endowed by their Creator with certain unalienable rights, that among these are Life, Liberty, and the pursuit of Happiness. That to secure these rights, Governments are instituted among Men, deriving their just powers from the consent of the governed. That whenever any Form of Government becomes destructive of these ends, it is the Right of the People to alter or to abolish it, and to institute new Government, laying its foundation on such principles and organizing its powers in such form, as to them shall seem most likely to effect their Safety and Happiness. Prudence, indeed, will dictate that Governments long established should not be changed for light and transient causes; and accordingly all experience hath shown, that mankind are more disposed to suffer, while evils are sufferable, than to right themselves by abolishing the forms to which they are accustomed. But when a long train of abuses and usurpations, pursuing invariably the same Object evinces a design to reduce them under absolute Despotism, it is their right, it is their duty, to throw off such Government, and to provide new Guards for their future security.—Such has been the patient sufferance of these Colonies; and such is now the necessity which constrains them to alter their former Systems of Government. The history of the present King of Great Britain is a history of repeated injuries and usurpations, all having in direct object the establishment of an absolute Tyranny over these States. To prove this, let Facts be submitted to a candid world.

He has refused his Assent to Laws, the most wholesome and necessary for the public good.

He has forbidden his Governors to pass Laws of immediate and pressing importance, unless suspended in their operation till his Assent should be obtained; and when so suspended, he has utterly neglected to attend to them.

He has refused to pass other Laws for the accommodation of large districts of people, unless those people would relinquish the right of Representation in the Legislature, a right inestimable to them and formidable to tyrants only.

He has called together legislative bodies at places unusual, uncomfortable, and distant from the depository of their public Records, for the sole purpose of fatiguing them into compliance with his measures.

He has dissolved Representative Houses repeatedly, for opposing with manly firmness his invasions on the rights of the people.

He has refused for a long time, after such dissolutions, to cause others to be elected; whereby the Legislative powers, incapable of Annihilation, have returned to the People at large for their exercise; the State remaining in the mean time exposed to all dangers of invasion from without, and convulsions within.

He has endeavoured to prevent the population of these States; for that purpose obstructing the Laws of Naturalization of Foreigners; refusing to pass others to encourage their migrations hither, and raising the conditions of new Appropriations of Lands.

He has obstructed the Administration of Justice, by refusing his Assent to Laws for establishing Judiciary powers.

He has made Judges dependent on his Will alone, for the tenure of their offices, and the amount and payment of their salaries.

He has erected a multitude of New Offices, and sent hither swarms of Officers to harass our People, and eat out their substance.

He has kept among us, in times of peace, Standing Armies without the Consent of our legislatures.

He has affected to render the Military independent of and superior to the Civil Power.

He has combined with others to subject us to a jurisdiction foreign to our constitution, and unacknowledged by our laws; giving his Assent to their Acts of pretended Legislation:

For quartering large bodies of armed troops among us:

For protecting them, by a mock Trial, from Punishment for any Murders which they should commit on the Inhabitants of these States:

For cutting off our Trade with all parts of the world:

For imposing taxes on us without our Consent:

For depriving us of many cases, of the benefits of Trial by jury:

For transporting us beyond Seas to be tried for pretended offences:

For abolishing the free System of English Laws in a neighbouring Province, establishing therein an Arbitrary government, and enlarging its

Boundaries so as to render it at once an example and fit instrument for introducing the same absolute rule into these Colonies:

For taking away our Charters, abolishing our most valuable Laws, and altering fundamentally the Forms of our Governments:

For suspending our own Legislatures, and declaring themselves in vested with Power to legislate for us in all cases whatsoever.

He has abdicated Government here, by declaring us out of his Protection and waging War against us.

He has plundered our seas, ravaged our Coasts, burnt our towns, and destroyed the lives of our people.

He is at this time transporting large armies of foreign mercenaries to compleat the works of death, desolation, and tyranny, already begun with circumstances of Cruelty & perfidy scarcely paralleled in the most barbarous ages, and totally unworthy the Head of a civilized nation.

He has constrained our fellow Citizens taken Captive on the high Seas to bear Arms against their Country, to become the executioners of their friends and Brethren, or to fall themselves by their Hands.

He has excited domestic insurrections amongst us, and has endeavoured to bring on the inhabitants of our frontiers, the merciless Indian Savages, whose known rule of warfare, is an undistinguished destruction of all ages, sexes, and conditions.

In every stage of these Oppressions We have Petitioned for Redress in the most humble terms: Our repeated Petitions have been answered only by repeated injury. A Prince, whose character is thus marked by every act which may define a Tyrant, is unfit to be the ruler of a free people.

Nor have We been wanting in attention to our British brethren. We have warned them from time to time of attempts by their legislature to extend an unwarrantable jurisdiction over us. We have reminded them of the circumstances of our emigration and settlement here. We have appealed to their native justice and magnanimity, and we have conjured them by the ties of our common kindred to disavow these usurpations, which, would inevitably interrupt our connections and correspondence. They too must have been deaf to the voice of justice and of consanguinity. We must, therefore, acquiesce in the necessity, which denounces our Separation, and hold them, as we hold the rest of mankind, Enemies in War, in Peace Friends.

WE, THEREFORE, the Representatives of the UNITED STATES OF AMERICA, in General Congress, Assembled, appealing to the Supreme Judge of the world for the rectitude of our intentions, do, in the Name, and by Authority of the good People of these Colonies, solemnly publish and declare, That these United Colonies are, and of Right ought to be FREE AND INDEPENDENT STATES; that they are Absolved from all Allegiance to the

British Crown, and that all political connection between them and the State of Great Britain, is and ought to be totally dissolved; and that as Free and Independent States, they have full Power to levy War, conclude Peace, contract Alliances, establish Commerce, and to do all other Acts and Things which Independent States may of right do. And for the support of this Declaration, with a firm reliance on the Protection of Divine Providence, we mutually pledge to each other our Lives, our Fortunes, and our sacred Honor.

The foregoing Declaration was, by order of Congress, engrossed, and signed by the following members:

John Hancock

NEW HAMPSHIRE
Josiah Bartlett
William Whipple
Matthew Thornton

MASSACHUSETTS BAY
Samuel Adams
John Adams
Robert Treat Paine
Elbridge Gerry

RHODE ISLAND
Stephen Hopkins
William Ellery

CONNECTICUT
Roger Sherman
Samuel Huntington
William Williams
Oliver Wolcott

NEW YORK
William Floyd
Philip Livingston
Francis Lewis
Lewis Morris

NEW JERSEY
Richard Stockton
John Witherspoon
Francis Hopkinson
John Hart
Abraham Clark

PENNSYLVANIA
Robert Morris
Benjamin Rush
Benjamin Franklin
John Morton
George Clymer
James Smith
George Taylor
James Wilson
George Ross

DELAWARE
Caesar Rodney
George Read
Thomas M'Kean

MARYLAND
Samuel Chase
William Paca
Thomas Stone
Charles Carroll, of Carrollton

VIRGINIA
George Wythe
Richard Henry Lee
Thomas Jefferson
Benjamin Harrison
Thomas Nelson, Jr.
Francis Lightfoot Lee
Carter Braxton

NORTH CAROLINA
William Hooper
Joseph Hewes
John Penn

SOUTH CAROLINA
Edward Rutledge
Thomas Heyward, Jr.
Thomas Lynch, Jr.
Arthur Middleton

GEORGIA
Button Gwinnett
Lyman Hall
George Walton

Resolved, that copies of the declaration be sent to the several assemblies, conventions, and committees, or councils of safety, and to the several commanding officers of the continental troops; that it be proclaimed in each of the united states, at the head of the army.

ARTICLES OF
CONFEDERATION (1778)

To all to whom these Presents shall come, we the undersigned Delegates of the States affixed to our Names send greeting.

Whereas the Delegates of the United States of America in Congress assembled did on the fifteenth day of November in the Year of our Lord One Thousand Seven Hundred and Seventy-seven, and in the Second Year of the Independence of America agree to certain articles of Confederation and per-petual Union between the States of Newhampshire, Massachusetts-bay, Rhodeisland and Providence Plantations, Connecticut, New York, New Jersey, Pennsylvania, Delaware, Maryland, Virginia, North-Carolina, South-Carolina and Georgia in the Words following, viz.

Articles of Confederation and perpetual Union between the States of Newhampshire, Massachusetts-bay, Rhodeisland and Providence Planta-tions, Connecticut, New-York, New-Jersey, Pennsylvania, Delaware, Mary-land, Virginia, North-Carolina, South-Carolina and Georgia.

Article I. The stile of this confederacy shall be "The United States of America."

Article II. Each State retains its sovereignty, freedom and independence, and every power, jurisdiction and right, which is not by this confederation expressly delegated to the United States, in Congress assembled.

Article III. The said States hereby severally enter into a firm league of friend-ship with each other, for their common defence, the security of their liberties, and their mutual and general welfare, binding themselves to assist each other, against all force offered to, or attacks made upon them, or any of them, on account of religion, sovereignty, trade or any other pretence whatever.

ARTICLE IV. The better to secure and perpetuate mutual friendship and intercourse among the people of the different States in this Union, the free inhabitants of each of these States, paupers, vagabonds and fugitives from justice excepted, shall be entitled to all privileges and immunities of free citizens in the several States; and the people of each State shall have free ingress and regress to and from any other State, and shall enjoy therein all the privileges of trade and commerce, subject to the same duties, impositions and restrictions as the inhabitants thereof respectively, provided that such restrictions shall not extend so far as to prevent the removal of property imported into any State, to any other State of which the owner is an inhabitant; provided also that no imposition, duties or restriction shall be laid by any State, on the property of the United States, or either of them.

If any person guilty of, or charged with treason, felony, or other high misdemeanor in any State, shall flee from justice, and be found in any of the United States, he shall upon demand of the Governor or Executive power, of the State from which he fled, be delivered up and removed to the State having jurisdiction of his offence.

Full faith and credit shall be given in each of these States to the records, acts and judicial proceedings of the courts and magistrates of every other State.

ARTICLE V. For the more convenient management of the general interests of the United States, delegates shall be annually appointed in such manner as the legislature of each State shall direct, to meet in Congress on the first Monday in November, in every year, with a power reserved to each State, to recall its delegates, or any of them, at any time within the year, and to send others in their stead, for the remainder of the year.

No State shall be represented in Congress by less than two, nor by more than seven members; and no person shall be capable of being a delegate for more than three years in any term of six years; nor shall any person, being a delegate, be capable of holding any office under the United States, for which he, or another for his benefit receives any salary, fees or emolument of any kind.

Each State shall maintain its own delegates in a meeting of the States, and while they act as members of the committee of the States.

In determining questions in the United States, in Congress assembled, each State shall have one vote.

Freedom of speech and debate in Congress shall not be impeached or questioned in any court, or place out of Congress, and the members of Congress shall be protected in their persons from arrests and imprisonments, during the time of their going to and from, and attendance on Congress, except for treason, felony, or breach of the peace.

ARTICLE VI. No State without the consent of the United States in Congress assembled, shall send any embassy to, or receive any embassy from, or enter into any conference, agreement, alliance or treaty with any king, prince or state; nor shall any person holding any office of profit or trust under the United States, or any of them, accept of any present, emolument, office or title of any kind whatever from any king, prince or foreign state; nor shall the United States in Congress assembled, or any of them, grant any title of nobility.

No two or more States shall enter into any treaty, confederation or alliance whatever between them, without the consent of the United States in Congress assembled, specifying accurately the purposes for which the same is to be entered into, and how long it shall continue.

No State shall lay any imposts or duties, which may interfere with any stipulations in treaties, entered into by the United States in Congress assembled, with any king, prince or state, in pursuance of any treaties already proposed by Congress, to the courts of France and Spain.

No vessels of war shall be kept up in time of peace by any State, except such number only, as shall be deemed necessary by the United States in Congress assembled, for the defence of such State, or its trade; nor shall any body of forces be kept up by any State, in time of peace, except such number only, as in the judgment of the United States, in Congress assembled, shall be deemed requisite to garrison the forts necessary for the defence of such State; but every State shall always keep up a well regulated and disciplined militia, sufficiently armed and accoutred, and shall provide and constantly have ready for use, in public stores, a due number of field pieces and tents, and a proper quantity of arms, ammunition and camp equipage.

No State shall engage in any war without the consent of the United States in Congress assembled, unless such State be actually invaded by enemies, or shall have received certain advice of a resolution being formed by some nation of Indians to invade such State, and the danger is so imminent as not to admit of a delay, till the United States in Congress assembled can be consulted: nor shall any State grant commissions to any ships or vessels of war, nor letters of marque or reprisal, except it be after a declaration of war by the United States in Congress assembled, and then only against the kingdom or state and the subjects thereof, against which war has been so declared, and under such regulations as shall be established by the United States in Congress assembled, unless such State be infested by pirates, in which case vessels of war may be fitted out for that occasion, and kept so long as the danger shall continue, or until the United States in Congress assembled shall determine otherwise.

ARTICLE VII. When land-forces are raised by any State of the common defence, all officers of or under the rank of colonel, shall be appointed by the Legislature of each State respectively by whom such forces shall be raised, or in such manner as such State shall direct, and all vacancies shall be filled up by the State which first made the appointment.

ARTICLE VIII. All charges of war, and all other expenses that shall be incurred for the common defence or general welfare, and allowed by the United States in Congress assembled, shall be defrayed out of a common treasury, which shall be supplied by the several States, in proportion to the value of all land within each State, granted to or surveyed for any person, as such land and the buildings and improvements thereon shall be estimated according to such mode as the United States in Congress assembled, shall from time to time direct and appoint.

The taxes for paying that proportion shall be laid and levied by the authority and direction of the Legislatures of the several States within the time agreed upon by the United States in Congress assembled.

ARTICLE IX. The United States in Congress assembled, shall have the sole and exclusive right and power of determining on peace and war, except in the cases mentioned in the sixth article—of sending and receiving ambassadors— entering into treaties and alliances, provided that no treaty of commerce shall be made whereby the legislative power of the respective States shall be restrained from imposing such imposts and duties on foreigners, as their own people are subjected to, or from prohibiting the exportation or importation of and species of goods or commodities whatsoever—of establishing rules for deciding in all cases, what captures on land or water shall be legal, and in what manner prizes taken by land or naval forces in the service of the United States shall be divided or appropriated—of granting letters of marque and reprisal in times of peace—appointing courts for the trial of piracies and felonies committed on the high seas and establishing courts for receiving and determining finally appeals in all cases of captures, provided that no member of Congress shall be appointed a judge of any of the said courts.

The United States in Congress assembled shall also be the last resort on appeal in all disputes and differences now subsisting or that hereafter may arise between two or more States concerning boundary, jurisdiction or any other cause whatever; which authority shall always be exercised in the manner following. Whenever the legislative or executive authority or lawful agent of any State in controversy with another shall present a petition to Congress, stating the matter in question and praying for a hearing, notice thereof shall be given by order of Congress to the legislative or executive authority of the other State in controversy, and a day assigned for the appearance of the parties by their lawful agents, who shall then be directed to appoint by joint consent, commissioners or judges to constitute a court for hearing and determining the matter in question: but if they cannot agree, Congress shall name three persons out of each of the United States, and from the list of such persons each party shall alternately strike out one, the petitioners beginning, until the number shall be reduced to thirteen; and from that number not less than seven, nor more than nine names as Congress shall direct, shall in the presence of Congress be drawn out by lot, and the persons whose names shall be so drawn or any five of them, shall be commissioners or judges, to hear and finally determine the controversy, so always as a major part of the judges who shall hear the cause shall agree in the determination: and if either party shall neglect to attend at the day appointed, without reasons, which Congress shall judge sufficient, or being present shall refuse to strike, the Congress shall proceed to nominate three persons out of each State, and the Secretary of Congress shall strike in behalf of such party absent or refusing; and the judgment and sentence of the court to be appointed, in the manner before prescribed, shall be final and conclusive; and if any of the parties shall refuse to submit to the authority of such court, or to appear or defend their claim or cause, the court shall nevertheless proceed to pronounce sentence, or judgment, which shall in like manner be final and decisive, the judgment or sentence and other proceedings being in either case transmitted to Congress, and lodged among the acts of Congress for the security of the parties concerned: provided that every commissioner, before he sits in judgment, shall take an oath to be administered by one of the judges of the supreme or superior court of the State where the case shall be tried, "well and truly to hear and determine the matter in question, according to the best of his judgment, without favour, affection or hope of reward:" provided also that no State shall be deprived of territory for the benefit of the United States.

All controversies concerning the private right of soil claimed under different grants of two or more States, whose jurisdiction as they may respect such lands, and the states which passed such grants are adjusted, the said grants or either of them being at the same time claimed to have originated antecedent to such settlement of jurisdiction, shall on the petition of either party to the Congress of the United States, be finally determined as near as may be in the same manner as is before prescribed for deciding disputes respecting territorial jurisdiction between different States.

The United States in Congress assembled shall also have the sole and exclusive right and power of regulating the alloy and value of coin struck by their own authority, or by that of the respective States—fixing the standard of weights and measures throughout the United States—regulating the trade and managing all affairs with the Indians, not members of any of the States, provided that the legislative right of any State within its own limits be not infringed or violated—establishing and regulating post-offices from one State to another, throughout all of the United States, and exacting such postage on the papers passing thro' the same as may be requisite to defray the expenses of the said office—appointing all officers of the land forces, in the service of the United States, excepting regimental officers—appointing all the officers of the naval forces, and commissioning all officers whatever in the service of the United States—making rules for the government and regulation of the said land and naval forces, and directing their operations.

The United States in Congress assembled shall have authority to appoint a committee, to sit in the recess of Congress, to be denominated "a Committee of the States," and to consist of one delegate from each State; and to appoint such other committees and civil officers as may be necessary for managing the general affairs of the United States under their direction—to appoint one of their number to preside, provided that no person be allowed to serve in the office of president more than one year in any term of three years; to ascertain the necessary sums of money to be raised for the service of the United States, and to appropriate and apply the same for defraying the public expenses—to borrow money, or emit bills on the credit of the United States, transmitting every half year to the respective States an account of the sums of money so borrowed or emitted,—to build and equip a navy—to agree upon the number of land forces, and to make requisitions from each State for its quota, in proportion to the number of white inhabitants in such State; which requisition shall be binding, and thereupon the Legislature of each State shall appoint the regimental officers, raise the men and cloath, arm and equip them in a soldier like manner, at the expense of the United States; and the officers and men so cloathed, armed and equipped shall march to the place appointed, and within the time agreed on by the United States in Congress assembled: but if the United States in Congress assembled shall, on consideration of circumstances judge proper that any State should not raise men, or should raise a smaller number of men than the quota thereof, such extra number shall be raised, officered, cloathed, armed and equipped in the same manner as the quota of such State, unless the legislature of such State shall judge that such extra number cannot be safely spared out of the same, in which case they shall raise officer, cloath, arm and equip as many of such extra number as they judge can be safely spared. And the officers and men so cloathed, armed and equipped, shall march to the place appointed, and within the time agreed on by the United States in Congress assembled.

The United States in Congress assembled shall never engage in a war, nor grant letters of marque and reprisal in time of peace, nor enter into any treaties or alliances, nor coin money, nor regulate the value thereof, nor ascertain the sums and expenses necessary for the defence and welfare of the United States, or any of them, nor emit bills, nor borrow money on the credit of the United States, nor appropriate money, nor agree upon the number of vessels to be built or purchased, or the number of land or sea forces to be raised, nor appoint a commander in chief of the army or navy, unless nine States assent to the same: nor shall a question on any other point, except for adjourning from day to day be determined, unless by the votes of a majority of the United States in Congress assembled.

The Congress of the United States shall have power to adjourn to any time within the year, and to any place within the United States, so that no period of adjournment be for a longer duration than the space of six months, and shall publish the journal of their proceedings monthly, except such parts thereof relating to treaties, alliances or military operations, as in their judgment require secresy; and the yeas and nays of the delegates of each State on any question shall be entered on the Journal, when it is desired by any delegate; and the delegates of a State, or any of them, at his or their request shall be furnished with a transcript of the said journal, except such parts as are above excepted, to lay before the Legislatures of the several States.

ARTICLE X. The committee of the States, or any nine of them, shall be authorized to execute, in the recess of Congress, such of the powers of Congress as the United States in Congress assembled, by the consent of nine States, shall from time to time think expedient to vest them with; provided that no power be delegated to the said committee, for the exercise of which, by the articles of confederation, the voice of nine States in the Congress of the United States assembled is requisite.

ARTICLE XI. Canada acceding to this confederation, and joining in the measures of the United States, shall be admitted into, and entitled to all the advantages of this Union: but no other colony shall be admitted into the same, unless such admission be agreed to by nine States.

Article XII. All bills of credit emitted, monies borrowed and debts contracted by, or under the authority of Congress, before the assembling of the United States, in pursuance of the present confederation, shall be deemed and considered as a charge against the United States, for payment and satisfaction whereof the said United States, and the public faith are hereby solemnly pledged.

Article XIII. Every State shall abide by the determinations of the United States in Congress assembled, on all questions which by this confederation are submitted to them. And the articles of this confederation shall be inviolably observed by every State, and the Union shall be perpetual; nor shall any alteration at any time hereafter be made in any of them; unless such alteration be agreed to in a Congress of the United States, and be afterwards confirmed by the Legislatures of every State.

And whereas it has pleased the Great Governor of the world to incline the hearts of the Legislatures we respectively represent in Congress, to approve of, and to authorize us to ratify the said articles of confederation and perpetual union. Know ye that we the undersigned delegates, by virtue of the power and authority to us given for that purpose, do by these presents, in the name and in behalf of our respective constituents, fully and entirely ratify and confirm each and every of the said articles of confederation and perpetual union, and all and singular the matters and things therein contained: and we do further solemnly plight and engage the faith of our respective constituents, that they shall abide by the determinations of the United States in Congress assembled, on all questions, which by the said confederation are submitted to them. And that the articles thereof shall be inviolably observed by the States we respectively represent, and that the Union shall be perpetual.

In witness thereof we have hereunto set our hands in Congress. Done at Philadelphia in the State of Pennsylvania the ninth day of July in the year of our Lord one thousand seven hundred and seventy-eight, and in the third year of the independence of America.

THE CONSTITUTION OF THE UNITED STATES (1787)

We the People of the United States, in order to form a more perfect Union, establish Justice, insure domestic Tranquility, provide for the common defence, promote the general Welfare, and secure the Blessings of Liberty to ourselves and our Posterity, do ordain and establish this Constitution for the United States of America.

Article. I.

Section. 1. All legislative Powers herein granted shall be vested in a Congress of the United States, which shall consist of a Senate and House of Representatives.

Section. 2. The House of Representatives shall be composed of Members chosen every second Year by the People of the several States, and the Electors in each State shall have the Qualifications requisite for Electors of the most numerous Branch of the State Legislature.

No Person shall be a Representative who shall not have attained to the Age of twenty five Years, and been seven Years a Citizen of the United States, and who shall not, when elected, be an Inhabitant of that State in which he shall be chosen.

Representatives and direct Taxes shall be apportioned among the several States which may be included within this Union, according to their respective Numbers, which shall be determined by adding to the whole Number of free Persons, including those bound to Service for a Term of Years, and excluding Indians not taxed, three fifths of all other Persons. The actual Enumeration shall be made within three Years after the first Meeting of the Congress of the United States, and within every subsequent Term of ten Years, in such

Manner as they shall by Law direct. The Number of Representatives shall not exceed one for every thirty Thousand, but each State shall have at Least one Representative; and until such enumeration shall be made, the State of New Hampshire shall be entitled to chuse three, Massachusetts eight, Rhode-Island and Providence Plantations one, Connecticut five, New-York six, New Jersey four, Pennsylvania eight, Delaware one, Maryland six, Virginia ten, North Carolina five, South Carolina five, and Georgia three.

When vacancies happen in the Representation from any state, the Executive Authority thereof shall issue Writs of Election to fill such Vacancies.

The House of Representatives shall chuse their Speaker and other Officers; and shall have the sole Power of Impeachment.

Section. 3. The Senate of the United States shall be composed of two Senators from each State, chosen by the legislature thereof, for six Years; and each Senator shall have one Vote.

Immediately after they shall be assembled in Consequence of the first Election, they shall be divided as equally as may be into three Classes. The Seats of the Senators of the first Class shall be vacated at the Expiration of the second Year, of the second Class at the Expiration of the fourth Year, and of the third Class at the Expiration of the sixth Year, so that one third maybe chosen every second Year; and if Vacancies happen by Resignation, or otherwise, during the Recess of the Legislature of any State, the Executive thereof may make temporary Appointments until the next Meeting of the Legislature, which shall then fill such Vacancies.

No Person shall be a Senator who shall not have attained to the Age of thirty Years, and been nine Years a Citizen of the United States, and who shall not, when elected, be an Inhabitant of that State for which he shall be chosen.

The Vice President of the United States shall be President of the Senate, but shall have no Vote, unless they be equally divided.

The Senate shall chuse their other Officers, and also a President pro tempore, in the Absence of the Vice President, or when he shall exercise the Office of President of the United States.

The Senate shall have the sole Power to try all Impeachments. When sitting for that Purpose, they shall be on Oath or Affirmation. When the President of the United States is tried, the Chief Justice shall preside: And no Person shall be convicted without the Concurrence of two thirds of the Members present.

Judgment in Cases of Impeachment shall not extend further than to removal from Office, and disqualification to hold and enjoy any Office of honor, Trust or Profit under the United States: but the Party convicted shall nevertheless be liable and subject to Indictment, Trial, Judgment and Punishment, according to Law.

Section. 4. The Times, Places and Manner of holding Elections for Senators and Representatives, shall be prescribed in each State by the Legislature thereof; but the Congress may at any time by Law make or alter such Regulations, except as to the Places of chusing Senators.

The Congress shall assemble at least once in every Year, and such Meeting shall be on the first Monday in December, unless they shall by Law appoint a different Day.

Section. 5. Each House shall be the Judge of the Elections, Returns and Qualifications of its own Members, and a Majority of each shall constitute a Quorum to do Business; but a smaller Number may adjourn from day to day, and may be authorized to compel the Attendance of absent Members, in such Manner, and under such Penalties as each House may provide.

Each House may determine the Rules of its Proceedings, punish its Members for disorderly Behaviour, and, with the Concurrence of two thirds, expel a Member.

Each House shall keep a Journal of its Proceedings, and from time to time publish the same, excepting such Parts as may in their Judgment require Secrecy; and the Yeas and Nays of the Members of either House on any question shall, at the Desire of one fifth of those Present, be entered on the Journal.

Neither House, during the Session of Congress, shall, without the Consent of the other, adjourn for more than three days, not to any other Place than that in which the two Houses shall be sitting.

Section. 6. The Senators and Representatives shall receive a Compensation for their Services, to be ascertained by Law, and paid out of the Treasury of the United States. They shall in all Cases, except Treason, Felony and Breach of the Peace, be privileged from Arrest during their Attendance at the Session of their respective Houses, and in going to and returning from the same; and for any Speech or Debate in either House, they shall not be questioned in any other Place.

No Senator or Representative shall, during the Time for which he was elected, be appointed to any civil Office under the Authority of the United States, which shall have been created, or the Emoluments whereof shall have been encreased during such time; and no Person holding any Office under the United States, shall be a Member of either House during his Continuance in Office.

Section. 7. All Bills for raising Revenue shall originate in the House of Representatives; but the Senate may propose or concur with Amendments as on other Bills.

Every Bill which shall have passed the House of Representatives and the Senate shall, before it become a Law, be presented to the President of the United States; If he approve he shall sign it, but if not he shall return it, with his Objections to that House in which it shall have originated, who shall enter the Objections at large on their Journal, and proceed to reconsider it. If after such Reconsideration two thirds of that House shall agree to pass the Bill, it shall be sent, together with the Objections, to the other House, by which it shall likewise be reconsidered, and if approved by two thirds of that House, it shall become a Law. But in all such Cases the Votes of both Houses shall be determined by yeas and Nays, and the Names of the Persons voting for and against the Bill shall be entered on the Journal of each House respectively. If any Bill shall not be returned by the President within ten Days (Sundays excepted) after it shall have been presented to him, the Same shall be a Law, in like Manner as if he had signed it, unless the Congress by their Adjournment prevent its Return, in which Case it shall not be a Law.

Every Order, Resolution, or Vote to which the Concurrence of the Senate and House of Representatives may be necessary (except on a question of Adjournment) shall be presented to the President of the United States; and before the Same shall take Effect, shall be approved by him, or being disapproved by him, shall be repassed by two thirds of the Senate and House of Representatives, according to the Rules and Limitations prescribed in the Case of a Bill.

Section. 8. The Congress shall have Power To lay and collect Taxes, Duties, Imposts and Excises, to pay the Debts and provide for the common Defence and general Welfare of the United States; but all Duties, Imposts and Excises shall be uniform throughout the United States;

To borrow Money on the credit of the United States;

To regulate Commerce with foreign Nations, and among the several States, and with the Indian Tribes;

To establish an uniform Rule of Naturalization, and uniform Laws on the subject of Bankruptcies throughout the United States;

To coin Money, regulate the Value thereof, and of foreign Coin, and fix the Standard of Weights and Measures;

To provide for the Punishment of counterfeiting the Securities and current Coin of the United States;

To establish Post Offices and Post Roads;

To promote the Progress of Science and useful Arts, by securing for limited Times to Authors and Inventors the exclusive Right to their respective Writings and Discoveries;

To constitute Tribunals inferior to the supreme Court;

To define and punish Piracies and Felonies committed on the high Seas, and Offences against the Law of Nations;

To declare War, grant Letters of Marque and Reprisal, and make Rules concerning Captures on land and Water;

To raise and support Armies, but no Appropriation of Money to that Use shall be for a longer Term than two Years;

To provide and maintain a Navy;

To make Rules for the Government and Regulation of the land and naval Forces;

To provide for calling forth the Militia to execute the Laws of the Union, suppress Insurrections and repel Invasions;

To provide for organizing, arming, and disciplining, the Militia, and for governing such Part of them as may be employed in the Service of the United States, reserving to the States respectively, the Appointment of the Officers, and the Authority of training the Militia according to the discipline prescribed by Congress.

To exercise exclusive Legislation in all Cases whatsoever, over such District (not exceeding ten Miles square) as may, by Cession of Particular States, and the Acceptance of Congress, become the Seat of the Government of the United States, and to exercise like Authority over all Places purchased by the Consent of the Legislature of the State in which the Same shall be, for the Erection of Forts, Magazines, Arsenals, dock-Yards, and other needful Buildings;—And

To make all Laws which shall be necessary and proper for carrying into Execution the foregoing Powers, and all other Powers vested by this Constitution in the Government of the United States, or in any Department or Officer thereof.

Section. 9. The Migration or Importation of such Persons as any of the States now existing shall think proper to admit, shall not be prohibited by the Congress prior to the Year one thousand eight hundred and eight, but a Tax or duty may be imposed on such Importation, not exceeding ten dollars for each Person.

The Privilege of the Writ of Habeas Corpus shall not be suspended, unless when in Cases of Rebellion or Invasion the public Safety may require it.

No Bill of Attainder or ex post facto Law shall be passed.

No Capitation, or other direct, Tax shall be laid, unless in Proportion to the Census or Enumeration herein before directed to be taken.

No Tax or Duty shall be laid on Articles exported from any State.

No Preference shall be given by any Regulation of Commerce or Revenue to the Ports of one State over those of another: nor shall Vessels bound to, or from, one State, be obliged to enter, clear, or pay Duties in another.

No Money shall be drawn from the Treasury, but in Consequence of Appropriations made by Law; and a regular Statement and Account of the Receipts and Expenditures of all public Money shall be published from time to time.

No Title of Nobility shall be granted by the United States: And no Person holding any Office of Profit or trust under them, shall, without the Consent of the Congress, accept of any present, Emolument, Office, or Title, of any kind whatever, from any King, Prince, or foreign State.

Section 10. No State shall enter into any Treaty, Alliance, or Confederation; grant Letters of Marque and Reprisal; coin Money; emit Bills of Credit; make any Thing but gold and silver Coin a Tender in Payment of Debts; pass any Bill of Attainder, ex post facto Law, or Law impairing the Obligation of Contracts, or grant any Title of Nobility.

No State shall, without the Consent of the Congress, lay any Imposts or Duties on Imports or Exports, except what may be absolutely necessary for executing its inspection Laws: and the net Produce of all Duties and Imposts, laid by any State on Imports or Exports, shall be for the Use of the Treasury of the United States; and all such Laws shall be subject to the Revision and Controul of the Congress.

No State shall, without the Consent of Congress, lay any Duty of Tonnage, keep Troops, or Ships of War in time of Peace, enter into any Agreement or Compact with another State, or with a foreign Power, or engage in War, unless actually invaded, or in such imminent Danger as will not admit of delay.

ARTICLE. II.

Section. 1. The executive Power shall be vested in a President of the United States of America. He shall hold his Office during the term of four Years, and, together with the Vice President, chosen for the same Term, be elected, as follows:

Each State shall appoint, in such Manner as the Legislature thereof may direct, a Number of Electors, equal to the whole Number of Senators and Representatives to which the State may be entitled in the Congress: but no Senator or Representative, or Person holding an Office of Trust or Profit under the United States, shall be appointed an Elector.

The Electors shall meet in their respective States, and vote by Ballot for two Persons, of whom one at least shall not be an Inhabitant of the same State with themselves. And they shall make a List of all the Persons voted for, and of the Number of Votes for each; which List they shall sign and certify, and transmit sealed to the Seat of the Government of the United States, directed to the President of the Senate. The President of the Senate shall, in the Presence of the Senate and House of Representatives, open all the Certificates, and the Votes shall then be counted. The Person having the greatest Number of Votes shall be the President, if such Number be a Majority of the whole Number of Electors appointed; and if there be more than one who have such Majority, and have an equal Number of Votes, then the House of Representatives shall immediately chuse by Ballot one of them for President; and if no Person have a Majority, then from the five highest on the List the said House shall in like Manner chuse the President. But in chusing the President, the Votes shall be taken by States, the Representation from each State having one Vote; A quorum for this Purpose shall consist of a Member or Members from two thirds of the States, and a Majority of all the States shall be necessary to a Choice. In every Case, after the Choice of the President, the Person having the greatest Number of Votes of the Electors shall be the Vice President. But if there should remain two or more who have equal Votes, the Senate shall chuse from them by Ballot the Vice President.

The Congress may determine the Time of chusing the Electors, and the Day on which they shall give their Votes; which Day shall be the same throughout the United States.

No Person except a natural born Citizen, or a Citizen of the United States, at the time of the Adoption of this Constitution, shall be eligible to the Office of President; neither shall any Person be eligible to that Office who shall not have attained to the Age of thirty five Years, and been fourteen Years a Resident within the United States.

In Case of the Removal of the President from Office, or of his Death, Resignation, or Inability to discharge the Powers and Duties of the said Office, the Same shall devolve on the Vice President, and the Congress may by Law provide for the Case of Removal, Death, Resignation or Inability, both of the President and Vice President, declaring what Officer shall then act as President, and such Officer shall act accordingly, until the Disability be removed, or a President shall be elected.

The President shall, at stated Times, receive for his Services, a Compensation, which shall neither be encreased or diminished during the Period for which he shall have been elected, and he shall not receive within that Period any other Emolument from the United States, or any of them.

Before he enters on the Execution of his Office, he shall take the following Oath or Affirmation:—"I do solemnly swear (or affirm) that I will faithfully execute the Office of President of the United States, and will to the best of my Ability, preserve, protect and defend the Constitution of the United States."

Section. 2. The President shall be Commander in Chief of the Army and Navy of the United States, and of the Militia of the several States, when called into the actual Service of the United States; he may require the Opinion, in writing, of the principal Officer in each of the executive Departments, upon any Subject relating to the Duties of their respective Offices, and he shall have Power to grant Reprieves and Pardons for Offences against the United States, except in Cases of Impeachment.

He shall have Power, by and with the Advice and Consent of the Senate, to make Treaties, provided two thirds of the Senators present concur; and he shall nominate, and by and with the Advice and Consent of the Senate, shall appoint Ambassadors, other public Ministers and Consuls, Judges of the supreme Court, and all other Officers of the United States, whose Appointments are not herein otherwise provided for, and which shall be established by Law; but the Congress may by Law vest the Appointment of such inferior Officers, as they think proper, in the President alone, in the Courts of Law, or in the Heads of Departments.

The President shall have Power to fill up all Vacancies that may happen during the Recess of the Senate, by granting Commissions which shall expire at the End of their next Session.

Section. 3. He shall from time to time give to the Congress Information of the State of the Union, and recommend to their Consideration such Measures as he shall judge necessary and expedient; he may, on extraordinary Occasions, convene both Houses, or either of them, and in Case of Disagreement between them, with Respect to the Time of Adjournment, he may adjourn them to such Time as he shall think proper; he shall receive Ambassadors and other public Ministers; he shall take Care that the Laws be faithfully executed, and shall Commission all the Officers of the United States.

Section. 4. The President, Vice President and all civil Officers of the United States, shall be removed from Office on Impeachment for, and Conviction of, Treason, Bribery, or other high Crimes and Misdemeanors.

ARTICLE. III.

Section. 1. The judicial Power of the United States, shall be vested in one supreme Court, and in such inferior Courts as the Congress may from time to time ordain and establish. The Judges, both of the supreme and inferior Courts, shall hold their Offices during good Behavior, and shall, at stated Times, receive for their Services, a Compensation, which shall not be diminished during their Continuance in Office.

Section. 2. The judicial Power shall extend to all Cases, in Law and Equity, arising under this Constitution, the Laws of the United States, and Treaties made, or which shall be made, under their Authority;—to all Cases affecting Ambassadors, other public Ministers and Consuls;—to all Cases of admiralty and maritime Jurisdiction;—the Controversies to which the United States shall be a Party;—to Controversies between two or more States;—between a State and Citizens of another State;—between Citizens of different States;—between Citizens of the same State claiming Lands under Grants of different States, and between a State, or the Citizens thereof, and foreign States, Citizens or Subjects.

In all cases affecting Ambassadors, other public Ministers and Consuls, and those in which a State shall be Party, the supreme Court shall have original Jurisdiction. In all the other Cases before mentioned, the supreme Court shall have appellate Jurisdiction, both as to Law and Fact, with such Exceptions, and under such Regulations as the Congress shall make.

The Trial of all Crimes, except in Cases of Impeachment, shall be by Jury; and such Trial shall be held in the State where the said Crimes shall have been committed; but when not committed within any State, the Trial shall be at such Place or Places as the Congress may by Law have directed.

Section. 3. Treason against the United States, shall consist only in levying War against them, or in adhering to their Enemies, giving them Aid and Comfort. No Person shall be convicted of Treason unless on the Testimony of two Witnesses to the same overt Act, or on Confession in open Court.

The Congress shall have Power to declare the Punishment of Treason, but no Attainder of Treason shall work Corruption of Blood, or Forfeiture except during the Life of the Person attainted.

ARTICLE. IV.

Section. 1. Full Faith and Credit shall be given in each State to the public Acts, Records, and judicial Proceedings of every other State. And the Congress may by general Laws prescribe the Manner in which such Acts, Records and Proceedings shall be proved, and the Effect thereof.

Section. 2. The Citizens of each State shall be entitled to all Privileges and Immunities of Citizens in the several States.

A Person charged in any State with Treason, Felony, or other Crime, who shall flee from Justice, and be found in another State, shall on Demand of the executive Authority of the State from which he fled, be delivered up, to be removed to the State having Jurisdiction of the Crime.

No Person held to Service or Labour in one State, under the Laws thereof, escaping into another, shall, in Consequence of any Law or Regulation therein, be discharged from such Service or Labour, but shall be delivered up on Claim of the Party to whom such Service or Labour may be due.

Section. 3. New States may be admitted by the Congress into this Union; but no new State shall be formed or erected within the Jurisdiction of any other State; nor any State be formed by the Junction of two or more States, or Parts of States, without the consent of the Legislatures of the States concerned as well as of the Congress.

The Congress shall have Power to dispose of and make all needful Rules and Regulations respecting the Territory or other Property belonging to the United States; and nothing in this Constitution shall be so construed as to Prejudice any Claims of the United States, or of any particular States.

Section. 4. The United States shall guarantee to every State in this Union a Republican Form of Government, and shall protect each of them against Invasion; and on Application of the Legislature, or of the Executive (when the Legislature cannot be convened) against domestic Violence.

ARTICLE. V.

The Congress, whenever two thirds of both Houses shall deem it necessary, shall propose Amendments to this Constitution, or, on the Application of the

Legislatures of two thirds of the several States, shall call a Convention for proposing Amendments, which, in either Case, shall be valid to all Intents and Purposes, as Part of this Constitution, when ratified by the Legislatures of three fourths of the several States, or by Conventions in three fourths thereof, as the one or the other Mode of Ratification may be proposed by the Congress; Provided that no Amendment which may be made prior to the Year One thousand eight hundred and eight shall in any Manner affect the first and fourth Clauses in the Ninth Section of the first Article; and that no State, without its Consent, shall be deprived of its equal Suffrage in the Senate.

ARTICLE. VI.

All Debts contracted and Engagements entered into, before the Adoption of this Constitution, shall be as valid against the United States under this Constitution, as under the Confederation.

This Constitution, and the Laws of the United States which shall be made in Pursuance thereof; and all Treaties made, or which shall be made, under the Authority of the United States, shall be the supreme Law of the Land; and the Judges in every State shall be bound thereby, any Thing in the Constitution or Laws of any State to the Contrary notwithstanding.

The Senators and Representatives before mentioned, and the Members of the several State Legislatures, and all executive and judicial Officers, both of the United States and of the several States, shall be bound by Oath or Affirmation, to support this Constitution; but no religious Test shall ever be required as a Qualification to any Office or public Trust under the United States.

ARTICLE. VII.

The Ratification of the Conventions of nine States, shall be sufficient for the Establishment of this Constitution between the States so ratifying the Same.

Done in Convention by the Unanimous Consent of the States present the Seventeenth Day of September in the Year of our Lord one thousand seven hundred and Eighty seven and of the Independence of the United States of America the Twelfth. In witness thereof We have hereunto subscribed our Names,

Go. WASHINGTON—Presdt.
and deputy from Virginia.

New Hampshire ⎰ John Langdon
⎱ Nicholas Gilman

Massachusetts ⎰ Nathaniel Gorham
⎱ Rufus King

Connecticut ⎰ Wm Saml Johnson
⎱ Roger Sherman

New York: . . .   Alexander Hamilton

New Jersey ⎰ Wil: Livingston
David A. Brearley.
Wm Paterson.
⎱ Jona: Dayton

Pennsylvania ⎰ B Franklin
Thomas Mifflin
Robt Morris
Geo. Clymer
Thos FitzSimons
Jared Ingersoll
James Wilson
⎱ Gouv Morris

Delaware ⎰ Geo: Read
Gunning Bedford jun
John Dickinson
Richard Bassett
⎱ Jaco: Broom

Maryland ⎰ James McHenry
Dan of St Thos Jenifer
⎱ Danl Carroll

Virginia ⎰ John Blair—
⎱ James Madison Jr.

North Carolina ⎰ Wm Blount
Richd Dobbs Spaight.
⎱ Hu Williamson

South Carolina ⎰ J. Rutledge
Charles Cotesworth
Pinckney
Charles Pinckney
⎱ Pierce Butler.

Georgia ⎰ William Few
⎱ Abr Baldwin

AMENDMENTS TO THE
CONSTITUTION

ARTICLES IN ADDITION TO, and Amendment of the Constitution of the United States of America, proposed by Congress, and ratified by the Legislatures of the several States, pursuant to the fifth Article of the original Constitution.

AMENDMENT I.

Congress shall make no law respecting an establishment of religion, or prohibiting the free exercise thereof; or abridging the freedom of speech, or of the press; or the right of the people peaceably to assemble, and to petition the Government for a redress of grievances.

AMENDMENT II.

A well regulated Militia, being necessary to the security of a free State, the right of the people to keep and bear Arms, shall not be infringed.

AMENDMENT III.

No Soldier shall, in time of peace be quartered in any house, without the consent of the Owner, nor in time of war, but in a manner to be prescribed by law.

AMENDMENT IV.

The right of the people to be secure in their persons, houses, papers, and effects, against unreasonable searches and seizures, shall not be violated, and no Warrants shall issue, but upon probable cause, supported by Oath or affirmation, and particularly describing the place to be searched, and the persons or things to be seized.

AMENDMENT V.

No person shall be held to answer for a capital, or otherwise infamous crime, unless on a presentment or indictment of a Grand Jury, except in cases arising in the land or naval forces, or in the Militia, when in actual service in time of War or public danger; nor shall any person be subject for the same offence to be twice put in jeopardy of life or limb; nor shall be compelled in any criminal case to be a witness against himself, nor be deprived of life, liberty, or property, without due process of law; nor shall private property be taken for public use, without just compensation.

AMENDMENT VI.

In all criminal prosecutions, the accused shall enjoy the right to a speedy and public trial, by an impartial jury of the State and district wherein the crime shall have been committed, which district shall have been previously ascertained by law, and to be informed of the nature and cause of the accusation; to be confronted with the witnesses against him; to have compulsory process for obtaining witnesses in his favor, and to have the Assistance of Counsel for his defence.

AMENDMENT VII.

In Suits at common law, where the value in controversy shall exceed twenty dollars, the right of trial by jury shall be preserved, and no fact tried by a jury, shall be otherwise re-examined in any Court of the United States, than according to the rules of the common law.

AMENDMENT VIII.

Excessive bail shall not be required, nor excessive fines imposed, nor cruel and unusual punishments inflicted.

AMENDMENT IX.

The enumeration in the Constitution, of certain rights, shall not be construed to deny or disparage others retained by the people.

AMENDMENT X.

The powers not delegated to the United States by the Constitution, nor prohibited by it to the States, are reserved to the States respectively, or to the people. [The first ten amendments went into effect December 15, 1791.]

AMENDMENT XI.

The Judicial power of the United States shall not be construed to extend to any suit in law or equity, commenced or prosecuted against one of the United States by Citizens of another State, or by Citizens or Subjects of any Foreign State. [January 8, 1798.]

AMENDMENT XII.

The Electors shall meet in their respective states, and vote by ballot for President and Vice-President, one of whom, at least, shall not be an inhabitant of the same state with themselves; they shall name in their ballots the person voted for as President, and in distinct ballots the person voted for as Vice-President, and they shall make distinct lists of all persons voted for as President, and of all persons voted for as Vice President, and of the number of votes for each, which lists they shall sign and certify, and transmit sealed to the seat of the government of the United States, directed to the President of the Senate;—The President of the Senate shall, in the presence of the Senate and House of Representatives, open all the certificates and the votes shall then be counted;—The person having the greatest number of votes for President, shall be the President, if such number be a majority of the whole number of Electors appointed; and if no person have such majority, then from the persons having the highest numbers not exceeding three on the list of those voted for as President, the House of Representatives shall choose immediately, by ballot, the President. But in choosing the President, the votes shall be taken by states, the representation from each state having one vote; a quorum for this purpose shall consist of a member or members from two-thirds of the states, and a majority of all the states shall be necessary to a choice. And if the House of Representatives shall not choose a President whenever the right of choice shall devolve upon them, before the fourth day of March next following, then the Vice-President shall act as President, as in the case of the death or other constitutional disability of the President.— The person having the greatest number of votes as Vice-President, shall be the Vice-President, if such number be a majority of the whole number of Electors appointed, and if no person have a majority, then from the two highest numbers on the list, the Senate shall choose the Vice-President; a quorum for the purpose shall consist of two-thirds of the whole number of Senators, and a majority of the whole number shall be necessary to a choice. But no person constitutionally ineligible to the office of President shall be eligible to that of Vice-President of the United States. [September 25, 1804.]

Amendment XIII.

Section 1. Neither slavery nor involuntary servitude, except as a punishment for crime whereof the party shall have been duly convicted, shall exist within the United States, or any place subject to their jurisdiction.

Section 2. Congress shall have power to enforce this article by appropriate legislation. [December 18, 1865.]

Amendment XIV.

Section 1. All persons born or naturalized in the United States, and subject to the jurisdiction thereof, are citizens of the United States and of the State wherein they reside. No State shall make or enforce any law which shall abridge the privileges or immunities of citizens of the United States; nor shall any State deprive any person of life, liberty, or property, without due process of law; nor deny to any person within its jurisdiction the equal protection of the laws.

Section 2. Representatives shall be apportioned among the several States according to their respective numbers, counting the whole number of persons in each State, excluding Indians not taxed. But when the right to vote at any election for the choice of electors for President and Vice President of the United States, Representatives in Congress, the Executive and Judicial officers of a State, or the members of the Legislature thereof, is denied to any of the male inhabitants of such State, being twenty-one years of age, and citizens of the United States, or in any way abridged, except for participation in rebellion, or other crime, the basis of representation therein shall be reduced in the proportion which the number of such male citizens shall bear to the whole number of male citizens twenty-one years of age in such State.

Section 3. No person shall be a Senator or Representative in Congress, or elector of President and Vice President, or hold any office, civil or military, under the United States, or under any State, who, having previously taken an oath, as a member of Congress, or as an officer of the United States, or as a member of any State legislature, or as an executive or judicial officer of any State, to support the Constitution of the United States, shall have engaged in insurrection or rebellion against the same, or given aid or comfort to the enemies thereof. But Congress may by a vote of two-thirds of each House, remove such disability.

Section 4. The validity of the public debt of the United States, authorized by law, including debts incurred for payment of pensions and bounties for services in suppressing insurrection or rebellion, shall not be questioned. But neither the United States nor any State shall assume or pay any debt or obligation incurred in aid of insurrection or rebellion against the United States, or any claim for the loss or emancipation of any slave; but all such debts, obligations and claims shall be held illegal and void.

Section 5. The Congress shall have power to enforce, by appropriate legislation, the provisions of this article. [July 28, 1868.]

AMENDMENT XV.

Section 1. The right of citizens of the United States to vote shall not be denied or abridged by the United States or by any State on account of race, color, or previous condition of servitude—

Section 2. The Congress shall have power to enforce this article by appropriate legislation.—[March 30, 1870.]

AMENDMENT XVI.

The Congress shall have power to lay and collect taxes on incomes, from whatever source derived, without apportionment among the several

States, and without regard to any census or enumeration. [February 25, 1913.]

AMENDMENT XVII.

The Senate of the United States shall be composed of two senators from each State, elected by the people thereof, for six years; and each Senator shall have one vote. The electors in each State shall have the qualifications requisite for electors of the most numerous branch of the State legislature.

When vacancies happen in the representation of any State in the Senate, the executive authority of such State shall issue writs of election to fill such vacancies: *Provided,* That the legislature of any State may empower the executive thereof to make temporary appointments until the people fill the vacancies by election as the legislature may direct.

This amendment shall not be so construed as to affect the election or term of any senator chosen before it becomes valid as part of the Constitution. [May 31, 1913.]

AMENDMENT XVIII.

After one year from the ratification of this article, the manufacture, sale, or transportation of intoxicating liquors within, the importation thereof into, or the exportation thereof from the United States and all territory subject to the jurisdiction thereof for beverage purposes is hereby prohibited.

The Congress and the several States shall have concurrent power to enforce this article by appropriate legislation.

This article shall be inoperative unless it shall have been ratified as an amendment to the Constitution by the legislatures of the several States, as provided in the Constitution, within seven years from the date of the submission thereof to the States by Congress. [January 29, 1919.]

AMENDMENT XIX.

The right of citizens of the United States to vote shall not be denied or abridged by the United States or by any State on account of sex.

The Congress shall have power by appropriate legislation to enforce the provisions of this article. [August 26, 1920.]

Amendment XX.

Section 1. The terms of the President and Vice-President shall end at noon on the twentieth day of January, and the terms of Senators and Representatives at noon on the third day of January, of the years in which such terms would have ended if this article had not been ratified; and the terms of their successors shall then begin.

Section 2. The Congress shall assemble at least once in every year, and such meeting shall begin at noon on the third day of January, unless they shall by law appoint a different day.

Section 3. If, at the time fixed for the beginning of the term of the President, the President-elect shall have died, the Vice-President-elect shall become President. If a President shall not have been chosen before the time fixed for the beginning of his term, or if the President-elect shall have failed to qualify, then the Vice-President-elect shall act as President until a President shall have qualified; and the Congress may by law provide for the case wherein neither a President-elect nor a Vice-President-elect shall have qualified, declaring who shall then act as President, or the manner in which one who is to act shall be selected, and such person shall act accordingly until a President or Vice-President shall have qualified.

Section 4. The Congress may by law provide for the case of the death of any of the persons from whom the House of Representatives may choose a President whenever the right of choice shall have devolved upon them, and for the case of the death of any of the persons from whom the Senate may choose a Vice-President whenever the right of choice shall have devolved upon them.

Section 5. Sections 1 and 2 shall take effect on the 15th day of October following the ratification of this article.

Section 6. This article shall be inoperative unless it shall have been ratified as an amendment to the Constitution by the legislatures of three-fourths of the several States within seven years from the date of its submission. [February 6, 1933.]

Amendment XXI.

Section 1. The eighteenth article of amendment to the Constitution of the United States is hereby repealed.

Section 2. The transportation or importation into any State, Territory or possession of the United States for delivery or use therein of intoxicating liquors, in violation of the laws thereof, is hereby prohibited.

Section 3. This article shall be inoperative unless it shall have been ratified as an amendment to the Constitution by convention in the several States, as provided in the Constitution, within seven years from the date of the submission thereof to the States by the Congress. [December 5, 1933.]

Amendment XXII.

Section 1. No person shall be elected to the office of the President more than twice, and no person who has held the office of President, or acted as President, for more than two years of a term to which some other person was elected President shall be elected to the office of the President more than once. But this Article shall not apply to any person holding the office of President when this Article was proposed by the Congress, and shall not prevent any person who may be holding the office of President, or acting as President, during the term within which this Article becomes operative from holding the office of President or acting as President during the remainder of such term.

Section 2. This article shall be inoperative unless it shall have been ratified as an amendment to the Constitution by the legislatures of three-fourths of the several states within seven years from the date of its submission to the States by the Congress. [February 27, 1951.]

Amendment XXIII.

Section 1. The District constituting the seat of government of the United States shall appoint in such manner as the Congress may direct:

A number of electors of President and Vice-President equal to the whole number of Senators and Representatives in Congress to which the District would be entitled if it were a State, but in no event more than the least populous State; they shall be in addition to those appointed by the States, but they shall be considered, for the purposes of the election of President and Vice-President, to be electors appointed by a State; and they shall meet in the District and perform such duties as provided by the twelfth article of amendment.

Section 2. The Congress shall have the power to enforce this article by appropriate legislation. [March 29, 1961.]

AMENDMENT XXIV.

Section 1. The right of citizens of the United States to vote in any primary or other election for President or Vice President, for electors for President or Vice President, or for Senator or Representative in Congress, shall not be denied or abridged by the United States or any State by reason of failure to pay any poll tax or other tax.

Section 2. The Congress shall have power to enforce this article by appropriate legislation. [January 23, 1964.]

AMENDMENT XXV.

Section 1. In case of the removal of the President from office or of his death or resignation, the Vice President shall become President.

Section 2. Whenever there is a vacancy in the office of Vice President, the President shall nominate a Vice President who shall take office upon confirmation by a majority vote of both Houses of Congress.

Section 3. Whenever the President transmits to the President pro tempore of the Senate and the Speaker of the House of Representatives his written declaration that he is unable to discharge the powers and duties of his office, and until he transmits to them a written declaration to the contrary, such powers and duties shall be discharged by the Vice President as Acting President.

Section 4. Whenever the Vice President and a majority of either the principal officers of the executive departments or of such other body as Congress may by law provide, transmit to the President pro tempore of the Senate and the Speaker of the House of Representatives their written declaration that the President is unable to discharge the powers and duties of his office, the Vice President shall immediately assume the powers and duties of the office as Acting President.

Thereafter, when the President transmits to the President pro tempore of the Senate and the Speaker of the House of Representatives his written declaration that no inability exists, he shall resume the powers and duties of his office unless the Vice President and a majority of either the principal officers of the executive departments or of such other body as Congress may by law provide, transmit within four days to the President pro tempore of the Senate and the Speaker of the House of Representatives their written declaration that the President is unable to discharge the powers and duties of his office. Thereupon Congress shall decide the issue, assembling within forty-eight hours for that purpose if not in session. If the Congress, within twenty-one days after receipt of the latter written declaration, or, if Congress is not in session, within twenty-one days after Congress is required to assemble, determines by two-thirds vote of both Houses that the President is unable to discharge the powers and duties of his office, the Vice President shall continue to discharge the same as Acting President; otherwise, the President shall resume the powers and duties of his office. [February 10, 1967.]

AMENDMENT XXVI.

Section 1. The right of citizens of the United States, who are eighteen years of age or older, to vote shall not be denied or abridged by the United States or by any State on account of age.

Section 2. The Congress shall have power to enforce this article by appropriate legislation [June 30, 1971.]

AMENDMENT XXVII.

No law, varying the compensation for the services of the Senators and Representatives shall take effect, until an election of Representatives shall have intervened. [May 8, 1992.]

PRESIDENTIAL ELECTIONS

Year	Number of States	Candidates	Parties	Popular Vote	% of Popular Vote	Electoral Vote	% Voter Participation
1789	11	**GEORGE WASHINGTON**	No party designations			69	
		John Adams				34	
		Other candidates				35	
1792	15	**GEORGE WASHINGTON**	No party designations			132	
		John Adams				77	
		George Clinton				50	
		Other candidates				5	
1796	16	**JOHN ADAMS**	Federalist			71	
		Thomas Jefferson	Democratic-Republican			68	
		Thomas Pinckney	Federalist			59	
		Aaron Burr	Democratic-Republican			30	
		Other candidates				48	
1800	16	**THOMAS JEFFERSON**	Democratic-Republican			73	
		Aaron Burr	Democratic-Republican			73	
		John Adams	Federalist			65	
		Charles C. Pinckney	Federalist			64	
		John Jay	Federalist			1	
1804	17	**THOMAS JEFFERSON**	Democratic-Republican			162	
		Charles C. Pinckney	Federalist			14	

Year	Number of States	Candidates	Party	Popular Vote	% of Popular Vote	Electoral Vote	% Voter Participation
1808	17	**JAMES MADISON**	Democratic-Republican			122	
		Charles C. Pinckney	Federalist			47	
		George Clinton	Democratic-Republican			6	
1812	18	**JAMES MADISON**	Democratic-Republican			128	
		DeWitt Clinton	Federalist			89	
1816	19	**JAMES MONROE**	Democratic-Republican			183	
		Rufus King	Federalist			34	
1820	24	**JAMES MONROE**	Democratic-Republican			231	
		John Quincy Adams	Independent			1	
1824	24	**JOHN QUINCY ADAMS**	Democratic-Republican	108,740	30.5	84	26.9
		Andrew Jackson	Democratic-Republican	153,544	43.1	99	
		Henry Clay	Democratic-Republican	47,136	13.2	37	
		William H. Crawford	Democratic-Republican	46,618	13.1	41	
1828	24	**ANDREW JACKSON**	Democratic	647,286	56.0	178	57.6
		John Quincy Adams	National-Republican	508,064	44.0	83	

Year	Number of States	Candidates	Parties	Popular Vote	% of Popular Vote	Electoral Vote	% Voter Participation
1832	24	**ANDREW JACKSON**	Democratic	688,242	54.5	219	55.4
		Henry Clay	National-Republican	473,462	37.5	49	
		William Wirt	Anti-Masonic	101,051	8.0	7	
		John Floyd	Democratic			11	
1836	26	**MARTIN VAN BUREN**	Democratic	765,483	50.9	170	57.8
		William H. Harrison	Whig			73	
		Hugh L. White	Whig	739,795	49.1	26	
		Daniel Webster	Whig			14	
		W. P. Mangum	Whig			11	
1840	26	**WILLIAM H. HARRISON**	Whig	1,274,624	53.1	234	80.2
		Martin Van Buren	Democratic	1,127,781	46.9	60	
1844	26	**JAMES K. POLK**	Democratic	1,338,464	49.6	170	78.9
		Henry Clay	Whig	1,300,097	48.1	105	
		James G. Birney	Liberty	62,300	2.3		
1848	30	**ZACHARY TAYLOR**	Whig	1,360,967	47.4	163	72.7
		Lewis Cass	Democratic	1,222,342	42.5	127	
		Martin Van Buren	Free Soil	291,263	10.1		
1852	31	**FRANKLIN PIERCE**	Democratic	1,601,117	50.9	254	69.6
		Winfield Scott	Whig	1,385,453	44.1	42	
		John P. Hale	Free Soil	155,825	5.0		
1856	31	**JAMES BUCHANAN**	Democratic	1,832,955	45.3	174	78.9
		John C. Frémont	Republican	1,339,932	33.1	114	
		Millard Fillmore	American	871,731	21.6	8	

Year	Number of States	Candidates	Parties	Popular Vote	% of Popular Vote	Electoral Vote	% Voter Participation
1860	33	**ABRAHAM LINCOLN**	Republican	1,865,593	39.8	180	81.2
		Stephen A. Douglas	Democratic	1,382,713	29.5	12	
		John C. Breckinridge	Democratic	848,356	18.1	72	
		John Bell	Constitutional Union	592,906	12.6	39	
1864	36	**ABRAHAM LINCOLN**	Republican	2,206,938	55.0	212	73.8
		George B. McClellan	Democratic	1,803,787	45.0	21	
1868	37	**ULYSSES S. GRANT**	Republican	3,013,421	52.7	214	78.1
		Horatio Seymour	Democratic	2,706,829	47.3	80	
1872	37	**ULYSSES S. GRANT**	Republican	3,596,745	55.6	286	71.3
		Horace Greeley	Democratic	2,843,446	43.9	66	
1876	38	Rutherford B. Hayes	Republican	4,036,572	48.0	185	81.8
		Samuel J. Tilden	Democratic	4,284,020	51.0	184	
1880	38	**JAMES A. GARFIELD**	Republican	4,453,295	48.5	214	79.4
		Winfield S. Hancock	Democratic	4,414,082	48.1	155	
		James B. Weaver	Greenback-Labor	308,578	3.4		
1884	38	**GROVER CLEVELAND**	Democratic	4,879,507	48.5	219	77.5
		James G. Blaine	Republican	4,850,293	48.2	182	
		Benjamin F. Butler	Greenback-Labor	175,370	1.8		
		John P. St. John	Prohibition	150,369	1.5		
1888	38	**BENJAMIN HARRISON**	Republican	5,477,129	47.9	233	79.3
		Grover Cleveland	Democratic	5,537,857	48.6	168	
		Clinton B. Fisk	Prohibition	249,506	2.2		
		Anson J. Streeter	Union Labor	146,935	1.3		

Year	Number of States	Candidates	Parties	Popular Vote	% of Popular Vote	Electoral Vote	% Voter Participation
1892	44	**GROVER CLEVELAND**	Democratic	5,555,426	46.1	277	74.7
		Benjamin Harrison	Republican	5,182,690	43.0	145	
		James B. Weaver	People's	1,029,846	8.5	22	
		John Bidwell	Prohibition	264,133	2.2		
1896	45	**WILLIAM MCKINLEY**	Republican	7,102,246	51.1	271	79.3
		William J. Bryan	Democratic	6,492,559	47.7	176	
1900	45	**WILLIAM MCKINLEY**	Republican	7,218,491	51.7	292	73.2
		William J. Bryan	Democratic; Populist	6,356,734	45.5	155	
		John C. Wooley	Prohibition	208,914	1.5		
1904	45	**THEODORE ROOSEVELT**	Republican	7,628,461	57.4	336	65.2
		Alton B. Parker	Democratic	5,084,223	37.6	140	
		Eugene V. Debs	Socialist	402,283	3.0		
		Silas C. Swallow	Prohibition	258,536	1.9		
1908	46	**WILLIAM H. TAFT**	Republican	7,675,320	51.6	321	65.4
		William J. Bryan	Democratic	6,412,294	43.1	162	
		Eugene V. Debs	Socialist	420,793	2.8		
		Eugene W. Chafin	Prohibition	253,840	1.7		
1912	48	**WOODROW WILSON**	Democratic	6,296,547	41.9	435	58.8
		Theodore Roosevelt	Progressive	4,118,571	27.4	88	
		William H. Taft	Republican	3,486,720	23.2	8	
		Eugene V. Debs	Socialist	900,672	6.0		
		Eugene W. Chafin	Prohibition	206,275	1.4		

Year	Number of States	Candidates	Parties	Popular Vote	% of Popular Vote	Electoral Vote	% Voter Participation
1916	48	**WOODROW WILSON**	Democratic	9,127,695	49.4	277	61.6
		Charles E. Hughes	Republican	8,533,507	46.2	254	
		A. L. Benson	Socialist	585,113	3.2		
		J. Frank Hanly	Prohibition	220,506	1.2		
1920	48	**WARREN G. HARDING**	Republican	16,143,407	60.4	404	49.2
		James M. Cox	Democratic	9,130,328	34.2	127	
		Eugene V. Debs	Socialist	919,799	3.4		
		P. P. Christensen	Farmer-Labor	265,411	1.0		
1924	48	**CALVIN COOLIDGE**	Republican	15,718,211	54.0	382	48.9
		John W. Davis	Democratic	8,385,283	28.8	136	
		Robert M. La Follette	Progressive	4,831,289	16.6	13	
1928	48	**HERBERT C. HOOVER**	Republican	21,391,993	58.2	444	56.9
		Alfred E. Smith	Democratic	15,016,169	40.9	87	
1932	48	**FRANKLIN D. ROOSEVELT**	Democratic	22,809,638	57.4	472	56.9
		Herbert C. Hoover	Republican	15,758,901	39.7	59	
		Norman Thomas	Socialist	881,951	2.2		
1936	48	**FRANKLIN D. ROOSEVELT**	Democratic	27,752,869	60.8	523	61.0
		Alfred M. Landon	Republican	16,674,665	36.5	8	
		William Lemke	Union	882,479	1.9		
1940	48	**FRANKLIN D. ROOSEVELT**	Democratic	27,307,819	54.8	449	62.5
		Wendell L. Willkie	Republican	22,321,018	44.8	82	
1944	48	**FRANKLIN D. ROOSEVELT**	Democratic	25,606,585	53.5	432	55.9
		Thomas E. Dewey	Republican	22,014,745	46.0	99	

Year	Number of States	Candidates	Parties	Popular Vote	% of Popular Vote	Electoral Vote	% Voter Participation
1948	48	HARRY S. TRUMAN	Democratic	24,179,345	49.6	303	53.0
		Thomas E. Dewey	Republican	21,991,291	45.1	189	
		J. Strom Thurmond	States' Rights	1,176,125	2.4	39	
		Henry A. Wallace	Progressive	1,157,326	2.4		
1952	48	DWIGHT D. EISENHOWER	Republican	33,936,234	55.1	442	63.3
		Adlai E. Stevenson	Democratic	27,314,992	44.4	89	
1956	48	DWIGHT D. EISENHOWER	Republican	35,590,472	57.6	457	60.6
		Adlai E. Stevenson	Democratic	26,022,752	42.1	73	
1960	50	JOHN F. KENNEDY	Democratic	34,226,731	49.7	303	62.8
		Richard M. Nixon	Republican	34,108,157	49.5	219	
1964	50	LYNDON B. JOHNSON	Democratic	43,129,566	61.1	486	61.9
		Barry M. Goldwater	Republican	27,178,188	38.5	52	
1968	50	RICHARD M. NIXON	Republican	31,785,480	43.4	301	60.9
		Hubert H. Humphrey	Democratic	31,275,166	42.7	191	
		George C. Wallace	American Independent	9,906,473	13.5	46	
1972	50	RICHARD M. NIXON	Republican	47,169,911	60.7	520	55.2
		George S. McGovern	Democratic	29,170,383	37.5	17	
		John G. Schmitz	American	1,099,482	1.4		

Year	Number of States	Candidates	Parties	Popular Vote	% of Popular Vote	Electoral Vote	% Voter Participation
1976	50	**JIMMY CARTER**	Democratic	40,830,763	50.1	297	53.5
		Gerald R. Ford	Republican	39,147,793	48.0	240	
1980	50	**RONALD REAGAN**	Republican	43,901,812	50.7	489	52.6
		Jimmy Carter	Democratic	35,483,820	41.0	49	
		John B. Anderson	Independent	5,719,437	6.6		
		Ed Clark	Libertarian	921,188	1.1		
1984	50	**RONALD REAGAN**	Republican	54,451,521	58.8	525	53.1
		Walter F. Mondale	Democratic	37,565,334	40.6	13	
1988	50	**GEORGE H. W. BUSH**	Republican	47,917,341	53.4	426	50.1
		Michael Dukakis	Democratic	41,013,030	45.6	111	
1992	50	**BILL CLINTON**	Democratic	44,908,254	43.0	370	55.0
		George H. W. Bush	Republican	39,102,343	37.4	168	
		H. Ross Perot	Independent	19,741,065	18.9		
1996	50	**BILL CLINTON**	Democratic	47,401,185	49.0	379	49.0
		Bob Dole	Republican	39,197,469	41.0	159	
		H. Ross Perot	Independent	8,085,295	8.0		
2000	50	**GEORGE W. BUSH**	Republican	50,455,156	47.9	271	50.4
		Al Gore	Democrat	50,997,335	48.4	266	
		Ralph Nader	Green	2,882,897	2.7		
2004	50	**GEORGE W. BUSH**	Republican	62,040,610	50.7	286	60.7
		John F. Kerry	Democrat	59,028,444	48.3	251	
2008	50	**BARACK OBAMA**	Democrat	69,456,897	52.92%	365	63.0
		John McCain	Republican	59,934,814	45.66%	173	

Candidates receiving less than 1 percent of the popular vote have been omitted. Thus the percentage of popular vote given for any election year may not total 100 percent.

Before the passage of the Twelfth Amendment in 1804, the electoral college voted for two presidential candidates; the runner-up became vice president.

ADMISSION OF STATES

Order of Admission	State	Date of Admission
1	Delaware	December 7, 1787
2	Pennsylvania	December 12, 1787
3	New Jersey	December 18, 1787
4	Georgia	January 2, 1788
5	Connecticut	January 9, 1788
6	Massachusetts	February 7, 1788
7	Maryland	April 28, 1788
8	South Carolina	May 23, 1788
9	New Hampshire	June 21, 1788
10	Virginia	June 25, 1788
11	New York	July 26, 1788
12	North Carolina	November 21, 1789
13	Rhode Island	May 29, 1790
14	Vermont	March 4, 1791
15	Kentucky	June 1, 1792
16	Tennessee	June 1, 1796
17	Ohio	March 1, 1803
18	Louisiana	April 30, 1812
19	Indiana	December 11, 1816
20	Mississippi	December 10, 1817
21	Illinois	December 3, 1818
22	Alabama	December 14, 1819
23	Maine	March 15, 1820
24	Missouri	August 10, 1821
25	Arkansas	June 15, 1836
26	Michigan	January 26, 1837
27	Florida	March 3, 1845
28	Texas	December 29, 1845
29	Iowa	December 28, 1846
30	Wisconsin	May 29, 1848
31	California	September 9, 1850
32	Minnesota	May 11, 1858
33	Oregon	February 14, 1859
34	Kansas	January 29, 1861
35	West Virginia	June 30, 1863
36	Nevada	October 31, 1864
37	Nebraska	March 1, 1867
38	Colorado	August 1, 1876
39	North Dakota	November 2, 1889
40	South Dakota	November 2, 1889
41	Montana	November 8, 1889
42	Washington	November 11, 1889
43	Idaho	July 3, 1890
44	Wyoming	July 10, 1890
45	Utah	January 4, 1896
46	Oklahoma	November 16, 1907
47	New Mexico	January 6, 1912
48	Arizona	February 14, 1912
49	Alaska	January 3, 1959
50	Hawaii	August 21, 1959

POPULATION OF THE UNITED STATES

Year	Number of States	Population	% Increase	Population per Square Mile
1790	13	3,929,214		4.5
1800	16	5,308,483	35.1	6.1
1810	17	7,239,881	36.4	4.3
1820	23	9,638,453	33.1	5.5
1830	24	12,866,020	33.5	7.4
1840	26	17,069,453	32.7	9.8
1850	31	23,191,876	35.9	7.9
1860	33	31,443,321	35.6	10.6
1870	37	39,818,449	26.6	13.4
1880	38	50,155,783	26.0	16.9
1890	44	62,947,714	25.5	21.1
1900	45	75,994,575	20.7	25.6
1910	46	91,972,266	21.0	31.0
1920	48	105,710,620	14.9	35.6
1930	48	122,775,046	16.1	41.2
1940	48	131,669,275	7.2	44.2
1950	48	150,697,361	14.5	50.7
1960	50	179,323,175	19.0	50.6
1970	50	203,235,298	13.3	57.5
1980	50	226,504,825	11.4	64.0
1985	50	237,839,000	5.0	67.2
1990	50	250,122,000	5.2	70.6
1995	50	263,411,707	5.3	74.4
2000	50	281,421,906	6.8	77.0
2008	50	304,059,724	8.0	79.6

IMMIGRATION TO THE UNITED STATES, FISCAL YEARS 1820–2008

Year	Number	Year	Number	Year	Number	Year	Number
1820–1989	55,457,531	1871–80	2,812,191	1921–30	4,107,209	1971–80	4,493,314
1820	8,385	1871	321,350	1921	805,228	1971	370,478
1821–30	143,439	1872	404,806	1922	309,556	1972	384,685
1821	9,127	1873	459,803	1923	522,919	1973	400,063
1822	6,911	1874	313,339	1924	706,896	1974	394,861
1823	6,354	1875	227,498	1925	294,314	1975	386,914
1824	7,912	1876	169,986	1926	304,488	1976	398,613
1825	10,199	1877	141,857	1927	335,175	1976	103,676
1826	10,837	1878	138,469	1928	307,255	1977	462,315
1827	18,875	1879	177,826	1929	279,678	1978	601,442
1828	27,382	1880	457,257	1930	241,700	1979	460,348
1829	22,520	1881–90	5,246,613	1931–40	528,431	1980	530,639
1830	23,322	1881	669,431	1931	97,139	1981–90	7,338,062
1831–40	599,125	1882	788,992	1932	35,576	1981	596,600
1831	22,633	1883	603,322	1933	23,068	1982	594,131
1832	60,482	1884	518,592	1934	29,470	1983	559,763
1833	58,640	1885	395,346	1935	34,956	1984	543,903
1834	65,365	1886	334,203	1936	36,329	1985	570,009
1835	45,374	1887	490,109	1937	50,244	1986	601,708
1836	76,242	1888	546,889	1938	67,895	1987	601,516
1837	79,340	1889	444,427	1939	82,998	1988	643,025
1838	38,914	1890	455,302	1940	70,756	1989	1,090,924
1839	68,069	1891–1900	3,687,564	1941–50	1,035,039	1990	1,536,483
1840	84,066	1891	560,319	1941	51,776	1991–2000	9,090,857
1841–50	1,713,251	1892	579,663	1942	28,781	1991	1,827,167
1841	80,289	1893	439,730	1943	23,725	1992	973,977
1842	104,565	1894	285,631	1944	28,551	1993	904,292
		1895	258,536	1945	38,119	1994	804,416
		1896	343,267	1946	108,721		

Year	Number	Year	Number	Year	Number	Year	Number
1843	52,496	1897	230,832	1947	147,292	1995	720,461
1844	78,615	1898	229,299	1948	170,570	1996	915,900
1845	114,371	1899	311,715	1949	188,317	1997	798,378
1846	154,416	1900	448,572	1950	249,187	1998	660,477
1847	234,968					1999	644,787
1848	226,527	**1901–10**	**8,795,386**	**1951–60**	**2,515,479**	2000	841,002
1849	297,024	1901	487,918	1951	205,717	**2001–8**	**8,330,011**
1850	369,980	1902	648,743	1952	265,520	2001	1,058,902
		1903	857,046	1953	170,434	2002	1,059,356
1851–60	**2,598,214**	1904	812,870	1954	208,177	2003	705,827
1851	379,466	1905	1,026,499	1955	237,790	2004	957,883
1852	371,603	1906	1,100,735	1956	321,625	2005	1,122,373
1853	368,645	1907	1,285,349	1957	326,867	2006	1,266,129
1854	427,833	1908	782,870	1958	253,265	2007	1,052,415
1855	200,877	1909	751,786	1959	260,686	2008	1,107,126
1856	200,436	1910	1,041,570	1960	265,398		
1857	251,306						
1858	123,126	**1911–20**	**5,735,811**	**1961–70**	**3,321,677**		
1859	121,282	1911	878,587	1961	271,344		
1860	153,640	1912	838,172	1962	283,763		
		1913	1,197,892	1963	306,260		
1861–70	**2,314,824**	1914	1,218,480	1964	292,248		
1861	91,918	1915	326,700	1965	296,697		
1862	91,985	1916	298,826	1966	323,040		
1863	176,282	1917	295,403	1967	361,972		
1864	193,418	1918	110,618	1968	454,448		
1865	248,120	1919	141,132	1969	358,579		
1866	318,568	1920	430,001	1970	373,326		
1867	315,722						
1868	138,840						
1869	352,768						
1870	387,203						

Source: U.S. Department of Homeland Security.

IMMIGRATION BY REGION AND SELECTED COUNTRY OF LAST RESIDENCE, FISCAL YEARS 1820–2008

Region and country of last residence	1820 to 1829	1830 to 1839	1840 to 1849	1850 to 1859	1860 to 1869	1870 to 1879	1880 to 1889	1890 to 1899
Total	128,502	538,381	1,427,337	2,814,554	2,081,261	2,742,137	5,248,568	3,694,294
Europe	99,272	422,771	1,369,259	2,619,680	1,877,726	2,251,878	4,638,677	3,576,411
Austria-Hungary	—	—	—	—	3,375	60,127	314,787	534,059
Austria	—	—	—	—	2,700	54,529	204,805	268,218
Hungary	—	—	—	—	483	5,598	109,982	203,350
Belgium	28	20	3,996	5,765	5,785	6,991	18,738	19,642
Bulgaria	—	—	—	—	—	—	—	52
Czechoslovakia	—	—	—	—	—	—	—	—
Denmark	173	927	671	3,227	13,553	29,278	85,342	56,671
Finland	—	—	—	—	—	—	—	—
France	7,694	39,330	75,300	81,778	35,938	71,901	48,193	35,616
Germany	5,753	124,726	385,434	976,072	723,734	751,769	1,445,181	579,072
Greece	17	49	17	32	51	209	1,807	12,732
Ireland	51,617	170,672	656,145	1,029,486	427,419	422,264	674,061	405,710
Italy	430	2,225	1,476	8,643	9,853	46,296	267,660	603,761
Netherlands	1,105	1,377	7,624	11,122	8,387	14,267	52,715	29,349
Norway-Sweden	91	1,149	12,389	22,202	82,937	178,823	586,441	334,058
Norway	—	—	—	—	16,068	88,644	185,111	96,810
Sweden	—	—	—	—	24,224	90,179	401,330	237,248
Poland	19	366	105	1,087	1,886	11,016	42,910	107,793
Portugal	177	820	196	1,299	2,083	13,971	15,186	25,874
Romania	—	—	—	—	—	—	5,842	6,808
Russia	86	280	520	423	1,670	35,177	182,698	450,101
Spain	2,595	2,010	1,916	8,795	6,966	5,540	3,995	9,189
Switzerland	3,148	4,430	4,819	24,423	21,124	25,212	81,151	37,020
United Kingdom	26,336	74,350	218,572	445,322	532,956	578,447	810,900	328,759
Yugoslavia	—	—	—	—	—	—	—	—
Other Europe	3	40	79	4	9	590	1,070	145

Asia	34	55	121	36,080	54,408	134,128	71,151	61,285
China	3	8	32	35,933	54,028	133,139	65,797	15,268
Hong Kong	9	38	33	42	50	166	247	102
India	—	—	—	—	—	—	—	102
Iran	—	—	—	—	—	—	—	—
Israel	—	—	—	—	—	—	—	—
Japan	—	—	—	—	138	193	1,583	13,998
Jordan	—	—	—	—	—	—	—	—
Korea	—	—	—	—	—	—	—	—
Philippines	—	—	—	—	—	—	—	—
Syria	—	—	—	—	—	—	—	—
Taiwan	—	—	—	—	—	—	—	—
Turkey	19	8	45	94	129	382	2,478	27,510
Vietnam	—	—	—	—	—	—	—	—
Other Asia	3	1	11	11	63	248	1,046	4,407
America	9,655	31,905	50,516	84,145	130,292	345,010	524,826	37,350
Canada and Newfoundland	2,297	11,875	34,285	64,171	117,978	324,310	492,865	3,098
Mexico	3,835	7,187	3,069	3,446	1,957	5,133	2,405	734
Caribbean	3,061	11,792	11,803	12,447	8,751	14,285	27,323	31,480
Cuba	—	—	—	—	—	—	—	—
Dominican Republic	—	—	—	—	—	—	—	—
Haiti	—	—	—	—	—	—	—	—
Jamaica	—	—	—	—	—	—	—	—
Other Caribbean	3,061	11,792	11,803	12,447	8,751	14,285	27,323	31,480
Central America	57	94	297	512	70	173	279	649
Belize	—	—	—	—	—	—	—	—
Costa Rica	—	—	—	—	—	—	—	—
El Salvador	—	—	—	—	—	—	—	—
Guatemala	—	—	—	—	—	—	—	—
Honduras	—	—	—	—	—	—	—	—
Nicaragua	—	—	—	—	—	—	—	—
Panama	—	—	—	—	—	—	—	—
Other Central America	57	94	297	512	70	173	279	649
South America	405	957	1,062	3,569	1,536	1,109	1,954	1,389
Argentina	—	—	—	—	—	—	—	—
Bolivia	—	—	—	—	—	—	—	—

Region and country of last residence	1820 to 1829	1830 to 1839	1840 to 1849	1850 to 1859	1860 to 1869	1870 to 1879	1880 to 1889	1890 to 1899
Brazil	—	—	—	—	—	—	—	—
Chile	—	—	—	—	—	—	—	—
Colombia	—	—	—	—	—	—	—	—
Ecuador	—	—	—	—	—	—	—	—
Guyana	—	—	—	—	—	—	—	—
Paraguay	—	—	—	—	—	—	—	—
Peru	—	—	—	—	—	—	—	—
Suriname	—	—	—	—	—	—	—	—
Uruguay	—	—	—	—	—	—	—	—
Venezuela	—	—	—	—	—	—	—	—
Other South America	405	957	1,062	3,569	1,536	1,109	1,954	1,389
Other America	—	—	—	—	—	—	—	—
Africa	15	50	61	84	407	371	763	432
Egypt	—	—	—	—	4	29	145	51
Ethiopia	—	—	—	—	—	—	—	—
Liberia	1	8	5	7	43	52	21	9
Morocco	—	—	—	—	—	—	—	—
South Africa	—	—	—	—	35	48	23	9
Other Africa	14	42	56	77	325	242	574	363
Oceania	3	7	14	166	187	9,996	12,361	4,704
Australia	2	1	2	15	—	8,930	7,250	3,098
New Zealand	—	—	—	—	—	39	21	12
Other Oceania	1	6	12	151	187	1,027	5,090	1,594
Not Specified	19,523	83,593	7,366	74,399	18,241	754	790	14,112

Total	8,202,388	6,347,380	4,295,510	699,375	856,608	2,499,268	3,213,749	6,244,379
Europe	7,572,569	4,985,411	2,560,340	444,399	472,524	1,404,973	1,133,443	668,866
Austria-Hungary	2,001,376	1,154,727	60,891	12,531	13,574	113,015	27,590	20,437
Austria	532,416	589,174	31,392	5,307	8,393	81,354	17,571	15,374
Hungary	685,567	565,553	29,499	7,224	5,181	31,661	10,019	5,063
Belgium	37,429	32,574	21,511	4,013	12,473	18,885	9,647	7,028
Bulgaria	34,651	27,180	2,824	1,062	449	97	598	1,124
Czechoslovakia	—	—	101,182	17,757	8,475	1,624	2,758	5,678
Denmark	61,227	45,830	34,406	3,470	4,549	10,918	9,797	4,847
Finland	—	—	16,922	2,438	2,230	4,923	4,310	2,569
France	67,735	60,335	54,842	13,761	36,954	50,113	46,975	32,066
Germany	328,722	174,227	386,634	119,107	119,506	576,905	209,616	85,752
Greece	145,402	198,108	60,774	10,599	8,605	45,153	74,173	37,729
Ireland	344,940	166,445	202,854	28,195	15,701	47,189	37,788	22,210
Italy	1,930,475	1,229,916	528,133	85,053	50,509	184,576	200,111	55,562
Netherlands	42,463	46,065	29,397	7,791	13,877	46,703	37,918	11,234
Norway-Sweden	426,981	192,445	170,329	13,452	17,326	44,224	36,150	13,941
Norway	182,542	79,488	70,327	6,901	8,326	22,806	17,371	3,835
Sweden	244,439	112,957	100,002	6,551	9,000	21,418	18,779	10,106
Poland	—	—	223,316	25,555	7,577	6,465	55,742	63,483
Portugal	65,154	82,489	44,829	3,518	6,765	13,928	70,568	42,685
Romania	57,322	13,566	67,810	5,264	1,254	914	2,339	24,753
Russia	1,501,301	1,106,998	61,604	2,463	605	453	2,329	33,311
Spain	24,818	53,262	47,109	3,669	2,774	6,880	40,793	22,783
Switzerland	32,541	22,839	31,772	5,990	9,904	17,577	19,193	8,316
United Kingdom	469,518	371,878	341,552	61,813	131,794	195,709	220,213	153,644
Yugoslavia	—	—	49,215	6,920	2,039	6,966	17,990	16,267
Other Europe	514	6,527	22,434	9,978	5,584	11,756	6,845	3,447
Asia	299,836	269,736	126,740	19,231	34,532	135,844	358,605	2,391,356
China	19,884	20,916	30,648	5,874	16,072	8,836	14,060	170,897
Hong Kong	—	—	—	—		13,781	67,047	112,132
India	3,026	3,478	2,076	554	1,692	1,850	18,638	231,649
Iran	—	—	208	198	1,144	3,195	9,059	98,141
Israel	—	—	—	—	98	21,376	30,911	43,669

Region and country of last residence	1900 to 1909	1910 to 1919	1920 to 1929	1930 to 1939	1940 to 1949	1950 to 1959	1960 to 1969	1980 to 1989
Japan	139,712	77,125	42,057	2,683	1,557	40,651	40,956	44,150
Jordan	—	—	—	—	—	4,899	9,230	28,928
Korea	—	—	—	—	83	4,845	27,048	322,708
Philippines	—	—	—	391	4,099	17,245	70,660	502,056
Syria	—	—	5,307	2,188	1,179	1,091	2,432	14,534
Taiwan	—	—	—	—	—	721	15,657	119,051
Turkey	127,999	160,717	40,450	1,327	754	2,980	9,464	19,208
Vietnam	—	—	—	—	—	290	2,949	200,632
Other Asia	9,215	7,500	5,994	6,016	7,854	14,084	40,494	483,601
America	277,809	1,070,539	1,591,278	230,319	328,435	921,610	1,674,172	2,695,329
Canada and Newfoundland	123,067	708,715	949,286	162,703	160,911	353,169	433,128	156,313
Mexico	31,188	185,334	498,945	32,709	56,158	273,847	441,824	1,009,586
Caribbean	100,960	120,860	83,482	18,052	46,194	115,661	427,235	790,109
Cuba	—	—	12,769	10,641	25,976	73,221	202,030	132,552
Dominican Republic	—	—	—	1,026	4,802	10,219	83,552	221,552
Haiti	—	—	—	156	823	3,787	28,992	121,406
Jamaica	—	—	—	—	—	7,397	62,218	193,874
Other Caribbean	100,960	120,860	70,713	6,229	14,593	21,037	50,443	120,725
Central America	7,341	15,692	16,511	6,840	20,135	40,201	98,560	339,376
Belize	77	40	285	193	433	1,133	4,185	14,964
Costa Rica	—	—	—	431	1,965	4,044	17,975	25,017
El Salvador	—	—	—	597	4,885	5,094	14,405	137,418
Guatemala	—	—	—	423	1,303	4,197	14,357	58,847
Honduras	—	—	—	679	1,874	5,320	15,078	39,071
Nicaragua	—	—	—	405	4,393	7,812	10,383	31,102
Panama	—	—	—	1,452	5,282	12,601	22,177	32,957
Other Central America	7,264	15,652	16,226	2,660	—	—	—	—

South America	15,253	39,938	43,025	9,990	19,662	78,418	250,754	399,862
Argentina	—	—	—	1,067	3,108	16,346	49,384	23,442
Bolivia	—	—	—	50	893	2,759	6,205	9,798
Brazil	—	—	4,627	1,468	3,653	11,547	29,238	22,944
Chile	—	—	—	347	1,320	4,669	12,384	19,749
Colombia	—	—	—	1,027	3,454	15,567	68,371	105,494
Ecuador	—	—	—	244	2,207	8,574	34,107	48,015
Guyana	—	—	—	131	596	1,131	4,546	85,886
Paraguay	—	—	—	33	85	576	1,249	3,518
Peru	—	—	—	321	1,273	5,980	19,783	49,958
Suriname	—	—	—	25	130	299	612	1,357
Uruguay	—	—	—	112	754	1,026	4,089	7,235
Venezuela	—	—	—	1,155	2,182	9,927	20,758	22,405
Other South America	15,253	39,938	38,398	4,010	7	17	28	61
Other America	—	—	29	25	25,375	60,314	22,671	83
Africa	6,326	8,867	6,362	2,120	6,720	13,016	23,780	141,990
Egypt	—	—	1,063	781	1,613	1,996	5,581	26,744
Ethiopia	—	—	—	10	28	302	804	12,927
Liberia	—	—	—	35	37	289	841	6,420
Morocco	—	—	—	73	879	2,703	2,880	3,471
South Africa	6,326	8,867	5,299	312	1,022	2,278	4,360	15,505
Other Africa	—	—	—	909	3,141	5,448	9,314	76,923
Oceania	12,355	12,339	9,860	3,306	14,262	11,353	23,630	41,432
Australia	11,191	11,280	8,404	2,260	11,201	8,275	14,986	16,901
New Zealand	—	—	935	790	2,351	1,799	3,775	6,129
Other Oceania	1,164	1,059	521	256	710	1,279	4,869	18,402
Not Specified	33,493	488	930	—	135	12,472	119	305,406

Region and country of last residence	1990 to 1999	2000	2001	2002	2003	2004	2005	2006	2007	2008
Total	9,775,398	841,002	1,058,902	1,059,356	703,542	957,883	1,122,257	1,266,129	1,052,415	1,107,126
Europe	1,348,612	131,920	176,892	177,059	102,546	135,663	180,396	169,156	120,759	121,146
Austria-Hungary	27,529	2,009	2,303	4,004	2,176	3,689	4,569	2,991	2,057	2,576
Austria	18,234	986	996	2,650	1,160	2,442	3,002	1,301	849	1,505
Hungary	9,295	1,023	1,307	1,354	1,016	1,247	1,567	1,690	1,208	1,071
Belgium	7,077	817	997	834	515	746	1,031	891	733	829
Bulgaria	16,948	4,779	4,273	3,476	3,706	4,042	5,451	4,690	3,766	2,805
Czechoslovakia	8,970	1,407	1,911	1,854	1,472	1,871	2,182	2,844	1,851	1,650
Denmark	6,189	549	732	651	435	568	714	738	505	551
Finland	3,970	377	497	365	230	346	549	513	385	287
France	35,945	4,063	5,379	4,567	2,926	4,209	5,035	4,945	3,680	5,246
Germany	92,207	12,230	21,992	20,977	8,061	10,270	12,864	10,271	8,640	8,456
Greece	25,403	5,113	1,941	1,486	900	1,213	1,473	1,544	1,152	943
Ireland	65,384	1,264	1,531	1,400	1,002	1,518	2,083	2,038	1,599	1,499
Italy	75,992	2,652	3,332	2,812	1,890	2,495	3,179	3,406	2,682	2,738
Netherlands	13,345	1,455	1,888	2,296	1,321	1,713	2,150	1,928	1,482	1,423
Norway-Sweden	17,825	1,967	2,544	2,082	1,516	2,011	2,264	2,111	1,604	1,557
Norway	5,211	508	582	460	385	457	472	532	388	386
Sweden	12,614	1,459	1,962	1,622	1,131	1,554	1,792	1,579	1,216	1,171
Poland	172,249	9,750	12,308	13,274	11,004	14,048	14,836	16,704	9,717	7,896
Portugal	25,497	1,373	1,611	1,301	808	1,062	1,084	1,439	1,054	781
Romania	48,136	6,506	6,206	4,515	3,305	4,078	6,431	6,753	5,240	4,563
Russia	433,427	43,156	54,838	55,370	33,513	41,959	60,344	59,720	41,593	45,092
Spain	18,443	1,390	1,875	1,588	1,102	1,453	2,002	2,387	1,810	1,970
Switzerland	11,768	1,339	1,786	1,493	862	1,193	1,465	1,199	885	936
United Kingdom	156,182	14,427	20,118	17,940	11,155	16,680	21,956	19,984	16,113	16,189
Yugoslavia	57,039	11,960	21,854	28,051	8,270	13,213	19,249	11,066	6,364	5,812
Other Europe	29,087	3,337	6,976	6,723	6,377	7,286	9,485	10,994	7,847	7,347

Asia	2,859,899	254,932	336,112	325,749	235,339	319,025	382,707	411,746	359,387	369,339
China	342,058	41,804	50,677	55,901	37,342	50,280	64,887	83,590	70,924	75,410
Hong Kong	116,894	7,181	10,282	7,938	5,015	5,421	5,004	4,514	4,450	4,389
India	352,528	38,938	65,673	66,644	47,032	65,507	79,139	58,072	55,371	59,728
Iran	76,899	6,481	8,003	7,684	4,696	5,898	7,306	9,829	8,098	9,920
Israel	41,340	3,871	4,892	4,907	3,686	5,206	6,963	6,667	4,999	6,682
Japan	66,582	7,688	10,424	9,106	6,702	8,655	9,929	9,107	7,213	7,510
Jordan	42,755	4,476	5,106	4,774	4,008	5,186	5,430	5,512	5,516	5,692
Korea	179,770	15,107	19,728	19,917	12,076	19,441	26,002	24,472	21,278	26,155
Philippines	534,338	40,465	50,644	48,493	43,133	54,651	57,654	71,133	68,792	52,391
Syria	22,906	2,255	3,542	3,350	2,046	2,549	3,350	3,080	2,550	3,310
Taiwan	132,647	9,457	12,457	9,932	7,168	9,314	9,389	8,545	9,053	9,237
Turkey	38,687	2,702	3,463	3,914	3,318	4,491	6,449	6,433	4,728	4,953
Vietnam	275,379	25,159	34,537	32,372	21,227	30,074	30,832	29,701	27,510	29,807
Other Asia	637,116	49,348	56,684	50,817	37,890	52,352	70,373	91,091	68,905	74,155
America	5,137,743	392,461	470,794	477,363	305,936	408,972	432,726	548,812	434,272	491,045
Canada and Newfoundland	194,788	21,289	29,991	27,142	16,447	22,439	29,930	23,913	20,324	22,366
Mexico	2,757,418	171,445	204,032	216,924	114,758	173,711	157,992	170,042	143,180	188,015
Caribbean	1,004,687	84,250	96,384	93,914	67,498	82,116	91,371	144,477	114,318	134,744
Cuba	159,037	17,897	25,832	27,435	8,685	15,385	20,651	44,248	25,441	48,057
Dominican Republic	359,818	17,373	21,139	22,386	26,112	30,063	27,365	37,997	27,875	31,801
Haiti	177,446	21,977	22,470	19,151	11,924	13,695	13,491	21,625	29,978	25,522
Jamaica	177,143	15,603	15,031	14,507	13,045	13,581	17,774	24,538	18,873	18,077
Other Caribbean	181,243	11,400	11,912	10,435	7,732	9,392	12,090	16,069	12,151	11,287
Central America	610,189	60,331	72,504	66,298	53,283	61,253	52,629	74,244	53,834	49,741
Belize	12,600	774	982	983	616	888	901	1,263	1,089	1,113
Costa Rica	17,054	1,390	1,863	1,686	1,322	1,811	2,479	3,459	2,722	2,287
El Salvador	273,017	22,301	30,876	30,472	27,854	29,297	20,891	31,258	20,009	18,937
Guatemala	126,043	9,861	13,399	15,870	14,195	18,655	16,466	23,674	17,198	15,791
Honduras	72,880	5,851	6,546	6,355	4,582	5,339	6,825	8,036	7,300	6,389

Region and country of last residence	1990 to 1999	2000	2001	2002	2003	2004	2005	2006	2007	2008
Nicaragua	80,446	18,258	16,908	9,171	3,503	3,842	3,196	4,035	3,587	3,486
Panama	28,149	1,896	1,930	1,761	1,211	1,421	1,869	2,519	1,929	1,738
Other Central America	—	—	—	—	—	—	—	—	—	—
South America	570,624	55,143	67,880	73,082	53,946	69,452	100,803	136,134	102,616	96,178
Argentina	30,065	2,472	3,426	3,791	3,193	4,672	6,945	7,239	5,375	5,170
Bolivia	18,111	1,744	1,804	1,660	1,365	1,719	2,164	4,000	2,326	2,350
Brazil	50,744	6,767	9,391	9,034	6,108	10,247	16,329	17,741	13,546	11,813
Chile	18,200	1,660	1,881	1,766	1,255	1,719	2,354	2,727	2,202	1,988
Colombia	137,985	14,125	16,234	18,409	14,400	18,055	24,705	42,017	32,055	29,349
Ecuador	81,358	7,624	9,654	10,524	7,022	8,366	11,528	17,624	12,011	11,541
Guyana	74,407	5,255	7,835	9,492	6,373	5,721	8,771	9,010	5,288	6,302
Paraguay	6,082	394	464	413	222	324	523	725	518	489
Peru	110,117	9,361	10,838	11,737	9,169	11,369	15,205	21,300	17,056	14,873
Suriname	2,285	281	254	223	175	170	287	341	193	225
Uruguay	6,062	396	516	499	470	750	1,110	1,639	1,340	1,380
Venezuela	35,180	5,052	5,576	5,529	4,190	6,335	10,870	11,758	10,696	10,689
Other South America	28	12	7	5	4	5	12	13	10	9
Other America	37	3	3	3	4	1	1	2	—	1
Africa	346,416	40,790	50,009	56,002	45,559	62,623	79,697	112,100	89,277	100,881
Egypt	44,604	4,323	5,333	6,215	3,928	6,590	10,296	13,163	10,178	10,728
Ethiopia	40,097	3,645	4,620	6,308	5,969	7,180	8,378	13,390	11,340	11,703
Liberia	13,587	1,225	1,477	1,467	1,081	1,540	1,846	3,736	3,771	3,478
Morocco	15,768	3,423	4,752	3,188	2,969	3,910	4,165	4,704	4,311	4,187
South Africa	21,964	2,814	4,046	3,685	2,088	3,335	4,425	3,173	2,842	2,638
Other Africa	210,396	25,360	29,781	35,139	29,524	40,068	50,587	73,934	56,835	68,147
Oceania	56,800	5,928	7,201	6,495	5,076	6,954	7,432	8,000	6,639	5,926
Australia	24,288	2,694	3,714	3,420	2,488	3,397	4,090	3,770	3,026	3,031
New Zealand	8,600	1,080	1,347	1,364	1,030	1,420	1,457	1,344	1,234	1,092
Other Oceania	23,912	2,154	2,140	1,711	1,558	2,137	1,885	2,886	2,379	1,803
Not Specified	25,928	14,971	17,894	16,688	9,086	24,646	39,299	16,315	42,081	18,789

— Represents zero or not available.

PRESIDENTS, VICE PRESIDENTS, AND SECRETARIES OF STATE

	President	*Vice President*	*Secretary of State*
1.	George Washington, Federalist 1789	John Adams, Federalist 1789	Thomas Jefferson 1789 Edmund Randolph 1794 Timothy Pickering 1795
2.	John Adams, Federalist 1797	Thomas Jefferson, Dem.-Rep. 1797	Timothy Pickering 1797 John Marshall 1800
3.	Thomas Jefferson, Dem.-Rep. 1801	Aaron Burr, Dem.-Rep. 1801 George Clinton, Dem.-Rep. 1805	James Madison 1801
4.	James Madison, Dem.-Rep. 1809	George Clinton, Dem.-Rep. 1809 Elbridge Gerry, Dem.-Rep. 1813	Robert Smith 1809 James Monroe 1811
5.	James Monroe, Dem.-Rep. 1817	Daniel D. Tompkins, Dem.-Rep. 1817	John Q. Adams 1817
6.	John Quincy Adams, Dem.-Rep. 1825	John C. Calhoun, Dem.-Rep. 1825	Henry Clay 1825
7.	Andrew Jackson, Democratic 1829	John C. Calhoun, Democratic 1829 Martin Van Buren, Democratic 1833	Martin Van Buren 1829 Edward Livingston 1831 Louis McLane 1833 John Forsyth 1834
8.	Martin Van Buren, Democratic 1837	Richard M. Johnson, Democratic 1837	John Forsyth 1837
9.	William H. Harrison, Whig 1841	John Tyler, Whig 1841	Daniel Webster 1841

	President	Vice President	Secretary of State
10.	John Tyler, Whig and Democratic 1841	None	Daniel Webster 1841 Hugh S. Legaré 1843 Abel P. Upshur 1843 John C. Calhoun 1844
11.	James K. Polk, Democratic 1845	George M. Dallas, Democratic 1845	James Buchanan 1845
12.	Zachary Taylor, Whig 1849	Millard Fillmore, Whig 1848	John M. Clayton 1849
13.	Millard Fillmore, Whig 1850	None	Daniel Webster 1850 Edward Everett 1852
14.	Franklin Pierce, Democratic 1853	William R. King, Democratic 1853	William L. Marcy 1853
15.	James Buchanan, Democratic 1857	John C. Breckinridge, Democratic 1857	Lewis Cass 1857 Jeremiah S. Black 1860
16.	Abraham Lincoln, Republican 1861	Hannibal Hamlin, Republican 1861 Andrew Johnson, Unionist 1865	William H. Seward 1861
17.	Andrew Johnson, Unionist 1865	None	William H. Seward 1865
18.	Ulysses S. Grant, Republican 1869	Schuyler Colfax, Republican 1869 Henry Wilson, Republican 1873	Elihu B. Washburne 1869 Hamilton Fish 1869
19.	Rutherford B. Hayes, Republican 1877	William A. Wheeler, Republican 1877	William M. Evarts 1877

	President	Vice President	Secretary of State
20.	James A. Garfield, Republican 1881	Chester A. Arthur, Republican 1881	James G. Blaine 1881
21.	Chester A. Arthur, Republican 1881	None	Frederick T. Frelinghuysen 1881
22.	Grover Cleveland, Democratic 1885	Thomas A. Hendricks, Democratic 1885	Thomas F. Bayard 1885
23.	Benjamin Harrison, Republican 1889	Levi P. Morton, Republican 1889	James G. Blaine 1889 John W. Foster 1892
24.	Grover Cleveland, Democratic 1893	Adlai E. Stevenson, Democratic 1893	Walter Q. Gresham 1893 Richard Olney 1895
25.	William McKinley, Republican 1897	Garret A. Hobart, Republican 1897 Theodore Roosevelt, Republican 1901	John Sherman 1897 William R. Day 1898 John Hay 1898
26.	Theodore Roosevelt, Republican 1901	Charles Fairbanks, Republican 1905	John Hay 1901 Elihu Root 1905 Robert Bacon 1909
27.	William H. Taft, Republican 1909	James S. Sherman, Republican 1909	Philander C. Knox 1909
28.	Woodrow Wilson, Democratic 1913	Thomas R. Marshall, Democratic 1913	William J. Bryan 1913 Robert Lansing 1915 Bainbridge Colby 1920
29.	Warren G. Harding, Republican 1921	Calvin Coolidge, Republican 1921	Charles E. Hughes 1921
30.	Calvin Coolidge, Republican 1923	Charles G. Dawes, Republican 1925	Charles E. Hughes 1923 Frank B. Kellogg 1925

	President	Vice President	Secretary of State
31.	Herbert Hoover, Republican 1929	Charles Curtis, Republican 1929	Henry L. Stimson 1929
32.	Franklin D. Roosevelt, Democratic 1933	John Nance Garner, Democratic 1933 Henry A. Wallace, Democratic 1941 Harry S. Truman, Democratic 1945	Cordell Hull 1933 Edward R. Stettinius, Jr. 1944
33.	Harry S. Truman, Democratic 1945	Alben W. Barkley, Democratic 1949	Edward R. Stettinius, Jr. 1945 James F. Byrnes 1945 George C. Marshall 1947 Dean G. Acheson 1949
34.	Dwight D. Eisenhower, Republican 1953	Richard M. Nixon, Republican 1953	John F. Dulles 1953 Christian A. Herter 1959
35.	John F. Kennedy, Democratic 1961	Lyndon B. Johnson, Democratic 1961	Dean Rusk 1961
36.	Lyndon B. Johnson, Democratic 1963	Hubert H. Humphrey, Democratic 1965	Dean Rusk 1963
37.	Richard M. Nixon, Republican 1969	Spiro T. Agnew, Republican 1969 Gerald R. Ford, Republican 1973	William P. Rogers 1969 Henry Kissinger 1973
38.	Gerald R. Ford, Republican 1974	Nelson Rockefeller, Republican 1974	Henry Kissinger 1974
39.	Jimmy Carter, Democratic 1977	Walter Mondale, Democratic 1977	Cyrus Vance 1977 Edmund Muskie 1980

	President	Vice President	Secretary of State
40.	Ronald Reagan, Republican 1981	George H. W. Bush, Republican 1981	Alexander Haig 1981 George Schultz 1982
41.	George H. W. Bush, Republican 1989	J. Danforth Quayle, Republican 1989	James A. Baker 1989 Lawrence Eagleburger 1992
42.	William J. Clinton, Democratic 1993	Albert Gore, Jr., Democratic 1993	Warren Christopher 1993 Madeleine Albright 1997
43.	George W. Bush, Republican 2001	Richard B. Cheney, Republican 2001	Colin L. Powell 2001 Condoleezza Rice 2005
44.	Barack Obama, Democratic 2009	Joseph R. Biden, Democratic 2009	Hillary Rodham Clinton 2009

FURTHER READINGS

CHAPTER 18

The most comprehensive treatment of Reconstruction is Eric Foner's *Reconstruction: America's Unfinished Revolution, 1863–1877* (1988). On Andrew Johnson, see Hans L. Trefousse's *Andrew Johnson: A Biography* (1989). An excellent brief biography of Grant is Josiah Bunting III's *Ulysses S. Grant* (2004).

Scholars have been sympathetic to the aims and motives of the Radical Republicans. See, for instance, Herman Belz's *Reconstructing the Union: Theory and Policy during the Civil War* (1969) and Richard Nelson Current's *Those Terrible Carpetbaggers: A Reinterpretation* (1988). The ideology of the Radicals is explored in Michael Les Benedict's *A Compromise of Principle: Congressional Republicans and Reconstruction, 1863–1869* (1974). On the black political leaders, see Phillip Dray's *Capitol Men: The Epic Story of Reconstruction through the Lives of the First Black Congressmen* (2008).

The intransigence of southern white attitudes is examined in Michael Perman's *Reunion without Compromise: The South and Reconstruction, 1865–1868* (1973) and Dan T. Carter's *When the War Was Over: The Failure of Self-Reconstruction in the South, 1865–1867* (1985). Allen W. Trelease's *White Terror: The Ku Klux Klan Conspiracy and Southern Reconstruction* (1971) covers the various organizations that practiced vigilante tactics. On the massacre of African Americans, see Charles Lane's *The Day Freedom Died: The Colfax Massacre, the Supreme Court, and the Betrayal of Reconstruction* (2008). The difficulties former slaves had in adjusting to the new labor system are documented in James L. Roark's *Masters without Slaves: Southern Planters in the Civil War and Reconstruction* (1977). Books on southern politics during Reconstruction include Michael Perman's *The Road to Redemption: Southern Politics, 1869–1879* (1984), Terry L. Seip's *The South Returns to Congress: Men, Economic Measures, and Intersectional Relationships, 1868–1879* (1983), and Mark W. Summers's *Railroads, Reconstruction, and the Gospel of Prosperity: Aid under the Radical Republicans, 1865–1877* (1984).

Numerous works study the freed blacks' experience in the South. Start with Leon F. Litwack's *Been in the Storm So Long: The Aftermath of Slavery* (1979). Joel Williamson's *After Slavery: The Negro in South Carolina during Reconstruction, 1861–1877* (1965) argues that South Carolina blacks took an active role in pursuing their political and economic rights. The Freedmen's Bureau is explored in William S. McFeely's *Yankee Stepfather: General O. O. Howard and the Freedmen* (1968). The situation of freed slave women is discussed in Jacqueline Jones's *Labor of Love, Labor of Sorrow: Black Women, Work and the Family, from Slavery to the Present* (1985).

The politics of corruption outside the South is depicted in William S. McFeely's *Grant: A Biography* (1981). The political maneuvers of the election of 1876 and the resultant crisis and compromise are explained in C. Vann Woodward's *Reunion and Reaction: The Compromise of 1877 and the End of Reconstruction* (1951) and in William Gillette's *Retreat from Reconstruction, 1869–1879* (1979). The role of religion in determining the fate of Reconstruction is the focus of Edward J. Blum's *Reforging the White Republic: Race, Religion, and American Nationalism, 1865–1898* (2005).

CHAPTER 19

The classic study of the emergence of the New South remains C. Vann Woodward's *Origins of the New South, 1877–1913* (1951). A more recent treatment of southern society after the end of Reconstruction is Edward L. Ayers's *Southern Crossing: A History of the American South, 1877–1906* (1995). A good survey of industrialization in the South is James C. Cobb's *Industrialization and Southern Society, 1877–1984* (1984).

C. Vann Woodward's *The Strange Career of Jim Crow*, commemorative ed. (2002), remains the standard on southern race relations. Some of Woodward's points are challenged in Howard N. Rabinowitz's *Race Relations in the Urban South, 1865–1890* (1978). Leon F. Litwack's *Trouble in Mind: Black Southerners in the Age of Jim Crow* (1998) treats the rise of legal segregation, while Michael Perman's *Struggle for Mastery: Disfranchisement in the South, 1888–1908* (2001) surveys efforts to keep African Americans from voting. An award-winning study of white women and the race issue is Glenda Elizabeth Gilmore's *Gender and Jim Crow: Women and the Politics of White Supremacy in North Carolina, 1896–1920* (1996). On W. E. B. Du Bois, see David Levering Lewis's *W. E. B. Du Bois: Biography of a Race, 1868–1919* (1993).

For stimulating reinterpretations of the frontier and the development of the West, see William Cronon's *Nature's Metropolis: Chicago and the Great*

West (1991), Patricia Nelson Limerick's *The Legacy of Conquest: The Unbroken Past of the American West* (1987), Richard White's *"It's Your Misfortune and None of My Own": A New History of the American West* (1991), and Walter Nugent's *Into the West: The Story of Its People* (1999). An excellent overview is James M. McPherson's *Into the West: From Reconstruction to the Final Days of the American Frontier* (2006).

The role of African Americans in western settlement is the focus of William Loren Katz's *The Black West: A Documentary and Pictorial History of the African American Role in the Westward Expansion of the United States,* rev. ed. (2005), and Nell Irvin Painter's *Exodusters: Black Migration to Kansas after Reconstruction* (1977). The best account of the conflicts between Indians and whites is Robert M. Utley's *The Indian Frontier of the American West, 1846–1890* (1984). On Sitting Bull, see Utley's *The Lance and the Shield: The Life and Times of Sitting Bull* (1993). For a presentation of the Native American side of the story, see Peter Nabokov's *Native American Testimony: A Chronicle of Indian-White Relations from Prophecy to the Present, 1492–2000,* rev. ed. (1999). On the demise of the buffalo herds, see Andrew C. Isenberg's *The Destruction of the Bison: An Environmental History, 1750–1920* (2000).

CHAPTER 20

For masterly syntheses of post–Civil War industrial development, see Walter Licht's *Industrializing America: The Nineteenth Century* (1995) and Maury Klein's *The Genesis of Industrial America, 1870–1920* (2007). On the growth of railroads, see Albro Martin's *Railroad Triumphant: The Growth, Rejection, and Rebirth of a Vital American Force* (1992). A monumental study of the transcontinental railroad is David Haward Bain's *Empire Express: Building the First Transcontinental Railroad* (1999). On the 1877 railroad strike, see David O. Stowell's *Streets, Railroad, and the Great Strike of 1877* (1999).

On entrepreneurship in the iron and steel sector, and Thomas J. Misa's *A Nation of Steel: The Making of Modern America, 1865–1925* (1995). The best biographies of the leading business tycoons are Ron Chernow's *Titan: The Life of John D. Rockefeller, Sr.* (1998), David Nasaw's *Andrew Carnegie* (2006), and Jean Strouse's *Morgan: American Financier* (1999). Nathan Rosenberg's *Technology and American Economic Growth* (1972) documents the growth of invention during the period.

Much of the scholarship on labor stresses the traditional values and the culture of work that people brought to the factory, Hebert G. Gutman's *Work, Culture, and Society in Industrializing America: Essays in American*

Working-Class and Social History (1975) best introduces these themes. The leading survey remains David Montgomery's *The Fall of the House of Labor: The Workplace, the State, and American Labor Activism, 1865–1925* (1987).

For the role of women in the changing workplace, see Alice Kessler-Harris's *Out to Work: A History of Wage-Earning Women in the United States* (1982) and Susan E. Kennedy's *If All We Did Was to Weep at Home: A History of White Working-Class Women in American* (1979).

As for the labor unions, Gerald N. Grob's *Workers and Utopia: A Study of Ideological Conflict in the American Labor Movement, 1865–1900* (1961) examines the difference in outlook between the Knights of Labor and the American Federation of Labor. For the Knights, see Leon Fink's *Workingmen's Democracy: The Knights of Labor and American Politics* (1983). Also useful is Susan Levine's *Labor's True Woman: Carpet Weavers, Industrialization, and Labor Reform in the Gilded Age* (1984), on the role of women in the Knights. On Mother Jones, see Elliott J. Gorn's *Mother Jones: The Most Dangerous Woman in America* (2001). To trace the rise of socialism among organized workers, see Nick Salvatore's *Eugene V. Debs: Citizen and Socialist* (1982). The key strikes are discussed in Paul Arvich's *The Haymarket Tragedy* (1984) and Paul Krause's *The Battle for Homestead, 1880–1892: Politics, Culture, and Steel* (1992).

CHAPTER 21

For a survey of urbanization, see David R. Goldfield's *Urban America: A History*, 2nd ed. (1989). Gunther Barth discusses the emergence of a new urban culture in *City People: The Rise of Modern City Culture in Nineteenth-Century America* (1980). John Bodnar offers a synthesis of the urban immigrant experience in *The Transplanted: A History of Immigrants in Urban America* (1985). See also Roger Daniels's *Guarding the Golden Door: American Immigration Policy and Immigrants since 1882* (2004). Walter Nugent's *Crossings: The Great Transatlantic Migrations, 1870–1914* (1992) provides a wealth of demographic information and insight. Efforts to stop Chinese immigration are described in Erika Lee's *At America's Gates: Chinese Immigration during the Exclusion Era* (2003).

On urban environments and sanitary reforms, see Martin V. Melosi's *The Sanitary City: Urban Infrastructure in America from Colonial Times to the Present* (2000), Joel A. Tarr's *The Search for the Ultimate Sink: Urban Pollution in Historical Perspective* (1996), and Suellen Hoy's *Chasing Dirt: The American Pursuit of Cleanliness* (1995).

For the growth of urban leisure and sports, see Roy Rosenzweig's *Eight Hours for What We Will: Workers and Leisure in an Industrial City, 1870–1920* (1983) and Steven A. Riess's *City Games: The Evolution of American Urban Society and the Rise of Sports* (1989). Saloon culture is examined in Madelon Powers's *Faces along the Bar: Lore and Order in the Workingman's Saloon, 1870–1920* (1998).

Richard Hofstadter's *Social Darwinism in American Thought*, rev. ed. (1969), and Cynthia Eagle Russett's *Darwin in America: The Intellectual Response, 1865–1912* (1976) examine the impact of the theory of evolution. On the rise of realism in thought and the arts during the second half of the nineteenth century, see David E. Shi's *Facing Facts: Realism in American Thought and Culture, 1850–1920* (1995). Pragmatism is the focus of Louis Menand's *The Metaphysical Club: A Story of Ideas in America* (2001).

Eleanor Flexner and Ellen Fitzpatrick's *Century of Struggle: The Woman's Rights Movement in the United States,* enl. ed. (1996), surveys the condition of women in the late nineteenth century. The best study of the settlement house movement is Jean Bethke Elshtain's *Jane Addams and the Dream of American Democracy: A Life* (2002).

CHAPTER 22

A good overview of the Gilded Age is Vincent P. De Santis's *The Shaping of Modern America, 1877–1916* (1973). Nell Irvin Painter's *Standing at Armageddon: The United States, 1877–1919* (1987) focuses on the experience of the working class. For a stimulating overview of the political, social, and economic trends during the Gilded Age, see Jack Beatty's *Age of Betrayal: The Triumph of Money in America, 1865–1900* (2007). On the development of city rings and bosses, see Kenneth D. Ackerman's *Boss Tweed: The Rise and Fall of the Corrupt Pol Who Conceived the Soul of Modern New York* (2005). Excellent presidential biographies include Hans L. Trefousse's *Rutherford B. Hayes* (2002), Zachary Karabell's *Chester Alan Arthur* (2004), Henry F. Graff's *Grover Cleveland* (2002), and Kevin Phillips's *William McKinley* (2003).

Scholars have also examined various Gilded Age issues and interest groups. Gerald W. McFarland's *Mugwumps, Morals, and Politics, 1884–1920* (1975) examines the issue of reforming government service. Tom E. Terrill's *The Tariff, Politics, and American Foreign Policy, 1874–1901* (1973) lends clarity to that complex issue. The finances of the Gilded Age are covered in Walter T. K. Nugent's *Money and American Society, 1865–1880* (1968).

One of the most controversial works on populism is Lawrence Goodwyn's *The Populist Movement: A Short History of the Agrarian Revolt in America* (1978). A more balanced account is Robert C. McMath Jr.'s *American Populism: A Social History, 1877–1898* (1992). On the role of religion in the agrarian protest movements, see Joe Creech's *Righteous Indignation: Religion and the Populist Revolution* (2006). The best biography of Bryan is Michael Kazin's *A Godly Hero: The Life of William Jennings Bryan* (2006).

CHAPTER 23

An excellent survey of the diplomacy of the era is Charles S. Campbell's *The Transformation of American Foreign Relations, 1865–1900* (1976). For background on the events of the 1890s, see Walter LaFeber's *The American Search for Opportunity, 1865–1913* (1993) and David Healy's *U.S. Expansionism: The Imperialist Urge in the 1890s* (1970). The dispute over American policy in Hawaii is covered in Thomas J. Osborne's *"Empire Can Wait": American Opposition to Hawaiian Annexation, 1893–1898* (1981).

Ivan Musicant's *Empire by Default: The Spanish-American War and the Dawn of the American Century* (1998) is the most comprehensive volume on the conflict. For the war's aftermath in the Philippines, see Stuart Creighton Miller's *"Benevolent Assimilation": The American Conquest of the Philippines, 1899–1903* (1982). Robert L. Beisner's *Twelve against Empire: The Anti-Imperialists, 1898–1900* (1968) handles the debate over annexation. On the Philippine-American War, see David J. Silbey's *A War of Frontier and Empire: The Philippine-American War, 1899–1902* (2007).

A good introduction to American interest in China is Michael H. Hunt's *The Making of a Special Relationship: The United States and China to 1914* (1983). Kenton J. Clymer's *John Hay: The Gentleman as Diplomat* (1975) examines the role of this key secretary of state in forming policy.

For U.S. policy in the Caribbean and Central America, see Walter LaFeber's *Inevitable Revolutions: The United States in Central America*, 2nd ed. (1993). David McCullough's *The Path between the Seas: The Creation of the Panama Canal, 1870–1914* (1977) presents the fullest account of how the United States secured the Panama Canal.

CHAPTER 24

A splendid analysis of progressivism is John Whiteclay Chambers II's *The Tyranny of Change: America in the Progressive Era, 1890–1920*, rev. ed.

(2000). On Ida Tarbell and the muckrakers, see Steve Weinberg's *Taking on the Trust: The Epic Battle of Ida Tarbell and John D. Rockefeller* (2008). The evolution of government policy toward business is examined in Martin J. Sklar's *The Corporate Reconstruction of American Capitalism, 1890–1916: The Market, the Law, and Politics* (1988). Mina Carson's *Settlement Folk: Social Thought and the American Settlement Movement, 1885–1930* (1990) and Jack M. Holl's *Juvenile Reform in the Progressive Era: William R. George and the Junior Republic Movement* (1971) examine the social problems in the cities. An excellent study of the role of women in progressivism's emphasis on social justice is Kathryn Kish Sklar's *Florence Kelley and the Nation's Work: The Rise of Women's Political Culture, 1830–1900* (1995). On the tragic fire at the Triangle Shirtwaist Company, see David Von Drehle's *Triangle: The Fire That Changed America* (2003).

There is a rich body of scholarship focused on the conservation movement. See especially Rebecca Conard's *Places of Quiet Beauty: Parks, Preserves, and Environmentalism* (1997), Samuel P. Hays's *Conservation and the Gospel of Efficiency: The Progressive Conservation Movement, 1890–1920* (1959), Karl Jacoby's *Crimes against Nature: Squatters, Poachers, Thieves, and the Hidden History of American Conservation* (2001), John F. Reiger's *American Sportsmen and the Origins of Conservation* (1975), and Ted Steinberg's *Down to Earth: Nature's Role in American History* (2002). Robert Kanigel's *The One Best Way: Frederick Winslow Taylor and the Enigma of Efficiency* (1997) highlights the role of efficiency in the Progressive Era.

On the pivotal election of 1912, see James Chace's *1912: Wilson, Roosevelt, Taft, and Debs—The Election That Changed the Country* (2004). Excellent biographies include Kathleen Dalton's *Theodore Roosevelt: A Strenuous Life* (2002) and H. W. Brands's *Woodrow Wilson* (2003). For banking developments, see Allan H. Meltzer's *A History of the Federal Reserve*, vol. 1, *1913–1951* (2003).

CHAPTER 25

A lucid overview of international events covered in this chapter is Robert H. Ferrell's *Woodrow Wilson and World War I, 1917–1921* (1985). On Wilson's stance toward war, see Ross Gregory's *The Origins of American Intervention in the First World War* (1971). An excellent brief biography is H. W. Brands's *Woodrow Wilson* (2003).

Edward M. Coffman's *The War to End All Wars: The American Military Experience in World War I* (1968) is a detailed presentation of America's military involvement. See also Gary Mead's *The Doughboys: America and the*

First World War (2000). David M. Kennedy's *Over Here: The First World War and American Society* (1980) surveys the impact of the war on the home front, as does Meirion Harries and Susie Harries's *The Last Days of Innocence: America at War, 1917–1918* (1997). One of the best overviews of the European context of the war is John Keegan, *The First World War* (1998). Maurine Weiner Greenwald's *Women, War, and Work: The Impact of World War I on Women Workers in the United States* (1980) discusses the role of women. Ronald Schaffer's *America in the Great War: The Rise of the War Welfare State* (1991) shows the effect of war mobilization on business organization. Richard Polenberg's *Fighting Faiths: The Abrams Case, the Supreme Court, and Free Speech* (1987) examines the prosecution of a case under the 1918 Sedition Act.

How American diplomacy fared in the making of peace has received considerable attention. Thomas J. Knock interrelates domestic affairs and foreign relations in his explanation of Wilson's peacemaking in *To End All Wars: Woodrow Wilson and the Quest for a New World Order* (1992).

The problems of the immediate postwar years are chronicled by a number of historians. The best overview is Ann Hagedorn's *Savage Peace: Hope and Fear in America, 1919* (2007). On the Spanish flu, see John M. Barry's *The Great Influenza: The Epic Story of the Deadliest Plague in History* (2004). Labor tensions are examined in David E. Brody's *Labor in Crisis: The Steel Strike of 1919* (1965) and Francis Russell's *A City in Terror: Calvin Coolidge and the 1919 Boston Police Strike* (1975). On racial strife, see William M. Tuttle Jr.'s *Race Riot: Chicago in the Red Summer of 1919* (1970). The fear of Communists is analyzed in Robert K. Murray's *Red Scare: A Study in National Hysteria, 1919–1920* (1955).

CHAPTER 26

For a lively survey of the social and cultural changes during the interwar period, start with William E. Leuchtenburg's *The Perils of Prosperity, 1914–32,* 2nd ed. (1993). The best introduction to the culture of the 1920s remains Loren Baritz's *The Culture of the Twenties* (1970). See also Lynn Dumenil's *The Modern Temper: American Culture and Society in the 1920s* (1995).

John Higham's *Strangers in the Land: Patterns of American Nativism, 1860–1925,* 2nd ed. (2002) details the story of immigration restriction. The controversial Sacco and Vanzetti case is thoroughly explored in *Kill Now, Talk Forever: Debating Sacco and Vanzetti,* edited by Richard Newby (2001). For analysis of the revival of Klan activity, see Nancy MacLean's *Behind the Mask of Chivalry: The Making of the Second Ku Klux Klan* (1994). The best analysis of the Scopes trial is Edward J. Larson's *Summer for the Gods: The Scopes Trial and America's Continuing Debate over Science and Religion* (1997). On Prohibition, see Michael A. Lerner's *Dry Manhattan: Prohibition in New York City* (2007).

Women's suffrage is treated extensively in Eleanor Flexner and Ellen Fitzpatrick's *Century of Struggle: The Woman's Rights Movement in the United States,* enlarged ed. (1996). The best study of the birth-control movement is Ellen Chesler's *Woman of Valor: Margaret Sanger and the Birth Control Movement in America* (1992). See Charles Flint Kellogg's *NAACP: A History of the National Association for the Advancement of Colored People* (1967) for his analysis of the pioneering court cases against racial discrimination. Nathan Irvin Huggins's *Harlem Renaissance* (1971) assesses the cultural impact of the Great Migration on New York City. The emergence of jazz is ably documented in Burton W. Peretti's *The Creation of Jazz: Music, Race, and Culture in Urban America* (1992). On the African American migration to Chicago, see James R. Grossman's *Land of Hope: Chicago, Black Southerners, and the Great Migration* (1989). Nicholas Lemann's *The Promised Land: The Great Black Migration and How It Changed America* (1991) is a fine exposition of the changes brought about by the migration in both the South and the North.

On southern modernism, see Daniel Joseph Singal's *The War Within: From Victorian to Modernist Thought in the South, 1919–1945* (1982). Stanley Coben's *Rebellion against Victorianism: The Impetus for Cultural Change in 1920s America* (1991) surveys the appeal of modernism among writers, artists, and intellectuals.

CHAPTER 27

A fine synthesis of events immediately following the First World War is Ellis W. Hawley's *The Great War and the Search for a Modern Order: A History of the American People and Their Institutions, 1917–1933,* 2nd ed. (1992). On the election of 1920, see David Pietrusza, *1920: The Year of the Six Presidents* (2006).

On Harding, see Robert K. Murray's *The Harding Era: Warren G. Harding and His Administration* (1969). On Coolidge, see Robert H. Ferrell's *The Presidency of Calvin Coolidge* (1998). On Hoover, see Martin L. Fausold's *The Presidency of Herbert C. Hoover* (1985). The Democratic candidate for president in 1928 is explored in Robert A. Slayton's *Empire Statesman: The Rise and Redemption of Al Smith* (2001). The influential secretary of the Treasury during the 1920s is ably analyzed in David Cannadine's *Mellon: An American Life* (2006).

Overviews of the depressed economy are found in Charles P. Kindle-berger's *The World in Depression, 1929–1939*, rev. and enlarged ed. (1986) and Peter Fearon's *War, Prosperity, and Depression: The U.S. Economy, 1917–1945* (1987). John A. Garraty's *The Great Depression: An Inquiry into the Causes, Course, and Consequences of the Worldwide Depression of the Nineteen-Thirties* (1986) describes how people survived the Depression. On the removal of the Bonus Army, see Paul Dickson and Thomas B. Allen's *The Bonus Army: An American Epic* (2004).

CHAPTER 28

A comprehensive overview of the New Deal is David M. Kennedy's *Freedom from Fear: The American People in Depression and War, 1929–1945* (1999). On the critics of the New Deal, see Alan Brinkley's *Voices of Protest: Huey Long, Father Coughlin, and the Great Depression* (1982).

James N. Gregory's *American Exodus: The Dust Bowl Migration and Okie Culture in California* (1989) describes the migratory movement's effect on American culture. On the environmental and human causes of the dust bowl, see Donald Worster, *Dust Bowl: The Southern Plains in the 1930s* (1979).

CHAPTER 29

The best overview of interwar diplomacy remains Selig Adler's *The Uncertain Giant, 1921–1941: American Foreign Policy between the Wars* (1965). Joan Hoff's *American Business and Foreign Policy, 1920–1933* (1971) highlights the efforts of Republican administrations during the 1920s to promote international commerce. Robert Dallek's *Franklin D. Roosevelt and American Foreign Policy, 1932–1945* (1979) provides a judicious assessment of Roosevelt's foreign policy during the 1930s.

A noteworthy study is Waldo Heinrichs's *Threshold of War: Franklin D. Roosevelt and American Entry into World War II* (1988). See also David Reynolds's *From Munich to Pearl Harbor: Roosevelt's America and the Origins of the Second World War* (2001). Bruce M. Russett's *No Clear and Present Danger: A Skeptical View of the United States Entry into World War II*, 25th anniversary ed. (1997), provides a critical account of American actions.

On Pearl Harbor, see Gordon W. Prange's *Pearl Harbor: The Verdict of History* (1986). Japan's perspective is described in Akira Iriye's *The Origins of the Second World War in Asia and the Pacific* (1987).

CHAPTER 30

John Keegan's *The Second World War* (1989) surveys the European conflict, while Charles B. MacDonald's *The Mighty Endeavor: The American War in Europe* (1986) concentrates on U.S. involvement. Roosevelt's wartime leadership is analyzed in Eric Larrabee's *Commander in Chief: Franklin Delano Roosevelt, His Lieutenants, and Their War* (1987).

Books on specific European campaigns include Stephen E. Ambrose's *D-Day, June 6, 1944: The Climactic Battle of World War II* (1994) and Charles B. MacDonald's *A Time for Trumpets: The Untold Story of the Battle of the Bulge* (1985). On the Allied commander, see Carlo D'Este's *Eisenhower: A Soldier's Life* (2002).

For the war in the Far East, see John Costello's *The Pacific War, 1941–1945* (1981), Ronald H. Spector's *Eagle against the Sun: The American War with Japan* (1985), John W. Dower's award-winning *War without Mercy: Race and Power in the Pacific War* (1986), and Dan van der Vat's *The Pacific Campaign: The U.S.-Japanese Naval War, 1941–1945* (1991).

An excellent overview of the war's effects on the home front is Michael C. C. Adams's *The Best War Ever: America and World War II* (1994). On economic effects, see Harold G. Vatter's *The U.S. Economy in World War II* (1985).

Susan M. Hartmann's *The Home Front and Beyond: American Women in the 1940s* (1982) treats the new working environment for women. Neil A. Wynn looks at the participation of blacks in *The Afro-American and the Second World War* (1976). The story of the oppression of Japanese Americans is told in Peter Irons's *Justice at War: The Story of the Japanese American Internment Cases* (1983).

A sound introduction to U.S. diplomacy during the conflict can be found in Gaddis Smith's *American Diplomacy during the Second World War, 1941–1945* (1965). To understand the role that Roosevelt played in policy making, consult Warren F. Kimball's *The Juggler: Franklin Roosevelt as Wartime Statesman* (1991).

The issues and events that led to the deployment of atomic weapons are addressed in Martin J. Sherwin's *A World Destroyed: The Atomic Bomb and the Grand Alliance* (1975).

CHAPTER 31

The cold war remains a hotly debated topic. The traditional interpretation is best reflected in John Lewis Gaddis's *The United States and the Origins* of the Cold War, 1941–1947 (1972) and We Now Know: Rethinking Cold War History (1997). Both superpowers, Gaddis argues, were responsible for causing the cold war, but the Soviet Union was more culpable. The revisionist perspective is represented by Gar Alperovitz's Atomic Diplomacy: Hiroshima and Potsdam: The Use of the Atomic Bomb and the American Confrontation with Soviet Power, 2nd ed. (1994). Alperovitz places primary responsibility for the conflict on the United States. Also see H. W. Brands's The Devil We Knew: Americans and the Cold War (1993) and Melvyn P. Leffler's A Preponderance of Power: National Security, the Truman Administration, and the Cold War (1992). On the architect of containment, see David Mayers's George Kennan and the Dilemmas of U.S. Foreign Policy (1988).

Arnold A. Offner indicts Truman for clumsy statesmanship in Another Such Victory: President Truman and the Cold War, 1945–1953 (2002). For a positive assessment of Truman's leadership, see Alonzo L. Hamby's Beyond the New Deal: Harry S. Truman and American Liberalism (1973). The domestic policies of the Fair Deal are treated in William C. Berman's The Politics of Civil Rights in the Truman Administration (1970), Richard M. Dalfiume's Desegregation of the U.S. Armed Forces: Fighting on Two Fronts, 1939–1953 (1969), and Maeva Marcus's Truman and the Steel Seizure Case: The Limits of Presidential Power (1977). The most comprehensive biography of Truman is David McCullough's Truman (1992).

For an introduction to the tensions in Asia, see Akira Iriye's The Cold War in Asia: A Historical Introduction (1974). For the Korean conflict, see Callum A. MacDonald's Korea: The War before Vietnam (1986) and Max Hasting's The Korean War (1987).

The anti-Communist syndrome is surveyed in David Caute's The Great Fear: The Anti-Communist Purge under Truman and Eisenhower (1978). Arthur Herman's Joseph McCarthy: Reexamining the Life and Legacy of America's Most Hated Senator (2000) covers McCarthy himself. For a well-documented account of how the cold war was sustained by superpatriotism, intolerance, and suspicion, see Stephen J. Whitfield's The Culture of the Cold War, 2nd ed. (1996).

CHAPTER 32

Two excellent overviews of social and cultural trends in the postwar era are William H. Chafe's The Unfinished Journey: America since World War II, 6th ed. (2006), and William E. Leuchtenburg's A Troubled Feast: America since 1945, rev. ed. (1979). For insights into the cultural life of the

1950s, see Jeffrey Hart's *When the Going Was Good! American Life in the Fifties* (1982) and David Halberstam's *The Fifties* (1993).

The baby boom generation and its impact are vividly described in Paul C. Light's *Baby Boomers* (1988). The emergence of the television industry is discussed in Erik Barnouw's *Tube of Plenty: The Evolution of American Television*, 2nd rev. ed. (1990), and Ella Taylor's *Prime-Time Families: Television Culture in Postwar America* (1989).

A comprehensive account of the process of suburban development is Kenneth T. Jackson's *Crabgrass Frontier: The Suburbanization of the United States* (1985). Equally good is Tom Martinson's *American Dreamscape: The Pursuit of Happiness in Postwar Suburbia* (2000).

The middle-class ideal of family life in the 1950s is examined in Elaine Tyler May's *Homeward Bound: American Families in the Cold War Era*, rev. ed. (2008). Thorough accounts of women's issues are found in Wini Breines's *Young, White, and Miserable: Growing Up Female in the Fifties* (1992). For an overview of the resurgence of religion in the 1950s, see George M. Marsden's *Religion and American Culture*, 2nd ed. (2000).

A lively discussion of movies of the 1950s can be found in Peter Biskind's *Seeing Is Believing: How Hollywood Taught Us to Stop Worrying and Love the Fifties* (1983). The origins and growth of rock and roll are surveyed in Carl Belz's *The Story of Rock*, 2nd ed. (1972). Thoughtful interpretive surveys of postwar literature include Josephine Hendin's *Vulnerable People: A View of American Fiction since 1945* (1978) and Malcolm Bradbury's *The Modern American Novel* (1983). The colorful Beats are brought to life in Steven Watson's *The Birth of the Beat Generation: Visionaries, Rebels, and Hipsters, 1944–1960* (1995).

CHAPTER 33

Scholarship on the Eisenhower years is extensive. A carefully balanced overview of the period is Chester J. Pach, Jr. and Elmo Richardson's *The Presidency of Dwight D. Eisenhower*, rev. ed. (1991). For the manner in which Eisenhower conducted foreign policy, see Robert A. Divine's *Eisenhower and the Cold War* (1981). Tom Wicker deems Eisenhower a better person than a president in *Dwight D. Eisenhower* (2002).

For the buildup of U.S. involvement in Indochina, consult Lloyd C. Gardner's *Approaching Vietnam: From World War II through Dienbienphu, 1941–1954* (1988) and David L. Anderson's *Trapped by Success: The Eisenhower Administration and Vietnam, 1953–61* (1991). How the Eisenhower Doctrine came to be implemented is traced in Stephen E. Ambrose and Douglas G. Brinkley's *Rise to Globalism: American Foreign Policy since 1938*, 8th ed. (1997).

The impact of the Supreme Court during the 1950s is the focus of Archibald Cox's *The Warren Court: Constitutional Decision as an Instrument of Reform* (1968). A masterly study of the important Warren Court decision on school desegregation is James T. Patterson's *Brown v. Board of Education: A Civil Rights Milestone and Its Troubled Legacy* (2001).

For the story of the early years of the civil rights movement, see Taylor Branch's *Parting the Waters: America in the King Years, 1954–1963* (1988) and Robert Weisbrot's *Freedom Bound: A History of America's Civil Rights Movement* (1990).

CHAPTER 34

A dispassionate analysis of John Kennedy's life is Thomas C. Reeves's *A Question of Character: A Life of John F. Kennedy* (1991). The best study of the Kennedy administration's domestic policies is Irving Bernstein's *Promises Kept: John F. Kennedy's New Frontier* (1991). For details on the still swirling conspiracy theories about the assassination, see David W. Belin's *Final Disclosure: The Full Truth about the Assassination of President Kennedy* (1988).

The most comprehensive biography of Johnson is Robert Dallek's two-volume work, *Lone Star Rising: Lyndon Johnson and His Times, 1908–1960* (1991) and *Flawed Giant: Lyndon Johnson and His Times, 1961–1973* (1998). On the Johnson administration, see Vaughn Davis Bornet's *The Presidency of Lyndon B. Johnson* (1984).

Among the works that interpret liberal social policy during the 1960s, John E. Schwarz's *America's Hidden Success: A Reassessment of Twenty Years of Public Policy* (1983) offers a glowing endorsement of Democratic programs. For a contrasting perspective, see Charles Murray's *Losing Ground: American Social Policy, 1950–1980*, rev. ed. (1994).

On foreign policy, see *Kennedy's Quest for Victory: American Foreign Policy, 1961–1963* (1989), edited by Thomas G. Paterson. To learn more about Kennedy's problems in Cuba, see Mark J. White's *Missiles in Cuba: Kennedy, Khrushchev, Castro and the 1962 Crisis* (1997). See also Aleksandr Fursenko and Timothy Naftali's *"One Hell of a Gamble": Khrushchev, Castro and Kennedy, 1958–1964* (1997).

American involvement in Vietnam has received voluminous treatment from all political perspectives. For an excellent overview, see Larry Berman's *Planning a Tragedy: The Americanization of the War in Vietnam* (1983) and

Lyndon Johnson's War: The Road to Stalemate in Vietnam (1989), as well as Stanley Karnow's *Vietnam: A History,* 2nd rev. ed. (1997). An analysis of policy making concerning the Vietnam War is David M. Barrett's *Uncertain Warriors: Lyndon Johnson and His Vietnam Advisors* (1993). A fine account of the military involvement is Robert D. Schulzinger's *A Time for War: The United States and Vietnam, 1941–1975* (1997). On the legacy of the Vietnam War, see Arnold R. Isaacs's *Vietnam Shadows: The War, Its Ghosts, and Its Legacy* (1997).

Many scholars have dealt with various aspects of the civil rights movement and race relations in the 1960s. See especially Carl M. Brauer's *John F. Kennedy and the Second Reconstruction* (1977), David J. Garrow's *Bearing the Cross: Martin Luther King, Jr., and the Southern Christian Leadership Conference* (1986), and Adam Fairclough's *To Redeem the Soul of America: The Southern Christian Leadership Conference and Martin Luther King, Jr.* (1987). William H. Chafe's *Civilities and Civil Rights: Greensboro, North Carolina, and the Black Struggle for Freedom* (1980) details the original sit-ins. An award-winning study of racial and economic inequality in a representative American city is Thomas J. Sugrue's *The Origins of the Urban Crisis: Race and Inequality in Postwar Detroit* (1996).

CHAPTER 35

An engaging overview of the cultural trends of the 1960s is Maurice Isserman and Michael Kazin's *America Divided: The Civil War of the 1960s,* 3rd ed. (2007). The New Left is assessed in Irwin Unger's *The Movement: A History of the American New Left, 1959–1972* (1974). On the Students for a Democratic Society, see Kirkpatrick Sale's *SDS* (1973) and Allen J. Matusow's *The Unraveling of America: A History of Liberalism in the 1960s* (1984). Also useful is Todd Gitlin's *The Sixties: Years of Hope, Days of Rage,* rev. ed. (1993).

Two influential assessments of the counterculture by sympathetic commentators are Theodore Roszak's *The Making of a Counter-culture: Reflections on the Technocratic Society and Its Youthful Opposition* (1969) and Charles A. Reich's *The Greening of America: How the Youth Revolution Is Trying to Make America Livable* (1970). A good scholarly analysis that takes the hippies seriously is Timothy Miller's *The Hippies and American Values* (1991).

The best study of the women's liberation movement is Ruth Rosen's *The World Split Open: How the Modern Women's Movement Changed America,* rev. ed. (2006). The organizing efforts of Cesar Chavez are detailed in Ronald B. Taylor's *Chavez and the Farm Workers* (1975). The struggles of Native

Americans for recognition and power are sympathetically described in Stan Steiner's *The New Indians* (1968).

On Nixon, see Melvin Small's *The Presidency of Richard Nixon* (1999). For a solid overview of the Watergate scandal, see Stanley I. Kutler's *The Wars of Watergate: The Last Crisis of Richard Nixon* (1990). For the way the Republicans handled foreign affairs, consult Tad Szulc's *The Illusion of Peace: Foreign Policy in the Nixon Years* (1978).

The loss of Vietnam and the end of American involvement there are traced in Larry Berman's *No Peace, No Honor: Nixon, Kissinger, and Betrayal in Vietnam* (2001). William Shawcross's *Sideshow: Kissinger, Nixon and the Destruction of Cambodia*, rev. ed. (2002), deals with the broadening of the war, while Larry Berman's *Planning a Tragedy: The Americanization of the War in Vietnam* (1982) assesses the final impact of U.S. involvement. The most comprehensive treatment of the anti-war movement is Tom Wells's *The War Within: America's Battle over Vietnam* (1994).

A comprehensive treatment of the Ford administration is contained in John Robert Greene's *The Presidency of Gerald R. Ford* (1995). The best overview of the Carter administration is Burton I. Kaufman's *The Presidency of James Earl Carter, Jr.*, 2nd rev. ed. (2006). A work more sympathetic to the Carter administration is John Dumbrell's *The Carter Presidency: A Re-evaluation*, 2nd ed. (1995). Gaddis Smith's *Morality, Reason, and Power: American Diplomacy in the Carter Years* (1986) provides an overview. Background on how the Middle East came to dominate much of American policy is found in William B. Quandt's *Decade of Decisions: American Policy toward the Arab-Israeli Conflict, 1967–1976* (1977).

CHAPTER 36

Two brief accounts of Reagan's presidency are David Mervin's *Ronald Reagan and the American Presidency* (1990) and Michael Schaller's *Reckoning with Reagan: America and Its President in the 1980s* (1992). A more substantial biography is John Patrick Diggins's *Ronald Reagan: Fate, Freedom, and the Making of History* (2007). An excellent analysis of the 1980 election is Andrew E. Busch's *Reagan's Victory: The Presidential Election of 1980 and the Rise of the Right* (2005). A more comprehensive summary of the Reagan years is Sean Wilentz's *The Age of Reagan: A History, 1974–2008* (2008).

On Reaganomics, see David A. Stockman's *The Triumph of Politics: Why the Reagan Revolution Failed* (1986) and Robert Lekachman's *Greed Is Not Enough: Reaganomics* (1982). On the issue of arms control, see Strobe Talbott's

Deadly Gambits: The Reagan Administration and the Stalemate in Nuclear Arms Control (1984).

For Reagan's foreign policy in Central America, see James Chace's *Endless War: How We Got Involved in Central America—and What Can Be Done* (1984) and Walter LaFeber's *Inevitable Revolutions: The United States in Central America*, 2nd ed. (1993). Insider views of Reagan's foreign policy are offered in Alexander M. Haig Jr.'s *Caveat: Realism, Reagan, and Foreign Policy* (1984) and Caspar W. Weinberger's *Fighting for Peace: Seven Critical Years in the Pentagon* (1990).

On Reagan's second term, see Jane Mayer and Doyle McManus's *Landslide: The Unmaking of the President, 1984–1988* (1988). For a masterly work on the Iran-Contra affair, see Theodore Draper's *A Very Thin Line: The Iran Contra Affairs* (1991). Several collections of essays include varying assessments of the Reagan years. Among these are *The Reagan Revolution?* (1988), edited by B. B. Kymlicka and Jean V. Matthews; *The Reagan Presidency: An Incomplete Revolution?* (1990), edited by Dilys M. Hill, Raymond A. Moore, and Phil Williams, and *Looking Back on the Reagan Presidency* (1990), edited by Larry Berman.

On the 1988 campaign, see Jack W. Germond and Jules Witcover's *Whose Broad Stripes and Bright Stars? The Trivial Pursuit of the Presidency, 1988* (1989) and Sidney Blumenthal's *Pledging Allegiance: The Last Campaign of the Cold War* (1990). For a social history of the decade, see John Ehrman's *The Eighties: America in the Age of Reagan* (2005).

CHAPTER 37

On George H. W. Bush's presidency, see *Leadership and the Bush Presidency: Prudence or Drift in an Era of Change?*, edited by Ryan J. Barilleaux and Mary E. Stuckey (1992), and Charles Tiefer's *The Semi-Sovereign Presidency: The Bush Administration's Strategy for Governing without Congress* (1994). Among the journalistic accounts of the presidential election of 1992, the best narrative is Jack W. Germond and Jules Witcover's *Mad as Hell: Revolt at the Ballot Box, 1992* (1993). The best scholarly study is Theodore J. Lowi and Benjamin Ginsberg's *Democrats Return to Power: Politics and Policy in the Clinton Era* (1994).

Analysis of the Clinton years can be found in Joe Klein's *The Natural: The Misunderstood Presidency of Bill Clinton* (2002). Clinton's impeachment is assessed in Richard A. Posner's *An Affair of State: The Investigation, Impeachment, and Trial of President Clinton* (1999).

On changing demographic trends, see Sam Roberts's *Who We Are Now: The Changing Face of America in the Twenty-First Century* (2004). On social and cultural life in the 1990s, see Haynes Johnson's *The Best of Times: America in the Clinton Years* (2001). The onset and growth of the AIDS epidemic are traced in *And the Band Played On: Politics, People, and the AIDS Epidemic,* 20th anniversary ed. (2007), by Randy Shilts.

Aspects of fundamentalist and apocalyptic movements are the subject of Paul Boyer's *When Time Shall Be No More: Prophecy Belief in Modern American Culture* (1992), George M. Marsden's *Understanding Fundamentalism and Evangelicalism,* new ed. (2006), and Ralph E. Reed's *Politically Incorrect: The Emerging Faith Factor in American Politics* (1994).

On the invention of the computer and the Internet, see Paul E. Ceruzzi's *A History of Modern Computing,* 2nd ed. (2003), and Janet Abbate's *Inventing the Internet* (1999). The booming economy of the 1990s is well analyzed in Joseph E. Stiglitz's *The Roaring Nineties: A New History of the World's Most Prosperous Decade* (2003). On the rising stress within the workplace, see Jill Andresky Fraser's *White-Collar Sweatshop: The Deterioration of Work and Its Rewards in Corporate America* (2001). Aspects of corporate restructuring and downsizing are the subject of Bennett Harrison's *Lean and Mean: The Changing Landscape of Corporate Power in the Age of Flexibility* (1994).

For further treatment of the end of the cold war, see Michael R. Beschloss and Strobe Talbott's *At the Highest Levels: The Inside Story of the End of the Cold War* (1993) and Richard Crockatt's *The Fifty Years War: The United States and the Soviet Union in World Politics, 1941–1991* (1995). On the Persian Gulf conflict, see Lester H. Brune's *America and the Iraqi Crisis, 1990–1992: Origins and Aftermath* (1993). On the transformation of American foreign policy, see James Mann's *Rise of the Vulcans: The History of Bush's War Cabinet* (2004), Claes G. Ryn's *America the Virtuous: The Crisis of Democracy and the Quest for Empire* (2003), and Stephen M. Walt's *Taming American Power: The Global Response to U.S. Primacy* (2005).

The disputed 2000 presidential election is the focus of Jeffrey Toobin's *Too Close to Call: The Thirty-Six-Day Battle to Decide the 2000 Election* (2001). On the attacks of September 11, 2001, and their aftermath, see *The Age of Terror: America and the World after September 11,* edited by Strobe Talbott and Nayan Chanda (2001).

On the environmental history of New Orleans, see Craig E. Colten's *An Unnatural Metropolis: Wresting New Orleans from Nature* (2004). For a devastating account of the Bush administration by a White House insider, see Scott McClellan's *What Happened: Inside the Bush White House and Washington's Culture of Deception* (2008). On the historic 2008 election, see Michael Nelson's *The Elections of 2008* (2009).

CREDITS

CHAPTER 18: p. 702, Library of Congress; **p. 704,** Library of Congress; **p. 705,** Library of Congress; **p. 706,** Library of Congress; **p. 709,** Bettmann/Corbis; **p. 710,** Library of Congress; **p. 712,** Library of Congress; **p. 713,** Library of Congress; **p. 714,** Library of Congress; **p. 718,** National Archives; **p. 721,** Granger Collection; **p. 722,** Bettmann/Corbis; **p. 723,** Library of Congress; **p. 727,** Library of Congress; **p. 728,** Library of Congress; **p. 731,** Library of Congress; **p. 733,** Library of Congress; **p. 736,** Library of Congress.

PART 5: p. 743, Granger Collection; **p. 744,** Granger Collection.

CHAPTER 19: p. 747, Library of Congress; **p. 749,** Special Collections, Duke University; **p. 752,** The Granger Collection; **p. 755,** Granger Collection; **p. 757,** Library of Congress; **p. 758,** Warder Collection; **p. 761,** Special Collections, University of Chicago library; **p. 762,** Library of Congress; **p. 763,** Warder Collection; **p. 765,** Kansas State Historical Society; **p. 766,** Bettmann/Corbis; **p. 770,** Library of Congress; **p. 772,** Warder Collection; **p. 774,** SPC Plateau Nez Perce NAA 4876 00942000, Smithsonian Institution National Anthropological Archives; **p. 776,** Bettmann/Corbis; **p. 778,** National Archives; **p. 780,** Corbis; **p. 782,** Western Historical Collections University of Oklahoma Library.

CHAPTER 20: p. 786, Library of Congress; **p. 788;** Alfred Stieglitz, The Hand of Man 1902, Photogravure, P.1978.112, Amon Carter Museum; **p. 789,** Bettmann/Corbis; **p. 791,** Union Pacific Museum; **p. 793,** Collection of the New-York Historical Society; **p. 794,** National Archives; **p. 795,** The Granger Collection; **p. 796,** Warder Collection; **p. 797,** American Petroleum Institute Historical Photo Collection; **p. 799,** Carnegie Library of Pittsburgh; **p. 800,** Keystone-Mast Collection [WX13101]; **p. 801,** Pierpont Morgan Library; **p. 802,** Carnegie Library of Pittsburgh; **p. 803,** Granger Collection; **p. 805,** Bettmann/Corbis; **p. 808,** Granger Collection; **p. 809,** T. V. Powderly Photographic Collection, The American Catholic History Research Center University Archives, The Catholic University of America, Washington, D.C.; **p. 812,** Bettmann/Corbis; **p. 813,** Museum of the City of New York/Corbis; **p. 815,** Library of Congress; **p. 817,** Bettmann/Corbis; **p. 819,** Walter P. Reuther Library, Wayne State University.

CHAPTER 21: **p. 824,** Library of Congress; **p. 828,** The Art Archive/Culver Pictures; **p. 830,** Bettmann/Corbis; **p. 832,** The Bryon Collection, Museum of the City of New York; **p. 833,** William Williams Papers, Manuscripts and Archives Division, The New York Public Library, Astor, Lenox and Tilden Foundations; **p. 835,** Library of Congress; **p. 836,** The Denver Public Library, Western History Collection; **p. 838,** Bettmann/Corbis; **p. 839,** Granger Collection; **p. 841,** Brown Brothers; **p. 842,** Old York Library; **p. 843,** Library of Congress; **p. 845,** Corbis; **p. 846,** Special Collections, Vassar College Libraries; **p. 848,** American Museum of Natural History; **p. 849,** John Carter Brown Library; **p. 850,** National Library of Medicine; **p. 851,** Time Life Pictures/Getty Images; **p. 854,** The Salvation Army National Archives; **p. 856,** University of Illinois at Chicago; **p. 857,** Granger Collection.

CHAPTER 22: **p. 864,** Library of Congress; **p. 865,** Library of Congress; **p. 869,** Library of Congress; **p. 871,** Bettmann/Corbis; **p. 873,** Warder Collection; **p. 874,** Warder Collection; **p. 877,** Bettmann/Corbis; **p. 878,** Warder Collection; **p. 879,** Bettmann/Corbis; **p. 881,** Library of Congress; **p. 883,** Library of Congress; **p. 885,** Wooten Studios; **p. 887,** Kansas State Historical Society; **p. 888,** Nebraska State Historical Society; **p. 891,** Library of Congress; **p. 894,** Library of Congress.

PART 6: **p. 901,** Library of Congress; **p. 903,** Library of Congress.

CHAPTER 23: **p. 905,** Bettmann/Corbis; **p. 909,** Bettmann/Corbis; **p. 910,** Hawaii State Archives; **p. 912,** Brown Brothers; **p. 913,** Library of Congress; **p. 914,** Bettmann/Corbis; **p. 921,** National Archives; **p. 922,** Photo: Corporal George J. Vennage; Courtesy of OSU Rare Books & Manuscripts Library; **p. 925,** Library of Congress; **p. 927,** Granger Collection; **p. 928,** Bettmann/Corbis; **p. 930,** Granger Collection; **p. 932,** Bettmann/Corbis; **p. 934.** Bettmann/Corbis.

CHAPTER 24: **p. 940,** Library of Congress; **p. 943,** Granger Collection; **p. 946,** Library of Congress; **p. 947,** Bettmann/Corbis; **p. 948,** Corbis; **p. 952,** Collection of the New-York Historical Society; **p. 952,** Library of Congress; **p. 953,** Bettmann/Corbis; **p. 956,** Library of Congress; **p. 958,** Bettmann/Corbis; **p. 959,** Bettmann/Corbis; **p. 960,** Library of Congress; **p. 961,** Library of Congress, **p. 964,** Granger Collection; **p. 965,** Library of Congress; **p. 967,** Library of Congress; **p. 968,** Warder Collection; **p. 974,** Warder Collection; **p.976,** Corbis.

CHAPTER 25: **p. 982,** Library of Congress; **p. 985,** Bettmann/Corbis; **p. 988,** Alamy; **p. 989,** Warder Collection; **p. 991,** The New York Times; **p. 992,** Rollin Kirby; **p. 995,** Bettmann/Corbis; **p. 998,** Swim Ink 2, LLC/Corbis; **p. 1000,** Bettmann/Corbis; **p. 1001,** Everett Collection; **p. 1003,** National Archives; **p. 1004,** Bettmann/Corbis; **p. 1006,** National Archives; **p. 1008,** Warder Collection; **p. 1010,** Mary Evans Picture Library; **p. 1011,** Courtesy of the Ding Darling Wildlife Society; **p. 1016,** Bettmann/Corbis; **p. 1017,** Chicago History Museum.

CHAPTER 26: **p. 1022,** Bettmann/Corbis; **p. 1024,** Digital Image, The Museum of Modern Art/Licensed by SCALA/Art Resource, NY. © Estate of Ben Shahn/Licensed by VAGA, New York, NY; **p. 1025,** Bettmann/Corbis; **p. 1027,** Bettmann/Corbis; **p. 1029,** Bettmann/Corbis; **p. 1031,** Ramsey Archive; **p. 1032,** Bettmann/Corbis; **p. 1033,** Bettmann/Corbis; **p. 1035,** Bettmann/Corbis; **p. 1036,** University of Chicago; **p. 1037,** AP Photos; **p. 1040,** Warder Collection; **p. 1042,** Image copyright © The Metropolitan Museum of Art/Art Resource, NY. © 2009 Estate of Pablo Picasso/Artists Rights Society (ARS), New York; **p. 1043,** Brown Brothers; **p. 1044,** Brown Brothers.

CHAPTER 27: **p.1048,** Bettmann/Corbis; **p. 1051,** Hulton Archives/Getty Images; **p. 1053,** The Washington Post. Reprinted with permission; **p. 1055,** Hulton Archives/ Getty Images; **p. 1058,** Bettmann/Corbis; **p. 1059,** Bettmann/Corbis; **p.1060,** Library of Congress; **p. 1062,** From the Collections of The Henry Ford Museum; **p. 1063,** Gehl Company/Corbis; **p. 1066,** Bettmann/Corbis; **p. 1067,** David J. & Janice L. Frent Collection/Corbis; **p. 1069,** Herbert Hoover Presidential Library; **p. 1071,** AP Photos; **p. 1074,** Bettmann/Corbis; **p. 1076,** New York Daily News.

CHAPTER 28: **p. 1080,** Bettmann/Corbis; **p. 1083,** AP Photos; **p. 1087,** National Archives; **p. 1088,** Bettmann/Corbis; **p. 1090,** Robert Holmes/Corbis; **p. 1093,** Library of Congress; **p. 1094,** Bettmann/Corbis; **p. 1097,** Library of Congress; **p. 1098,** National Archives; **p. 1100,** Library of Congress; **p. 1101,** Bettmann/Corbis; **p. 1104,** Bettmann/ Corbis; **p. 1105,** Hulton Archives/Getty Images; **p. 1107,** Bettmann/Corbis; **p. 1108,** Bettmann/Corbis; **p. 1110,** Library of Congress; **p. 1112,** Corbis; **p. 1114,** 1936, The Washington Post; **p. 1116,** Bettmann/Corbis; **p. 1119,** Granger Collection; **p. 1122,** Bettmann/Corbis.

CHAPTER 29: **p. 1126,** Bettmann/Corbis; **p. 1129,** AP Photo; **p. 1131,** Bettmann/ Corbis; **p. 1133,** Granger Collection; **p. 1135,** National Archives; **p. 1139,**1938, The Washington Post; **p.1140,** Imperial War Museum London; **p. 1142,** British Information Services; **p. 1143,** Granger Collection; **p. 1146,** Bettmann/Corbis; **p. 1150,** Bettmann/ Corbis; **p. 1152,** Library of Congress.

CHAPTER 30: **p. 1156,** Bettmann/Corbis; **p. 1157,** Warder Collection; **p. 1160,** Swim Ink 2, LLC/Corbis; **p. 1163,** Granger Collection; **p. 1164,** Library of Congress; **p. 1165,** AP Photo; **p. 1167,** Bettmann/Corbis; **p. 1168,** Russell Lee/Getty Images; **p. 1174,** AP Photo; **p. 1175,** Copyright 1945 by Bill Mauldin. Reprinted courtesy of the William Mauldin Estate; **p. 1177,** Eisenhower Presidential Library; **p. 1178,** National Archives; **p. 1184,** National Archives; **p. 1186,** Hulton Archives/Getty Images; **p.1187,** National Archives; **p. 1190,** National Archives; **p. 1191,** National Archives; **p. 1193,** Bettmann/Corbis; **p. 1195,** Hulton Archives/Getty Images.

PART 7: **p. 1201,** Bill Eppridge/Getty Images; **p. 1203,** Peter Turnley/Corbis.

CHAPTER 31: **p. 1205,** Bettmann/Corbis; **p. 1207,** University of Louisville; **p. 1210,** Collections of the New York Public Library, Astor, Lenox and Tilden Foundations;

p. 1210, Granger Collection; **p. 1213,** Bettmann/Corbis; **p. 1215,** Herman Landshoff; **p. 1217,** Library of Congress; **p. 1218,** Hartford Courant; **p. 1221,** Hy Peskin/Getty Images; **p. 1222,** 1948, Washington Post; **p. 1223,** Bettmann/Corbis; **p. 1224,** AP Photo; **p. 1225,** Bettmann/Corbis; **p. 1231,** Bettmann/Corbis; **p. 1234,** Bettmann/Corbis; **p. 1235,** Yale Joel/Getty Images.

CHAPTER 32: **p. 1240,** Hulton Archives/Getty Images; **p. 1242,** William Joseph O'Keefe Collection, Veterans History Project, Library of Congress; **p. 1243,** AP Photo; **p. 1245,** AP Photo; **p. 1246,** New York Public Library; **p. 1247,** Hulton Archives/Getty Images; **p. 1249,** Library of Congress; **p. 1250,** Image copyright © The Metropolitan Museum of Art/Art Resource, NY; **p. 1251,** Fogg Art Museum, Harvard University; **p. 1253,** PNI/Archive Museum of Art; **p. 1255,** William Gottlieb/Corbis; **p.1257,** Culver Pictures; **p. 1257,** Bernard Gotfryd/Getty Images; **p. 1259,** AP Photos; **p. 1260,** Art Shay/Time Life Pictures/Getty Images; **p. 1261,** Hulton Archives/Getty Images; **p. 1262,** AP Photos.

CHAPTER 33: **p. 1266,** Bettmann/Corbis; **p. 1269,** Library of Congress; **p. 1272,** Bettmann/Corbis; **p. 1273,** AP Photo; **p. 1275,** "Don't Be Afraid—I Can Always Pull You Back" from Herblock's *Special for Today* (Simon & Schuster 1958); **p. 1276,** Photoworld; **p. 1277,** AP Photo; **p. 1284,** Bettmann/Corbis; **p. 1286,** Detroit News; **p. 1287,** AP Photo; **p. 1289,** AP Photo; **p. 1290,** University of Louisville; **p. 1293,** Black Star/Stock Photo; **p. 1294,** Joseph Scherschel/Time Life Pictures/Getty Images.

CHAPTER 34: **p. 1300,** Bettmann/Corbis; **p. 1303,** National Archives; **p. 1307,** National Archives; **p. 1309,** National Archives; **p. 1311,** Hulton Archives/Getty Images; **p. 1312,** Bettmann/Corbis; **p. 1314,** National Archives; **p. 1316,** Hulton Archives/Getty Images; **p. 1318,** National Archives; **p. 1319,** Time Life Pictures; **p. 1320,** AP Photo; **p. 1322,** The New Statesman; **p. 1325,** Bettmann/Corbis; **p. 1327,** National Archives; **p. 1329,** Newark Star-Ledger; **p. 1333,** Bettmann/Corbis; **p. 1334,** Jack Kightlinger, Lyndon Baines Johnson Library and Museum; **p. 1336,** Bettmann/Corbis.

CHAPTER 35: **p. 1340,** Bettmann/Corbis; **p. 1342,** Ted Streshinsky/Corbis; **p. 1344,** AP Photos; **p. 1345,** Magnum Photos; **p. 1348,** John Dominis/Getty Images; **p. 1349,** Warder Collection; **p. 1350,** Bettmann/Corbis; **p. 1351,** H. William Tetlow/Getty Images; **p. 1354,** AP Photos, **p. 1356,** Bettmann/Corbis; **p. 1358,** National Archives; **p. 1360,** Howard Ruffner/Time Life Pictures/Getty Images; **p. 1363,** Nik Wheeler/Corbis; **p. 1365,** Bettmann/Corbis; **p. 1367,** Bettmann/Corbis; **p. 1369,** AP Photo; **p. 1370,** NASA Kennedy Space Center; **p. 1372,** John Dominis/Getty Images; **p. 1373,** AP Photo; **p. 1376,** AP Photo; **p. 1377,** AP Photo; **p. 1380,** Wally McNamee/Corbis; **p. 1383,** White House; **p. 1384,** AP Photo; **p. 1386,** Kaveh Kazemi/Corbis.

CHAPTER 36: **p. 1390,** Bettmann/Corbis; **p. 1392,** Bettmann/Corbis; **p. 1394,** Bettmann/Corbis; **p. 1397,** Wally McNamee/Corbis; **p. 1399,** Bettmann/Corbis; **p. 1401,** Los Angeles Times Syndicate; **p. 1405,** Bettmann/Corbis; **p. 1406,** Bettmann/Corbis;

p. **1408,** Black Star/Stock Photo; **p. 1409,** AP Photo; **p. 1411,** Black Star/Stock Photo; **p. 1414,** Woodfin Camp; **p. 1415,** AP Photo; **p. 1418,** Bettmann/Corbis.

CHAPTER 37: **p. 1422,** Smiley N. Pool/Dallas Morning News/Corbis; **p. 1424,** AP Photo; **p. 1425,** Library of Congress; **p. 1427,** Durand-Hudson-Langevin-Orban/Sygma/Corbis; **p. 1430,** Chris Wilkins/Getty Images; **p. 1431,** AP Photo; **p. 1432,** AP Photo; **p. 1435,** AP Photo; **p. 1438,** Hartford Courant; **p. 1439,** AP Photo; **p. 1441,** AP Photo; **p. 1445,** Najlah Feanny/Corbis; **p. 1448,** Sean Adair/Reuters/Corbis; **p. 1450,** AP Photo; **p. 1451,** Reuters/Corbis; **p. 1452,** Reuters/Corbis; **p. 1454,** Bettmann/Corbis; **p. 1456,** Brooks Kraft/Corbis; **p. 1459,** Reuters/Corbis; **p. 1461,** AP Photo; **p. 1462,** AP Photo; **p. 1463,** AP Photo; **p. 1465,** AP Photo; **p. 1466,** Michael Ainsworth/Dallas Morning News/Corbis; **p. 1467,** AP Photo; **p. 1468,** Shawn Thew/epa/Corbis; **p. 1469,** AP Photo; **p. 1471,** Jim Young/Reuters/Corbis.

INDEX

Page numbers in *italics* refer to illustrations.

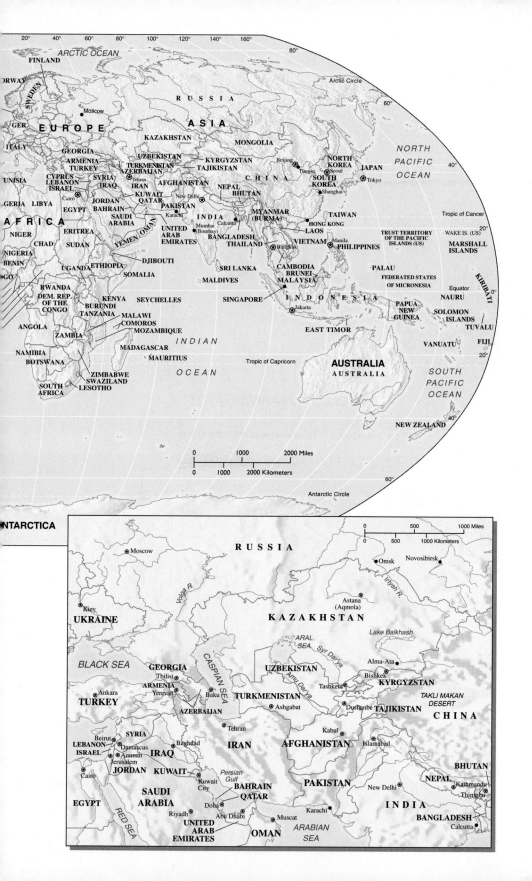